C000242118

STREET ATLAS

North Essex

First published in 1999 by

Philip's, a division of
Octopus Publishing Group Ltd
2–4 Heron Quays, London E14 4JP

Second edition 2003
First impression 2003

ISBN 0-540-08285-6 (spiral)

© Philip's 2003

 Ordnance Survey®

This product includes mapping data licensed
from Ordnance Survey® with the permission of
the Controller of Her Majesty's Stationery Office.
© Crown copyright 2003. All rights reserved.
Licence number 100011710.

Printed and bound in Spain
by Cayfosa-Quebecor

Contents

III	**Key to map symbols**
IV	**Key to map pages**
VI	**Route planning**
VIII	**Administrative and Postcode boundaries**
1	**Street maps** at 3½ inches to 1 mile
222	**Index** of towns and villages
223	**Index** of streets, hospitals, industrial estates, railway stations, schools, shopping centres, universities and places of interest

Digital Data

The exceptionally high-quality mapping found in this atlas is available as digital data in TIFF format, which is easily convertible to other bitmapped (raster) image formats.

The index is also available in digital form as a standard database table. It contains all the details found in the printed index together with the National Grid reference for the map square in which each entry is named.

For further information and to discuss your requirements, please contact Philip's on 020 7644 6932 or james.mann@philips-maps.co.uk

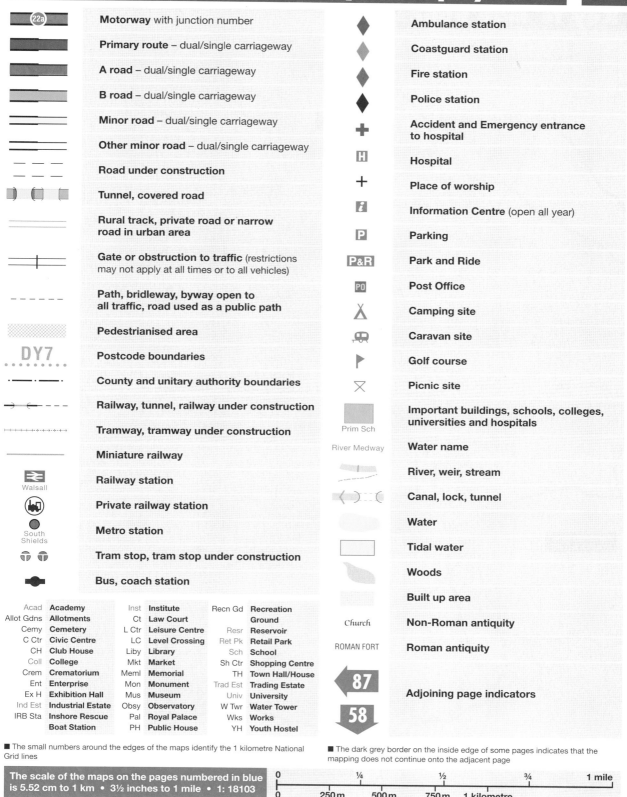

	Motorway with junction number
	Primary route – dual/single carriageway
	A road – dual/single carriageway
	B road – dual/single carriageway
	Minor road – dual/single carriageway
	Other minor road – dual/single carriageway
	Road under construction
	Tunnel, covered road
	Rural track, private road or narrow road in urban area
	Gate or obstruction to traffic (restrictions may not apply at all times or to all vehicles)
	Path, bridleway, byway open to all traffic, road used as a public path
	Pedestrianised area
DY7	**Postcode boundaries**
	County and unitary authority boundaries
	Railway, tunnel, railway under construction
	Tramway, tramway under construction
	Miniature railway
Walsall	**Railway station**
	Private railway station
South Shields	**Metro station**
	Tram stop, tram stop under construction
	Bus, coach station

◆	**Ambulance station**
◆	**Coastguard station**
◆	**Fire station**
◆	**Police station**
✚	**Accident and Emergency entrance to hospital**
H	**Hospital**
+	**Place of worship**
i	**Information Centre** (open all year)
P	**Parking**
P&R	**Park and Ride**
PO	**Post Office**
⋏	**Camping site**
	Caravan site
▶	**Golf course**
⊠	**Picnic site**
Prim Sch	**Important buildings, schools, colleges, universities and hospitals**
River Medway	**Water name**
	River, weir, stream
	Canal, lock, tunnel
	Water
	Tidal water
	Woods
	Built up area
Church	**Non-Roman antiquity**
ROMAN FORT	**Roman antiquity**
87 / 58	**Adjoining page indicators**

Acad	**Academy**	Inst	**Institute**	Recn Gd	**Recreation Ground**
Allot Gdns	**Allotments**	Ct	**Law Court**		
Cemy	**Cemetery**	L Ctr	**Leisure Centre**	Resr	**Reservoir**
C Ctr	**Civic Centre**	LC	**Level Crossing**	Ret Pk	**Retail Park**
CH	**Club House**	Liby	**Library**	Sch	**School**
Coll	**College**	Mkt	**Market**	Sh Ctr	**Shopping Centre**
Crem	**Crematorium**	Meml	**Memorial**	TH	**Town Hall/House**
Ent	**Enterprise**	Mon	**Monument**	Trad Est	**Trading Estate**
Ex H	**Exhibition Hall**	Mus	**Museum**	Univ	**University**
Ind Est	**Industrial Estate**	Obsy	**Observatory**	W Twr	**Water Tower**
IRB Sta	**Inshore Rescue Boat Station**	Pal	**Royal Palace**	Wks	**Works**
		PH	**Public House**	YH	**Youth Hostel**

■ The small numbers around the edges of the maps identify the 1 kilometre National Grid lines

■ The dark grey border on the inside edge of some pages indicates that the mapping does not continue onto the adjacent page

The scale of the maps on the pages numbered in blue is 5.52 cm to 1 km • 3½ inches to 1 mile • 1: 18103

0	¼	½	¾	1 mile
0	250 m	500 m	750 m	1 kilometre

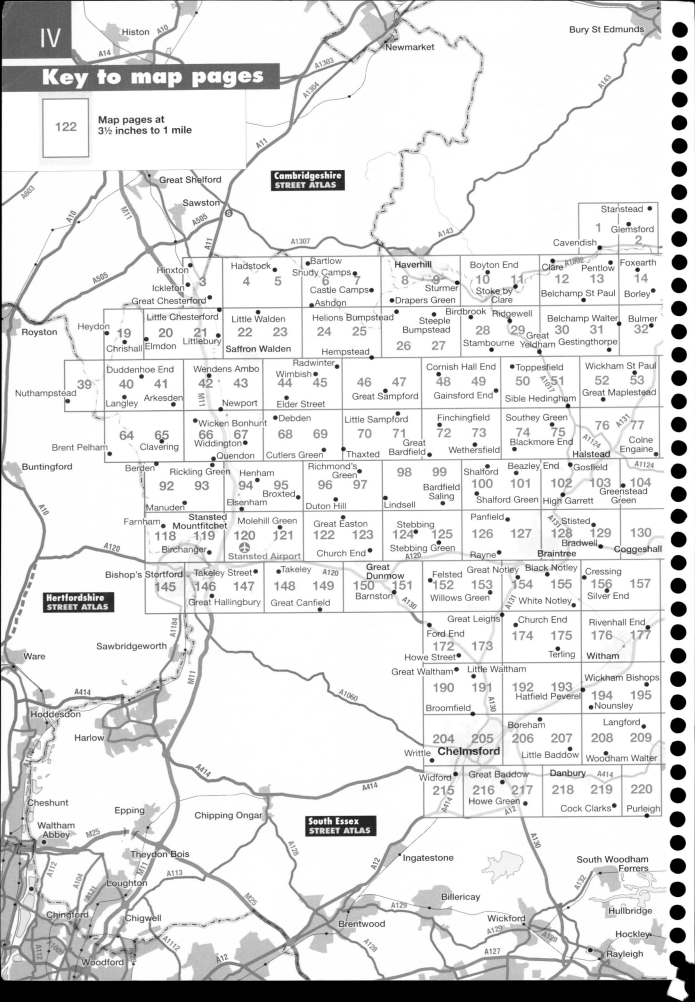

IV

Key to map pages

| 122 | Map pages at 3½ inches to 1 mile |

Cambridgeshire STREET ATLAS

Bury St Edmunds

Histon

Newmarket

Great Shelford

Sawston

Stanstead •

| | | | | 1 | Glemsford | |
| | | | Cavendish | | 2 | |

Hinxton

Ickleton

Great Chesterford

Hadstock		Bartlow		Haverhill		Boyton End		Clare	Pentlow	Foxearth
3	4	5	Shudy Camps		8	9	10	11	12	13	14
			6	7							

Castle Camps

Ashdon

Sturmer

Drapers Green

Stoke by Clare

Belchamp St Paul

Borley

Heydon

Royston

Little Chesterford

| | Little Chesterford | | | Little Walden | | Helions Bumpstead | | Birdbrook | Ridgewell | Belchamp Walter | Bulmer |
| 19 | 20 | 21 | 22 | 23 | 24 | 25 | | 28 | 29 | 30 | 31 | 32 |

Chrishall Elmdon

Littlebury

Saffron Walden

Hempstead

Steeple Bumpstead

26 27

Stambourne

Great Yeldham

Gestingthorpe

Nuthampstead

Radwinter

Wimbish

Cornish Hall End

Toppesfield

Wickham St Paul

| | Duddenhoe End | | Wendens Ambo | | | | | Cornish Hall End | | Toppesfield | | Wickham St Paul | |
| 39 | 40 | 41 | 42 | 43 | 44 | 45 | 46 | 47 | 48 | 49 | 50 | 51 | 52 | 53 |

Langley Arkesden

Newport

Elder Street

Great Sampford

Gainsford End

Sible Hedingham

Great Maplestead

Brent Pelham

Buntingford

Berden

Wicken Bonhunt

Debden

Little Sampford

Finchingfield

Southey Green

| | | | Wicken Bonhunt | | Debden | | Little Sampford | | Finchingfield | | Southey Green | | | |
| 64 | 65 | 66 | 67 | 68 | 69 | 70 | 71 | 72 | 73 | 74 | 75 | 76 | 77 |

Widdington

Quendon

Cutlers Green

Thaxted

Great Bardfield

Wethersfield

Blackmore End

Halstead

Colne Engaine

Rickling Green

Henham

Richmond's Green

Shalford

Beazley End

Gosfield

| | Rickling Green | Henham | | Richmond's Green | | | | Shalford | Beazley End | Gosfield | | |
| 92 | 93 | 94 | 95 | 96 | 97 | 98 | 99 | 100 | 101 | 102 | 103 | 104 |

Manuden

Broxted

Elsenham

Duton Hill

Lindsell

Bardfield Saling

Shalford Green

High Garrett

Greenstead Green

Farnham

Stansted Mountfitchet

Molehill Green

Great Easton

Stebbing

Panfield

Stisted

| | Stansted Mountfitchet | Molehill Green | | Great Easton | | Stebbing | | Panfield | | | Stisted | | |
| 118 | 119 | 120 | 121 | 122 | 123 | 124 | 125 | 126 | 127 | 128 | 129 | 130 |

Birchanger

Stansted Airport

Church End

Stebbing Green

Rayne

Bradwell

Braintree

Coggeshall

Bishop's Stortford

Hertfordshire STREET ATLAS

Takeley Street

Takeley

Great Dunmow

Felsted

Great Notley

Black Notley

Cressing

| 145 | 146 | 147 | 148 | 149 | 150 | 151 | 152 | 153 | 154 | 155 | 156 | 157 |

Great Hallingbury

Great Canfield

Barnston

Willows Green

White Notley

Silver End

Ware

Sawbridgeworth

Great Leighs

Church End

Rivenhall End

									Church End		Rivenhall End	
						Ford End			174	175	176	177
						172	173			Terling	Witham	

Howe Street

Great Waltham

Little Waltham

Wickham Bishops

| | | | | | Great Waltham | Little Waltham | | | | | Wickham Bishops | |
| | | | | | 190 | 191 | 192 | 193 | | | 194 | 195 |

Hoddesdon

Harlow

Broomfield

Hatfield Peverel

Nounsley

Boreham

Langford

| | | | | | | | Boreham | | | Langford | |
| | | | | | 204 | 205 | 206 | 207 | 208 | 209 |

Writtle

Chelmsford

Little Baddow

Woodham Walter

Cheshunt

Epping

Widford

Great Baddow

Danbury

| | | | | Widford | Great Baddow | | Danbury | | |
| | | | | 215 | 216 | 217 | 218 | 219 | 220 |

Howe Green

Cock Clarks

Purleigh

Waltham Abbey

Chipping Ongar

South Essex STREET ATLAS

Theydon Bois

Ingatestone

South Woodham Ferrers

Loughton

Billericay

Chingford

Chigwell

Brentwood

Wickford

Hullbridge

Woodford

Hockley

Rayleigh

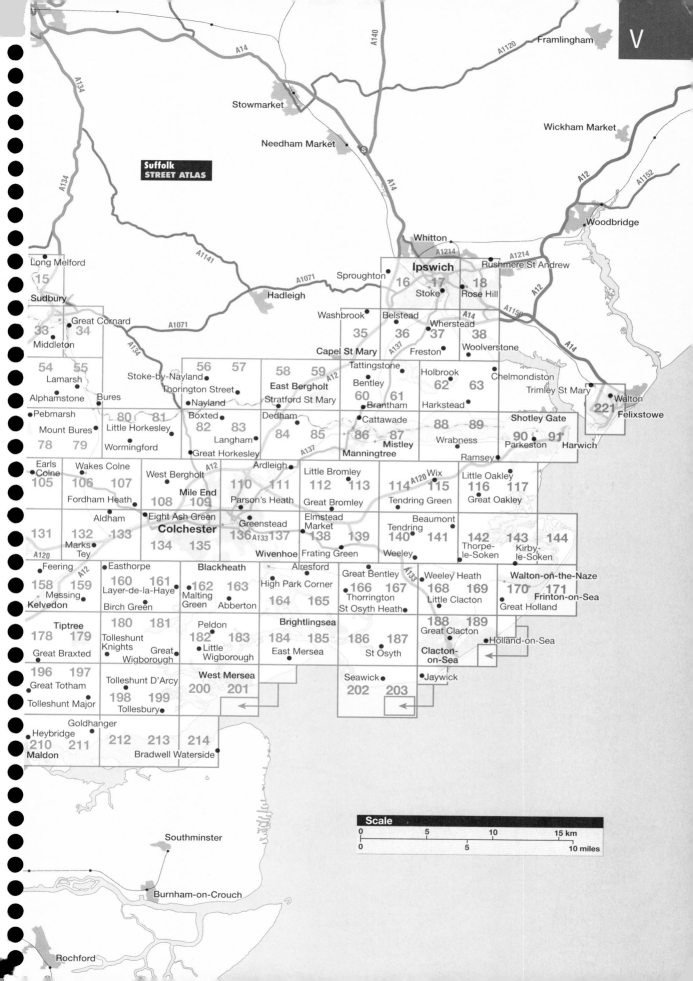

Suffolk
STREET ATLAS

Framlingham

Wickham Market

Woodbridge

Stowmarket

Needham Market

Whitton

Ipswich

Rushmere St Andrew

Sproughton

16   17   18
Stoke   Rose Hill

Hadleigh

Washbrook   Belstead   Wherstead

Long Melford
15

35   36   37   38

Sudbury

Capel St Mary   Freston   Woolverstone

Great Cornard

33   34

Middleton

Tattingstone   Holbrook

54   55   56   57   58   59   60   61   62   63

Lamarsh   Stoke-by-Nayland   East Bergholt   Bentley   Chelmondiston

Alphamstone   Bures   Thorington Street   Stratford St Mary   Trimley St Mary

Nayland   Brantham   Walton

Pebmarsh   Boxted   Dedham   Harkstead   221   Felixstowe

Mount Bures   80   81   82   83   84   85   86   87   88   89   90   91

78   79   Little Horkesley   Langham   Cattawade   Shotley Gate

Wormingford   Great Horkesley   Mistley   Wrabness   Parkeston   Harwich

Manningtree   Ramsey

Earls
Colne   Wakes Colne   West Bergholt   Ardleigh   Little Bromley   Wix   Little Oakley

105   106   107   108   109   110   111   112   113   114   115   116   117

Fordham Heath   Mile End   Parson's Heath   Great Bromley   Tendring Green   Great Oakley

Aldham   Eight Ash Green   Greenstead   Elmstead   Beaumont

Market   Tendring

131   132   133   134   135   136   137   138   139   140   141   142   143   144

Marks
Tey   Colchester   Wivenhoe   Frating Green   Weeley   Thorpe-
le-Soken   Kirby-
le-Soken

Feering   Eastthorpe   Blackheath   Alresford   Great Bentley   Weeley Heath   Walton-on-the-Naze

158   159   160   161   162   163   High Park Corner   166   167   168   169   170   171

Messing   Layer-de-la-Haye   Malting   Abberton   164   165   Thorrington   Little Clacton   Frinton-on-Sea

Kelvedon   Birch Green   Green   St Osyth Heath   Great Holland

Tiptree   180   181   Peldon   Brightlingsea   188   189

178   179   Tolleshunt   182   183   184   185   186   187   Great Clacton   Holland-on-Sea

Knights   Great   Little   East Mersea   St Osyth   Clacton-
on-Sea

Great Braxted   Wigborough   Wigborough

196   197   Tolleshunt D'Arcy   West Mersea   Seawick   Jaywick

Great Totham   198   199   200   201   202   203

Tolleshunt Major   Tollesbury

Goldhanger

Heybridge   210   211   212   213   214

Maldon   Bradwell Waterside

Southminster

Scale
0   5   10   15 km
0   5   10 miles

Burnham-on-Crouch

Rochford

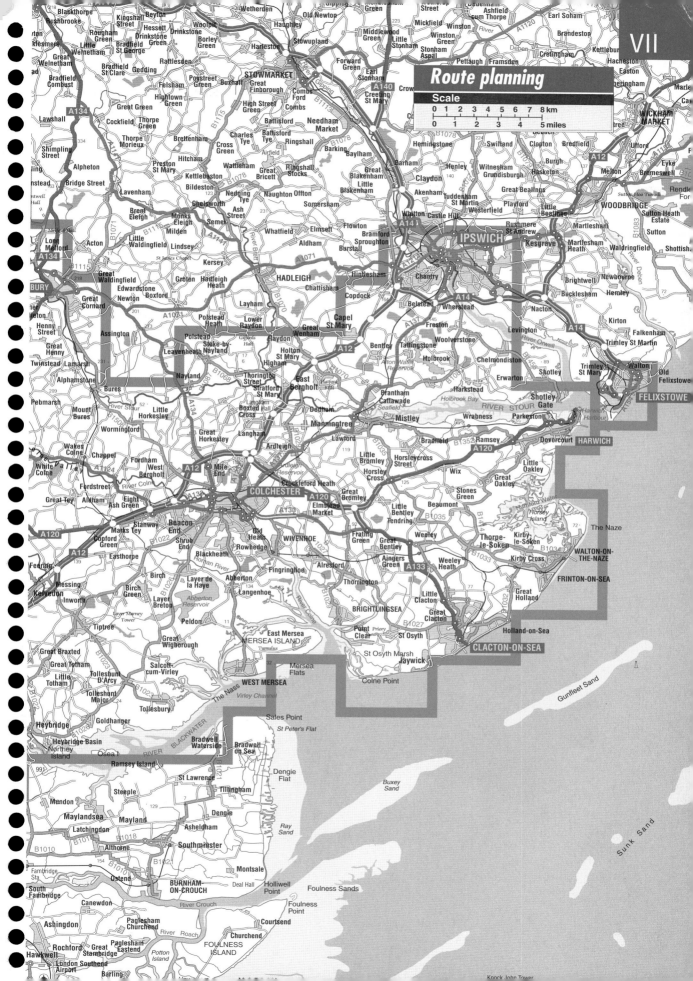

Route planning

Scale

0 1 2 3 4 5 6 7 8 km
0 1 2 3 4 5 miles

Major administrative and Postcode boundaries

Scale
0 5 10 15 km
0 5 10 miles

County and unitary authority boundaries
District boundaries
Postcode boundaries
Area covered by this atlas

Cambridgeshire
Suffolk
Hertfordshire
Essex
Kent
London
Medway

Felixstowe
IP11
Harwich
Walton-on-the-Naze
Frinton-on-Sea
Clacton-on-Sea
CO14
CO12
CO13
CO15
CO16
Great Oakley
Manningtree
Tendring
Holbrook
Ipswich
IP1 IP4 IP5 IP2 IP3 IP10 IP9 IP7
CO11
CO7
Wivenhoe
Ardleigh
East Bergholt
Brightlingsea
St Osyth
West Mersea
Colchester
CO4 CO1 CO2 CO3 CO5
Layer-de-la-Haye
Tiptree
Bures
CO6
CO8
Earls Colne
Coggeshall
Witham
CM8
CM77
Tollesbury
CM9
Tillingham
Maldon
CMO
Southminster
Burnham-on-Crouch
Glemsford
Sudbury
Haverhill
Clare
Belchamp St Paul
CO10
Castle Hedingham
Halstead
Braintree
CO9
Great Bardfield
CM7
Steeple Bumpstead
CB9
CB1
Great Sampford
Stebbing
Thaxted
CM6
Great Dunmow
Saffron Walden
CM10
Great Chesterford
Newport
Clavering
CB11
Stansted Mountfitchet
Elsenham
CM24
CM22
CM23
Hatfield Heath
Bishop's Stortford
CM21
Sawbridgeworth
SG12
SG9
SG8
Harlow
CM20 CM19 CM18 CM17
Hatfield Peverel
Great Leighs
Broomfield
CM3
Danbury
Cold Norton
Chelmsford
CM1 CM2
Stock
Billericay
CM12
CM11
East Hanningfield
Wickford
SS11
SS12
Basildon
SS13 SS14 SS15 SS16
Maldon
Canewdon
Rochford
SS4
SS5
SS6
Hayleigh
Great Wakering
SS3
SS2
SS1 SS0 SS9
Southend-on-Sea
Southend-on-Sea
Canvey Island
SS7 SS8
Castle Point
Stanford-le-Hope
SS17
Tilbury
RM18
RM16 RM17 RM15 RM19 RM20
DA1 DA9 DA DA10 DA11 DA12
DA8
DA18 DA17
Brentwood
CM15
CM14
CM13
Ingrave
Upminster
RM14
RM13
RM12 RM10 RM11
Romford
RM1 RM3 RM2
RM7 RM6 RM5 RM4
Barking
RM9
RM8
Chipping Ongar
CM5
CM4
Abridge
Loughton
IG10
IG7
Epping Forest
Epping
CM16
Waltham Abbey
EN9
EN8 EN3
EN11 EN10
Chingford
E4 E18 E17
IG9 IG8 IG6 IG5 IG4 IG2 IG1 IG3 IG11
E11 E7 E12 E6
Brentwood
Utlesford
Braintree
Colchester
Chelmsford
Basildon
Rochford
Maldon

Haverhill
Great Chesterford

TL TM
TM TR
TQ TR
TL TQ

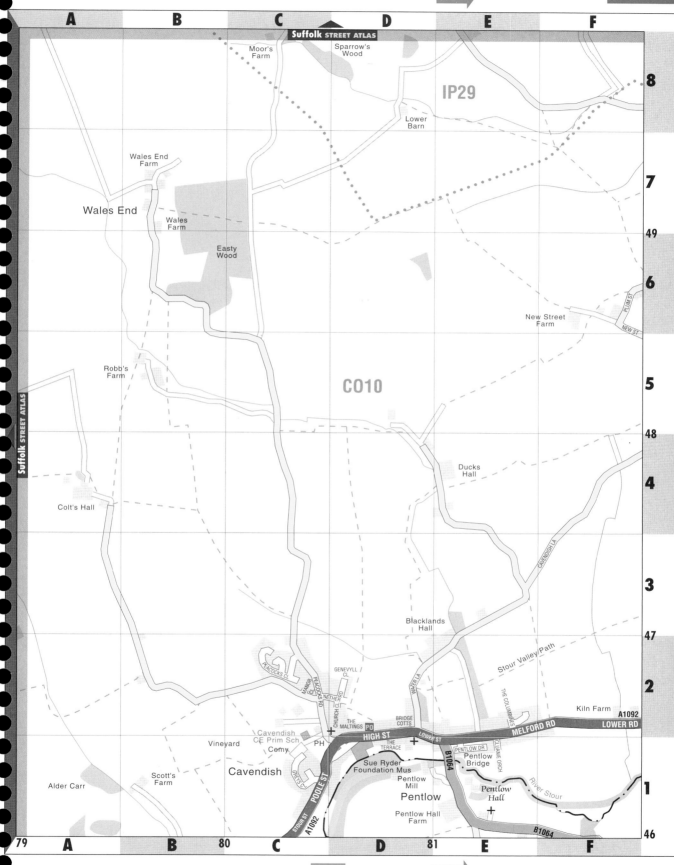

Suffolk STREET ATLAS

IP29

CO10

Moor's Farm
Sparrow's Wood
Lower Barn
Wales End Farm
Wales End
Wales Farm
Easty Wood
New Street Farm
PLUM ST
NEW ST
Robb's Farm
Colt's Hall
Ducks Hall
Blacklands Hall
CAVENDISH LA
Stour Valley Path
Kiln Farm
A1092
PEACOCKS CL
MANOR
PEACOCKS RD
GENEVYLL CL
NETHER
CHURCH CL
WATER LA
THE COLUMBINES
LOWER RD
MELFORD RD
Cavendish CE Prim Sch
THE MALTINGS
PO
BRIDGE COTTS
PENTLOW DR
Vineyard
PH
Cemy
HIGH ST
LOWER ST
THE TERRACE
PENTLOW DR
CLUANIE DRGH
Pentlow Bridge
B1064
Pentlow Hall
River Stour
Alder Carr
Scott's Farm
ST CAR
Sue Ryder Foundation Mus
Pentlow Mill
Cavendish
POOLE ST
Pentlow
Pentlow Hall Farm
STOUR ST
A1092
B1064

13
2
2

79   80   81

A   B   C   D   E   F

8   7   49   6   5   48   4   3   47   2   1   46

Suffolk STREET ATLAS

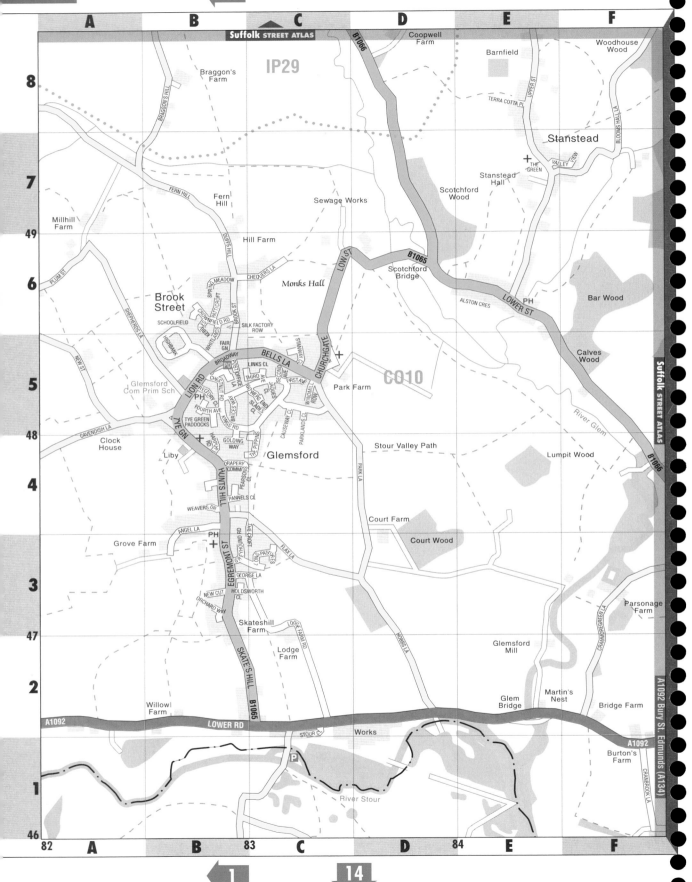

Suffolk STREET ATLAS

IP29

CO10

Suffolk STREET ATLAS

A1092 Bury St. Edmunds (A134)

Coopwell Farm

Braggon's Farm

BRAGGON'S HILL

Woodhouse Wood

Barnfield

TERRA COTTA PL

UPPER ST

BLOOMS HALL LA

Stanstead

Millhill Farm

FERN HILL

Fern Hill

Hill Farm

DUFFS HILL

Sewage Works

Scotchford Wood

Stanstead Hall

THE GREEN

VALLEY VIEW

PLUM ST

SHEPHERDS LA

Brook Street

SPRING MEADOW

CHEQUERS LA

CROMPFIELD RD

Monks Hall

LOW ST

B1065

Scotchford Bridge

ALSTON CRES

LOWER ST

PH

Bar Wood

SCHOOLFIELD

NEW ST

HIGHBANK

WHITLOCKS LA

KING'S RD

FAIR GN

SILK FACTORY ROW

PATTICROFT

STANWAY CT

CHURCHGATE

Calves Wood

River Glem

LION RD

BROADWAY

PO

BELLS LA

LINKS CL

THIRD AVE

SECOND CL

FIRST AVE

JACQUES CL

WINDMILL ROW

Park Farm

Glemsford Com Prim Sch

PH

CHESTNUT LA

REGENT RD

FOURTH AVE

KINGS RD

BRIDGE ST

BOWERS END

STABLES

CAUSEWAY CL

PARKLANDS CL

CAVENDISH LA

Clock House

TYE GREEN PADDOCKS

HARPER'S RD

GOLDING WAY

TYE PIPPINS

TYE GN

Liby

DRAPERY COMMON

PEARSONS CL

Glemsford

Stour Valley Path

Lumpit Wood

HUNTS HILL

PANNELS CL

PARK LA

WEAVERS DR

ANGEL LA

PH

CHURCHYARD RD

THE CROFT

LONG PASTURES

FLAX LA

Court Farm

Grove Farm

EGREMONT ST

GEORGE LA

HOLDSWORTH CL

NEW CUT

ORCHARD WAY

Court Wood

Parsonage Farm

CRANMOREGREEN LA

Skateshill Farm

LODGE FARM RD

Lodge Farm

HOBBS LA

Glemsford Mill

SKATE'S HILL

B1065

Willowl Farm

Glem Bridge

Martin's Nest

Bridge Farm

A1092

LOWER RD

STOUR C

Works

P

River Stour

A1092

Burton's Farm

CRANBROOK LA

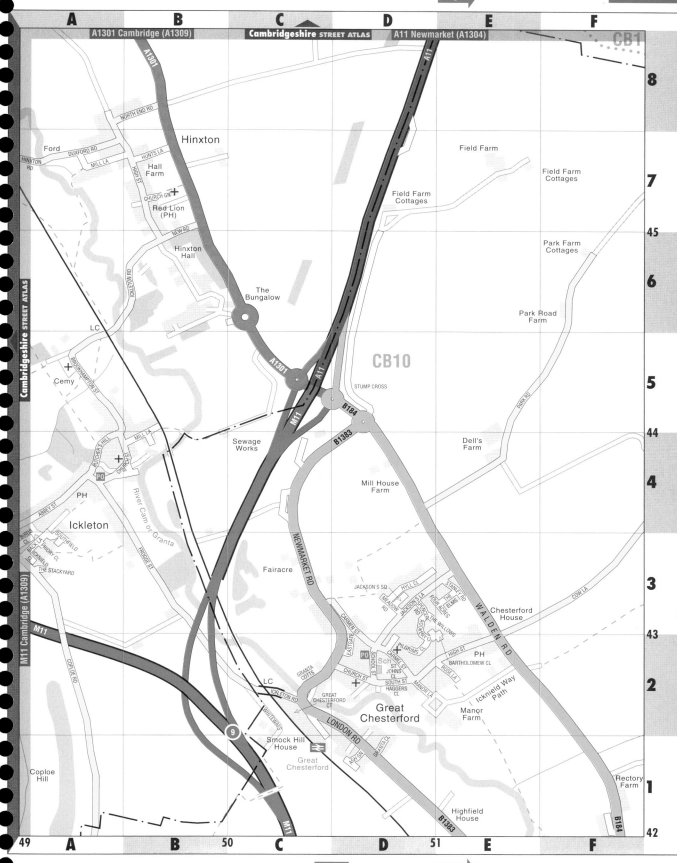

A | B | C | D | E | F

A1301 Cambridge (A1309) **Cambridgeshire** STREET ATLAS A11 Newmarket (A1304) CB1

8

Hinxton

Field Farm

North End Rd

Ford Duxford Rd
Hinxton Rd Mill La Hunts La
Hall Farm High St
Church Gn

Field Farm Cottages

Field Farm Cottages

7

45

Red Lion (PH) New Rd

Hinxton Hall

Ickleton Rd

Park Farm Cottages

The Bungalow

6

LC

Park Road Farm

Broadhampton St

Cemy

A1301

CB10

Park Rd

5

Stump Cross

M11

A11

B184

B1383

Dell's Farm

44

Butcher's Hill Mill La
PO 1st St Church St

Sewage Works

Mill House Farm

4

PH

Abbey St

River Cam or Granta

Ickleton

Birds Cl Priory Cl Southfield
Back La Hornie Cl
The Stackyard Frogge St

Fairacre

Jackson's Sq Hyll Cl

Newmarket Rd

Meadow Rd Jackson Spence The Willows
Stanley Rd Four Acres The Elms Rookery Cl
Carmel St Eastgate PO St Johns Cl
Pilgrims Cl High St PH Bartholomew Cl
Sch Carmel St South St Haggers Cl Rose La Manor La

Cow La

Chesterford House

Walden Rd

3

A1309) Cambridge (A1309

43

M11

Coploe Rd

LC

Ickleton Rd Whiteways

Granta Cotts

Great Chesterford Ct

Church St

Great Chesterford

Icknield Way Path

Manor Farm

2

9

Smock Hill House

London Rd

Granta Cl Ash Gn

Great Chesterford

B1383

Highfield House

Rectory Farm

B184

1

Coploe Hill

42

49 | A | B | 50 | C | D | 51 | E | F

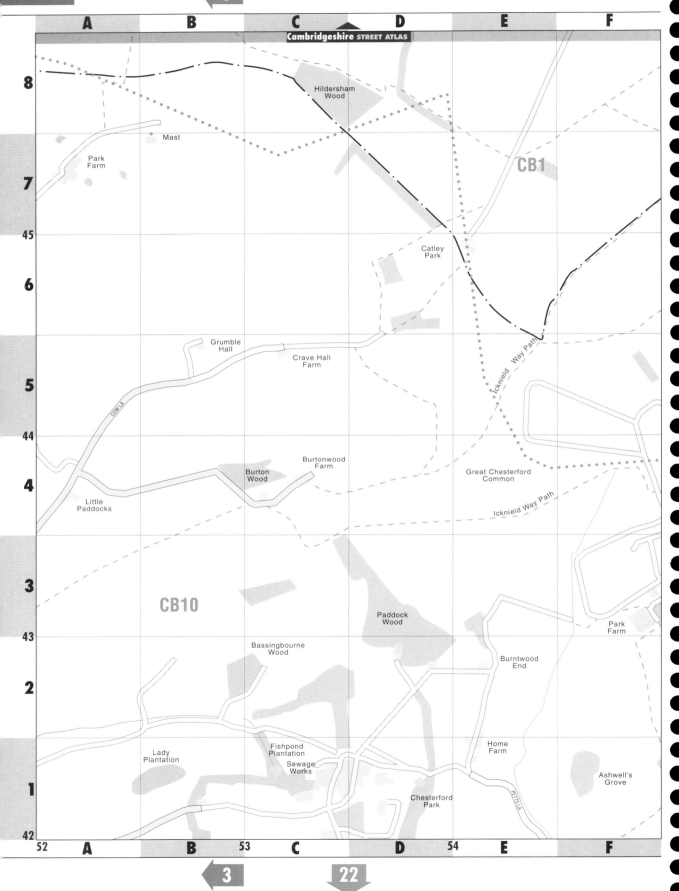

Cambridgeshire STREET ATLAS

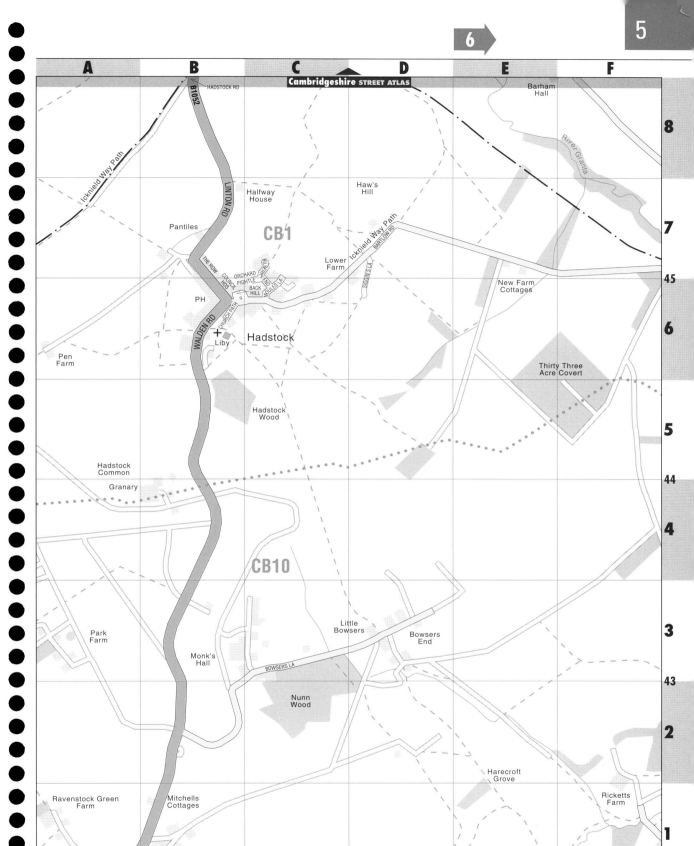

Cambridgeshire STREET ATLAS

Barham Hall

River Granta

Ickneild Way Path

B1052
HADSTOCK RD

Halfway House

Haw's Hill

Pantiles

CB1

LINTON RD

Ickneild Way Path

BARTLOW RD

Lower Farm

New Farm Cottages

THE ROW

ORCHARD
PIGHTLE

COUNCIL
HOS

BACK
HILL

BILLITER
END

YOULES LA

SIGGINS LA

PH

WALDEN RD

CHURCH PATH

+ Liby

Hadstock

Pen Farm

Thirty Three Acre Covert

Hadstock Wood

Hadstock Common

Granary

CB10

Park Farm

Little Bowsers

Bowsers End

Monk's Hall

BOWSERS LA

Nunn Wood

Harecroft Grove

Ricketts Farm

Ravenstock Green Farm

Mitchells Cottages

Mitchells

B1052

Ashton Street Farm

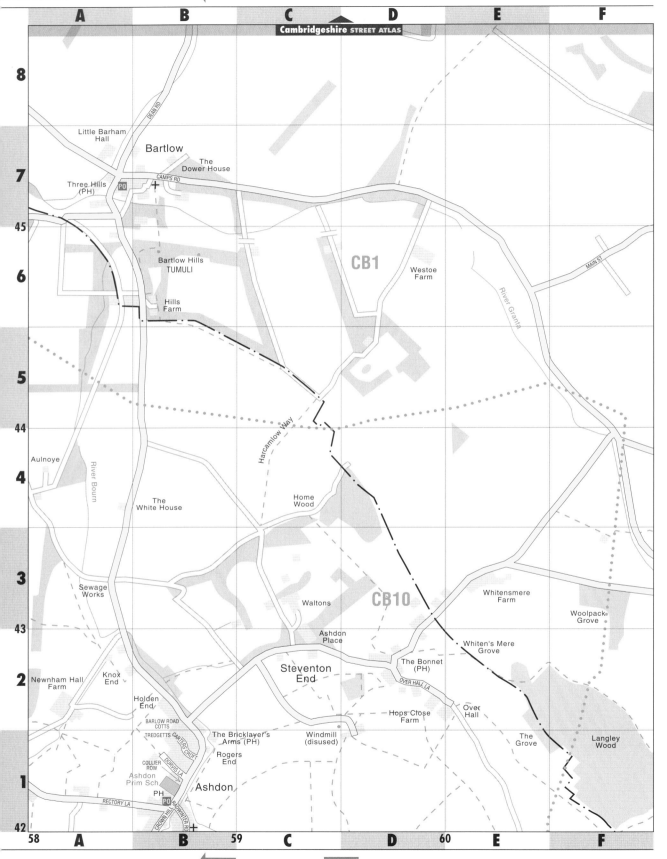

A   B   C   D   E   F

8

Little Barham Hall

Bartlow

The Dower House

7

Three Hills (PH)

PO

CAMPS RD

45

Bartlow Hills TUMULI

6

CB1

Westoe Farm

Hills Farm

River Granta

MAIN ST

5

Harcamlow Way

44

Aulnoye

River Bourn

4

The White House

Home Wood

3

Sewage Works

Waltons

CB10

Whitensmere Farm

Woolpack Grove

43

Ashdon Place

Whiten's Mere Grove

Newnham Hall Farm

Knox End

2

Steventon End

The Bonnet (PH)

OVER HALL LA

Over Hall

Holden End

BARLOW ROAD COTTS

TREDGETTS

CARTERS CROFT

The Bricklayer's Arms (PH)

Rogers End

Windmill (disused)

Hops Close Farm

The Grove

Langley Wood

COLLIER ROW

DORVIS LA

Ashdon Prim Sch

PH

PO

Ashdon

RECTORY LA

CROWN HILL

RADWINTER RD

1

42

58   A   B   59   C   D   60   E   F

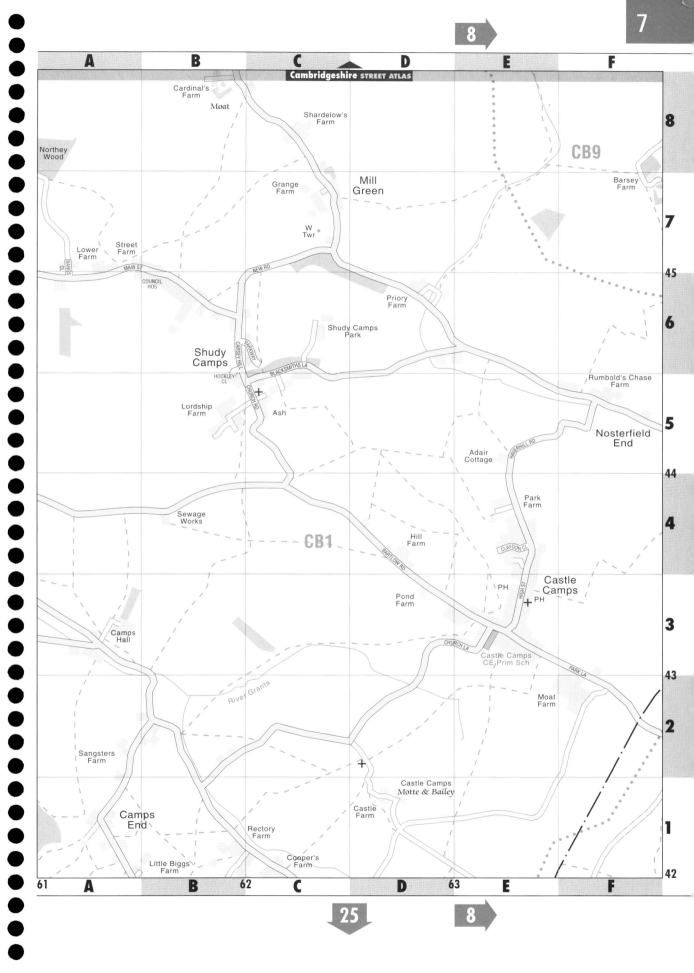

8 →

Cambridgeshire STREET ATLAS

CB9

Northey Wood

Cardinal's Farm

Moat

Shardelow's Farm

Mill Green

Barsey Farm

Grange Farm

W Twr

Lower Farm

Street Farm

MAIN ST

BANKS CL

COUNCIL HOS

NEW RD

Priory Farm

Shudy Camps Park

Shudy Camps

CARSEY HILL

PARKWAY

HOCKLEY CL

BLACKSMITHS LA

CHURCH RD

Rumbold's Chase Farm

Nosterfield End

Lordship Farm

Ash

Adair Cottage

HAVERHILL RD

Park Farm

CB1

Sewage Works

Hill Farm

CLAYDON CL

BARTLOW RD

Pond Farm

PH

HIGH ST

PH

Castle Camps

Camps Hall

CHURCH LA

Castle Camps CE Prim Sch

PARK LA

River Granta

Moat Farm

Sangsters Farm

Castle Camps Motte & Bailey

Camps End

Castle Farm

Rectory Farm

Cooper's Farm

Little Biggs Farm

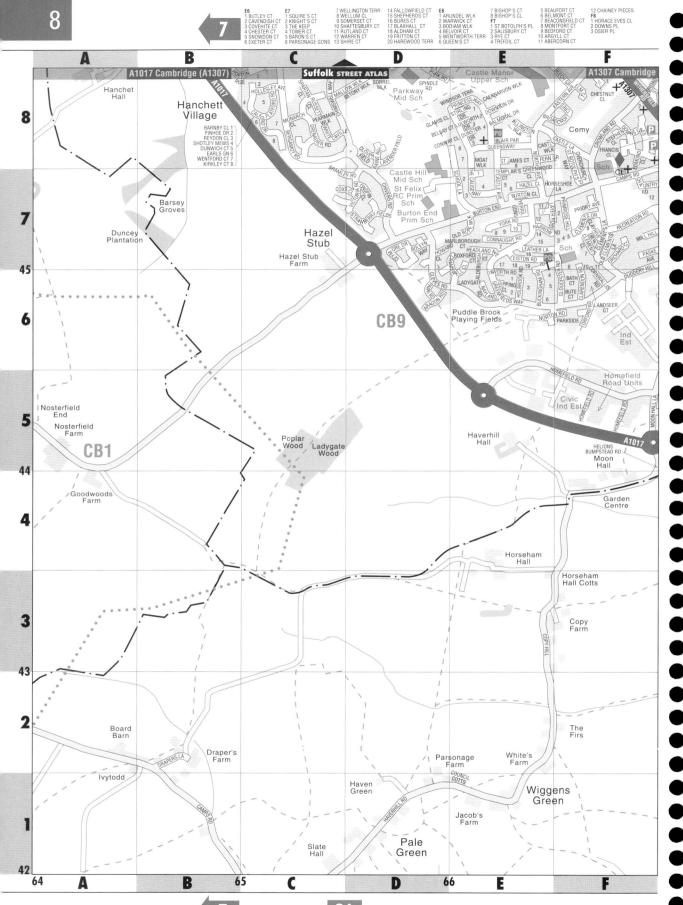

7

E6
1 BUTLEY CT
2 CAVENDISH CT
3 COVEHITE CT
4 CHESTER CT
5 SNOWDON CT
6 EXETER CT

E7
1 SQUIRE'S CT
2 KNIGHT'S CT
3 THE KEEP
4 TOWER CT
5 BARON'S CT
6 PARSONAGE GDNS

7 WELLINGTON TERR
8 WELLUM CL
9 SOMERSET CT
10 SHAFTESBURY CT
11 RUTLAND CT
12 WARREN CT
13 SHIRE CT

14 FALLOWFIELD CT
15 SHEPHERDS CT
16 BURES CT
17 BLAXHALL CT
18 ALDHAM CT
19 FRITTON CT
20 HAREWOOD TERR

E8
1 ARUNDEL WLK
2 WARWICK CT
3 BODIAM WLK
4 BELVOIR CT
5 WENTWORTH TERR
6 QUEEN'S CT

7 BISHOP'S CT
8 BISHOP'S CL
F7
1 ST BOTOLPH'S PL
2 SALISBURY CT
3 RYE CT
4 TREFOIL CT

5 BEAUFORT CT
6 BELMONT CT
7 BEACONSFIELD CT
8 MONTFORT CT
9 BEDFORD CT
10 ARGYLL CT
11 ABERCORN CT

12 CHAINEY PIECES
F8
1 HORACE EVES CL
2 DOWNS PL
3 OSIER PL

A1017 Cambridge (A1307)

Suffolk STREET ATLAS

A1307 Cambridge

Hanchet Hall

Hanchett Village

BARNBY CL 1
PINHOE DR 2
REYDON CL 3
SHOTLEY MEWS 4
DUNWICH CT 5
EARLS GN 6
WENTFORD CT 7
KIRKLEY CT 8

Barsey Groves

Duncey Plantation

Hazel Stub

Hazel Stub Farm

Castle Manor Upper Sch

Parkway Mid Sch

Castle Hill Mid Sch

St Felix RC Prim Sch

Burton End Prim Sch

Cemy

Puddle Brook Playing Fields

CB9

Homefield Road Units

Civic Ind Est

Nosterfield End

Nosterfield Farm

CB1

Poplar Wood

Ladygate Wood

Haverhill Hall

Moon Hall

HELIONS BUMPSTEAD RD

A1017

Goodwoods Farm

Garden Centre

Horseham Hall

Horseham Hall Cotts

Copy Farm

Board Barn

Draper's Farm

The Firs

Ivytodd

DRAPERS LA

White's Farm

Parsonage Farm

Haven Green

COUNCIL COTTS

Wiggens Green

Jacob's Farm

Slate Hall

Pale Green

7 26

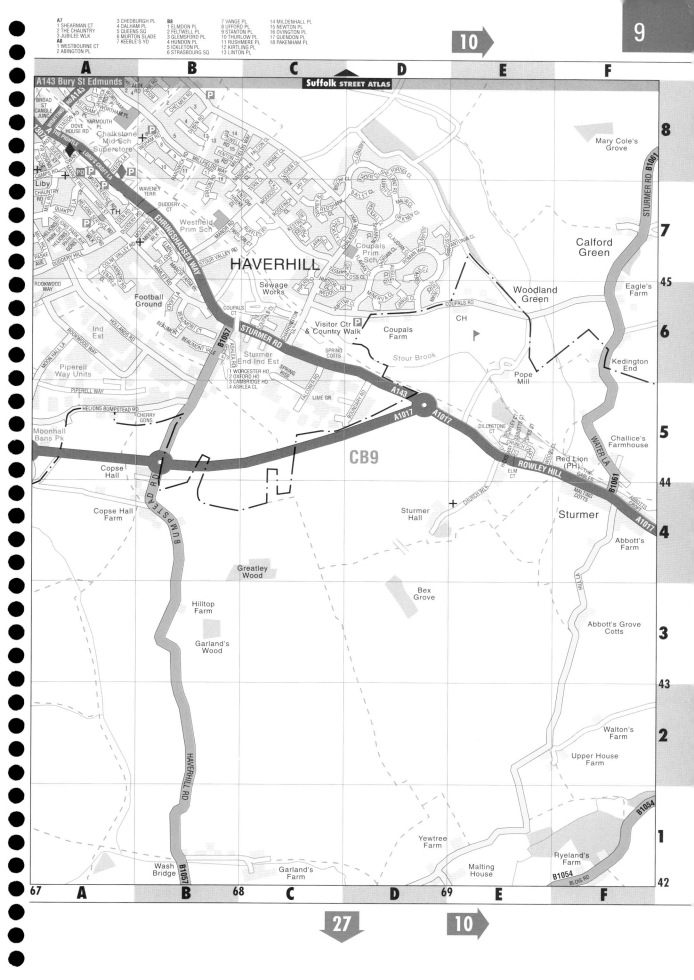

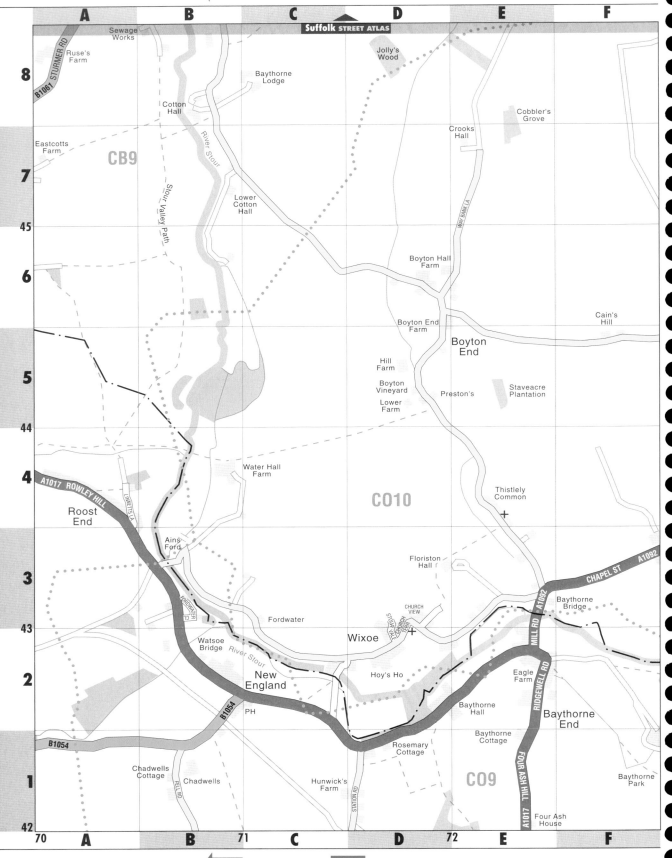

Suffolk STREET ATLAS

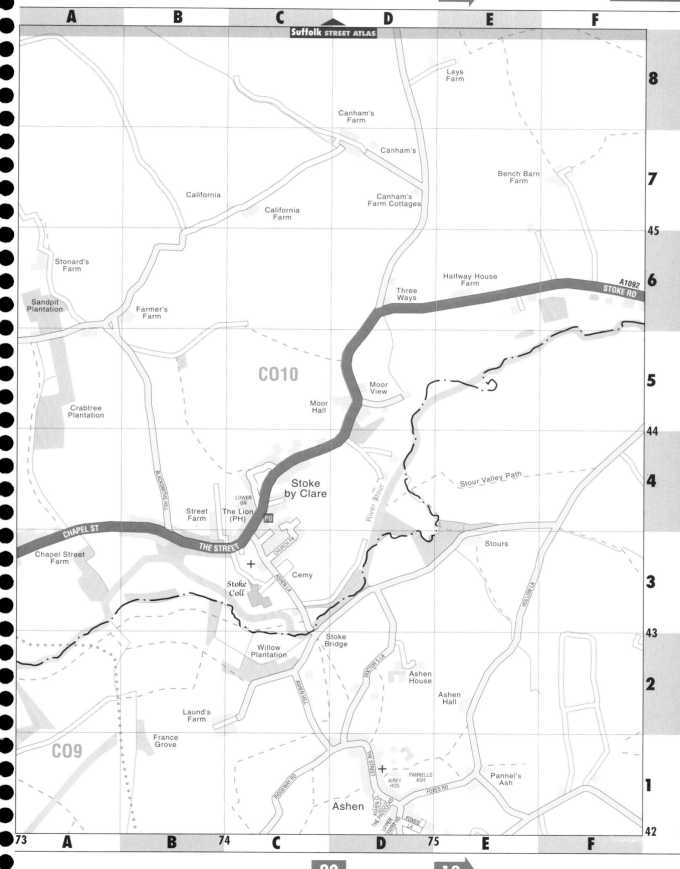

A   B   C   D   E   F

8

7

45

6

5

44

4

3

43

2

1

42

Sheepgate La
Clare Camp
Lower Common
Clarence Rd
Bridewell Ind Est
Upper Common
Clare Com Prim Sch
Common St
Gilbert Rd
Bridewell St
B1063
Callis Ct
Clare Mid Sch
Clare Hill Farm
CAVENDISH RD
A1092
Sewage Works
Clare
Mus
Drury Pl
Gosford Cl
Church St
B1063
Hill Terr
Cemy
Liby
St Peters Ct
Pashlers Alley 1
Bucks La 2
Church La 3
High St
TH
Park View
Riverbank
Highfield
Mill Rd
Bailey La
River Stour
Half Moon Yd
PO
Station Rd
Clare Castle Country Park
The Mill House
Stone Hall
Clifton's Fam Th
Nethergate St
Well La
Market Hill
Malting La
P
P
New Cut
Hickford Hill
Hickford Hill
Lindsells Farm
Westfield
The Grange
Lotus Cl
Stour Vale
Stour Gdn
Priory (remains of)
A1092
STOKE RD
Daneum Holt
CH
Mill Farm
Ashen Rd
Claredown Farm
Mast
Langley Wood

CO10

Claret Hall
Bradleyhill Farm
Long Lane
Butler's Farm
Loveland's Farm
Ovington Hall
Cutbush Farm
Donkey House
The Studio
Baker's Rd
Upper Farm
Ovington
Ovington Grange
Hall
Ashen Rd
Hole Farm
Gage's Rd

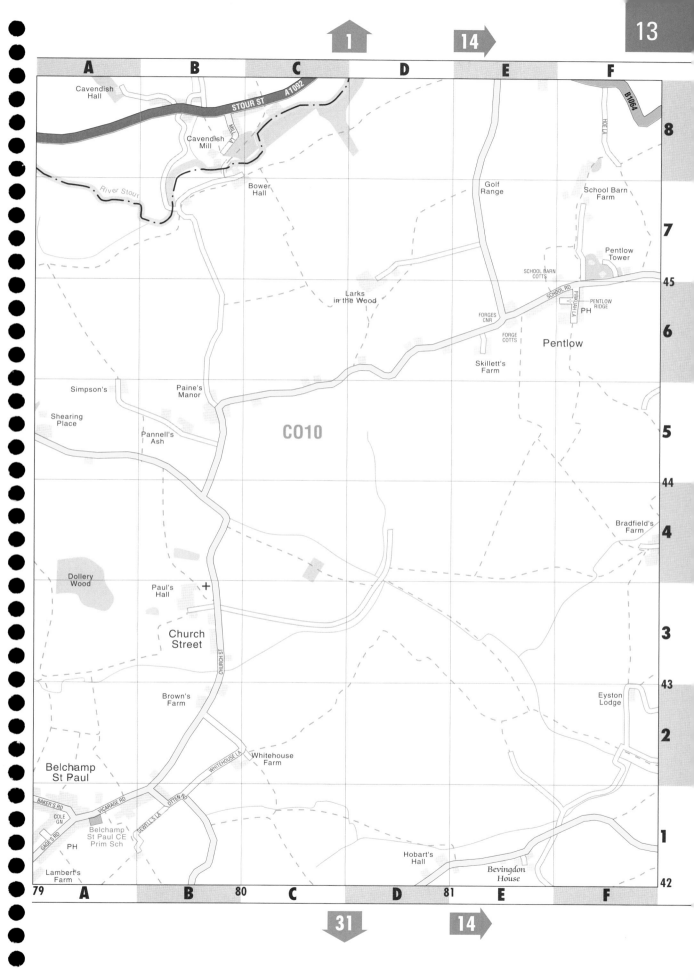

13
2

A   B   C   D   E   F

8

B1064
THE STREET
Pentlow
Street
PENTLOW HILL

7

45

Roper's
Farm
Bunting's
Farm

Constable's
Farm

Weston
Hall

Liston
Gardens

Works

Hartsbuckle
Farm

Park
Farm

Liston
Hall

6

Foxearth
Hall
THE STREET
THE CHASE
Foxearth
SCHOOL ST

Cardinal's
Farm

Huntsman's

CLAPPITS LA

Hawk's
Farm

The
Plantation

5

MILL RD
Mill
Cottage

Bradfield's
Wood

44

CO10

Red
Cottages
B1064

4

Bellybones

Claypit
Hall

Brook
Hall

Temple End

Hubbard's
Farm

3

Borley
Place
Borley
HALL RD

43

Eyston Smyth's
Farm

Purkis
Farm

2

Borley Green

Borleylodge
Farm

Eyston
Hall

1

Bardfield
Bridge

42

82   A   B   83   C   D   84   E   F

13
32

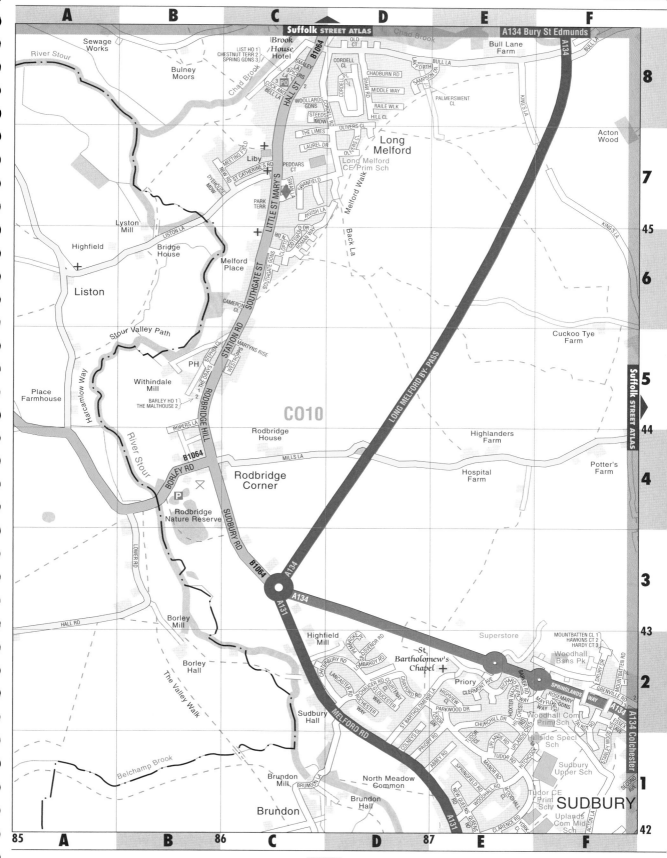

Suffolk STREET ATLAS

A134 Bury St Edmunds

Suffolk STREET ATLAS

A B C D E F

8

7

45

6

5

44

4

3

43

2

1

42

85   86   87

River Stour
Sewage Works
Bulney Moors
Chad Brook
Chad Brook
Brook House Hotel
LIST HO 1
CHESTNUT TERR 2
SPRING GDNS 3
OLD CT
CORDELL CL
CORDELL PL
CHADBURN RD
BULL LA
JAFFORTH
SAMPSON DR
Bull Lane Farm
B1064
HALL ST
SMALEY LA
SPICERS
WOOLLARDS GDNS
STEEDS MDW
CORRELL RD
SHAW RD
MIDDLE WAY
RAILE WLK
HILL CL
PALMERSWENT CL
KING'S LA
Acton Wood
THE LIMES
OLIVERS CL
Long Melford
LAUREL DR
OLIVERS CL
Liby
MEETING FIELD
NEW RD
ST CATHERINE'S RD
LITTLE ST MARY'S
PEDDARS CT
SWANFIELD
Long Melford CE/Prim Sch
Melford Walk
KING'S LA
DYEHOUSE MDW
PARK TERR
DR WAY
RUSH LA
Lyston Mill
LISTON LA
Melford Place
SOUTHGATE ST
HO PL
Back La
Highfield
Bridge House
SOUTHGATE GDNS
Liston
CAMERON CL
STATION RD
Cuckoo Tye Farm
Stour Valley Path
STEPPING
MARTYNS RISE
WESTROPPS
THE BRAYS
Harcamlow Way
Withindale Mill
PH
BARLEY HO 1
THE MALTHOUSE 2
RODBRIDGE HILL
CO10
Highlanders Farm
River Stour
ROPERS LA
Rodbridge House
MILLS LA
LONG MELFORD BY-PASS
Potter's Farm
Place Farmhouse
B1064
BORLEY RD
Rodbridge Corner
Hospital Farm
P
SUDBURY RD
Rodbridge Nature Reserve
B1064
A134
LOWER RD
A131
A134
Superstore
MOUNTBATTEN CL 1
HAWKINS CT 2
HARDY CT 3
HALL RD
Borley Mill
Highfield Mill
CANTERBURY RD
GROSVENOR RD
LOMBARDY RD
St Bartholomew's Chapel
Woodhall Bsns Pk
MOUNTBATTEN RD
DRURY RD
Borley Hall
LANCASTER RD
ROCHESTER RD
CHAUCER RD
CRAWFORD
COURTENAY
GLOUCESTER
ST BARTHOLOMEWS LA
Priory
HIGHVIEW
RICHARD BURN WAY
BARKER RD
CLERMONT AVE
SPRINGLANDS WAY
ROSEMARY WAY
MAYFLO GDNS
GRENVILLE RD
A134
The valley Walk
MELFORD RD
WAY
PARKWOOD DR
HOXTEN
HILLCREST
CHURCHILL DR
UPLANDS RD
UPLANDS CRES
HITCHCOCK
TALBOT
A134 Colchester
STANLEY WOOD AVE
Sudbury Hall
COLING CL
PRIORY RD
ABBEY RD
MANOR RD
TUDOR RD
Hillside Specl Sch
Sudbury Upper Sch
Tudor CE Prim Sch
SECOND AVE
Belchamp Brook
Brundon Mill
BRUNDON LA
North Meadow Common
NEW QUEENS RD
QUEENS RD
SPRINGFIELD RD
WOODHALL RD
WOODHALL RD
CLARENCE RD
YORK
SUDBURY
ACTON LA
Uplands Com Mid Sch
Brundon
Brundon Hall
A131

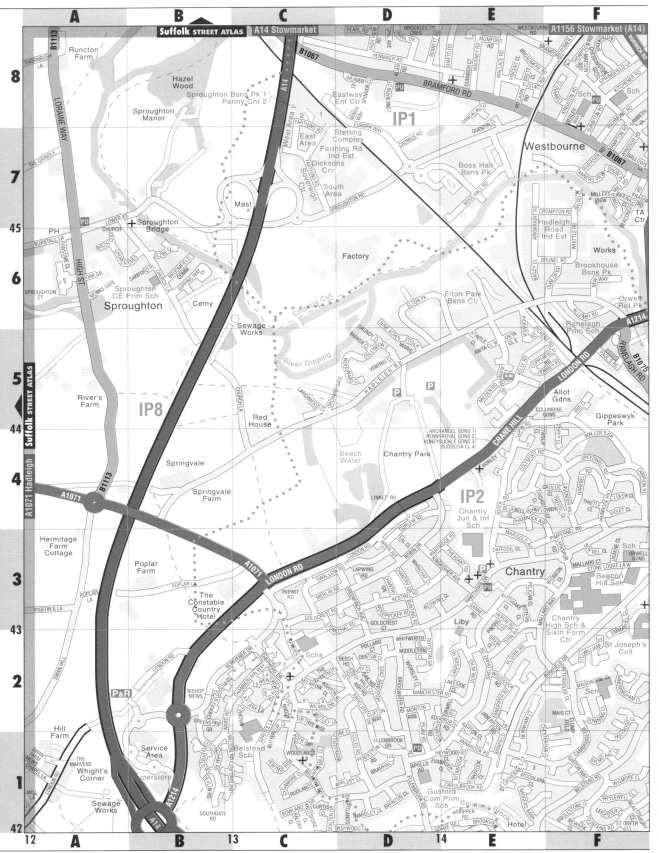

36

C2
1 BRAMBLEWOOD
2 LABURNUM CL
3 BROAD MEADOW
4 INNES END
5 PEACOCK CL
6 HALFORD CT
7 MERRION CL
8 MATLOCK CL
9 MOTTRAM CL

E1
1 DAWNBROOK CL
2 HILDABROOK CL
3 VINNICOMBE CT

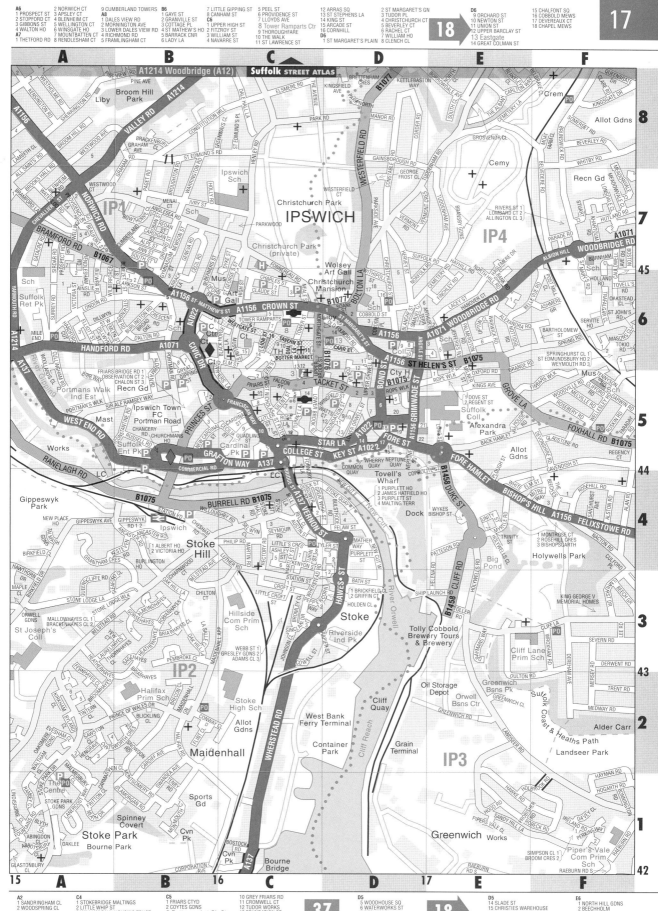

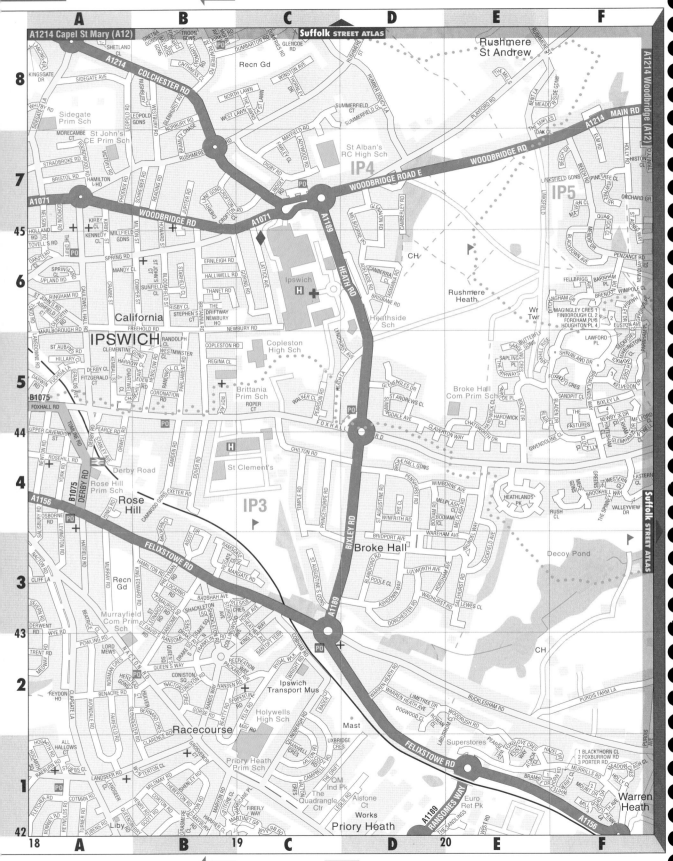

Suffolk STREET ATLAS

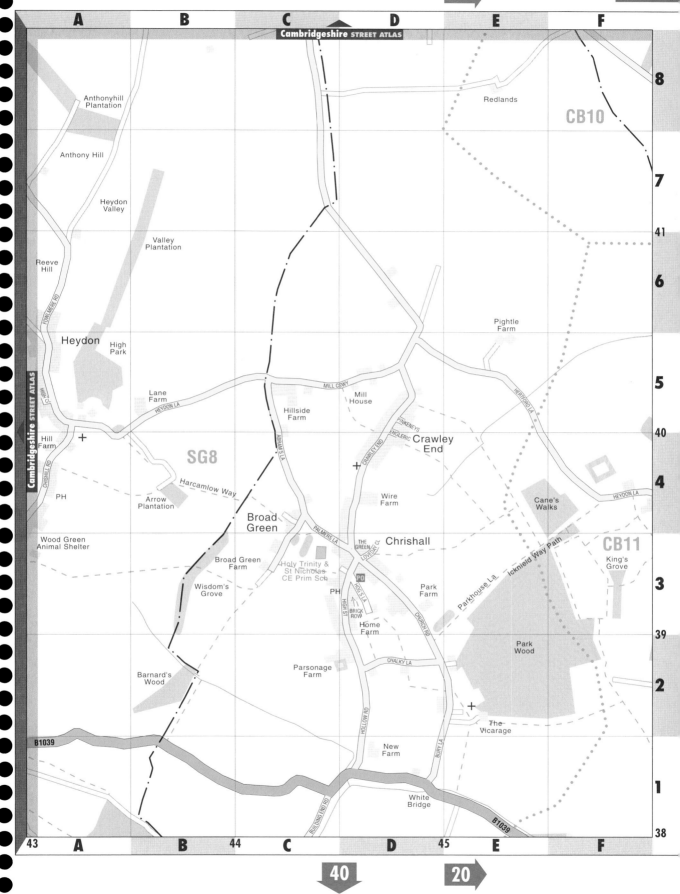

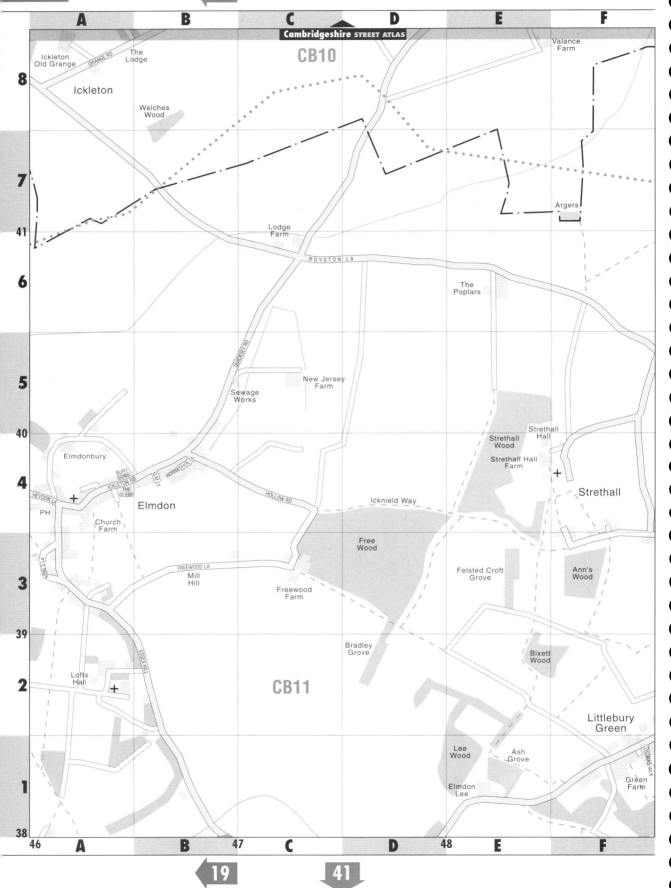

19

A   B   C   D   E   F

Cambridgeshire STREET ATLAS

CB10

Valance Farm

Ickleton Old Grange

GRANGE RD

The Lodge

8

Ickleton

Welches Wood

Argers

7

41

Lodge Farm

ROYSTON LA

6

The Poplars

QUICKSET RD

5

New Jersey Farm

Sewage Works

40

Strethall Wood

Strethall Hall

Strethall Hall Farm

4

Elmdonbury

BURY GDNS

ICKLETON RD

ELM CT

HORSESHOE CL

THE GLEBE

HEYDON LA

Elmdon

HOLLOW RD

Icknield Way

Strethall

PH

Church Farm

Free Wood

Felsted Croft Grove

Ann's Wood

FREEWOOD LA

Mill Hill

3

Freewood Farm

ESSEX HILL

39

Bradley Grove

Bixett Wood

Lofts Hall

2

CB11

Littlebury Green

Lee Wood

Ash Grove

THOMAS WLK

1

Elmdon Lee

Green Farm

38

46   A   B   47   C   D   48   E   F

19

41

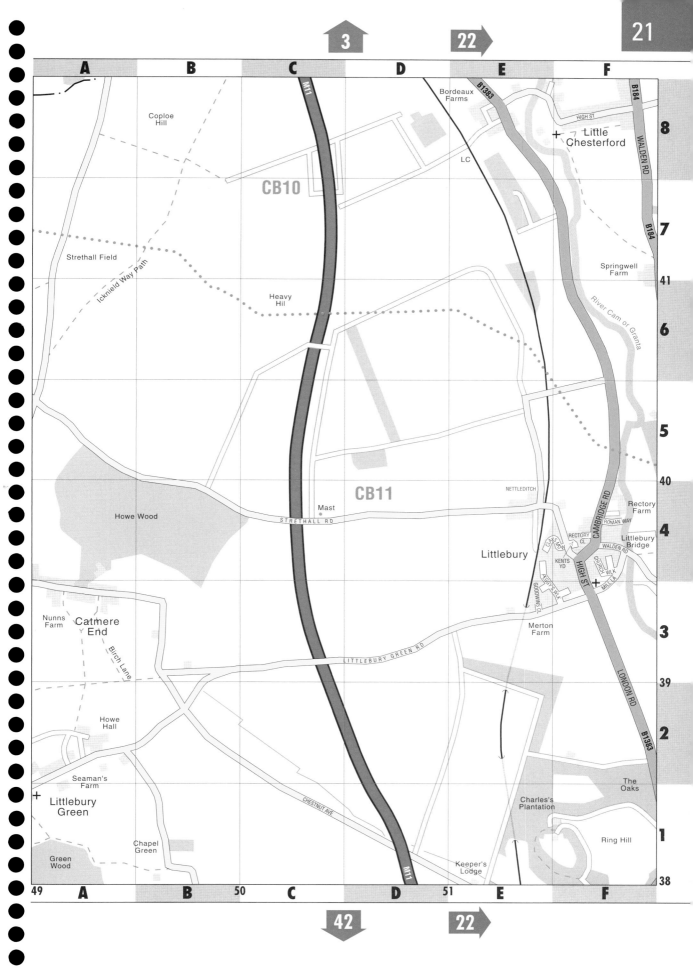

A B C D E F

8

Emanuel Cott

Emanuel Wood

Petlands

Little Walden

PETTIS LA

PH

B1052

7

Four Acre Grove

THE SLADE

The Slade

The Hall Farm

Joseph Farm

Bell Cotts

41

Springwell

Stone Bridge

B184

CB10

Stone Bridge Farm

6

Rowley Hill Farm

Protection Plantation

High Balks

Grimsditch Wood

LITTLE WALDEN RD

Westley wood

Mead Hall

5

Westley Farm

Byrds Farm

WESTLEY LA

SPRINGWELL RD

40

John's Acre

Brown's Plantation

The Slade

4

Northend Farm

NORTHEND

LITTLE WALDEN RD

Byrd's Farm La

Northend Lodge

Northend

SAFFRON WALDEN

Harcamlow Way

Spring Wood

The Vineyard

WINDMILL HILL

Catons La

RODES

THE GREEN

CROCUS FLDS

LIMEKILNS

3

39

Obelisk

CB11

River Cam or Granta

Duck Street

Home Farm

JOHNSONS YD 1
MARKET PL 2
MARKET ST 3
ROSE & CROWN WLK 4
MERCERS ROW 5
MARKET WLK 6
BUTCHERS ROW 7
MARKET ROW 8
CENTRAL ARC 9.

St Mary's CE Prim Sch

USTERDALE RD

BICKENHOE RD

HOWARD RD

THORNCROFT CL

WHITESHOT WAY

HARVEY WAY

1 DODDENHILL CL
2 CORNWALLIS PL
3 WYNYARD RD
4 COLYN PL

Saffron Bsns Ctr

2

CH

BELLINGHAM BLDGS LOWER SQ

Castle (rems of)

The Common

MABERLY

FITZPIERS CT

MARKING'S FIELD

Sch

ELIZABETH

B1383

Tea Bridge

Sir William's Plantation

Sewage Works

Mus

YH

WALDEN

Liby

EASTACRE 1
HATHERLEY CT 2

SHEPHERDS WAY

ROCHESTER

Nursery

CHURCH PATH 10
MYDOYLTON PL 11
EDWARD BAWDEN CT 12
KING EDWARD IV'S ALMHOUSES 13
THE MALTINGS 14
BARNARDS YD 15
BARLEY CT 16
SAFFRON CT 17

PRIME'S

Place Pond

HANOVER PL

CASTLE ST

CHURCH ST

EMSON

COMMON HILL

B1053

RADWINTER RD

B1053

CATES CNR

EAST ST

PO

HORN BOOK

1

Stable Bridge

LONDON RD

SPRING HILL

Audley End

Audley Park

PARKSIDE

ABBEY LA

HIGH ST

B184

B184

AUDLEY RD

THAXTED RD

TANNERY

RA Butler Jun & Inf Schs

Cemy

VICTORIA GDNS

B184

38

52 A 53 B C 53 D 54 E F

E1
1 NEWCROFT
2 ALPHA PL
3 FARMADINE CT
4 JOHN DANE PLAYER CT
5 FARMADINE HO

F2
1 BRADLEY MEWS
2 NIGHTINGALE MEWS
3 HAMILTON MEWS
4 HADLEIGH CT
5 ST JAMES CT
6 LAVENDER FIELD
7 THE SPIKE
8 CAVENDISH CT

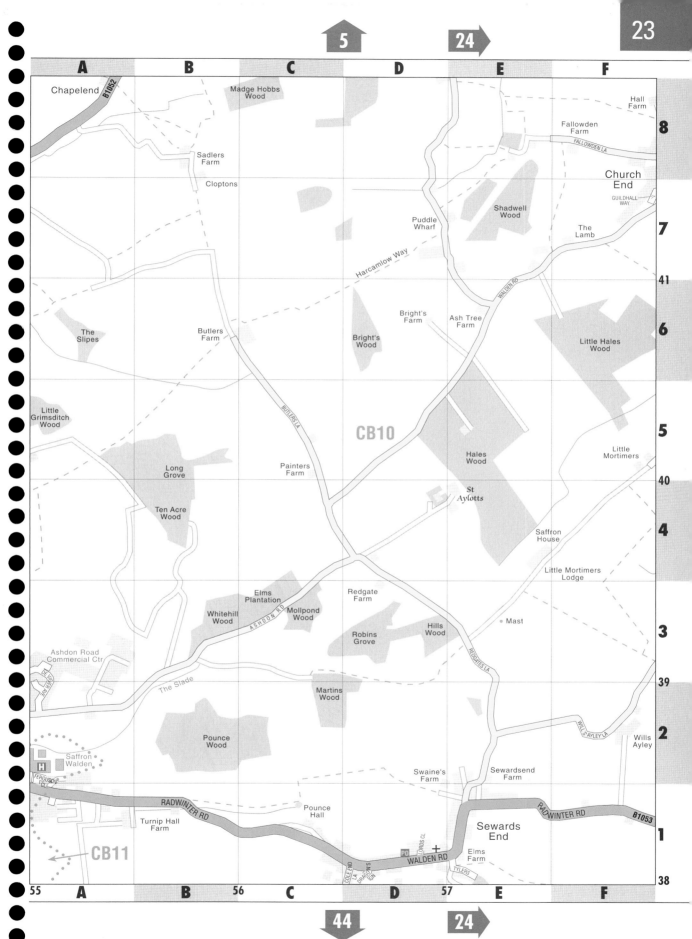

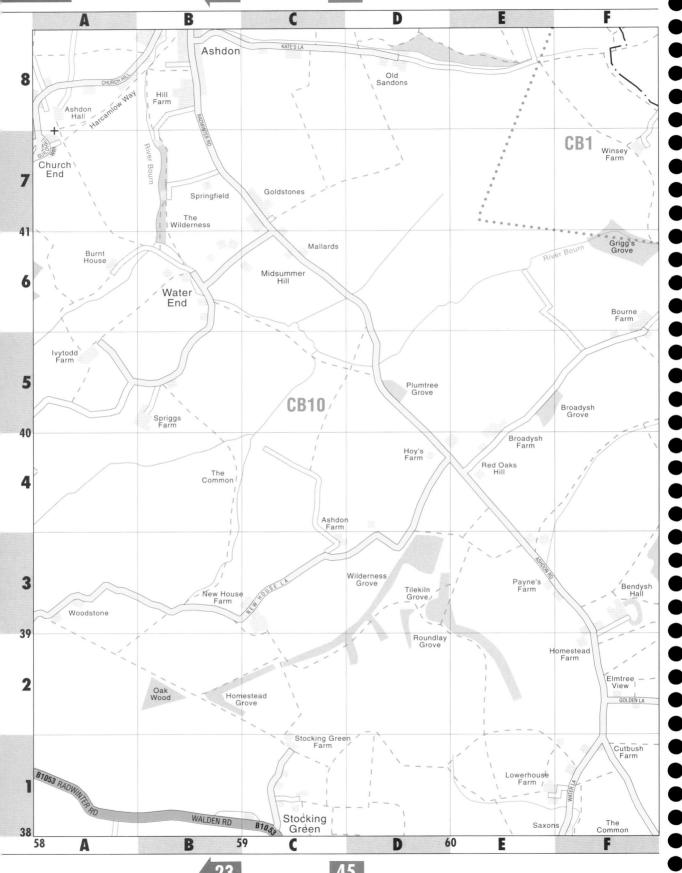

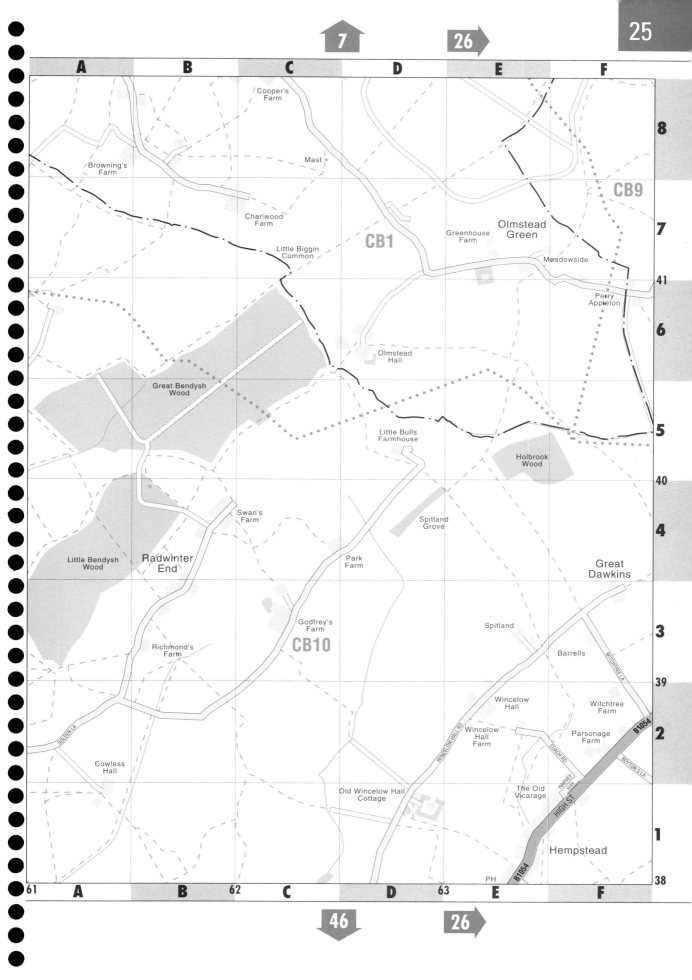

7

26

A   B   C   D   E   F

8

CB9

Cooper's Farm

Mast

Browning's Farm

Charlwood Farm

CB1

Greenhouse Farm

Olmstead Green

7

Little Biggin Common

Meadowside

41

Perry Appleton

6

Great Bendysh Wood

Olmstead Hall

Little Bulls Farmhouse

Holbrook Wood

5

40

Swan's Farm

Spitland Grove

4

Little Bendysh Wood

Radwinter End

Park Farm

Great Dawkins

Spitland

3

Richmond's Farm

Godfrey's Farm

CB10

Barrells

Witchtree Farm

WITCHTREE LA

39

Wincelow Hall

B1054

2

GOLDEN LA

Wincelow Hall Farm

Parsonage Farm

WINCELOW HALL RD

COACH RD

BOYTON'S LA

Cowless Hall

The Old Vicarage

HARVEY WAY

HIGH ST

Old Wincelow Hall Cottage

1

Hempstead

PH

B1054

38

61   A   B   62   C   D   63   E   F

46

26

25
8

A   B   C   D   E   F

8

Sage's End

Rolls Farm

CAMPS RD

CHURCH RISE

MILL RD

HAVERHILL RD

CHURCH HILL

Helions Bumpstead

SAGES END RD

PH

7

Helions

Oakfields

Bumpstead Hall

Bumpstead Hall Cottages

STEEPLE BUMPSTEAD RD

CB9

WATER LA

New House

41

6

Boblow Hill Cottages

Balance Wood

Boblow

Smith's Green Farm

5

B1054

40

Bull's Bridge Farm

Smith's Green

4

Little Bulls Farm

Fircones

Hillside Farm

3

Ruses

Hempstead Hall

Thurgood House Farm

CB10

39

The Limes

B1054

2

Hempstead Wood

Hophouse Farm

Lakehouse Grove

CM7

1

Boyton's Farm

BOYTON S LA

Homeleigh Poultry Farm

Mast

38

Lakehouse Farm

64 A   B 65 C   D 66 E   F

25
47

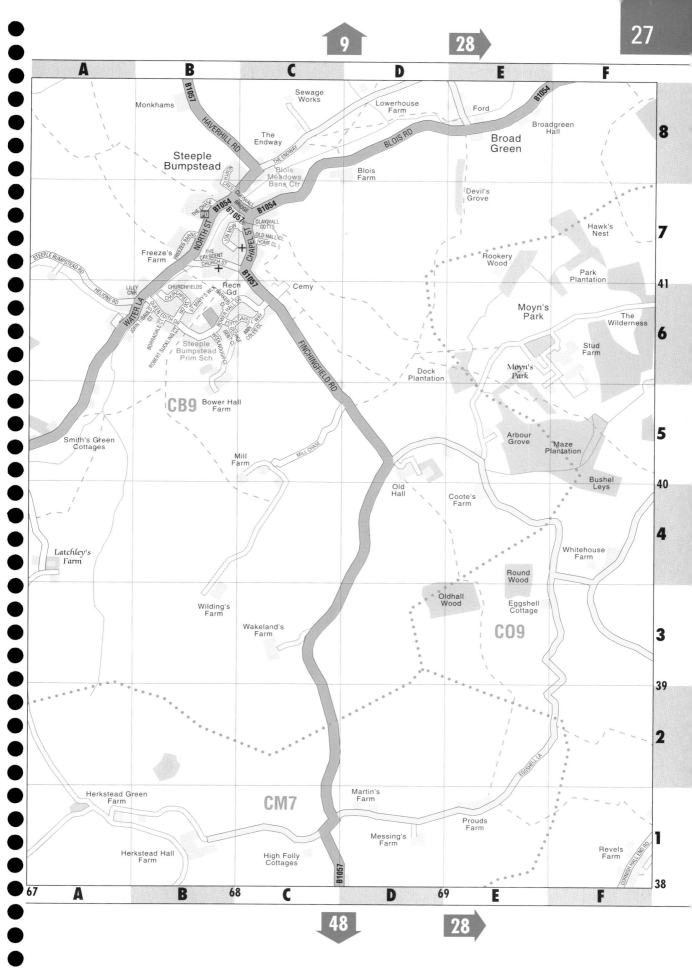

A B C D E F

8

CB9

Moyn's
Wood

Birdbrook

7

Birdbrook
Hall

Churchfield
Grove

The Plough
(PH)

41

MOAT
FARM

FELL RD

THE STREET

DAW ST

STATION RD

MOAT RD

A1017

FOUR ASH HILL

THE CAUSEWAY

A1017

Causeway
Hall

Whitley
House

6

Paddock
Belt

SCHOOLFIELD

The
Rectory

Wash
Bridge

Carter's
Bridge

Wash
Farm

Stubland's
Farm

Wash
Farm

Woodview

Three Chimneys
Wood

5

Highfield
Clump

Finkle
Green

Bailey Hill
Farm

Bailey
Hill

CO9

Three Chimneys
Farm

40

Essex Hall

STAMBOURNE RD

Pettyfield La

4

Park
Wood

Wesley End

WESLEY END RD

3

Warren
Farm

BIRDBROOK RD

Little Collin's
Farm

MILL RD

Hill
Farm

Stambourne

39

PO

CHAPEL END WAY

Stambourne
Hall

CHURCH RD

2

Slough
Farm

Chapelend
Way

Oldhouse
Farm

CORNISH HALL END RD

Stambourne
Grange

DYERS RD

Greenfield's
Farm

Mill
Farm

1

Moat Hall
Farm

Stambourne
Green

Dyer's
End

Great Tagley
Farm

FINCHINGFIELD RD

Elm's
Farm

38

70 A B 71 C D 72 E F

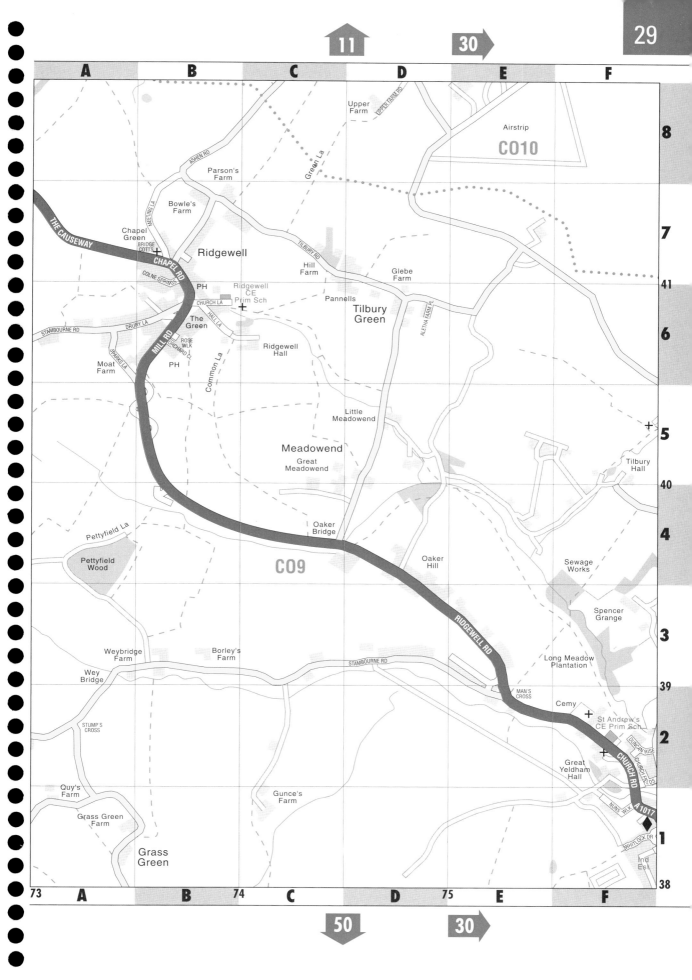

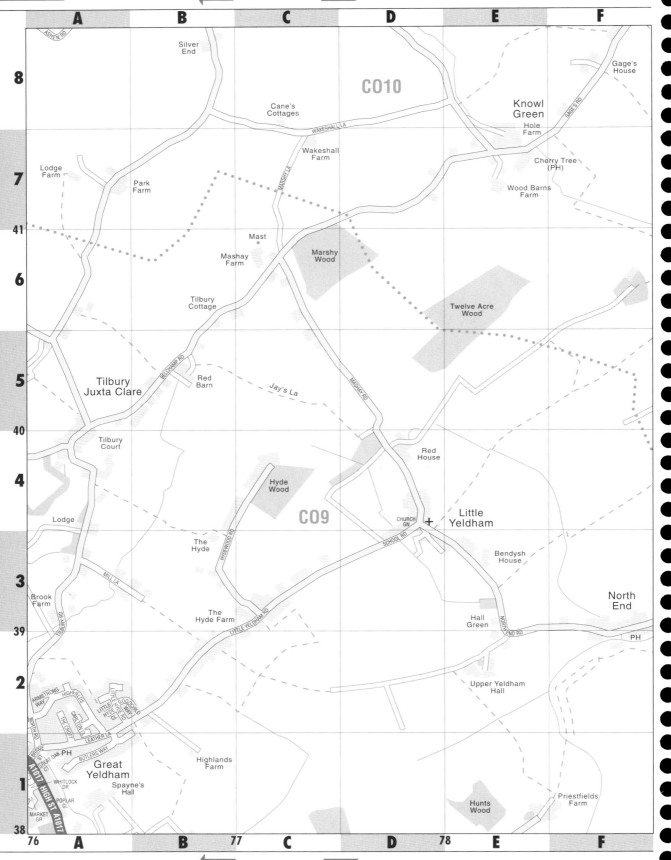

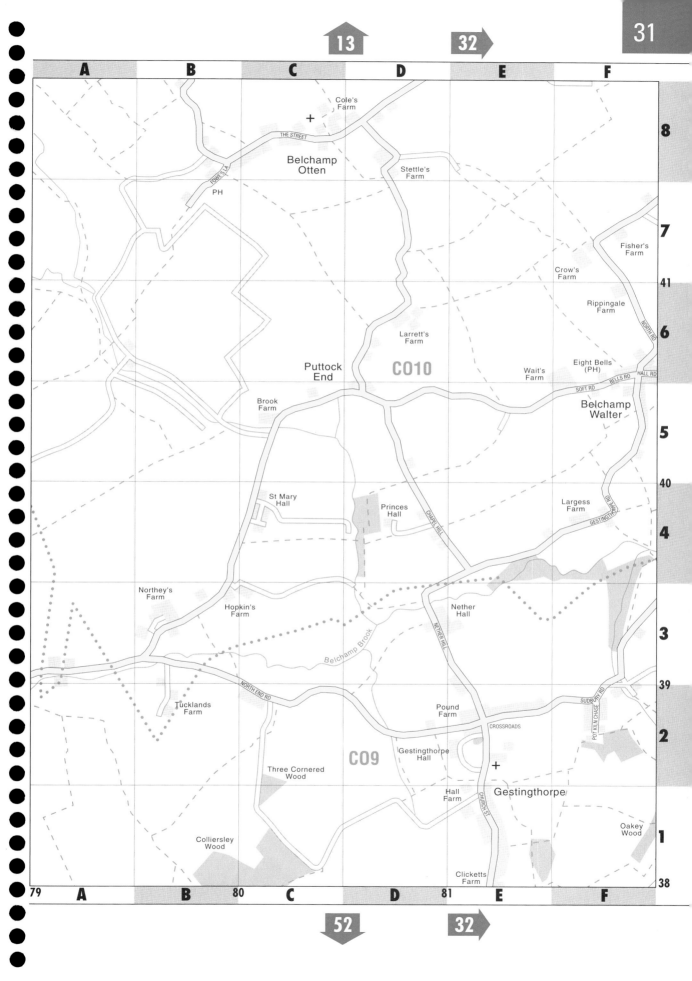

A B C D E F

8
7
41
6
5
40
4
3
39
2
1
38

Cole's Farm

THE STREET

FOWES LA

Belchamp Otten

PH

Stettle's Farm

Fisher's Farm

Crow's Farm

Rippingale Farm

NORTH RD

Larrett's Farm

CO10

Puttock End

Wait's Farm

Eight Bells (PH)

HALL RD

SOFT RD BELLS RD

Belchamp Walter

Brook Farm

St Mary Hall

Princes Hall

CHAPEL HILL

Largess Farm

GESTINGTHORPE RD

Northey's Farm

Hopkin's Farm

Belchamp Brook

Nether Hall

NETHER HILL

Tucklands Farm

NORTH END RD

Pound Farm

CROSSROADS

SUDBURY RD

POT KILN CHASE

CO9

Gestingthorpe Hall

Hall Farm

CHURCH ST

Gestingthorpe

Oakey Wood

Three Cornered Wood

Colliersley Wood

Clicketts Farm

79 A B 80 C D 81 E F

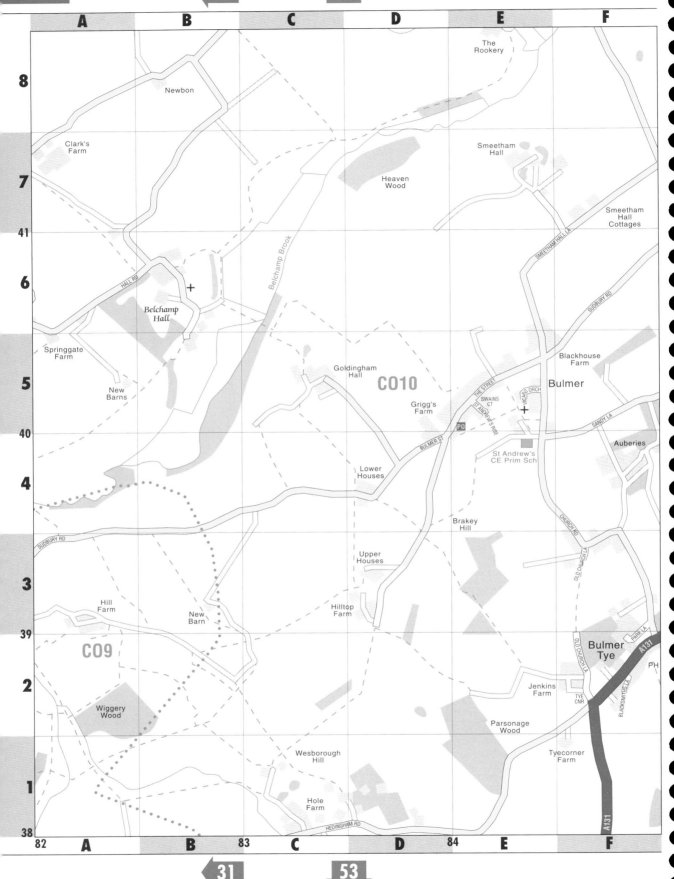

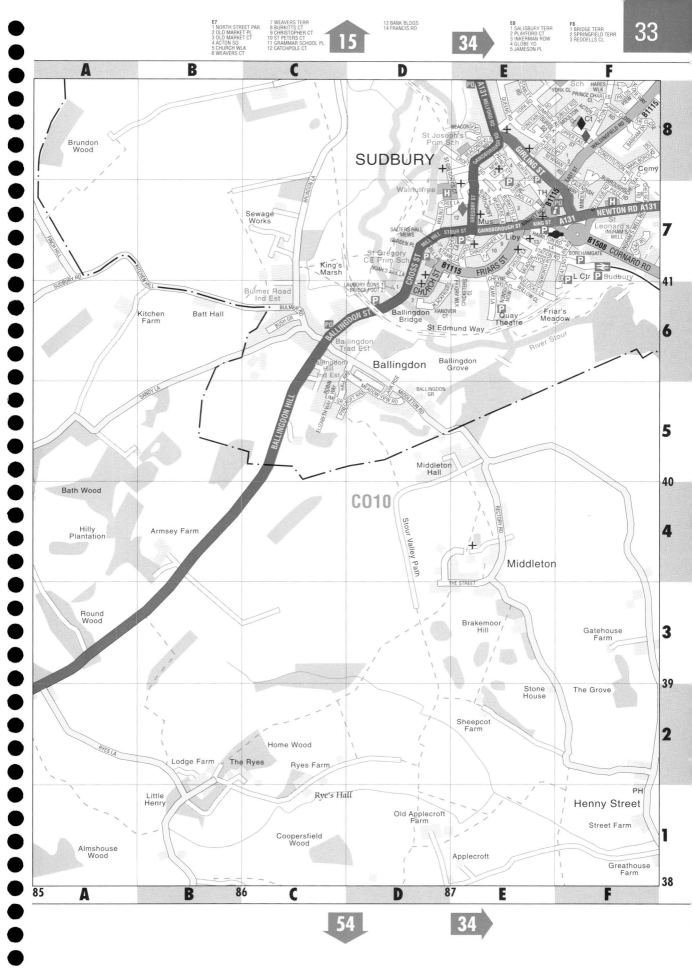

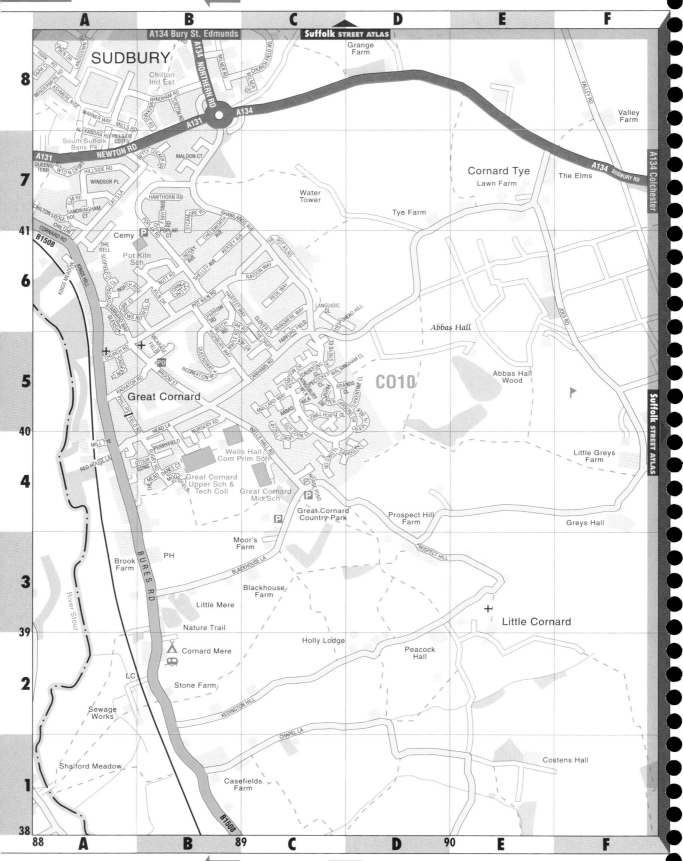

Suffolk STREET ATLAS

A B C D E F

A134 Bury St. Edmunds

SUDBURY

Chilton Ind Est

Grange Farm

8

Windham Rd

Milner Rd

Church Field Rd

Milner

A134

A131

NORTHERN RD

Valley Rd

Valley Farm

Warner Way

Mills Rd

South Suffolk Bsns Pk

Alexandra Rd

Hillside Cotts

Maldon Ct

NEWTON RD

Betty Cocker Gn

A131

Queens Terr

W TO N CROFT

Hillside Rd

Windsor Pl

Hawthorn Rd

Cat's La

7

Cornard Tye

Lawn Farm

The Elms

A134 Sudbury Rd

A134 Colchester

Water Tower

Tye Farm

41

Chilton Lodge Rd

Chilton

Cornard Rd

B1508

Cemy

Sandringham Ct

The Dell

Pot Kiln Sch

Poplar Ct

Sycamore Rd

Shawlands Ave

Chelsworth Ave

Poplar Ch

Firtree Rd

Lindsey Ave

Kersey Ave

Shelley Ave

Raydon Way

The Pot Kilns

6

Kings Meadow

North Rise

Butt Rd

Corner Cres

Kiln Dr

Pot Kiln Rd

Beech

Oak Rd

Maple Ash Dr

Highbury Way

Clover Cl

The Drift

Rede Way

Languidic Cl

Sheepshead Hill

Abbas Hall

Suffolk STREET ATLAS

Sparrow

Harvest Way

Mansmere Way

Tarford Field

Scofield Ct

Standish Way

Glensky

St Andrew's Rd

Rowel Cl

Church Rd

PO

Queensway

Canhams Rd

Greys Cl

Brands Cl

Walsingham Cl

CO10

Abbas Hall Wood

5

Radiator Rd

Broom St

Recreation Wk

Malard Way

Kennedy Way

Kingsbury Dr

Caulston Cl

Peddocks Wk

Byron Wk

Austin Wk

Turrentine Cl

Carsons Dr

Coleridge Cl

Lionel Hurst Cl

Abbas

Phillips Field Rd

Head La

Nursery Rd

Wells Hall Rd

Latell Croft

Guy Cook Cl

Crazy

Davos Cl

40

Mill Tye

Red House La

Perryfield

Stour Gdns

Mead

Danes Ct

Wood

Horsefield

Wells Hall Com Prim Sch

Horse Pond

Little Greys Farm

4

Great Cornard Upper Sch & Tech Coll

Great Cornard Mid Sch

Great Cornard Country Park

Prospect Hill Farm

Greys Hall

Moor's Farm

Blackhouse La

Prospect Hill

3

Brook Farm

PH

BURES RD

Blackhouse Farm

Little Mere

Nature Trail

Little Cornard

39

River Stour

Cornard Mere

Holly Lodge

Peacock Hall

LC

Stone Farm

2

Sewage Works

Kedington Hill

Chapel La

Costens Hall

1

Shalford Meadow

Casefields Farm

B1508

38

88 A B 89 C D 90 E F

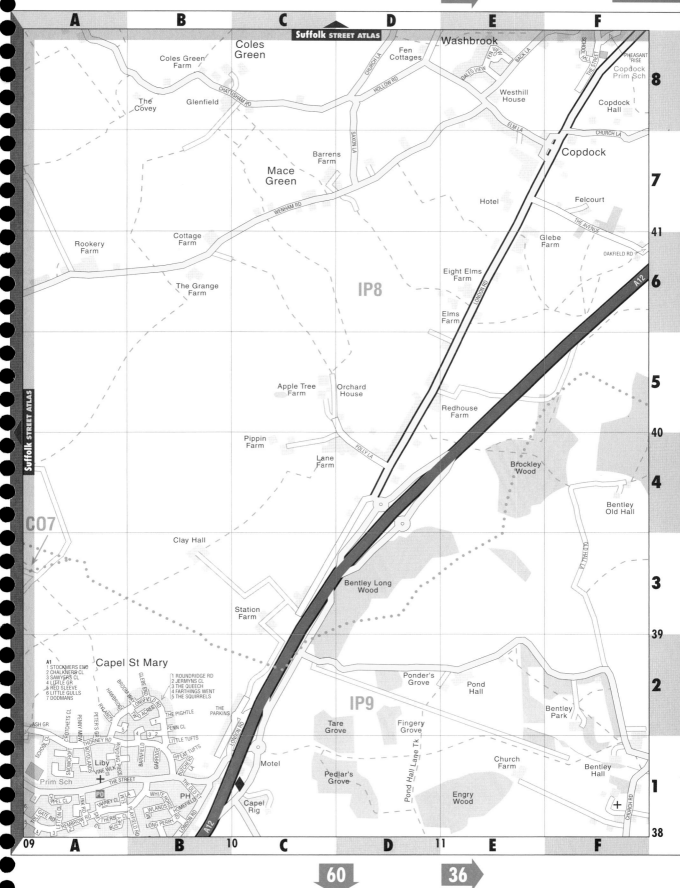

Suffolk STREET ATLAS

A B C D E F

Coles Green
Coles Green Farm
Fen Cottages
Washbrook

CHURCH LA
FEN VIEW
BACK LA
DALES VIEW
THE STREET
SCHOOL LA
PHEASANT RISE
Copdock Prim Sch
8

The Covey
Glenfield
CHATTISHAM RD
HOLLOW RD
SAXON LA
Westhill House
ELM LA
Copdock Hall
CHURCH LA

Mace Green
Barrens Farm
Copdock

WENHAM RD
7

Rookery Farm
Cottage Farm
Hotel
Felcourt
THE AVENUE
41

The Grange Farm
IP8
Eight Elms Farm
LONDON RD
Glebe Farm
OAKFIELD RD
6
A12

Elms Farm

Apple Tree Farm
Orchard House
Redhouse Farm
5

Pippin Farm
FOLLY LA
Brockley Wood
40

Lane Farm
Bentley Old Hall
4

Clay Hall
OLD HALL LA
CO7

Bentley Long Wood
3

Station Farm
39

Capel St Mary

A1
1 STOCKMERS END
2 CHALKNERS CL
3 SAWYERS CL
4 LITTLE GR
5 RED SLEEVE
6 LITTLE GULLS
7 DODMANS

1 ROUNDRIDGE RD
2 JERMYNS CL
3 THE QUEECH
4 FARTHINGS WENT
5 THE SQUIRRELS

Ponder's Grove
Pond Hall
Bentley Park
2

GLEBE END RD
LONGFIELD RD
BROOM WAY
HAMBRIDGE
TWO ACRES
THE PIGHTLE
THE PARKINS
IP9
Tare Grove
Fingery Grove
Church Farm
Bentley Hall

ASH GR
PENN MW
CHOTCHETS CL
SNOWCROFT
BOYDLANDS
PETER'S GR
THORNEY RD
BARNFIELD
WINDING PIECE
GARROODS
PENN CL
LITTLE TUFTS
GREAT TUFTS
BUTCHERS LA
THE OUTLET
LONDON RD
Motel
Pedlar's Grove
Pond Hall Lane Trk
Engry Wood

Prim Sch
Liby
VINE WLK
THE STREET
PO
PH
WHITE HORSE
HOMEFIELD RD
LONG PERRY
Capel Rig
CHURCH RD

CAPEL CL
GATE RD
TOLL GATE RD
LETTON CL
REMBROW RD
MYRLANDS
PLAYFIELD RD
BUSH...
A12
38

Suffolk STREET ATLAS

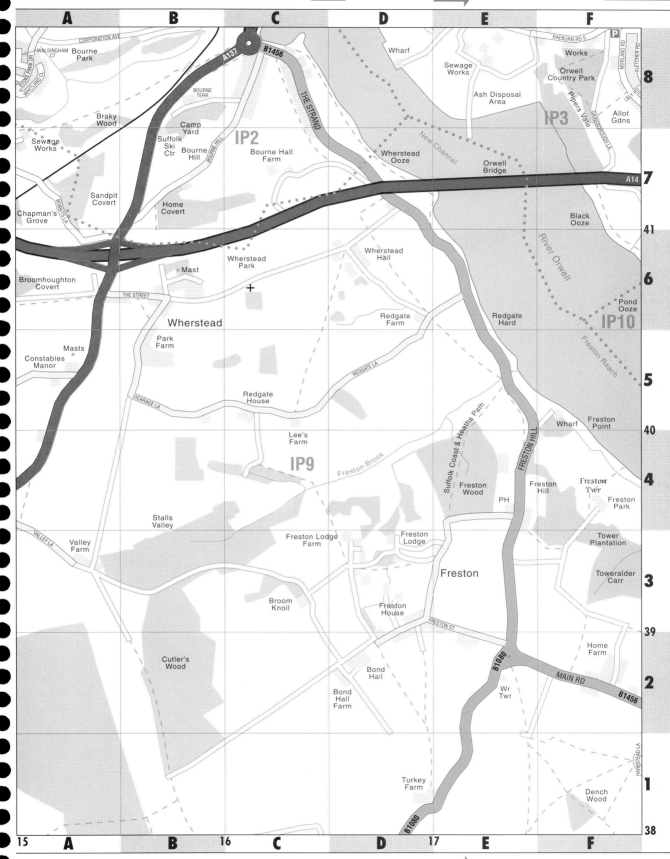

A B C D E F

8
7
41
6
5
40
4
3
39
2
1
38

CORPORATION AVE
Bourne Park
STOKE PARK DR
WALSINGHAM CT
WHITLAND CL
Braky Wood
Sewage Works
A137
BOBBITS LA
Chapman's Grove
Sandpit Covert
Broomhoughton Covert
THE STREET
Masts
Constables Manor
VALLEY LA
Valley Farm
VICARAGE LA
Park Farm
Wherstead
BOURNE TERR
Suffolk Ski Ctr
BOURNE HILL
Camp Yard
Bourne Hill
Home Covert
Mast
B1456
THE STRAND
Bourne Hall Farm
IP2
Wherstead Park
Redgate House
Lee's Farm
IP9
Stalls Valley
Cutler's Wood
Broom Knoll
Wharf
Sewage Works
Ash Disposal Area
Wherstead Ooze
New Channel
Orwell Bridge
Wherstead Hall
Redgate Farm
REDGATE LA
Freston Brook
Freston Lodge Farm
Freston Lodge
Bond Hall
Bond Hall Farm
Turkey Farm
B1080
RAEBURN RD S
P
Works
Orwell Country Park
MORLAND RD
FLETCHER RD
IP3
Pipers Vale
GAINSBOROUGH LA
LEY RD
Allot Gdns
A14
Black Ooze
River Orwell
Pond Ooze
IP10
Freston Reach
Redgate Hard
Suffolk Coast & Heaths Path
Freston Wood
FRESTON HILL
Wharf
Freston Point
Freston Hill
Freston Twr
Freston Park
PH
Tower Plantation
Toweralder Carr
Freston
FRESTON ST
Freston House
Home Farm
B1080
Wr Twr
MAIN RD
B1456
HARKSTEAD LA
Dench Wood

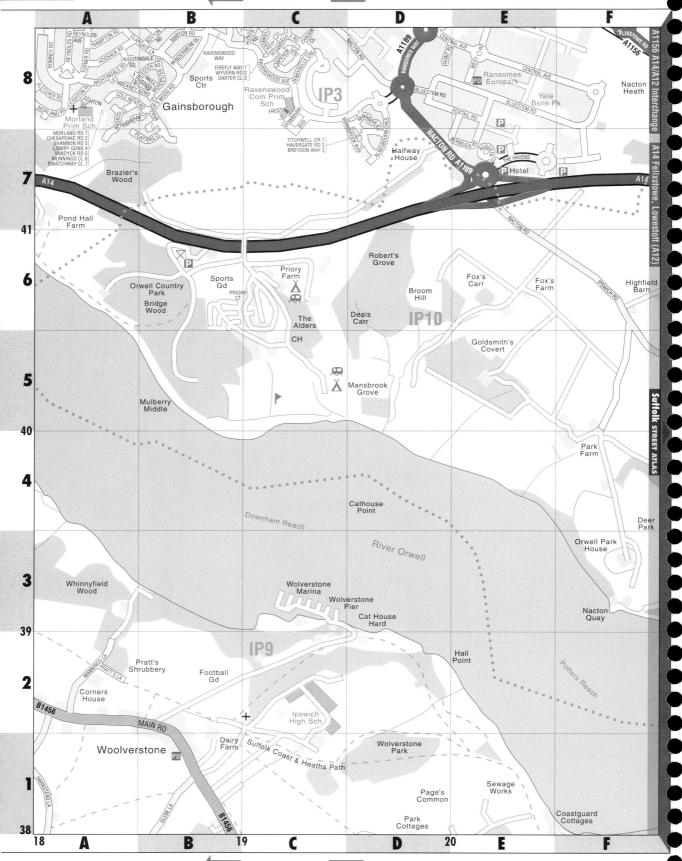

A14 A14/A12 Interchange
A1156
A14 Felixstowe, Lowestoft (A12)

Suffolk STREET ATLAS

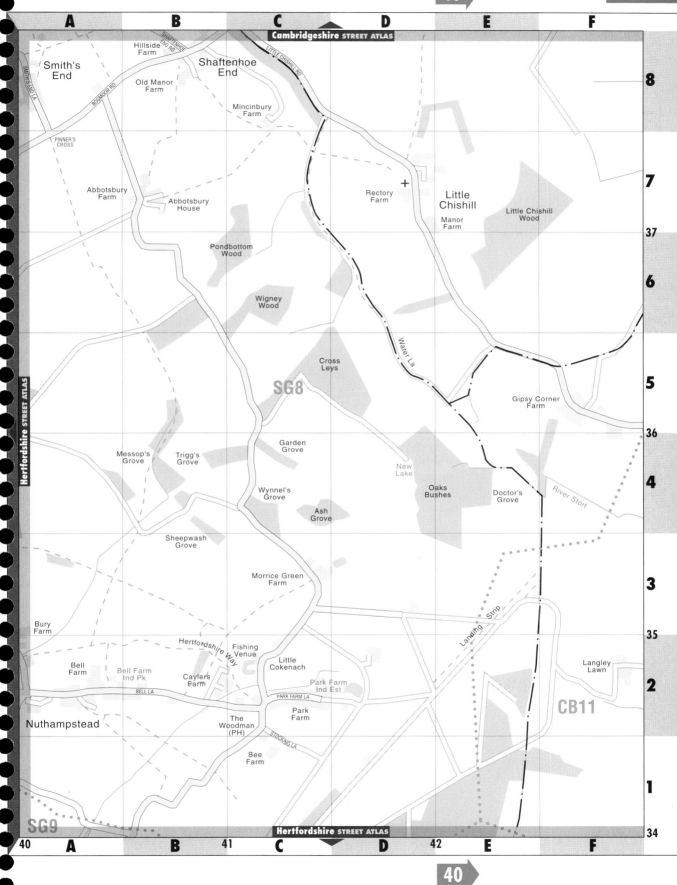

Smith's End

Hillside Farm

Shaftenhoe End

Old Manor Farm

Mincinbury Farm

BOGMOOR RD

SHAFTENHOE END RD

LITTLE CHISHILL RD

SMITH'S END LA

PINNER'S CROSS

Abbotsbury Farm

Abbotsbury House

Pondbottom Wood

Rectory Farm

Little Chishill

Manor Farm

Little Chishill Wood

Wigney Wood

Cross Leys

SG8

Water La

Garden Grove

New Lake

Gipsy Corner Farm

Messop's Grove

Trigg's Grove

Wynnel's Grove

Ash Grove

Oaks Bushes

Doctor's Grove

River Stort

Sheepwash Grove

Morrice Green Farm

Landing Strip

Bury Farm

Hertfordshire Way

Fishing Venue

Bell Farm

Bell Farm Ind Pk

Caylers Farm

Little Cokenach

Park Farm Ind Est

Langley Lawn

BELL LA

PARK FARM LA

CB11

Nuthampstead

The Woodman (PH)

Park Farm

STOCKING LA

Bee Farm

SG9

Hertfordshire STREET ATLAS

Hertfordshire STREET ATLAS

39

19

A B C D E F

8
Monkshole Wood
Building End
Lower Farm
BUILDING END RD
Chiswick Hall
Lower Pond Street
Hope Farm House
B1039

7
Upper Farm
BUILDING END RD
COMMON LA
SG8
Harcamlow Way
Mead Bushes Wood
Upper Pond Street
SCHOOL LA

37
Wicken Water

6
Duddenhoe End Farm
Hall
BROOKSIDES

Common La
Pickerton Green
High Wood
White Friars Farm

5
Chrishall Common
Roughway Wood
Oldfield Grove

36
Killem's Green
Lorking's La

4
Grange Farm
Cosh Farm

River Stort
Hall Grove
Duddenhoe Grange
CB11

3
The Hall
THE CAUSEWAY
Church Farm
Hall
Harcamlow Way
Upper Green

35
PARK LA
BULL LA
THE KANGELS
LONG LEY

2
Langley
HIGHFIELDS

The Bull (PH)

1
Lower Green
Ford
Bury Farm

34
Roper's La
WATERWICK HILL
New Farm

43 A B 44 C D 45 E F

39

64

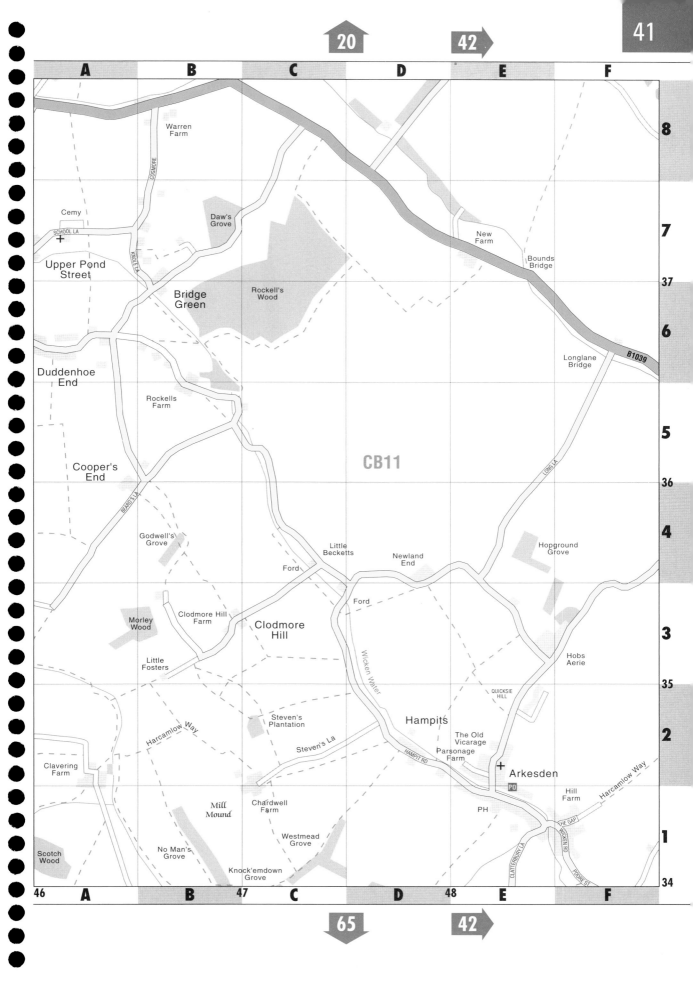

A B C D E F

8

Cups Grove

Bush Pasture Grove

The Triangle

Strawberry Close Belt

CHESTNUT AVE

The Willows

B1383

Cornwallis Hill

Mast

7

Neville Hill

LONDON RD

Red Leg Plantation

37

6

WALDEN RD

B1039

The Old Vicarage

Wenden Place Farm

NATS LA
THE BEECHES

RAILWAY COTTS

PH

B1039

STATION RD

MUTLOW CL

SILVER ROW

ROYSTON RD

CHURCH ST

PH

Mutlow Farm

Mutlow Hall

MUTLOW HILL

CB11

Wenden Hall

Bearwalden Bsns Pk

Audley End

5

Clanverend Farm

Clanverend Bridge

CHAWIEL LA

Wendens Ambo

DUCK ST

Rookery Farm

36

Norton End

ROOKERY LA

LC

4

Mill Farm

Duddenhoe La

Bulse Farm

Mill Hill

3

35

Whiteditch Farm

Tudhope Farm

LONDON RD

B1383

Harcamlow Way

Long Plantation

2

WHITEDITCH LA

Newport Free Gram Sch

BURY WATER LA

Nursery

BURYWATER COTTS

1

Severals Farm

BURY WATER LA

TENTERFIELDS

SCHOOL LA

GILBEY GN

34

M11

B1038

WICKEN RD

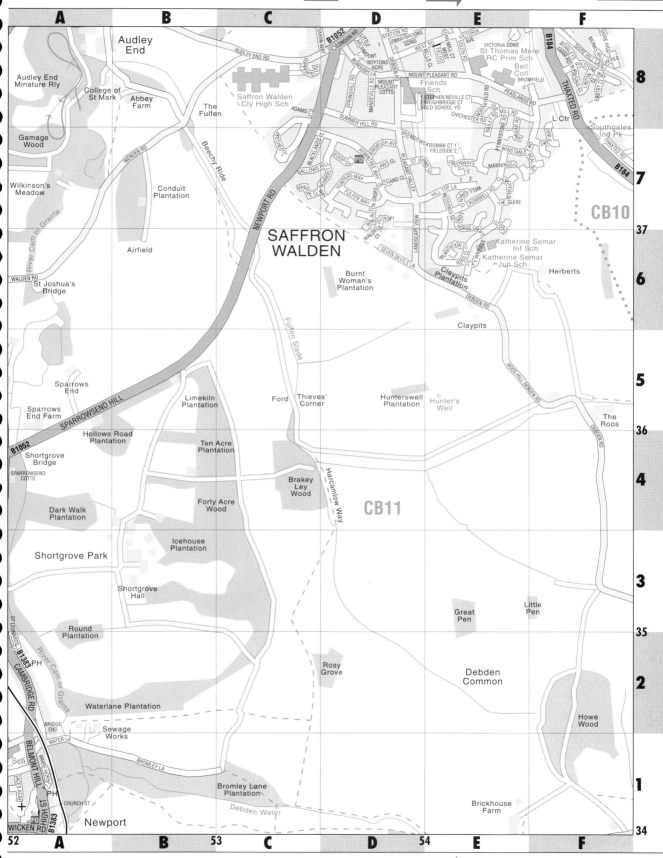

← 43

↑ 23

| | **A** | **B** | **C** | **D** | **E** | **F** |

8

Shire Hill Farm

SHIRE HILL LA

THE DREYS

Sewage Works

The Towers

Frogsgreen Farm

Tiptoft Farm

Bears Hall

COLE END LA

7

THAXTED RD

B184

Veerman Lodge

37

Brickkiln Leys Farm

Cole End

Cole End Farm

6

Wr Twr

Gunters

Thunderley Parsonage

The Old Pig And Whistle (PH)

COLE END LA

5

Thunderley Hall

Six Acre Wood

CB10

Harrison's Wood

36

Crowney Wood

4

THAXTED RD

New House Farm

Peverel's Wood

Parsonage Farm

Abbots Manor

Harleyfield Grove

3

Pamphillions

PARSONAGE LA

35

Purton End

Airfield (dis)

WIMBISH WLK

WIMBISH WLK

WALDEN AVE

Sewage Works

B184

2

Carver Barracks

PINKNEY CL

POWNEY CL

DEBDEN DR

AVE

Newhouse Farm

CB11

BROAD OAKES CL

Elder Street

Burnt House

Debden Manor

PEBELLS RD

Freemans

1

Ricketts

WATER LA

WYTOORS HILL

34

| **55** | **A** | **B** | **56** | **C** | **D** | **57** | **E** | **F** |

← 43

↓ 68

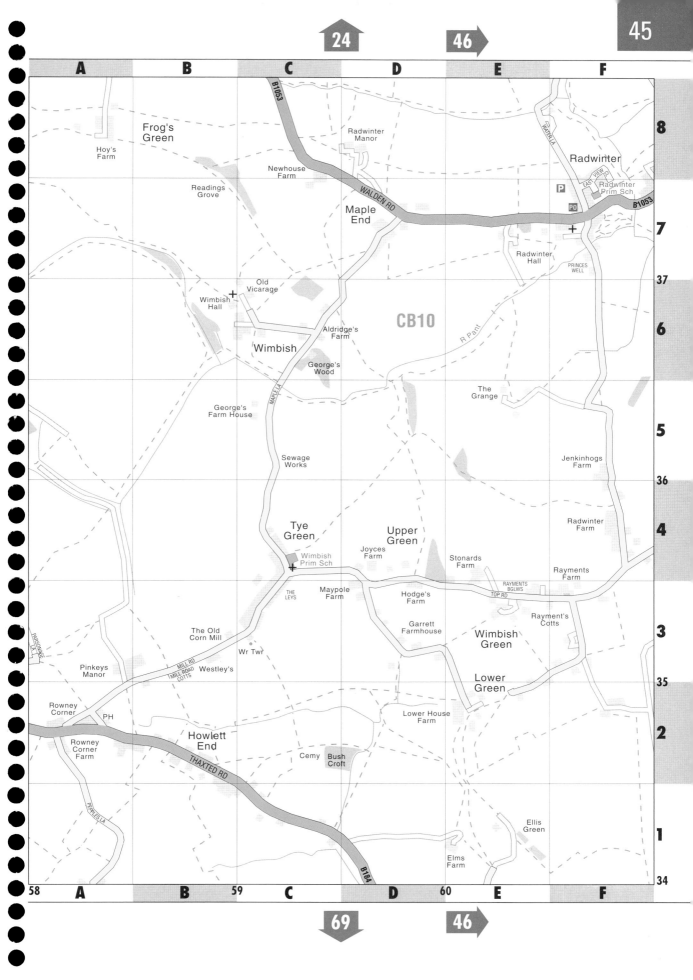

45
25

A **B** **C** **D** **E** **F**

WINCELOW HALL RD

HILL RD

B1054

B1054

HIGH ST

CHURCH RD

Church Farm

8

Shelland's Farm

Hill Farm

Longcroft

+

Equestrian Ctr

B1054

B1055

Pant Brook House

Prentice's Farm

B1053

PH

Sharp Crofts Wood

Moss's Farm

7

37

Hill Farm

Anso Corner Farm

6

B1053

B1055

Howses

Anser Gallows Farm

Long Thatch

Mortlock's Farm

Clay Wood

River Pant

CB10

5

36

B1053

Little Brockholds Farm

Sparrow's Hall

Moor End Farm

4

Different Part Grove

Great Brockholds

Goddards Farm

Ivytodd's Farm

Barleyfields

3

Byeball's Farm

35

Giffords Farm

Longmead

TINDON END RD

Broadfields

BUSH RD

Collins Cross

2

The Dovehouse

Bush Cottage

BUSH LA

Blackhouse Farm

Mill Farm House

B1051

South Fields

Hole Farm

Tindon Manor

Grassy Grove

1

Tindon End

Broadcroft Grove

Bush Farm

Market Farm

B1051

34

61 **A** 62 **B** **C** 63 **D** **E** **F**

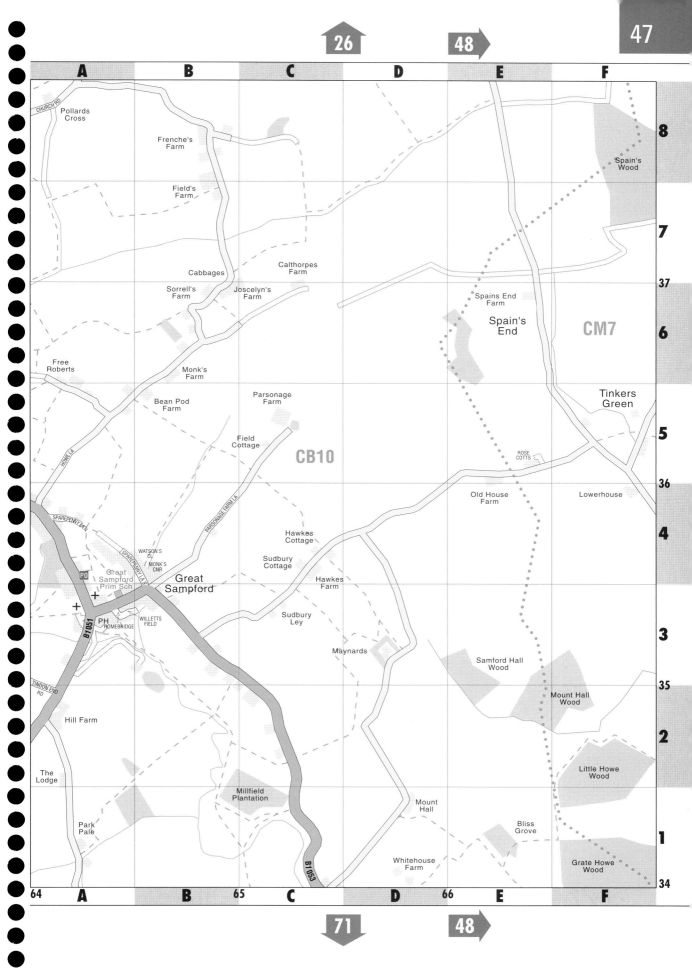

A B C D E F

8

Little Nortons

Old Robin

Great Nortons

CORNISH HALL END RD

CO9

7

Bushy Grove

Lopham's Farm

Rockall's Farm

Howsey Wood

37

Springlette

Shore Hall

The Grove

Rivett's Farm

White House Farm

Sewage Works

6

MILLERS ROW

HEARDS LA

Briar Cottages

PH

Cornish Hall End

HEARD'S LA

Heard's Farm

Hole Farm

5

CM7

Whitleys

36

Jekyll's Farm

4

Cornish Hall

JEKYLLS LA

Unwin's Farm

New Cover

Hobtoe's Farm

MILL LA

3

Little London

35

Rook Hall

Yeldhams

2

Howe Farm

Obourne's Farm

Howe Street

1

Spainshall Farm

Bumpstead Lodge

Spain's Hall

Tridgate Ley

B1057

34

67 A B 68 C D 69 E F

B1057

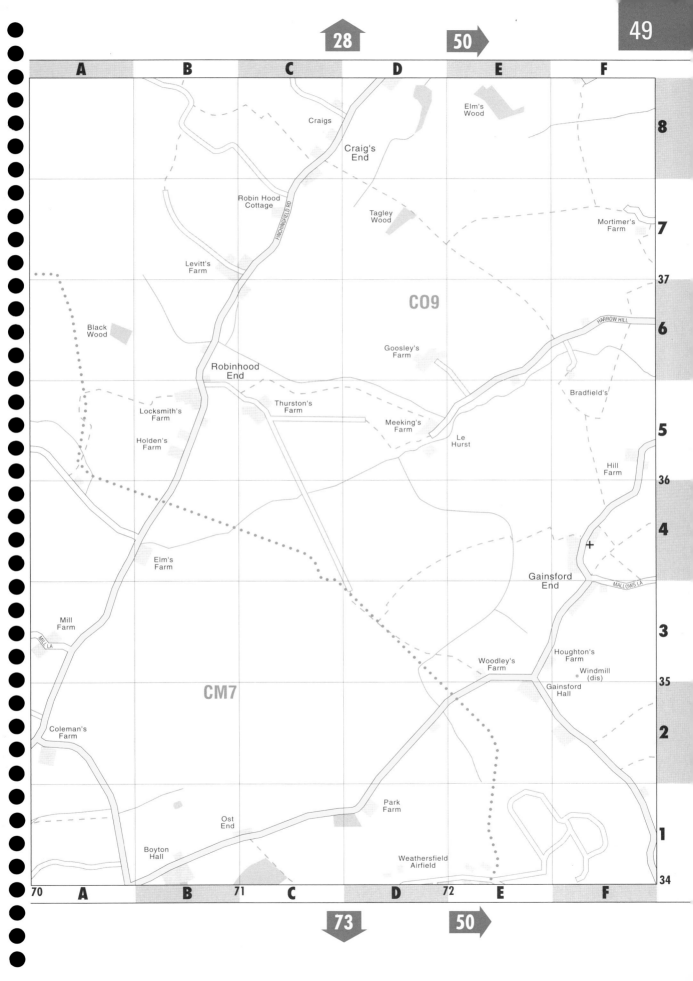

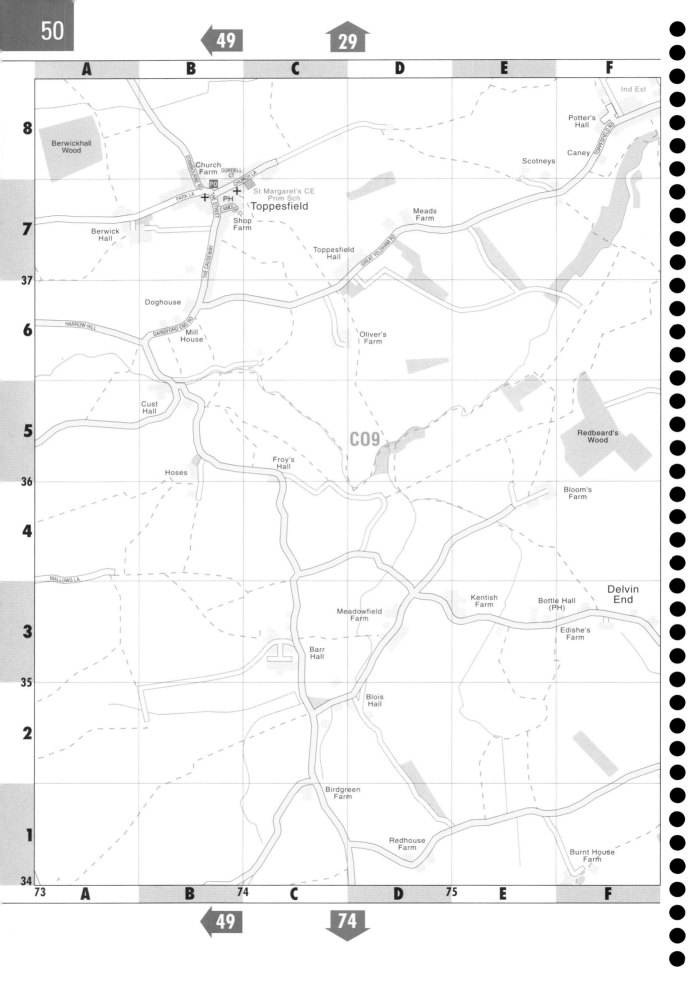

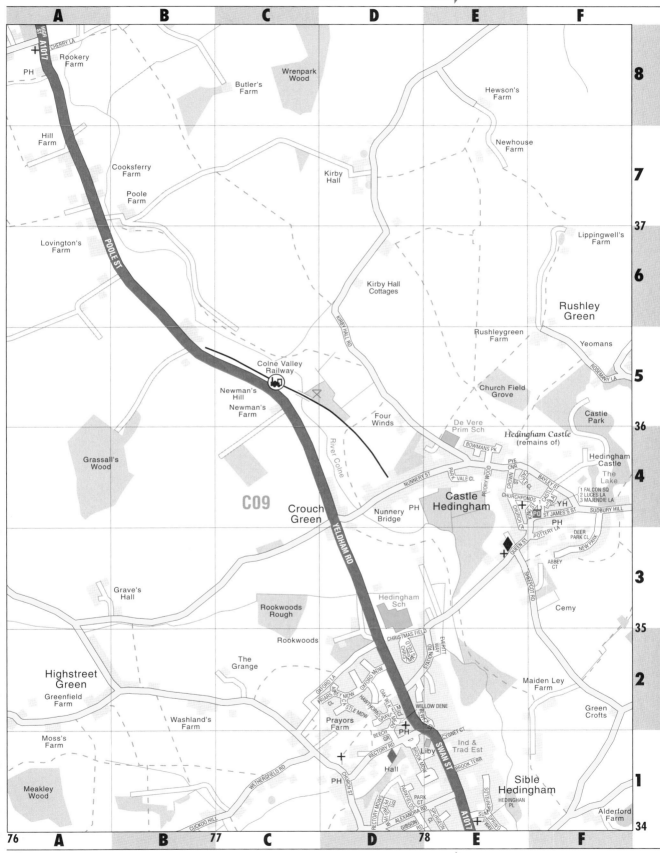

30
52

A　B　C　D　E　F

8
7
37
6
5
36
4
3
35
2
1
34

PH
High St
A1017
CHERRY LA
Rookery Farm
Hill Farm
Cooksferry Farm
Poole Farm
Lovington's Farm
POOLE ST

Butler's Farm
Wrenpark Wood

Hewson's Farm
Newhouse Farm

Kirby Hall
Kirby Hall Cottages

Lippingwell's Farm
Rushley Green
Rushleygreen Farm
Yeomans
ROSEMARY LA

Colne Valley Railway
Newman's Hill
Newman's Farm
Four Winds

Church Field Grove
De Vere Prim Sch
Hedingham Castle (remains of)
BOWMANS PK
Castle Park
Hedingham Castle
The Lake
Castle Hedingham
PYE CNR
PRIORY WOOD
PARK VALE CL
CASTLE CL
BAYLEY ST
CHURCHPONDS
NUNNERY ST
Nunnery Bridge
Nunnery St
PH
1 FALCON SQ
2 LUCES LA
3 MAJENDIE LA
YH
PO
PH
ST JAMES S ST
CHURCH ST
POTTERY LA
SUDBURY HILL
DEER PARK CL
NEW PARK
QUEEN ST
ABBEY CT

Grassall's Wood

CO9
Crouch Green
YELDHAM RD
River Colne

Grave's Hall
Rookwoods Rough
Rookwoods
The Grange

Hedingham Sch
SHEEPCOT RD
Cemy

Highstreet Green
Greenfield Farm
Moss's Farm
Meakley Wood
WETHERSFIELD RD
Washland's Farm

CHRISTMAS FIELD
STATION RD
EVERITT WAY
CHRIS
Maiden Ley Farm
Green Crofts

OXFORD LA
PRIARS
ABBEY MDW
CASTLE MDW
OXFORD MDW
HAWTHORNS
OAK WLK
GRAYS CL
ELM CL
WILLOW DENE
BEVOCK
Prayors Farm
BEECH GR
PH
SWAN ST
Ind & Trad Est
Sible Hedingham
HEDINGHAM PL
RECTORY RD
BROOK MDW
Liby
Hall
CYGNET CT
BROOK TERR
PH
CHURCH ST
RECTORY MDWS
ST
CRESTVALE
ALEXANDRA RD
GIBSON
PARK FIELDS
PARK CT
SPRINGER
SLANE
SPRING
WAY
SCHERFIELD
A1017
CUCKOO HILL
Alderford Farm

A   B   C   D   E   F

8

7

37

6

5

36

4

35

3

2

1

34

79   80   81

A   B   C   D   E   F

Ridley's Wood

Delvyn's Lane

CHURCH ST

Delvyn's Farm

Audley End

PH

Edeys Farm

Rectory Farm

Parkgate Farm

DELVYN'S LA

Crouch House

Great Lodge Farm

Branwhite's Grove

The Moat

CO9

Lawrence's Farm

Pannells Ash Farm

ROSEMARY LA

Rosemary Farm

SUDBURY RD

Pantile Cottage

Kendallscroft Grove

Little Chelmshoe House

Odewells

ST JAMES'S ST

Byham Hall

Little Lodge Farm

Chelmshoe House Farm

New Barn

Monks Lodge Farm

Monks Lodge

Hosden's Farm

MONKS LODGE RD

St Giles CE Prim Sch

ST GILES CL

Link Hills

Hopwell's Farm

STONE COTTS

Great Maplestead

Lucking Street

CHURCH ST

Luckinghouse Farm

Purls Cottage

Barrett's Hall

Little Lodge Farm

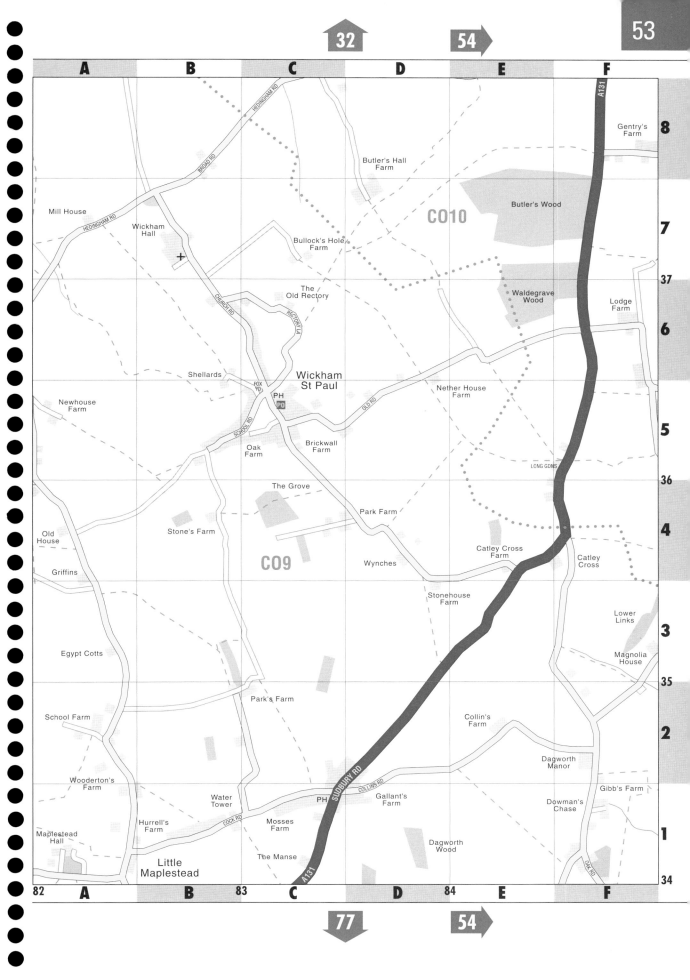

32
54

A B C D E F

8
Gentry's Farm

Butler's Hall Farm

Butler's Wood

CO10

7
Mill House

Wickham Hall

Bullock's Hole Farm

37

Waldegrave Wood

Lodge Farm

6
The Old Rectory

Shellards

Wickham St Paul

FOX YD
PH
PO

Nether House Farm

Newhouse Farm

Oak Farm

Brickwall Farm

5

LONG GDNS

The Grove

Park Farm

36

Stone's Farm

CO9

Wynches

Catley Cross Farm

Catley Cross

4

Old House

Griffins

Stonehouse Farm

Lower Links

3

Egypt Cotts

Magnolia House

35

Park's Farm

School Farm

Collin's Farm

2

Dagworth Manor

Wooderton's Farm

Water Tower

PH

Gallant's Farm

Gibb's Farm

Dowman's Chase

Hurrell's Farm

Mosses Farm

COCK RD
COLLINS RD
SUDBURY RD

Dagworth Wood

1

Maplestead Hall

Little Maplestead

The Manse

A131

OAK RD

34

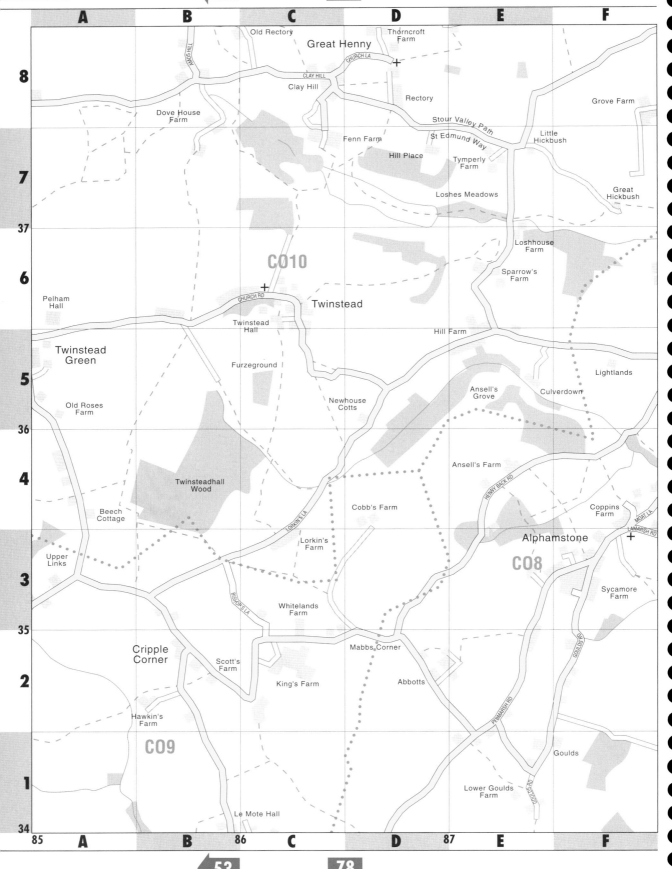

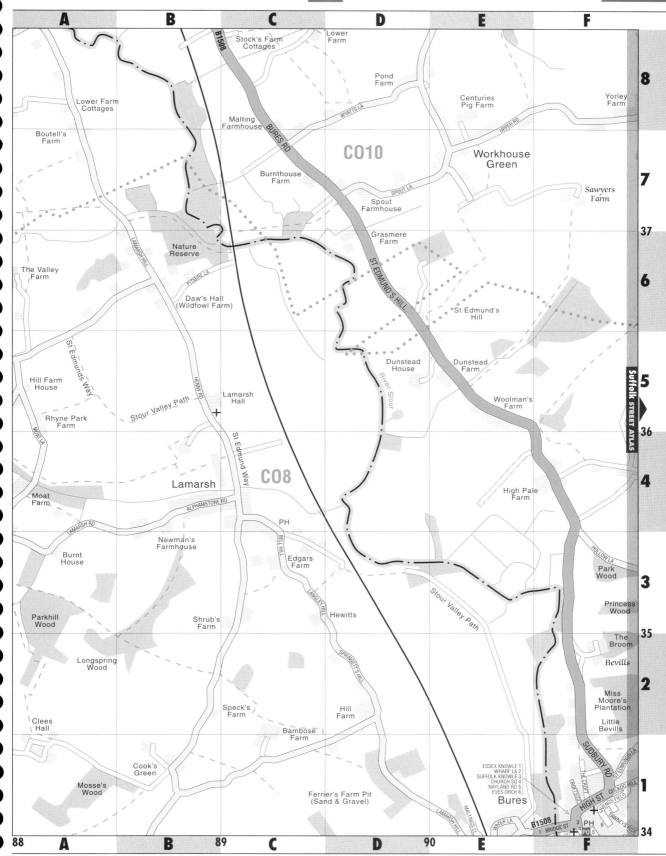

Suffolk STREET ATLAS

CO10

CO8

Lamarsh

Bures

Workhouse Green

Labels on map:

Stock's Farm Cottages
Lower Farm
Pond Farm
Centuries Pig Farm
Yorley Farm
Lower Farm Cottages
Boutell's Farm
Malting Farmhouse
Burnthouse Farm
Sawyers Farm
Spout Farmhouse
Spout La
Wyatts La
Upper Rd
Bures Rd
B1508
The Valley Farm
Nature Reserve
Grasmere Farm
Pitmire La
Lamarsh Hill
Daw's Hall (Wildfowl Farm)
St Edmund's Hill
St Edmund's Hill
Hill Farm House
St Edmunds Way
Stour Valley Path
Henry Rd
Lamarsh Hall
River Stour
Dunstead House
Dunstead Farm
Woolman's Farm
Rhyne Park Farm
Moat La
Moat Farm
St Edmund Way
Lamarsh Rd
Newman's Farmhouse
Alphamstone Rd
PH
Bell Hill
Edgars Farm
High Pale Farm
Hollow La
Park Wood
Burnt House
Shrub's Farm
Hewitts
Langley Hill
Stour Valley Path
Princess Wood
The Broom
Bevills
Parkhill Wood
Longspring Wood
Springett's Hill
Speck's Farm
Hill Farm
Miss Moore's Plantation
Little Bevills
Clees Hall
Bambose Farm
Cook's Green
Mosse's Wood
Ferrier's Farm Pit (Sand & Gravel)
Lamarsh Hill
Maltings Cl
Water La
Sudbury Rd
St Edmunds La
High St
Croftside
The Croft
Bridge St
B1508
PH
PO
Cuckoo Hill
Esends Field
Tawneys Ride

ESSEX KNOWLE 1
WHARF LA 2
SUFFOLK KNOWLE 3
CHURCH SQ 4
NAYLAND RD 5
EVES ORCH 6

Grid references (right): 8 7 37 6 5 36 4 3 35 2 1 34

Grid references (top): A B C D E F

Grid references (bottom): 88 A B 89 C D 90 E F 34

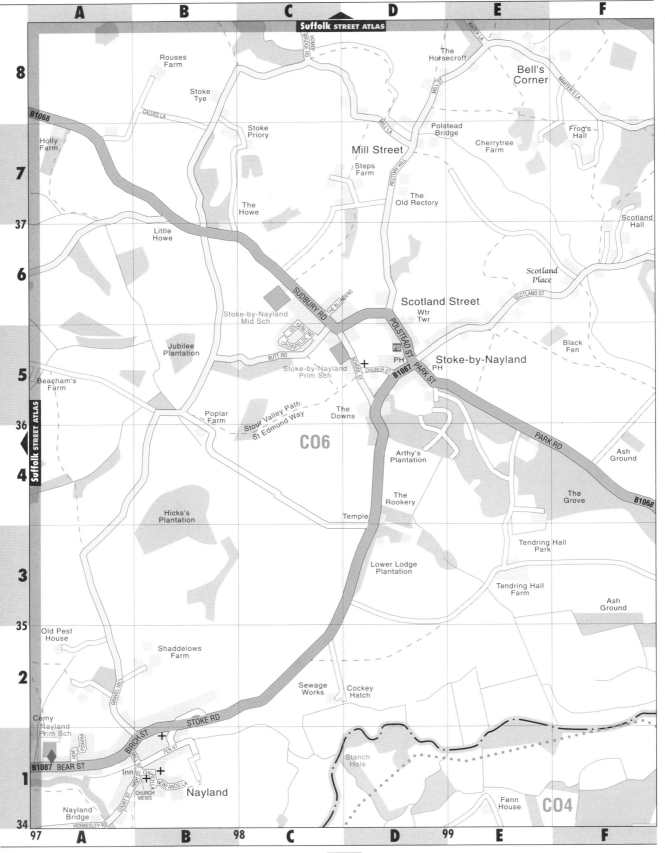

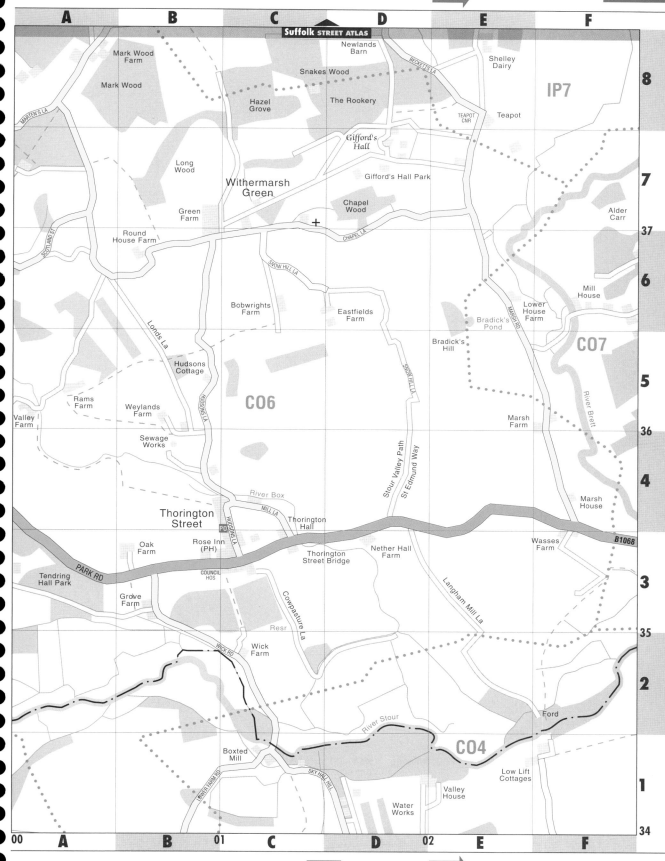

58 ➤

Suffolk STREET ATLAS

A B C D E F

8

IP7

7

37

6

Mark Wood Farm

Mark Wood

Snakes Wood

Newlands Barn

Shelley Dairy

MARTEN'S LA

Hazel Grove

The Rookery

BECKETT'S LA

TEAPOT CNR

Teapot

Gifford's Hall

Long Wood

Gifford's Hall Park

Withermarsh Green

Green Farm

Chapel Wood

SCOTLAND ST

Round House Farm

CHAPEL LA

Alder Carr

Mill House

SNOW HILL LA

Bobwrights Farm

Eastfields Farm

Bradick's Pond

Lower House Farm

CO7

MARSH RD

Lonals La

Bradick's Hill

River Brett

5

36

4

Hudsons Cottage

CO6

Rams Farm

Weylands Farm

HUDSONS LA

SNOW HILL LA

Marsh Farm

Valley Farm

Sewage Works

River Box

MILL LA

Stour Valley Path

St Edmund Way

Marsh House

Thorington Street

PO

Thorington Hall

Thorington Street Bridge

Nether Hall Farm

Wasses Farm

B1068

3

35

2

Oak Farm

Rose Inn (PH)

HUDSONS LA

COUNCIL HOS

Langham Mill La

PARK RD

Tendring Hall Park

Grove Farm

Resr

Cowpasture La

WICK RD

Wick Farm

Ford

River Stour

CO4

Low Lift Cottages

Boxted Mill

LOWER FARM RD

SKY HALL HILL

Water Works

Valley House

1

34

00 A B 01 C D 02 E F

58 ➤

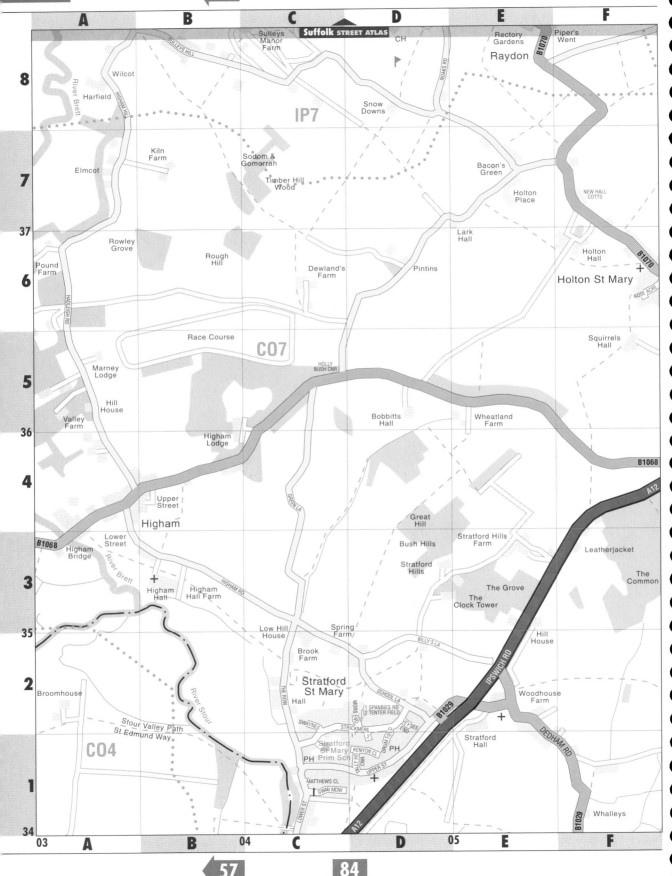

Suffolk STREET ATLAS

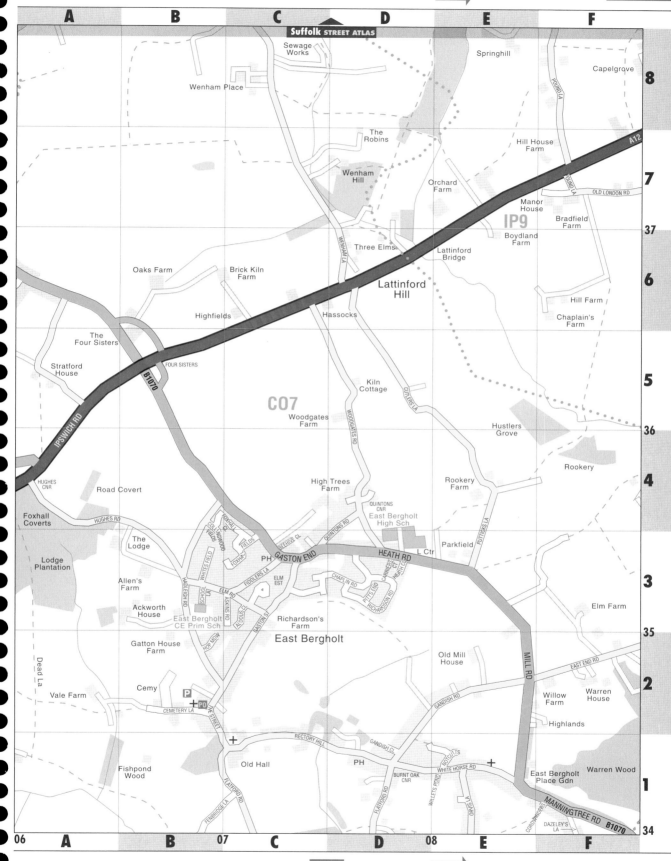

Suffolk STREET ATLAS

| | A | B | C | D | E | F | |

8
Sewage Works
Springhill
Capelgrove
Wenham Place
The Robins
Wenham Hill
Hill House Farm
7
Orchard Farm
Manor House
Old London Rd
POUND LA
A12
IP9
Bradfield Farm
37
Three Elms
Lattinford Bridge
Boydland Farm
WENHAM LA
Oaks Farm
Brick Kiln Farm
Lattinford Hill
Hill Farm
6
Highfields
Hassocks
Chaplain's Farm
The Four Sisters
FOUR SISTERS
Kiln Cottage
CUTLERS LA
Stratford House
B1070
WOODGATES RD
IPSWICH RD
Hustlers Grove
5
CO7
36
Woodgates Farm
HUGHES CNR
Road Covert
High Trees Farm
Rookery
4
Foxhall Coverts
Rookery Farm
QUINTONS CNR
East Bergholt High Sch
The Lodge
COLLINGWOOD
FOXHALL CL
FIELDS
QUINTONS RD
Parkfield
PUTTOCKS LA
HUGHES RD
Lodge Plantation
WHITES FIELD
FOXHALL
PH
BEEHIVE CL
GASTON END
HEATH RD
L Ctr
3
Allen's Farm
FIDDLERS LA
ELM EST
CHAPLIN RD
PITTS END
CARRIERS CT
HEATH CL
Elm Farm
HAULEIGH RD
ELM RD
RICHARDSON RD
ACKWORTH House
SCHOOL
ASKINS RD
PODSL CL
A
East Bergholt CE Prim Sch
GASTON ST
Richardson's Farm
35
Gatton House Farm
HOP MDW
East Bergholt
Old Mill House
EAST END RD
2
Dead La
Cemy
P
PO
GANDISH RD
MILL RD
Willow Farm
Warren House
Vale Farm
CEMETERY LA
THE STREET
Highlands
RECTORY HILL
GANDISH CL
WHITE HORSE RD
1
Fishpond Wood
Old Hall
PH
BURNT OAK CNR
NUTGALLS
WILLETS POND
East Bergholt Place Gdn
Warren Wood
FLATFORD RD
FENBRIDGE LA
FLATFORD RD
ORVIS LA
CORDWINDERS
MANNINGTREE RD
B1070
DAZELEY'S LA
34

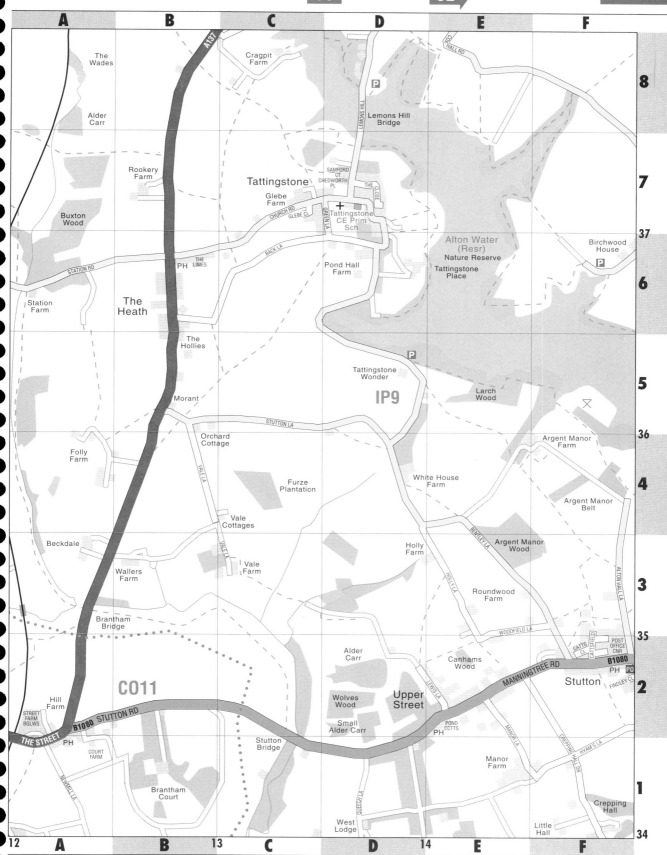

61
37

A B C D E F

8

Great Birch Wood

The Dower House

Potash Farm

B1080

The Woodlands

Woodlands Farm

7

Woodley Wood

Little Birch Wood

Hale's Grove

Halesgrove Cottage

Brown's Farm

Redhouse Farm

WOODLANDS RD

CLENCH RD

Freston Grove

Samford Cl

COUNCIL HOS

37

Holbrook High Sch

IPSWICH RD

6

Brook Farm

Clifton Wood

Broomhill Holbrook Prim Sch

The Street

HOLM DENMARK GDNS OAK

COACHMAN'S PADDOCK

Park House

BROOK FARM LA

GIFFORD CL

FIREBRONDS RD

READE RD

Ha'penny GDNS

EAST ROW

Holbrook Gardens

IP9

Crag Hall Covert

Walkgate Cottages

Brook

HYAM'S LA

RIVER VIEW

HEATHFIELD RD

MILL RISE

PO

Fish Pond

Holbrook

5

Old Alton Hall Farm

Alton Hall Cottages

FIVE ACRES

LITTLE ORCH

CHURCH RD

FISHPONDS LA

FIR TREE HILL

NEW LA

36

Alton Water (Resr) Nature Reserve

Sewage Works

BACK HILL

4

Water Sports Ctr

Chestnut Spinney

PRIMROSE HILL

Holbrook Mill

Park Covert

BRICK COTTS

Holbrook Lodge

Wall Farm

HARKSTEAD RD

Visitor Ctr

P

P

3

Royal Hospital Sch

Lower Holbrook

35

Stutton CE Prim Sch

LARKSFIELD RD

B1080

HOLBROOK RD

THE DRIFT

Wall Farm Wharf

P

2

FINDLEY CL

CHURCH RD

STUTTON CL

Bay Tree Farm

LOWER ST

Alton Wharf

The Hermitage

HYAM'S LA

Suffolk Coast and Heaths Path

STUTTON GN

Stutton House

Markwell's Farm

1

Lower Street

CROWE HALL LA

Crowe Hall

34

Crowe Hall Farm

15 A B 16 C D 17 E F

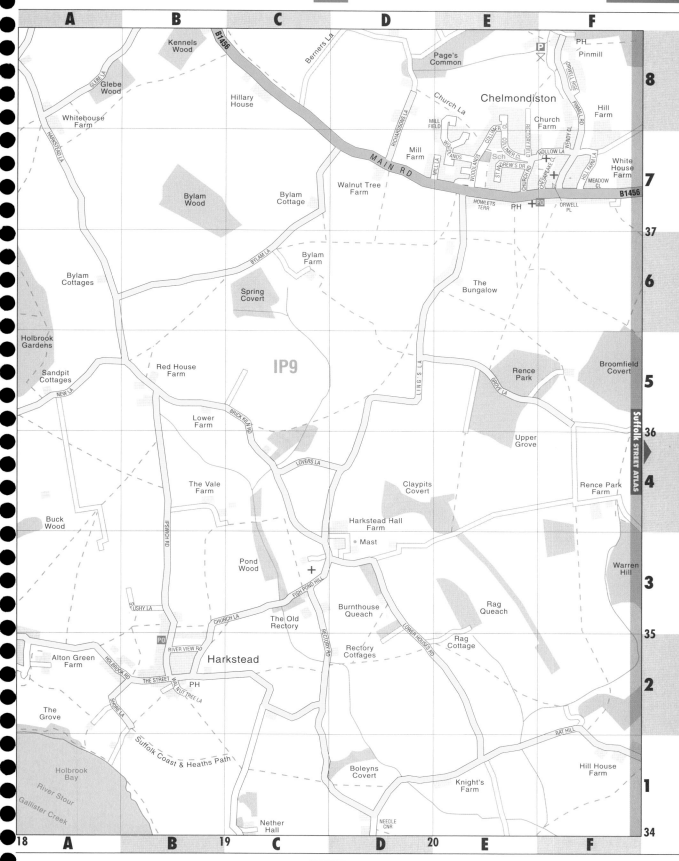

38

A   B   C   D   E   F

Kennels
Wood

B1456

Berners La

P
PH
Pinmill

Page's
Common

Glebe Wood

Glebe La

8

Whitehouse
Farm

Harkstead La

Hillary
House

Church La

Chelmondiston

Richardsons La

Church La

Mill
Field

Mill Field

Church
Farm

Collier Cl

Hill
Farm

Orwell Rise

Pinmill Rd

7

Bylam
Wood

Bylam
Cottage

MAIN RD

Walnut Tree
Farm

Mill
Farm

Mill La

Woodlands

St Andrew's Dr

Church Rd

Collier Cl

Sch

Hollow La

Wendy Cl

Chesapeake Cl

Hill Farm La

Meadow
Cl

White
House
Farm

B1456

7

Howlets
Terr

PH   PO

Orwell
Pl

37

Bylam La

Bylam
Farm

The
Bungalow

6

Bylam
Cottages

Spring
Covert

Rence
Park

Broomfield
Covert

5

Holbrook
Gardens

Red House
Farm

Ling's La

Grove La

Suffolk STREET ATLAS

Sandpit
Cottages

New La

IP9

Upper
Grove

36

Lower
Farm

Brick Kiln Rd

Lovers La

Claypits
Covert

Rence Park
Farm

4

Buck
Wood

The Vale
Farm

Ipswich Rd

Harkstead Hall
Farm

Warren
Hill

Pond
Wood

Mast

Rag
Queach

3

Fish Pond Hill

Burnthouse
Queach

Lower House Rd

Cushy La

Church La

The Old
Rectory

Rectory
Cottages

Rag
Cottage

35

PO

River View Rd

Harkstead

Rectory Rd

Alton Green
Farm

Holbrook Rd

The Street

Walnut Tree La

PH

2

The
Grove

Shore La

Bat Hill

Hill House
Farm

Suffolk Coast & Heaths Path

Holbrook
Bay

Boleyns
Covert

Knight's
Farm

1

River Stour

Gallister Creek

Nether
Hall

Needle
Cnr

34

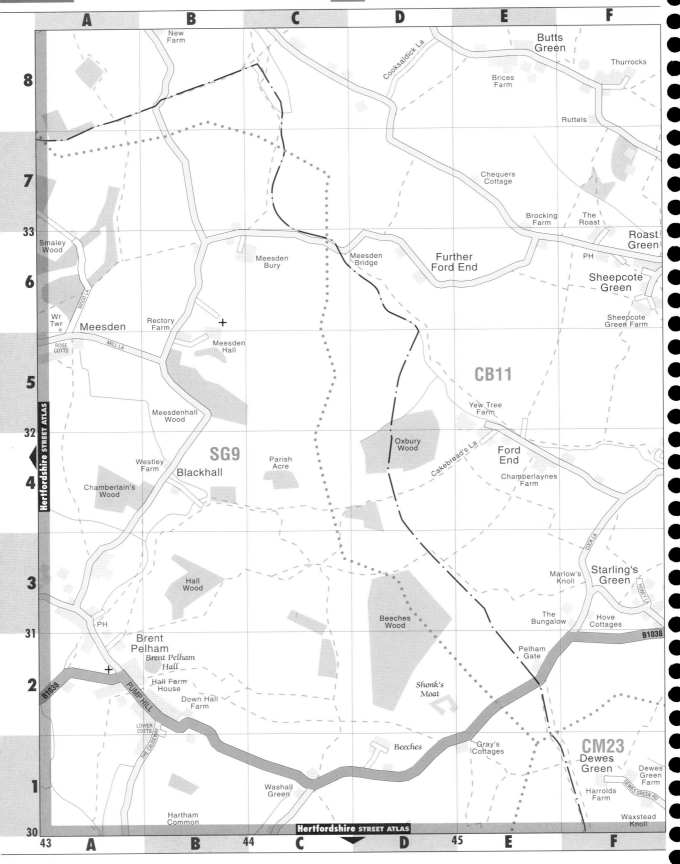

A | B | C | D | E | F

8

7

33

6

5

32

4

3

31

2

1

30

43 | A | B | 44 | C | D | 45 | E | F

New Farm

Butts Green

Thurrocks

Cooksaldick La

Brices Farm

Ruttels

Chequers Cottage

Brocking Farm

The Roast

Roast Green

Smaley Wood

Meesden Bury

Meesden Bridge

Further Ford End

PH

Sheepcote Green

WOOD LA

Wr Twr

Meesden

Rectory Farm

Meesden Hall

Sheepcote Green Farm

ROSE COTTS

MILL LA

CB11

Yew Tree Farm

Meesdenhall Wood

Oxbury Wood

Cakebread's La

Ford End

SG9

Parish Acre

Chamberlaynes Farm

Westley Farm

Blackhall

Chamberlain's Wood

Hall Wood

Beeches Wood

Marlow's Knoll

Starling's Green

COCK LA

HONEY LA

The Bungalow

Hove Cottages

B1038

PH

Brent Pelham

Brent Pelham Hall

Pelham Gate

Hall Farm House

PUMP HILL

Shonk's Moat

B1038

Down Hall Farm

LOWER COTTS

THE CAUSEWAY

Beeches

Gray's Cottages

CM23

Dewes Green

Dewes Green Farm

DEWES GREEN RD

Washall Green

Harrolds Farm

Waxstead Knoll

Hartham Common

Hertfordshire STREET ATLAS

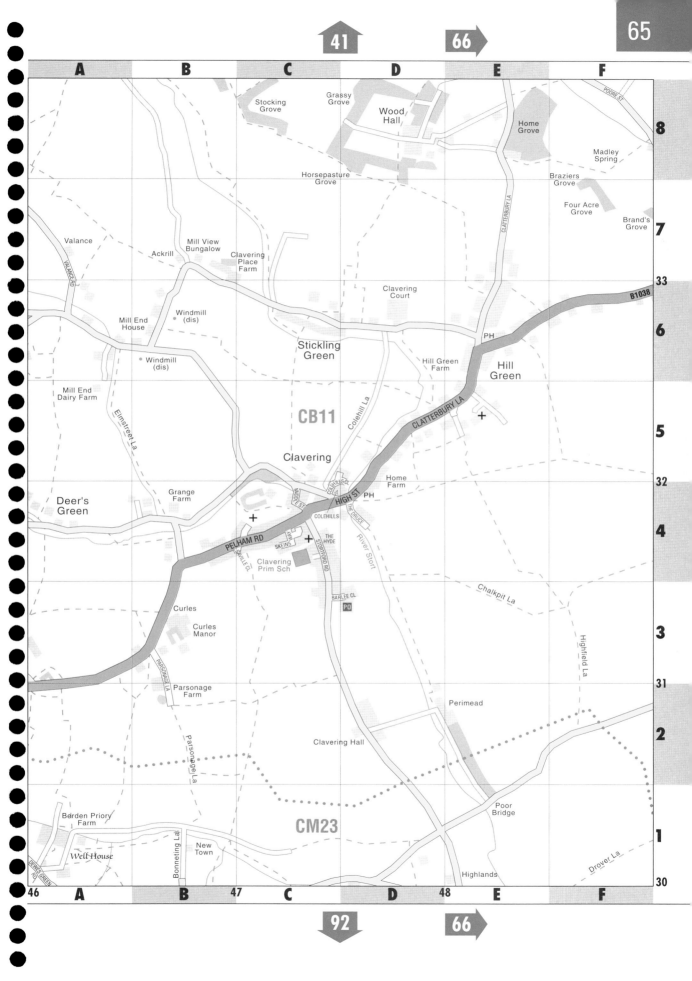

41

66

A B C D E F

8

Poore St

Stocking Grove

Grassy Grove

Wood Hall

Home Grove

Madley Spring

Horsepasture Grove

Braziers Grove

Four Acre Grove

Brand's Grove

7

Valance

Ackrill

Mill View Bungalow

Clavering Place Farm

Clavering Court

CLATTERBURY LA

33

B1038

VALANCE RD

Mill End House

Windmill (dis)

Stickling Green

PH

Hill Green

6

Windmill (dis)

Hill Green Farm

Hill Green

Mill End Dairy Farm

Elmstreet La

CB11

Colehill La

CLATTERBURY LA

+

5

Clavering

Home Farm

32

Deer's Green

Grange Farm

MIDDLE ST

GENTILISCL

HIGH ST

PH

+

+

SAVILLE CL

THE DRUCE

Chalkpit La

PELHAM RD

SKEINS

COLEHILLS

THE HYDE

River Stort

4

STORTFORD RD

Clavering Prim Sch

BARLEE CL.

PO

Highfield La

Curles

Curles Manor

3

PARSONAGE LA

Parsonage Farm

31

Perimead

Parsonage La

Clavering Hall

2

Berden Priory Farm

CM23

Poor Bridge

Bonneting La

Well House

New Town

Highlands

Drover La

DEWS GREEN RD

1

30

46 A 47 B C 48 D E F

92

66

| | A | B | C | D | E | F |

Newport

Cuckingstool End
BARNARD CL 1
HITCH COMMON RD 2
CHERRY GARDEN
BRAMBURY LA
ORCHARD CL

WICKEN RD
B1038
M11
Bonhunt Water
St Helen's Chapel
Bonhunt
Newport Prim Sch
Recn Gd

Works
Wicken Hall
PH
Howland Farm
Lower Farm
Wicken Bonhunt
THE MEADS
Brick House
B1038
Howland Farm House
Wicken Water
POORE ST

Bonhunt Springs

Bolsters

Fairwells
CB11
Broadfields
Harcamlow Way
Bushy Lays
Spring Close
Northcroft Spring

RICKLING RD

Coldhams Farm
Moat Farm
Mary Ann's Plantation

Tinney Springs
Tinney Spinney
Quendon Park
NEWPORT DR

Deer Park
Fireball Hill

Church End Farm
Fir Plantation
Rickling
Sibcopp's Wood
B1383

Codham Wood
Hanginghill
Dark Plantation

Pond Lay Plantation
Inn

CM23
BRICK KILN LA
Willis's La
Quendon

Coney Acre
Rickling Hall
Thistley Cres
GREYS HOLLOW
RICKLING GREEN RD
PO
B1383

49 A | B 50 C | D 51 E | F

A B C D E F

8

Debden Hall
Farm

IVY TODD HILL

Deynes
Farm

Harcamlow Way

CB10

Rowney Woods

Scabbard
Wood

MILL RD

PH THE
CAUSEWAY

DEYNES RD

THE CLOSE

HIGH ST

Debden CE
Prim Sch

CHURCH LA

PO

7

+

Debden

SMITHS GW

HIGH FIELDS

+

Barnards
Farm
(Riding Ctr)

Beck's
Wood

33

Brocton's
Plantation

TRAXTED RD

Tenddrings
Farm

6

Brocton
Farm

Rookend
Farm

ROOK END LA

CB11

Wieldbarns
Farm

Laceys

Debden
Green

5

Rook End

Sampson's La

32

Wigmore
Farm

Littley Wood
West

Monk's
Farm

Roother's
Farm

4

Littley Wood
East

Grove
Spring

River Cam or Granta

3

Thistley
Hall

HENHAM RD

Woodruff
Farm

Pinewood
Farm

Hamperden End

31

CORNELLS LA

Green Croft La

2

Amberden
Hall

Scotts
Farm

Duckett's
Farm

New Amberden
Hall

Leggatts
Farm

Staines
Farm

1

CM22

Mast

Wr Twr

CHICKNEY RD

CM6

30

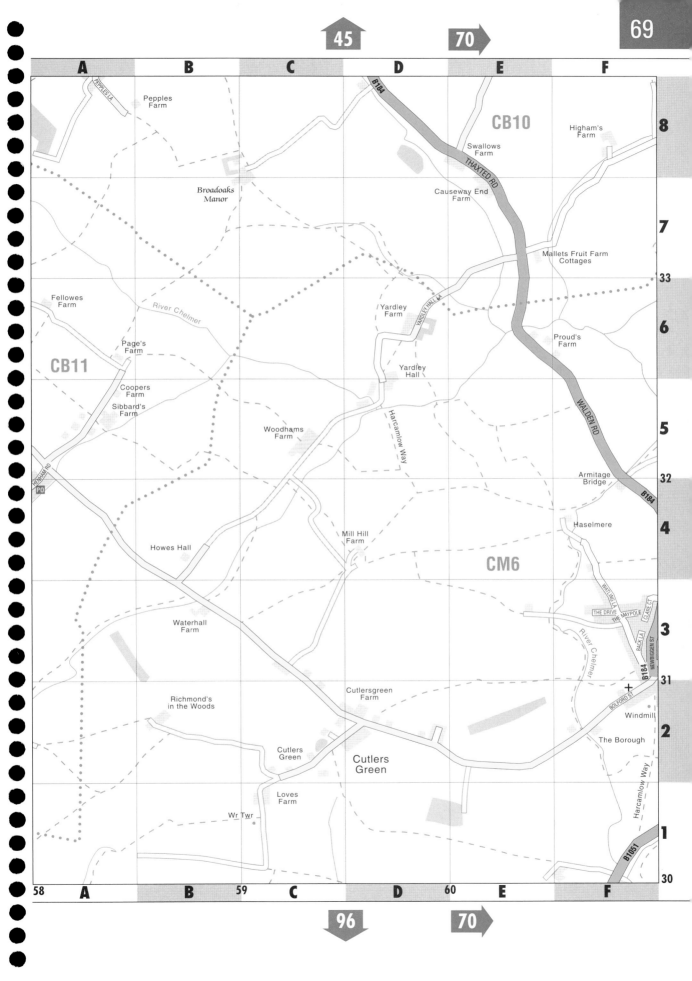

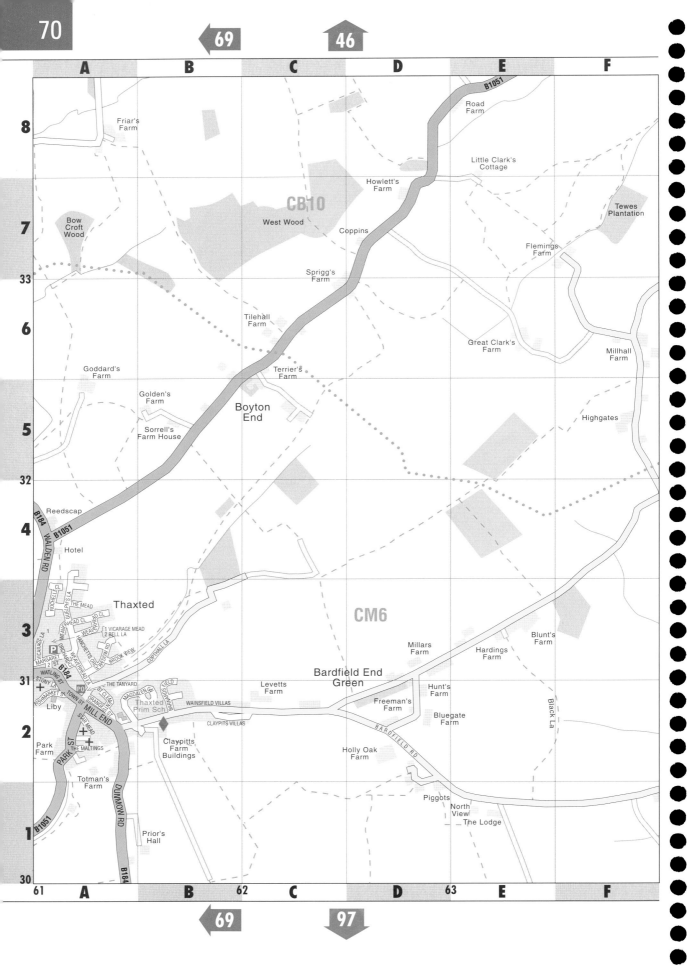

69
46

A B C D E F

8

Friar's Farm

B1051

Road Farm

7

Bow Croft Wood

CB10

West Wood

Howlett's Farm

Little Clark's Cottage

Tewes Plantation

Coppins

Flemings Farm

33

Sprigg's Farm

6

Tilehall Farm

Great Clark's Farm

Millhall Farm

Goddard's Farm

Terrier's Farm

Golden's Farm

Boyton End

Highgates

5

Sorrell's Farm House

32

Reedscap

4

B184

B1051

WALDEN RD

Hotel

ROCHELLE CL

THE MEAD

Thaxted

CM6

3

WEAVERHEAD CL

ST GUELPH'S LA

VICARAGE LA

1 VICARAGE MEAD
2 BELL LA

WEAVERHEAD LA

COPTHALL LA

BROOK VIEW

Millars Farm

Hardings Farm

Blunt's Farm

MARGARET ST

ORCHARD CL

VIEWTOWN RD

Bardfield End Green

31

STONY LA

B184

WATLING ST

THE TANYARD

HANCHETT'S DRICK

PO

FIELD SIDE

Levetts Farm

Hunt's Farm

FISHMARKET ST

TOWN ST

ST CLEAR

ORANGE CL

Thaxted Prim Sch

MAGDALEN CL

WAINSFIELD VILLAS

Freeman's Farm

Black La

Liby

MILL END

CLAYPITS VILLAS

Bluegate Farm

2

SAGE MEAD

Park Farm

PARK ST

THE MALTINGS

Claypitts Farm Buildings

Holly Oak Farm

BARDFIELD RD

Totman's Farm

DUNMOW RD

Piggots

North View

The Lodge

1

B1051

Prior's Hall

30

B184

69
97

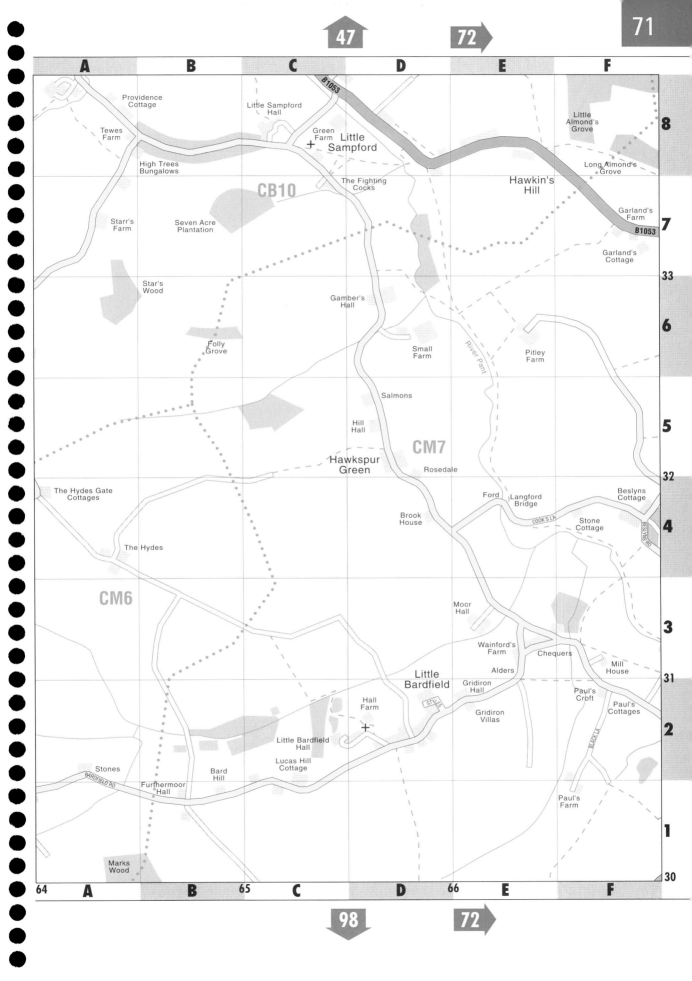

71 48

A B C D E F

8

Lodge

Darielay Farm

Mill End

Howe Hall

Fancy Covert

LITTLE LONDON HILL

B1057

The Thicket

The Round House

7

Spinney Lodge

The Moors

B1053

Brent Hall

33

BRENT HALL RD

TOM'S LA

Duck End

Windmill (dis)

Great Biggins Farm

Highbank

6

COACHMANS MEAD

PH

Mus

Church Hill

THE CAUSEWAY

VALLEY VIEW

KEMPE RD

VICARAGE RD

Finchingfield CE Prim Sch

Justice's Hill

BRIDGE ST

PO

THE OLD VICARAGE

B1053

WINSEY CHASE

STEPHEN MARSH AVE

THE PIGHTLE

THE HOPGROUNDS

Gatward's Farm

Winsey Chase

Finchingfield

Finchingfield Brook

5

Little Winceys Farm

The Mill House

MILL RD

Dynes Cottage

Daw Street Cottages

32

Beslyns

The Haven

Talavera

CM7

Normans

DAW ST

Daw Street

Petches

Petches Cottages

4

Pakes

Littles

BESLYNS RD

Robjohns Farm

The Briars

3

Bridge End

Champions

Sculpin's Bridge

Petches Bridge

Bridge Farm

NORTHFIELD

The Watermill

31

Brooklands

High Chimneys

Southcotts

Whinbush Farm

2

BRIDGE ST

MEADOW VIEW

RUTLAND PL

Windmill

Claypit Hall

School Farm

Waltham's Cross

NORTHAMPTON MDW

ST JOHN'S TERR

MILL CL

MILL RD

BELL LA

Cage

PH

PO

VW ST

CROWN ST

HIGH ST

BROOK ST

Great Bardfield Prim Sch

Great Bardfield

Cross Farm Cottage

DURHAM CL

HIGH ST

THE CORNICHE

Liby TH

The Cross Farm

1

Mus

Bardfield Ctr

BRAINTREE RD

ST MARY'S VILLAS

NEWLAND AVE

BENDYSHES RD

Lodge Wood

WEATHERVANE COTTS

ALIENOR AVE

HALL VILLAS

The Nutshell

30

B1057 DUNMOW RD

67 A B 68 C D 69 E F

71 99

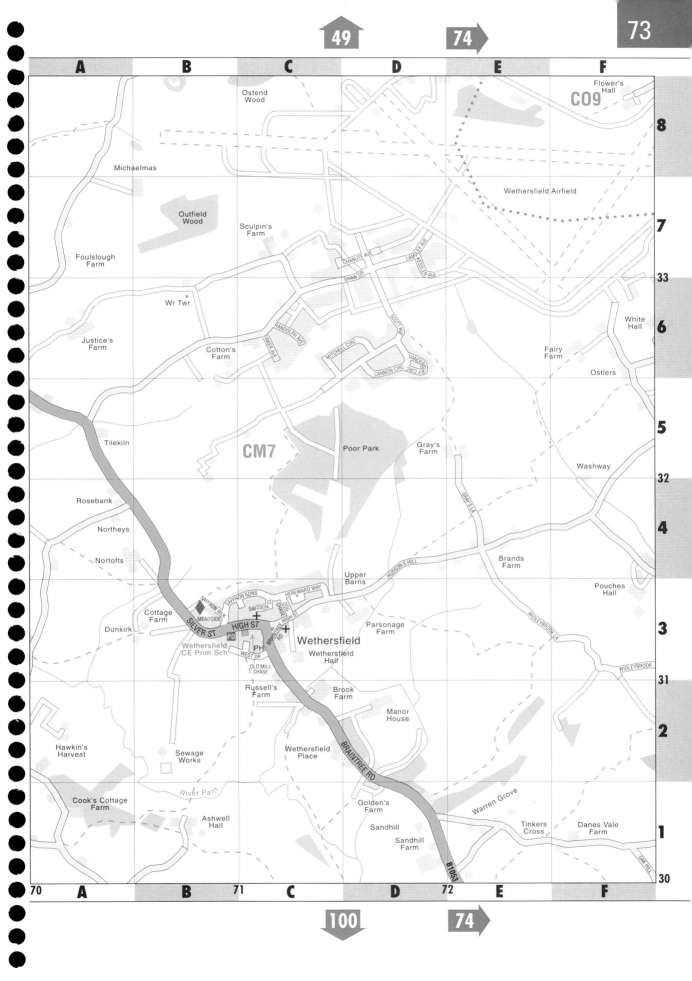

A B C D E F

8
7
33
6
32
5
4
3
31
2
1
30

Wethersfield Airfield
Welcome Slough Farm
Tattersall's Farm
Morris Green
Finch's Farm
Burnt House Farm
Almshouse Green
Deek's Farm
Moss Farm
SUGAR LA
Sugar Lane Farm
Barnard's Farm
Whitehall Farm
Upper Wright's Farm
Oak House
Runalong Farm
CO9
Runalong Wood
Thorley Grove
Thorley's Farm
Tredgell's Wood
Cherrytree Farm
Littley Wood
New Barns
CM7
Brickkiln Green
Lower Green
Lower Green
School Green
Lealands
Patten's Wood
Readings
Hawks Wood
Elms Farm
Patten's Farm
PH
The Readings Spinney
New Plantation
Baker's Farm
WIDLEYBROOK LA
Blackmore End
SYERS FIELD
Owl's Hall
HYDE LA
Shragg's Wood
FOUR ASHES
Waver's Farm
Hyde Farm
HYDE LA
Summer's Hall
Shinborough

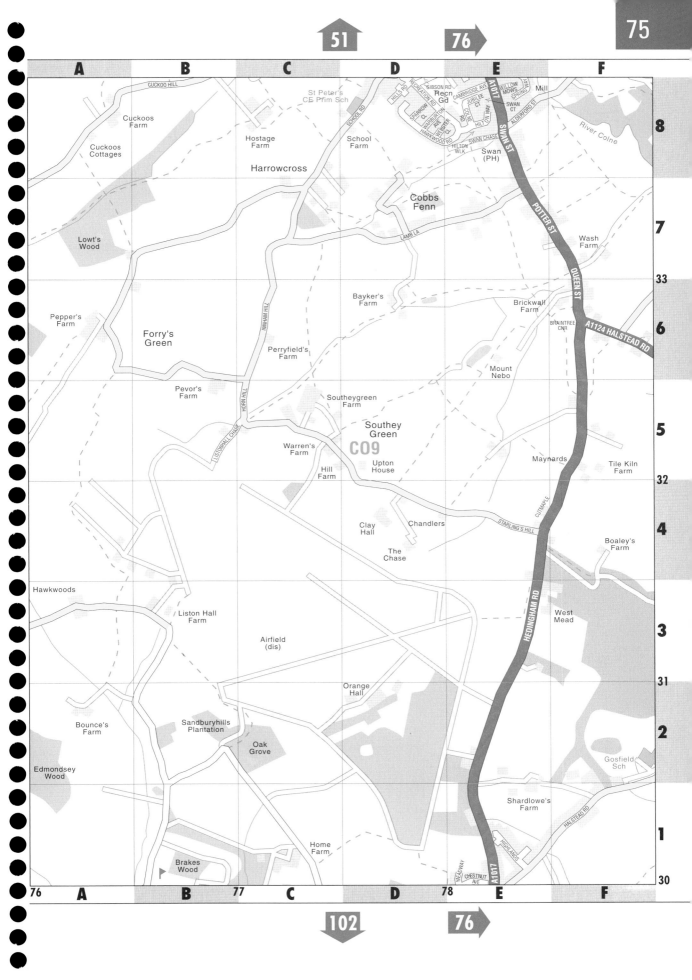

75 52 75 103

A B C D E F

8 7 33 6 5 32 4 3 31 2 1 30

Purlshill

Purlshill Plantation

Barretts Hall

Toldishall Cottages

Mill Farm

Hull's Mill Farm

Chestnut Grove

Mill

DYNE'S HALL RD

Dynes Hall

Sewage Works

Wallace's Farm

Dog House Grove

Pearman's Hill

A1124

HALSTEAD RD

Foxborough Hills Farm

Bennett's Farm

Bennett's Park

Fitz John's Farm

CO9

Hepworth Hall

Foxborough

DOE'S CNR

Fitz John's Grove

Brook Street Farm

HOWE CHASE

The Howe

Bradley's House

HEDINGHAM RD

ASHLONG GR

Wash Farm

Broak's Wood

Box Mill Plantation

CHURCHILL AVE

A131

Shardlowe's Wood

Woodcot

BOX MILL LA

COURTAULD HOMES OF REST

SUDBURY RD

Whitehouse Farm

Sloe House

Halstead

H

NORTH MILL PL

Sch

Whiteash Green

SLOE HILL

HALSTEAD

BELLEVUE TERR 1
PAPERMILL COTTS 2
RIVERSIDE CT 3
CAXTON PL 4
TRINITY CT 5.

MILL CHASE

BOIS FIELD TERR

FINSBURY PL

COLNE RD

Sch

Gosfield Sch

SLOUGH FARM RD

STANLEY RD

Trad Est

BAYS DR

CHAPEL ST

BROTON DR

UPPER ST

MORLEY RD

PRETORIA RD

EAST MILL

Cemy

HALSTEAD RD

THE PIP/INSPRIDGE RD

BUTLER RD

COLNE VALLEY CT

P

MARKET HILL

A1124 HIGH ST

HEAD ST

ST ANDREW'S ROAD

GARDEN TERR

HARVEY CT

COLCHESTER RD A1124

Crowbridge Farm

VICARAGE CT

P

P

CHAPEL HILL

Sch

WEAVERS CT

FACTORY TERR

FACTORY LA

WEAVERS ROW

MIDDLEFIELD

THE CENTRE

GARDENERS CT

YARFIELD CT

Great Spansey Wood

ORCHARD AVE RD

DOOLEY RD

Liby

i

FACTORY LA

SWALLOW WLK

KESTREL

KINGFISHER MDWS

Little Spansey Wood

WINDMILL RD

TRINITY ST

ADAMS CT

NEW ST

DORSET RD

KING'S RD

COURTAULD

P

RAVENS AVE

Russell's Farm

New Wood

Blamsters Farm

MOUNT HILL

A131

WILLOW RD

GODWIN CL

WARREN RD

OXFORD RD

TRINITY TERR

MANOR CL

UPPER MT PLEASANT

MOUNT PLEASANT

NEALE RD

CUTTING

MITCHELL AVE

PARK

FAIRFIELD WAY

TIDINGS HL

BALL'S CHASE

ELM DR

MEADOW CL

The Grange

Russell's Farm

RUSSELL'S RD

RAYNER WAY

KNOWLES

79 A B 80 C D 81 E F

River Colne

D1
1 SPANSEY CT
2 MONKLANDS CT
3 TRINITY TERR
4 MOUNT RISE
5 CLOVERS
6 TRYON CT
7 DE VERES RD
8 RAMSEY RD

F2
1 HIGHBURY TERR
2 CHIPPING HILL
3 CROFT HO
4 PARSONS CT

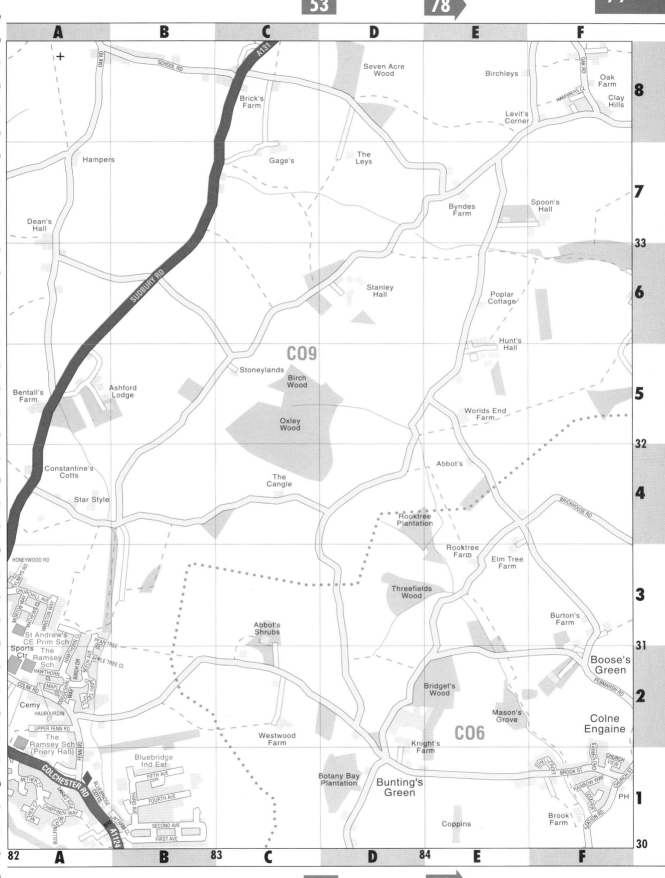

A B C D E F

8

OAK RD

SCHOOL RD

A131

Seven Acre Wood

Birchleys

HAMSHERS CL

OAK RD

Oak Farm

Clay Hills

Brick's Farm

Levit's Corner

Hampers

Gage's

The Leys

7

Byndes Farm

Spoon's Hall

33

Dean's Hall

SUDBURY RD

Stanley Hall

6

Poplar Cottage

CO9

Hunt's Hall

Stoneylands

Birch Wood

Worlds End Farm

5

Bentall's Farm

Ashford Lodge

Oxley Wood

32

Constantine's Cotts

Abbot's

Star Style

The Cangle

BRICKHOUSE RD

4

Rooktree Plantation

Rooktree Farm

Elm Tree Farm

HONEYWOOD RD

TYLERS RD

Threefields Wood

Burton's Farm

3

MORTOW WAY
MATHEWS CL
CHURCHILL AVE
WINSTON WAY

St Andrew's CE Prim Sch

PEAR TREE
APPLE TREE CL

Abbot's Shrubs

31

Sports Ctr

The Ramsey Sch

HAWTHORN CL
BIRCH DR
MAPLE CL
CHERRY CL
CLOSE SHAY WAY

Boose's Green

PEBMARSH RD

COLNE RD

Cemy

Bridget's Wood

Mason's Grove

2

HAUBOURDIN CT

Colne Engaine

UPPER FENN RD

CO6

The Ramsey Sch (Priory Hall)

FENN RD

Westwood Farm

Knight's Farm

SHELLEY CROFT

BROOK ST

SWAN'S CROFT
CHURCH VIEW
CHURCH ST

NETHER CT

COLCHESTER RD

Bluebridge Ind Est

FIFTH AVE
THIRD AVE
FOURTH AVE

Botany Bay Plantation

Bunting's Green

RAINBOW WAY

PH

NIC CL
WELL CL
CHAFFINCH WAY

BLUEBRIDGE COTTS
BRICK FARM CL

A1124

SECOND AVE
FIRST AVE

Brook Farm

STATION RD

BULLFINCH

Coppins

1

30

82 A B 83 C D 84 E F

Map grid

| | A | B | C | D | E | F |

8 — New Barn Farm, PH, St John The Baptist CE Prim Sch, Pebmarsh, Le Mote Hall, Cross End, PEBMARSH RD, Stapleford's Farm, Montague's Farm, CO8, Peyton Hall, CO9

Greathouse Farm, Hoblets, New Wood, Fishpits

7 — KINGS MEAD, THE STREET, MILL LA

33 — North Wood, Polstead's Farm, Valiants Farm, Garlands Farm

6 — Marvel's Garden, WATER LA, Cricks Farm, Lamarsh Park, DAWS CROSS, Daws Farm, Hill House

5 — Preston's Lake, Hungary Hall, Great Wheatley Wood, Poultry Farm

32 — Peverel's Farm, CO6, Baggaretts, Rye Fenn

4 — Nightingales Farm, The Privet, Manning's Farm, Bramble's Farm

3 — Brick House Farm, Bromptons, Crofts Wood, West Grove, Great Catley's Farm

31 — Countess Cross, Countesscross Farm, OVERHALL HILL

2 — THE GREEN, Colne Engaine CE Prim Sch, Black Bats, GREEN FARM RD, GREEN WAY, Over Hall, Chestnut Plantation, Mon, Shrive's Wood, Aldercar, PEBMARSH RD, HIGH ST, CHURCH ST

1 — Colne Park, Home Farm, Instep's Farm

30 — MILL LA, Lodge Farm, Millbrook Grove, LAWSHALL'S HILL

85 A B 86 C D 87 E F

	A	B	C	D	E	F

8

Lamarsh Hill
Station Hvl
New Cut
Woolpit Downs
The Paddocks
Parsonage Gr
Bures Ho
Bures
Colne Rd
B1508
P.O.
Square La
The Waldegraves
Mayland Rd
Claypits Ave
Bures CE Prim Sch
The Ferrier's
Ferrier's Farm
Bures
Bures
Parsonage Hall
Normandy Way
Cambridge Way
Colchester Rd
River Stour
Nether Hall

7
Baker's Hall
Brook House
Brook House Farm
B1508

33
Horne's Green
Ravensfield Farm
Peytonhall Wood
Butler's Farm
Hobb's Well
The Plantation
Boadicea Cotts
LC
Old Barn Rd

6
The Lodge
Pricketts Hall
CO8
Craig's Hill
Craigs La
Craig's

5
Nursery Farm
Lower Jennies Farm
Spentpenny Farm
Mount Bures
Bures Hall
Works
Hall Rd

32
White's Farm
Valley Green Farm
Cambridge Brook
Thatcher's Arms (PH)

4
Pannells

3
Morelands Farm
Little Loveney Hall
Great Loveney Hall
Abrams
Chappel Rd
Flint Field Farm
Robert's Hill
Fordham Rd
Dowling Rd
Norton Farm
Sergeant's Farm
CO6

31
Weirstock Farm
Wr Twr
Beak Farm

2
Reedings
Loveneys Farm
Inworth La
Middle Gn
Ball's Chace
Golden Square

1
Berewyk Hall
Normans Farm
Sturgeons Farm
Wakes Colne Green
Council Hos
Legerton Cotts
Lower Gn
Lane Rd
Jordans Farm
Pattricks Farm
Jupe's Hill
Rowneys Farm
Burnt House Farm

30

88	A	B	89	C	D	90	E	F

79

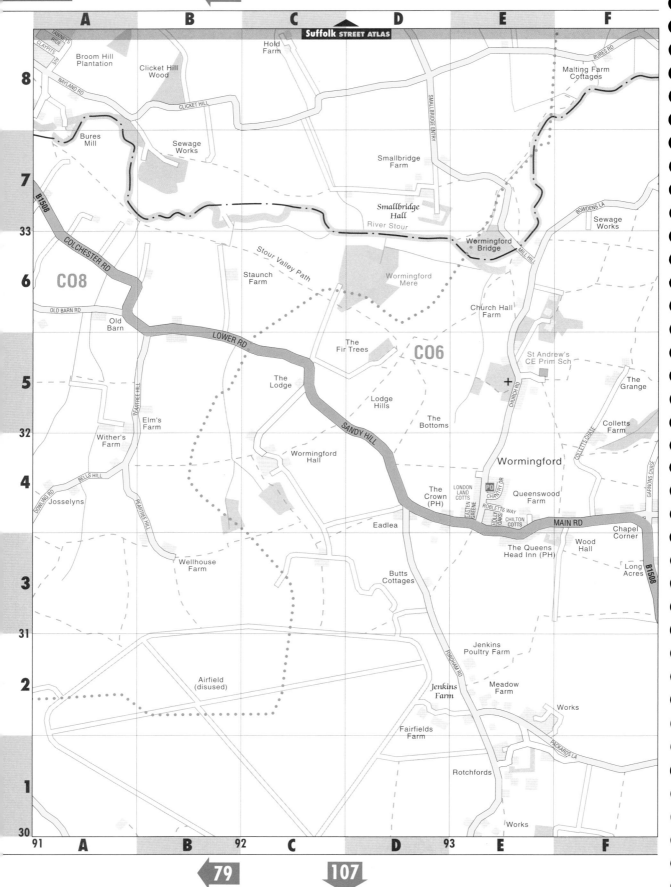

Suffolk STREET ATLAS

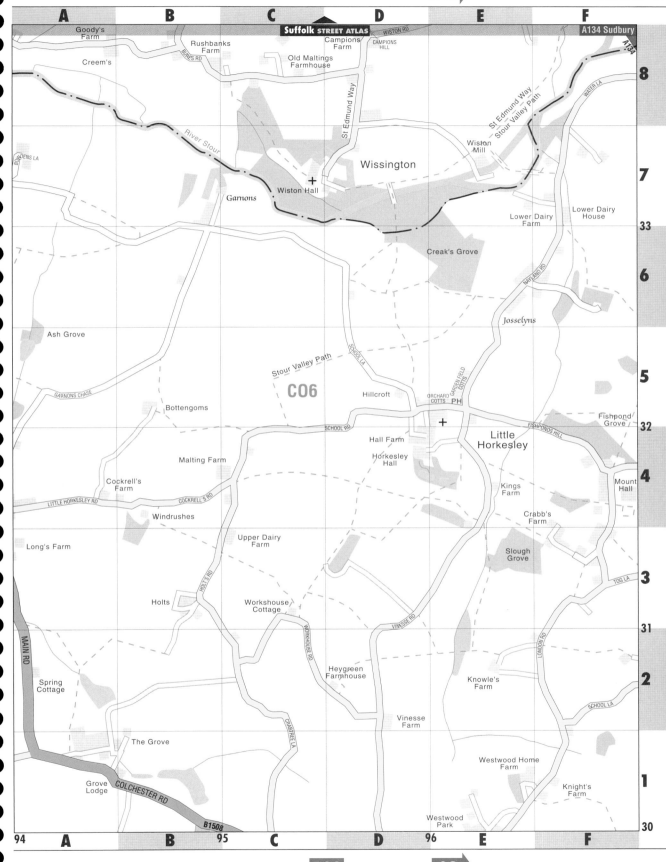

Suffolk STREET ATLAS

A134 Sudbury

82
108
82

A   B   C   D   E   F

Goody's Farm
Creem's
Rushbanks Farm
BURES RD
Old Maltings Farmhouse
Campions Farm
WISTON RD
CAMPIONS HILL
St Edmund Way
St Edmund Way
Stour Valley Path
A134
WATER LA
8

River Stour
BURDENS LA
Wissington
Wiston Mill
7

Garnons
Wiston Hall
Lower Dairy Farm
Lower Dairy House
33

Creak's Grove
MAYLAND RD
6

Ash Grove
Josselyns

Stour Valley Path
SCHOOL LA
CO6
Hillcroft
ORCHARD COTTS
GARDEN FIELD COTTS
PH
FISHPONDS HILL
Fishpond Grove
5
32

Garnons Chase
Bottengoms
School Rd
Hall Farm
Horkesley Hall
Little Horkesley
Mount Hall
4

Malting Farm
Cockrell's Farm
LITTLE HORKESLEY RD
COCKRELL'S RD
Windrushes
Kings Farm
Crabb's Farm
Slough Grove
TOG LA
3

Long's Farm
Upper Dairy Farm
HOLTS RD
Holts
Workshouse Cottage
WORKHOUSE RD
VINESSE RD
LONDON RD
31

MAIN RD
Spring Cottage
Heygreen Farmhouse
Knowle's Farm
SCHOOL LA
2

The Grove
CRABTREE LA
Vinesse Farm
Westwood Home Farm
Knight's Farm
1

Grove Lodge
COLCHESTER RD
B1508
Westwood Park
30

94   A   B   95   C   D   96   E   F

81
56

A   B   C   D   E   F

8

A134

WATER LA

River Stour

PARK RD

HORKESLEY HILL

Horkesley
Park

Littlegarth
Sch

King's Yard

BURNT DICK HILL

Boxtedhall
Great Wood

Gulsons

Boxted

Boxted CE
Prim Sch

CHURCH ST

7

Valley
Yard

Little Wood

Boxted Hall

33

Whitepark
Farm

Kerseys

CHURCH RD

6

South Lodge

CO4

Pond House

The
Chantry

GREENFIELD
COTTS

Ridgnalls

Potter's
Farm

Orchard
Farm

WET LA

5

Carter's Farm

Carters
Vineyard

Brook
Farm

Martins
PH

NAYLAND RD

CO6

Coveneys

BOXTED CHURCH RD

Horkesley
Green

GREEN LA

BROOK
COTTS

Boxted Lodge

LONDON RD

32

Holly Lodge
Farm

Workhouse
Hill

WORKHOUSE HILL

4

The
Grove

HOLLY LA

Barritts Farm

MILL RD

WINDMILL G

SCARFE'S
CNR

Nevards
Farm

Enfields Farm

Old Ellis
Farmhouse

ELLIS RD

Noakes
Farm

TOG LA

3

Altyre
House

Lodge Farm

BOXTED RD

Frost's
Grove

31

QUEEN'S HEAD RD

REDHOUSE LA

THE CAUSEWAY

Harrow
Corner

STRAIGHT RD

Priory Hall
Farm

OLD HOUSE LA

2

Breewood Hall

PO

Essex Way

Redhouse
Farm

SCHOOL LA

BROAD LA

Great Horkesley

PH

LINCOLN LA

Horkesley
Plantation

PEPPER'S RD

LANGHAM RD

1

OLD HOUSE RD

A134

THE
CRESCENT

MORLAND
CT

GR

GLENWAY
CT

GLEBELANDS

Spratt's Marsh

30

97   A   B   98   C   D   99   E   F

81
109

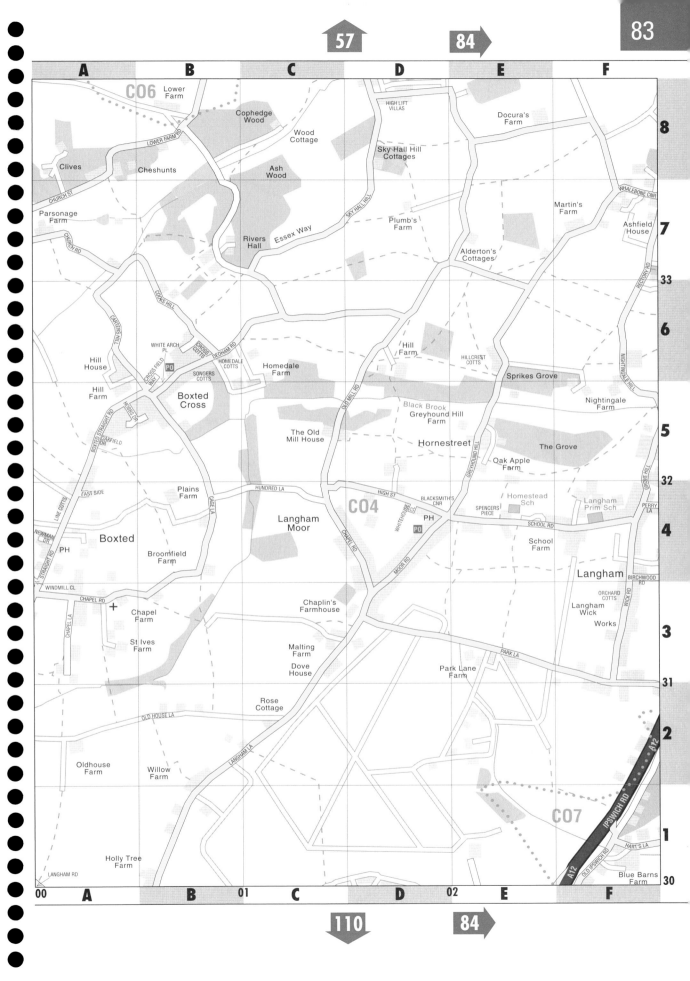

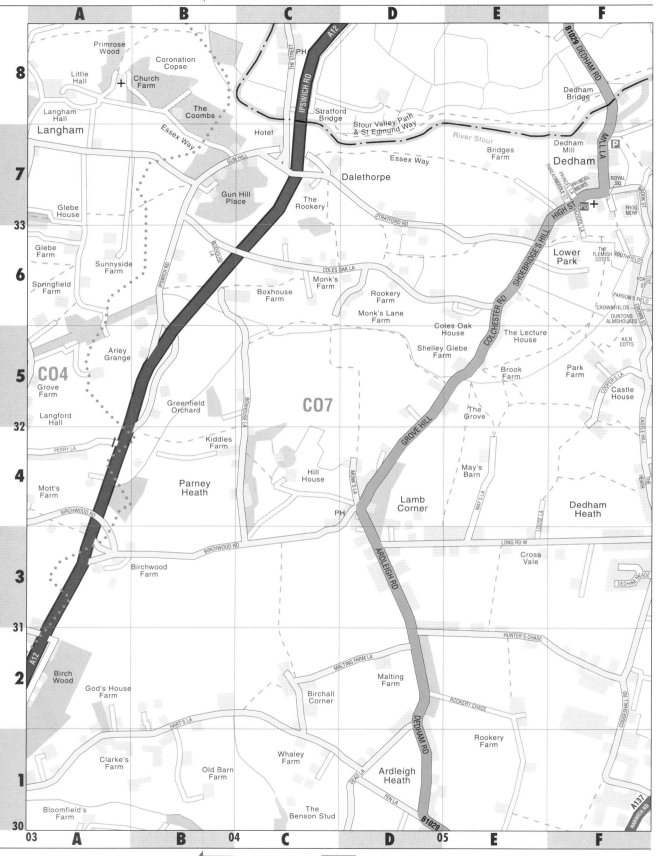

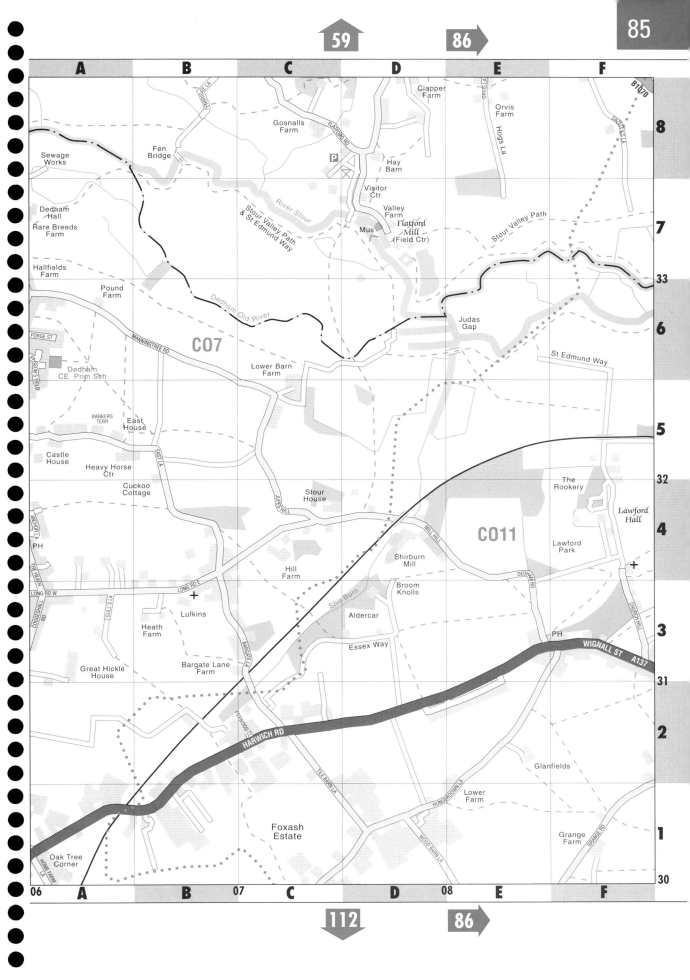

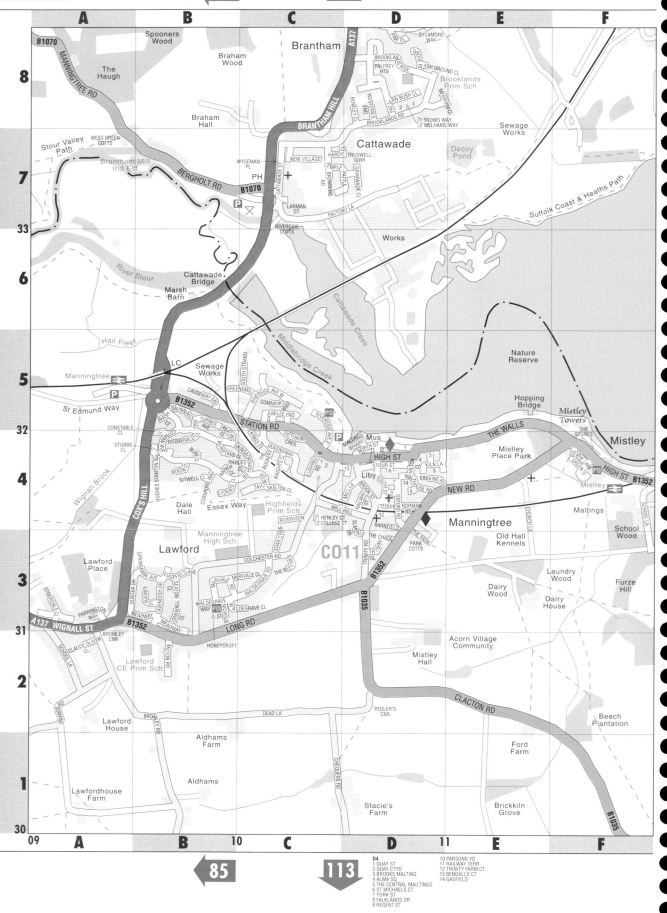

85
60

B1070

Spooners Wood

Braham Wood

Brantham

A137

PINE CL

SYCAMORE WAY

Brooklands Rise

GROVE RD

ASH GROUND CL

PALFREY HTS

WESTERS END

BRAN BUSH CL

Brooklands Prim Sch

MERRIAM CL

MANNINGTREE RD

The Haugh

Braham Hall

BRANTHAM HILL

ROWLEY CL

BROOKLANDS RD

1 SNOWS WAY
2 WELHAMS WAY

Sewage Works

Stour Valley Path

WEST GREEN COTTS

Brantham Mill Ind Est

BERGHOLT RD

WYSEMAN PL

PH

B1070

P

Cattawade

New Village

HARDY

TRUSWELL TERR

TEMPLE PATTLE

GRIMWADE CL

Decoy Pond

CATTAWADE ST

BROWNING RD

Suffolk Coast & Heaths Path

8

7

33

LARMAN CT

RIVERSIDE COTTS

FACTORY LA

Works

River Stour

Cattawade Bridge

Marsh Barn

Cattawade Creek

6

Hall Fleet

Middlebridge Creek

Nature Reserve

Manningtree

LC

Sewage Works

SOUTH STRAND

GREENSMILL

COMMERCE WAY

RIVERSIDE AVE W

Hopping Bridge

THE WALLS

Mistley Towers

THE STORES

Mistley

5

32

P

St Edmund Way

B1352

MUNNINGS WAY

TURNER AVE

CAUSEWAY END

KEATING

KINGS CL

STATION RD

JUBILEE END

VICTORIA CRES

RIVERSIDE AVE E

PO

P

MAERES

WHARF ST

NORTH ST

Mus

HIGH ST

STOUR ST

Mistley Place Park

THE GREEN

THE VILLAGE

PO

Mistley

High St

B1352

CONSTABLE CL

NASH

FITZGERALD

QUEENSWAY

THE ROMERY

GAINSBOROUGH

KNIGHTS

LISHINGS

Lib

Mistley

4

STUBBS CL

HUGHES STANTON WAY

MUNNINGS WAY

INNLOD

BLAKE

BARKER

LYDGATE CL

TAY

SKELTON CL

MILL LA

BROOKS

ST

KILN LA

ERSKINE RD

HOUSE RD

9

NORMAN RD

NEW RD

Maltings

School Wood

SCHOOL LA

Cox's Hill

DIXON

SITWELL CL

CORNFORD WAY

BURROWS CL

Dale Hall

Essex Way

Highfields Prim Sch

RIVERVIEW

HENLEY CT
COLLEGE CT

ELMDALE

THE CHASE

OXFORD RD

BARNFIELD

PARK COTTS

THE PARK

Manningtree

Old Hall Kennels

Wignall Brook

Lawford

CEDAR CRES

COLCHESTER RD

THE BEECH

MILL HILL

TRINITY RD

CO11

3

Lawford Place

SPRINGPARK AVE

EDGEFIELD AVE

SEATON CL

CORNWALL

MERIVALE RD

MERIVALE CL

WALDEGRAVE RD

B1352

B1035

Dairy Wood

Laundry Wood

Dairy House

Furze Hill

HUNTER DR

LINDYS

CAVENDISH DR

WALDEGRAVE WAY

NICHOLS

PO

W4LDEGRAVE CL

Acorn Village Community

2

PARRINGTON WAY

BROMLEY CNR

Lawford CE Prim Sch

MILTON RD

HONEYCROFT

LONG RD

Mistley Hall

CLACTON RD

31

A137 WIGNALL ST

B1352

MEADWAY

SCHOOL LA

CLAUDE OLIVER CL

GRABER RD

Lawford House

BROMLEY RD

DEAD LA

PEDLER'S CNR

CHEQUERS RD

Aldhams Farm

Aldhams

Stacie's Farm

Ford Farm

Beech Plantation

1

Lawfordhouse Farm

Brickkiln Grove

B1035

30

09

10

11

85
113

D4
1 QUAY ST
2 QUAY CTYD
3 BROOKS MALTING
4 ALMA SQ
5 THE CENTRAL MAILTINGS
6 ST MICHAELS CT
7 YORK ST
8 FALKLANDS DR
9 REGENT ST
10 PARSONS YD
11 RAILWAY TERR
12 TRINITY FARM CT
13 BENDALLS CT
14 GASFIELD

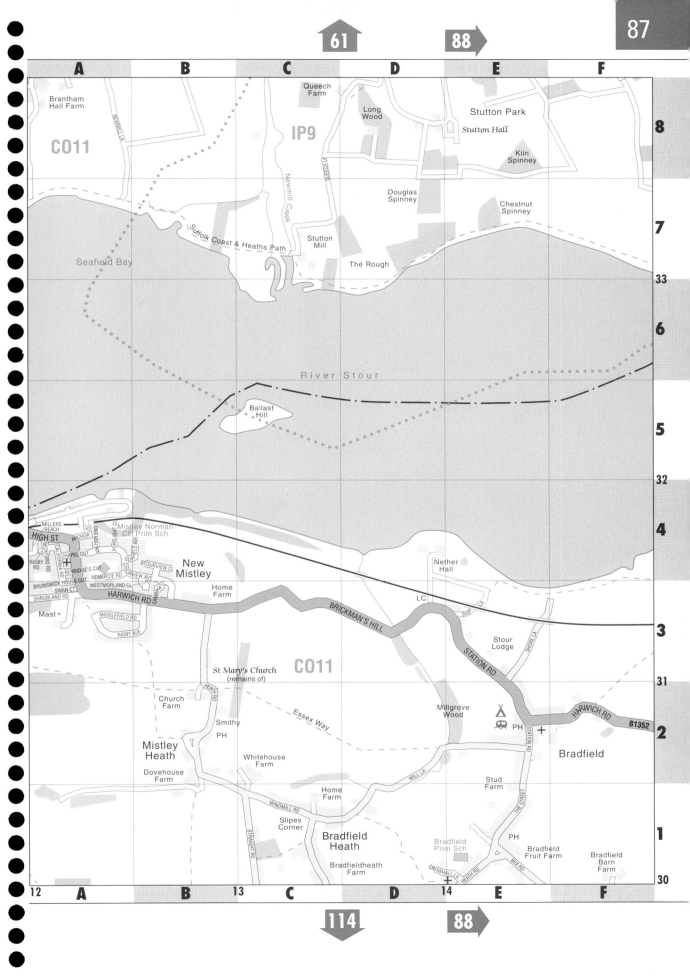

61
88
114
88

87
62

A   B   C   D   E   F

8

IP9

Backhouse
Ley

Holbrook Bay

7

Graham's
Wharf

Suffolk Coast
and
Heaths Path

33

Stutton
Ness

Dovehouse
Point

River Stour

6

Stone
Point

5

Wrabness
Point

Shore
Farm

32

Jacques Bay

Essex Way

Oakfield
Wood

Wrabness
Hall

4

Wrabness
Local Nature
Reserve

WALL LA

Cemy

Lower
Farm

Wrabness

CHURCH RD

STONE LA

P

P

Ragmarsh
Farm

WHEATSHEAF CL

STATION RD

Brakey
Grove

Dimbols
Farm

3

Jacques
Hall

WHEATSHEAF LA

31

Gateways

Foxes
Farm

Domine
Farm

CO11

B1352

2

B1352 HARWICH RD

Lonbarn

PH

HARWICH RD

Priory
Farm

COOK'S
CORNER

The
Firs

LONBARN HILL

Lonbarn
Bridge

SPINWEL'S HILL

Spinnel's
Farm

Windmill

SPINNEL'S LA

BUTLER'S LA

Butler's
Farm

1

Pondhall
Wood

Bluehouse
Farm

30

15   A   16   B   C   16   D   17   E   F

87
115

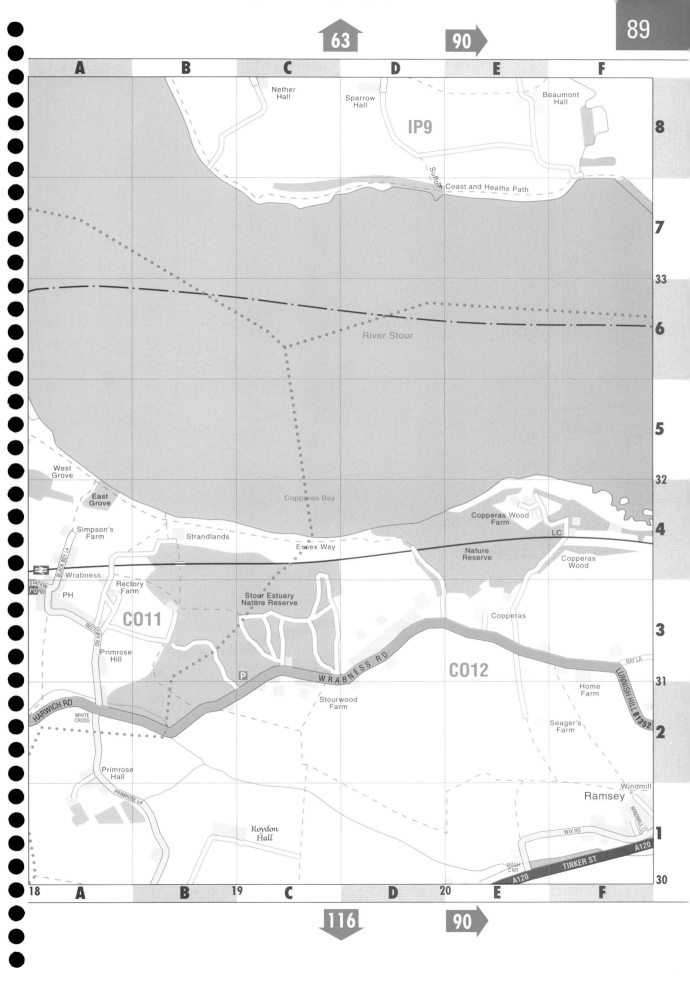

A B C D E F

8

IP9

Nether
Hall

Sparrow
Hall

Beaumont
Hall

Suffolk Coast and Heaths Path

7

33

6

River Stour

5

West
Grove

32

East
Grove

Copperas Bay

Copperas Wood
Farm

4

Simpson's
Farm

Strandlands

Essex Way

Nature
Reserve

LC

Copperas
Wood

Wrabness

Rectory
Farm

Stour Estuary
Nature Reserve

CO11

Copperas

3

STATION
RD

PO

PH

BLACK BOY LA

RECTORY RD

Primrose
Hill

P

WRABNESS RD

CO12

RAY LA

UNNISH HILL B1352

31

Home
Farm

HARWICH RD

WHITE
CROSS

Stourwood
Farm

Seager's
Farm

2

Primrose
Hall

PRIMROSE LA

Windmill

WINDMILL LA

Ramsey

1

Roydon
Hall

WIX RD

WASH
CNR

A120

TINKER ST

A120

30

18 A B 19 C D 20 E F

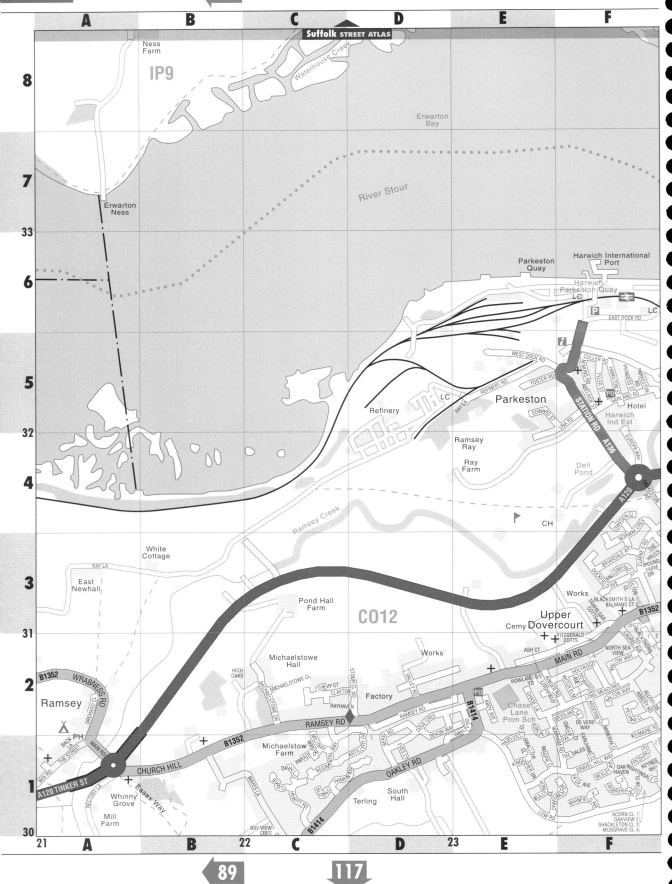

Suffolk STREET ATLAS

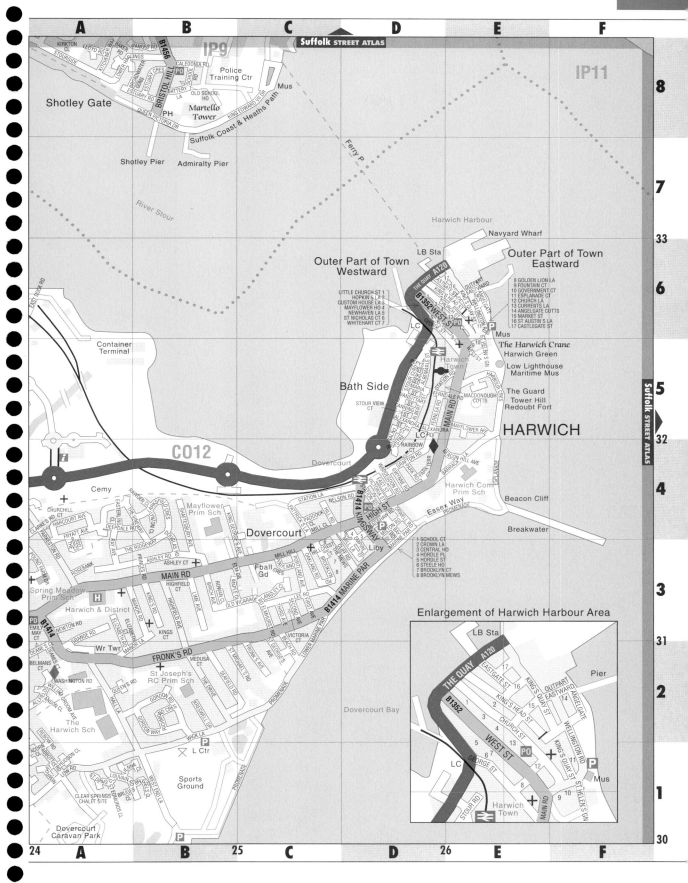

65

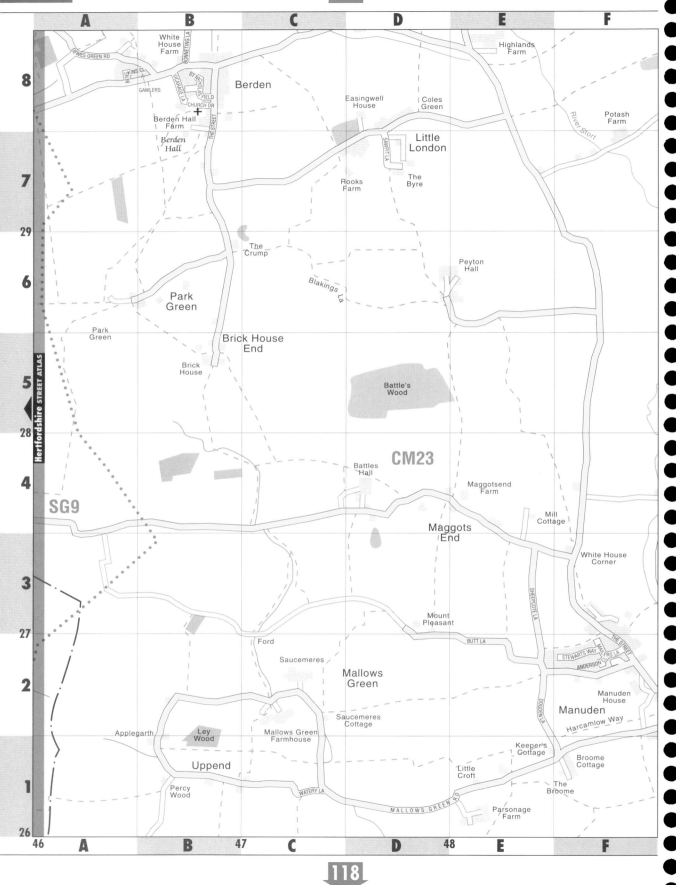

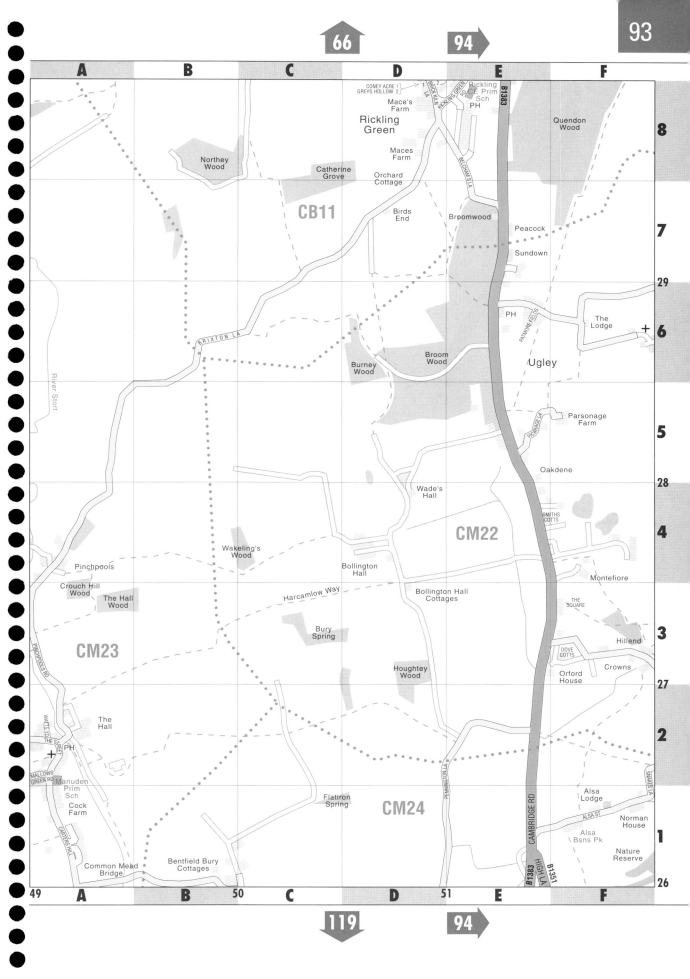

93
67

A B C D E F

8

CB11

Fivefoot Bridge

NORTH HALL RD

CH
LC

The White House

River Cam or Granta

Sheepcote La

7

Meadside

29

Ugley Hall Farm Cottages

Birds Farm

The Cock (PH)

Henham

6

Ugley Hall Farm

Down Hall House

CHURCH ST

THE CHASE

HIGH ST

PO

STAR RD

HALL CL

HIGHFIELDS

Parsonage Farm

CROWN ST

CARTERS LA

SAGES

The Vicarage

5

Hazelmoor Common

OLD MEAD RD

Birch Grove

CM22

Bacons Farm

PIMBLETT ROW

SCHOOL LA

Henham & Ugley Prim Sch

28

Old Mead

VERN

MILL RD

Playing Field

Church Common

Old Mead La

4

Mast

Fieldgate Farm House

Works

Byculla

The Mill House

Mill Pond Farm

Ugley Green

Hudsons Farm

FIELD GATE LA

3

Ugley Park

Bedwell Common

MILL RD

B1051

The Hermitage

BEDWELL RD

DELLONS VW

MAYTREE GDNS

SPENCER CL

Golds Nursery Bsns Pk

P

LC

Elsenham

Sand Pit

Pennington Hall

27

JENKINS PK

NEW RD

HUNTERS CT

FENMAN CT

SHAKES LA

ALSA LEYS

ALSA GDNS

CRANMORE CL

HENHAM RD

2

Harewood

BROOM FARM RD

ELM CL

STATION RD

RIDLEY CL

OTTERS

MARKWELLS

CORIANDER DR

PARK LA

HAILES WOOD

Driving Range

CH

Alsa Wood

PAGET CL

THE GLEBE

The Crown (PH)

Elsenham Palace

Stansted Brook

Mast

Elsenham

Playing Field

LEIGH DR

FOURWAYS

STANSTED RD

PO

GLEBE END

ROBIN HOOD RD

MILL

RUSH LA

HIGH ST

HAILES WOOD CL

Elsenham CE Prim Sch

ELSENHAM CROSS

HALL RD

1

Alsa Wood Cottage

May Tree Farm

B1051

GILBEY COTTS

SAUNDERS CL

Nursery

The Old Vicarage

Abbotsford Bridge

MAY WLK

CM24

M11

26

52 A 53 B C 53 D 54 E F

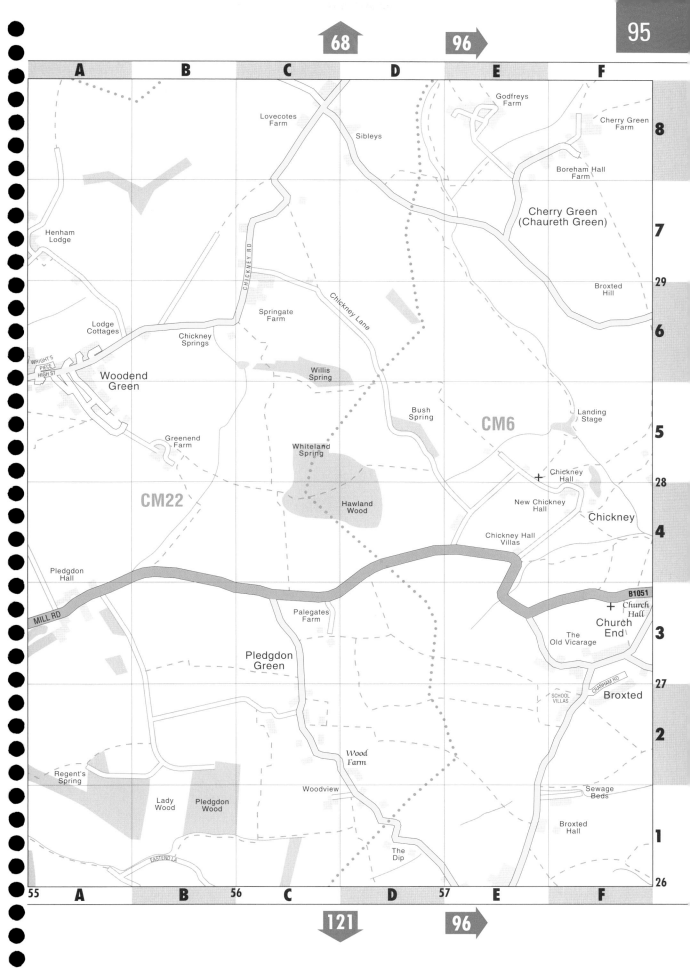

68
96

A B C D E F

Godfreys
Farm

Cherry Green
Farm

8

Lovecotes
Farm

Sibleys

Boreham Hall
Farm

Cherry Green
(Chaureth Green)

7

Henham
Lodge

Broxted
Hill

29

6

Lodge
Cottages

Chickney
Springs

Springate
Farm

Chickney Lane

CHICKNEY RD

WRIGHT'S
PIECE
HIGH ST

Woodend
Green

Willis
Spring

Bush
Spring

Landing
Stage

CM6

5

Greenend
Farm

Whiteland
Spring

Chickney
Hall

28

CM22

Hawland
Wood

New Chickney
Hall

Chickney

4

Chickney Hall
Villas

Pledgdon
Hall

B1051

Church
Hall

MILL RD

Palegates
Farm

The
Old Vicarage

Church
End

3

Pledgdon
Green

CRANHAM RD

27

SCHOOL
VILLAS

Broxted

Regent's
Spring

Wood
Farm

2

Lady
Wood

Pledgdon
Wood

Woodview

Sewage
Beds

Broxted
Hall

1

EASTEND LA

The
Dip

26

55 A 56 B C 57 D E F

121
96

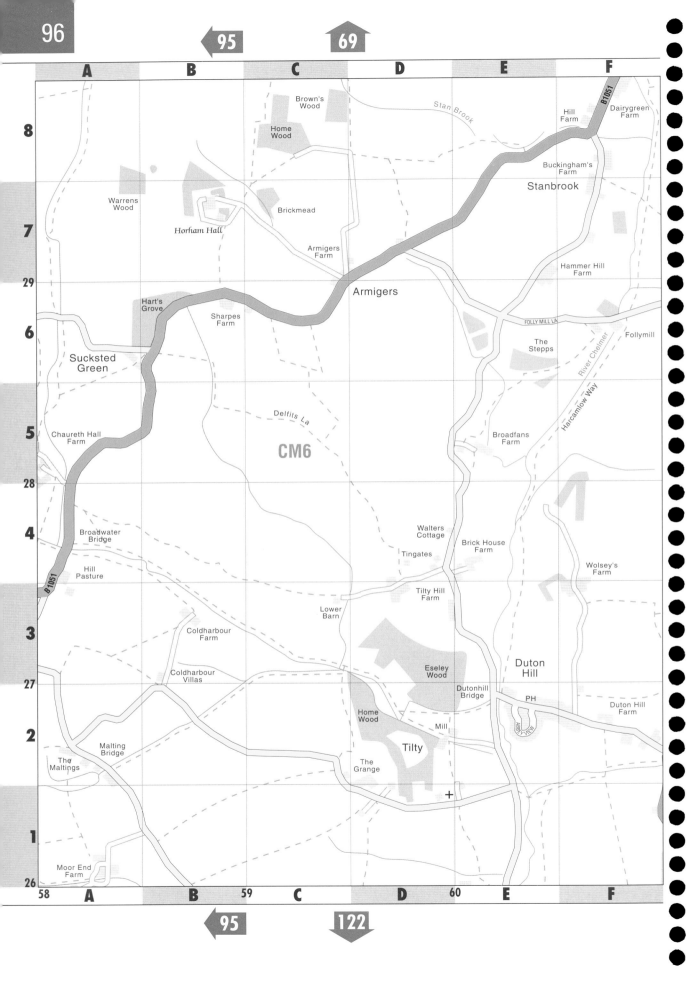

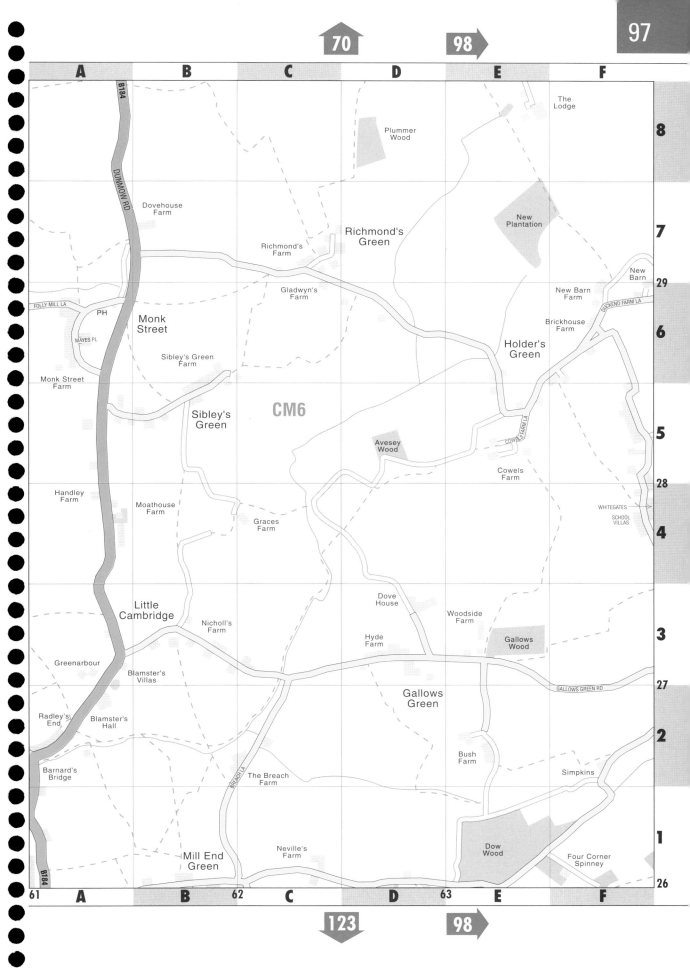

A   B   C   D   E   F

8

7

CM7

29

Markswood
Farm

Charity
Farm

DUNMOW RD

B1057

Duck End
Farm

The Grove

6

Bustard Green Lane

Oxen
End

Bustard
Green

Fann's
Farm

Coft
Hall

5

Porridge
Hall

Frenches
Farm

Daisyley Brook

28

Brazenhead
Farm

Templars

DAISYLEY RD

4

CM6

Page's
Farm

Tolladay's
Farm

Pratt's
Farm

LUBBERHEDGES LA

3

Lindsell

Church
End

GALLOWS GREEN RD

LINDSELL LA

Poplar
Farm

27

Goland's
Bridge

Carter's
Farm

Hill
Farm

2

Holt's
Farm

Stebbing Brook

Lashley
Hall

1

Duck End

B1057

26
64   A   B   65   C   D   66   E   F

Drakeswell

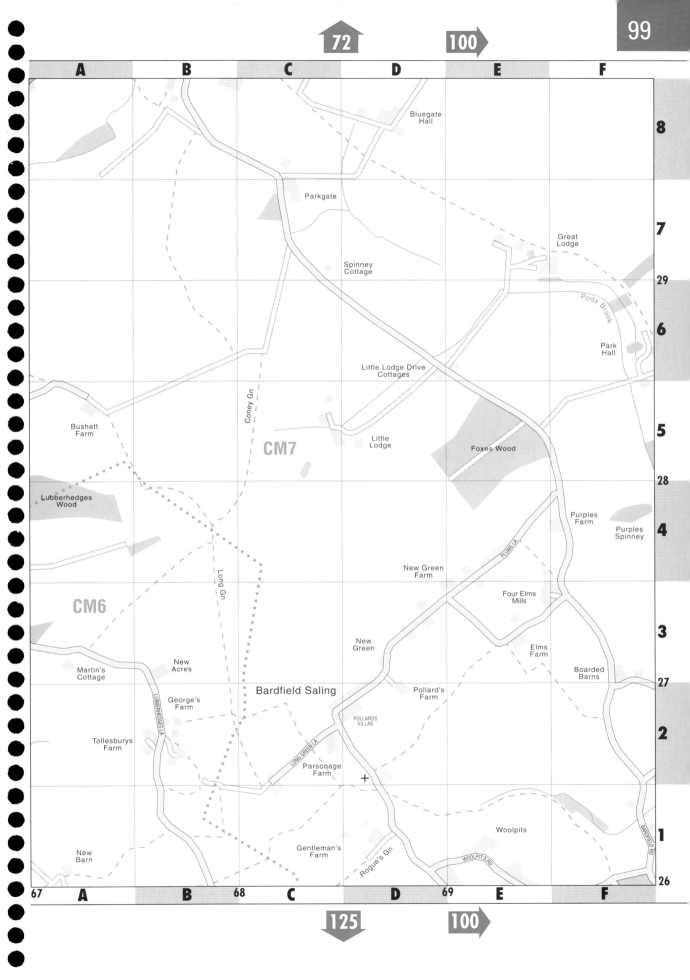

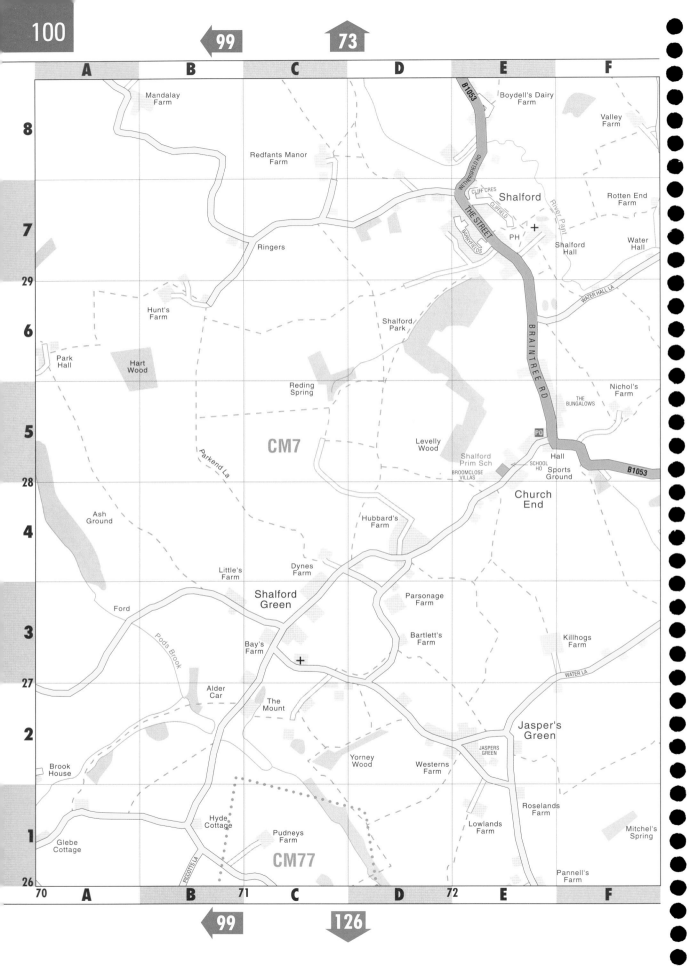

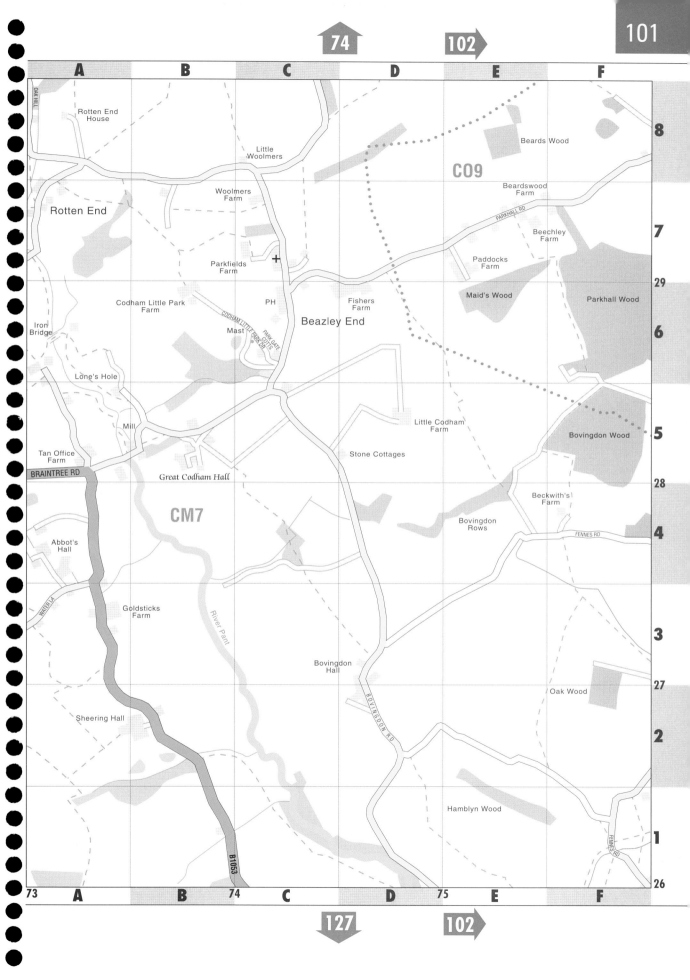

74
102
127
102

A B C D E F

8
7
29
6
5
28
4
3
27
2
1
26

OAK HILL

Rotten End
House

Little
Woolmers

Beards Wood

CO9

Beardswood
Farm

Rotten End

Woolmers
Farm

PARKHALL RD

Beechley
Farm

Parkfields
Farm

Paddocks
Farm

Codham Little Park
Farm

PH

Fishers
Farm

Maid's Wood

Parkhall Wood

CODHAM LITTLE PARK DR

Mast

Beazley End

PARK GATE COTTS

Iron
Bridge

Lone's Hole

Little Codham
Farm

Bovingdon Wood

Mill

Stone Cottages

Tan Office
Farm

BRAINTREE RD

Great Codham Hall

Beckwith's
Farm

CM7

Bovingdon
Rows

FENNES RD

Abbot's
Hall

WATER LA

Goldsticks
Farm

River Pant

Oak Wood

Bovingdon
Hall

BOVINGDON RD

Sheering Hall

Hamblyn Wood

FENNES RD

B1053

73 A B 74 C D 75 E F

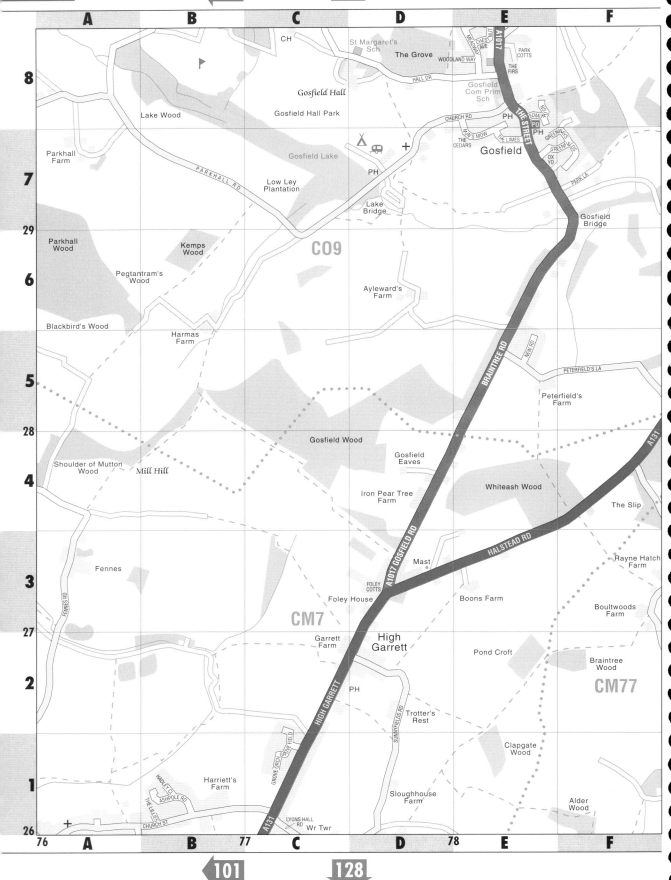

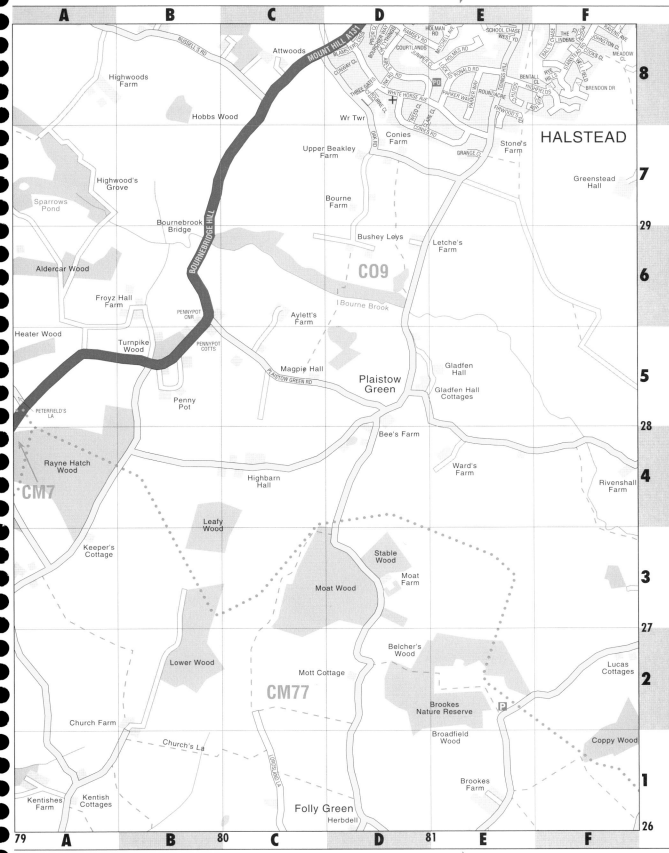

103
77

A B C D E F

8

7

29

6

5

28

4

3

27

2

1

26

A1124
COLCHESTER RD

Blue Bridge

Bluebridge
Farmhouse

Langley Mill

Elms Hall

ELMS HALL RD

Munn's Farm

River Colne

Riverside
Bsns Pk

STATION RD

DE VERE RD

Sewage
Works

Sewage
Works

Lodge

Stonebridge
Hill

STONEBRIDGE HILL

Stone Bridge

HALSTEAD RD

A1124

GREEN CT

ATLAS RD

DUDLEY RD

HUNT RD

Parley Beams
Farm

Stanstead
Hall

The
Kennels

Bullock Wood

Don Johns

Greenstead
Green

CHURCH RD

+

Ash
Bottom

Warren
Farm

CO6

Nightingale
Hall

Homely Ash
Grounds

NEWHOUSE RD

Greensteadhall
Farm

CROCKLANDS

CO9

BURTON'S GREEN RD

New Wood

Bourne Brook

PH

P0

The
Grange

Whitings

Nightingale
Hall Farm

Keepers

Lodge
Farm

Landing
Strip

Home
Farm

Perces

Airfield

Tyler's
Wood

Long Ley
Grove

27

Ind Est

LANCASTER WAY

CH

Burton's Green

Villa Farm

Mann's
Farm

HALIFAX WAY

Clavering's
Farm

Riefields

Cleveland
Wood

Markshall Wood

NUNTY'S LA

Great Nunty's
Farm

Nunty's Wood

Lily Wood

Deer Park

Thrift Wood

82 A B 83 C D 84 E F

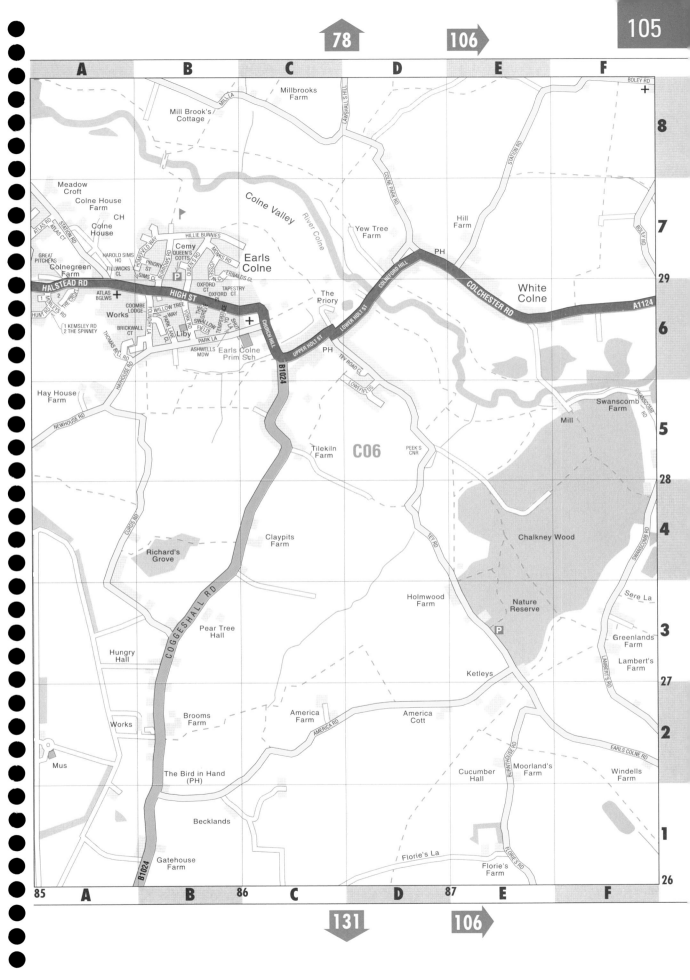

78
106

A B C D E F

BOLEY RD

8

Millbrooks
Farm

Mill Brook's
Cottage

MILL LA

LAWSHALL'S HILL

COLNE PARK RD

STATION RD

7

Meadow
Croft

Colne House
Farm

CH

Colne
House

Colne Valley

River Colne

Yew Tree
Farm

Hill
Farm

BOLEY RD

Great
Pitchers

ATLAS RD
STATION RD
ATLAS CT

Colnegreen
Farm

HILLIE BUNNIES

Cemy

QUEEN'S
COTTS

HAROLD SIMS HO

HORNFIELD WAY

PRIORY ST

TILLWICKS CL

SIMS CL

BURROWS RD

MONKS RD

QUEEN'S RD

FERNALDS CL

Earls
Colne

COLNEFORD HILL

PH

White
Colne

COLCHESTER RD

29

HALSTEAD RD

HIGH ST

P

ATLAS BGLWS

OXFORD CT

OXFORD CT

TAPESTRY CT

The Priory

LOWER HOLT ST

A1124

6

1 MOLLYS RD
2 THE CROFT

HUN

1 KEMSLEY RD
2 THE SPINNEY

Works

COOMBE LODGE

BRICKWALL CT

THOMAS BELL RD

FOUNDRY LA

PARK LA

WILLOW TREE WAY

YORK RD

PARK LA

THE SWALLOW FIELD

TEMPERANCE

SHUT LA

Liby

CHURCH HILL

UPPER HOLT ST

PH

TEY ROAD CL

ASHWELLS MDW

Earls Colne
Prim Sch

B1024

LOWER CL

Hay House
Farm

NEWHOUSE RD

HAYHOUSE RD

Swanscomb
Farm

SWANSCOMBE RD

Mill

5

Tilekiln
Farm

C06

PEEK'S
CNR

28

CURDS RD

Richard's
Grove

Claypits
Farm

Chalkney Wood

TEY RD

4

COGGESHALL RD

Pear Tree
Hall

Holmwood
Farm

Nature
Reserve

Sere La

P

Greenlands
Farm

3

LAMBERT'S RD

Lambert's
Farm

Hungry
Hall

Ketleys

27

Works

Brooms
Farm

America
Farm

AMERICA RD

America
Cott

EARLS COLNE RD

2

Mus

BURNTHOUSE RD

Moorland's
Farm

Windells
Farm

The Bird in Hand
(PH)

Cucumber
Hall

FLORIE'S RD

1

Becklands

B1024

Gatehouse
Farm

Florie's La

Florie's
Farm

26

85 A B 86 C D 87 E F

131
106

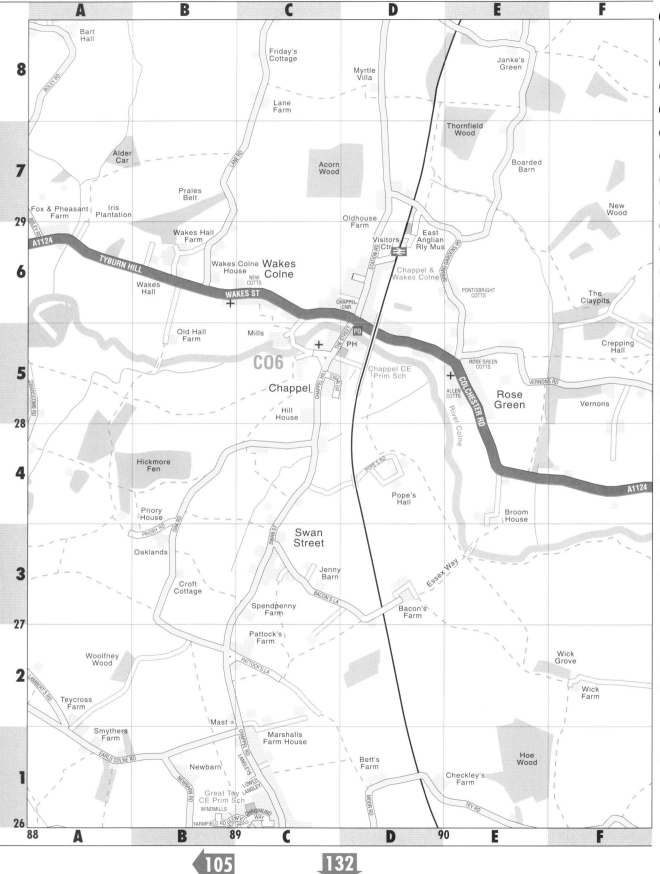

A B C D E F

8

7

29

6

5

28

4

3

27

2

1

26

88 89 90

Bart Hall

Friday's Cottage

Myrtle Villa

Janke's Green

BOLEY RD

Lane Farm

Thornfield Wood

Alder Car

LANE RD

Acorn Wood

Boarded Barn

Prales Belt

Iris Plantation

New Wood

Fox & Pheasant Farm

Oldhouse Farm

Wakes Hall Farm

Visitors Ctr

STATION RD

East Anglian Rly Mus

A1124

TYBURN HILL

Wakes Colne House

NEW COTTS

Wakes Colne

Chappel & Wakes Colne

SPRING GARDENS RD

PONTISBRIGHT COTTS

The Claypits

Wakes Hall

WAKES ST

CHAPPEL CNR

Old Hall Farm

Mills

THE STREET

PO

PH

Rose Green Cotts

Crepping Hall

SWANSCOMB RD

CO6

CHAPPEL HILL

SWAN GR

Chappel CE Prim Sch

Rose Green

VERNONS RD

Chappel

Hill House

ALLEN COTTS

COLCHESTER RD

Vernons

Hickmore Fen

River Colne

Priory House

PRIORY RD

OAK RD

SWAN ST

Pope's Rd

Pope's Hall

Broom House

A1124

Oaklands

Swan Street

Essex Way

Croft Cottage

Jenny Barn

BACON'S LA

Bacon's Farm

Spendpenny Farm

Woolfney Wood

Pattock's Farm

PATTOCK'S LA

Wick Grove

LAMBERT'S RD

Teycross Farm

Wick Farm

Smythers Farm

Mast

CHAPPEL RD

Marshalls Farm House

Bett's Farm

Hoe Wood

EARLS COLNE RD

Newbarn

LANGLEY'S

LOWER LANGLEY

Checkley's Farm

NEWBARN RD

Great Tey CE Prim Sch

WINDMILLS

CHRISMUND WAY

MOOR RD

TEY RD

FARMFIELD RD

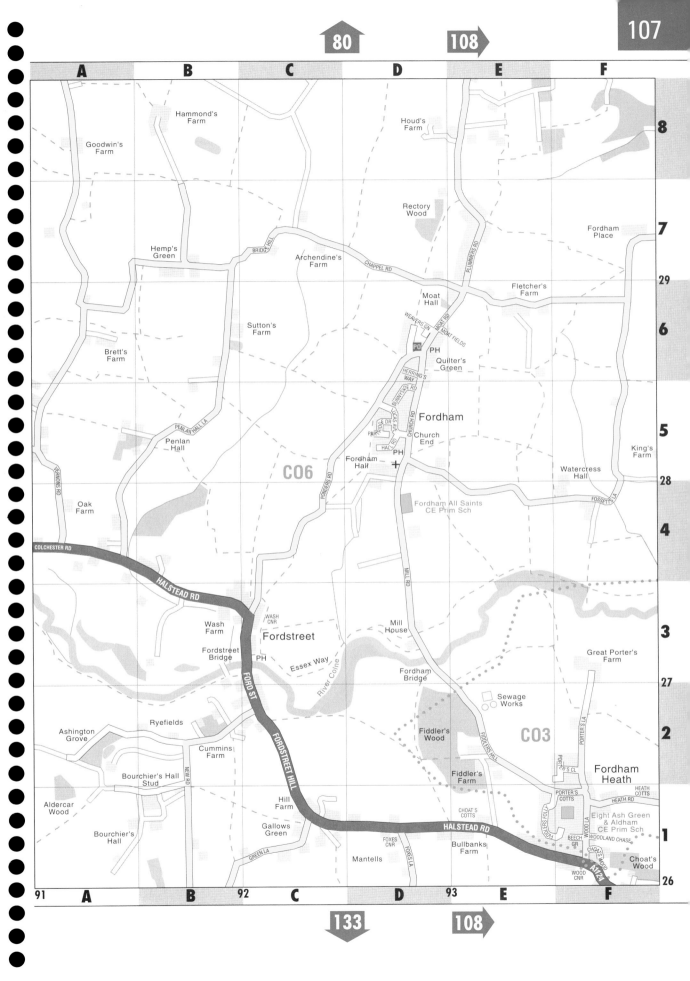

80
108
133
108

A B C D E F

8
7
29
6
5
28
4
3
27
2
1
26

Goodwin's Farm
Hammond's Farm
Houd's Farm
Rectory Wood
Fordham Place
Hemp's Green
BRIDGE HILL
Archendine's Farm
CHAPPEL RD
Moat Hall
Fletcher's Farm
PLUMMERS RD
Sutton's Farm
WEAVERS GN
MOAT RD
Moat Fields
PO
PH
Quilter's Green
Brett's Farm
HERRING'S WAY
SWANS RD
DUKE RD
Fordham
PENLAN HALL LA
LUCAS AVE
CHURCH RD
Church End
Penlan Hall
PARK DR
PRIDE E DR
PH
King's Farm
CO6
HALL
Fordham Hall
+
Watercress Hall
FOSSETT'S LA
Oak Farm
PONDERS RD
Fordham All Saints CE Prim Sch
COLCHESTER RD
HALSTEAD RD
MILL RD
Mill House
Great Porter's Farm
WASH CNR
Fordstreet
Wash Farm
Fordham Bridge
Fordstreet Bridge
PH
Essex Way
River Colne
Sewage Works
CO3
VERNONS RD
FORD ST
Ashington Grove
Ryefields
Fiddler's Wood
PORTER'S LA
Fordham Heath
Cummins Farm
NEW RD
FIDDLERS HALL
Fiddler's Farm
POBER'S CL
HEATH COTTS
FORDSTREET HILL
Bourchier's Hall Stud
PORTER'S COTTS
HEATH RD
Aldercar Wood
Hill Farm
CHOAT'S COTTS
WOOD LA
Eight Ash Green & Aldham CE Prim Sch
FIDLERS FOLLY
Bourchier's Hall
Gallows Green
GREEN LA
Mantells
FOXES CNR
FOXES LA
HALSTEAD RD
Bullbanks Farm
BEECH GR
WOODLAND CHASE
CHOATSWOOD
Choat's Wood
WOOD CNR
A124

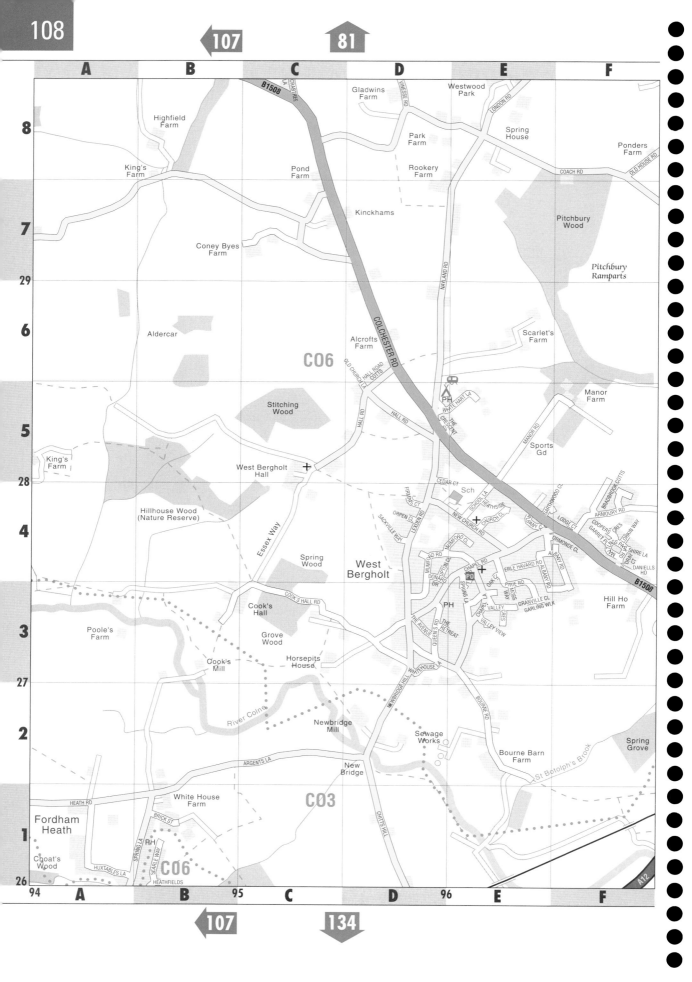

A   B   C   D   E   F

8

Highfield
Farm

Gladwins
Farm

Westwood
Park

B1508
CRABTREE LA

VINESSE RD

LONDON RD

Spring
House

Ponders
Farm

OLD HOUSE RD

King's
Farm

Pond
Farm

Park
Farm

Rookery
Farm

COACH RD

7

Coney Byes
Farm

Kinckhams

NAYLAND RD

Pitchbury
Wood

29

Pitchbury
Ramparts

6

Aldercar

Alcrofts
Farm

Scarlet's
Farm

CO6

OLD CHURCH LA
HALL ROAD COTTS

COLCHESTER RD

WHITE HART LA
PH

THE CRESCENT

Manor
Farm

5

Stitching
Wood

OLD HALL RD

HALL RD

MANOR RD

Sports
Gd

King's
Farm

West Bergholt
Hall

CEDAR CT
Sch
HEATHSIDE
SCHOOL LA

GREYNWOOD CL
LODGE CT

BRADBROOK COTTS

ARMOURY RD

COOPERS CRES
CORNIN WAY
GARRET PL
SHIRE LA
DRANS
DRAW CL

28

Hillhouse Wood
(Nature Reserve)

Essex Way

FIRMANS CT
ORPEN CL
LENDER RD
SACKVILLE WAY

NEW CHURCH RD
CHURCH CL
DAINY CT

ORMONDE CL
ADANY RD

DANIELLS
HO

4

Spring
Wood

West
Bergholt

MUMFORD CL
MUMFORD RD
UPTON CL
DONARD DR

CHAPEL RD
SPRING LA
OAK CL

ERLE HAVARD RD
ALBANY RD
PRIE RD

GRANVILLE CL
GARLING WLK

Hill Ho
Farm

3

Poole's
Farm

COOK'S HALL RD
Cook's
Hall

Grove
Wood

PH

THE AVENUE
QUEEN'S RD
CHAPEL LA
VALLEY VIEW
MYSS CRES
VALLEY CRES

27

Cook's
Mill

Horsepits
House

WHITE HOUSE LA
WHITEHOUSE HILL

BOURNE RD

2

River Colne

Newbridge
Mill

Sewage
Works

Bourne Barn
Farm

St Botolph's Brook

Spring
Grove

ARGENTS LA

New
Bridge

CHITTS HILL

CO3

1

HEATH RD

White House
Farm

BRICK ST

Fordham
Heath

SPRING LA
PH
SEARLE WAY

CO6

A12

Choat's
Wood

HUXTABLES LA
HEATHFIELDS

26

94   A   B   95   C   D   96   E   F

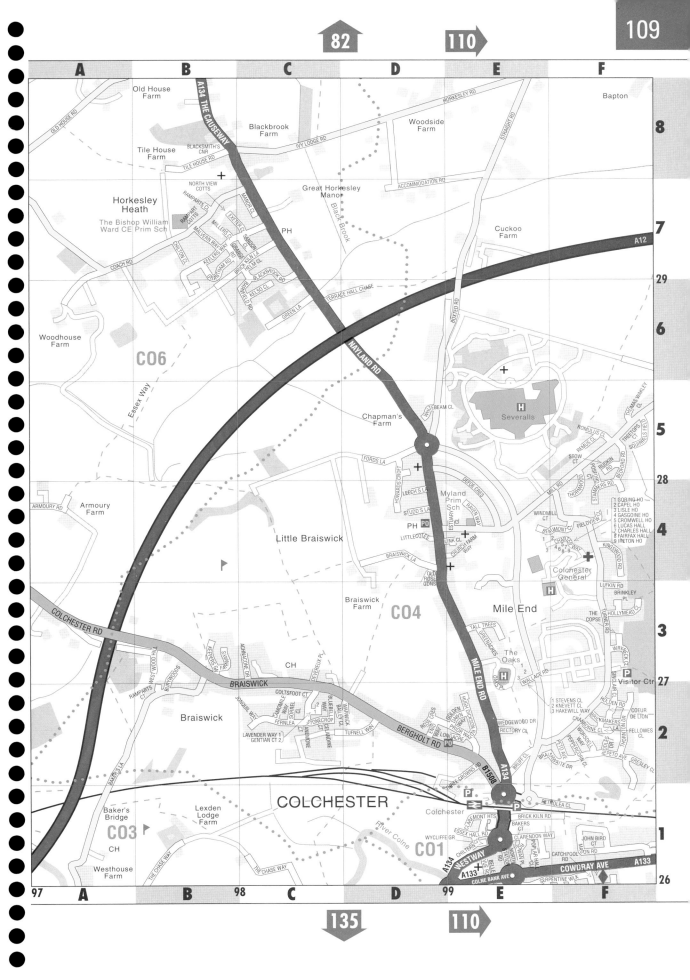

82
110

A B C D E F

8

Old House Farm
Old House Farm
A134 THE CAUSEWAY
Blackbrook Farm
Bapton
Woodside Farm
HORKESLEY RD
IVY LODGE RD
STRAIGHT RD

Tile House Farm
BLACKSMITH'S CNR
TILE HOUSE RD
ACCOMMODATION RD

NORTH VIEW COTTS
Great Horkesley Manor

Horkesley Heath
RAMPARTS CL
RAMPART COTTS
EXETER CL
MANOR CL
MILLERS CL
SAMSON
PH

7

The Bishop William Ward CE Prim Sch
MALVERN WAY
GRANGE RD
BRICK KILN LA
HELM CL
Cuckoo Farm
A12

CHILTON CL
KEELERS WAY
GRANTHAM RD
Black Brook
BOXTED RD

COACH RD
GREEN LA
WARFIELD RD
KELSO CL
BLACKBROOK RD

29

TERRACE HALL CHASE
GREEN LA

6

Woodhouse Farm
NAYLAND RD
Severalls
H

CO6

Essex Way

Chapman's Farm
WHITEBEAM CL
ROMULUS CL
REMUS CL
TRETOPS CL
SQUIRRELS FIELD
5

FORDS LA
DEFOE CRES
STOW CT
RUDKIN
POSTGROVE
DOWNING
BEDFORD RD
THORNWAY
STAMMERS RD

28

Armoury Farm
HOWARDS CROFT
LEECH'S LA
WINDMILL CT
1 GOBING HO
2 CAPEL HO
3 LISLE HO
4 GASGOINE HO
5 CROMWELL HO
6 LUCAS HALL
7 CHARLES HALL
8 FAIRFAX HALL
9 IRETON HO

ARMOURY RD
STUDD'S LA
Myland Prim Sch
ESTUARY CL
BEAUMONT
FIELDVIEW
4

Little Braiswick
LITTLECOTES
RAVEN WAY
CHARLES WAY
KINGSWOOD RD

PH
PO
LINK CL
CHURCH FARM WAY
Colchester General
H

BRAISWICK LA
LUFKIN RD
BRINKLEY PL

COLCHESTER RD
OLD ROSE GDNS
THE COPSE
HOLLYMEAD
3

Braiswick Farm
CO4
Mile End
WRYNECK CL
TURNER RD

KEEPERS CL
WEST WOOD HILL
ACHNACONE DR
DEVEREUX PL
CH
TALL TREES
GREENACRES
The Oaks
H
SINCLAIR CL
P
Visitor Ctr

27

BRAISWICK
RAMPARTS CT
BURYWOODS
JONQUIL WAY
CAMOMILE WAY
COLTSFOOT CT
SORREL
BLUEBELL CL
BAILEY CL
WARWICK
GOLDEN
ENID CRES
PRIOR WAY
HUGH DICKSON RD
WALLACE RD
OAKS
1 STEVENS CL
2 KNEVETT CL
3 HAKEWILL WAY
HOLDEN RD
BRICKMAKERS
COEUR DE LION

Braiswick
FERNLEA
STONECROP
ANEMONE
CELANDINE WAY
LONGACRE
WEDGEWOOD DR
RECTORY CL
CRAMBORNE CL
WORSDELL
PEPPERCORN CL
FELLOWES CL
2

LAVENDER WAY 1
GENTIAN CT 2
TUFNELL WAY
BERGHOLT RD
PO
BRUFF CL
A134
BRAIZWRAITE DR
PETO AVE
RIDDLES
THORNTON DR
PEPPERCORN RD
GRESLEY CL

BAKERS LA
THREE CROWNS RD
B1508
RETROLEA CL

Baker's Bridge
CO3
Lexden Lodge Farm
COLCHESTER
P
P
P
Colchester
CLAREMONT HTS
BRICK KILN RD
BAKERS CT
1

River Colne
CO1
WYCLIFFE GR
ESSEX HALL RD
CLARENDON WAY
JOHN BIRD CL
MASON RD

CH
Westhouse Farm
THE CHASE WAY
THE CHASE WAY
A134
WESTWAY
CHILTERN
STATION
NORTH
BELLE VUE RD
POPLAR HALL
CATCHPOOL RD
COWDRAY AVE
A133

A133
COLNE BANK AVE
SERPENTINE WLK
26

97 A 98 B C 99 D E F

135
110

A B C D E F

8
Langham Rd
Langham La
Runkin's Corner
Langham Lodge
Lodge La
Wick La
A12

7
Whitehouse Farm
Salary Brook
Kiln Wood
PH
Gatehouse Farm
A12

29
The Crescent
Hale Way
Flood La
Gilberd Rd
Matchett Dr
A1232
Hotel
CO7
Crown La N

6
Comyns Cl
Oxley Parker Dr
Sports Ctr
Newcomen Way
Colchester Bsns Pk
Charter Ct
Clough Rd
Stephenson Rd
Telford Way
Seedbed Ctr
A1232
A120
Plains Farm Cl
Willow Cl
Harvey's Farm
Mill Rd
Magnus Dr
Valens Rd
Julian Way
Tibullus Way
Hadrian Cl
Vitullus Way
Antonius Way
Marcus Cl
Maximum Way
Caracalla Way
Gordian Wlk
Jackson Ho
Brunel Cl
Brunel Way
Heckworth Cl
Smeaton Cl
Wyncolls Rd
Crown Gate
Altbarn Cl

5
Otho Dr
Gavin Way
Lidius Cl
Petronius Way
Purvis Way
Honorius Way
Lilley Cl
Gavin Way
Asquith Dr
Brinkley Grove Prim Sch
The Gilberd Sch
Atwood Cl
Hanningfield Way
Jack Andrews Dr
Viscount Dr
Regents Cl
Princess Dr
Autoway
Bullock Wood Cl
Plains Farm
Brinkley Grove
Brinkley La
Brinkley Grove Rd

28
Brinkley Grove
Grassmere
Hanbury Gdns
Langdale Dr
Chinook
Hallcroft Chase
Elizabeth Cl
Berkeley Cl
Bignells Croft
Bullock Wood
Fen Farm
A120

4
High Woods Country Park
Princeton Mews 1
Tally Ho 2
Tynedale Ct 3
Alderman Howe Lodge 4
Ivor Brown Ct 5
Hurrell Dr
Northfield Gdns
Rosewood Cl
Kinlett Cl
Firtree Cl
Hunters Ridge
Sea King
Highclere Rd
Highwoods App
Sioux Cl
Leighton Croft
Cleveland Cl
Bilsdale Cl
Woodview Cl
Evergreen Dr
St John's CE Prim Sch
Fox Street
Fox Street
Heathcote Farm
PH
Harwich Rd
A137

3
High Woods
Aldergrove
Valley View Cl
Ridgeway
Victoria Gdns
Cotswold Ct
Craydel Dr
Arbour Way
CO4
Ipswich Rd
Arden Cl
Rossendale Cl
Glentress Cl
Bullace Cl
Buildings Farm

27
Reynolds
Harebell Cl
Eastwood Dr
West View
Alverton Way
Langham Pl
Greenwood Gr
Basin Cl
Greenwood Cl
Chalfont Rd
Glendale Gr
Kildermorie Cl
Delamere Rd
St John's Rd
Kentmere
Green La

Thistledown
The Brackens
Hillridge
Barnlow
Brireswood
Chatterell Cl
Copse End
The Spring
Myland Hall Chase
St Bartholomew Cl
Wilmington Rd
St Joseph Rd
St Cyrus Rd
St Mark's Rd
St Bernard Rd
Anthony Cl
Broadoaks Tk
Dunthorne Rd

2
Friar's Grove
Friars Grove Jun & Inf Schs
Friars Cl
Silcock Cl
St Christopher Ct
St Columb Ct
St Clement Rd
St Lawrence Rd
St Savour Rd
St Alde Gdns
St Judes Rd
Vale Cl
St Thomas Cl
Campbell Dr
Welshwood Park Rd
The Glade
Mountain Ash Cl
Upland
Tyburst
Porters Brook Wlk
St Faith
St Bride Ct
Parsons Heath CE Prim Sch
Stour Wlk
Parsons Heath

COLCHESTER
Mayfield Rd
Cloverlands
St Fillan Rd
St Monance Way
Temple Cl
Francis Cl
Welshwood Park
Pegasus Way
Southland Cl
Chaplin Dr
Thurlston
Baldwin Rd
Roach Vale
Orwell Cl
Debru Cl
Roach Vale Prim Sch

CO1

1
The Cowdray Ctr
Golne View Ret Pk
Havering Cl
Norfolk Cres
Wilson Marriage Rd
Barkstead Rd
The Causeway
Walter Porter Ct
Churnwood Rd
Bridgebrook
Pondfield Cl
St Paul's Rd
Spendlove Cl
Royal Cl
Hawthorn Ave
Longridge
PH
Rayleigh Cl
Ripple Way
Greswell Cl
Edison Gdns
St Anne's Prim Sch
Goring Rd
Barnardiston Rd
Ryloffe Rd
Churnwood Cl
Parson's Heath
Redwood Cl
Grayling Dr
Bream Cl
Bromley Cl
Owls Retreat
Merlin End

26
Cowdray Ave
A133
Romford Cl
Valentines Dr
A1232
A137
Harwich Rd
A133

84
112
137
112

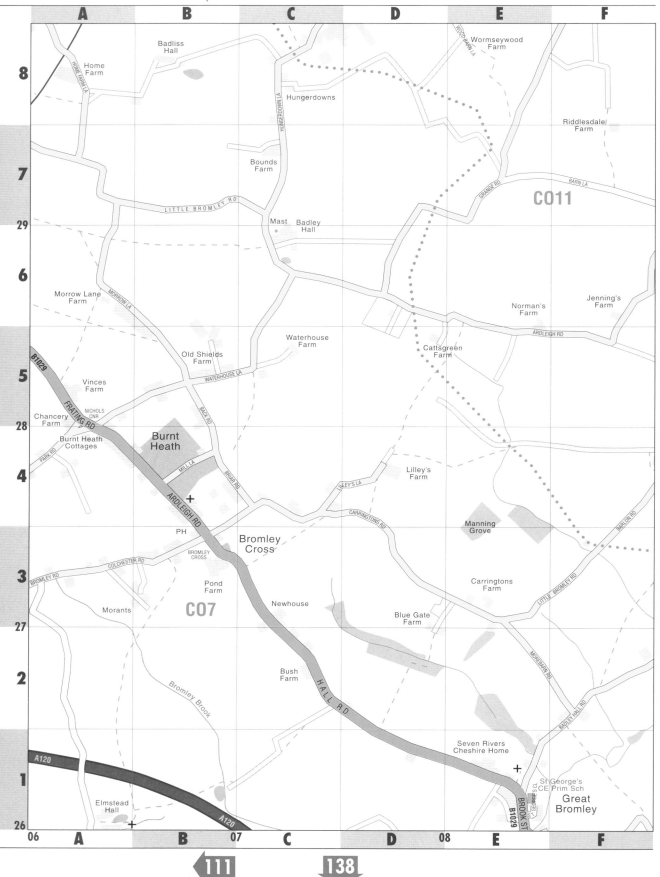

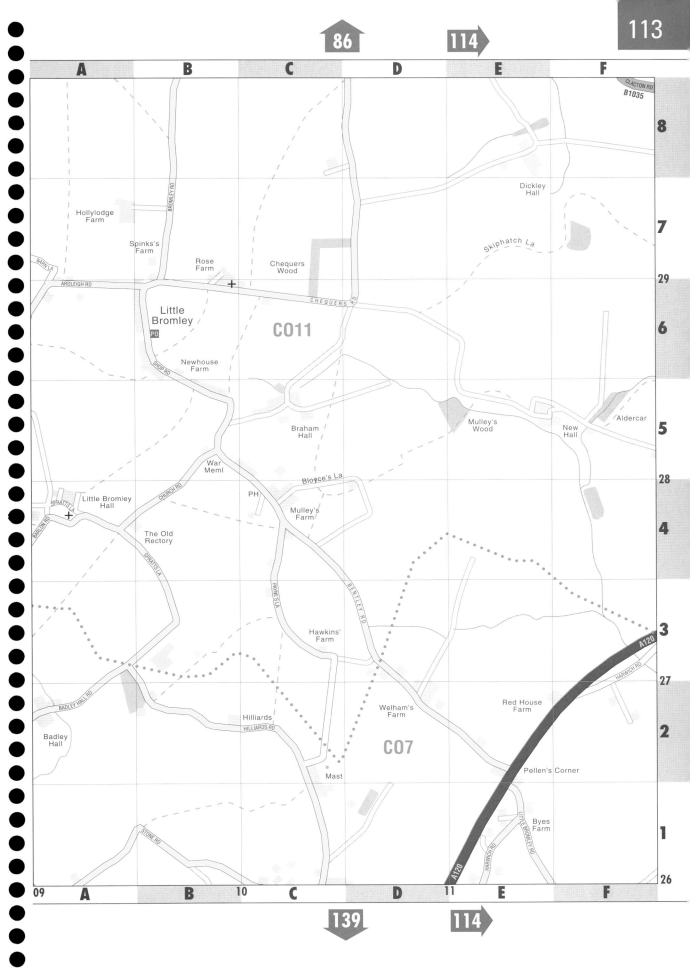

A B C D E F

B1035
CLACTON RD

8

Dickley
Hall

7

Skiphatch La

Hollylodge
Farm

BROMLEY RD

Spinks's
Farm

Rose
Farm

Chequers
Wood

29

BARN LA

ARDLEIGH RD

CHEQUERS RD

Little
Bromley

CO11

6

PO

SHOP RD

Newhouse
Farm

Mulley's
Wood

New
Hall

Aldercar

5

Braham
Hall

War
Meml

CHURCH RD

Bloyce's La

28

Little Bromley
Hall

PH

Mulley's
Farm

4

SPRATTS LA

BARTON RD

The Old
Rectory

SPRATTS LA

PAYNE'S LA

BENTLEY RD

A120

3

Hawkins'
Farm

HARWICH RD

27

BADLEY HALL RD

Welham's
Farm

Red House
Farm

2

Badley
Hall

Hilliards

HILLIARDS RD

CO7

Pellen's Corner

Mast

Byes
Farm

LITTLE BROMLEY RD

1

STONE RD

HARWICH RD

A120

26

113
87

A **B** **C** **D** **E** **F**

B1035

Old Mount

8

Mast

STEAM MILL RD

Steam Mill Corner

STRAIGHT RD

KING ST

DUNNING CL

WINDMILL RD

KING ST

PO

PH

HEATH RD

Bradfield Heath

WIX RD

7

Mayfield Cottages

BARRACK ST

ELLIS RD

DAIRHOUSE LA

Dairy House

29

Bradfield Hall

CO11

CANSEY LA

6

CLACTON RD

Horsleycross Street

PH

Goldenferry

Wix Lodge

5

Bradfield Lodge

Rosemary Cottage

Lipstone

A120

28

Crossman's Farm

CANSEY LA

Burrow's Farm

4

Wr Twr

Arch Cottages

COLCHESTER RD

Baker's Farm

Spring Farm

HONEYPOT LA

Abbott's Hall

PH

Burnt Ash Farm

Goose Green

3

A120

HORSLEY CROSS

HARWICH RD

CO12

27

Kellys Farm

Hempstall's Farm

New House Farm

Greentrees Fruit Farm

TENDRING RD

2

Knight's Farm

CO16

Brockett's Hall

Holland Brook

1

CO7

LITTLE BENTLEY RD

PH

HEATH RD

Tendring Heath

WOLVES HALL LA

26

Chy

Old Hall Farm

B1035

PARSONAGE LA

12 **A** **B** **13** **C** **D** **14** **E** **F**

113
140

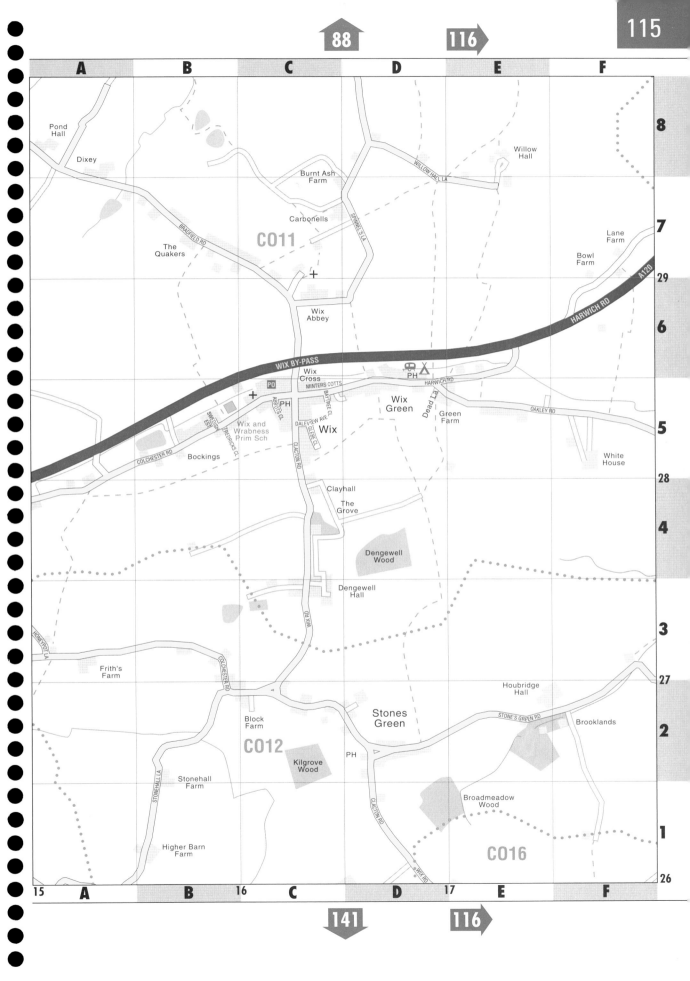

115
89

A B C D E F

8

7

29

6

CO11

5

28

4

CO12
Great
Oakley

3

27

2

1

26

18 A B 19 C D 20 E F

PRIMROSE LA
Poplar Hall
Ramsey Hall Cottages
Ramsey Hall
Model Cottages
HARWICH RD
TINKER ST
A120
THE MALTINGS
Hill House
HILL RD
Millpond Farm
A120
Brickkiln Farm
Southhouse Farm
Saltwater Bridge
RECTORY RD
Soilspond Bridge
Soils Wood
THE SOILS
Redhouse Farm
Great Oakley Lodge
Sparrow's Farm
Great Oakley Hall
Parkpail Farm
SPARROWS CNR
B1414
OAKLEY RD
Whitehouse Farm
Parkers Farm
HARWICH RD
PARTRIDGE CL
DOCK LA
Holt Farm
MILL HOUSE COTTS
HIGH ST
PO
PH
P
QUEEN ST
PICK LA
FARM RD
Mosses Farm
WIX RD
SCHOOL RD
HALFORD DR
ORCHARD CL
PESTHOUSE LA
THE AVENUE
All Saints CE Prim Sch
BEAUMONT RD
WORKHOUSE CNR
Brook Farm
STONE'S GREEN RD
WOODLANDS
RED BARN LA
Red Barn Farm
Cabbage Row
Marden's Farm
CROSS HILL
MOZE CROSS
Old Moze Hall
CO16
Buck's Farm
Holland's Farm
HARWICH RD
B1414

115
142

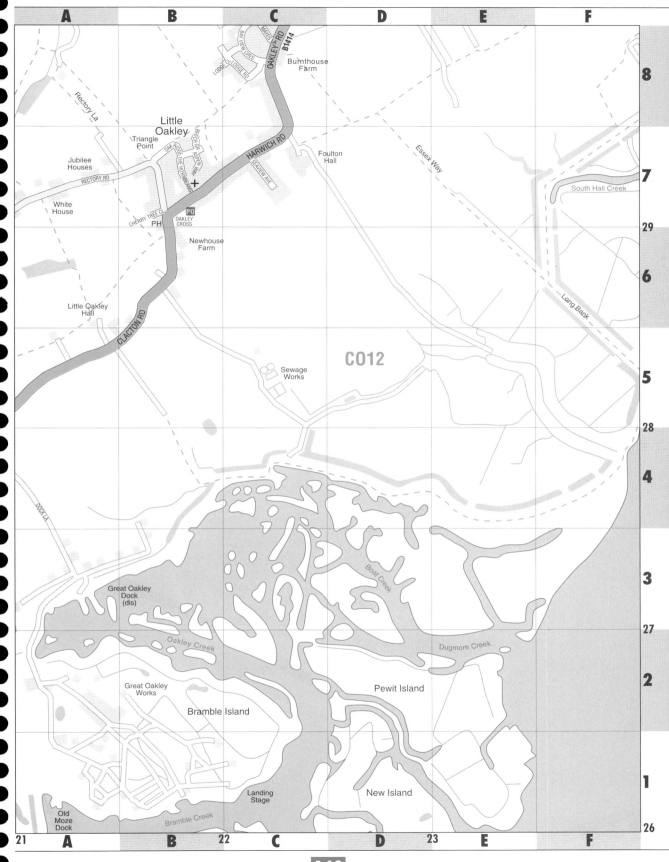

A B C D E F

8

Burnthouse
Farm

Rectory La

Little
Oakley

Triangle
Point

Foulton
Hall

Essex Way

7

South Hall Creek

Jubilee
Houses

RECTORY RD

29

White
House

CHERRY TREE CL

PH

OAKLEY
CROSS

Newhouse
Farm

6

Long Bank

Little Oakley
Hall

CLACTON RD

CO12

Sewage
Works

5

28

4

DOCK LA

Great Oakley
Dock
(dis)

Boat Creek

3

27

Oakley Creek

Dugmore Creek

Great Oakley
Works

Pewit Island

2

Bramble Island

Landing
Stage

New Island

1

Old
Moze
Dock

Bramble Creek

26

21 A 22 B C 22 D 23 E F

HARWICH RD

OAKLEY RD

B1414

BAY VIEW CRES

MAYES RD

LODGE CL

LODGE RD

BEECH GR

ASPEN WAY

OAK RIDGE

THE HORNBEAMS

SEAVIEW AVE

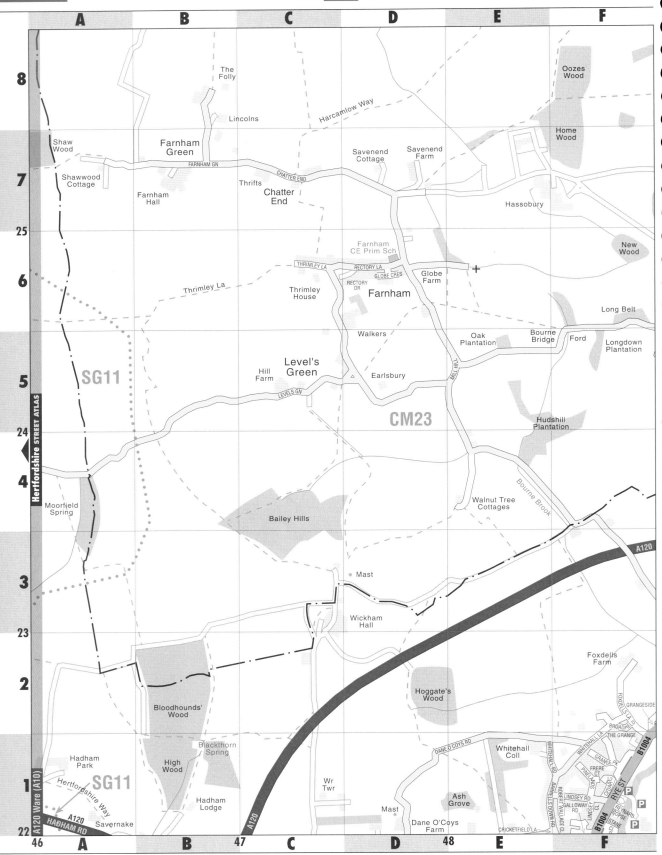

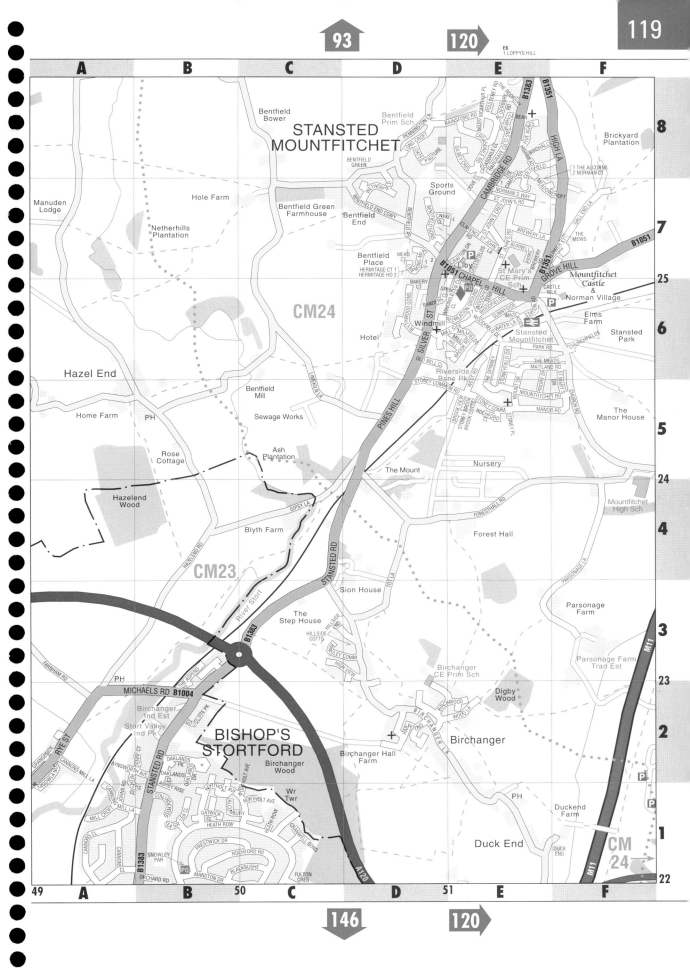

E6
1 LOPPYS HILL

A B C D E F

8

Bentfield
Bower

STANSTED
MOUNTFITCHET

Bentfield
Prim Sch

Brickyard
Plantation

THE ROOKERY

B1383 B1351

B1051

7

Manuden
Lodge

Hole Farm

Netherhills
Plantation

Bentfield
Green
Farmhouse

Bentfield
End

Bentfield
End Cswy

CAMBRIDGE RD

Sports
Ground

HIGH LA

1 THE ALCORNS
2 NORMAN CT

THE MEWS

25

CM24

Bentfield
Place
HERMITAGE CT 1
HERMITAGE HO 2

St Mary's
CE Prim
Sch

Mountfitchet
Castle
&
Norman Village

Elms
Farm

Stansted
Park

6

Hazel End

Bentfield
Mill

Sewage Works

Windmill

Hotel

SILVER ST

OLD BELL CL

Stansted
Mountfitchet

Riverside
Bsns Pk

THE MEADS
MAITLAND RD

PARK RD

CHURCHFIELDS

The
Manor House

5

Home Farm

PH

Rose
Cottage

Ash
Plantation

PINES HILL

The Mount

Nursery

Forest Hall

24

Hazelend
Wood

GIPSY LA

Blyth Farm

STANSTED RD

Mountfitchet
High Sch

4

CM23

River Stort

Sion House

TOT LA

PARSONAGE LA

Parsonage
Farm

Parsonage Farm
Trad Est

M11

3

B1383

PH

The
Step House

HILLSIDE
COTTS

HIGH VIEW

Birchanger
CE Prim Sch

Digby
Wood

23

THE ASPENS

MICHAELS RD B1004

Birchanger
Ind Est

Stort Valley
Ind Pk

RYE ST

STANSTED RD

BISHOP'S
STORTFORD

Birchanger
Wood

Wr
Twr

Birchanger Hall
Farm

BIRCHANGER LA

BIRCHWOOD
WOOD LA

Birchanger

PH

Duckend
Farm

2

Duck End

CM
24

M11

1

B1383

49 A B 50 C D 51 E F 22

119
94

A B C D E F

MAX WK
STANSTED RD
B1051
M11
Old Mill Farm
Fuller's End
Elsenham Stud
Hall Rd
Church La
Elsenham Hall
Park Wood

The Down Farm
Mill Wood
The Bungalow
Gaunt's End

Stansted House
Long Plantation
Jubilee Cottage
CM22

B1051
The Lodge
Durrel's Wood
Wilkin's Plantation
Mott's Hall

Stansted Park
Tye Green Rd
Tye Green Farm
Tye Green

Stansted Hall
The Bourne
Barley Common
Clapit Hill
Mast

Church Rd
Old Bury Lodge La
Burton Bower
Cvn Pks
Burton Bury
Burton End
Warman's Farm
Belmer Rd
Highfields Lodge

CM24
PH
Sixth Ave
Control Tower

M11
Burylodge Cottages
Bury Lodge La
Monks Farm
Pincey Rd
Thirtieth St
Twenty First St

Little Bury Lodge Farm
Eleventh Ave
Ninth Ave
Fourth Ave
First Ave
Fifth Ave
Seventh Ave
Third Ave
Works

Bury Lodge
Second Ave
Tenth Ave
Control Tower

Roman La
P
P
P
London Stansted Airport
Bassingbourn Rd

Hotel
Round Coppice Rd
Long Border Rd
Taylors End Rd

52 A B 53 C D 54 E F

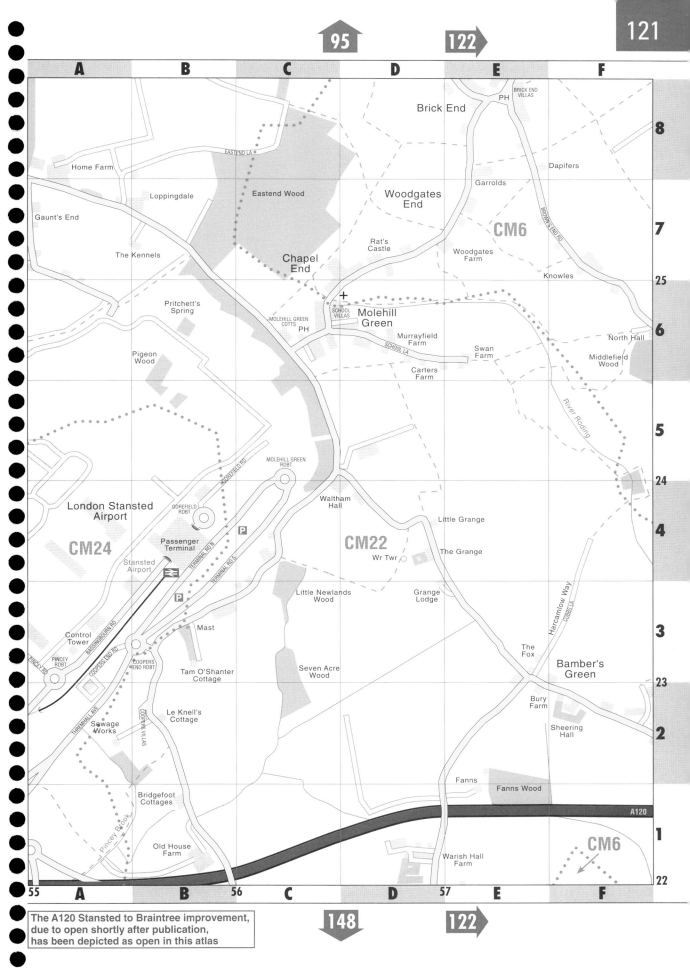

The A120 Stansted to Braintree improvement,
due to open shortly after publication,
has been depicted as open in this atlas

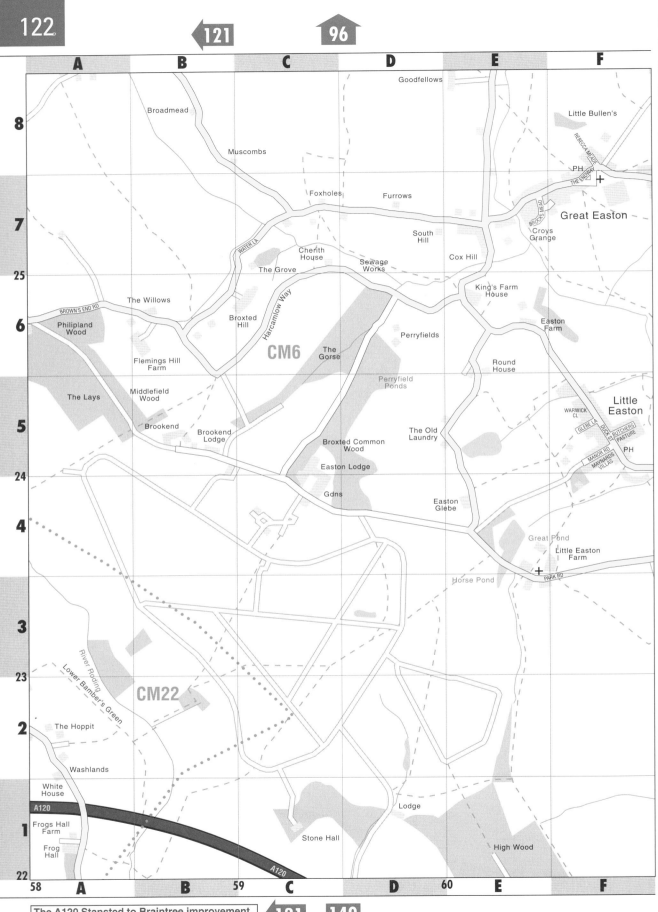

121

96

A B C D E F

8

Goodfellows

Broadmead

Little Bullen's

Muscombs

REBECCA MEADE

PH

THE ENDWAY

Great Easton

7

Foxholes

Furrows

BROOKS MEAD

Croys Grange

WATER LA

Cherith House

South Hill

Cox Hill

25

The Grove

Sewage Works

King's Farm House

The Willows

Harcamlow Way

BROWN'S END RD

Easton Farm

6

Philipland Wood

Broxted Hill

Perryfields

CM6

The Gorse

Round House

Flemings Hill Farm

Perryfield Ponds

Little Easton

Middlefield Wood

The Lays

WARWICK CL

GLEBE LA

DUCK ST

BUTCHERS PASTURE

5

Brookend

The Old Laundry

MANOR RD

MAYNARDS VILLAS

PH

Brookend Lodge

Broxted Common Wood

24

Easton Lodge

Easton Glebe

Gdns

Great Pond

4

Little Easton Farm

Horse Pond

PARK RD

River Roding

3

23

Lower Bamber's Green

CM22

2

The Hoppit

Washlands

White House

A120

Lodge

1

Frogs Hall Farm

Stone Hall

High Wood

Frog Hall

A120

22

58 A B 59 C D 60 E F

The A120 Stansted to Braintree improvement, due to open shortly after publication, has been depicted as open in this atlas

121 149

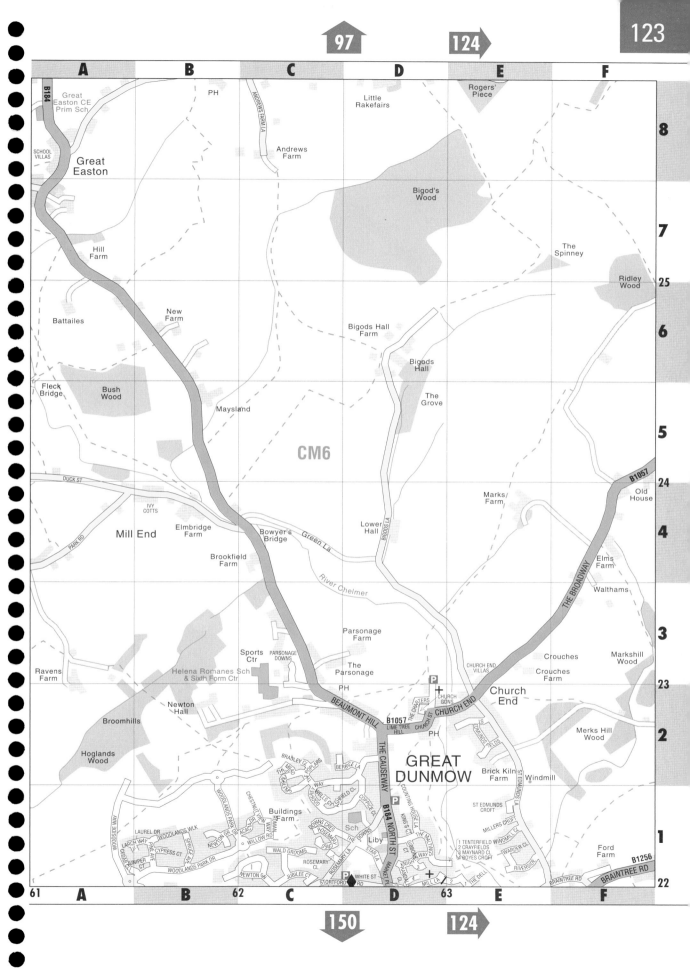

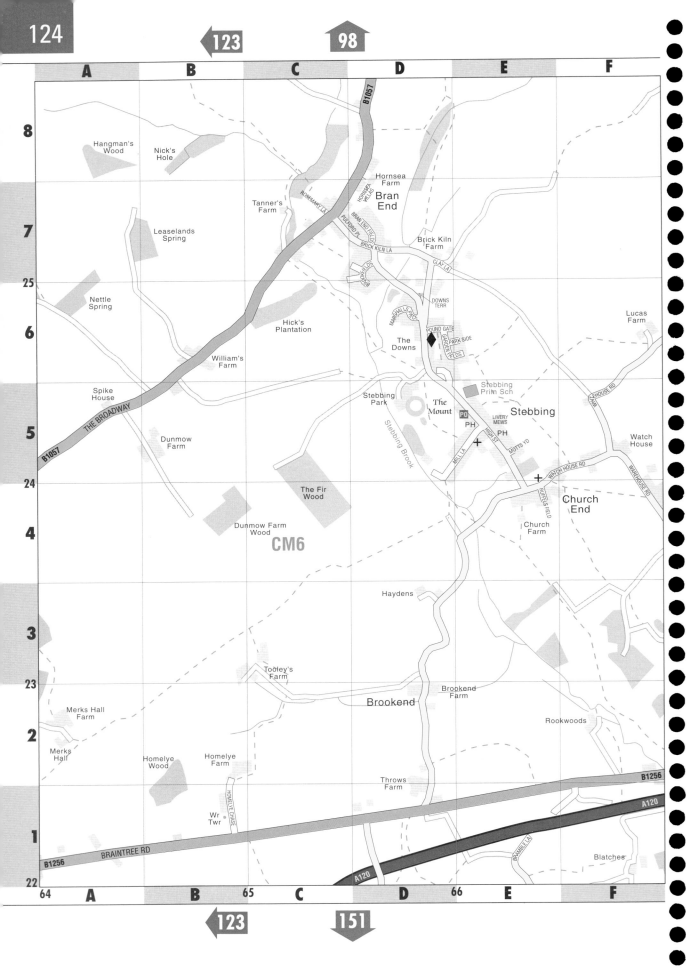
A   B   C   D   E   F

8   Hangman's Wood   Nick's Hole

B1057

Hornsea Farm

Bran End

Tanner's Farm

ROSEMARY LA

HORNSEA MILL ST

BRAN END FIELDS

PULFORD PL

7   Leaselands Spring

Brick Kiln Farm

BRICK KILN LA

CLAY LA

25   BRIDGE FIELDS

DOWNS TERR

Nettle Spring

MARSHALL'S PIECE

6   Hick's Plantation

POUND GATE

The Downs

PARK SIDE

GARDEN FIELDS

Lucas Farm

William's Farm

Stebbing Prim Sch

Spike House

THE BROADWAY

Stebbing Park

The Mount

LEHOUSE RD

LA

5   B1057

Dunmow Farm

PO

PH

LIVERY MEWS

Stebbing

Watch House

HIGH ST

PH

MOTTS YD

Stebbing Brook

MILL LA

WATCH HOUSE RD

24   The Fir Wood

✝

✝

RUFFELS FIELD

Church End

WAREHOUSE RD

4   Dunmow Farm Wood

CM6

Church Farm

3   Haydens

Tooley's Farm

23   Brookend Farm

Merks Hall Farm

Brookend

Rookwoods

2   Merks Hall

Homelye Wood

Homelye Farm

Throws Farm

B1256

HOMELYE CHASE

A120

1   Wr Twr

A120

BRAMBLE LA

Blatches

B1256   BRAINTREE RD

22

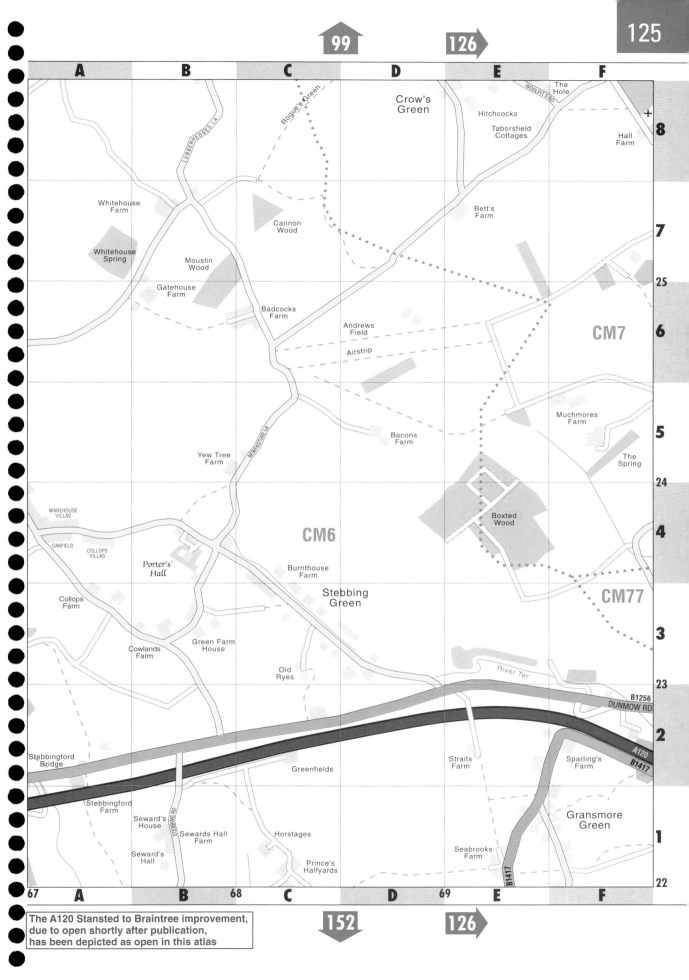

99
126
152
126

The A120 Stansted to Braintree improvement, due to open shortly after publication, has been depicted as open in this atlas

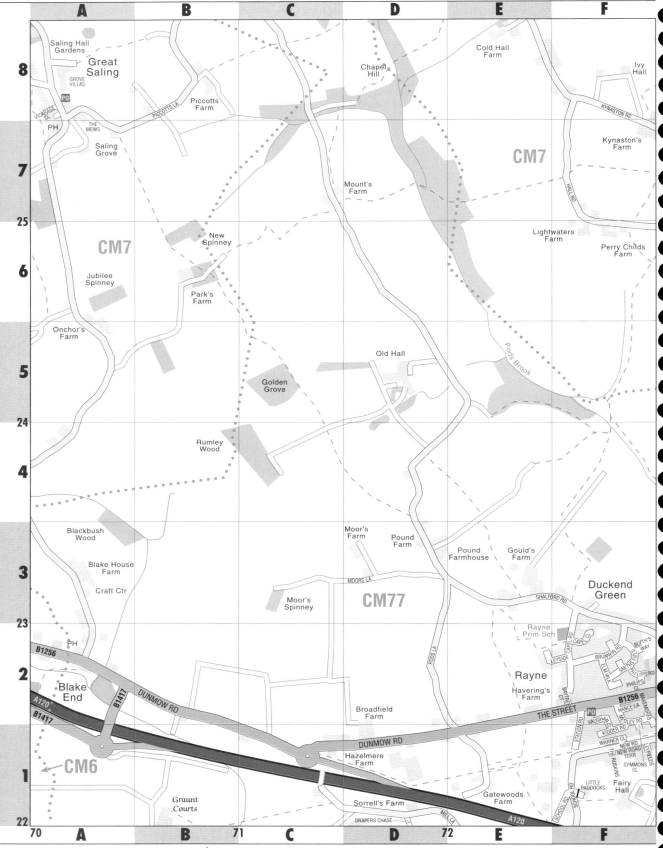

The A120 Stansted to Braintree improvement,
due to open shortly after publication,
has been depicted as open in this atlas

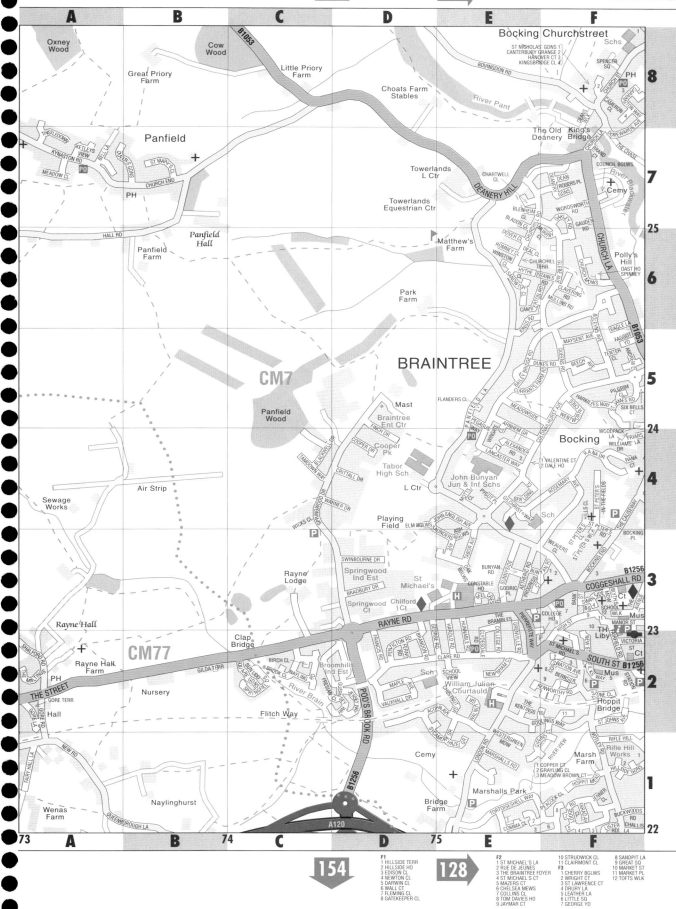

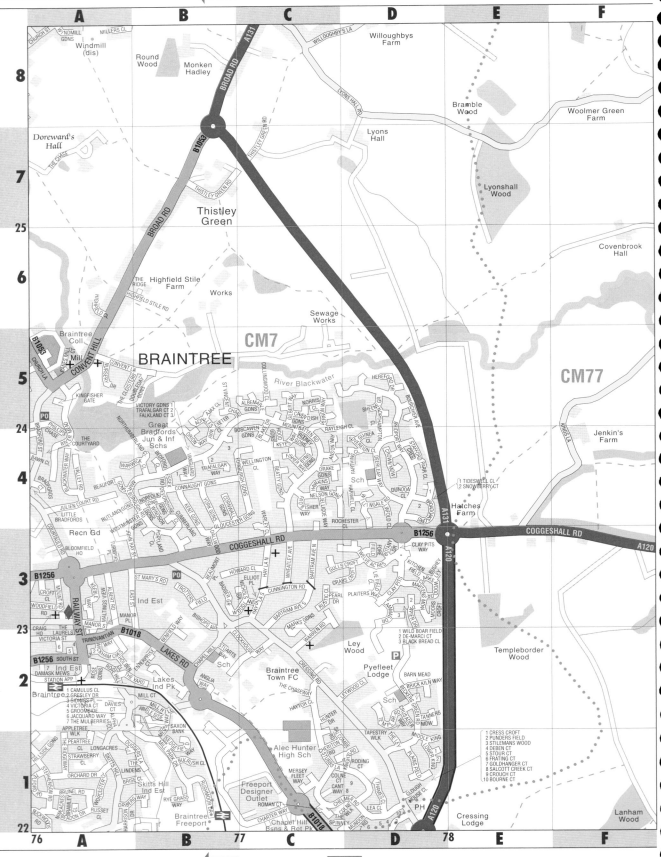

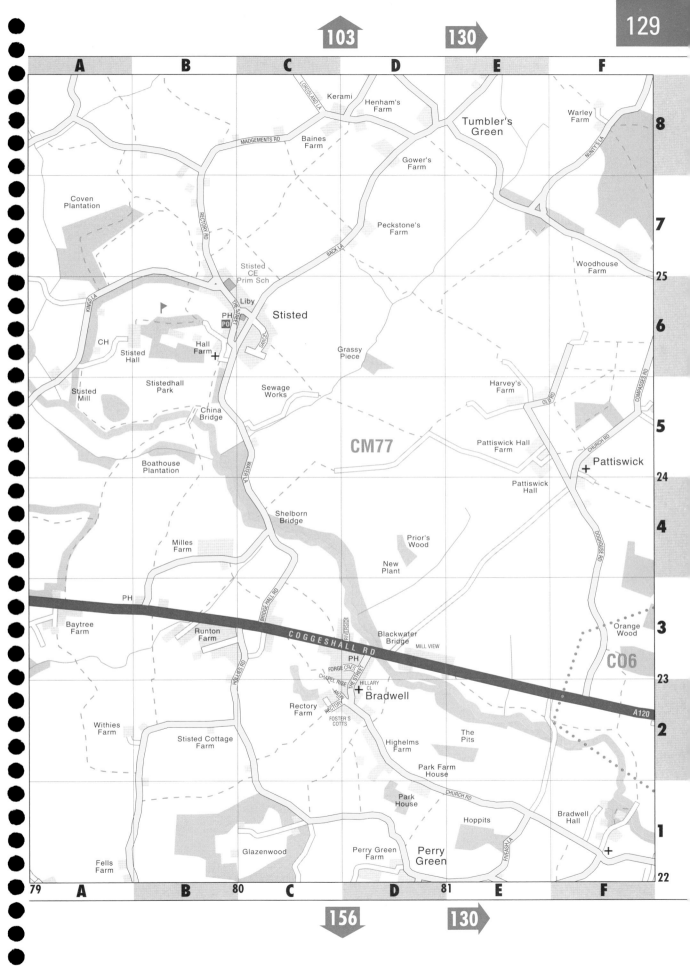

A B C D E F

8 7 25 6 5 24 4 3 23 2 22 1

Kerami
Henham's Farm
Tumbler's Green
Warley Farm
LORDS LAND LA
Baines Farm
MADGEMENTS RD
Gower's Farm
NUNTY'S LA
Coven Plantation
RECTORY RD
Peckstone's Farm
BACK LA
Woodhouse Farm
Stisted CE Prim Sch
Liby
PH PO
Stisted
THE STREET
SAND CT
Grassy Piece
Harvey's Farm
OLD RD
COMPASSES RD
CH
Hall Farm
Stisted Hall
Stistedhall Park
Sewage Works
CM77
Pattiswick Hall Farm
CHURCH RD
Pattiswick
Stisted Mill
China Bridge
Pattiswick Hall
KINGS LA
Boathouse Plantation
WALTER LA
Shelborn Bridge
Prior's Wood
DOGHOUSE RD
Milles Farm
New Plant
Orange Wood
PH
BRIDGE HALL RD
CO6
Baytree Farm
Runton Farm
COGGESHALL RD
RIVERSIDE
Blackwater Bridge
MILL VIEW
A120
HOLLIES RD
FORGE CRES
CHAPEL RISE
THE STREET
HILLARY CL
PH
Bradwell
Withies Farm
Rectory Farm
MOTT
RECTORY
FOSTER'S COTTS
Highelms Farm
The Pits
Stisted Cottage Farm
Park Farm House
CHURCH RD
Park House
Bradwell Hall
Hoppits
FIVEASH LA
Fells Farm
Glazenwood
Perry Green Farm
Perry Green

79 80 81

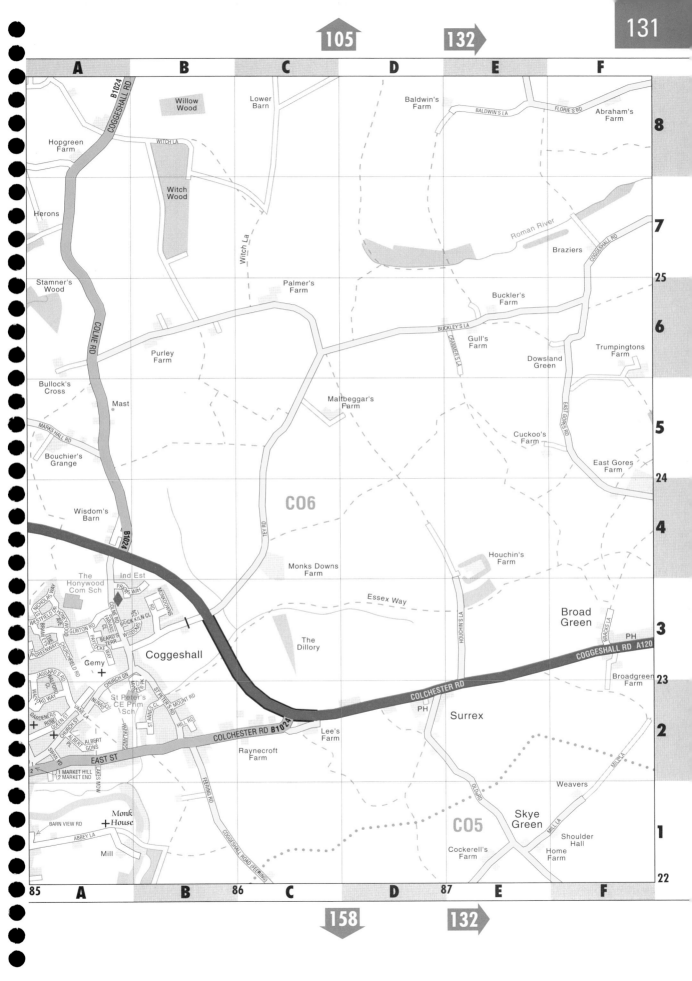

131 106

A B C D E F

8

FLORIE'S RD
Brookhouse
BROOKHOUSE RD
NEWBARN RD
HARVESTERS WAY
GREENFIELD DR
HOLLAND GRO
THE STREET
CHURCH RD
CHAPPEL RD
THE CHASE
MOOR RD
Great Tey
Moor Farm
PO
PH
WINDMILLS
TAMBOUR CL 2
Warrens Farm
NEW COTTS

7

Walcott's Farm
Walcott's Hall
COGGESHALL RD
Brick Kiln Cottage
BROOK RD
Hoe Farm
TEY RD
RECTORY RD
Church House Farm

25

Tey Brook Piggeries
Chase Cottage
LC

6

Essex Way
Teybrook Farm
Little Tey House

5

Sparrow Grove
Little Tey House Farm
Stonefield Grove

24

East Gores
EAST GORES RD
Knave's Farm
CO6

4

SALMON'S LA
Upp Hall Farm
CHURCH LA
Little Tey
Church Farm
GREAT TEY RD
Mott's Farm
MOTT'S LA
Marks Tey
A120
Godbolt's Farm
PH

3

A120
Buxton Cotts
SALMON'S CNR
Elm Farm
Honeylands Farm
COGGESHALL RD
NORMAN CL 1
ROXBOROUGH CL 2
STONE FIELD
GODMANS
HAWL MA
DOMSEY BANK
LEY FIELD
WEL
PATTEN CL
NURSERY CL
BURY CL
ASHBURY DR
MAYS LA
MAYBURY CL
1 KINGSBURY CL
2 STEELE CL
Wks
St Andrew's CE Prim Sch
HORN
WOOD CL
MANDEVILLE RD
BRIEF AVE
SANDERSON
PROCTOR
KEARS RD
CORNWALLIS DR
DOBBIES LA
LONDON RD
LC
A12
WILSON'S LA
MANTS CRES

23

2

ELM LA

1

Hornigals
CO5
LONDON RD
A12
Damyon's Farm

22

88 A B 89 C D 90 E F

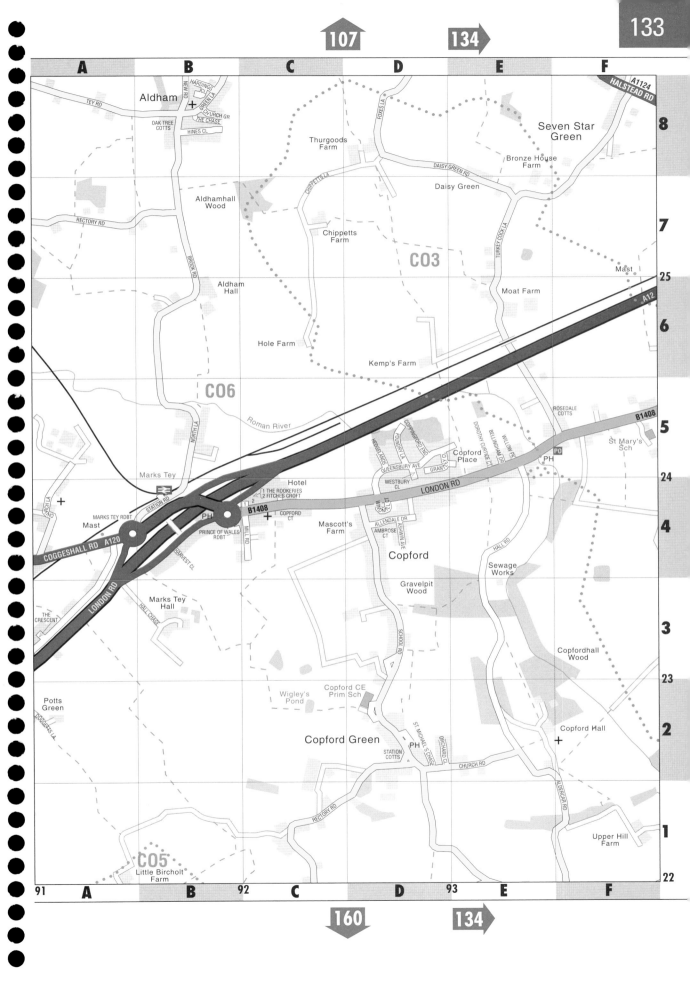

133 108

A · B · C · D · E · F

8

7

25

6

5

24

4

3

23

2

1

22

CO6

A1124

THE WALK
SPRING LA
HEATHFIELDS
THE RISE
PH
BLNDTS LA
PO
HALSTEAD RD
Newlands Farm
Eight Ash Green

Bridge Farm

Hotel
Abbots Hall
ABBOTS LA
DARNA CT
LY CL

Chitts Hills
LC

Chittshill Farm

Holmwood House Prep Sch

Seven Arches Farm

River Colne
A12
Maltings Farm House

COOK'S LA
FIRST DRIVE DR
COOK'S LA

1 COLUMBINE MEWS
2 SPRING SEDGE CL
3 DAWNFORD CT
4 DAWNFORD CT

IRON LATCH LA

HALSTEAD RD

Lexden Springs Sch

CYMBELINE WAY (COLCHESTER BY PASS)
A133
LEXDEN MEWS
P
LEXDEN RD A1124

A12
A12

ESSEX YEOMANRY WAY

COWSLIP CT
FLOWER CL
TUDOR ROSE CL

SWEET BRIAR RD
DAMASK CL
RUGOSA CL
PEACE RD

MUSK CL
RAMBLER CL

FRENSHAM CL

JUBILEE
NEW RD

LONDON RD

LEXDEN PL
NEWHYTHE
ASCOT GDNS

TRAFALGAR RD

NELSON RD

P
DATCHET HO
Victoria CT

HENLEY CT
NELSON AVE
CHALICE RD
COLCHIN CL

SHERIDAN CT
MARLOWE WAY
CHAUCER WAY
THE MOUNT

LUCY CL N
LUCY LA
PROVENCE RD
ALBERTINE CL

BEACON END CTYD
CORALIN WLK
NEW RD

Badgers Holt
Beacon End

COLLINGWOOD RD
COBBLE ROW
LANVALLEY RD

Lexden Prim Sch
VICTORY CT
GARDEN DR

WORDSWORTH RD
MASEFIELD DR
THOMPSON AVE

SHELLEY RD
BROWNING CL
KEATS AVE
SHAKESPEARE RD
BURNS AVE
MILTON CL

MEADOW GRASS

WOODRUSH END

B1408

Wyvern Farm

LONDON RD

TOLLGATE RDBT
A1124
B1408

TOLLGATE CT
TOLLGATE E
TOLLGATE W

Liby

VILLA HO
CHAPEL RD

Stanway Prim Sch

ELMWOOD

Gryme's Dyke

1 STIRRUP MEWS
2 SADDLE MEWS
RATCLIFFE RD

De Burgh Rd

St Teresa's RC Prim Sch

CLAIRMONT RD

Home Farm Prim Sch

HUNTERS CNR

HEATH RD
WOODLAND DR
CHERRY TREE
CHERRYWOOD DR
HEATHER CHASE
DR BAINES

RICHARDSON WLK
DALE WAY

Westside Ctr

B1408

CO3

Stanway

Oldhouse Farm

PARTRIDGE WAY

CHURCH LA

NURSERY CL
VILLARD
THE COPSE

DOVE TREE CT

The Stanway Sch

New Farm Lodge

The Heath Sch

SHEPHERDS CROFT
COPPERFIELDS

THRESHERS END
BRIDGEHALL END
FARRIERS END
CLOVER CT

MEADOW VIEW CL
WASHINGTON CT
PLOUGH END
ROW CL

JUNIPER RD
WINSTREE RD
GORSE WAY
HOLLY RD

ROBIN CL
CRANE AVE
CHURCHFIELDS
NIGHTINGALE PL
MALLARD WAY

BATLEY DALE
RISE AVE
BLACKBERRY RD
PO
ROW AN CL

Stanway Fiveways Prim Sch

Peartree Bsns Ctr
Jayrest Ctr

PEARTREE RD

BARLEY WAY
KALE CROFT
PERSHORE END
JEFFERSON RD

PRESIDENT RD
STERLING CL
STRAIGHT RD

MARSDEN CT
TWINING RD

CLARA REEVE CL

CARSHALTON
STONEBRIDGE PK

Tye Grove

Sand & Gravel Pit

CYGNET WLK
SANDMARTIN CRES
WRELL CL
DULVERTON COTTS

GRIEVES CT
EGREMONT CL
AMBOURNE CL

PEARIN WAY
YOEMAN

DYER'S RD

FIVE WAYS

GRYME'S DYKE WAY

HEATH RD
VALLEY CT
STANFIELD

FISON WAY
PILBROUGH WAY
WILLIS CL

LADELL CL

JAMES CARTER RD

DUGARD AVE
SALMON CL
WORTHINGTON WAY
ALAN WAY
REGENCY CL

AMBROSE AVE
THE WAY

Stanway Green

Bellhouse Farm

Furze Hill

WARREN LA

Sand & Gravel Pit

Mast

B1022
SHRUB END RD

Brickwall Farm

TUMULUS WAY
CUNOBELIN WAY
BARBOUR GDNS
P

Cheshunt Field

CO6

Hanging Wood

Warren Plantation

MALDON RD

CO2

FOUNTAIN LA
Gol Grove

B1022
Colchester Zoo

Stanway Hall Farm

Butcher's Wood

OLIVERS LA

94 · A · B · 95 · C · D · 96 · E · F

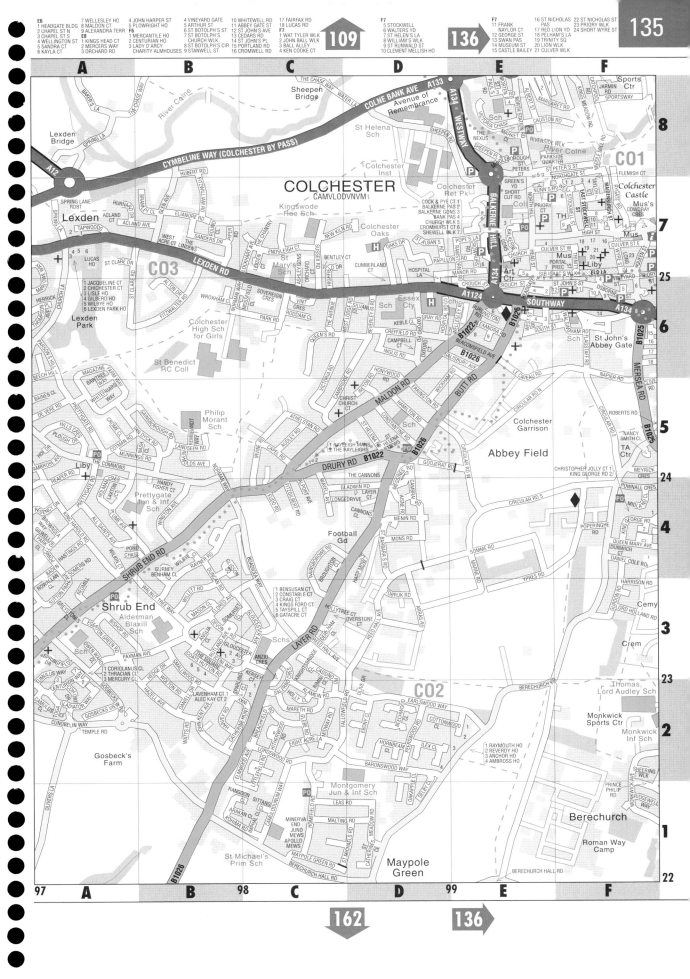

A6
1 JOHN KAVANAGH CT
2 WILLIAMSON HO
3 KENDALL'S ALMSHOUSES
4 WINNOCK'S ALMSHOUSES
5 WINNOCKS
6 SHRUBLAND RD
7 ATTLEE GDNS
8 PIONEER PL
9 TYMPERLEY CT
10 MILITARY CT
11 RAVENSWOOD
12 ROSE HO
13 SCHOOL HO

A6
14 WHEATSHEAF CT
C6
5 NEPTUNE CT
6 WINDSOR CT
7 ST LEONARDS TERR
8 ST LEONARDS SCHOOL HO
9 STANDARD RD

C8
1 DINSDALE CL
2 FAIRFIELD GDNS
3 ST ANDREWS CT
4 WHYBREWS
5 COMPTON MEWS
6 FAIRHEAD RD S

7 DANSIE CT
D7
1 FAIRBROTHER CT
2 GROOME CT
3 DEWBERRY CT
4 PURBECK CT
5 BENTLEIGH CT

6 THE CHASE
D8
1 WILLIAM BOYS CL
2 ROSEMARY CL
3 ASPEN WAY
4 DAPHNE CT

5 CAMELLIA CT
6 FUCHSIA CT
7 CORRY CT
8 DAMMANT CT
E8
1 WILLOW TREE CT
2 REDWOOD CT

3 SOLWAY CT
F8
1 OWLS RETREAT
2 WOODPECKER CL
3 TURNSTONE END
4 IMOGEN CL
5 CYPRESS GR

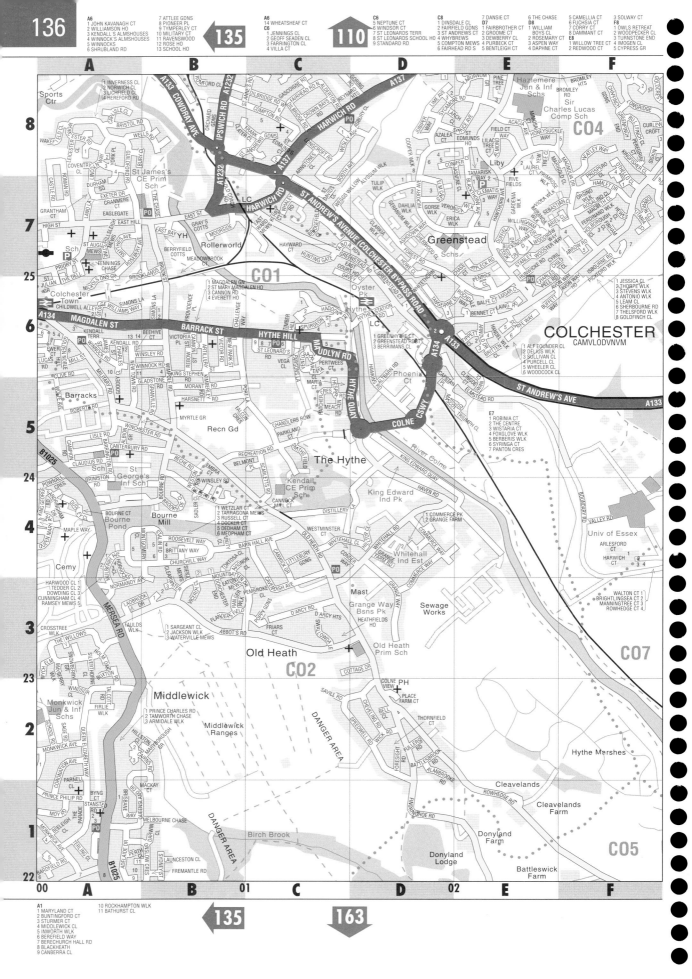

A1
1 MARYLAND CT
2 BUNTINGFORD CT
3 STURMER CT
4 MIDDLEWICK CL
5 INWORTH WLK
6 BEREFIELD WAY
7 BERECHURCH HALL RD
8 BLACKHEATH
9 CANBERRA CL
10 ROCKHAMPTON WLK
11 BATHURST CL

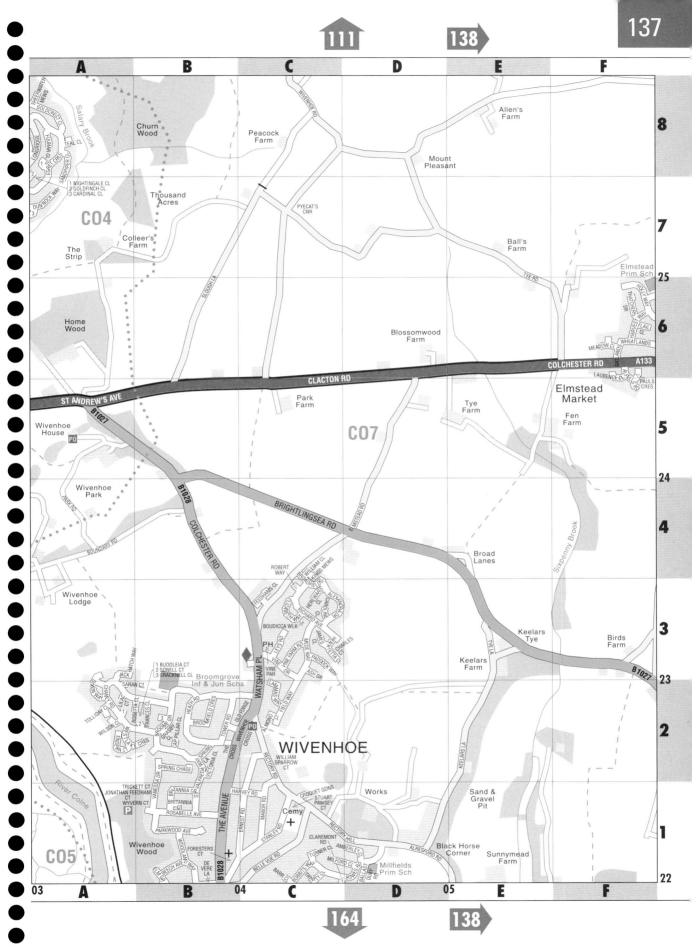

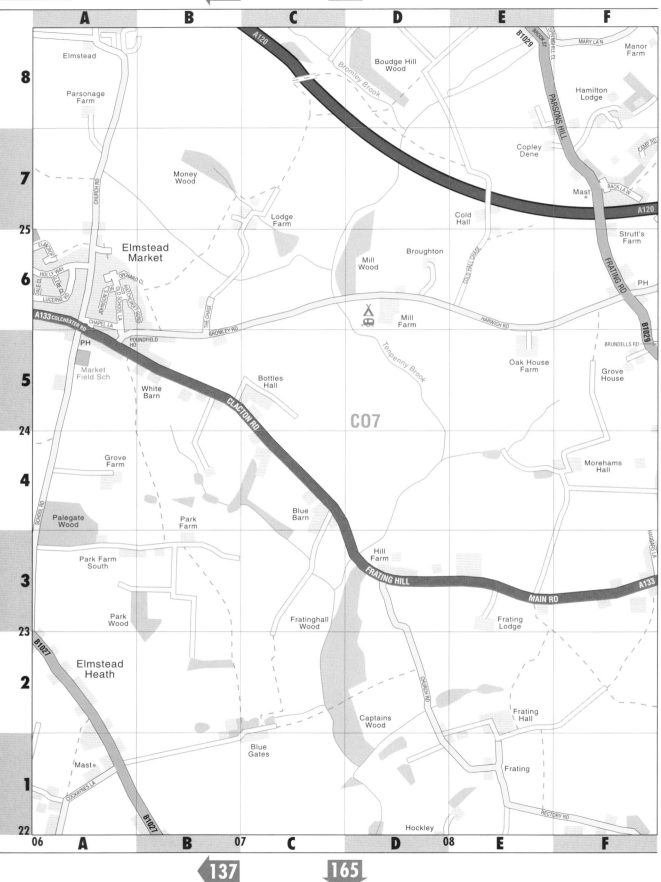

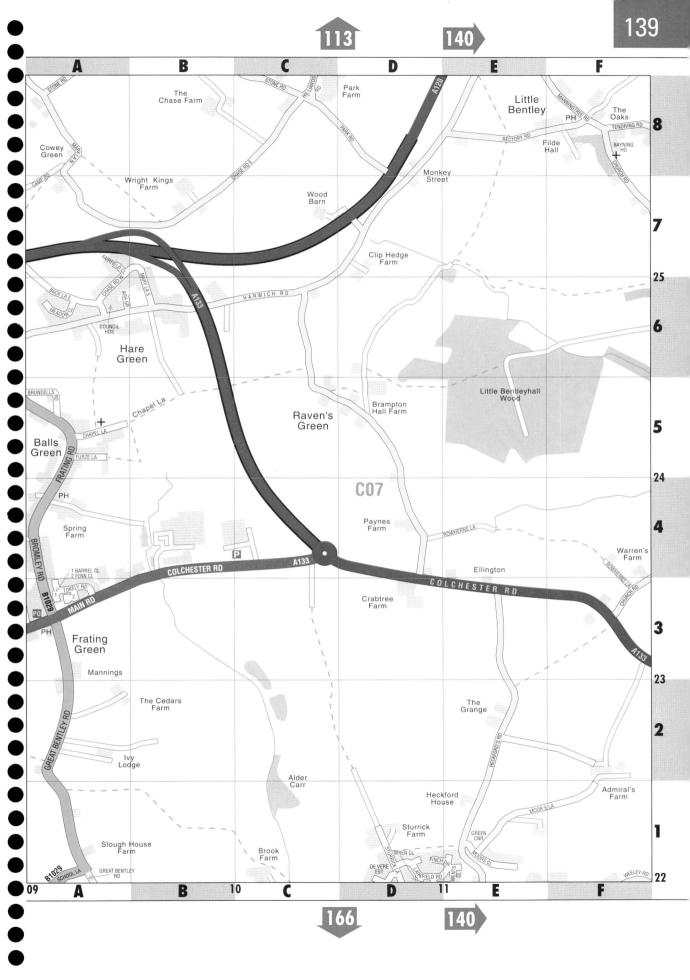

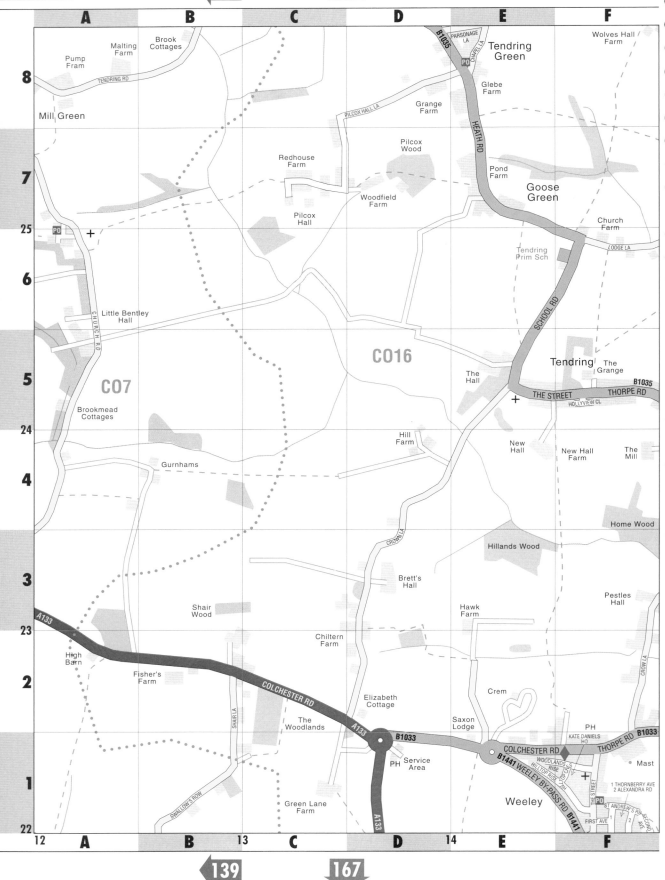

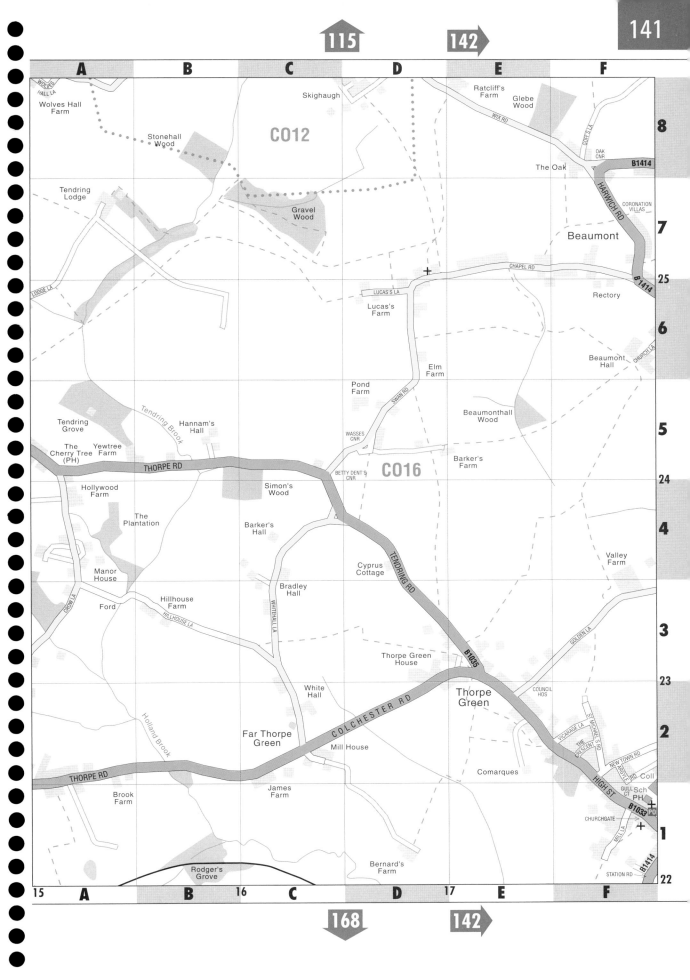

141
116

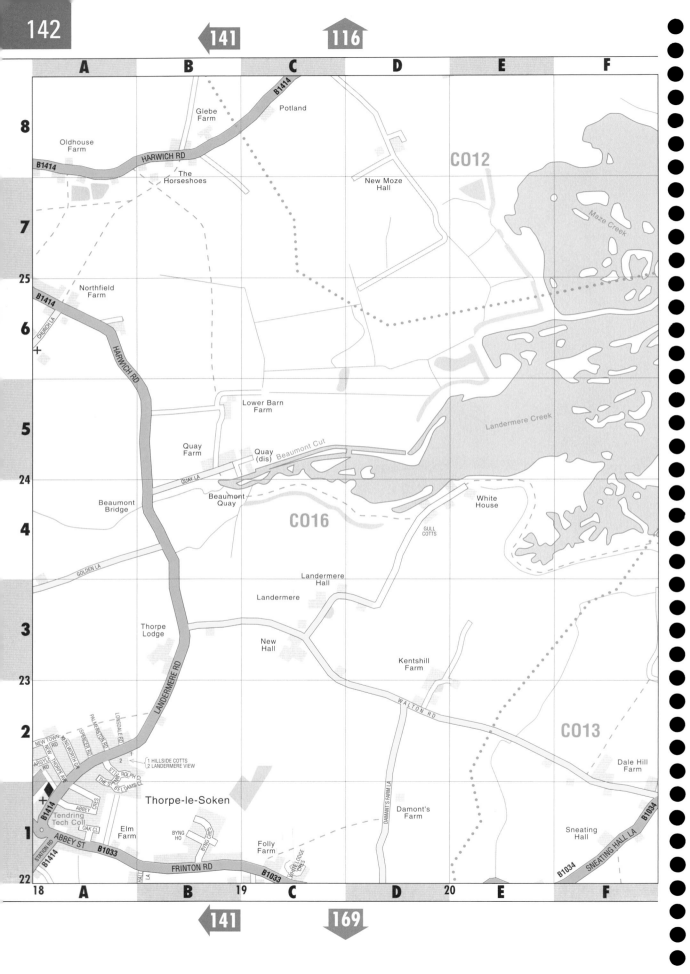

141
169

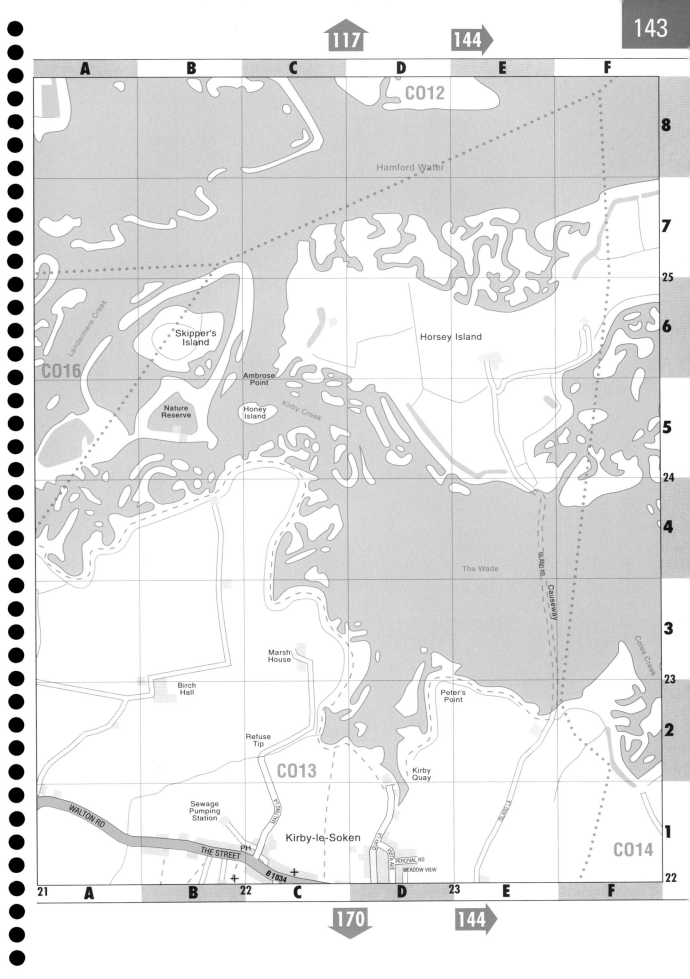

143

Stone Point

Stone Marsh

Stone Creek

Cormorant Creek

The Dardanelles

Standcreek Salts

Salt Fleet

The Naze Nature Reserve

Walton Channel

Sewage Works

THE NAZE

Hedge-end Island

Walton Hall Marshes

CREEK COTTS

The Naze Nature Trail

Walton Hall

CO14

The Naze Tower

P

NAZE CT

OLD HALL LA

SUNNY POINT

The Twizzle

ELIZABETH CT

LOUISE CL

P

PH

COLES LA

Titchmarsh Marina

HIGH TREE LA

SHAMFORD CL

FIRST AVE

SECOND AVE

THIRD AVE

NAZE PARK RD

P

Mabel Greville Breakwater

1 D'ARCY HO
2 RIVERS HO

SPENDEL

GREY CL

PO

Sole Creek

FLORENCE RD

CLIFF PAR

BEATRICE RD

Jubilee Beach

PERCIVAL RD

TUDOR CL

HALL LA

GREEN LA

WINFIELD TERR

Walton Mere

COASTGUARD COTTS

Walton Maritime Mus

PENRICE CT 1
EASTCLIFF HO 2
WATERFRONT TERR 3
KINGS REACH 4

EAST TERR

East Terrace Breakwater

CH

P

Walton Prim Sch

Martello Tower

BRIAN BISHOP CL

MILL LA

COLES LA

NORTH ST

NORTH ST

SAVILLE ST

STANDLEY RD

EAGLE AVE

PRINCE'S ESPL

B1034

171

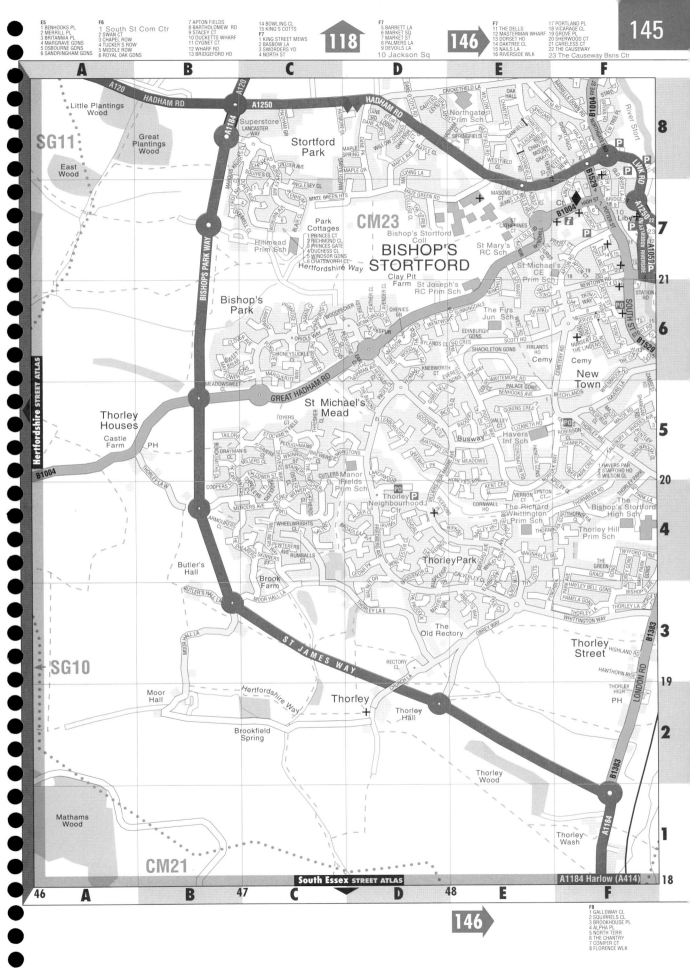

118

146

146

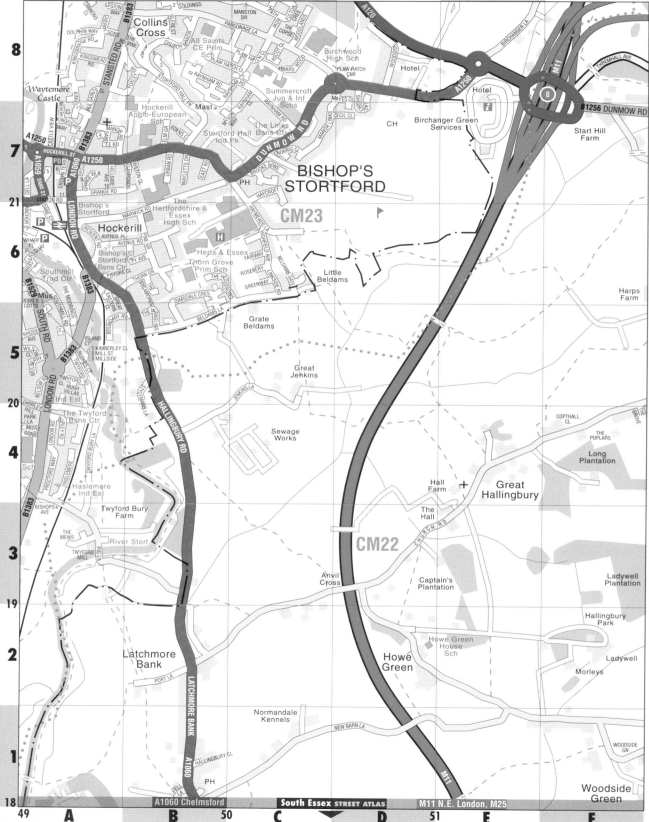

146

A7
1 THE CAUSEWAY
2 THE OLD MALTINGS
3 FULLER CT
4 LIMES CRES
5 RED LION CT
6 BAKERS CT

7 HOCKERILL CT
8 HARRINGTON CL
9 PRIORS
10 CLIFFORD CT
11 THOMAS HESKIN CT

B8
1 BOYD CL
2 HEATH ROW
3 STORTFORD HALL RD
4 GROSVENOR HO
5 EATON HO
6 BELGRAVE HO

145

119

Collins Cross

Waytemore Castle

Hockerill Anglo-European Sch

BISHOP'S STORTFORD

CM23

Hockerill

The Hertfordshire & Essex High Sch

Herts & Essex Thorn Grove Prim Sch

Southmill Trad Ctr

Bishop's Stortford Bsns Ctr

Little Beldams

Grate Beldams

Great Jehkins

Sewage Works

The Twyford Bsns Ctr

Haslemere Ind Est

Twyford Bury Farm

River Stort

Twyford Mill

Latchmore Bank

Normandale Kennels

Birchwood High Sch

Hotel

Hotel

8

Birchanger Green Services

Start Hill Farm

Harps Farm

Long Plantation

Great Hallingbury

Hall Farm

The Hall

CM22

Anvil Cross

Captain's Plantation

Ladywell Plantation

Hallingbury Park

Howe Green

Howe Green House Sch

Ladywell

Morleys

Woodside Green

The A120 Stansted to Braintree improvement, due to open shortly after publication, has been depicted as open in this atlas

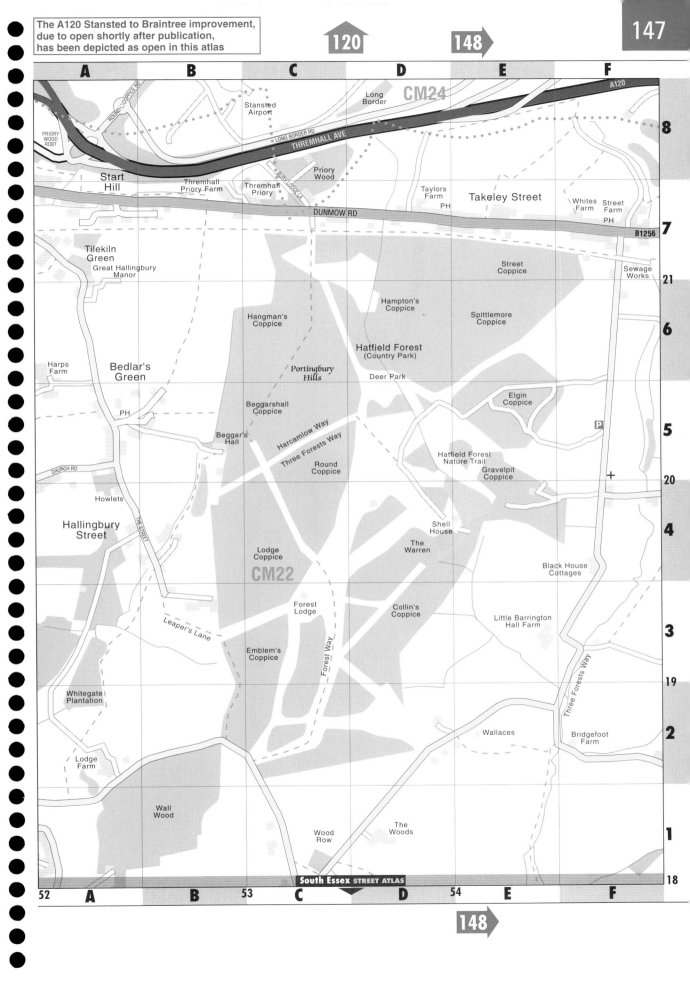

PRIORY WOOD RDBT

ROUND COPPICE RD

Stansted Airport

Long Border

CM24

A120

LONG BORDER RD

THREMHALL AVE

Start Hill

Thremhall Priory Farm

Thremhall Priory

BURY LODGE LA

Priory Wood

DUNMOW RD

Taylors Farm PH

Takeley Street

Whites Farm

Street Farm PH

B1256

Tilekiln Green

Great Hallingbury Manor

Street Coppice

Sewage Works

Hangman's Coppice

Hampton's Coppice

Spittlemore Coppice

Harps Farm

Bedlar's Green

Portingbury Hills

Hatfield Forest (Country Park)

Deer Park

Elgin Coppice

PH

Beggarshall Coppice

Beggar's Hall

Harcamlow Way

Three Forests Way

Hatfield Forest Nature Trail

Gravelpit Coppice

CHURCH RD

Round Coppice

Howlets

Hallingbury Street

THE STREET

Shell House

The Warren

Black House Cottages

Lodge Coppice

CM22

Leaper's Lane

Forest Lodge

Collin's Coppice

Little Barrington Hall Farm

Emblem's Coppice

Forest Way

Whitegate Plantation

Three Forests Way

Wallaces

Bridgefoot Farm

Lodge Farm

Wall Wood

Wood Row

The Woods

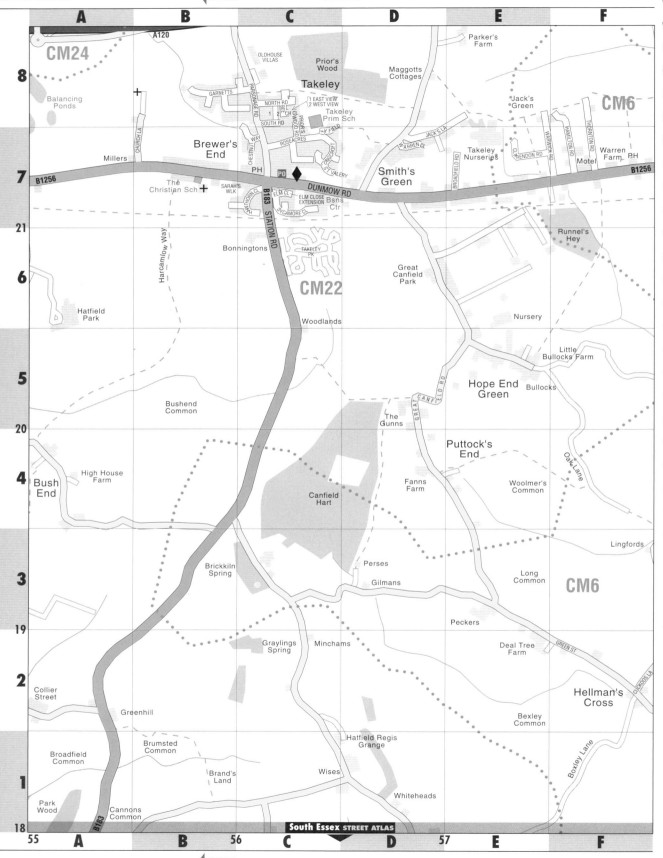

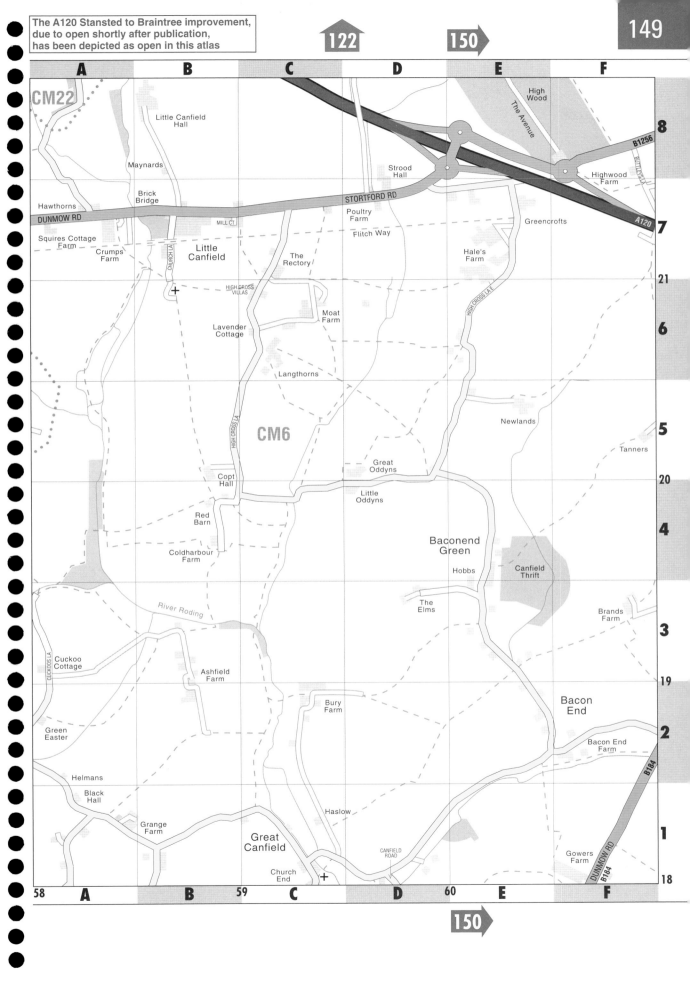

The A120 Stansted to Braintree improvement, due to open shortly after publication, has been depicted as open in this atlas

122
150

CM22

Little Canfield Hall

High Wood

The Avenue

B1256

8

Maynards

Strood Hall

Highwood Farm

Brick Bridge

STORTFORD RD

A120

7

Hawthorns

DUNMOW RD

Poultry Farm

Greencrofts

Squires Cottage Farm

MILL CT

Flitch Way

21

Crumps Farm

CHURCH LA

Little Canfield

The Rectory

Hale's Farm

HIGH CROSS LA

HIGH CROSS LA E

HIGH CROSS LA E

+

HIGH CROSS VILLAS

6

Lavender Cottage

Moat Farm

Langthorns

Newlands

Tanners

CM6

5

Copt Hall

Great Oddyns

20

Red Barn

Little Oddyns

Baconend Green

4

Coldharbour Farm

Hobbs

Canfield Thrift

River Roding

The Elms

Brands Farm

3

CUCKOOS LA

Cuckoo Cottage

Ashfield Farm

19

Green Easter

Bury Farm

Bacon End

Bacon End Farm

2

B184

Helmans

Black Hall

Haslow

Grange Farm

Great Canfield

CANFIELD ROAD

Gowers Farm

DUNMOW RD

1

Church End

+

B184

18

150

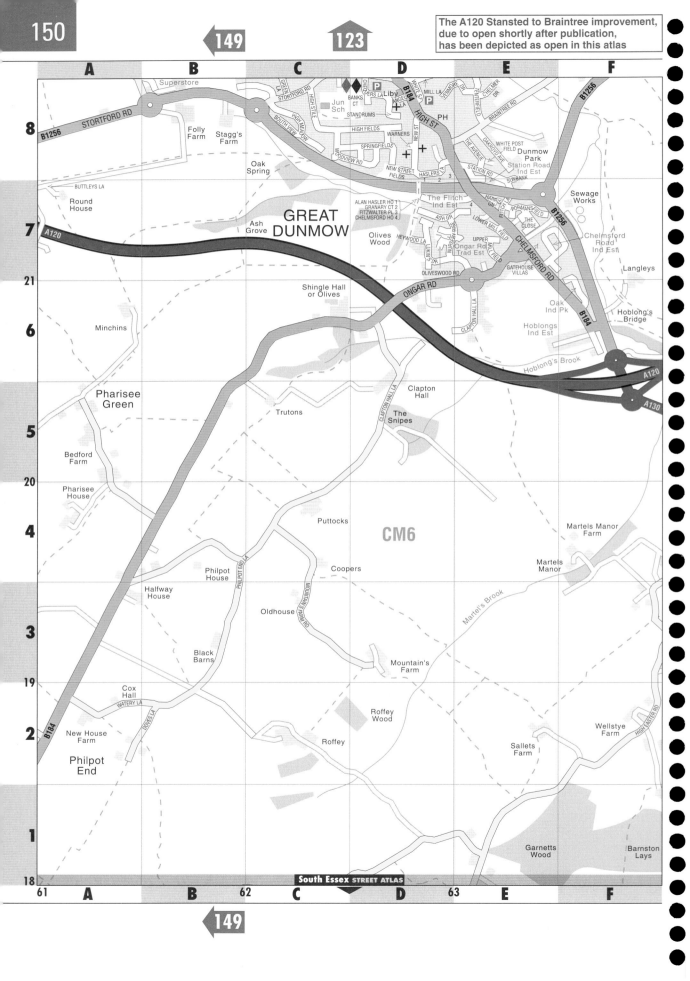

The A120 Stansted to Braintree improvement,
due to open shortly after publication,
has been depicted as open in this atlas

A B C D E F

8

STORTFORD RD

B1256

Superstore

GREEN LA
STORTFORD RD

HIGH STILE

South View

Folly
Farm

Stagg's
Farm

Oak
Spring

BUTTLEYS LA

Round
House

7

A120

Ash
Grove

GREAT
DUNMOW

Olives
Wood

Jun
Sch

BANKS
CT

STANDRUMS

HIGH FIELDS

WARNERS

SPRINGFIELDS

WOODVIEW RD

NEW STREET
FIELDS

CHELMERS LA

Liby

B184

MILL LA

HIGH ST

PH

VENMORE
DR

TENTERFIELD

BRAINTREE RD

B1256

White Post
Field

Dunmow
Park

Station Road
Ind Est

Sewage
Works

21

ALAN HASLER HO 1
GRANARY CT 2
FITZWALTER PL 3
CHELMSFORD HO 4

The Flitch
Ind Est

STATION RD

SUNBANK

HARRIS GN

NORMANSFIELD

THE CLOSE

LOWER MILL FIELD

B1256

Chelmsford
Road
Ind Est

Langleys

6

Minchins

Shingle Hall
or Olives

ONGAR RD

HEYWOOD LA

Ongar Rd
Trad Est

UPPER
MILL FIELD

OLIVESWOOD RD

GATEHOUSE
VILLAS

CLAPTON HALL LA

Oak
Ind Pk

Hoblongs
Ind Est

CHELMSFORD RD

B184

Hoblong's
Brook

Hoblong's
Bridge

A120

A130

5

Pharisee
Green

Trutons

CLAPTON HALL LA

The
Snipes

Clapton
Hall

20

Bedford
Farm

Pharisee
House

Puttocks

CM6

Martels Manor
Farm

4

Coopers

Philpot
House

PHILPOT END LA

Halfway
House

Oldhouse

MOUNTAIN'S FARM RD

Martel's Brook

Martels
Manor

19

3

Black
Barns

Mountain's
Farm

Cox
Hall

WATERY LA

DOVES LA

Roffey
Wood

Wellstye
Farm

HIGHEASTER LA

2

B184

New House
Farm

Roffey

Sallets
Farm

Philpot
End

Garnetts
Wood

Barnston
Lays

1

18

61 A 62 B C 62 D 63 E F

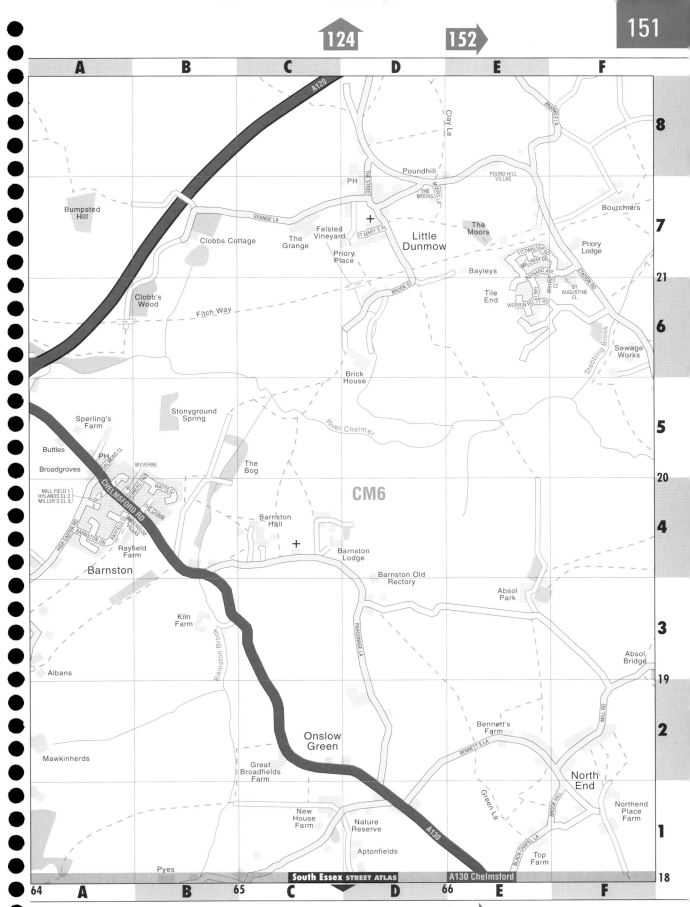

A120

8

Clay La

Poundhill

BRAMBLE LA

POUND HILL VILLAS

Bourchiers

7

THE MOORS

PH

THE STREET

MOORS LA

Little Dunmow

The Moors

Priory Lodge

Grange La

Clobbs Cottage

The Grange

Felsted Vineyard

ST MARY'S PL

Bumpsted Hill

FITZWALTER RD

MILDMAY CL

BARNARD AVE

BRITHC CL

STATION RD

ST AUGUSTINE CL

Priory Place

Bayleys

Tile End

WORRIN RD

HALE TT RD

21

Clobb's Wood

Fitch Way

Brook St

6

Stebbing Brook

Sewage Works

Brick House

Stonyground Spring

River Chelmer

5

Sperling's Farm

Buttles

PH

SALTONS CL

WYVERNE

The Bog

CM6

Broadgroves

BERNERS END

WATTS CL

20

MILL FIELD 1
HYLANDS CL 2
MILLER'S CL 3

CHELMSFORD RD

MILL HOUSE VILLAS

THE CHASE

Barnston Hall

4

HIGH EASTER RD

BARNSTON GN

HAYFIELD CL

Rayfield Farm

Barnston Lodge

Absol Park

Barnston

Barnston Old Rectory

Kiln Farm

Barnston Brook

PARSONAGE LA

Absol Bridge

3

Albans

19

MILL RD

Bennett's Farm

2

Mawkinherds

BENNETT'S LA

North End

Onslow Green

Green La

Great Broadfields Farm

Northend Place Farm

BROOK HILL

New House Farm

Nature Reserve

A130

BLACK CHAPEL LA

Top Farm

1

Aptonfields

Pyes

A130 Chelmsford

18

151
125

A B C D E F

8

Stebbing Brook

Brook Farm

Gifford House

Fitch Way

B1477

Great Greenfields

7

Miniature Rifle Range

STEBBING RD

Felmoor Farm

Sunnybrook Farm

Weavers Farm

Watch House Green

Felsted Cty Prim Sch

21

Wr Twr

CHESTNUT WLK

CHAFFIX CL

GARNETTS LA

CHAFFIX

Chaffix Farm

OXNEY VILLAS

RAVENS CRES

BANNISTER GREEN VILLAS

CRESSAGE CL

STEVENS LA

6

PLAYERS CT

Felsted Sch

ALDERTON CL

BRAINTREE RD

Chaffix

Chaffix

Oxney's Farm

BURNSTIE RD

PH

THE CLOSE

Bannister Green

Bury Farm

FELSTED ALMSHOUSES

GARNETTS VILLAS

THE ORCHARD

JOLYBOYS LN N

GARNETTS BGLWS

5

STATION RD

BURY FIELDS

PO

RICHE CL

CROMWELL PK

Felsted Pl

Felsted Prep Sch

Hotel

Felsted

Playing Field

CM6

Cleveland's Farm

20

Mariskalls

THE TERRACE

CHELMSFORD RD

BAKERS LA

Jollyboys

JOLLYBOYS LA S

Cock Green

Brick House Farm

4

Mill Moorings

MILL RD

BRICKBURN CL

Potash Farm

Cobler's Green

Pondpark Farm

Mill House

LADYSMITH COTTS

CAUSEWAY END RD

3

Causeway End

Glanfield's Farm

19

River Chelmer

Millbank's Farm

2

LEEZ LA

The Gate House

CM3

1

B1477

Prior's Green

CAUSEWAY

18

67 A   B   68   C   D   69   E   F

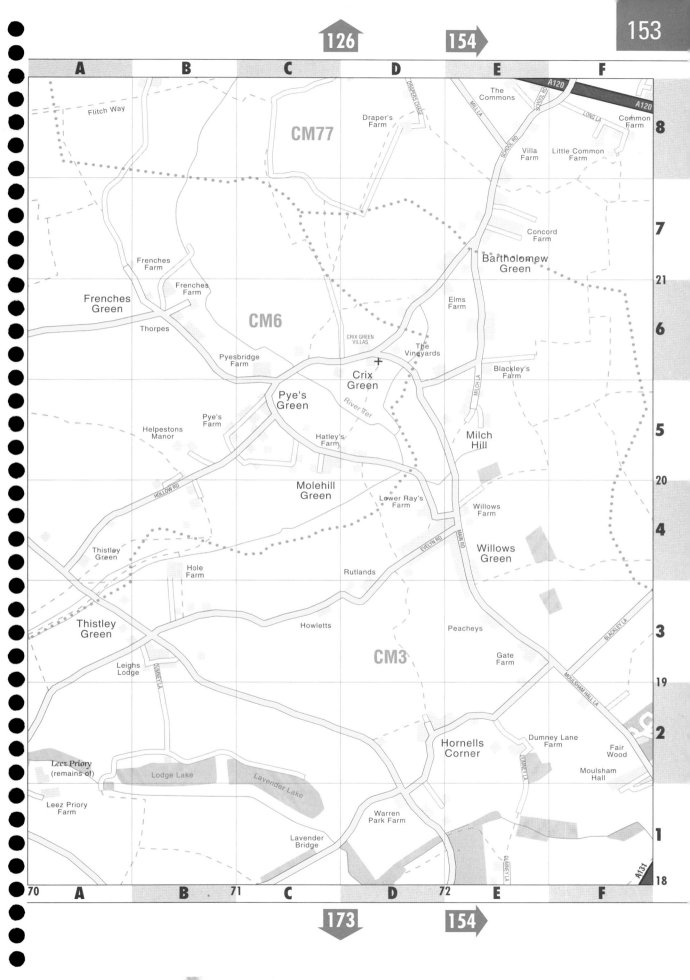

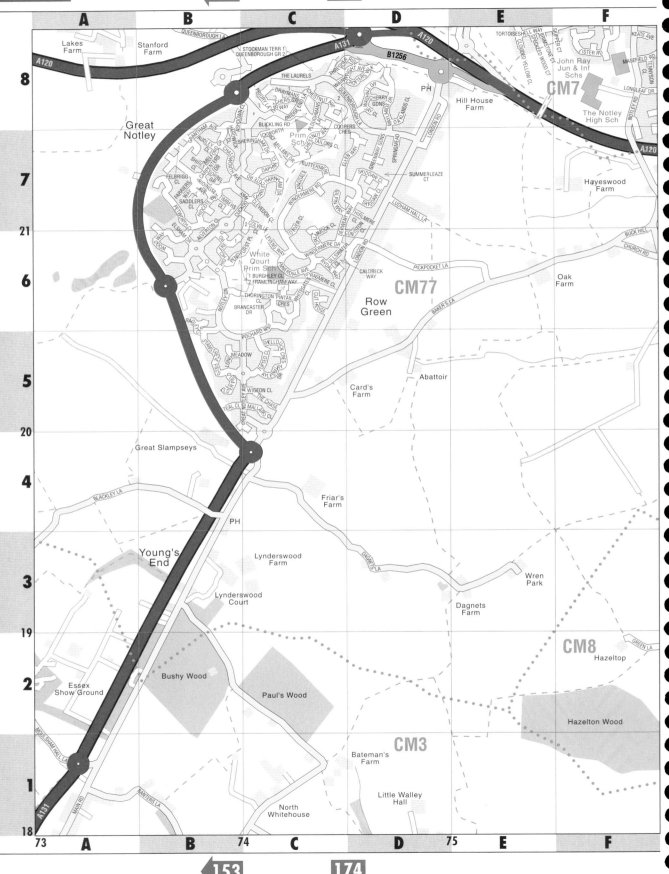

153
127

A   B   C   D   E   F

8

7

21

6

5

20

4

3

19

2

1

18

153
174

Lakes Farm
Stanford Farm
A120
Great Notley
QUEENBOROUGH LA
STOCKMAN TERR 1
QUEENBOROUGH GR 2
THE LAURELS
A131
B1256
A120
TORTOISESHELL WAY
CLOUDED YELLOW CL
SPECKLED WOOD CT
BRIMSTONE CT
SKIPPER CT
LISTER RO
KEATS AVE
John Ray Jun & Inf Schs
MASEFIELD
TENNYSON
LONGLEAF DR
CM7
NOTLEY RD
The Notley High Sch
A120

PH
Hill House Farm
Prim Sch
BLICKLING RD
GRANTHAM AVE
FELBRIGG CL
FARRIERS
SADDLERS CL
PELWORTH CT
ELSHAM DR
RAGLEY CL

Hayeswood Farm
BUCK HILL
CHURCH RD

SUMMERLEAZE CT
LUDHAM HALL LA

White Court Prim Sch
1 BURGHLEY CL
2 FRAMLINGHAM WAY
THORINGTON CL
BRANCASTER DR
PINTAIL CRES

CM77
Row Green

CALDBECK WAY
PICKPOCKET LA
Oak Farm
BAKER'S LA
Abattoir

MEADOW
POCHARD WY
GREAT NOTLEY AVE
SHELDUCK CRES
WISEON CL
TEAL CL
MALLARD CL
THE CHASE
AYLESBURY

Card's Farm

Great Slampseys
BLACKLEY LA
PH
Young's End

Friar's Farm
DAGNETS LA
Wren Park

Lynderswood Farm
Lynderswood Court

Dagnets Farm

CM8
Hazeltop
GREEN LA

Bushy Wood
Paul's Wood

Hazelton Wood

CM3
Bateman's Farm

Little Walley Hall

MIDDLE SHAM HALL LA
A131
MAIN RD
BANTERS LA
Essex Show Ground
North Whitehouse

155
129

A B C D E F

8

Lanham Manor Farm

Sand & Gravel Pit

Jubilee Plantation

Wr Twr

Lanham Green

Clapdog Green

LINK RD

Gosling's Farm

7

Ashes Farm

ASHES RD

PH

LANHAM GREEN RD

Schills Farm

Link's Farm

Link's Wood

Essex Way

21

6 Cressing

THE STREET

Wright's Farm

Airfield (disused)

POLECAT RD

Egypts Farm

Mast

Sheepcotes Farm

BOARS TYE RD

Rolph's Farmhouse

CHURCH RD

5 CM77

BROOMFIELD

SHEEPCOTES LA

20

COUNCIL HOUSES

WEAVERSFIELD

THE GOSLINGS

RUNNACLES ST

BROADWAY CT

BROADWAY

FRANCIS CT

WALTER WAY

SILVER ST

RACHAEL GDNS

WITHAM DR

Silver End

PETTIT

FRANCIS WAY

DANIEL WAY

CRITTALL RD

GROVES

REBECCA GDNS

4

NEW HOUSE

MANORS WAY

Liby

PO

THE SHOPS

Hotel

MANORS

Works

JOSEPH GDNS

GROOMS LA

Bower Hall

WESTERN RD

B1018

3

STATION RD

Sheepcote Wood

WITHAM RD

TEMPLE LA

VALENTINE WAY

MAGDALENE CRES

LEDGSTER CT

STRETFORD CT

BRISTOL CT

SCHOOL RD

Silver End Prim Sch

PH

WESTERN CL

WESTERN RD

CM8

Park House

19

Rivenhall Place

2

Cressing Temple Barns

Cressing Temple

Old Court Room

1

Sewage Works

Essex Way

B1018

Hungry Hall

Rivenhall Thicks

18

79 A B 80 C D 81 E F

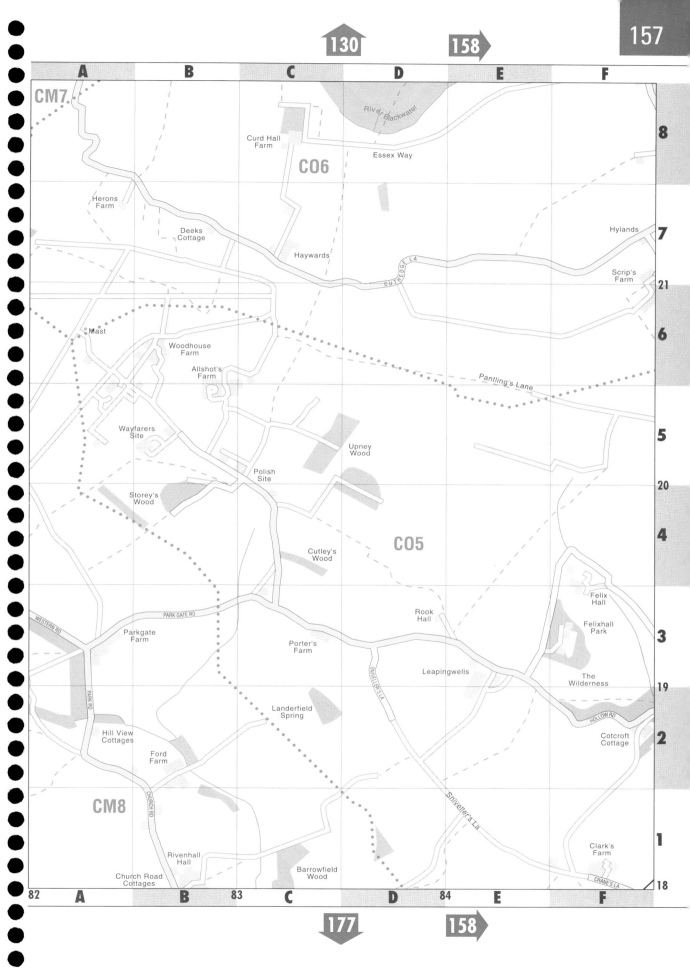

130
158

CM7

A B C D E F

8

CO6

River Blackwater

Curd Hall
Farm

Essex Way

Herons
Farm

Deeks
Cottage

Hylands

7

21

Haywards

CUTHEDGE LA

Scrip's
Farm

Mast

6

Woodhouse
Farm

Allshot's
Farm

Pantling's Lane

Wayfarers
Site

Upney
Wood

5

Polish
Site

Storey's
Wood

20

Cutley's
Wood

CO5

4

Felix
Hall

Felixhall
Park

WESTERN RD

Parkgate
Farm

PARK GATE RD

Rook
Hall

Porter's
Farm

Leapingwells

The
Wilderness

3

19

PARK RD

SNIVELLER'S LA

HOLLOW RD

Landerfield
Spring

Cotcroft
Cottage

2

Hill View
Cottages

Ford
Farm

CHURCH RD

CM8

Sniveller's La

Clark's
Farm

1

Rivenhall
Hall

Barrowfield
Wood

Church Road
Cottages

CRANE'S LA

18

82 A B 83 C D 84 E F

177
158

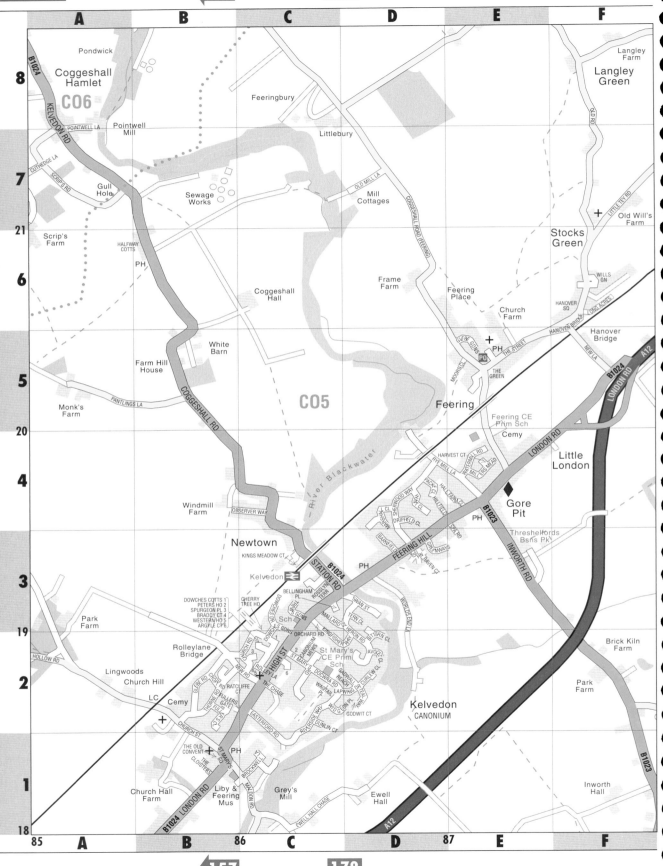

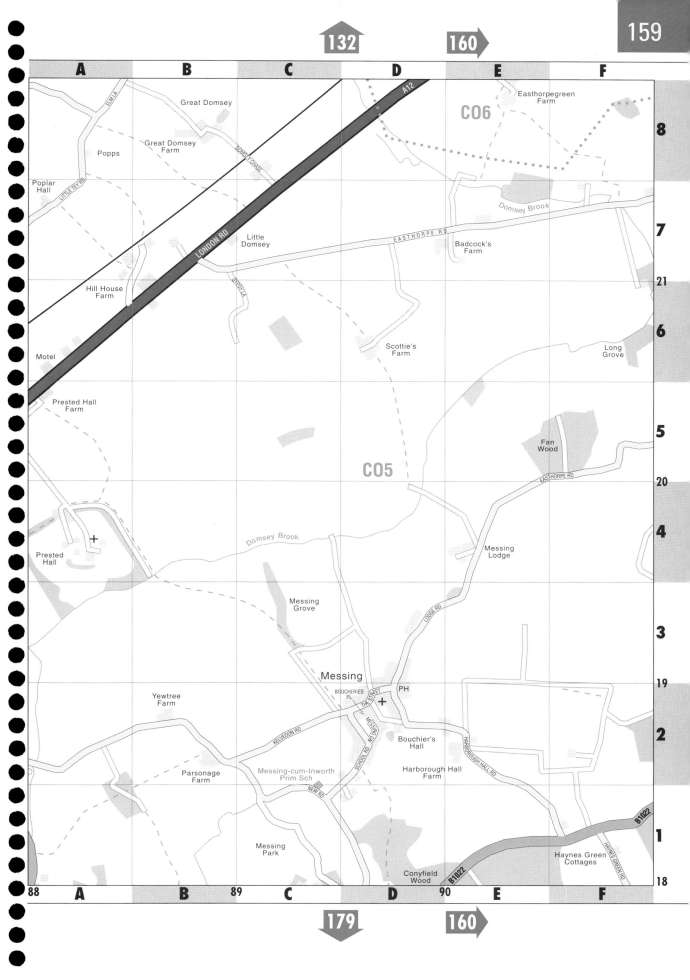

A B C D E F

8

Little Birch
Holt Farm

Boarded
Barn

CO6

St Mary's
Grange

Bockingham Hall
Farm

Easthorpe
Hall

EASTHORPE RD

PH ONSLOW
COTTS Easthorpe

CHURCHWELL AVE

Seller
Wood

Potash
Wood

7

21

Whitehouse
Farm

Hogget's
Farm

Hardy's
Green

Porters
Green

Hellens

Beckingham
Hall

6

WELL LA

Winterflood's
Farm

Sandfordhall
Green

Round
Grove

Shemmings
Farm

Glebe
Farm

Cantfield's
Farm

Greenacres

5

EASTHORPE RD

Radar
Spinney

CO2

B1022

20

Brake's
Farm

Sewage
Works

4

BLIND LA

Sand
Pit

MALDON RD

CAPEL LA

SCHOOL LA

3

Palmer's
Farm

ROUNDBUSH
CNR

MILL LA

19

Birch
Holt

2

Birch Holt
Cottages

CO5

ROUNDBUSH RD

Roundbush
Farm

Smythe's
Green

Pond
Farm

Duke's
Farm

B1022

Layerwood
Farm

POPLAR
COTTS

WINTER'S RD

WINTER'S HILL

1

Grassreasons
Farm

Thorrington's
Farm

Layer
Wood

18

91 A B 92 C D 93 E F

RECTORY RD

ALDERCAR RD

FOUNTAIN LA

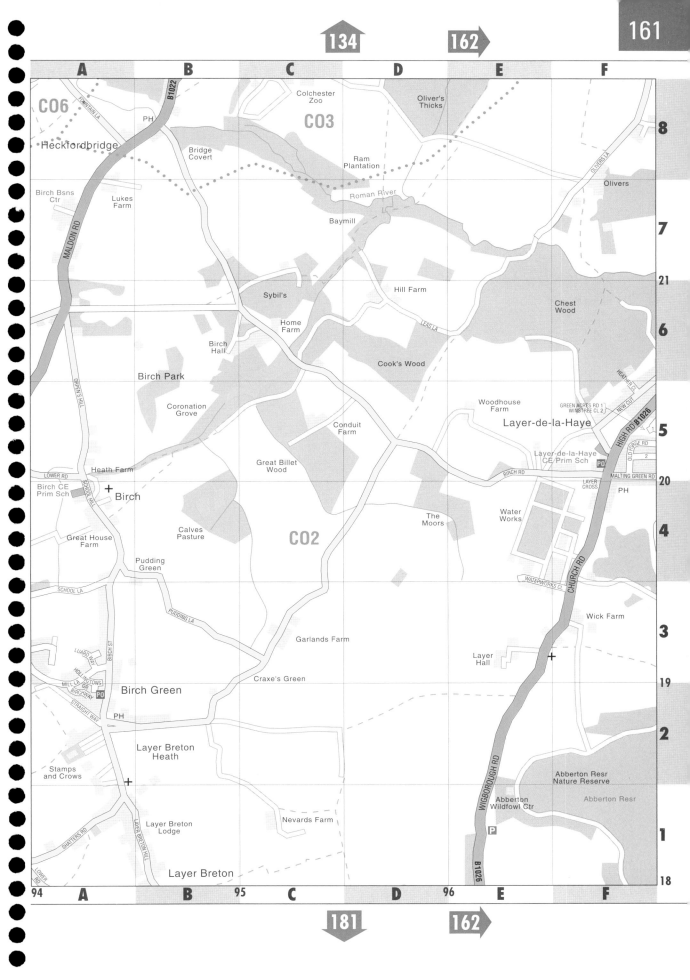

134
162

A B C D E F

8

CO6

Tomkin La

PH

Heckfordbridge

Bridge Covert

B1022

Colchester Zoo

CO3

Oliver's Thicks

Olivers La

8

Birch Bsns Ctr

Lukes Farm

Maldon Rd

Ram Plantation

Roman River

Baymill

Olivers

7

21

Owen's Hill

Sybil's

Home Farm

Birch Hall

Hill Farm

Leas La

Chest Wood

6

Birch Park

Cook's Wood

Heather Cl

Coronation Grove

Conduit Farm

Woodhouse Farm

Layer-de-la-Haye

Green Acres Rd 1
Winstree Cl 2

New Cut

High Rd B1026

5

Great Billet Wood

Layer-de-la-Haye CE Prim Sch

Old Forge Rd

2

20

Lower Rd

Heath Farm

School Hill

Birch Rd

Layer Cross

Malting Green Rd

PH

Birch CE Prim Sch

Birch

The Moors

Water Works

Church Rd

4

Great House Farm

Calves Pasture

CO2

Waterworks Cl

School La

Pudding Green

Wick Farm

Pudding La

Garlands Farm

Layer Hall

3

19

Luard Way

Hollingtons

Birch St

Mill La

Gr

Birchway

PO

Birch Green

Craxe's Green

Straight Way

PH

2

Stamps and Crows

Layer Breton Heath

Wigborough Rd

Abberton Resr Nature Reserve

Abberton Resr

Shatters Rd

Layer Breton Hill

Layer Breton Lodge

Nevards Farm

Abberton Wildfowl Ctr

P

1

Lower Rd

Layer Breton

B1026

18

94 A B 95 C D 96 E F

181
162

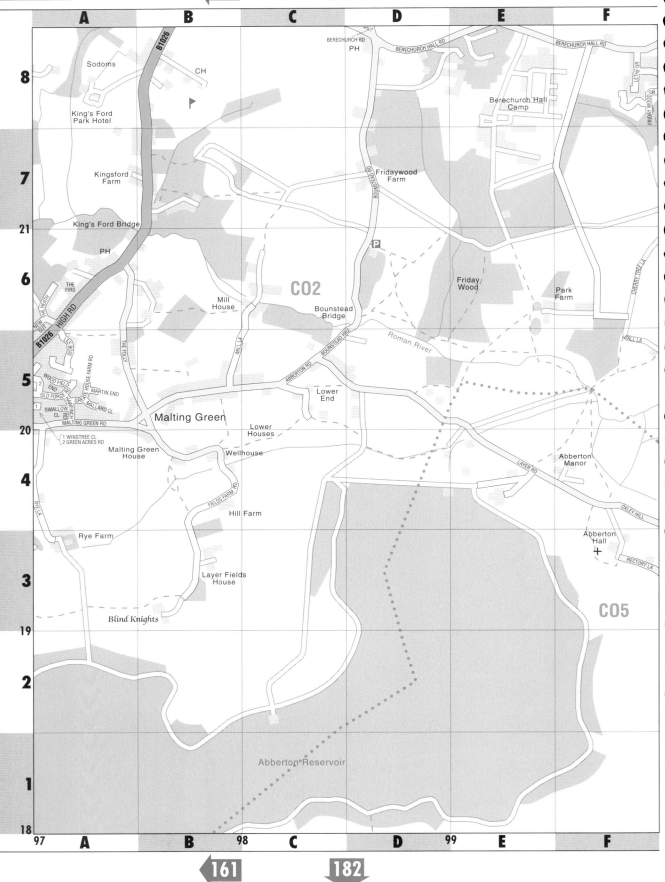

A   B   C   D   E   F

8

Sodoms

CH

King's Ford
Park Hotel

BERECHURCH RD
PH

BERECHURCH HALL RD

BERECHURCH HALL RD

Berechurch Hall
Camp

LETHE GR

FRIDAY WOOD RD

7

Kingsford
Farm

BOUNSTEAD RD

Fridaywood
Farm

21

King's Ford Bridge

P

Friday
Wood

Park
Farm

CHERRY TREE LA

PH

THE FIRS

CO2

6

Mill
House

Bounstead
Bridge

Roman River

BALL LA

NEW CUT

HIGH RD

B1026

THE FOLLY

MILL LA

BOUNSTEAD HILL

5

LES BOIS

GREAT HOUSE FARM RD

ABBERTON RD

Lower
End

Abberton
Manor

LAYER RD

WOOD FIELD END

MARTIN END

OLD FORGE

MALLARD CL

20

SWALLOW CL

Malting Green

Lower
Houses

MALTING GREEN RD

1 WINSTREE CL
2 GREEN ACRES RD

Malting Green
House

Wellhouse

OXLEY HILL

Abberton
Hall

4

RYE LA

FIELDS FARM RD

Hill Farm

+

RECTORY LA

Rye Farm

3

Layer Fields
House

CO5

19

Blind Knights

2

1

Abberton Reservoir

18

97   A   B   98   C   D   99   E   F

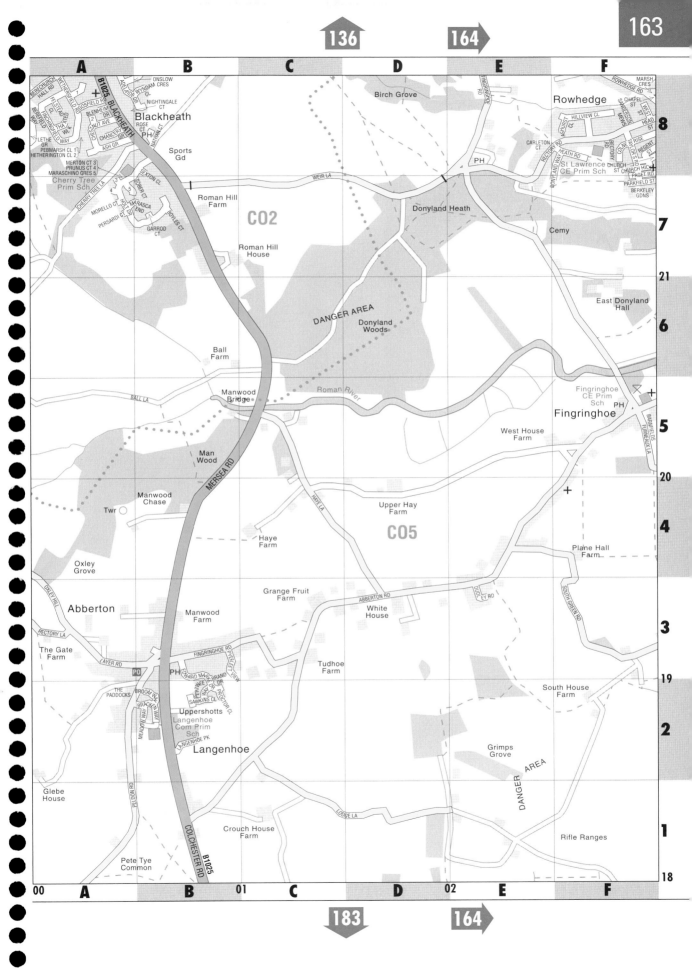

163 137

A **B** **C** **D** **E** **F**

ELM RD
DE VERE LA
CHAPEL RD 1
BLITHE CT 2
BLYTHE LA 3
ALMA ST 4
DENTON'S TERR 5
COLNE TERR 6
ALMSHOUSES 7
BELLE VUE RD 8

B1028 HIGH ST

Liby

IONA WLK
OXTON CL
1 HEAD ST
MARSH
CL
SUNBEAM
VELVET
VALONIA DR
DARKHOUSE
REGENT
CT
PH
CHURCH ST
THE OLD
SCHOOL HO
REGENT ST
HIGH ST
ALBION ST
STEPHEN
CRANFIELD
CL
2 PAGET RD
3 PARKFIELD ST

Wivenhoe
STATION
RD
PH
B1028
RONHEDGE FERRY RD
SPINDRIFT
WAY
ADMIRALS WLK
MEREDITHS
CL
MULBERRY
HARBOUR
WAY
WEST
QUAY
THE SHIPWRIGHTS
DRY DOCK
BATH ST
MICHOLLS AV
ROSE LA
OLD FERRY RD
CLIFTON TERR
TERN MEWS
HARDINGS YD 1
BLACK BUOY HILL
THE FOLLY
THE
QUAY

8

CROSS
FRIARS CL
RETWORTH CL
THE
ROBBITS WAY
DENHAM
CLEMON
CASTLEWARD CL
NOTTAGE
CL
THE DALE
VALLEY RD
BALLAST QUAY RD
QUEEN'S RD
PHILLIP RD
HAMILTON RD
PAGET RD
ARGLESEA RD
COOK ST
ST JOHN'S
WALTER RADCLIFFE WAY
REBOW
PARK RD
MALTING
PO
EAST ST
SANDFORD CL
SAXTON
MERSEA
Ballast Quay
Farm

ALRESFORD RD

Sewage
Works

WIVENHOE RD

CO7

FERRY RD

21

Sewage
Works

Ballast Quay
Farm

Marsh
Farm

Alresford
Grange

6

High Park
Corner

BALLAST QUAY RD

BROOK HALL RD
FERRY
FROG HALL CL
PYEFLEET CL

Lower Brickhouse
Farm

CO7

River Colne

Mill

ABBERTON RD

Fingringhoe
Hall
Tower

Holmwood
Farm

CO5

Alresford
Lodge

5

Sand Pit

20

4

Jaggers

SOUTH GREEN RD

South
Green

WICK LA

Fingringhoe Wick
Nature Reserve

P

3

Fingringhoe Wick
Conservation Centre

Aldboro
Point

19

DANGER AREA

NORTH GEEDON CREEK

DANGER AREA

2

1

Fingringhoe Ranges

Fingringhoe
Marsh

Geedon
Saltings

18

A 03 **B** 04 **C** **D** 05 **E** **F**

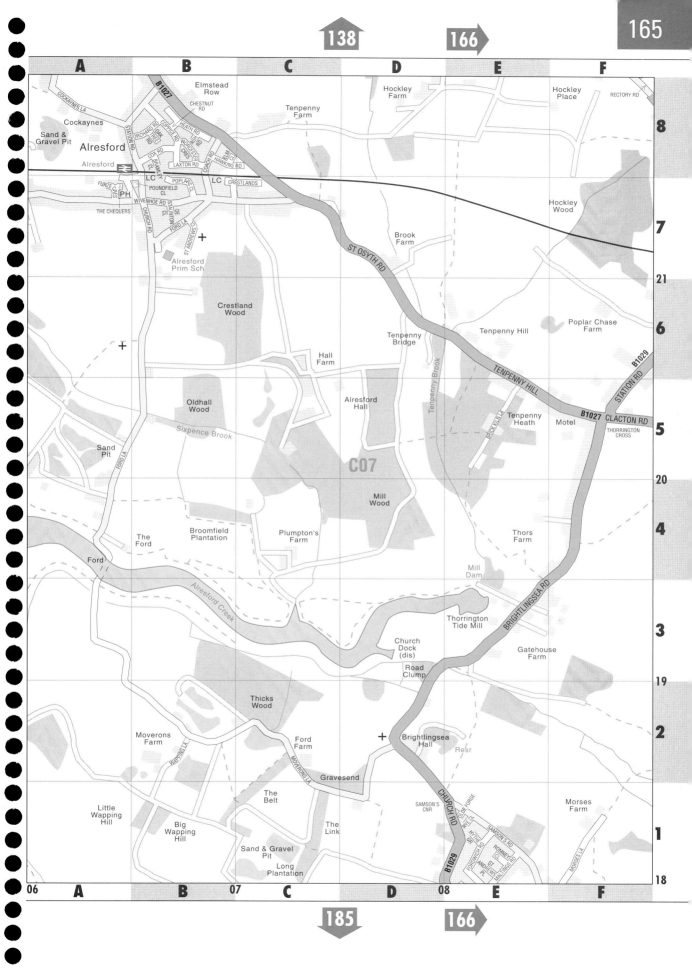

165
139

A B C D E F

8

School La
B1029
STATION RD
FRATING RD
Burr's Farm
GREAT BENTLEY RD
Lufkins Farm
Hill House Farm
THORRINGTON RD
Great Bentley
FRATING CROSS

WREN CL
DE VERE EST
STURRICK LA
ROBIN CL
LINNET WAY
CHERRY WOODS
THE PATH
HECKFORD'S RD
WEELEY RD
Bentley Green
LABURNUM CT
ROWAN CL
THE GREEN
PH
PO
MORELLA CL
SYCAMORE PL
BIRCH AVE
CEDAR WAY
ELM CL
PINE CL
NEW CUT
STATION RD
Great Bentley Prim Sch
HALL VIEW RD
LC
Great Bentley
Ind Est

7

GREAT BENTLEY RD
LC
KEEBLE CT
PLOUGH RD
St Mary's Farm

21

B1029
LC
Mast

6

STATION RD
The Talbots
Whitehouse Farm
CHURCH RD
FRATING ABBEY FARM RD
Frating Abbey
Bentley Brook
Lodge Plantation
COUNCIL HOUSES
WEELEY RD
ST MARY'S RD
ST MARY'S RD
AINGERS GREEN RD

5

B1027
HEATHLANDS
CLOVER DR
AXEL CL
HONEYSUCKLE WAY
ACORN WLK
CHAPEL LA
PO
Thorrington
ROSEMARY LA
PH
High Barns
Aingers Green
THE PADDOCKS
Thicket Grove
WOOD GREEN EST
Carpenter's Farm

20

Glebe Farm
Thorrington Hall
CLACTON RD
COLLES BROOK RD
Colles Brook
The Lodge

4

CO7
Thorringtonhall Wood
Saltwater Brook Cottages
Saltwater Bridge
DIAL RD
STRAIGHT RD
SOUTH HEATH RD

3

DIAL CNR
HOLLYBUSH HILL
Lady Wood
Kellands Farm

19

MARSH FARM LA
Saltwater Brook

2

Crocky Grove
Greatmarsh Farm
Cottage Farm
DEAD LA

1

FOLKARDS LA
HILL COTTS
Thorrington Creek
Holiday Centre
L Ctr
Dines Farm
FLAG HILL
B1027
CO16
Hollybush Hill

18

Lowermarsh Farm

09 A B 10 C D 11 E F

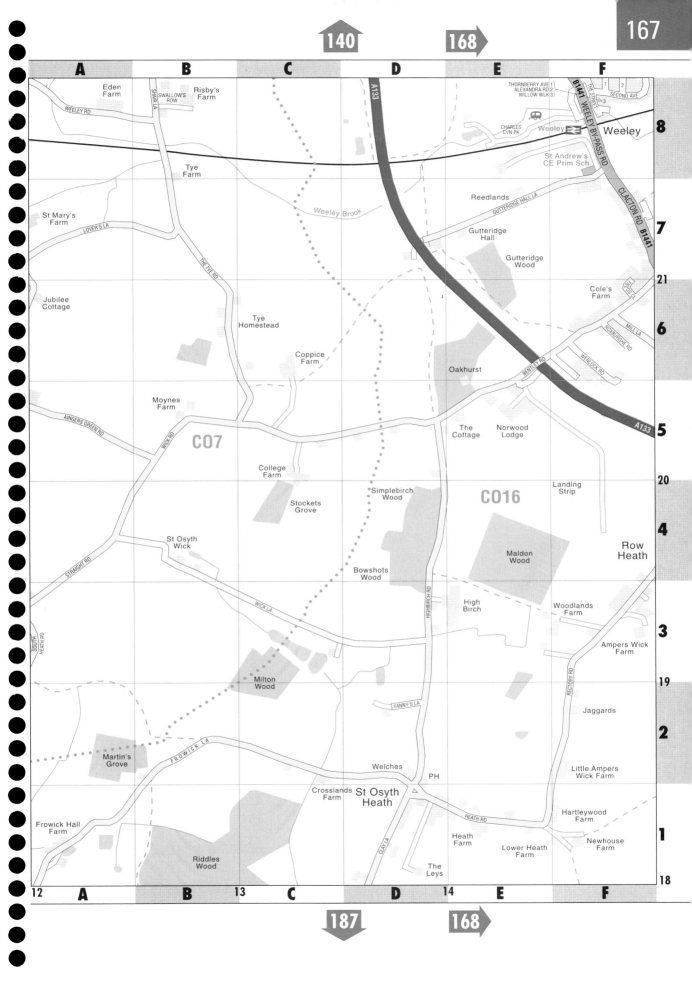

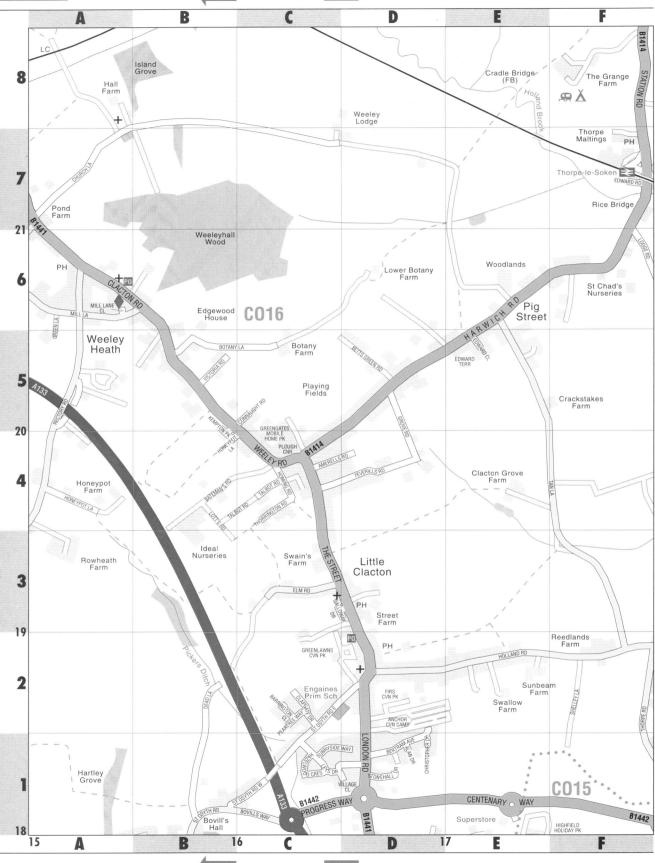

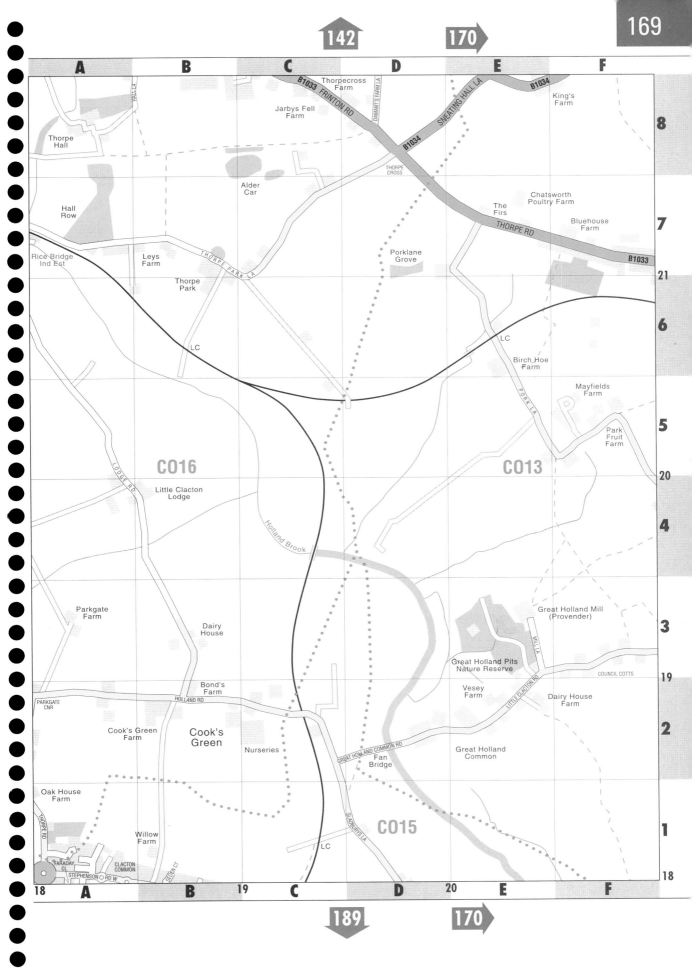

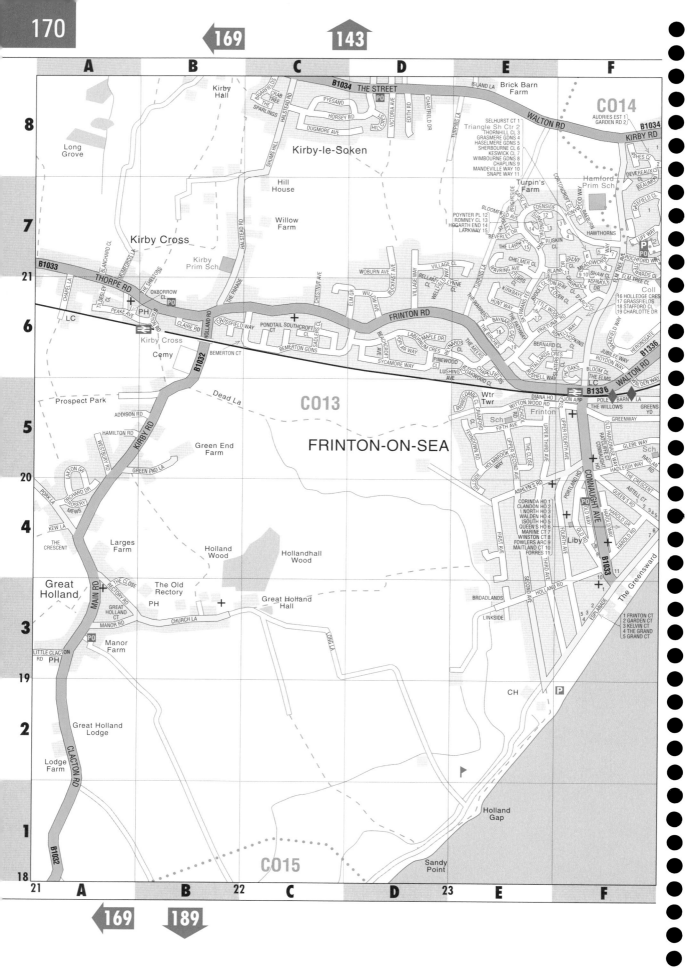

C8
1 MARINA MEWS
2 VICARAGE LA
3 HAVENCROFT CT
4 STRATFORD PL
5 NEWGATE ST
6 PATERNOSTER ROW
7 NEW PIER ST
8 MARTELLO RD
9 AGAR RD
10 AGAR ROAD APP
11 ST BOTOLPH'S TERR

144

WALTON-ON-THE-NAZE

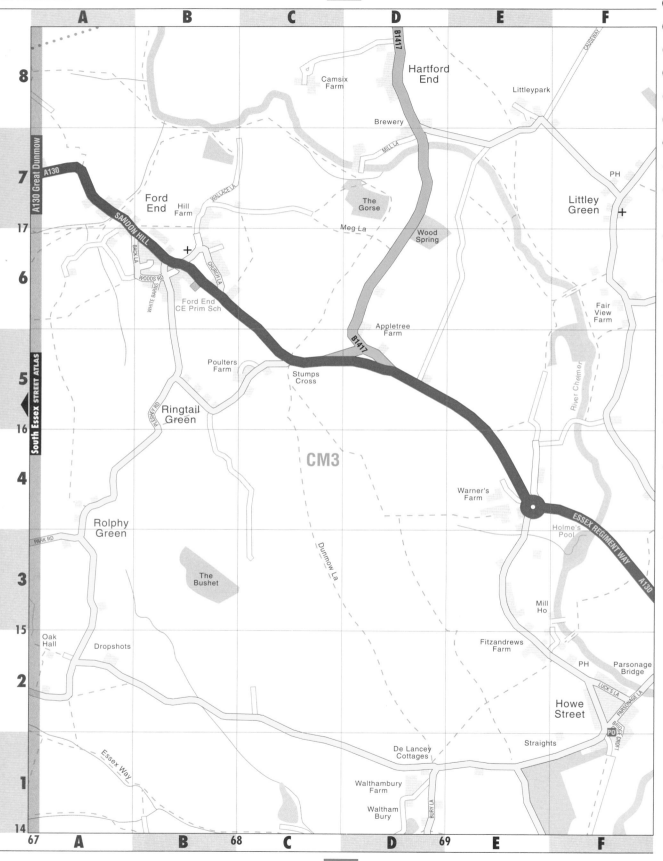

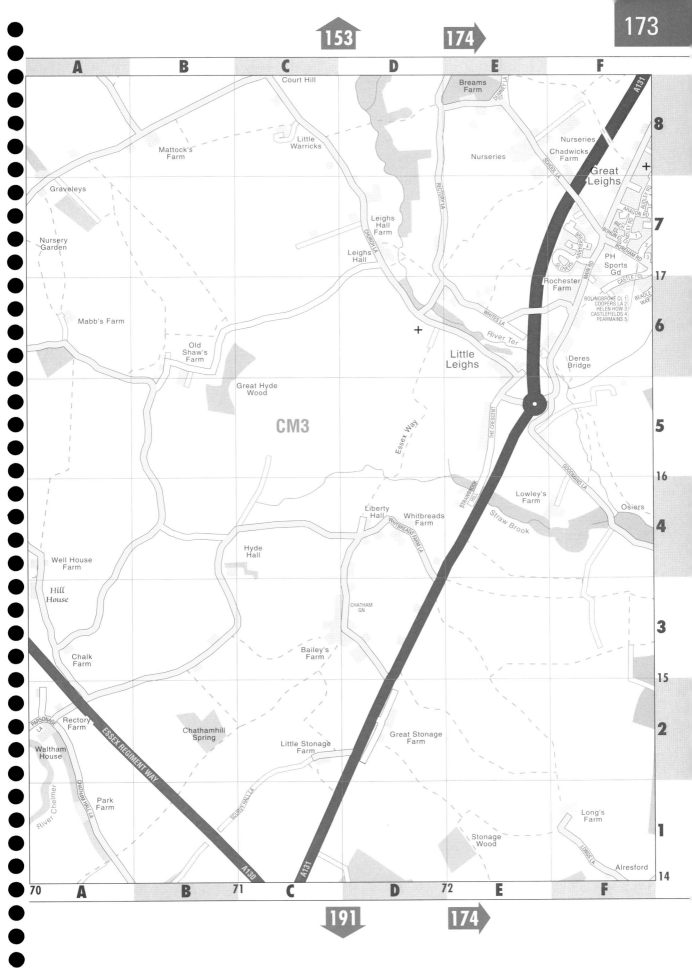

A **B** **C** **D** **E** **F**

PH

MAIN RD

8

Gubbion's Hall

Sandylay Wood

Shackle's Farm

Rank's Green

Blue Barns

Gubbion's Green

Blixes Farm

Dines Hall

BATTERS LA

MILL LA

1 KAY CL
2 WOODVIEW DR
3 FORTUNE CL

ARAGON RD.

Great Leighs Prim Sch

7

Endway

Mann Wood

Parson's Wood

Newneys Farm

Galleycable Wood

High Hall

Beauchamps

BOREHAM RD

17

Coles Farm

Fulbournes Farm

1 BEADLE WAY
2 CATHERINES CL

Bishop's Hall Farm

Queen's Wood

Fairsteadhall Wood

Brickhouse Wood

6

The Rectory

POULK HALL LA

Church End

Fairstead Lodge

Hookley Wood

5

Ashwells Farm

COLE HILL

CM3

Dobb's Croft

FAIRSTEAD HALL RD

16

PH

BRAINTREE RD

WHITE COTTS

Essex Way

Fuller Street

4

Lyons Hall

Hole Farm

+

Goodman's Farm

GOODMANS LA

River Ter

Essex Way

Ridley Hall

Sandy Wood

3

15

Leyland Farm

Wat Hob's Farm

DAGSLEYS LA

BOREHAM RD

2

Lyonshall Wood

Whitehouse Farm

Scarlett's Wood

Sparrow's Farm

Oak Piggeries

WALTHAM RD

Wakering's Farm

Scarlett's Farm

Little Weathers

TERLING HALL RD

1

Hasler's Farm

PH

Whitehouse Cottages

Noake's Farm

Hankins Farm

Roll's Farm

14

A 73 **B** 74 **C** **D** 75 **E** **F**

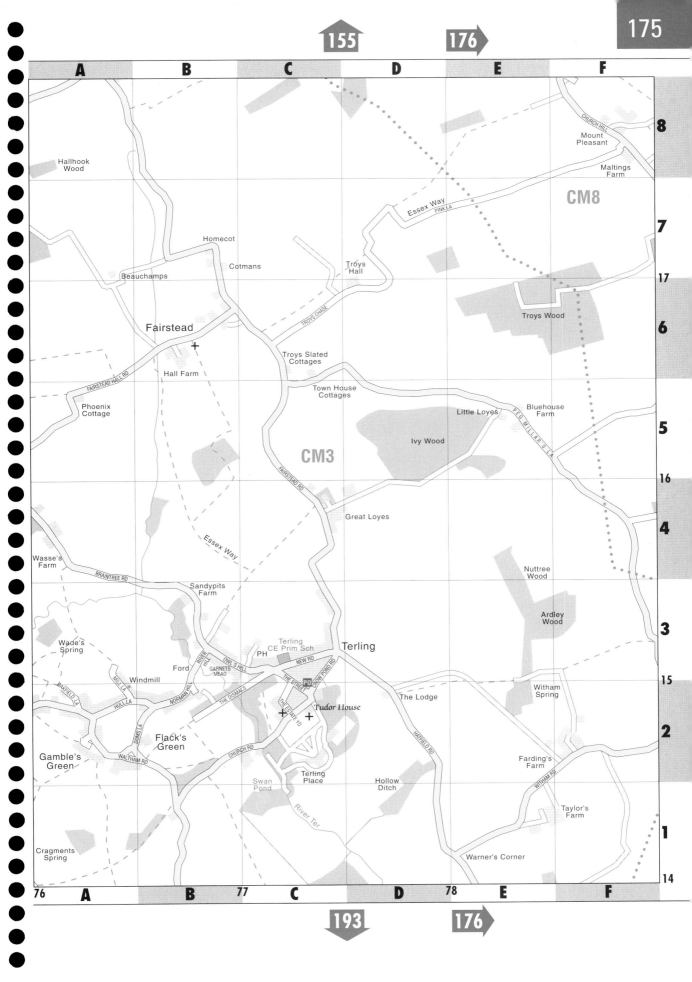

155
176
193
176

A B C D E F

8
7
17
6
5
16
4
3
15
2
1
14

76 77 78

CHURCH HILL
Mount Pleasant
Maltings Farm
CM8

Essex Way
PINK LA

Hallhook Wood

Homecot
Cotmans
Beauchamps
Troys Hall

TROYS CHASE

Troys Wood

Fairstead

Troys Slated Cottages

Hall Farm

Town House Cottages

Little Loyes
Bluehouse Farm
PEG MILLAR'S LA

FAIRSTEAD HALL RD

Phoenix Cottage

Ivy Wood

CM3

FAIRSTEAD RD

Great Loyes

Essex Way

Wasse's Farm
BRAINTREE RD

Nuttree Wood

Sandypits Farm

Ardley Wood

Wade's Spring

Terling CE Prim Sch
Terling

PH
Ford
River Hill
GARNETS MEAD
OWL'S HILL
NEW RD

Windmill
MILL LA
OAKFIELD LA
HULL LA
NORMAN HILL
THE DISMAL'S
THE STREET
PO
CROW POND RD

Witham Spring

The Lodge

DOMS LA
Flack's Green
THE ESTATE YD
Tudor House

HATFIELD RD

15

Gamble's Green
WALTHAM RO
CHURCH RD

Terling Place
Swan Pond
Hollow Ditch

Farding's Farm
WITHAM RD

Cragments Spring

River Ter

Warner's Corner

Taylor's Farm

175
156

A B C D E F

8

Essex Way
Whiteways
Godfry's Farm

Whitehead's Farm

B1018

Hole Farm

Tarecroft Wood

7

Oak Farm
CHURCH HILL
Grove Cottages

Faulkbourne

Hill Farm

17

CRESSING RD

COURT ONE 1
COURT TWO 2
COURT THREE 3
COURT FOUR 4
COURT FIVE 5
COURT SIX 6
COURT SEVEN 7
COURT EIGHT 8
COURT NINE 9
COURT TEN 10
COURT ELEVEN 11
COURT TWELVE 12
COURT THIRTEEN 13
COURT FOURTEEN 14
COURT FIFTEEN 15
COURT SIXTEEN 16
COURT SEVENTEEN 17
COURT EIGHTEEN 18
COURT NINETEEN 19
COURT TWENTY 20

The Rickstones Sch

6

Southview Sch

Elm Hall Farm

CONRAD RD
BLAKE RD
CAMPBELL RD
VIRGIL RD
SHAW
MUNRO RD
HEMINGWAY RD
BRONTE RD
DOROTHY SAYERS DR
ELM RISE

Templars Jun Sch

5

Troys Farm

Home Farm

Faulkbourne Hall

River Brain

Warren Farm

LONGFIELD
UPPER ACRES
CHESTNUT CR

CROSS RD
CHASEWAY

16

The Old Rectory

CM8

LARKSPUR CL 1
LAVENDER CL 2
BRAMBLE CT 3
PRIMROSE PL 4
BUTTERCUP WLK 5
CAMPION WAY 6
THYME MEWS 7

WITHAM

GLEBE CRES
SOUTHCOTE RD
ST NICHOLAS CL

4

HONEYSUCKLE WAY
OXLIP RD
BLACKTHORN RD
ORCHID AVE
BRAMBLE RD
BERTY RD
ROVE
BLUEBELL CL

CORNEL CL
BYRONY CL
SNOWDROP CL
TAVERNERS WLK
BRAMSTON GN
CHURCH ST
ST NICHOLAS CL
TEMPLARS
BRAMSTON WLK
CHIPPING
CHALKS RD

FAULKBOURNE RD
SPEEDWELL CL
FLORA RD
CALAMINT RD
HAREBELL DR
COVERDALE

Chipping Hill

Sch

BRAINTREE RD

3

Resr

Powers Hall

FOXGLOVE CL
LAVENDER
SAMPHIRE CL

Powers Hall End

PH

MOUNT RD
OAK RD
SAXON DR
WHITEWAYS CT
POWERS HALL END
THE CL

MOAT FARM CHASE
EARL
WHITE HORSE LA

CHIPPING HILL
TEMPLEMEAD
B1018

15

The Grove

CM3

PER MILLAR LA

TERLING RD

Powers Hall
Inf & Jun Sch

P
PO

EDEN CL
AVON WLK 5
HIGHFIELDS RD
CROMWELL WAY
GIMSON
VON RD
BARNARD RD
ARMOND RD

NICHOLAS CL

2

WITHAM RD
DANCING DICKS LA

HUMBER RD
OUSE CHASE
MEDWAY AVE
NESS WLK
TEIGN DR
DART CL
DON CT
CAM
CROUCH
DOUGLAS
BLYTH
BRENT CL
TAMAR AVE
RIBBLE
SPA RD
SHAMBLE
DENE CHASE
MERSEY RD
TRENT RD
CHELMER RD

GUITHAVON CT 1
OLD PARSONAGE CT 2
MILL VALE LO 3

GUITHAVON RD
GUITHAVON VALLEY
LOCKRAM LA
P

15

1

Dancing Dicks Cottages

Wheeler's

BLUNTS HALL RD

BLUNT'S HALL DR

Blunt's Hall

STEVENS RD

WHARFE CL 1
AIRE WLK 2
TEES CL 3
DEBEN CL 4
ORWELL WLK 5

Sports Gd

CUPPERS CL
HIGHFIELDS RD
MILLBRIDGE RD

HOLLYBANK
THE BUNGALOWS
MILL LA
ORCHARDS
CHASE
SPINKS LA
GUITHAVON ST

The John Bramston Sch

BARNFIELD PL 1
MOORFIELD CT 2

Sports Ctr
P

NEWLAND ST

14

1 SUTOR CL
2 PHILIP RD

TURSTAN RD
EPPING WAY

Bridge St
H
TUCKER DR

B1389
BRIDGE ST
LODGE CL
GUARD WAY

79 A 80 B C 80 D 81 E F

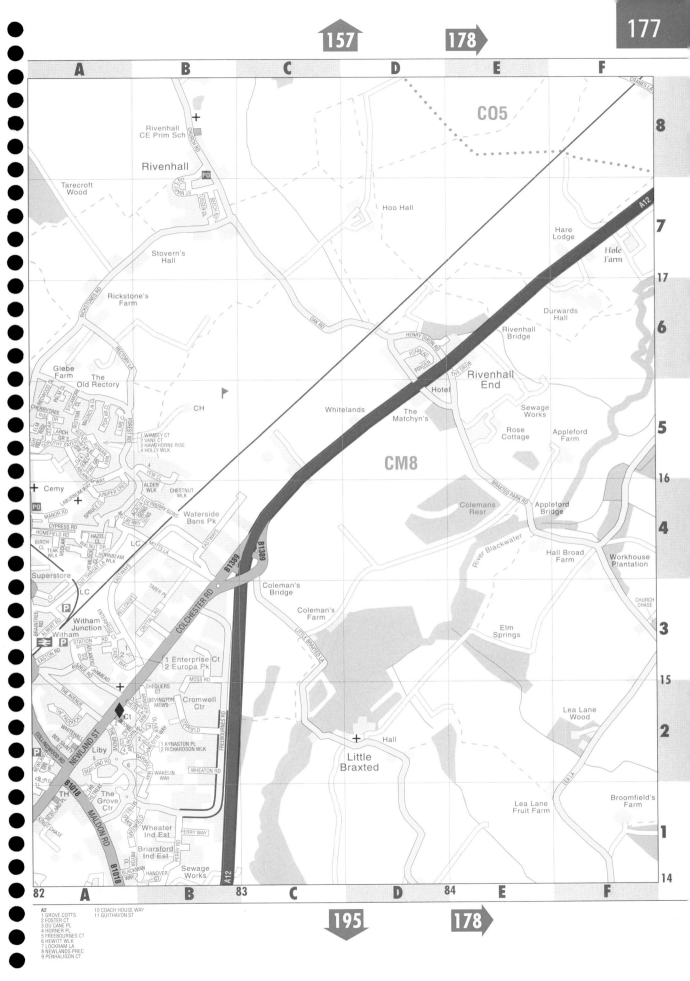

CO5

CM8

Rivenhall CE Prim Sch

Rivenhall

Tarecroft Wood

Stovern's Hall

Hoo Hall

Hare Lodge

Hole Farm

A12

Durwards Hall

Rickstone's Farm

Rivenhall Bridge

Glebe Farm

The Old Rectory

CH

Whitelands

Rivenhall End

Rivenhall Hotel

Sewage Works

Rose Cottage

Appleford Farm

The Matchyn's

1 WIMSEY CT
2 VANE CT
3 HAWTHORNE RISE
4 HOLLY WLK

Cemy

Waterside Bsns Pk

Colemans Resr

Appleford Bridge

River Blackwater

Hall Broad Farm

Workhouse Plantation

CHURCH CHASE

Superstore

Coleman's Bridge

Coleman's Farm

Elm Springs

Witham Junction

Witham

1 Enterprise Ct
2 Europa Pk

Lea Lane Wood

Chequers Ct
Bevington Mews

Cromwell Ctr

1 KYNASTON PL
2 RICHARDSON WLK

Hall

Liby

Little Braxted

The Grove Ctr

Wheater Ind Est

Briarsford Ind Est

Lea Lane Fruit Farm

Broomfield's Farm

Sewage Works

A2
1 GROVE COTTS
2 FOSTER CT
3 DU CANE PL
4 HORNER PL
5 FREEBOURNES CT
6 HEWITT WLK
7 LOCKRAM LA
8 NEWLANDS PREC
9 PENHALIGON CT
10 COACH HOUSE WAY
11 GUITHAVON ST

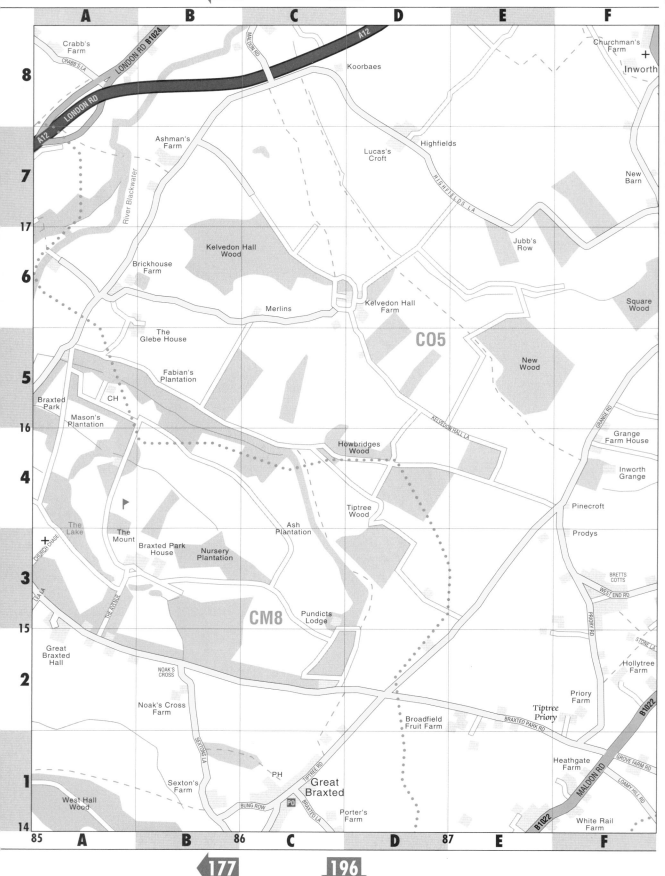

A   B   C   D   E   F

8

7

17

6

5

16

4

3

15

2

1

14

85   A   86   B   C   86   D   87   E   F

Crabb's Farm

LONDON RD B1024

MALDON RD

A12

Koorbaes

Churchman's Farm

Inworth

London Rd

A12

CRABB'S LA

Ashman's Farm

Lucas's Croft

Highfields

HIGHFIELDS LA

New Barn

River Blackwater

Kelvedon Hall Wood

Jubb's Row

Brickhouse Farm

Merlins

Kelvedon Hall Farm

Square Wood

The Glebe House

CO5

Fabian's Plantation

New Wood

Braxted Park

CH

Mason's Plantation

Howbridges Wood

KELVEDON HALL LA

GRANGE RD

Grange Farm House

Inworth Grange

The Lake

The Mount

Ash Plantation

Tiptree Wood

Pinecroft

Prodys

Church Chase

Braxted Park House

Nursery Plantation

BRETTS COTTS

WEST END RD

TEA LA

THE AVENUE

CM8

Pundicts Lodge

PRIORY RD

STONE LA

Great Braxted Hall

15

NOAK'S CROSS

Hollytree Farm

Noak's Cross Farm

Priory Farm

Tiptree Priory

B1022

SEXTONS LA

BRAXTED PARK RD

Broadfield Fruit Farm

Heathgate Farm

MALDON RD

GROVE FARM RD

West Hall Wood

Sexton's Farm

PH

BUNG ROW

PO

Great Braxted

TIPTREE RD

BRAXTED LA

Porter's Farm

LOAMY HILL RD

White Rail Farm

B1022

159 **180**

A B C D E F

PH
THE STREET

Hill
House

B1023

HAPPY
GDNS

Hill
Farm

Perry's
Wood

KELVEDON RD

Baynard's
Prim Sch

Hill Wood

WATERWORKS
COTTS

GRANGE RD

Vine
Farm

Windmill HIll

Sand & Gravel Pit

Villa
Farm

WEST END RD

SIMPSONS LA

Manor House
Farm

STONE LA

P Tiptree
Heath

GROVE FARM RD

LOAMY HILL RD

CM9

Hawthorn Farm

Messing
Park
Farm

NEW RD

Bishops
Cottage

COLCHESTER RD

The Elms

PH

Woodview
Farm

EATON
COTTS

Thurstable
Sch

Spinneyfields

HEATON WAY

Milldene
Prim Sch

Tiptree
Windmill

BARBROOK LA

MAYPOLE RD

SIMONS
FLATS

CEDAR AVE

Tiptree

1 DOWNTON WLK
2 ST JEAN WLK
3 ELEANOR WLK
4 TALISMAN WLK
5 GLOBE WLK
6 ELTON WLK

1 BROCK CL
2 OLLEY WLK

CHURCH RD

Liby

PO
BRYANITA
CT

Sch

THE
CENTRE

NEW RD

MORLEY RD

P

Factory

Tiptree
Mus

FACTORY HILL

Gate
House

STATION RD

Tiptree Heath
Prim Sch

MALDON RD

PH

HALL RD

ORCHARD
LODGE

Gorse La

CHERRY CHASE

Birch Wood

Brook Hall

STRAWBERRY LA

BROOK CL

BROOK RD
PO
KNIGHTS CL
THE FOLLY

Tolleshunt
Knight's

PH

D'ARCY RD

B1023

Oxley
Farm

Tiptree Hall La

Tiptree Hall

Layer Brook

TUDWICK RD

Venn Farm

Wilkin's
Grove

GREEN LA

Elmwood
Farm

Wr Twr

CM9

CO5

Poyston

Ransome's
Grove

Sewage
Works

Viners
Farm

Viners
Farm

NEWBRIDGE RD

FREDERICK
DR

BIRCHWOOD WAY

Napiers
Farm

Pods Wood

B1022

Haynes
Green

HAYNES GREEN RD

The Rampart

8

7

17

6

5

16

4

3

15

2

1

14

88 A B 89 C D 90 E F

197 **180**

179
160

A   **B**   **C**   **D**   **E**   **F**

Layer Woodlands Farm

White Lodge

8

HAYNES GREEN RD

WOODVIEW COTTS

Layer Marney

CO2

STOCKHOUSE RD

Parkhouse Farm

Layer Marney Tower

+

Wick Farm

7

Oak Farm

Parkgate Farm

Hall Farm

17

NEWBRIDGE RD

CO5

Layer Brook

6

Stockridge Farm

Silverthorn

Rockingham's Farm

5

Cadgers Wood

16

Long Wood

4

Park Farm

Beatbush Wood

CM9

PARK LA

3

Paternoster Heath

15

BROOK RD

HAWTHORN RD

BLACKTHORN WAY

STOCKHOUSE CL

Gobolt's Farm

Barn Hall Farm

2

ELIZABETH VILLAS

Tolleshunt Knights

BARNHALL RD

TOP RD

Palmers Farm

D'ARCY RD

RECTORY RD

1

B1023

The Plough Inn (PH)

BLIND LA

HONEYPOT LA

Wigborough Springs

Oxley Green

OXLEY HILL

Krissimon Farm

Manifold Wick Farm

14

Lovedowns Farm

91   **A**   **B**   92   **C**   **D**   93   **E**   **F**

179
198

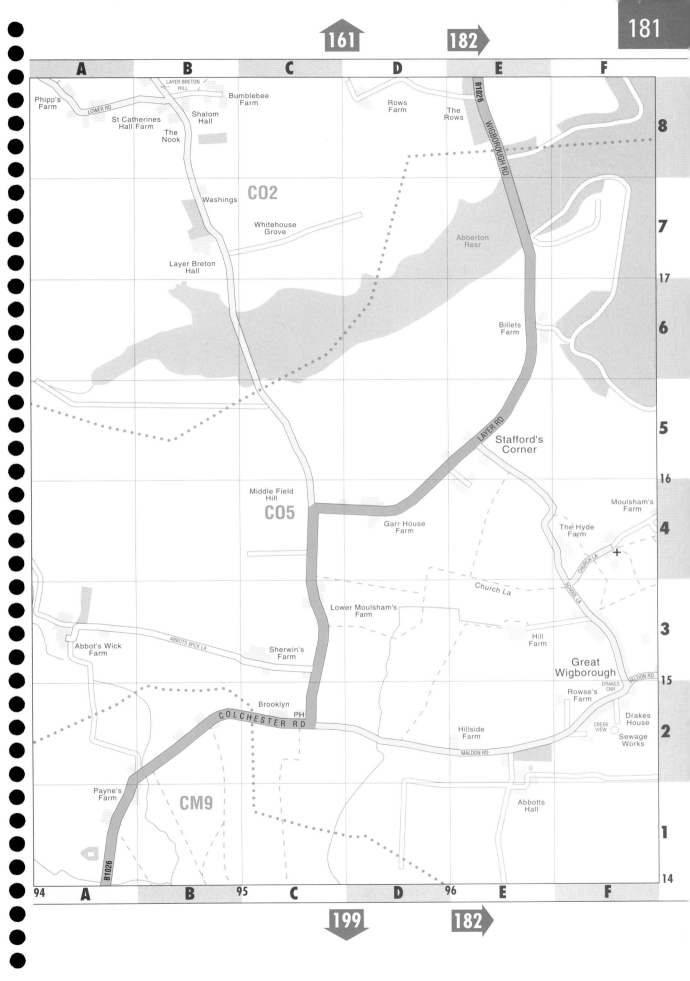

161
182
199
182

Phipp's Farm

LAYER BRETON HILL

LOWER RD

Bumblebee Farm

St Catherines Hall Farm

Shalom Hall

The Nook

Washings

CO2

Whitehouse Grove

Layer Breton Hall

Rows Farm

The Rows

B1026

WIGBOROUGH RD

Abberton Resr

Billets Farm

LAYER RD

Stafford's Corner

Middle Field Hill

CO5

Garr House Farm

Moulsham's Farm

The Hyde Farm

CHURCH LA

Church La

SCHOOL LA

Lower Moulsham's Farm

Hill Farm

Great Wigborough

PELDON RD

Abbot's Wick Farm

ABBOTS WICK LA

Sherwin's Farm

Rowse's Farm

DRAKES CNR

Brooklyn

PH

COLCHESTER RD

Hillside Farm

MALDON RD

CREEK VIEW

Drakes House

Sewage Works

Payne's Farm

CM9

B1026

Abbotts Hall

94   95   96

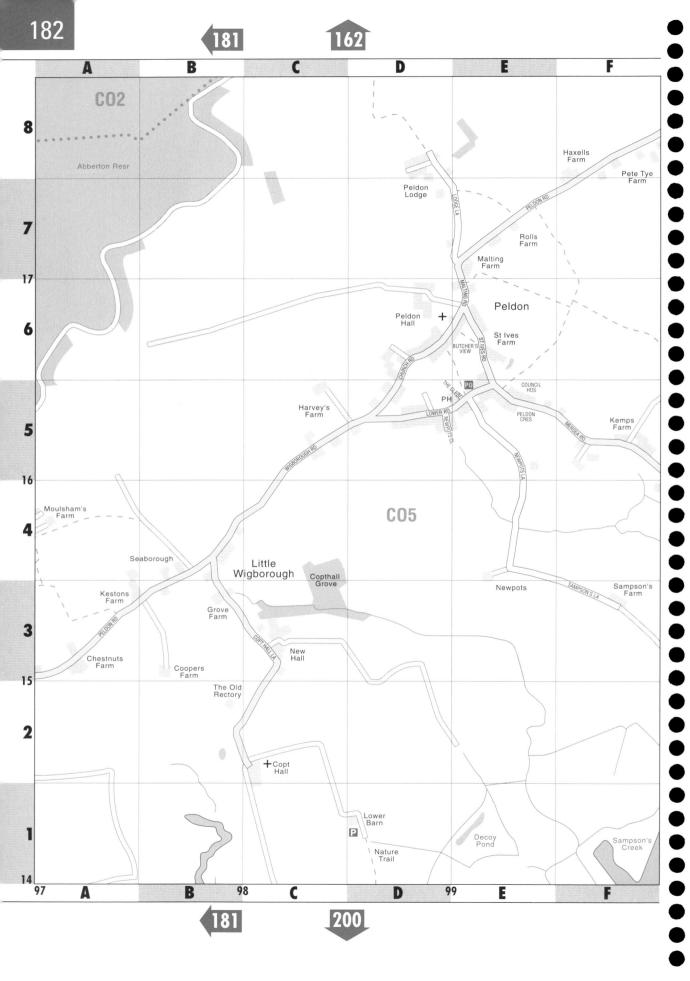

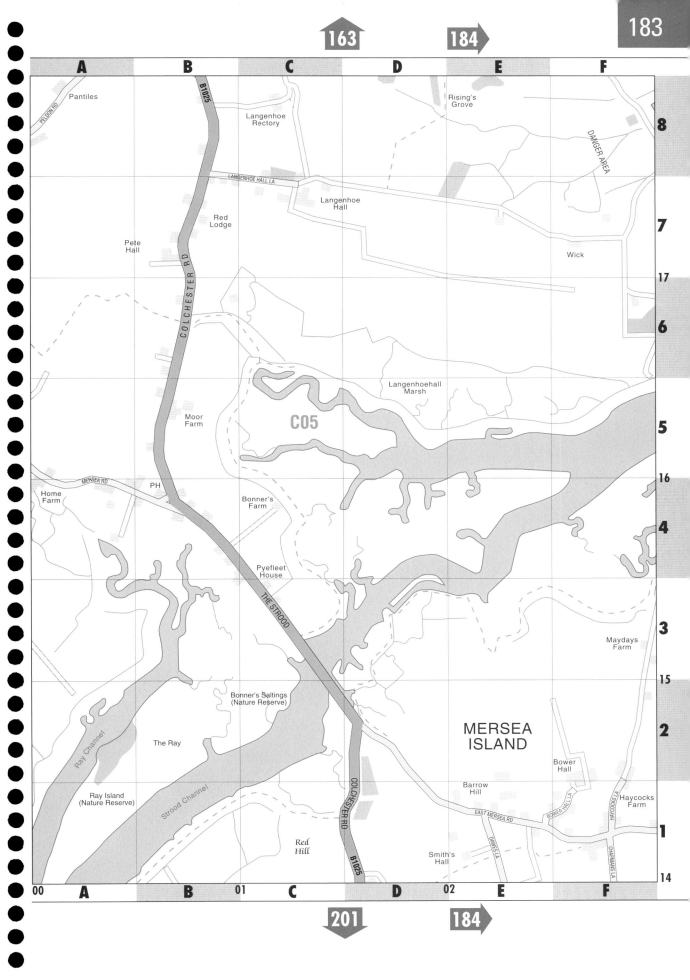

163 184

A B C D E F

Pantiles

PELDON RD

B1025

Langenhoe
Rectory

Rising's
Grove

DANGER AREA

8

Langenhoe Hall La

Langenhoe
Hall

Red
Lodge

7

Pete
Hall

COLCHESTER RD

Wick

17

6

Langenhoehall
Marsh

Moor
Farm

C05

5

MERSEA RD

PH

16

Home
Farm

Bonner's
Farm

4

Pyefleet
House

THE STROOD

3

Maydays
Farm

15

Bonner's Saltings
(Nature Reserve)

2

MERSEA
ISLAND

Bower
Hall

Ray Channel

The Ray

Barrow
Hill

BOWER HALL LA

HAYCOCKS LA

Haycocks
Farm

Ray Island
(Nature Reserve)

Strood Channel

COLCHESTER RD

EAST MERSEA RD

DAVIES LA

CHAPMANS LA

1

Red
Hill

Smith's
Hall

14

B1025

00 A B 01 C D 02 E F

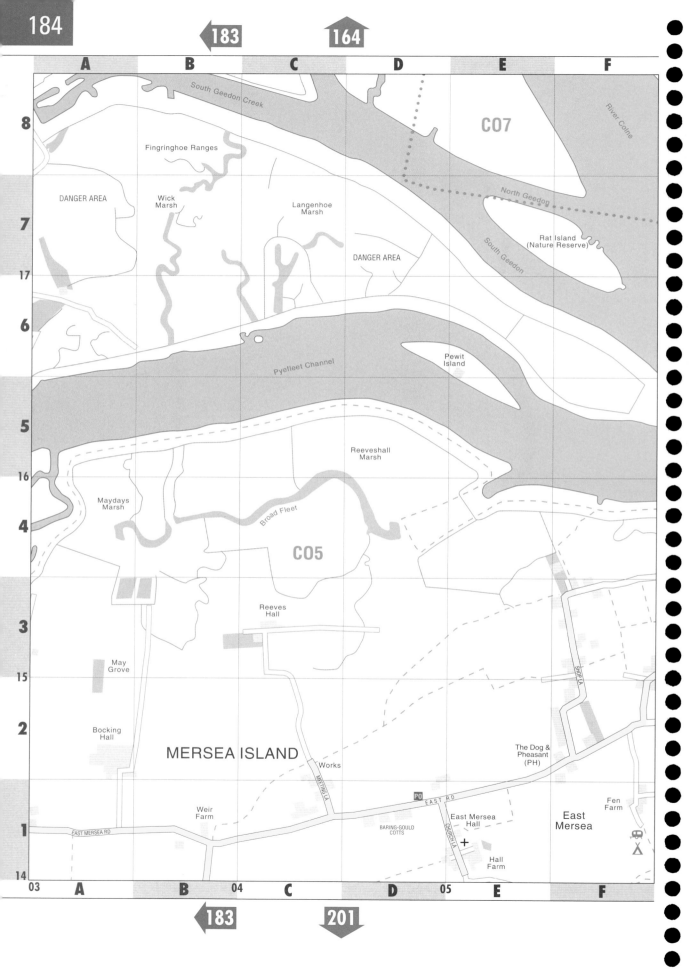

183
164

A B C D E F

8

South Geedon Creek

CO7

River Colne

Fingringhoe Ranges

DANGER AREA

Wick Marsh

Langenhoe Marsh

North Geedon

7

17

DANGER AREA

South Geedon

Rat Island (Nature Reserve)

6

Pyefleet Channel

Pewit Island

5

Reeveshall Marsh

16

Maydays Marsh

Broad Fleet

CO5

4

Reeves Hall

3

May Grove

15

Bocking Hall

2

MERSEA ISLAND

Works

The Dog & Pheasant (PH)

SHOP LA

Weir Farm

MEETING LA

PO

E A S T RD

East Mersea Hall

Fen Farm

East Mersea

1

EAST MERSEA RD

BARING-GOULD COTTS

CHURCH LA

Hall Farm

14

03 A B 04 C D 05 E F

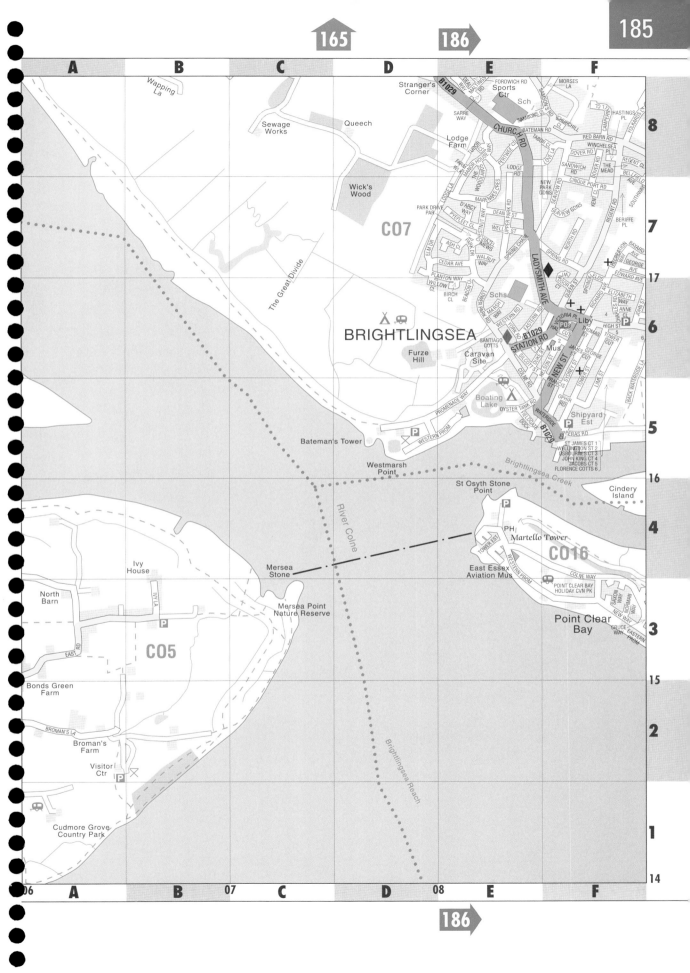

A B C D E F

8

Wapping La

Stranger's Corner

Sewage Works

Queech

Sports Ctr

Sch

FORDWICH RD

MORSES LA

Hastings PL

Lodge Farm

CHURCH RD

B1029

SARRE WAY

SAMSONS RD

CHURCHILL

RED BARN

WINCHELSEA

BATEMAN RD

TABOR CL

DOVER RD

SANDWICH RD

CINQUE PORT RD

KENT RD

REGENT RD

THE MEAD

BELLFIELD AVE

SOUTHVIEW

7

Wick's Wood

CO7

PARK DRIVE PAR

D'ARCY WAY

DEAN RD

PYEFLEET CL

WELL RD

UPPER PARK RD

NEW PARK GDNS

SEAVIEW GDNS

SEAVIEW RD

BERIFFE PL

BAYARD AVE

ST GEORGE AVE

EDWARD AVE

17

ELM DR

ASH CL

CEDAR AVE

PLANTON WAY

WILLOW CL

BIRCH CL

BEACON

LOWER PARK RD

EASTERN RD

MARSH WAY

WESTERN RD

Schs

SPRING CHASE

NORTH RD

LADYSMITH AVE

SPRING RD

QUEEN ST

JM

JASON CT

RICHARD RD

ELIZABETH WAY

ANNE

6

BRIGHTLINGSEA

Furze Hill

Caravan Site

Santiago Cotts

PO

STATION RD

B1029

NEW ST

Mus

JAMES GEORGE

FRANCIS ST

SYDNEY ST

OPHIR RD

TOWER ST

LIME ST

THOMAS ST

HIGH ST

TOWER CUT

P

Liby

BACK WATERSIDE LA

6

Boating Lake

OYSTER TANK RD

COLNE RD

WATERSIDE

TELEGATE DOCK

P

SILCO

WELSH ST

B1029

Shipyard Est

P

COPPERAS RD

5

Bateman's Tower

WESTERN PROM

WESTERN PROM

ST JAMES CT 1

WELLINGTON ST 2

USBOURNES CT 3

JOHN KING CT 4

JACOBS CT 5

FLORENCE COTTS 6

Westmarsh Point

St Osyth Stone Point

P

Brightlingsea Creek

Cindery Island

16

River Colne

PH

Martello Tower

East Essex Aviation Mus

TOWER EST

WESTERN PROM

CO16

4

Ivy House

IVY LA

P

Mersea Stone

Mersea Point Nature Reserve

COLNE WAY

POINT CLEAR BAY HOLIDAY CVN PK

Point Clear Bay

SAXON WAY

NORMAN WAY

NEW WAY

BRUCE WAY

EASTERN PROM

3

North Barn

EAST RD

CO5

15

Bonds Green Farm

BROMAN'S LA

2

Broman's Farm

Brightlingsea Reach

Visitor Ctr

P

Cudmore Grove Country Park

1

06 A B 07 C D 08 E F

14

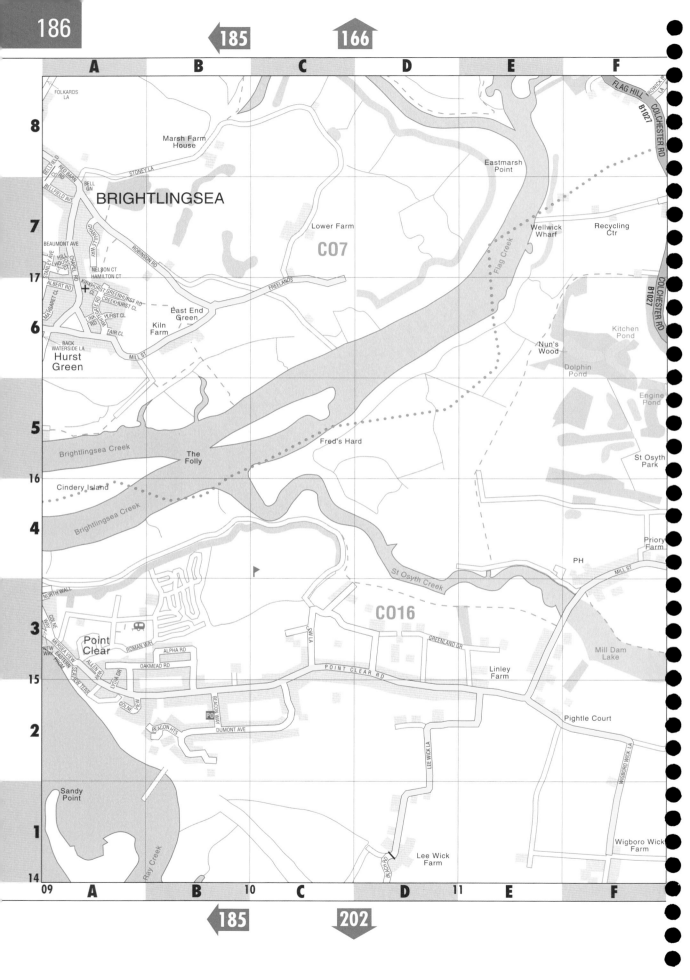

185
166

A B C D E F

8

FOLKARDS LA

Marsh Farm House

STONEY LA

BELL GN

BRIGHTLINGSEA

7

Lower Farm

CO7

Eastmarsh Point

Wellwick Wharf

Recycling Ctr

BEAUMONT AVE

HILL HOUSE CL

CHAPEL RD

ROBINSON RD

NELSON CT

HAMILTON CT

17

KIRKHURST CL

GREENHURST RD

CREEKHURST CL

FREELANDS

Flag Creek

B1027

COLCHESTER RD

FLAG HILL

B1027

FRIWICK RD

ALBERT RD

MARGARET CL

LINK RD

HURST CL

FAIR CL

East End Green

Kiln Farm

Kitchen Pond

6

BACK WATERSIDE LA

Hurst Green

MILL ST

Nun's Wood

Dolphin Pond

Engine Pond

5

Brightlingsea Creek

The Folly

Fred's Hard

St Osyth Park

16

Cindery Island

Brightlingsea Creek

St Osyth Park

4

Brightlingsea Creek

St Osyth Creek

PH

Priory Farm

MILL ST

NORTH WALL

CO16

3

COLNE WAY

ROMAN WAY

Point Clear

ALPHA RD

OAKMEAD RD

SW LA

GREENLAND GR

Mill Dam Lake

NEW WAY

MERSEA VIEW

EASTERN

SEAVIEW TERR

ALLEN WAY

LYDIA DR

COLNE VIEW

15

Linley Farm

BEACON WAY

PO

2

BEACON HTS

DUMONT AVE

Pightle Court

LEE WICK LA

WIGBORO WICK LA

Sandy Point

1

Ray Creek

BEACH RD

Lee Wick Farm

Wigboro Wick Farm

14

09 A B 10 C D 11 E F

185
202

167
188

A B C D E F

8

FROWICK LA

CO7

Riddles
Wood

Sandyhayes

Kiln
Cottage

High
Grove

B1027

COLCHESTER RD

Caravan
Park

7

17

CLAY LA

Wellwick
Farm

6

Park Farm
Cottages

Park Farm

Earls Hall

Lamb Farm

1 GOLDING WAY
2 TUNSTALL CL.

PARK CHASE

Cemy

COLCHESTER RD

Lower Barn

EARLS HALL DR

5

Deer
Park

PARK
COTTS

NEWTON
GDNS

1
2

NEWTON
WLK

BYPASS RD

Bush
Paddock

CO16

Nursery

Duchess
Farm

DEEPING

ST CLAIR'S
DR

WITHRICK
WLK

ST
CLAIR'S
RD

D'ARCY RD

MAYFIELD GDNS

JONES GDNS

NASSAU RD

ABBOTS
GDNS

Pump Hill
Farm

PUMP HILL
CVN PK

PUMP HILL

ST JOHN'S RD

B1027

16

BOTANICAL
WAY

BROADSTROOD

STANMORE
WAY

LONGFIELDS

CLACTON RD

ROCHFORD RD

THREE ACRES

PRIORY
PK

CASTLE

MAYPOLE
RD

KINCAID RD

LONGFIELDS
SOUTH

4

St Osyth
Priory

JOHNSON RD

MEADOW
VIEW

St Osyth

LODGE FARM LA

St Osyth Lodge
Farm

ROUSES LA

NORMAN C.

THE BURY

CHURCH
SQ

CHAPEL ST

St Osyth
CE Prim Sch

Rouses
Farm

MILL ST

OLD SCHOOL CL

KING ST

CHAPEL LA

BROOK VW

SPRING RD

DALTES LA

3

15

Warren
Farm

Brazier's
Farm

Daltes Farm

Botany La

2

WARREN LA

ST CLERES HALL LA

Reed
Pond

CO15

St Clere's
Hall

BEACH RD

LEICESTER
CL

SEYMOUR RD

FROBISHER DR

SOMERSET WAY

Top Barns

SPENSER WAY

Sch

1

PH

Sewage
Works

PARK SQ W

PARK SQ E

Whyers Hall
Farm

COCKETT WICK LA

Cockett Wick
Farm

TUDOR GV

14

A B C D E F

12 13 14

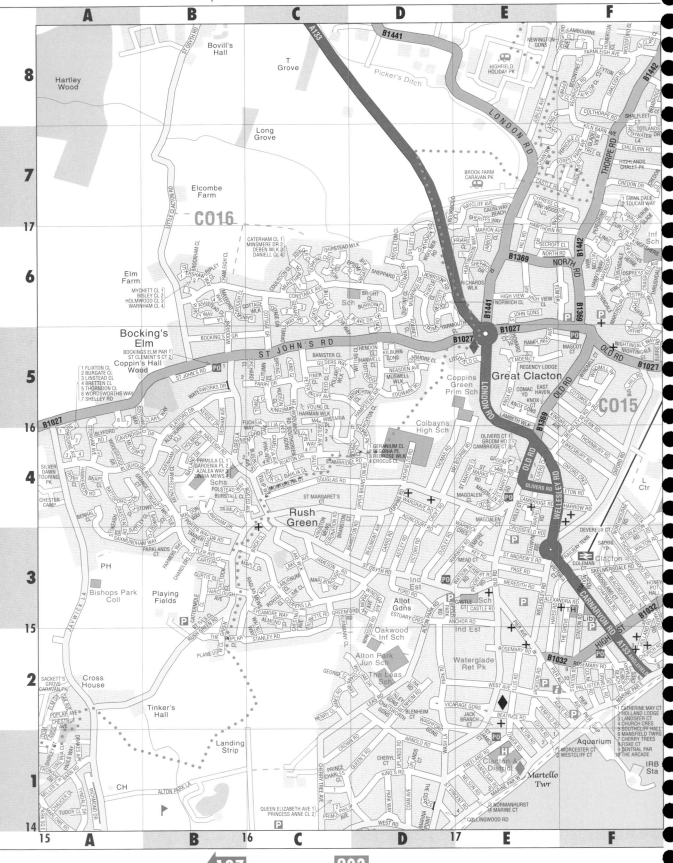

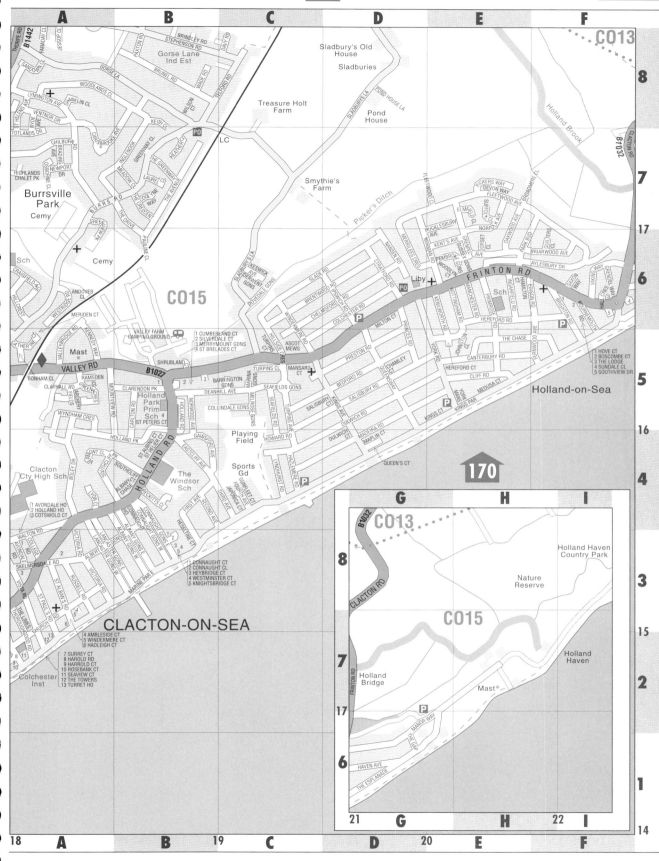

Main map labels:

Sladbury's Old House, Sladburies, Pond House, Pond House La, Sladbury's La, Treasure Holt Farm, Smythie's Farm, Picker's Ditch, Holland Brook

Burrsville Park, Cemy, Sch, Gorse Lane Ind Est

CO13, CO15

B1442, Thorpe Rd, Faraday Cl, Jessop Cl, Gorse La, Sandown Cl, St Helens Grn, Woodlands Cl, Lymington Ave, Franklin Cl, Ventnor Dr, Ryde Ave, Totlands Dr, Chilburn Rd, Brading Ave, Newport Dr, Osborne Rd, Highlands Chalet Pk, Craigfield Ave, Hillcrest Rd, Andover Cl, Meriden Ct, Heather Cl, Keith Cl, Brunel Rd, Wade Rd, Telford Rd, Davy Rd, Brindley Rd, Stephenson Rd, Paxton Rd, Wilson Ct, Greenway Cl, Inglenook, Meadow Cl, Laurel Cl, Coquine Way, The Greenway, The Crescent, The Avenue, The Drive, Green Way, Pauline Cl, Burrs Rd, Westruther, Valleybridge Rd, Kennedy Way, Mountview Rd, Carlton Rd, Clarendon Pk, Holland Pk, Norwood Ave, St Osyth Rd

Mast, Valley Rd, B1027, Bonham Cl, Clayhall Rd, Ramsden Rd, Greens Rd, Archery Fields, Wyndham Cres, Shrubland Rd, Barrington Gdns, Deanhill Ave, Collindale Gdns, Marina Gdns, Turpins Ct, Seafields Gdns, Melrose Gdns, Seafields Rd, Turpins Ave, Howard Rd, Lyndhurst Rd, Gunfleet Ave, Hazlemere Rd, Third Ave, Second Ave, First Ave, Eastcliff Ave, Gaws Cro Ave

Holland Park Prim Sch, St Peters Ct, St Aubins Ct, St Peter Ct, Fronks Rd, Chichester Rd, Southcliff, Beley Rd, Lyon Cl, Albany Gdns W, Connaught Gdns W, Lancaster Gdns W, Victoria Rd, Russell Rd, St Albans Rd, Walton Rd, College, Avondale Rd, Skelmersdale Rd, Vista Rd, St Paul's Rd, Church Rd, The Lines, Thoroughgood Rd, Colchester Inst

Clacton Cty High Sch, The Windsor Sch, Playing Field, Sports Gd

CLACTON-ON-SEA

Keswick Gdns, Derwent Gdns, Dovedale Gdns, Slade Rd, Brentwood Rd, Chelmsford Rd, Colchester Rd, Watermere Rd, Mansard Rd, Stratford Rd, Milton Rd, Princes Rd, Hillside Cres, Ascot Mews, Preston Rd, Bedford Rd, Chamley, Queensway, Salisbury Rd, Dulwich Rd, Maplin Ct, Madeira Rd, Queen's Ct, York Rd, Times Ave, Kenilworth Rd, Nottingham Rd, Manchester Rd, Hereford Rd, Canterbury Rd, Cliff Rd, Hereford Ct, The Chase, Johnston Cl, Fernwood Ave, Kings Par, Medusa Rd, Kings Ct, York Mans, Liby, PO, Sch

Frinton Rd, Pickers Way, Devon Way, Fleetwood Ave, Fleetwood Cl, Elmer Cl, Suffolk Ave, Norfolk Ave, Kent's Ave, Grenfell Ave, Sussex Gdns, Pembroke Ave, Woodbryn, Merrilees Cres, Park Byd, Oakwood Ave, Briarwood Ave, Aylesbury Dr, Quilters Cl, Broadmere Cl, Diamond Ave, Ingarfield Rd, Primrose Rd, Ennison Rd, Hamilton Rd, Brighton Cl, Viking Way, Grenier Way, Saxon Way, Hall Cres, Bournemouth, Holland-on-Sea

B1032, Clacton Rd

Numbered lists:
1 Cumberland Ct, 2 Silverdale Ct, 3 Merrymount Gdns, 4 St Brelades Ct

1 Avondale Ho, 2 Holland Ho, 3 Cotswold Ct

1 Connaught Ct, 2 Connaught Cl, 3 Heybridge Ct, 4 Westminster Ct, 5 Knightsbridge Ct

1 Hove Ct, 2 Boscombe Ct, 3 The Lodge, 4 Sundale Cl, 5 Southview Dr

4 Ambleside Ct, 5 Windermere Ct, 6 Hadleigh Ct, 7 Surrey Ct, 8 Harold Rd, 9 Harrold Ct, 10 Rosebank Ct, 11 Seaview Ct, 12 The Towers, 13 Turret Ho

Inset map (170): CO13, CO15, B1032, Clacton Rd, Frinton Rd, Holland Bridge, Holland Haven Country Park, Nature Reserve, Holland Haven, Mast, Manor Way, The Gap, Haven Ave, The Esplanade

170

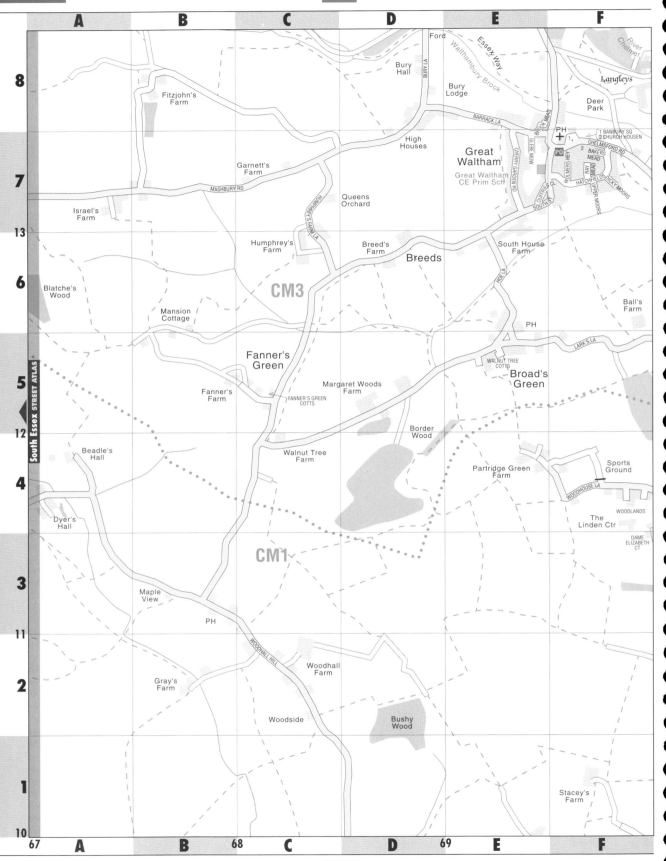

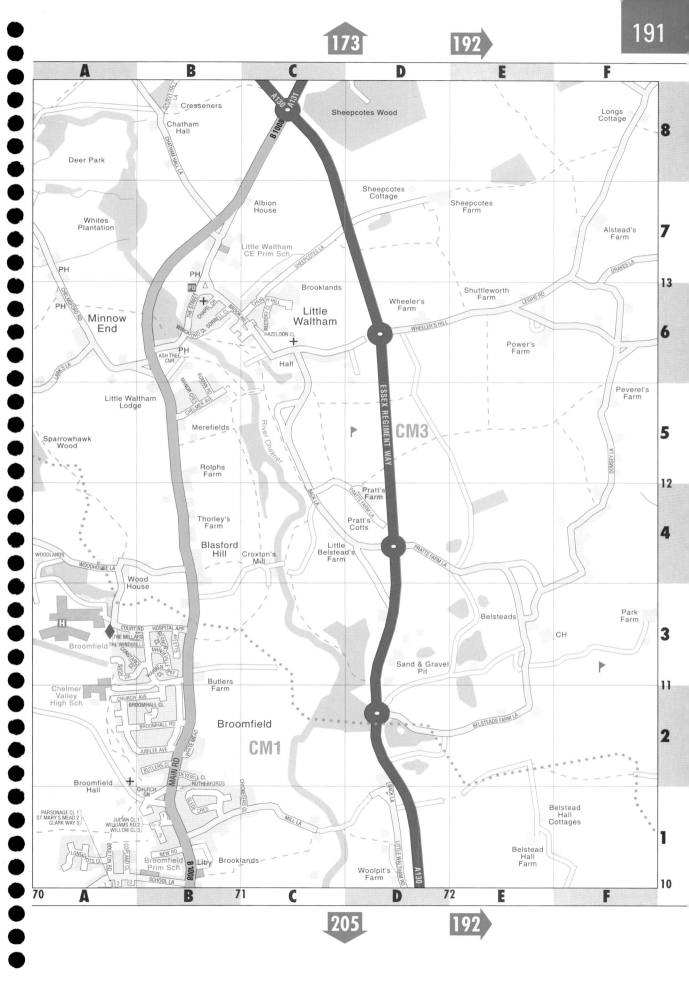

191
174

A B C D E F

8

Chopping's Wood

Noake's House

Lawns Farm

Noake's Farm

Ringer's Wood

Little Drakes

BOREHAM RD

Bird's Farm

7

DRAKES LA

Drake's Farm

Works

Russel Green House

13

Russell Green

6

Brent Hall

Stocks Farm

CM3

Stocks Cottages

Porter's Wood

5

Works

P

Little Holts

12

Boreham Airfield (disused)

Holts Farm

4

WALTHAM RD

Sand & Gravel Pit

Wallace's Farm Cottages

WALLACE'S LA

Park Farm

Walford House

Mount Maskall

3

11

2

Boreham Ind Est

Centenary Circle

GENERALS LA

The Grove

Brick House Farm

A12

B1137

SHEARERS

Bulls Lodge Cotts

GWYN CL 1
ROSEMARY COTTS 2
ARMONDE CL 3
MEADOWSIDE CT 4
SEABROOK GDNS 5

New Hall Sch

P

+

Bulls Lodge

MAIN RD

B1137

PLANTATION RD

ALLENS CL

1

CM1

A12

VILLIERS PL

ELM WAY

CLEVES

CLOAK COTTS

ST ANDREWS

CLAYPITS RD

10

73 A B 74 C D 75 E F

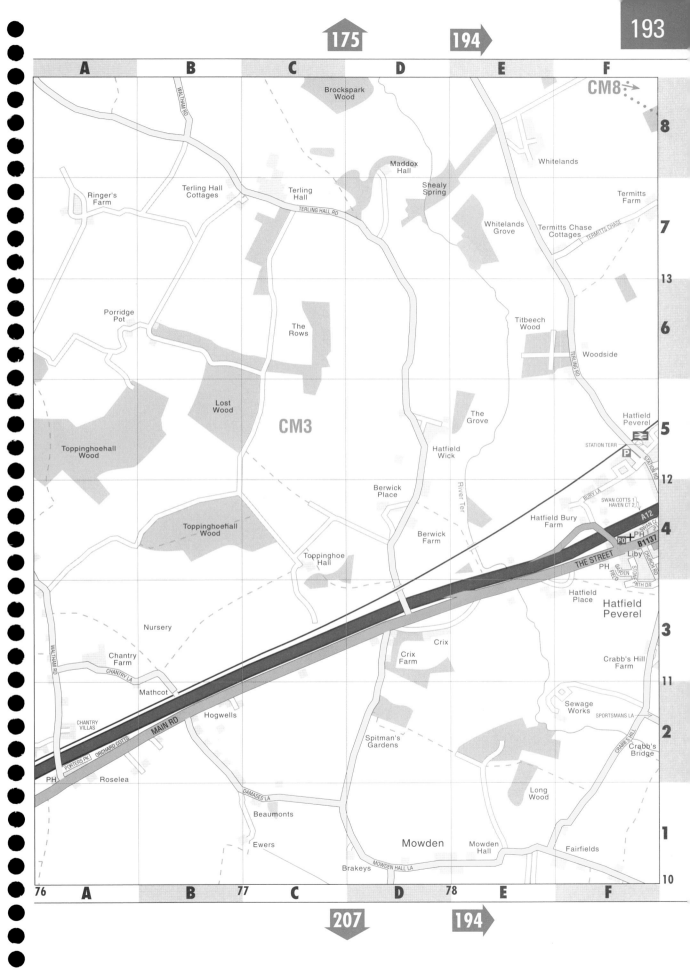

175
194

CM8

A **B** **C** **D** **E** **F**

8

Brockspark
Wood

Maddox
Hall

Whitelands

Terling Hall
Cottages

Terling
Hall

Shealy
Spring

Termitts
Farm

7

Ringer's
Farm

TERLING HALL RD

Whitelands
Grove

Termitts Chase
Cottages

TERMITTS CHASE

13

Porridge
Pot

The Rows

Titbeech
Wood

Woodside

TERLING RD

6

Lost
Wood

CM3

The
Grove

Hatfield
Peverel

5

Toppinghoehall
Wood

Hatfield
Wick

STATION TERR

P

STATION RD

12

Toppinghoehall
Wood

Berwick
Place

River Ter

Berwick
Farm

BURY LA

SWAN COTTS 1
HAVEN CT 2

A12

Hatfield Bury
Farm

SWAN CL

LPH

B1137

PO

4

Toppinghoe
Hall

THE STREET

Liby

PH

CHURCH RD

STONE

4TH DR

GARDEN
FIELDS

Hatfield
Place

Hatfield
Peverel

3

Nursery

Crix

Crabb's Hill
Farm

Chantry
Farm

CHANTRY LA

Crix
Farm

11

Mathcot

WALTHAM RD

Hogwells

Sewage
Works

SPORTSMANS LA

2

CHANTRY
VILLAS

MAIN RD

Spitman's
Gardens

CRABB'S HILL

Crabb's
Bridge

PORTERS PK

ORCHARD COTTS

PH

Roselea

DAMASES LA

Beaumonts

Long
Wood

1

Ewers

Mowden

Mowden
Hall

Fairfields

Brakeys

MOWDEN HALL LA

10

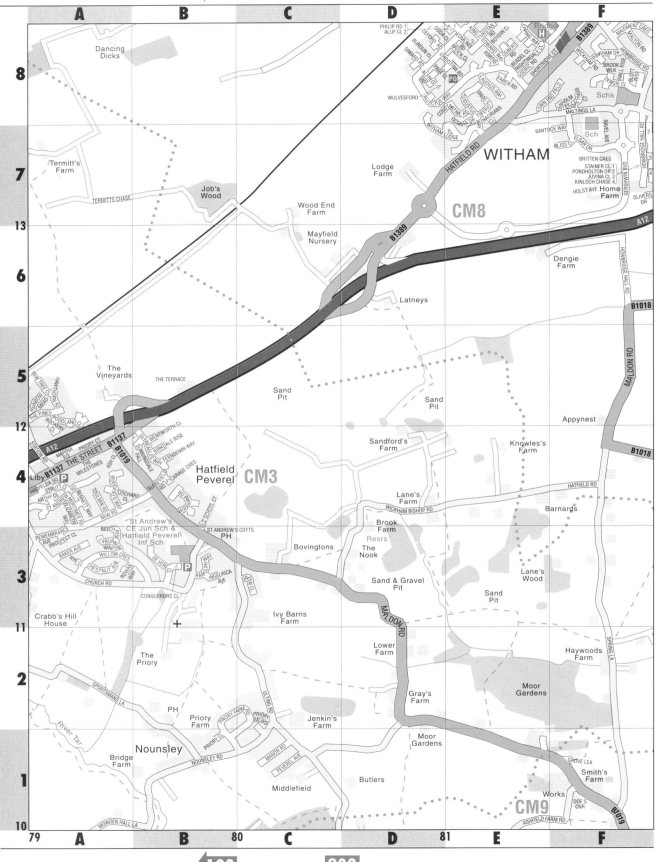

WITHAM

CM8

CM3

Hatfield Peverel

Nounsley

CM9

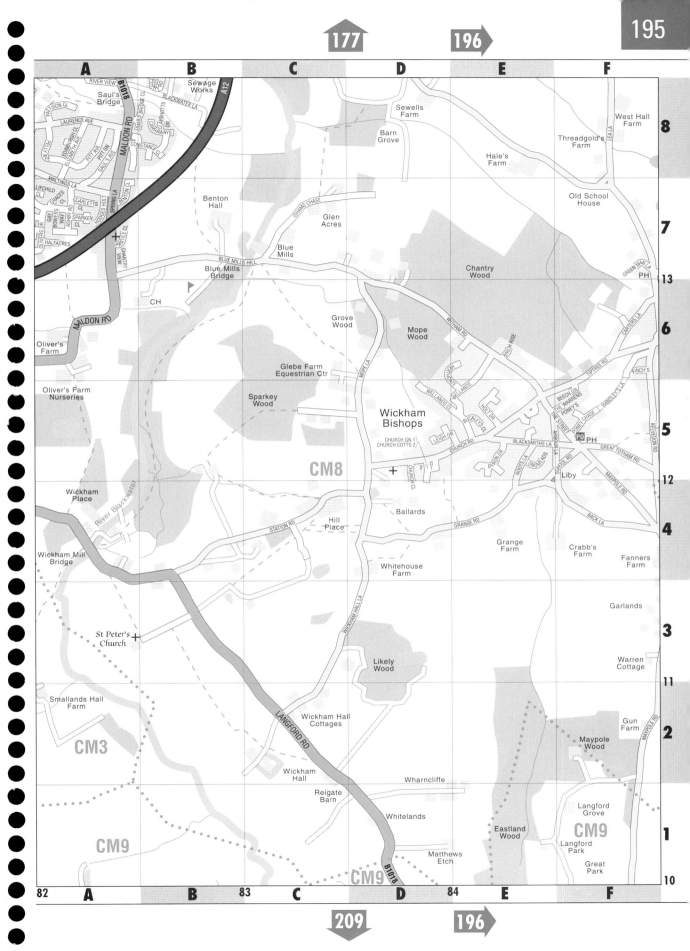

177
196
209
196

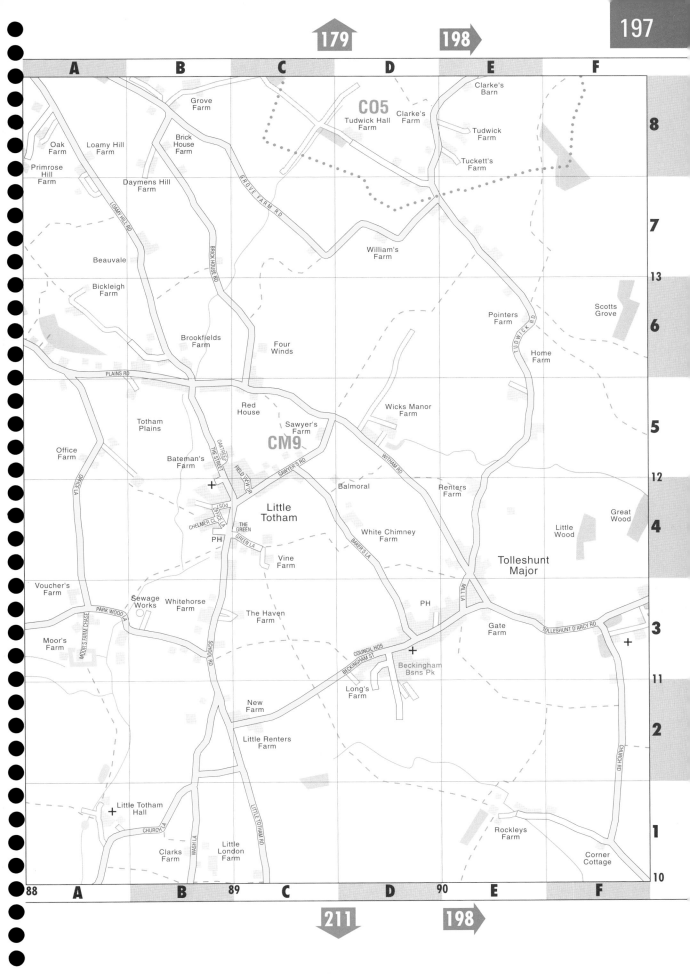

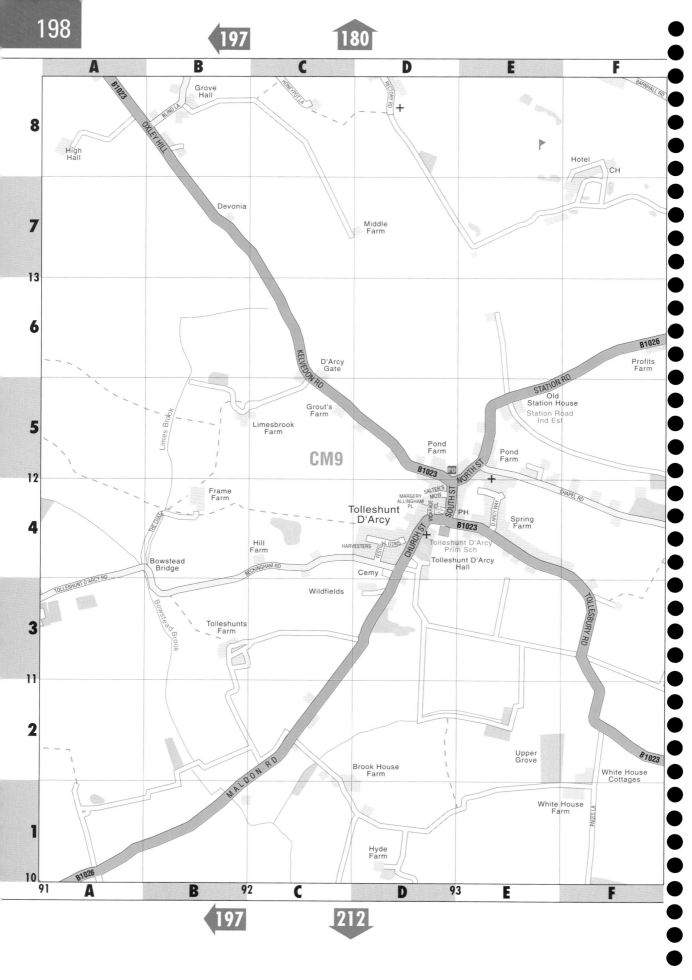

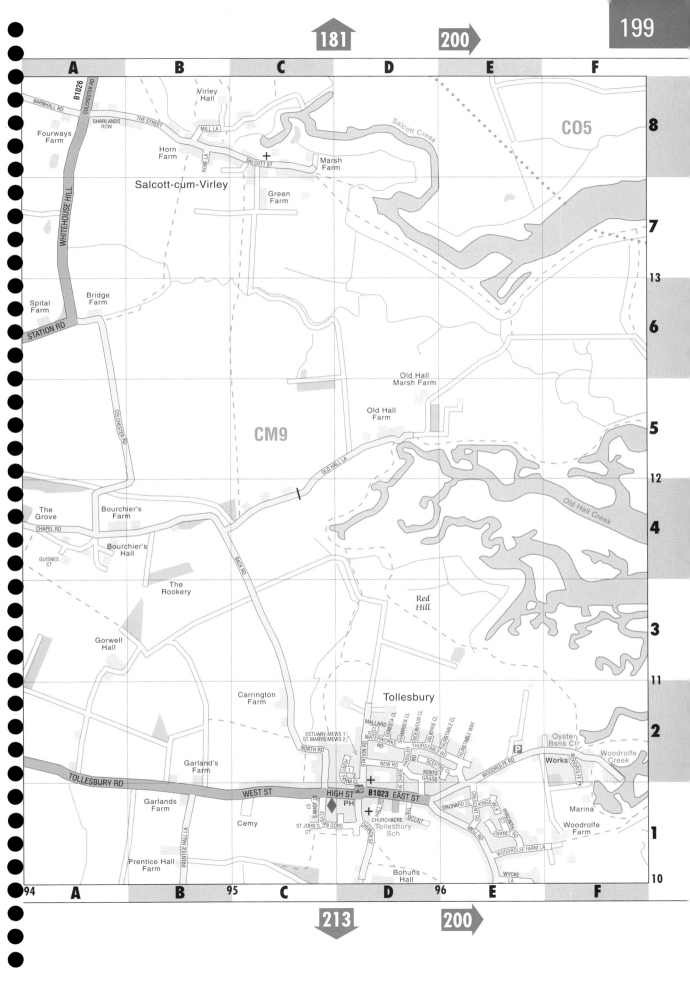

199
182

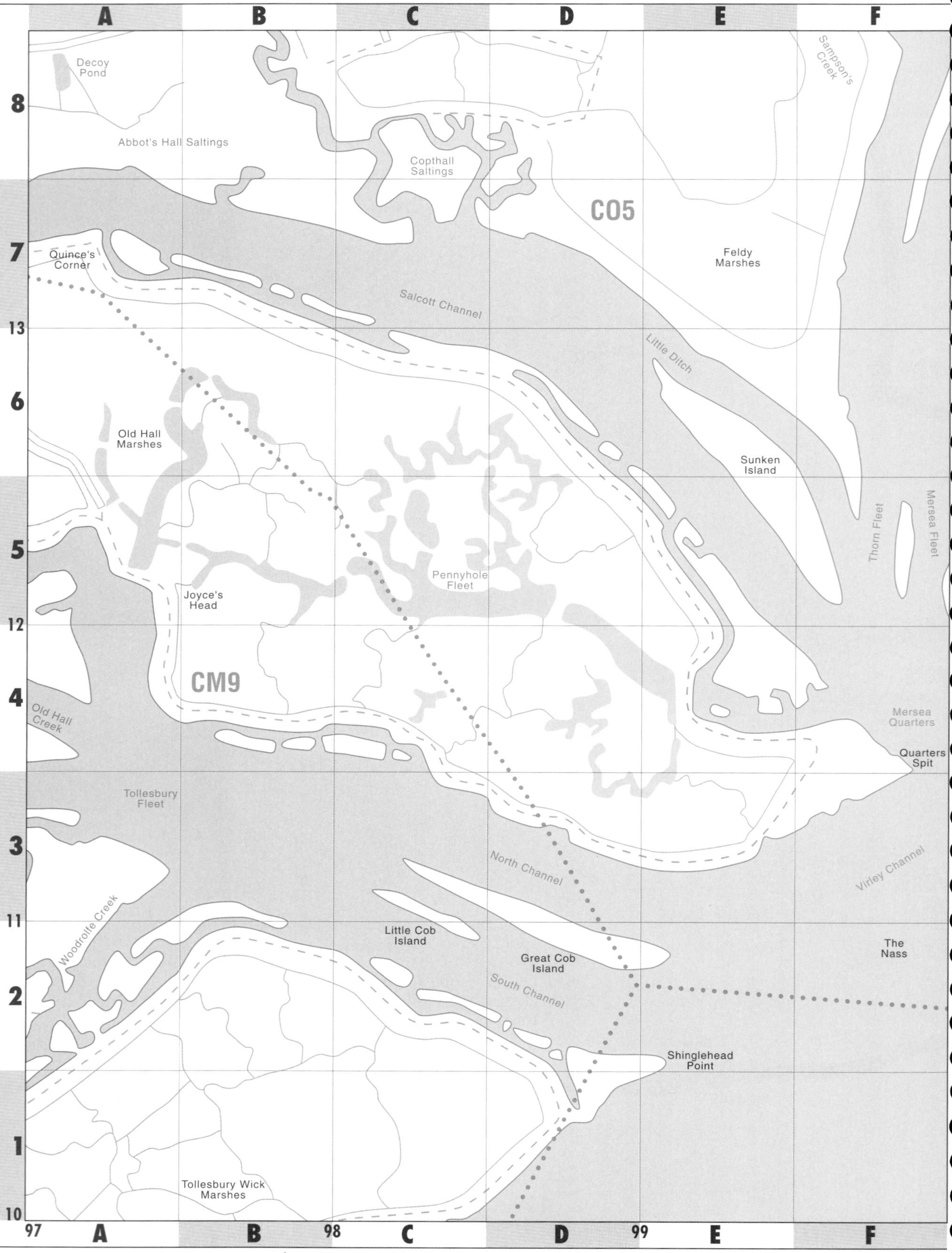

| | A | B | C | D | E | F |

Decoy Pond

Abbot's Hall Saltings

Sampson's Creek

Copthall Saltings

CO5

8

Quince's Corner

Feldy Marshes

7

Salcott Channel

Little Ditch

13

Old Hall Marshes

6

Sunken Island

Thorn Fleet

Mersea Fleet

Joyce's Head

Pennyhole Fleet

5

12

CM9

Mersea Quarters

4

Old Hall Creek

Quarters Spit

Tollesbury Fleet

Virley Channel

3

North Channel

11

Woodrolfe Creek

Little Cob Island

The Nass

Great Cob Island

2

South Channel

Shinglehead Point

1

Tollesbury Wick Marshes

10

199
214

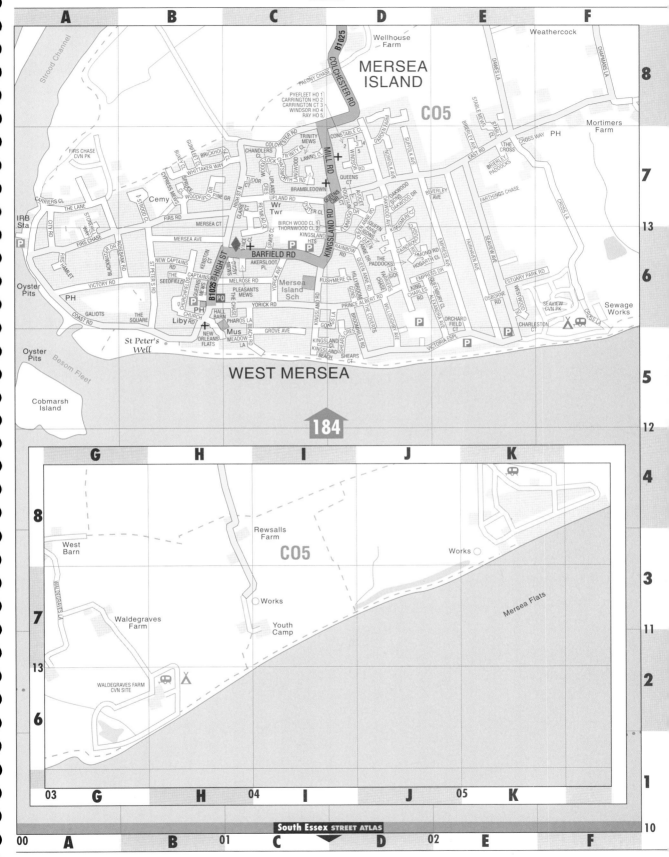

186

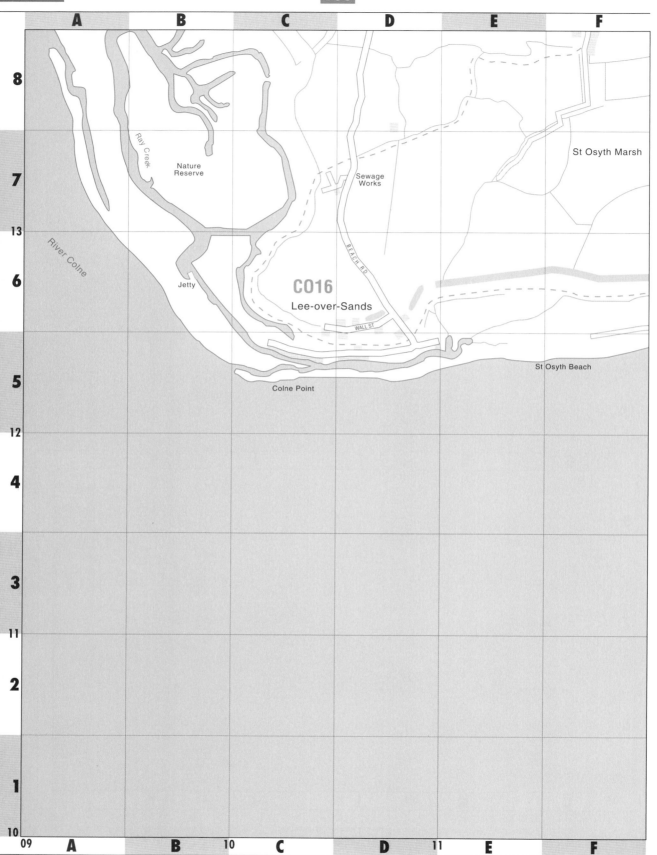

River Colne

Ray Creek

Nature
Reserve

Jetty

Sewage
Works

St Osyth Marsh

BEACH RD

CO16
Lee-over-Sands

WALL ST

Colne Point

St Osyth Beach

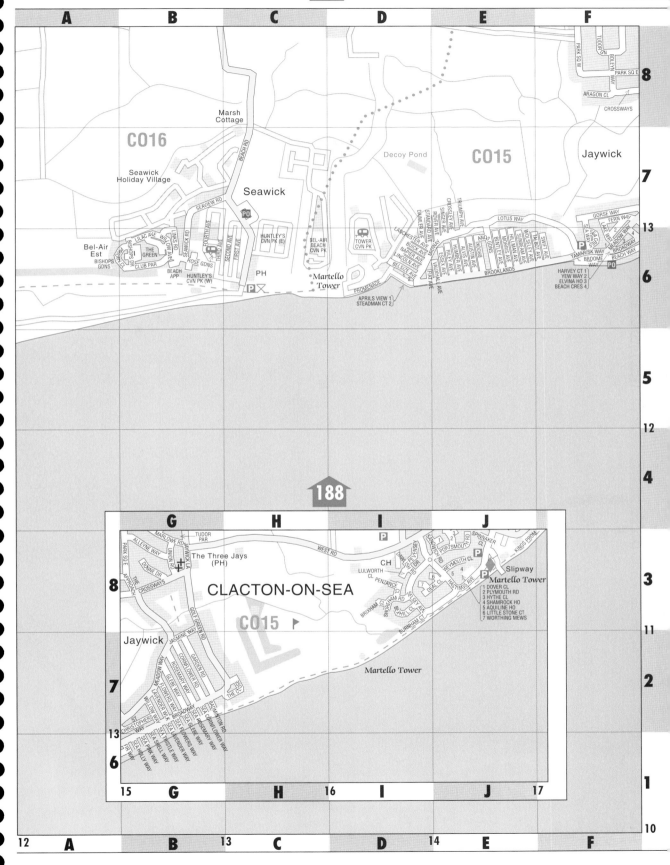

187
188

A B C D E F

8
7
13
6
5
12
4
11
2
3
1
10

CO16

Marsh Cottage

Seawick Holiday Village

Seawick

Bel-Air Est
BISHOPS GDNS

Decoy Pond

CO15

Jaywick

PARK SQ W
BOLEYN WAY
PARK SQ E
TUDOR GN
ARAGON CL
CROSSWAYS

LILAC AVE
WILLOW AVE
THE GREEN
CLUB PAR
BISHOPS DR
LINKS RD
SEAWICK RD
JAYWICK LA
ROSE GDNS
FOURTH AVE
THIRD AVE
SECOND AVE
FIRST AVE
SEAVIEW RD
BEACH RD

HUNTLEY'S CVN PK (E)

BEACH APP
HUNTLEY'S CVN PK (W)

PH

TOWER CVN PK

BEL-AIR BEACH CVN PK

Martello Tower

PROMENADE

APRILS VIEW 1
STEADMAN CT 2

LANCHESTER AVE
DAIMLER AVE
BUICK AVE
NAPIER AVE
LINCOLN AVE
BELSIZE AVE
VAUXHALL AVE
FIAT AVE
CRESSLEY AVE
SINGER AVE
ROVER AVE
TRIUMPH AVE
STANDARD AVE
RILEY AVE
ESSEX AVE
HUMBER AVE
AUSTIN AVE
ALVIS AVE
BENTLEY AVE
MORRIS AVE
SUNBEAM AVE
WOLSELEY AVE
SWIFT AVE
TALBOT AVE
SUN AVE
BROOKLANDS
LOTUS WAY

GORSE WAY
FERN WAY
LAKE WAY
MEADOW WAY
GROSE WAY
SEA WAY
TAMARISK WAY
BROADWAY
BEACH WAY
BROOME WAY

HARVEY CT 1
YEW WAY 2
ELVINA HO 3
BEACH CRES 4

CLACTON-ON-SEA

CO15

Jaywick

G H I J

TUDOR PAR
MARLOWE RD
ALLEYNE WAY
PARK SQ E
THE APPROACH
DONNE DR
UNION RD
THE CROSSWAYS

The Three Jays (PH)

WEST RD

LULWORTH CL
PENZANCE
BRIXHAM CL
SHOREHAM CL
BEXHILL CL
BURNHAM CL
CH
SANDWICH CL
DEAL CL
ASHBY DR
DANE ST FLEUR
SELSEY RD
WEYMOUTH CL
PORTSMOUTH CL
HASTINGS AVE
SPINNAKER CL
KINGS PROM

Slipway
Martello Tower

1 DOVER CL
2 PLYMOUTH RD
3 HYTHE CL
4 SHAMROCK HO
5 AQUILINE HO
6 LITTLE STONE CT
7 WORTHING MEWS

GOLF GREEN RD
JASMINE WAY
MEADOW WAY
GLEBE WAY
LOWER WAY
CORNFLOWER RD
GARDEN RD
ROSEMARY WAY
BROADWAY
BADMINTON RD
CORNFLOWER WAY
ST CHRISTOPHERS WAY
WILLOW WAY
LAVENDER WAY
SEA THISTLE WAY
SEA FLOWERS WAY
SEA GLEBE WAY
SEA PINK WAY
SEA HOLLY WAY
SEA SHELL WAY
FIR WAY

Martello Tower

15 G H 16 I J 17

12 A B 13 C D 14 E F

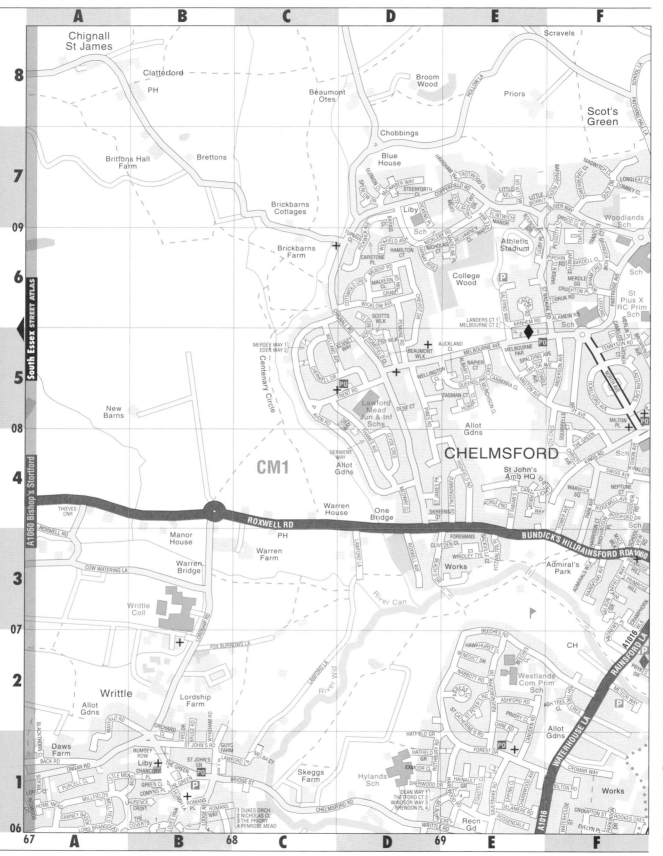

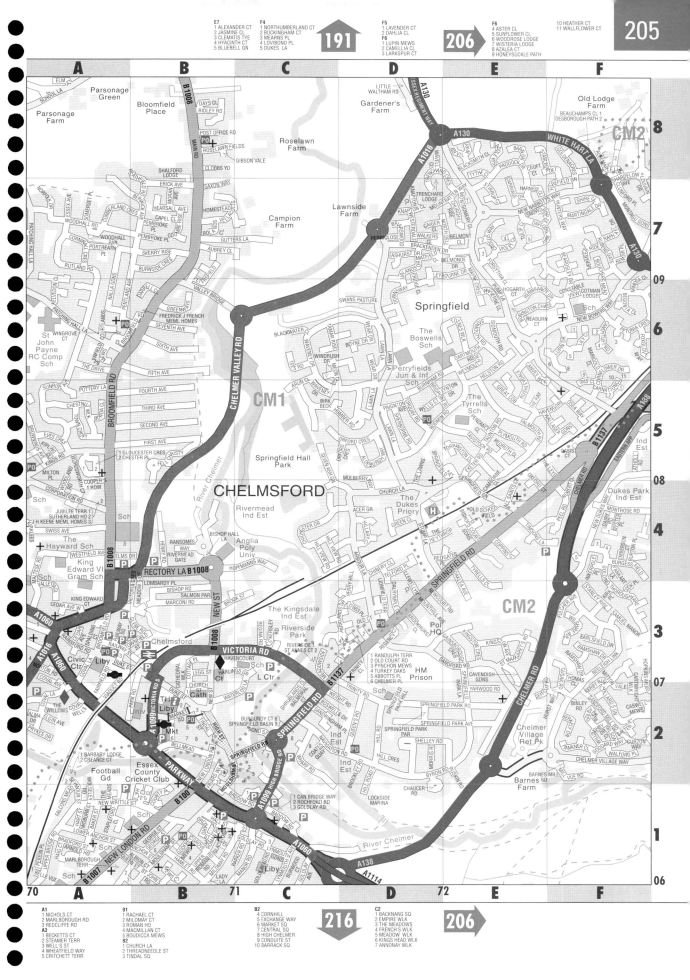

205 192

A B C D E F

8

CM1

A12
B1137
GENERALS LA
CHELMER RD
MAIN RD
OAK COTTS
VILLERS PL
CROMPTONS
ST ANDREWS
SUSSEX CL
HULTON CL
BUTTERFIELD RD
FALKLAND RD
FITZWALTER RD
HASELFOOT RD
Sch
PLANTATION RD
BOONS CL
OLD FORGE RD
TRELAWN
PH
PO
RIVER COTTS
TYSSEN MEAD
LEWIN PL
HOWARDS CL
THE LAGRES
THE WILLOWS
JUNIPER RD
CHURCH RD
ABERCORN HO
COOPERS
LODGE CRES
Tyrell Cottage
Boreham
The Old Rectory
CHURCH GN
Old Hall

7

A138
A130
Hotel
Service Area
Boreham House

09

WHITE HART LA
CHELMER RD
COLCHESTER RD
WINSFORD WAY
JACARANDA CL
OAK LODGE TYE
BEAULIE RD
MAULDEN GN
SIDNEY PL
BILLERS CHASE
FRANCES
BURRELL GATE
JONGE LINK
WARTON DR
B1137
ALYSSUM CL
LOBELIA CL
POPPY GN
PRIMULA WAY
DAISY CT
A130
PH
FORDSON RD
Boreham Hall

6

COLCHESTER RD
B1137
WHITE HART COTTS
SPRINGFIELD LYONS APP
Hedgerows Bsns Pk
Sheepcotes
SHEEPCOTES
Little Baddow Lock

5

TA Ctr
Springfield Lyons
CM2
Stonham's Lock

08

Dukes Park Ind Est
CUTON HALL LA
NEW DUKES WAY
BEAUFORT RD
MONTROSE RD
RICHMOND RD
SUFFOLK DR
ARGYLL RD
Cuton Hall
MAGGY TYE
TOWNSEND
ALBRA MEAD
BRYANT LINK
ABELL WAY
WRIGHT MEAD
CORNELIUS VALE
CHASE RD
ALERN
WIGGINS VIEW
CM3
Chelmer & Blackwater Navigation
Whitwell's Farm

4

HERRINGHAM GN
WILKINSONS
CANNONBURY CL
POCKLINGTON CL
GRAFTON PL
BARTLEY
MURIEL GN
BARLOW'S REACH
TWIN OAKS
SHEPPARD DR
BANK
QUALL RD
CHANCELLOR AVE
WARD
CRESS RD
SELDON
COWDRIE WAY
Chelmer Village
Cuton Lock
Phillow's Farm

3

LITTELL TWEED
HENIKER GATE
HOLLIS CL
WOODROFFE CL
CLARENCE
BLACK'S LA
Schs
PO
PETERBROOK
WEBB CL
WHITMORE CT
BENNIE PLS
PORTWAY
GORDON DR
1 CROZIER TERR
2 PEERS SQ
Brookend
BROOK END RD
Centenary Circle
Hammond's Farm
HURRELLS LA
Ford
Waterhall Meadows Nature Reserve

07

CHELMET VILLAGE WAY
LEAPINGWELL CL
COLYERS REACH
HOPKINS MEAD
FAIRFAX MEAD
PALMERS CROFT
VILLAGE GATE
YELDHAM LOCK
YELDHAM GATE
POLLARD'S GN
HAMMONDS RD

2

CURZON WAY
HOWARD DR
SANDFORD MILL RD
STORMS WAY
SAYWELL REACH
SANDFORD BROOK LA
Sewage Works
Grace's Wlk

1

Sandford Mill Bridge
Works
SANDFORD MILL RD
Rumbold's Farm

06

73 A B 74 C D 75 E F

A12

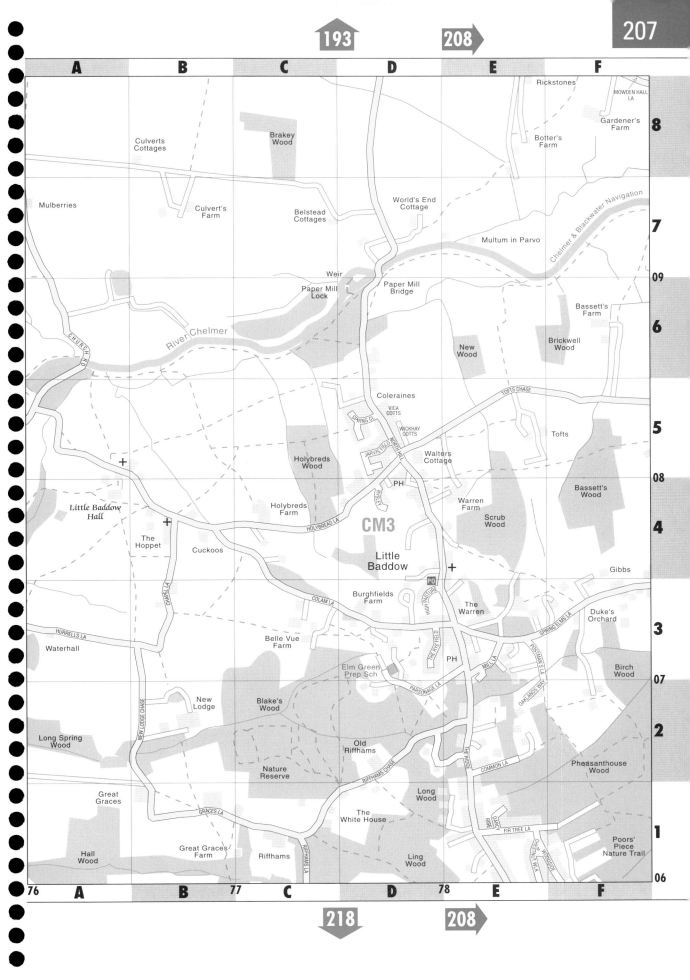

207
194

MALDON RD
B1019

8

MOWDEN HALL LA

Cardfield's Farm

Crouchman's

Fairwinds Farm

Ashfield Cottage

ULTING RD

ASHFIELD FARM RD

Ulting Grove

River Ter

BUMFORDS LA

Bamfields

Wick Wood

CROUCHMAN'S FARM RD

ULTING HALL RD

7

Bumfords Bridge

Stammer's Farm

09

CHURCH RD

Ulting Wick

Ulting Hall

Southland's Farm

Ulting

6

Chelmer & Blackwater Navigation

ULTING LA

River Chelmer

TOFTS CHASE

Retreat Farm

5

Hoemill Bridge

MANOR RD

Bassetts

Hoe Mill Barns

Manor Farm

08

Hoe Mill

HOE MILL RD

CM3

BASSETTS LA

Raven's Farm

LITTLE LONDON LA

Blue Mill

HOP GARDENS LA

4

WEST BOWERS RD

Little London Farm

West Bowers Farm

West Bowers Hall

Glendale

BLUE MILL LA

SPRING ELMS LA

Crossways

MEAD PASTURES

CURLING TYE LA

3

Spring Elms Poultry Farm

STILE'S RD

CM9

RECTORY RD

Whitehouse Farm

COMMON LA

CH

LITTLE BADDOW RD

Gun Hill Farm

TOP RD

Woodham Walter CE Prim Sch

07

Woodhall

BROOK CL

PH

THE STREET

PO

The Wilderness

2

Woodham Walter Common Nature Reserve

CH

CHURCH HILL

Woodham Walter

CHURCH CNR

OAK FARM RD

The Warren House

Gravel Pit

1

Twitty Fee

TWITTY FEE

HERBAGE PARK RD

Oak Farm

OLD LONDON RD

06

207
219

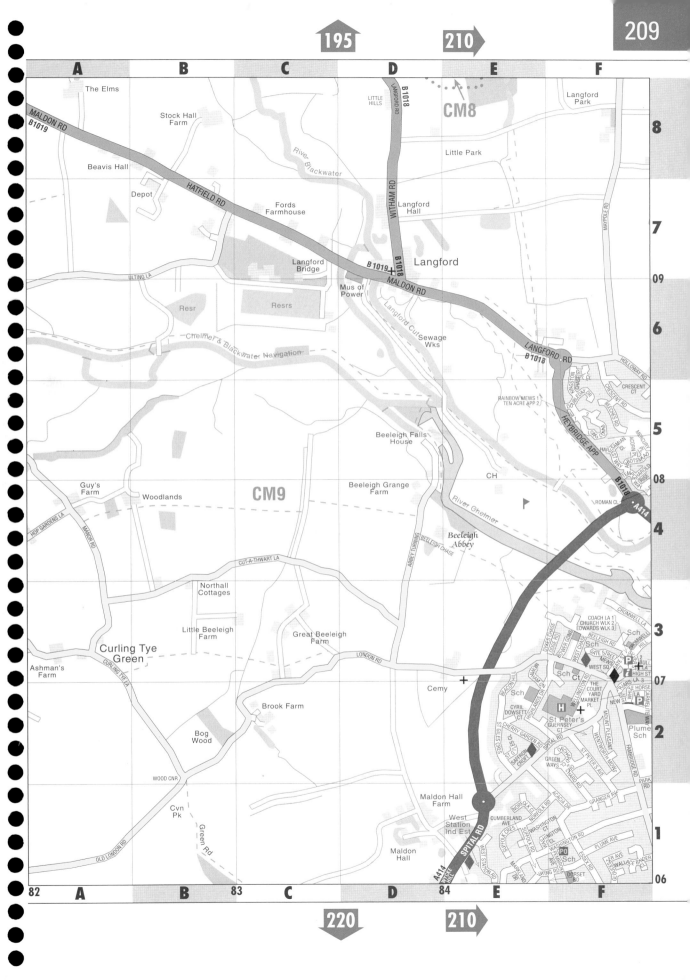

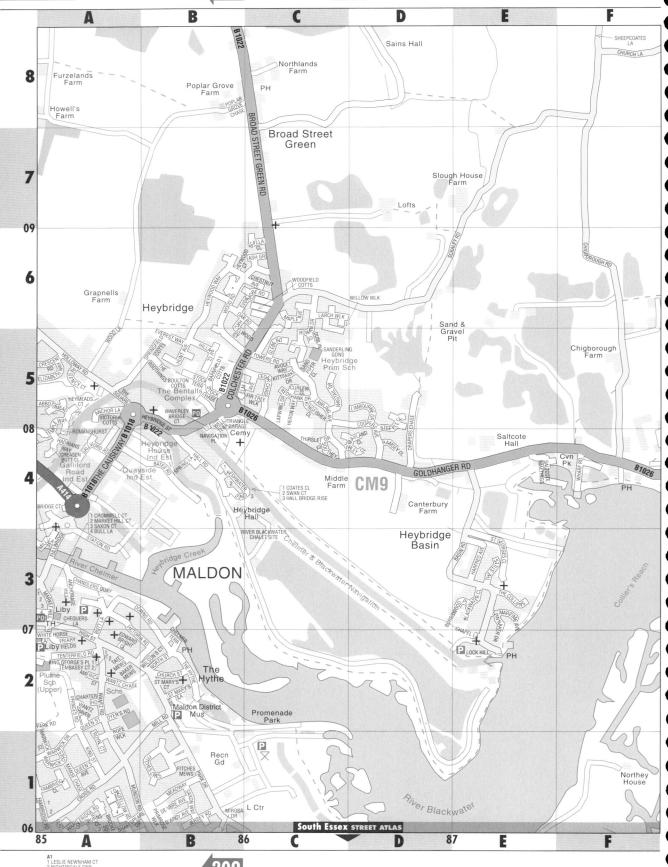

A1
1 LESLIE NEWNHAM CT
2 NIGHTINGALE CNR
3 SASSOON WAY
4 DRAYTON CL

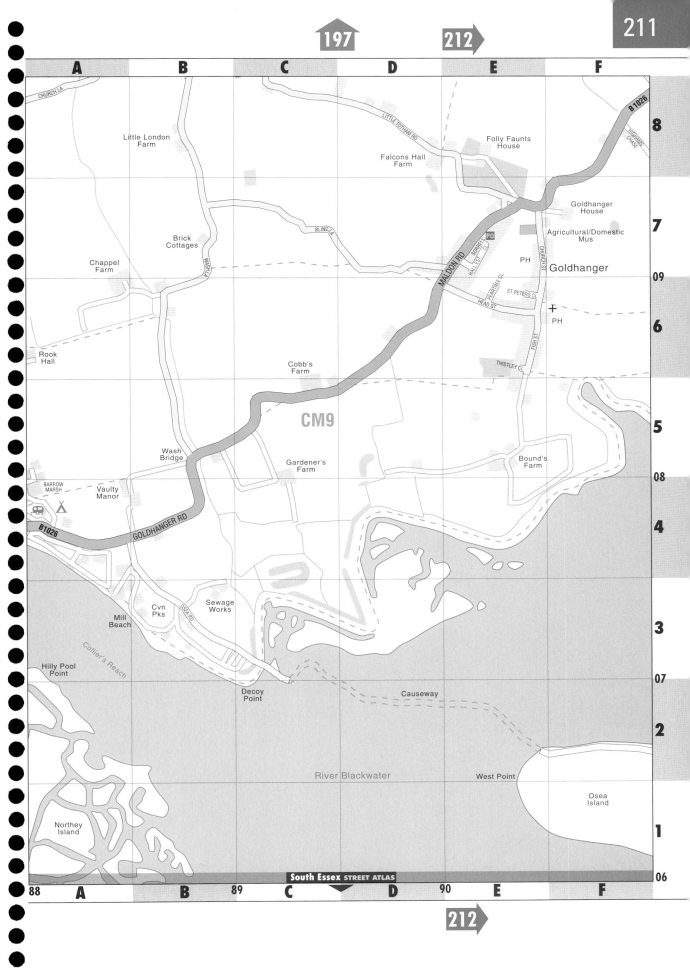

A B C D E F

8

CHURCH LA

LITTLE TOTHAM RD

Little London
Farm

Falcons Hall
Farm

Folly Faunts
House

B1026

HIGHAMS CHASE

7

Brick
Cottages

BLIND LA

WASH LA

MALDON RD

Goldhanger
House

Agricultural/Domestic
Mus

PO

SORREL CL

HALL ST CL

PH

CHURCH ST

Goldhanger

09

Chappel
Farm

PEARTREE CL

HEAD ST

ST PETERS CL

HIGH ST

+
PH

6

Rook
Hall

Cobb's
Farm

THISTLEY CL

CM9

5

Wash
Bridge

Gardener's
Farm

Bound's
Farm

08

BARROW
MARSH

Vaulty
Manor

4

B1026

GOLDHANGER RD

Cvn
Pks

OSEA RD

Sewage
Works

Mill
Beach

Collier's Reach

3

Hilly Pool
Point

07

Decoy
Point

Causeway

2

River Blackwater

West Point

Osea
Island

Northey
Island

1

06

88 A B 89 C D 90 E F

A **B** **C** **D** **E** **F**

MALDON RD
B1026

Lower
Grove

8

New
Barn

JOYCE'S CHASE

HIGHAMS CHASE

PAGES LA

Wycke
Farm

7

Highams
Farm

Longwick
Farm

Bowstead Brook

09

JOYCE'S CHASE

6

Joyce's
Farm

Lauriston
Farm

LAURISTON
BGLWS

5

CM9

Gore
Saltings

08

4

Goldhanger Creek

River Blackwater

3

The Stumble

07

2

Osea
Island

Works

THE CHASE

1

Osea
Farm

East
Point

06

Wr
Twr

91 **A** 92 **B** **C** **D** 93 **E** **F**

199
214

A B C D E F

8

Bohuns
Hall

MELL RD

MONKS WLK

WYCKE LA

Tollesbury

Wick
Farm

Mell
Farm

Thistly Rd

PRENTICE HALL A

Boreham & Profits
Farm

CM9

7

09

Mill Creek

Decoy
Farm

Mill Farm
Marshes

6

Rolls
Farm

Left Decoy
Marshes

Mill
Point

5

08

4

River Blackwater

3

07

2

1

St Lawrence

The
Stone

CM0

SEA VIEW PROM

SPA

MOUNTVIEW PH
CRES

OYSTER
COTTS

RIVERTON DR

TINNOCKS LA

ST LAWRENCE DR

MAIN RD

SEA VIEW
PAS

06

214

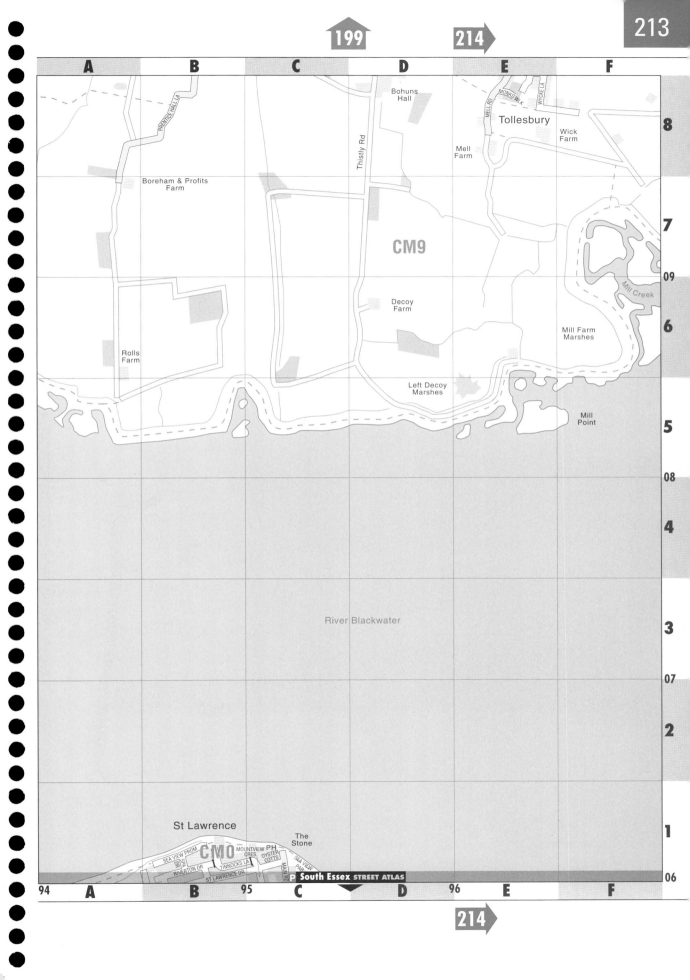

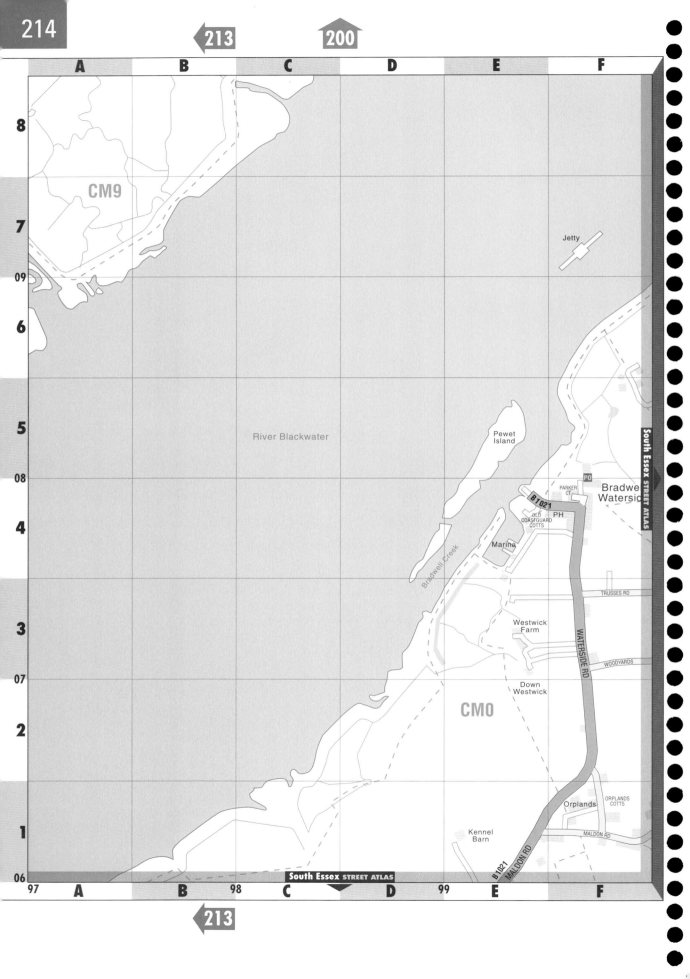

A   B   C   D   E   F

8

CM9

7

09

6

Jetty

5

River Blackwater

Pewet
Island

08

Bradwe
Watersid

PO

PARKER
CT

B1021

OLD
COASTGUARD
COTTS

PH

Marina

4

Bradwell Creek

TRUSSES RD

3

Westwick
Farm

WATERSIDE RD

WOODYARDS

07

Down
Westwick

CMO

2

ORPLANDS
COTTS

Orplands

1

Kennel
Barn

MALDON RD

B1021

MALDON RD

06

South Essex STREET ATLAS

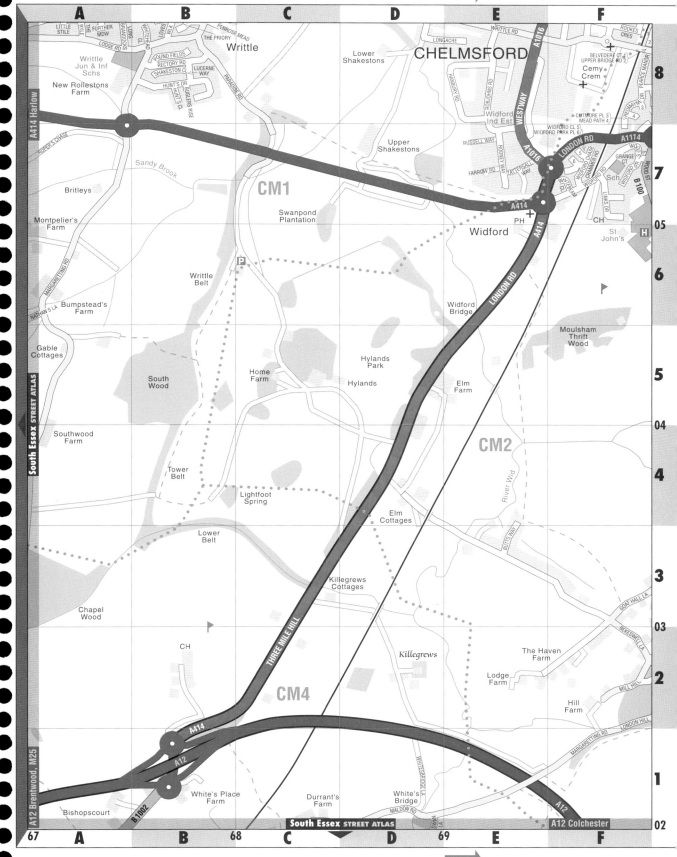

216

A8
1 CHERRYGARDEN LA
2 UPPER CHASE
3 DOUGLAS WLK
4 LAUREL GR

215   205

CHELMSFORD

Moulsham

Great Baddow

CM2

Galleyend

Galleywood

Lower Green

Chelmer Park

Moulsham High Sch

Moulsham Jun & Inf Schs

Mildmay Jun & Inf Schs

Lathcoats Farm

Galleywood Hall

Great Baddow High Sch

Beehive Lane Prim Sch

Carlton Riding Sch

Thriftwood Sch

Galleywood Inf Sch

The Horse & Groom (PH)

Seabrights Barn (PH)

Great Seabrights

Willow Cottage

Duffield's Farm

Research Laboratories

Cemy   Mast

Whiss-Stocks

Brook Farm

Mushroom Farm

Baddow Park

Canon-Leys Farm

Parklands Farm

Pond's Farm

Wood Farm

Glebe Farm

Galleywood Common

The Lodge

Superstore

Sports Gd

Recn Gd

BEEHIVE LA

GALLEYWOOD RD

STOCK RD

NEW LONDON RD B1007

PRINCES RD

A1114

A1009

A12

B1007

B1009

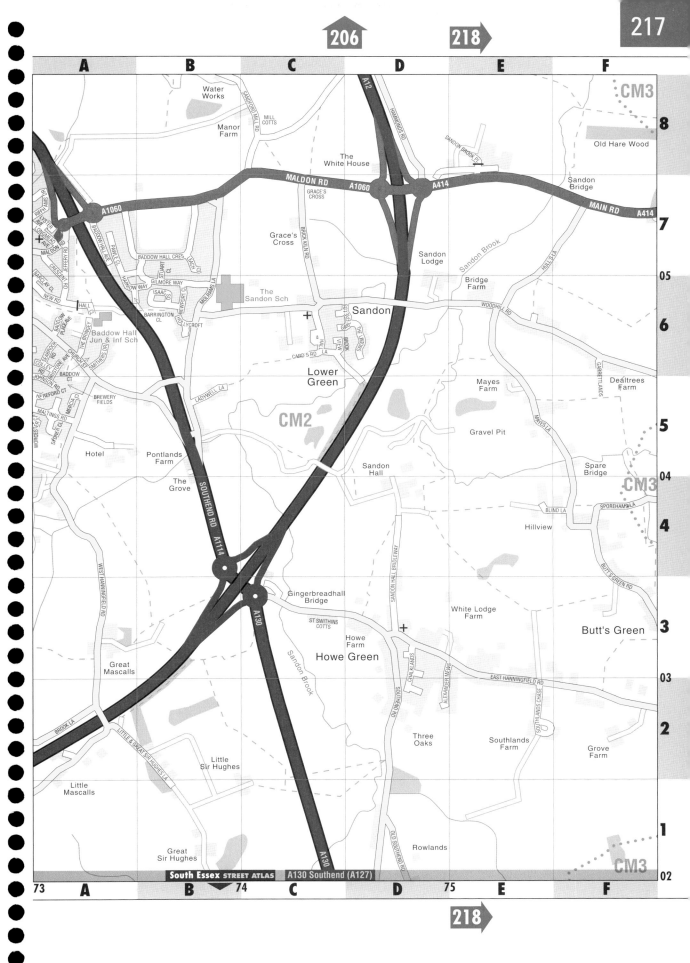

A   B   C   D   E   F

CM3

8

Water Works

Old Hare Wood

Manor Farm

The White House

Sandon Bridge

MALDON RD   A1060   A414

Sandon Brook Pl

MAIN RD   A414

GRACE'S CROSS

A1060

7

Grace's Cross

Sandon Lodge

Sandon Brook

05

Bridge Farm

The Sandon Sch

Sandon

WOODHILL RD

6

Lower Green

Dealtrees Farm

Mayes Farm

CM2

Gravel Pit

5

MAYES LA

GARRETTLANDS

Spare Bridge

CM3

04

BLIND LA

SPOREHAMS LA

Hotel

Sandon Hall

Hillview

BUTT'S GREEN RD

4

Pontlands Farm

The Grove

SOUTHEND RD

A1114

Gingerbreadhall Bridge

White Lodge Farm

Butt's Green

3

WEST HANNINGFIELD RD

A130

ST SWITHINS COTTS

Howe Farm

Howe Green

SANDON HALL BRIDLEWAY

CHALKLANDS

EAST HANNINGFIELD RD

03

Great Mascalls

Sandon Brook

ALEXANDER MEWS

OLD SOUTHEND RD

SOUTHLANDS CHASE

Southlands Farm

Grove Farm

2

BROOK LA

Three Oaks

Little Sir Hughes

LITTLE & GREAT SIR HUGHES LA

Little Mascalls

1

Great Sir Hughes

A130

Rowlands

CM3

02

73   A   B   74   C   D   75   E   F

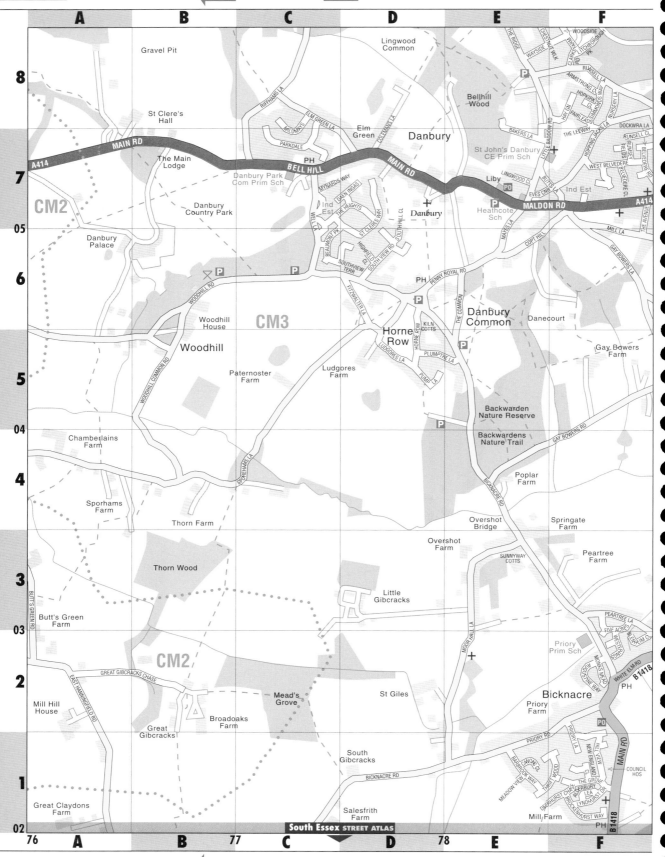

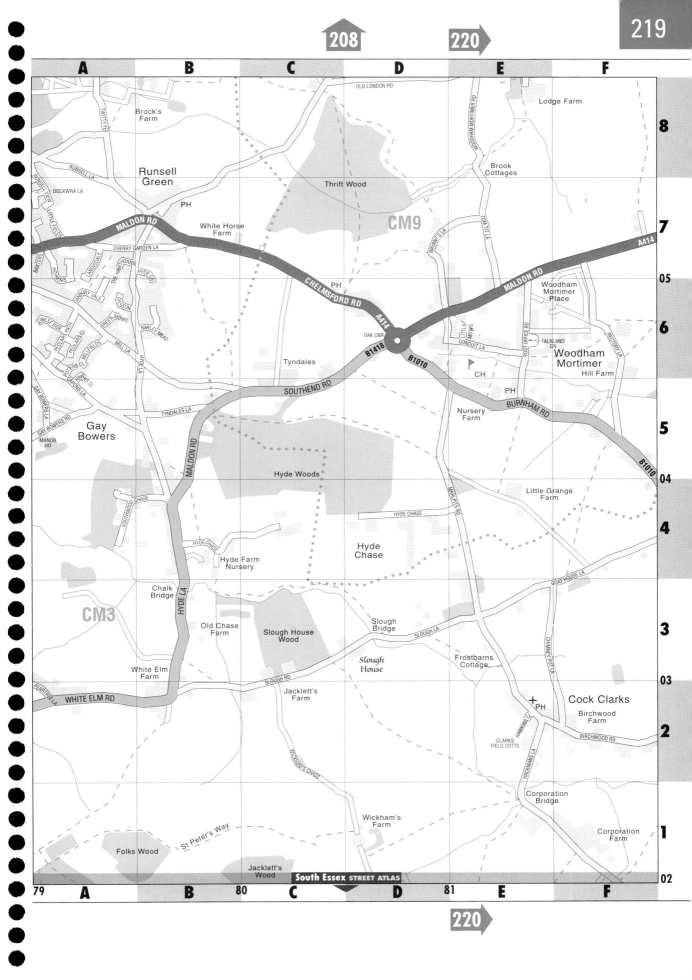

A B C D E F

8

7

05

6

5

04

4

3

03

2

1

02

79 A B 80 C D 81 E F

OLD LONDON RD

Lodge Farm

Brock's Farm

Runsell Green

Thrift Wood

CM9

Brook Cottages

WOODHAM MORTIMER RD

RUNSELL LA

DOCKWRA LA

TWITTY FEE

LITTLE FIELDS

RUNSELL VIEW

MALDON RD

White Horse Farm

PH

A414

MALDON RD

TOM TIT LA

BRYANT'S LA

CHELMSFORD RD

PH

A414

Woodham Mortimer Place

CHERRY GARDEN LA

THE HAWTHORNS

HYDE GRN

BAXTERS

HOYACKS

LANDSDALE

DANBURY VALE

LISTON

Woodham Mortimer

Hill Farm

RECTORY LA

POST OFFICE RD

FALKLAND GN

CONDUIT LA

LITTLE MDWS

OAK CNR

B1418

B1010

JUBILEE RISE

PEDLARS PATH

PEDLARS CL

GREEN MDWS

BARLEY MEAD

MILL LA

MILLFIELDS

POTTERS CL

BANKS CL

CAPONS LA

Tyndales

SOUTHEND RD

Nursery Farm

CH

PH

BURWHAM RD

Gay Bowers

MANOR HO

GAY BOWERS RD

GAY BOWERS LA

TYNDALES LA

MALDON RD

Little Grange Farm

B1010

Hyde Woods

MARLPITS RD

HYDE LA

SOUTHWOOD CHASE

HYDE CHASE

HYDE CHASE

Hyde Chase

GOAT HOUSE LA

CM3

Chalk Bridge

Hyde Farm Nursery

Old Chase Farm

Slough House Wood

Slough Bridge

SLOUGH LA

CHIMNEY POT LA

Frostbarns Cottage

+ PH

Cock Clarks

Birchwood Farm

White Elm Farm

SLOUGH RD

Jacklett's Farm

Slough House

BIRCHWOOD RD

PEARTREE LA

WHITE ELM RD

CLARKS FIELD COTTS

HAWKINS CL

HACKMANS LA

Corporation Bridge

WICKHAM'S CHASE

Wickham's Farm

Corporation Farm

Folks Wood

St Peter's Way

Jacklett's Wood

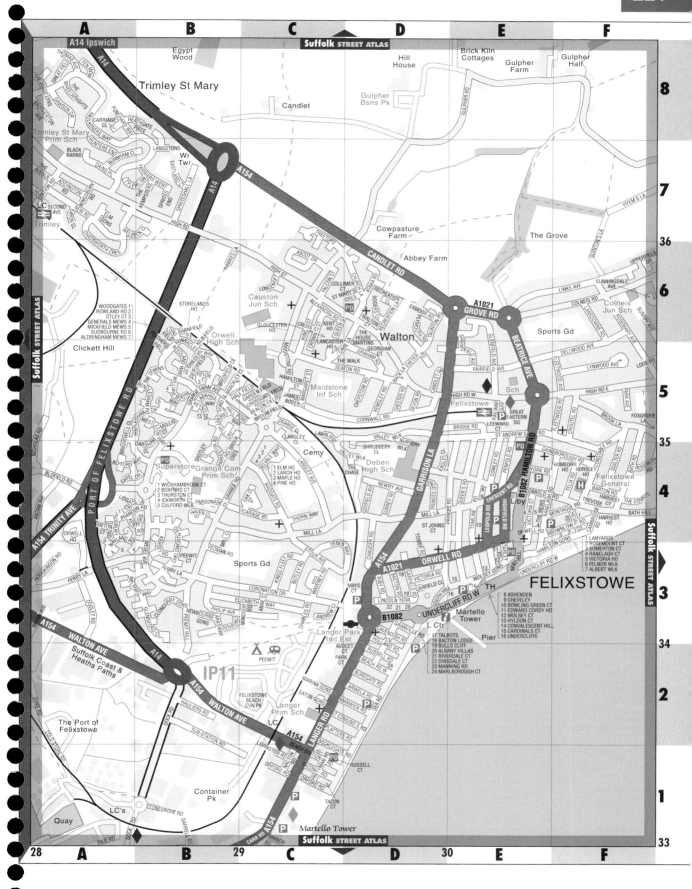

Index

Church Rd **6** Beckenham BR2..........**53** C6

Place name	Location number	Locality, town or village	Postcode district	Page and grid square
May be abbreviated on the map	Present when a number indicates the place's position in a crowded area of mapping	Shown when more than one place has the same name	District for the indexed place	Page number and grid reference for the standard mapping

Public and commercial buildings are highlighted in magenta   **Places of interest** are highlighted in blue with a star★

Abbreviations used in the index

Acad	**Academy**	Comm	**Common**	Gd	**Ground**	L	**Leisure**	Prom	**Prom**
App	**Approach**	Cott	**Cottage**	Gdn	**Garden**	La	**Lane**	Rd	**Road**
Arc	**Arcade**	Cres	**Crescent**	Gn	**Green**	Liby	**Library**	Recn	**Recreation**
Ave	**Avenue**	Cswy	**Causeway**	Gr	**Grove**	Mdw	**Meadow**	Ret	**Retail**
Bglw	**Bungalow**	Ct	**Court**	H	**Hall**	Meml	**Memorial**	Sh	**Shopping**
Bldg	**Building**	Ctr	**Centre**	Ho	**House**	Mkt	**Market**	Sq	**Square**
Bsns, Bus	**Business**	Ctry	**Country**	Hospl	**Hospital**	Mus	**Museum**	St	**Street**
Bvd	**Boulevard**	Cty	**County**	HQ	**Headquarters**	Orch	**Orchard**	Sta	**Station**
Cath	**Cathedral**	Dr	**Drive**	Hts	**Heights**	Pal	**Palace**	Terr	**Terrace**
Cir	**Circus**	Dro	**Drove**	Ind	**Industrial**	Par	**Parade**	TH	**Town Hall**
Cl	**Close**	Ed	**Education**	Inst	**Institute**	Pas	**Passage**	Univ	**University**
Cnr	**Corner**	Emb	**Embankment**	Int	**International**	Pk	**Park**	Wk, Wlk	**Walk**
Coll	**College**	Est	**Estate**	Intc	**Interchange**	Pl	**Place**	Wr	**Water**
Com	**Community**	Ex	**Exhibition**	Junc	**Junction**	Prec	**Precinct**	Yd	**Yard**

Index of localities, towns and villages

Abberton 163 A3
Aldham 133 B8
Alphamstone 54 F3
Alresford 165 A8
Ardleigh 111 E7
Arkesden 41 E2
Ashdon 6 B1
Ashen 11 D1
Bardfield Saling 99 C2
Barnston 151 A4
Bartlow 6 B7
Beaumont 141 F7
Beazley End 101 C6
Belchamp St Paul 13 A2
Belchamp Walter 31 F5
Belstead 36 C7
Bentley 60 B7
Berden 92 C8
Bicknacre 218 F2
Birch 161 A4
Birchanger 119 E2
Birdbrook 28 B7
Bishop's Stortford 145 D7
Blackheath 163 B8
Black Notley 155 B5
Boreham 206 E8
Borley 14 F3
Boxted 82 F7
Bradfield 87 F7
Bradwell 129 D2
Bradwell Waterside . . .214 F4
Braintree 128 B5
Brantham 60 E1
Brightlingsea 185 E6
Broomfield 191 B8
Bulmer 32 E5
Bulmer Tye 32 F2
Bures 79 E8
Capel St Mary 35 B2
Castle Camps 7 E3
Castle Hedingham 51 E4
Cavendish 1 C1
Chappel 106 C5
Chelmondiston 63 E8
Chelmsford 205 C4
Chrishall 19 D3
Clacton-on-Sea 189 B3
Clare 12 C6
Clavering 65 C5
Cock Clarks 219 F2

Coggeshall 131 B3
Colchester 135 D7
Colne Engaine 77 F2
Copford 133 D4
Cressing 156 A6
Danbury 218 D7
Debden 68 B7
Dedham 84 F7
Duddenhoe End 41 A6
Earls Colne 105 C7
East Bergholt 59 C5
Easthorpe 160 A7
East Mersea 184 F1
Eight Ash Green 134 A8
Elder Street 44 E1
Elmdon 20 B4
Elmstead 138 A6
Elsenham 94 C1
Farnham 118 D6
Feering 158 A5
Felixstowe 221 F3
Felsted 152 B5
Finchingfield 72 C5
Fingringhoe 163 F5
Ford End 172 B7
Fordham 107 D5
Fordham Heath 107 F2
Foxearth 14 C6
Frating 139 A3
Frinton-on-Sea 170 D5
Galleywood 216 D2
Gestingthorpe 31 E1
Glemsford 2 C4
Goldhanger 211 F7
Gosfield 102 E8
Great Baddow 216 E7
Great Bardfield 72 C1
Great Bentley 166 D8
Great Braxted 178 C1
Great Bromley 112 F1
Great Canfield 149 C1
Great Chesterford 3 D2
Great Cornard 34 B5
Great Dunmow 150 C7
Great Easton 122 F7
Great Hallingbury 146 E4
Great Henny 54 C8
Great Holland 170 A3
Great Horkesley 82 B1
Great Leighs 173 F7

Great Maplestead 52 D2
Great Notley 154 B7
Great Oakley 116 C4
Great Sampford 47 B3
Great Tey 132 C8
Great Totham 196 B4
Great Waltham 190 E7
Great Wigborough 181 F3
Great Yeldham 30 A1
Greenstead Green 104 A5
Hadstock 5 C6
Halstead 76 D2
Harkstead 63 B2
Harwich 91 E5
Hatfield Peverel 194 B4
Haverhill 9 C7
Helions Bumpstead . . .26 C8
Hempstead 25 F1
Henham 94 F6
Heybridge 210 B6
Heybridge Basin 210 D3
Heydon 19 A5
Hinxton 3 B7
Holbrook 62 C5
Holland-on-Sea 189 F5
Howe Green 217 D3
Howe Street 172 F2
Ickleton 3 A4
Ipswich 17 C7
Jaywick 203 F7
Kelvedon 158 D2
Kirby Cross 170 B7
Kirby-le-Soken 170 C8
Lamarsh 55 B4
Langford 209 D7
Langham 83 F4
Langley 40 C2
Lawford 86 B3
Layer-de-la-Haye 161 F5
Lindsell 98 A3
Little Baddow 207 D4
Little Bentley 139 E8
Little Bromley 113 B6
Littlebury 21 E4
Little Clacton 168 D3
Little Dunmow 151 D7
Little Easton 122 F5
Little Horkesley 81 E4
Little Leighs 173 E6
Little Maplestead 53 B1

Little Oakley 117 B7
Little Totham 197 C4
Little Waltham 191 C6
Little Yeldham 30 E4
Long Melford 15 D7
Maldon 210 B3
Manningtree 86 E4
Manuden 92 F2
Marks Tey 132 E4
Messing 159 D3
Mistley 86 F4
Nayland 56 B1
New Mistley 87 B4
Newport 43 A1
North End 151 F2
Nuthampstead 39 A2
Panfield 127 B7
Pattiswick 129 F5
Pebmarsh 78 B7
Peldon 182 E6
Pentlow 13 F6
Point Clear Bay 185 F3
Purleigh 220 D1
Quendon 66 F2
Radwinter 45 F8
Ramsey 89 F1
Rayne 126 E2
Rickling Green 93 D8
Ridgewell 29 B7
Rivenhall 177 B8
Rowhedge 163 F8
Rushmere St Andrew . .18 E8
Saffron Walden 22 E3
St Lawrence 213 B1
St Osyth 187 B4
Salcott-cum-Virley 199 B8
Seawick 203 C7
Sewards End 23 E1
Shalford 100 E7
Shotley Gate 91 A8
Shudy Camps 7 B6
Sible Hedingham 51 E1
Silver End 156 E4
Sproughton 16 B6
Stambourne 28 D3
Stanstead 2 F7
Stansted Mountfitchet .119 C8
Stebbing 124 E5
Steeple Bumpstead 27 B8
Stisted 129 C6

Stoke by Clare 11 C4
Stoke-by-Nayland 56 E5
Stratford St Mary 58 C2
Sturmer 9 F4
Stutton 61 F2
Sudbury 33 D8
Takeley 148 C8
Tattingstone 61 C7
Tendring 140 F5
Terling 175 C3
Thaxted 70 A3
Thorington Street 57 B4
Thorpe-le-Soken 142 B1
Thorrington 166 A5
Tiptree 179 D5
Tollesbury 199 D2
Tolleshunt D'arcy 198 D4
Tolleshunt Knights 180 A2
Tolleshunt Major 197 E4
Toppesfield 50 C7
Trimley St Mary 221 B8
Ugley 93 E6
Ulting 208 C6
Wakes Colne 106 C6
Walton-on-the-Naze . .171 D8
Washbrook 35 E8
Weeley 140 E1
Weeley Heath 168 A5
Wendens Ambo 42 E5
West Bergholt 108 D4
West Mersea 201 C5
Wethersfield 73 C3
Wherstead 37 B6
White Colne 105 E6
White Notley 155 E1
Wicken Bonhunt 66 C5
Wickham Bishops 195 D5
Wickham St Paul 53 C5
Widdington 67 E4
Wimbish 45 C6
Witham 176 E4
Wivenhoe 137 C2
Wix 115 C5
Woodham Mortimer . . .219 F6
Woodham Walter 208 E2
Woolverstone 38 B1
Wormingford 80 E4
Wrabness 88 C4
Writtle 204 A2

A

Abbas Wlk CO10 ....34 C5
Abberton Rd
Fingringhoe CO5 ....163 D3
Layer-de-l-H CO2 ....162 C5
Abberton Resr Nature Reserve★ CO2 ....161 F2
Abberton Wildfowl Ctr★ CO2 ....161 E1
Abbess Cl CM1 ....204 E2
Abbey Cres CO16 ....142 A1
Abbey Ct CO9 ....51 F3
Abbey Gate St 11 CO2 ....135 F6
Abbey La Coggeshall CO6 131 A1
Saffron Walden CB10 ....22 D1
Abbey Mdw CO9 ....51 D2
Abbey Rd CO10 ....15 E1
Abbey St Ickleton CB10 ....3 A4
Thorpe-le-S CO16 ....142 A1
Abbey Turning CM9 ....209 D4
Abbey View CM6 ....96 E2
Abbot's Rd CO2 ....136 B3
Abbots Cl
Clacton-on-S CO15 ....188 E6
Wix CO11 ....115 C5
Abbots Gdns CO16 ....187 C4
Abbots La CO6 ....134 A7
Abbots Wick La CO5 ....181 B3
Abbotsbury Cl IP2 ....17 A1
Abbotsmead CM9 ....209 F5
Abbott Rd CO12 ....90 F2
Abbotts Croft CB9 ....9 F4
Abbotts Ct CB9 ....9 E5
Abbotts Pl CM2 ....205 D3
Abbotts Way CM23 ....145 E3
Abdy Ave CO12 ....90 E2
Abell Way CM2 ....206 B4
Abels Rd CO9 ....103 D8
Abercorn Ct 11 CB9 ....8 F7
Abercorn Ho CM3 ....206 E8
Abercorn Way CM8 ....177 A2
Abingdon Cl IP2 ....17 A1
Abinger Cl CO16 ....188 C6
Abington Pl 2 CB9 ....9 A8
Abraham Dr CM8 ....156 E4
Abram's La SG8 ....19 C4
Acacia Ave CO4 ....136 E8
Acacia Cl IP3 ....18 E1
Acacia Ct CO11 ....60 D1
Acacia Dr
Great Dunmow CM6 ....123 C1
Maldon CM9 ....209 F1
Acacia Gdns CM8 ....177 B4
Accommodation Rd CO4 ....109 D7
Acer Gr Chelmsford CM1 .205 D4
Ipswich IP8 ....16 C1
Achilles Way CM7 ....128 B5
Achnacone Dr CO4 ....109 C3
Acland Ave CO3 ....135 B7
Acland Ct CO3 ....135 A7
Acorn Ave Braintree CM7 127 E2
Halstead CO9 ....76 D1
Acorn Cl Colchester CO4 .110 D4
Harwich CO12 ....90 F1
Ipswich IP2 ....16 C2
Acorn Pl CM9 ....209 F5
Acorn Wlk CO7 ....166 A5
Acres End CM1 ....204 E4
Acton Cl CO10 ....33 F8
Acton Gn CO10 ....33 E7
Acton La CO10 ....33 F8
Acton Sq 4 CO10 ....33 E7
Adair Rd IP1 ....16 D8
Adams Cl IP2 ....17 C3
Adams Ct Halstead CO9 ....76 D2
Saffron Walden CB11 ....43 C8
Adderley Rd CM23 ....145 F7
Addington Rd IP11 ....221 A7
Addison Rd
Great Holland CO13 ....170 B5
Sudbury CO10 ....34 B8
Adelaide Dr CO2 ....136 A1
Adelaide Rd IP4 ....18 D6
Adelaide St CO12 ....90 F5
Admiral Rd IP8 ....36 E8
Admirals Wlk
Chelmsford CM1 ....204 F3
Wivenhoe CO7 ....164 B8
Aetheric Rd CM7 ....127 E3
Affleck Rd CO4 ....136 E7
Agar Rd 9 CO14 ....171 C8
Agar Road App 10 CO14 171 C8
Agate Rd CO15 ....188 F2
Agincourt Rd CO15 ....188 D4
Agricultural/Domestic Mus★ CM9 ....211 E7
Ainger Rd CO12 ....90 E2
Aingers Green Rd CO7 .167 A5
Ainslie Rd IP1 ....17 A6
Aire Wlk CM8 ....176 E2
Airey Hos CO10 ....11 D1
Aisne Rd CO2 ....135 D4
Ajax Cl CM7 ....128 B5
Akersloot Pl CO5 ....201 C6
Alamein Rd
Chelmsford CM1 ....204 F6
Colchester CO2 ....135 C2
Alan Dr CO16 ....168 D1
Alan Hasler Ho CM6 ....150 D7
Alan Rd Ipswich IP3 ....17 F4
Witham CM8 ....176 E1
Alan Way CO3 ....134 F4
Alanbrooke Rd CO2 ....136 D2
Albany Chase CO15 ....189 B4
Albany Cl
Chelmsford CM1 ....204 E5
West Bergholt CO6 ....108 E4
Albany Gdns E CO15 ....189 B3
Albany Gdns W CO15 ....189 B3
Albany Rd CO6 ....108 E4
Albany The IP4 ....17 E8
Albany Villas IP11 ....221 D3
Albemarle Gdns CM7 ....128 C5
Albemarle Link CM2 ....205 F8
Albemarle St CO12 ....91 D5
Albert Cotts CO7 ....60 C2
Albert Gdns
Clacton-on-S CO15 ....189 B3
Coggeshall CO6 ....131 A2
Albert Ho IP2 ....17 B4
Albert Pl CO6 ....131 A2
Albert Rd Braintree CM7 .128 A3
Brightlingsea CO7 ....186 A6
Witham CM8 ....177 A3
Albert St Colchester CO1 .135 E8
Harwich CO12 ....91 D5
Albert Wlk IP11 ....221 E4
Albertine Cl CO3 ....134 C6
Albion Ct CM2 ....205 B1
Albion Gr CO2 ....136 A5
Albion Hill IP4 ....17 F7
Albion St CO5 ....164 A8
Albra Mead CM2 ....206 B4
Albrighton Croft CO4 ....110 C4
Alconbury CM23 ....119 B1
Alcorns The CM24 ....119 E7
Alde Rd CB9 ....9 A8
Aldeburgh Cl
Clacton-on-S CO16 ....188 B4
Haverhill CB9 ....8 E7
Aldeburgh Gdns CO4 ....110 B4
Aldeburgh Way CM1 ....205 D5
Alder Cl CM23 ....145 D4
Alder Dr CM2 ....216 B6
Alder Way CO10 ....33 F8
Alder Wlk CM8 ....177 B4
Alderbury Lea CM3 ....218 F1
Alderbury Rd CM24 ....119 E8
Aldercar Rd CO6 ....133 F1
Alderford St CO9 ....75 E8
Alderlee IP2 ....36 F8
Alderman Blaxhill Sch CO2 ....135 B3
Alderman Howe Lodge CO4 ....110 B4
Alderman Rd IP1 ....17 B5
Alderton Cl CM6 ....152 C6
Alderton Rd CO4 ....136 C8
Aldham Ct 18 CB9 ....8 E7
Aldon Cl CO12 ....90 C1
Aldous Cl CO7 ....59 C3
Aldridge Cl CM2 ....206 A4
Aldringham Mews IP11 221 B5
Alec Hunter High Sch CM7 ....128 C1
Alec Kay Ct CO2 ....135 C2
Aletha Farm Pl CO9 ....29 D6
Alexander Ct 1 CM1 ....205 E7
Alexander Mews CM2 ....217 D2
Alexander Rd CM7 ....127 E4
Alexandra Ave CO5 ....201 E6
Alexandra Dr CO7 ....137 C3
Alexandra Rd
Clacton-on-S CO15 ....188 F3
Colchester CO3 ....135 E6
Felixstowe IP11 ....221 C6
Harwich CO12 ....91 D5
Ipswich IP4 ....17 E6
Sible Hedingham CO9 ....51 D1
Sudbury CO10 ....34 A7
Weeley CO16 ....140 F1
Alexandra St CO12 ....91 D5
Alexandra Terr 9 CO3 ....135 E6
Alf Eounder Cl CO4 ....136 E6
Alfells Rd CO7 ....137 F6
Alfred Terr CO14 ....171 C8
Alfreg Rd CM8 ....194 D8
Alienor Ave CM7 ....72 B1
All Hallows Ct IP3 ....18 A1
All Saints Ave CO3 ....135 A4
All Saints CE Prim Sch
Bishop's Stortford CM23 .146 B8
Great Oakley CO12 ....116 C3
Harwich CO12 ....90 F3
All Saints Cl
Bishop's Stortford CM23 .146 A8
Chelmsford CM1 ....205 E4
All Saints Maldon CE Prim Sch CM9 ....209 E2
All Saints' Rd IP1 ....17 A8
Allectus Way CM8 ....194 D8
Allen Cotts CO6 ....106 E5
Allen Way
Chelmsford CM2 ....206 B4
Point Clear B CO16 ....186 A3
Allenby Rd IP2 ....16 F6
Allendale Dr CO6 ....133 D4
Allens Cl CM3 ....192 F1
Alleyne Way CO15 ....203 G8
Allfields CO12 ....91 A2
Allington Cl IP4 ....17 F7
Allington Wlk CB9 ....8 E8
Alma Dr CM1 ....205 A2
Alma Sq 4 CO11 ....86 D4
Alma St CO7 ....164 B8
Almond Cl
Clacton-on-S CO15 ....188 C3
Tiptree CO5 ....179 C6
Wivenhoe CO7 ....137 C2
Almond Way CO4 ....136 E8
Almondhayes IP2 ....17 B3
Almshouses CO7 ....164 B8
Alnesbourn Cres IP3 ....38 D7
Alpe St IP1 ....17 B7
Alpha Cl CM7 ....128 A2
Alpha Pl
4 Bishop's Stortford CM23 ....145 F8
2 Saffron Walden CB11 ....22 E1
Alpha Rd CO16 ....186 B3
Alphamstone Rd CO8 ....55 B4
Alport Ave CO2 ....135 C4
Alresford Prim Sch CO7 165 B7
Alresford Rd CO7 ....164 E8
Alresford Sta CO7 ....165 A8
Alsa Bsns Pk CM24 ....93 F1
Alsa Gdns CM22 ....94 C2
Alsa Leys CM22 ....94 C2
Alsa St CM24 ....93 F1
Alston Cres CO10 ....2 E6
Alston Rd IP3 ....17 F4
Alstone Ct IP3 ....18 D1
Altbarn Cl CO4 ....110 C5
Altbarn Rd CO2 ....136 D5
Alton Dr CO3 ....135 B6
Alton Hall La IP9 ....61 F3
Alton Park Jun Sch CO15 ....188 D2
Alton Park La CO15 ....188 B1
Alton Park Rd CO15 ....188 D3
Alton Rd CO15 ....188 C1
Alton Water (Resr)★ IP9 62 A4
Alton Water Visitor Ctr★ IP9 ....62 B3
Aluf Cl CM8 ....194 E8
Alverton Cl CM77 ....154 B6
Alverton Way CO4 ....110 B3
Alvis Ave CO15 ....203 E6
Alyssum Cl CM1 ....206 A6
Alyssum Wlk CO4 ....136 D8
Amberley Cl CO7 ....137 D1
Ambleside Ct CO15 ....189 A3
Ambridge Rd CO6 ....130 E3
Ambrose Ave CO3 ....134 F4
Ambrose Ct CO6 ....133 D4
Ambross Ho CO2 ....135 D2
Amcotes Pl CM2 ....216 C8
Amerells Rd CO16 ....168 C4
America Rd CO6 ....105 C2
America St CM9 ....210 A2
Amos Hill CO10 ....54 B8
Amoss Rd CM2 ....216 F8
Ancaster Rd IP2 ....17 B4
Anchor Cvn Camp CO16 168 D2
Anchor End CO11 ....87 A4
Anchor Hill CO7 ....164 B7
Anchor Ho CO2 ....135 E2
Anchor La Dedham CO7 ....85 A4
Heybridge CM9 ....210 A5
New Mistley CO11 ....87 A4
Anchor Rd
Clacton-on-S CO15 ....188 E3
Tiptree CO5 ....179 C4
Anchor St
Bishop's Stortford CM23 .146 A6
Chelmsford CM2 ....205 B1
Anchorage Hill CM9 ....210 A3
Anderson Ave CM1 ....204 F5
Anderson Cl CM23 ....92 F2
Andover Cl CO15 ....189 A6
Andrew Cl Braintree CM7 127 F5
Felixstowe IP11 ....221 C3
Andrews Farm La CM6 .123 C8
Andrews Pl CM1 ....204 F3
Andros Cl IP3 ....38 A8
Anemone Ct CO4 ....109 C2
Angel La Glemsford CO10 ....2 B4
Great Dunmow CM6 ....150 D8
18 Ipswich IP4 ....17 D5
Angelgate CO12 ....91 E6
Angelgate Cotts CO12 ....91 E6
Angle Side CM7 ....128 B2
Anglefield CO15 ....188 F2
Anglesea Rd Ipswich IP1 .17 B7
Wivenhoe CO7 ....164 C8
Anglesey Cl CM23 ....145 C7
Anglia Cl CO2 ....135 B3
Anglia Poly Univ
Chelmsford CM1 ....205 B2
Chelmsford CM1 ....205 B4
Anglia Way CM7 ....128 B2
Anita Cl E IP2 ....16 E5
Anita Cl W IP2 ....16 E5
Anjou Gn CM1 ....206 A7
Ann Coles Cl CB9 ....27 C6
Ann St IP1 ....17 B7
Annbrook Rd IP2 ....16 E1
Anne Cl CO7 ....185 F6
Anne St IP11 ....221 C3
Annonay Wlk 7 CM2 ....205 C2
Ansgar Rd CB11 ....43 E7
Anson Cl CO12 ....91 A2
Anson Way CM7 ....128 C4
Anthony Cl CO4 ....110 D2
Antonia Cl CB9 ....9 E7
Antonio Wlk CO4 ....136 F7
Antonius Way CO4 ....110 B6
Anvil Way CM1 ....205 E8
Anzani Ave IP11 ....221 A4
Anzio Cres CO2 ....135 C3
Apollo Ho IP2 ....16 D1
Apollo Mews CO2 ....135 C1
Apple Tree Cl CO9 ....77 A2
Apple Way CM2 ....216 D6
Appleby Cl IP2 ....16 D1
Appleton Fields CM23 ....145 E4
Appletree Cl CM77 ....155 F5
Appletree Wlk CM7 ....128 A1
Approach The CO15 ....203 G8
Aprils View CO15 ....203 D6
Apsley Cl CM23 ....145 F4
Apsley Ct 3 IP1 ....17 A7
Apton Ct CM23 ....145 F7
Apton Fields 7 CM23 ....145 F6
Apton Rd CM23 ....145 F7
Aquiline Ho CO15 ....203 J8
Aragon Cl CO15 ....203 F8
Aragon Rd
Great Leighs CM3 ....173 F7
Haverhill CB9 ....8 D6
Arakan Cl CO2 ....135 B1
Arbour La
Chelmsford CM1 ....205 D4
Wickham Bishops CM8 ....195 F5
Arbour Way CO4 ....110 C4
Arbutus Cl CM2 ....216 B6
Arcade St 15 IP1 ....17 C6
Arcade The CO15 ....188 F2
Archangel Gdns IP2 ....16 E4
Archer Cres CO5 ....179 E5
Archers Way CM2 ....216 C2
Archery Fields CO15 ....189 A5
Arden Cl CO4 ....110 C3
Arderne Cl CO12 ....90 F2
Ardleigh Ct CO7 ....111 E8
Ardleigh Rd Dedham CO7 .84 D3
Great Bromley CO7 ....112 B4
Little Bromley CO11 ....112 E5
Argents La CO3 ....108 C2
Argyle Ct CO5 ....158 C2
Argyle Rd CO16 ....141 F2
Argyle St IP4 ....17 D6
Argyll Ct 10 CB9 ....8 F7
Argyll Rd CM2 ....206 A5
Ariel Cl CO4 ....136 F7
Arkwright Rd IP2 ....16 E7
Arlesford Ct CO4 ....136 F4
Armidale Wlk CO2 ....136 A2
Armiger Way CM8 ....177 B2
Armond Rd CM8 ....176 F3
Armonde Cl CM3 ....192 E1
Armourers Cl CM23 ....145 B4
Armoury Rd CO6 ....108 F4
Armstrong Cl CM3 ....218 F8
Armstrong Way CO9 ....30 A2
Arnhem Gr CM7 ....127 E5
Arnhem Rd CM1 ....204 E6
Arnold Dr CO4 ....136 E6
Arnold Ho CM2 ....205 A1
Arnold Rd CO15 ....188 D1
Arnold Villas CO5 ....179 C6
Arnold Way CM2 ....216 C3
Arnstones Cl CO4 ....136 C8
ARP Shelter Mus★ IP4 ....17 F5
Arras Rd CO2 ....135 D3
Arras Sq 12 IP1 ....17 C6
Arrow Rd CO4 ....136 F7
Arthur Ct CM1 ....204 F5
Arthur St 5 CO2 ....135 F6
Arthur's Terr IP4 ....17 E6
Arthy Cl CM3 ....194 A4
Artillery Dr CO12 ....90 D1
Artillery St CO1 ....136 B6
Arun Cl CM1 ....205 C5
Arundel Way IP3 ....18 E3
Arundel Wlk 1 CB9 ....8 E8
Arwela Rd IP11 ....221 D2
Asbury Cl CO4 ....136 D8
Asbury Dr CO6 ....132 F3
Ascot Cl CM23 ....146 C8
Ascot Dr Felixstowe IP11 221 C6
Ipswich IP3 ....18 B4
Ascot Gdns CO3 ....134 E7
Ascot Mews CO15 ....189 C5
Ash Bglws CM7 ....127 E3
Ash Cl Brightlingsea CO7 .185 E7
Clacton-on-S CO15 ....188 C3
Hatfield Peverel CM3 ....194 A4
Ipswich IP3 ....18 F1
Ash Ct CO12 ....90 E2
Ash Fall CM8 ....177 A5
Ash Gn CB10 ....3 D1
Ash Gr Blackheath CO2 .163 A8
Capel St M IP9 ....35 A2
Chelmsford CM2 ....216 D7
Great Bromley CO7 ....139 A6
Great Cornard CO10 ....34 C5
Great Dunmow CM6 ....150 D7
Heybridge CM9 ....210 C6
Wivenhoe CO7 ....137 C3
Ash Ground Cl CO11 ....86 D8
Ash Ho IP2 ....16 D2
Ash Rd CO7 ....165 B8
Ash Rise CO9 ....103 F8
Ash Tree Cl CM1 ....204 F2
Ash Tree Cnr CM3 ....191 B6
Ash Tree Cres CM1 ....204 F2
Ash Way CO3 ....134 F3
Ashby Rd CM8 ....195 A7
Ashby Rise CM23 ....119 B1
Ashdale CM23 ....145 D4
Ashdon Prim Sch CB10 ....6 B1
Ashdon Rd Ashdon CB10 ....24 E3
Saffron Walden CB10 ....23 C3
Ashdon Road Commercial Ctr CB10 ....23 A3
Ashdown Cl CM77 ....154 B8
Ashdown Way
Colchester CO4 ....136 D7
Ipswich IP3 ....18 D3
Ashen Cl CO10 ....11 D1
Ashen Hill CO10 ....11 C2
Ashen La CO10 ....11 C3
Ashen Rd Ashen CO10 ....12 A1
Clare CO10 ....12 B5
Ridgewell CO9 ....29 B8
Ashenden IP11 ....221 E4
Ashes Cl CO14 ....170 F8
Ashes Rd CM77 ....155 F7
Ashfield Cl CM6 ....123 C1
Ashfield Ct IP4 ....18 A6
Ashfield Farm Rd CM9 .208 D8
Ashford Rd CM1 ....204 E2
Ashlea Cl CB9 ....9 B6
Ashlea Rd CB9 ....9 B6
Ashley Ct CO12 ....91 B3
Ashley Gdns CO3 ....135 C6
Ashley Rd CO12 ....91 B3
Ashley St IP2 ....17 C4
Ashlong Gr CO9 ....76 E3
Ashlyn's Rd CO13 ....170 E4
Ashmere Gr IP4 ....17 F6
Ashmere Rise CO10 ....34 A8
Ashmole Dr CO13 ....170 F6
Ashpole Rd CM7 ....102 B1
Ashstead Cl CO16 ....188 B6
Ashton Cl IP2 ....16 C2
Ashton Pl CM2 ....206 A3
Ashurst Cl CO5 ....163 F8
Ashurst Dr CM1 ....205 D7
Ashwells Mdw CO6 ....105 B6
Ashwin Ave CO6 ....133 D4
Askins Rd CO7 ....59 C3
Aspen Way
3 Colchester CO4 ....136 D8
Little Oakley CO12 ....117 B7
Aspens The CM23 ....119 B3
Aspin Mews CB10 ....22 E3
Asquith Dr CO4 ....110 C5
Astell Ct CO13 ....170 F4
Aster Cl
Bishop's Stortford CM23 .145 D6
4 Chelmsford CM1 ....205 F6
Clacton-on-S CO16 ....188 C4
Aster Rd IP2 ....16 E4
Astley Rd CO15 ....188 D3
Ataka Rd IP11 ....221 D6
Athelstan Rd CO3 ....135 C5
Atherton Rd IP2 ....16 D2
Atholl Rd CM2 ....205 F5
Atlantic Sq CM8 ....177 A3
Atlas Bglws CO6 ....105 A6
Atlas Ct CO6 ....105 A7
Atlas Ho 3 IP4 ....17 E6
Atlas Rd CO6 ....104 F7
Attlee Gdns 7 CO1 ....136 A6
Attwood Cl CO4 ....110 B5
Attwoods Cl CM2 ....216 C3
Aubrey Cl CM1 ....205 B7
Auckland Cl CM1 ....204 E5
Audley Cl CM77 ....154 B7
Audley End★ CB11 ....22 B1
Audley End Miniature Rly★ CB11 ....43 A8
Audley End Rd CB11 ....43 C8
Audley End Sta CB11 ....42 F5
Audley Rd
Colchester CO3 ....135 C5
Great Leighs CM3 ....173 F7
Saffron Walden CB11 ....22 E1
Audley Way CO13 ....171 B6
Audrey Gdns CM23 ....145 F4
Audries Est CO14 ....171 A8
Augusta Cl IP3 ....38 E7
Augustine Way CM3 ....218 F2
Augustus Cl
Colchester CO4 ....110 B6
Haverhill CB9 ....9 D7
Augustus Way CM8 ....194 E8
Austen Cl CM7 ....155 A8
Austin Ave CO15 ....203 E6
Austin St IP2 ....17 C4
Auton Croft CB11 ....43 D7
Autoway CO4 ....110 C5
Autumn Cl CO16 ....188 C5
Aveley Way CM9 ....220 F8
Aveline Rd CO7 ....111 E7
Avenue Pl CM23 ....146 A6
Avenue Rd
Bishop's Stortford CM23 .146 B6
Chelmsford CM2 ....216 D7
Witham CM8 ....177 A3
Avenue The
Braintree CM7 ....127 F3
Clacton-on-S CO15 ....189 B7
Colchester CO3 ....135 C6
Danbury CM3 ....218 F7
Great Braxted CM8 ....178 A3
Great Dunmow CM6 ....150 E8
Great Oakley CO12 ....116 B3
Ipswich IP1 ....17 C8
Trimley St M IP11 ....221 A7
Washbrook IP8 ....35 F7
West Bergholt CO6 ....108 D3
Witham CM8 ....177 A2
Wivenhoe CO7 ....137 B1
Avignon Cl CO2 ....136 B4
Avila Chase CM2 ....216 B1
Avocet Cl
Frinton-on-S CO13 ....170 E6
Kelvedon CO5 ....158 D2
West Mersea CO5 ....201 D7
Avocet Ct IP11 ....221 D2
Avocet Way CM9 ....210 C5
Avon Rd CM1 ....204 C5
Avon Way CO4 ....136 F6
Avon Way Ho CO4 ....136 F6
Avon Wlk CM8 ....176 E3
Avondale Ho CO15 ....189 A3
Avondale Rd
Clacton-on-S CO15 ....189 A3
Ipswich IP3 ....18 A2

Aylesbury Dr
Great Notley CM77 ......154 C5
Holland-on-S CO15 ...189 F6
Ayletts CM1 ....191 B3
Ayloffe Rd CO4 ....110 C1
Aynsworth Ave CM23 ...119 B2
Azalea Ct
8 Chelmsford CM1 ....205 F6
Colchester CO4 ....136 D8
Azalea Way CO16 ......188 C4

B

Back Hamlet IP3 ....17 E5
Back Hill Hadstock CB1 ...5 B6
Holbrook IP9 ....62 E4
Back La Broomfield CM1 .191 D1
Colchester CO3 ....134 E7
Felixstowe IP11 ......221 D5
Ford End CM3 ....172 B6
Great Oakley CO12 ...116 C4
Ickleton CB10 ....3 A3
Little Waltham CM3 ...191 C4
Ramsey CO12 ....90 A1
Stisted CM7 ....129 C7
Tattingstone IP9 ......61 C6
Thaxted CM6 ....69 F3
Washbrook IP8 ....35 E8
Wickham Bishops CM8 .195 F6
Back La E CO7 ....139 A6
Back La W CO7 ....138 F7
Back Rd Ardleigh CO7 ..112 B5
Tollesbury CM9 ....199 C4
Writtle CM1 ....204 A1
Back Waterside La CO7 .185 F5
Backnang Sq 1 CM2 ..205 C2
**Backwardens Nature
Reserve★** CM3 ....218 E5
Backwardens Nature Trail★
CM3 ....218 E4
Bacon's La CO6 ....106 C3
Bacton Lodge IP11 ....221 D3
Bacton Rd IP11 ....221 D3
Baddow Ct CM2 ....217 A6
Baddow Hall Ave CM2 .217 A7
Baddow Hall Cres CM2 .217 B7
Baddow Hall Jun & Inf Sch
CM2 ....217 A6
Baddow Place Ave CM2 217 A6
Baddow Rd
Chelmsford CM2 ......205 C1
Great Baddow CM2 ...216 E7
Baden Powell Dr CO3 ..135 A4
Bader Cl IP3 ....18 C2
Badger Gr CM7 ....128 B3
Badgers CM23 ....145 E5
Badgers Bank IP2 ......16 E1
Badgers Cl CM2 ....216 B1
Badgers Gn CO6 ....132 E3
Badgers Gr CO6 ....82 B1
Badgers Holt CO3 .....134 D6
Badley Hall Rd CO7 ...112 F2
Badminton Rd CO15 ...203 G7
Badshah Ave IP3 ....18 B3
Bagshaw Rd CO12 ......91 D4
Bailey Bridge Rd CM7 .127 D5
Bailey Cl Haverhill CB9 ...9 D7
Ipswich IP2 ....16 E6
Bailey Dale CO3 ....134 C4
Bailey La CO10 ....12 C7
Bainbridge Dr CO5 ....179 D4
Baines Cl CO3 ....135 A5
Baird Cl IP2 ....16 F7
Baker Ave CM3 ....194 A3
Baker Mews CM9 ......210 A2
Baker Rd IP9 ....91 A8
Baker St CM2 ....205 A1
Baker's La
Colchester CO4 ....109 A2
Great Notley CM77 ...154 D6
Tolleshunt Major CM9 .197 D4
Baker's Rd CO10 ....12 F2
Bakers Ct
6 Bishop's Stortford
CM23 ....146 A7
Colchester CO1 ......109 E1
Bakers La Danbury CM3 .218 E7
Felsted CM6 ....152 C4
Bakers Mead CM3 .....190 F7
Bakery Ct CM24 ....119 D6
Baldry Cl IP8 ....16 C1
Baldwin's La CO6 .....131 E8
Bale Cl CO3 ....134 E4
Balfe Ct CO4 ....136 E6
Balkerne Gdns CO1 ...135 E7
Balkerne Hill CO3 .....135 E7
Balkerne Pas CO1 ....135 E7
Ball Alley 3 CO1 .....135 F7
Ball La Abberton CO2 ..162 F5
Blackheath CO2 ......163 B5
Ball's Chace CO8 ......79 F2
Ball's Chase CO9 .....76 F1
Ballast Quay Rd
Fingringhoe CO5 ......164 B6
Wivenhoe CO7 ....137 D1
Ballingdon Gr CO10 ....33 D5
Ballingdon Hill CO10 ...33 C5
Ballingdon Hill Ind Est
CO10 ....33 D6
Ballingdon St CO10 ....33 D6
Ballingdon Trad Est
CO10 ....33 C6
Balmoral Ave CO15 ...188 D3
Balmoral Cl IP2 ....16 F1
Balmoral Ct CM2 ......205 C2
Balmoral Dr CB9 ....8 E8
Balton Way CO12 ....90 F2
Bangs Cl CB1 ....7 A7
Banham Dr CO10 ....33 F8
Banister Cl CO16 ......188 C5
Bank Bldgs 13 CO10 ...33 E7
Bank Pas CO1 ....135 E7
Bank Rd IP4 ....17 E6
Bank St CM7 ....127 F3
Bankart La CM2 ......205 F4
Banks Ct CM6 ....150 D8
Bannister Green Villas
CM6 ....152 E6
Banters La CM3 ....154 B1
Bantock Way CM8 .....194 F7
Bantoft Terr IP3 ....18 C2
Barbary Lodge CM2 ...205 A2
Barbel Rd CO4 ....110 F1
Barbour Gdns CO2 ....134 F2
Barbrook La CO5 ......179 D6
Barbrook Way CM3 ...218 E1
Barclay CM7 ....217 A6
Bardell Cl CM1 ....204 F6
Bardfield Ctr CM7 ......72 B1
Bardfield Rd
Bardfield Saling CM7 ...99 F1
Colchester CO2 ......136 A1
Thaxted CM6 ....70 D2
Bardfield Way CO13 ...170 F6
Barfield Rd CO5 ......201 C6
Bargate La CO7 ....85 C3
Baring-Gould Cotts
CO5 ....184 D1
Barker Cl Ipswich IP2 ...16 D5
Lawford CO11 ....86 B4
Steeple Bumpstead CB9 ..27 B6
Barker Rd CO10 ....15 E2
Barkers Terr CO7 ....85 A5
Barkis Cl CM1 ....204 D7
Barkstead Rd CO4 ....110 C1
Barlee Cl CB11 ....65 C3
Barley Cl CB11 ....22 D1
Barley Fields CM8 .....177 A1
Barley Hills CM23 .....145 E4
Barley Ho CO10 ....15 B5
Barley Mead CM3 .....219 B6
Barley Way CO3 ......134 C5
Barlow Rd CO11 ......112 F4
Barlow Road Cotts CB10 ..6 B2
Barlow's Reach CM2 ..206 A4
Barn Fields CO3 ......134 C6
Barn Gn CM1 ....205 E8
Barn Hall Ave CO2 ...136 C4
Barn La CO11 ....112 F7
Barn Mead CM7 ......128 D2
Barn View Rd CO6 ....131 A1
Barnaby Rudge CM1 ..204 F7
Barnard Cl CB11 ......66 F8
Barnard Rd CM2 ......216 C2
Barnardiston Rd CO4 ..110 C1
Barnardiston Way CM8 .176 F3
Barnards Field CM6 ....70 B2
Barnards Yd CB10 .....22 D1
Barnby Cl IP9 ....8 C8
Barncroft Cl CO4 .....110 B3
Barnes Farm Jun & Inf Schs
CM2 ....206 A3
Barnes Mill Rd CM2 ..205 F2
Barnfield Capel St M IP9 ..35 B1
Feering CO5 ....158 D3
Felixstowe IP11 ......221 B6
Manningtree CO11 .....86 D4
Barnfield Cotts CM1 ...210 B5
Barnfield Mews CM1 ..205 A6
Barnfield Pl CM8 ......176 F1
Barnfield Rd CO6 .....109 C6
Barnfields CO5 ....163 F5
Barnhall Rd CM9 ......180 D2
Barnham Pl IP5 ....18 F6
Barnston Gn CM6 .....151 B4
Baron's Ct 5 CB9 ......8 E7
Baron's La CM3,CM9 ...220 E1
Baronia Croft CO4 ....110 C3
Barons The CM23 .....145 D5
Baronswood Way CO2 .135 D2
Barr Cl CO7 ....137 C1
Barrack Cnr 5 IP1 .....17 B6
Barrack La
Great Waltham CM3 ..190 E8
Harwich CO12 ....91 E4
Ipswich IP1 ....17 B6
Barrack Sq 10 CM2 ...205 B2
Barrack St
Bradfield CO11 ....114 D8
Colchester CO1 ......136 B6
Barrel Cl CO7 ....139 A3
Barrells Down Rd CM23 .118 E1
Barrett La 5 CM23 ....145 F7
Barrington Cl
Great Baddow CM2 ...217 A6
Little Clacton CO16 ...168 C2
Barrington Gdns CO15 .189 C5
Barrington Rd CO2 ....136 A5
Barrow Chase CM2 ....206 B4
Barrow Marsh CM9 ...211 A4
Barryfields CM7 ......100 E2
Bartholomew Cl CB10 ...3 E2
Bartholomew Rd 8
CM23 ....145 F6
Bartholomew St IP4 ...17 F6
Bartletts CB10 ....22 D1
Bartlow Rd
Castle Camps CB1 ......7 D4
Hadstock CB1 ....5 D7
Barton Cl IP2 ....16 E2
Barton Rd IP11 ....221 F4
Bartram Ave N CM7 ...128 C3
Bartram Ave S CM7 ...128 C3
Barwell Way CM8 .....177 B2
Basbow La 2 CM23 ...145 F7
Basin Rd CM9 ....210 E3
Bassetts CM3,CM9 ....208 A4
Bassingbourn Rd CM24 .121 A3
Bassingham Cres CO5 .179 F5
Bateman Rd CO7 ......185 E8
Bateman's Rd CO16 ...168 B4
Bates Rd CM9 ....210 B4
Bath Ct CB9 ....8 F6
Bath Hill IP11 ....221 F4
Bath Rd IP11 ....221 F4
Bath St Ipswich IP2 ...17 D3
Wivenhoe CO7 ....164 B8
Bathurst Cl 11 CO2 ...136 A1
Battery La IP9 ....91 B8
Battisford Dr CO16 ...188 A4
Battlesbrook Rd CO2 ..136 D2
Bawden Way CM2 .....216 D8
Bawdsey Cl CO16 .....188 B3
Bawn Cl CM7 ....128 A4
Bawtree Way CO3 ....135 A5
Baxters CM3 ....219 A7
Bay Rd CO12 ....91 D4
Bay View Cres
Harwich CO12 ....90 C1
Little Oakley CO12 ...117 C8
Bayard Ave CO7 ......185 F7
Bayley St CO9 ....51 F4
Baynard Ave CM6 .....151 E7
Baynard's Prim Sch
CO5 ....179 B7
Baynards Cres CO13 ..170 E6
Bayning Ho CO7 ......139 F8
Bays Dr CO9 ....76 E2
Baytree Cl CO11 ......115 C5
Baytree Ct CM77 .....126 F2
Beach App CO16 ......203 B6
Beach Cres CO15 .....203 F6
Beach Rd
Clacton-on-S CO15 ...188 F2
Harwich CO12 ....91 C2
Point Clear B CO16 ...202 D6
St Osyth CO16 ....187 B2
West Mersea CO5 ....201 C5
Beach Rd W IP11 .....221 C1
Beach Station Rd IP11 .221 C1
Beach's Dr CM1 ......204 D3
Beachcroft Ave CO13 .170 D6
Beacon Cl CO7 ....185 E6
Beacon End Ctyd CO3 .134 C6
Beacon Field IP11 ....221 C5
Beacon Hill Maldon CM9 .209 E2
Wickham Bishops CM8 .196 A6
Beacon Hill Ave CO12 ..91 E4
Beacon Hill Sch IP2 ....16 F3
Beacon Hts CO16 .....186 B2
Beacon Way
Colchester CO3 ......134 C6
Point Clear B CO16 ...186 B2
Beaconsfield Cl CO10 ..33 E8
Beaconsfield Ct 7 CB9 ..8 F7
Beaconsfield Rd
Clacton-on-S CO15 ...188 F3
Ipswich IP1 ....16 F7
Sudbury CO10 ....33 E8
Beadel Cl CM8 ....194 E8
Beadon Dr CM7 ......128 A1
Bear St CO6 ....56 A1
Beard's La CB11 ....41 A4
Beard's Terr CO6 ....131 A3
Beardsley Dr CM1 ....205 F7
Bearwalden Bsns Pk
CB11 ....42 F5
Beatrice Ave IP11 ....221 E5
Beatrice Cl IP3 ....18 A3
Beatrice Rd
Clacton-on-S CO15 ...188 E2
Walton-on-t-N CO14 ..144 D2
Beatty Gdns CM7 ....128 C4
Beatty Rd IP3 ....18 B2
Beauchamps Cl CM1 ..205 F8
Beaufort Ct 5 CB9 ......8 F7
Beaufort Gdns CM7 ...128 A4
Beaufort Rd CM2 .....206 A4
Beaufort St IP1 ....17 A7
Beaulieu Bvd CM1 ....206 A7
Beaumont Ave
Brightlingsea CO7 ....186 A7
Clacton-on-S CO15 ...188 D3
Beaumont Cl
Colchester CO4 ......109 F4
Walton-on-t-N CO14 ..170 F7
Beaumont Ct CB9 ......9 B6
Beaumont Hill CM6 ...123 D2
Beaumont Pk CM3 ....218 C6
Beaumont Pl CM7 ....128 B3
Beaumont Rd CO12 ...116 C2
Beaumont Vale CB9 ....9 B6
Beaumont Wlk CM1 ...204 D5
Beaver Cl CO3 ....134 E7
Beche Rd CO2 ....136 B5
Beck Rd CB11 ....22 D1
Becker Rd CO3 ....134 E4
Beckers Green Prim Sch
CM7 ....128 D2
Beckers Green Rd CM7 .128 D2
Becketts Ct CM1 .....205 A3
Becketts La IP7 ....57 D8
Beckford Rd CO11 .....87 A4
Beckingham Bsns Pk
CM9 ....197 D3
Beckingham Rd
Great Totham CM9 ...196 D5
Beckingham Rd continued
Tolleshunt D'arcy CM9 .198 C4
Beckingham St CM9 ..197 D3
Becontree Cl CO15 ...188 F8
Bedells Ave CM77 ....155 B5
Bedford Cl
Braintree CM7 ....128 B4
Tiptree CO5 ....179 D5
Bedford Ct 9 CB9 ......8 F7
Bedford Rd
Colchester CO4 ......109 F5
Holland-on-S CO15 ...189 D5
Bedford St IP1 ....17 B6
Bedwell Rd CM22 ......94 B3
Beech Ave Braintree CM7 127 F5
Halstead CO9 ....77 A2
Wivenhoe CO7 ....137 B1
Beech Cl Sproughton IP8 ..16 A6
Takeley CM22 ....148 C8
Beech Gn CM8 ....195 F5
Beech Gr
Fordham Heath CO3 ..107 F1
Haverhill CB9 ....8 F8
Ipswich IP3 ....17 F3
Little Oakley CO12 ...117 B7
Rushmere St A IP5 ....18 F7
Sible Hedingham CO9 .51 D1
Beech Hill CO3 ....135 A6
Beech Ho IP2 ....16 D2
Beech Rd
Great Cornard CO10 ...34 B6
Rivenhall CM8 ....177 B7
Rushmere St A IP5 ....18 F7
Beech Rise CM3 ......194 A3
Beeches Cl
Chelmsford CM1 .....204 E2
Saffron Walden CB11 ..43 C7
Beeches Rd
Chelmsford CM1 .....204 E2
Heybridge CM9 ....94 A2
Beeches The Ipswich IP3 .17 F4
Lawford CO11 ....86 C3
Wendens Ambo CB11 ..42 F5
Beechholm 2 IP4 ......17 E6
Beechlands CM23 .....145 F5
Beechwood Cl CO2 ...135 D2
Beehive Cl CO7 ....59 C3
Beehive Ct CO1 ......136 A6
Beehive La CM2 ......216 C5
Beehive Lane Prim Sch
CM2 ....216 C2
Beeleigh Chase CM9 ..209 D4
Beeleigh Cl CO2 ......136 A1
Beeleigh Link CM2 ....205 F3
Beeleigh Rd CM9 .....209 F3
Begonia Cl CM1 ......205 F6
Begonia Pl CO16 .....188 C4
Bekeswell La CM2 ....216 C2
Bekeswell Pl CM2 ....216 C2
Bel-Air Beach Cvn Pk
CO15 ....203 C6
Bel-Air Est CO16 .....203 A6
Belcham's La CB11 ....93 E8
Belchamp Rd CO9 .....30 B5
Belchamp St Paul CE Prim
Sch CO10 ....13 A1
Beldams Cl CO16 .....142 A1
Beldams Gate CM23 ..146 C6
Beldams La CM23 .....146 B5
Belgrave Cl
Chelmsford CM2 .....216 D7
Ipswich IP4 ....17 E8
Belgrave Ho 6 CM23 .146 B8
Bell Cl Colchester CO2 ..136 D2
Ipswich IP2 ....17 C4
Bell Coll CB11 ....43 E8
Bell Gn CO7 ....186 A7
Bell Hill Danbury CM3 .218 C7
Lamarsh CO8 ....55 C3
Bell La Great Bardfield CM7 72 A2
Ipswich IP2 ....17 C4
Nuthampstead SG8 ....39 B2
Panfield CM7 ....127 A7
Thaxted CM6 ....70 A3
Bell St CM2 ....216 F6
Bellamy Cl CO13 .....170 D6
Bellcroft CM8 ....177 A3
Belle Vue CM2 ....205 A1
Belle Vue Rd
Colchester CO1 ......109 E1
Ipswich IP4 ....17 F8
Sudbury CO10 ....33 F7
Wivenhoe CO7 ....137 C1
Bellevue Terr CO9 .....76 E2
Bellfield Ave CO7 ....186 A7
Bellfield Cl CO7 ......186 A8
Bellingham Bldgs CB10 ..22 D2
Bellingham Dr CO6 ...133 E5
Bellingham Pl CO5 ...158 C3
Bellmead CM1 ....205 B2
Bells Chase CM2 .....216 E6
Bells Cl CB11 ....43 E8
Bells Hill
Bishop's Stortford CM23 .145 E7
Bures CO8 ....80 A4
Bells La CO10 ....2 C1
Bells Rd CO10 ....31 F6
Belmans Ct CO2 ....91 A2
Belmer Rd CM24 .....120 D4
Belmonde Dr CM1 ....205 E7
Belmont Cl CM1 .....205 E7
Belmont Cres CO4 ....110 C3
Belmont Ct 6 CB9 .....8 F7
Belmont Hill CB11 .....43 A1
Belmont Pl CO1 ......136 C5
Belmont Rd IP2 ....16 C1
Belsay Ct CB9 ....8 D8
Belsize Ave CO15 ....203 D6
Belstead Ave IP2 ......17 B3
Belstead Rd IP2 ....17 A3
Belstead Sch IP8 ......16 C2
Belsteads Farm La CM3 191 E2
Belvawney Cl CM1 ....204 E6
Belvedere Cl CM3 ....218 F7
Belvedere Ct
Chelmsford CM2 .....215 F8
Maldon CM9 ....220 F8
Belvedere Pl CM9 ....220 F8
Belvedere Rd
Danbury CM3 ....218 F7
Ipswich IP4 ....17 F7
Belvoir Ct 4 CB9 ....8 E8
Bembridge Cl CO15 ...188 F8
Bemerton Ct CO13 ...170 B6
Bemerton Gdns CO13 .170 C6
Ben Sainty Ct CM8 ...177 A2
Benacre Rd IP3 ....18 A2
Bendalls Ct 13 CO11 ...86 D4
Bendlowes Rd CM7 ....72 C1
Benedict Dr CM1 .....204 E2
Benezet St IP1 ....17 B6
Benfield Way CM7 ....128 B2
Benhall Cl CO16 ......188 A4
Benhooks Ave CM23 ..145 E5
Benhooks Pl 1 CM23 .145 E5
Bennet Ct CO4 ....136 E6
Bennett Cl
Braintree CM7 ....155 A8
Walton-on-t-N CO14 ..171 A8
Bennett Rd IP1 ....16 D8
Bennett Way CM3 ....194 A4
Bennett's La CM6 .....151 E2
Benskins Cl CM23 .....92 A8
Bensusan Ct CO2 .....135 B3
Bent Hill IP11 ....221 E3
Bent La IP4 ....18 E8
Bentall Cl CO9 ....103 E8
Bentalls Complex The
CM9 ....210 B5
Bentfield End Cswy
CM24 ....119 D7
Bentfield Gdns CM24 ..119 D7
Bentfield Gn CM24 ...119 D8
Bentfield Prim Sch
CM24 ....119 D8
Bentfield Rd CM24 ...119 D7
Bentleigh Ct 5 CO1 ..136 D7
Bentley Ave CO15 ....203 D7
Bentley CE Prim Sch IP9 60 F7
Bentley Cl CM23 .....145 F5
Bentley Ct CO3 ....135 C7
Bentley La Belstead IP8 ..36 C6
Stutton IP9 ....61 E3
Bentley Rd
Little Bromley CO11 ..113 D3
Weeley Heath CO7,CO16 .167 E6
Witham CM8 ....194 E4
Benton Cl Cressing CM77 155 E6
Witham CM8 ....195 A7
Berberis Wlk 5 CO4 ..136 E7
Berbice La CM6 ......123 D2
Berechurch Hall Rd
CO2 ....162 D8
Berechurch Rd CO2 ...135 E2
Berefield Way 6 CO2 .136 A1
Bergamot Rd CB9 ......8 C8
Bergen Ct CM9 ......220 E8
Bergholt Rd
Brantham CO11 ....86 B7
Colchester CO4 ......109 D2
Beridge Rd CO9 ....76 D2
Beriffe Pl CO7 ....185 F7
Berkeley Cl IP4 ....17 E8
Berkeley Gdns CO5 ...163 F7
Berkeley Rd CO15 ....188 F5
Berkely Dr CM2 ....205 F2
Berkley Cl CO4 ....110 C4
Bermuda Rd IP3 ....38 E7
Bernard Cl CO13 .....170 E6
Bernard Cres IP3 ......18 B2
Berners End CM6 .....151 B4
Berners St IP1 ....17 B6
Bernside CM7 ....127 F2
Berrimans Cl CO4 ....136 D6
Berry Cl IP3 ....18 F1
Berryfield Cotts CO1 ..136 B7
Bertram Ave CO16 ...168 D1
Berwick Ave CM1 ....205 B7
Beryl Rd CO12 ....90 D1
Beslyns Rd CM7 ....72 A3
Betjeman Cl CM7 .....155 A8
Betony Wlk CB9 ....8 D8
Betts Green Rd CO10 .168 D5
Betty Cocker Gr CO10 ..34 B7
Betty Dent's Cnr CO10 .141 C5
Beverley Ave CO5 ....201 E7
Beverley Ct 5 IP4 .....17 D6
Beverley Dr CO13 ....170 E7
Beverley Rd
Colchester CO4 ......135 D6
Ipswich IP4 ....17 F8
Bevington Mews CM8 .177 B2
Bewick Ct CO9 ....51 E2
Bexhill Cl CO15 ......203 I8
Bexley Ave CO12 ......90 F1
Bibb Way IP1 ....17 A5
Bicknacre Rd CM3 ...218 A4
Bignells Croft CO4 ....110 C4
Bigods La CM6 ....123 D4
Bijou Ct CO5 ....179 D6
Bilberry End CB1 ....5 C7
Billers Chase CM1 ....206 A7
Billy's La CO7 ....58 D2
Bilsdale Cl CO4 ....110 C4
Bilton Rd CM1 ....204 F1

Binley Rd CM2 ....205 F2
Birch Ave
  Great Bentley CO7 ......166 E8
  Harwich CO12 ....91 B3
Birch Bsns Ctr CO2 ....161 A7
Birch CE Prim Sch CO2 161 A4
Birch Cl Braintree CM7 ..127 C2
  Brightlingsea CO7 ......185 E6
  Clacton-on-S CO15 ......188 C3
  Witham CM8 ....177 A4
Birch Dr Brantham CO11 ..60 D1
  Halstead CO9 ....77 A4
Birch Rd CO2 ....161 E5
Birch Rise CM8 ....195 E6
Birch St Birch CO2 .....161 A3
  Nayland CO6 ....56 A1
Birch Wood Cl CO5 ....201 D6
Birchalls CM24 ....119 E8
Birchanger CE Prim Sch
  CM23 ....119 D2
Birchanger Ind Est
  CM23 ....119 B2
Birchanger La CM23 ....119 D2
Birches The CO13 ......170 E6
Birches Wlk CM2 ....216 A2
Birchway CO2 ....161 A2
Birchwood CM23 ....119 D2
Birchwood Cl CO5 .....179 F5
Birchwood High Sch
  CM23 ....146 C8
Birchwood Rd
  Cock Clarks CM3 ....219 F2
  Dedham CO7 ....84 B3
  Langham CO4 ....84 A4
Birchwood Way CO5 ...179 F5
Bird La CO5 ....179 E4
Birdbrook Rd CO9 ......28 A3
Birdbush Ave CB11 .....43 D7
Birds Cl CB10 ....3 A3
Birk Beck CM1 ....205 C5
Birkdale Rise CM3 .....194 B4
Birkfield Cl IP2 ....17 A4
Birkfield Dr IP2 ....16 F2
Birkin Cl CO5 ....179 C3
Biscay Cl CB9 ....9 C7
Bishop Hall La CM1 ....205 B4
Bishop Mews IP8 ......16 B2
Bishop Rd
  Chelmsford CM1 ....205 B3
  Colchester CO2 ....135 A3
Bishop William Ward CE
  Prim Sch The CO6 ......109 B7
Bishop's Ave CM23 ....145 F3
Bishop's Cl 8 CB9 ......8 E8
Bishop's Ct 7 CB9 .....8 E8
Bishop's Hill IP3 ......17 E4
Bishop's La CO9 ....54 B3
Bishop's Stortford Bsns Ctr
  CM23 ....146 A6
Bishop's Stortford Coll
  CM23 ....145 E7
Bishop's Stortford High Sch
  The CM23 ....145 F4
Bishop's Stortford Mus★
  CM23 ....146 A6
Bishop's Stortford Sta
  CM23 ....146 A6
Bishops Ave CM7 ......128 B3
Bishops Court Gdns
  CM2 ....205 E4
Bishops Dr CO16 ......203 B6
Bishops Gdns CO16 ....203 A6
Bishops La CO5 ....179 C7
Bishops Park Coll CO16 188 A3
Bishops Park Way
  CM23 ....145 B7
Bishopsgarth IP3 ....17 F4
Bisley Cl CO16 ....188 B6
Bittern Cl Ipswich IP2 ...16 E3
  Kelvedon CO5 ....158 D2
Bixley Dr IP4 ....18 E5
Bixley La IP4 ....18 F5
Bixley Rd IP3 ....18 D3
Black Arches IP8 ....36 E8
Black Barns IP11 ......221 A4
Black Boy La CO11 .....89 A4
Black Bread Cl CM7 ...128 D3
Black Buoy Hill CO7 ...164 B7
Black Chapel La CM6 ..151 E1
Black Horse La IP1 .....17 C6
Black La CM7 ....71 C4
Blackberry Rd CO3 ....134 C4
Blackbrook Rd CO6 ....109 C1
Blackbushe CM23 ......119 C1
Blackdown Ave IP5 .....18 F6
Blackfriars CO10 ....33 D6
Blackfriars Ct 8 IP4 ...17 D5
Blackheath CO2 ....163 A8
Blackhouse La CO10 ...34 C3
Blacklands Cl CB11 ....43 D4
Blackley La
  Braintree CM3 ....153 F3
  Great Notley CM77 .....154 A4
Blacklock CM2 ....206 A3
Blackman Way CM8 ...177 A1
Blacksmith Cl CM1 ....205 E8
Blacksmith's Cnr CO6 .109 B8
Blacksmith's Cnr CO4 ..83 D4
Blacksmith's La CO12 ..90 F2
Blacksmiths Cl CM23 .145 B5
Blacksmiths Hill CO10 ..11 B4
Blacksmiths La
  Bulmer Tye CO10 ....32 F2
  Shudy Camps CB1 ....7 C6
  Wickham Bishops CM8 ..195 E5
Blackthorn Ave CO4 ...136 E7

Blackthorn Cl Ipswich IP3 18 E1
  Writtle CM1 ....204 A1
Blackthorn Rd
  Harwich CO12 ....90 F2
  Witham CM8 ....176 E4
Blackthorn Way CM9 ..180 A2
Blackwater Ave CO4 ...110 E1
Blackwater Cl
  Chelmsford CM1 ....205 C6
  Heybridge Basin CM9 ..210 E3
Blackwater Dr CO5 ....201 A6
Blackwater La CM8 ....195 B8
Blackwater Way CM7 ..128 A4
Blackwell Dr CM7 .....127 C4
Bladen Dr IP4 ....18 F5
Bladon Cl Braintree CM7 .127 E2
  Tiptree CO5 ....179 E5
Blaine Dr CO13 ....170 F7
Blair Cl
  Bishop's Stortford CM23 .145 C7
  Rushmere St A IP4 .....18 E5
Blair Par CB9 ....8 E8
Blake Cl CO11 ....86 B4
Blake Dr Braintree CM7 .128 C4
  Clacton-on-S CO16 ....188 D6
Blake Rd CM8 ....176 F1
Blamsters Cres CO9 ...103 D8
Blanchard Cl CO13 ....170 A7
Blanche St IP4 ....17 D6
Blandford Rd IP3 ......18 D3
Blaxhall Cl 17 CB9 ......8 E7
Blenheim Cl
  Bicknacre CM3 ....218 F2
  Braintree CM7 ....127 E2
  Brantham CO11 ....60 D1
Blenheim Ct
  Bishop's Stortford CM23 .145 C7
  Clacton-on-S CO15 ....188 D2
  4 Ipswich IP1 ....17 A7
Blenheim Dr CO2 .....163 A8
Blenheim Rd
  Clacton-on-S CO15 ....188 D2
  Ipswich IP1 ....17 A7
Blenheim Way CO5 ...179 F5
Blickling Cl IP2 ....17 B2
Blickling Rd CM77 ....154 C8
Blind La Easthorpe CO2 .160 B4
  Eight Ash G CO6 ......134 A8
  Goldhanger CM9 ....211 C2
  Howe Green CM2 ......217 F4
  Tolleshunt Knights CM9 .180 B1
Bliss Cl CM8 ....194 F7
Blithe Ct CO7 ....164 B8
Blofield Rd IP11 ....221 A4
Blois Meadows Bsns Ctr
  CB9 ....27 C8
Blois Rd
  Steeple Bumpstead CB9 ..27 D8
  Sturmer CB9 ....9 F1
Bloom Cl CO13 ....170 F6
Bloomfield Ave CO13 ..170 E7
Bloomfield Ho CM7 ...128 A3
Bloomfield St IP4 ......18 B6
Blooms Hall La CO10 ....2 F1
Blott Rise CM8 ....194 F8
Blue Mill La CM9 .....208 E4
Blue Mills Hill CM8 ...195 B7
Blue Rd CO5 ....179 C5
Bluebell Ave CO16 ....188 C4
  Witham CM8 ....176 E3
Bluebell Cl Ipswich IP2 ..16 E4
Bluebell Gn 5 CM1 ...205 E7
Bluebell Way CO4 ....109 C2
Bluebridge Cotts CO9 ..77 B1
Bluebridge Ind Est CO9 ..77 B1
Bluegate La IP9 ....60 B7
Bluehouse Ave CO16 ..188 A4
Bluestem Rd IP3 ....38 E8
Blundens The CO6 .....56 C6
Blunt's Hall Dr CM8 ..176 D1
Blunts Hall Rd CM8 ...176 D1
Blyford Rd CO16 ......188 A4
Blyford Way IP11 .....221 A4
Blyth Cl IP2 ....17 A1
Blyth's Mdw CM7 ....127 F3
Blyth's Way CM77 ....126 F3
Blythe La CO7 ....164 B8
Blythwood Gdns CM24 .119 D6
Boadicea Cotts CO8 ....79 F6
Boadicea Way CO2 ...135 C4
Boars Tye Rd CM8 ...156 D6
Boatman Ct IP8 ....36 E8
Bobbits La IP9 ....36 F8
Bobbits Way CO7 .....164 C8
Bober Ct CO2 ....163 B7
Bocking Church Street Prim
  Sch CM7 ....127 F3
Bocking End CM7 .....127 F3
Bocking Pl CM7 ....127 F3
Bocking's Gr CO16 ....188 B5
Bockings Elm Par CO16 188 B5
Bodiam Cl IP3 ....18 D4
Bodiam Rd IP3 ....18 D4
Bodiam Wlk 3 CB9 .....8 E8
Bodmin Rd CM1 ......205 D5
Bogmoor Rd SG8 ......39 A8
Bohun Ct CM3 ....173 F7
Bois Field Terr CO9 ....76 E2
Bois Hall Gdns CO9 ....76 F3
Boley Dr CO15 ....189 A4
Boley Rd CO6 ....106 A8
Boleyn Way
  Boreham CM3 ....192 F1
  Clacton-on-S CO15 ....203 F8
  Haverhill CB9 ....8 D7
Boleyns Ave CM7 .....127 F6
Bolford St CM6 ....69 C2
Bolingbroke Cl CM3 ..173 F7

Bolton La 1P4 ....17 D6
Bond St Chelmsford CM2 .205 C2
  Ipswich 1P4 ....17 D5
Bonham Cl CO15 ......189 A5
Bonington Chase CM1 .205 E6
Bonneting La CM23 ....92 B8
Bonnington Rd IP3 .....17 F1
Boone Pl CM8 ....177 A2
Boons Cl CM3 ....206 E8
Booth Ave CO4 ....136 C8
Borda Cl CM1 ....205 A5
Boreham Ind Est CM3 .192 F2
Boreham Prim Sch CM3 206 F8
Boreham Rd
  Great Leighs CM3 ......174 B7
  Little Waltham CM3 ....174 B2
Borehamgate CO10 .....33 F7
Borley Rd CO10 ....15 A4
Borough La CB11 ......43 D8
Borradale Ct CB9 ......27 B6
Borrowdale Ave IP4 ....17 B6
Boscawen Gdns CM7 .128 C4
Boscombe Ct CO15 ...189 F6
Boss Hall Bsns Pk IP1 ..16 E7
Boss Hall Rd IP1 ....16 E7
Bostock Rd IP2 ....17 C1
Boston Rd IP4 ....17 F7
Boswells Dr CM2 .....205 C2
Boswells Sch The CM1 205 D6
Botanical Way CO16 ..187 A3
Botany Dr CM7 ....128 D3
Botany La CO16 ......168 B5
Boucheries Pl CO5 ....159 D2
Bouchers Mead CM1 ..205 E7
Bouchiers Barn Visitors Ctr★
  CO6 ....130 D7
Boudicca Mews 5 CM2 205 B1
Boudicca Wlk CO7 ....137 C3
Boulton Cotts CM9 ...210 B5
Boundary Rd
  Bishop's Stortford CM23 .146 A5
  Colchester CO4 ....136 F4
  Sturmer CB9 ....9 D5
  Wivenhoe CO7 ....137 A4
Bounderby Gr CM1 ...204 E7
Bounstead Hill CO2 ...162 C5
Bounstead Rd CO2 ...162 D7
Bourchier Ave CM7 ..128 D5
Bourchier Way CO9 ..103 D8
Bourne Cl CO9 ....103 D8
Bourne Ct Braintree CM7 128 D1
  Colchester CO2 ....136 A4
Bourne Hill IP2 ....37 B7
Bourne Mill★ CO2 ...136 B4
Bourne Rd
  Colchester CO2 ....136 B4
  Haverhill CB9 ....9 B8
  West Bergholt CO6 ....108 C2
Bourne Terr IP2 ....37 B8
Bourne The CM23 ....146 A8
Bournebridge Hill CO9 .103 B6
Bournemouth Rd CO15 189 F6
Bouverie Rd CM2 .....216 B8
Bovills Way CO16 .....168 C1
Bovingdon Rd CM7 ...101 D2
Bowdens La CO6 ....80 F7
Bower Gdns CM9 .....209 F3
Bower Hall Dr CB9 .....27 B6
Bower Hall La CO5 ...183 F1
Bowers Cl CM8 ....156 F5
Bowes Rd CO7 ....137 C1
Bowland Dr IP8 ....16 C1
Bowling Cl 14 CM23 ..145 F6
Bowling Green Ct IP11 221 E4
Bowmans Pk CO9 ......51 E4
Bowsers La CB10 ....5 C3
Bowthorpe Cl IP1 ......17 B7
Box Mill La CO9 ....76 E3
Boxford Ct
  Felixstowe IP11 ....221 A4
  Haverhill CB9 ....8 E7
Boxhouse La CO7 ......84 C5
Boxted Ave CO16 .....188 C4
Boxted CE Prim Sch 82 F7
Boxted Church Rd CO6 ..82 C5
Boxted Rd
  Colchester CO4 ....109 E6
  Great Horkesley CO6 ...82 B5
Boxted Straight Rd CO4 .83 A5
Boyd Cl 1 CM23 ....146 B8
Boydell's Dairy Farm★
  CM7 ....100 E8
Boydin Cl CM8 ....194 E8
Boydlands IP9 ....35 A1
Boyes Croft CM6 .....123 D1
Boyles Ct CO2 ....163 B7
Boyton Rd IP3 ....18 B1
Boyton Vineyard★ CO10 .10 D5
Boyton's La CB10 ......26 A1
Boytons Acre CB11 ....43 D8
Bracken Way CO5 ....163 B2
Brackenbury Cl IP1 ....17 B8
Brackenden Dr CM1 ..205 D7
Brackenhayes Cl IP2 ...17 B3
Brackens The CO4 ....110 B3
Brackley Cl IP11 ......221 C5
Bracks La CO6 ....131 F7
Bradbrook Cotts CO6 .108 F4
Bradbury Dr CM7 .....127 D3
Braddy Ct CO5 ....158 C2
Bradfield Prim Sch CM1 87 E1
Bradfield Rd CO11 ....115 B7
Bradford St
  Braintree CM7 ....128 A4
  Chelmsford CM2 ....205 A1
Bradfords Ct CM7 ....128 A4
Brading Ave CO15 ....189 A7

Bradley Cl CM6 ....123 C2
Bradley Comm CM23 .119 C3
Bradley Mews 1 CB10 ..22 F2
Bradley St 7 IP2 ....17 C4
Bradwell Ct CM77 ....155 C8
Braemar Ave CM2 ....216 B8
Braemore Cl CO4 .....110 D3
Brain Rd CM8 ....176 E3
Brain Valley Ave CM77 155 B6
Braintree Cnr CO9 .....75 F6
Braintree Coll CM7 ...128 A5
Braintree Ent Ctr CM7 127 D5
Braintree Foyer The 3
  CM7 ....127 F2
Braintree Freeport Sta
  CM77 ....128 B1
Braintree Mus & Heritage
  Ctr★ CM7 ....127 F3
Braintree Rd
  Cressing CM77 ....155 E7
  Felsted CM6 ....152 C6
  Gosfield CO9 ....102 E5
  Great Bardfield CM7 ....72 B1
  Great Dunmow CM6 ...124 A1
  Shalford CM7 ....100 E6
  Terling CM3 ....174 E5
  Wethersfield CM7 ......73 D2
  Witham CM8 ....176 F4
Braintree Sta CM7 ....128 A2
Braintree Town FC CM7 128 C2
Braiswick CO4 ....109 C2
Braiswick La CO4 ....109 D4
Braithwaite Dr CO4 ..109 F2
Bramble Cl CM8 ......176 E4
Bramble Dr IP3 ....18 E1
Bramble La CM6 ......151 F8
Bramble Rd CM8 .....176 E4
Brambledown CO5 ...201 C7
Brambles CO14 ......171 B7
Brambles The
  Bishop's Stortford CM23 .145 C6
  Braintree CM7 ....127 E3
  Colchester CO3 ....134 F3
Bramblewood 1 IP8 ..16 C2
Bramford La IP1 ....16 F8
Bramford Rd IP1 ......16 E8
Bramhall Cl IP2 ....16 D1
Bramley Chase IP4 .....18 B7
Bramley Cl Alresford CO7 165 B8
  Braintree CM7 ....128 A1
  Colchester CO3 ....135 B7
Bramley Pl CM2 ......216 D7
Bramley Rd CB9 ....8 D7
Bramleys The CO6 ...131 A3
Bramston Cl CM2 ....216 F8
Bramston Gn CM8 ...176 A4
Bramston Wlk CM8 ..176 A4
Bramwoods Rd CM2 .216 E8
Bran End Fields CM6 .124 D7
Brancaster Dr CM77 .154 C6
Brand Ct CM7 ....127 F7
Brand Dr CO5 ....163 B3
Brandon Rd
  Braintree CM7 ....127 D2
  Felixstowe IP11 ....221 A4
Brands Cl CO10 ....34 C5
Bransby Gdns IP4 .....17 E7
Branscombe Cl CO13 .170 E5
Branston Cl CO16 ....188 C3
Branston Rd CO15 ...188 D3
Brantham Hill CO11 ...86 A7
Brantham Mill Ind Est
  CO11 ....86 B7
Braxted La
  Great Braxted CM8 ....178 C1
  Great Totham CM8,CM9 .196 D8
Braxted Park Rd
  Rivenhall CM8 ....177 E4
  Tiptree CO5 ....178 E2
Braxted Rd CM8 ......196 A6
Braybrooke Gdns CB11 ..43 D8
Brazier's Wood Rd IP3 ..38 B8
Braziers Cl CM2 ......216 C3
Braziers Quay CM23 ..146 A6
Breach La CM6 ....97 B2
Breachfield Rd CO2 ...135 C2
Bream Ct CO4 ....110 F1
Brecon Ct IP2 ....17 B2
Bredfield Cl IP11 .....221 B5
Bree Ave CO6 ....132 E3
Brendon Ct CO5 .....179 D4
Brendon Dr
  Halstead CO9 ....103 F8
  Rushmere St A IP5 .....18 F6
Brendon Pl CM1 .....204 E1
Brent Cl
  Frinton-on-S CO13 ....170 F7
  Witham CM8 ....176 F2
Brent Hall Rd CM7 ....72 B6
Brentwood Rd CO15 .189 C6
Brett Cl IP1 ....16 E8
Bretten Cl CO16 ......188 A4
Brettenham Cres IP4 ..17 D8
Bretts Cotts CO5 .....178 F3
Brewers Cl CM23 .....145 C5
Brewery Fields CM2 ..217 A5
Brewery La CM24 .....119 E6
Brewery Yd CM24 ....119 E6
Breydon Way IP3 ......38 D7
Brian Bishop Cl CO14 .171 B8
Brian Cl CM2 ....216 B6
Briar Rd CO7 ....112 A4
Briardale Ave CO12 ...90 F3
Briarfields CO13 .....170 C6
Briarhayes IP2 ....17 B2
Briarhayes Cl IP2 .....17 B3
Briarsford Ind Est CM8 177 B1

Briarswood CM1 .....205 D7
Briarwood Ave CO15 .189 F6
Briarwood End CO4 ..110 B3
Brices Way CO9 ....2 B5
Brick Cotts IP9 ....62 F4
Brick End Villas CM6 .121 E8
Brick House La CM3 ..192 E1
Brick House Rd CM9 ..197 B7
Brick Kiln Cl CO6 ....131 A3
Brick Kiln La
  Great Horkesley CO6 ..109 C7
  Rickling Green CB11 ...66 D1
  Stebbing CM6 ....124 D7
  Thorrington CO7 ......165 E5
Brick Kiln Rd
  Chelmsford CM2 ....217 C7
  Colchester CO1 ....109 E1
  Harkstead IP9 ....63 C5
Brick Kiln Way CM7 ..128 D2
Brick Row SG8 ....19 D3
Brick St CO3 ....108 B1
Brickbarns CM3 ......173 F7
Brickburn Cl CM3 ....152 C4
Brickfield Cl IP2 ......17 D3
Brickhouse Cl CO5 ...201 B7
Brickhouse Rd CO6 ...78 A3
Brickmakers La CO4 .109 F2
Brickman's Hill CO11 .87 D3
Brickspring La CM9 ..196 D2
Brickwall Ct CO6 ....105 B6
Bridewell Ind Est CO10 .12 C8
Bridewell St CO10 ....12 C8
Bridge Cotts
  Cavendish CO10 ....1 D2
  Ridgewell CO9 ....29 B7
Bridge Croft CM3 ....172 B2
Bridge Ct CM9 ......210 A3
Bridge End CB11 ......43 A2
Bridge End La CM77 .154 C8
Bridge Foot CO10 .....33 D6
Bridge Hall Rd CM7 ..129 C3
Bridge Hill CO6 ......107 C7
Bridge Hospl CM8 ...194 E8
Bridge Rd IP11 ....221 E5
Bridge St
  Bishop's Stortford CM23 .145 F7
  Bures CO8 ....55 F1
  Coggeshall CO6 ....130 F1
  Finchingfield CM7 ......72 C6
  Great Bardfield CM7 ....72 B2
  Great Yeldham CO9 ....30 A1
  Halstead CO9 ....76 E2
  Ipswich IP1 ....17 C4
  Saffron Walden CB10 ..22 D2
  Witham CM8 ....176 F1
  Writtle CM1 ....204 C1
Bridge Terr 1 CO10 ...33 F8
Bridgebrook Cl CO4 ..110 C5
Bridgefield Cl CO4 ...136 C7
Bridgeford Ho 13 CM23 145 F6
Bridgwater Rd IP2 ....16 D2
Bridlewalk CO3 ......134 D6
Bridport Ave IP3 ......18 D3
Bridport Rd CM1 .....205 D5
Bridport Way CM7 ...128 D4
Brierley Ave CO5 ....201 E7
Brierley Paddocks CO5 201 E7
Bright Cl CO16 ......188 D6
Brightlingsea Ct CO7 .136 F4
Brightlingsea Inf Sch
  CO7 ....185 E6
Brightlingsea Jun Sch
  CO7 ....185 E6
Brightlingsea Mus CO7 185 F6
Brightlingsea Rd
  Thorrington CO7 ....165 E3
  Wivenhoe CO7 ....137 C4
Brighton Rd CO15 ....189 F6
Brightside CO13 ......170 E7
Brightwell Cl IP11 ....221 A4
Brimstone Ct CM7 ...154 E4
Brimstone Rd IP8 ......36 E8
Brindley Rd CO15 ....189 B8
Bringey The CM2 .....217 A6
Brinkley Cres CO4 ...110 D2
Brinkley Grove Prim Sch
  CO4 ....110 B5
Brinkley Grove Rd CO4 .110 A5
Brinkley La CO4 ......110 B5
Brinkley Pl CO4 ......109 F3
Brisbane Rd IP4 ......18 D6
Brisbane Way CO2 ...136 A1
Brise Cl CM7 ....128 A1
Bristol Ct CM8 ....156 E3
Bristol Hill IP9 ....91 B8
Bristol Rd
  Colchester CO1 ....136 A8
  Ipswich IP4 ....18 A7
Bristowe Ave CM2 ...217 A6
Britannia Cres CO7 ..137 B1
Britannia Ct CO7 ....137 B1
Britannia Pl 3 CM23 .145 E6
Britannia Rd IP4 ......18 B6
Britric Cl CM6 ....151 F6
Brittania Prim Sch IP4 .18 B5
Brittany Way CO2 ....136 B4
Britten Cl CO4 ....136 E6
Britten Cres
  Great Baddow CM2 ....216 F8
  Witham CM8 ....194 F7
Brixham Ct CO15 ....203 I8
Brixton La CB11,CM23 .93 B6
Broad La CO6 ....82 C2
Broad Mdw 3 IP8 ....16 C2
Broad Oakes Cl CB10 .44 E2

226 Bro – Car

Broad Oaks Pk CO4 110 E3
Broad Oke IP1 17 B6
Broad Rd Braintree CM7 128 B7
Wickham St P CO9 53 B8
Broad Street Green Rd
CM9 210 C7
Broadcroft Cres CB9 8 F8
Broadfield CM23 118 F2
Broadfield Rd CM22 148 E7
Broadfields CO7 137 C3
Broadlands CO13 170 E3
Broadlands Way
Colchester CO4 110 B1
Rushmere St A IP4 18 F5
Broadleaf Ave CM23 145 D4
Broadmead Rd CO4 110 E1
Broadmere Cl CO15 189 E7
Broadmere Rd IP1 16 E8
Broadoaks Cres CM7 128 D4
Broadstrood CO16 187 B5
Broadwater Gdns IP9 91 A8
Broadway
Clacton-on-S CO15 203 G7
Glemsford CO10 2 B5
Silver End CM8 156 D4
Broadway Ct CM8 156 D5
Broadway The CM6 123 F3
Brock Cl Tiptree CO5 179 E6
Witham CM8 194 E8
Brockenhurst Way CM3 218 F1
Brockham Cl CO16 188 B6
Brockley Cres IP1 16 D8
Brockley Rd CM2 205 D2
Brocks Mead CM6 122 E7
Brockwell La CO5 158 C1
Brograve Cl CM2 216 D3
Broke Hall Com Prim Sch
IP4 18 E5
Broke Hall Gdns IP3 18 D4
Broman's La CO5 185 A2
Bromfield CB11 43 E8
Bromley Cl
Clacton-on-S CO16 188 D4
Ipswich IP2 17 C3
Bromley Cnr CO11 86 A2
Bromley Cross CO7 112 B3
Bromley Hts CO4 136 F8
Bromley La CB11 43 B1
Bromley Rd
Colchester CO7,CO4 111 C2
Elmstead CO7 138 B5
Frating CO7 139 A4
Lawford CO11 86 B2
Brompton Gdns CM9 220 E8
Bronte Cl CM7 155 A8
Bronte Rd CM8 176 F5
Brook Cl Braintree CM7 127 C2
Great Totham CM9 196 A3
Tiptree CO5 179 F3
Woodham Walter CM9 208 D2
Brook Cotts Boxted CO4 82 E5
Stansted Mountfitchet
CM24 119 E5
Brook End Rd N CM2 206 A4
Brook End Rd S CM2 206 B3
Brook Farm Caravan Pk
CO15 188 E7
Brook Farm Cl CO9 77 A1
Brook Farm La IP9 62 D6
Brook Hall Rd CO5 164 B5
Brook Hill
Little Waltham CM3 191 B6
North End CM6 151 F1
Brook La Chelmsford CM2 206 B2
Felixstowe IP11 221 F5
Galleywood CM2 216 E3
Brook Mdw CO9 51 D1
Brook Mdws CO5 179 C4
Brook Mead CM3 190 E8
Brook Rd Aldham CO6 133 B7
Great Tey CO6 132 C7
Stansted Mountfitchet
CM24 119 E6
Tiptree CO5 179 F3
Tolleshunt Knights CM9,
CO5 180 A2
Brook Service Rd CB9 9 A7
Brook St Chelmsford CM1 205 B3
Colchester CO1 136 B7
Colne Engaine CO6 77 F1
Dedham CO7 84 F7
Glemsford CO10 2 B6
Great Bardfield CM7 72 B2
Great Bromley CO7 112 E1
Little Dunmow CM6 151 D6
Manningtree CO11 86 D4
Wivenhoe CO7 164 C8
Brook Terr CO9 51 E1
Brook Vale CO16 187 B3
Brook View
Chelmsford CM2 217 C6
Stansted Mountfitchet
CM24 119 E5
Thaxted CM6 70 A3
Brook Wlk CM8 194 F8
Brookbank CM2 216 E8
Brooke Ave CB10 22 E2
Brooke Gdns CM23 146 C7
Brooke Sq CM9 210 A1
Brookes Nature Reserve*
CM77 103 E2
Brookfield Rd IP1 16 F8
Brookfields CM6 124 D7
Brookhampton St CB10 3 A5
Brookhill Way IP4 18 F4
Brookhouse Bsns Pk IP2 16 F6
Brookhouse Pl 3 CM23 145 F8
Brookhouse Rd CO6 132 B8
Brookhurst Cl CM2 205 D3
Brookland CO5 179 C4
Brooklands
Clacton-on-S CO15 203 E6
Colchester CO1 136 B7
Brooklands Gdns CO15 203 E6
Brooklands Prim Sch
CO11 86 D8
Brooklands Rd CO11 86 D8
Brooklands Rise CO11 86 D8
Brooklands Wlk CM2 216 A7
Brooklyn Ct CO12 91 C3
Brooklyn Mews CO12 91 C3
Brooklyn Rd CO12 91 C3
Brooks Hall Rd IP1 17 A7
Brooks Malting 3 CO11 86 D4
Brookside Cl CO2 136 B4
Brooksies CB11 40 F6
Brookview IP2 36 E8
Broom Cres IP3 17 F1
Broom Farm Rd CM22 94 C2
Broom Field IP11 221 C5
Broom Hill Rd IP1 17 A8
Broom Knoll CO7 60 C2
Broom St CO10 34 B5
Broom Way
Abberton CO5 163 B2
Capel St M IP9 35 B2
Broomclose Villas CM7 100 E5
Broome Gr CO7 137 B2
Broome Way CO15 203 F6
Broomfield CM8 156 C5
Broomfield Comm IP8 16 B6
Broomfield Cres CO7 137 B2
Broomfield Hospl CM1 191 A3
Broomfield Prim Sch
CM1 191 B1
Broomfield Rd CM1 205 A5
Broomgrove Inf & Jun Schs
CO7 137 B2
Broomhall Cl CM1 191 B2
Broomhall Rd CM1 191 B2
Broomhayes IP2 17 A2
Broomhill IP9 62 D6
Broomhills Ind Est CM7 127 D2
Broomhills Rd CO5 201 D5
Brotherton Ave IP11 221 A8
Broton Dr CO9 76 E2
Brougham Glades CO3 134 D5
Broughton Cl CO2 135 C4
Broughton Rd IP1 17 B7
Brown's End Rd CM6 121 F7
Browning Cl CO3 134 F6
Browning Rd
Braintree CM7 155 A8
Brantham CO11 86 C7
Brownings Ave CM1 205 A5
Brownlow Rd IP11 221 F4
Brownsea Way CO3 135 A4
Bruce Gr CM2 216 A7
Bruce Rd CM1 204 B1
Bruff Cl CO4 109 E2
Bruff Dr CO14 171 A7
Bruges Cl CO12 91 A1
Brundells Rd CO7 139 A5
Brundon La CO10 33 C7
Brunel Ct CO4 110 C6
Brunel Rd Braintree CM7 128 A1
Clacton-on-S CO15 189 B8
Ipswich IP2 16 F6
Brunel Way CO4 110 C6
Brunswick House Cut
CO11 87 A3
Brunswick Rd IP4 17 F8
Brunwin Rd CM77 126 F2
Brussels Cl CO12 91 B1
Bryan Rd CM23 145 F8
Bryanita Ct CO5 179 D5
Bryanstone Mews CO3 134 E5
Bryant Link CM2 206 B4
Bryant's La CM9 219 D7
Bryon Ave IP11 221 A3
Buchan Cl CM7 155 A8
Buck Hill CM77 154 F6
Buck's Horns La IP8 36 B6
Buckenhoe Rd CB10 22 E3
Buckfast Ave CO13 170 D6
Buckfast Cl 5 IP2 17 A2
Buckingham Ct 2 CM2 205 F4
Buckingham Dr CO4 136 E7
Buckingham Rd CB9 8 E6
Bucklesham Rd IP3 18 E2
Buckley's La CO6 131 E6
Buckleys CM2 216 F7
Buckleys Cl CM8 195 E5
Bucks La CO10 12 B7
Buckwoods Rd CM7 128 A1
Buddleia Cl IP2 16 E4
Buddleia Ct CO7 137 A2
Buffett Way CO4 136 E6
Buglers Rise CM1 215 B8
Buick Ave CO15 203 D6
Building End Rd
Chrishall SG8 19 C1
Duddenhoe End SG8 40 B8
Bulford La CM77 155 C5
Bulford Mill La CM77 155 D5
Bull Hill Rd CO15 188 F5
Bull La Langley CB11 40 C2
Long Melford CO10 15 E8
Maldon CM9 210 A3
Tiptree CO5 179 C3
Bullace Cl CO4 110 D3
Bullen Wlk CM2 216 C3
Bullfields CB11 67 A8
Bullfinch Cl
Colchester CO4 136 F8
Harwich CO12 90 E1
Bullfinch Dr CO9 77 A1
Bullock Wood Cl CO4 110 D4
Bullocks La CO10 33 E6
Bulls Cliff IP11 221 D3
Bulls Lodge Cotts CM3 192 B1
Bulmer Rd CO10 33 C6
Bulmer Road Ind Est
CO10 33 C6
Bulmer St CO10 32 D4
Bulrush Cl CM7 128 B1
Bulstrode Rd IP2 17 D4
Bulwer Rd IP1 17 A6
Bumfords La CM3,CM9 208 A7
Bumpstead Rd CB9 9 B4
Bundick's Hill CM1 204 F3
Bung Row CM8 178 C1
Bungalows The CM8 176 F1
Bunting Cl CM2 216 B5
Bunting Rd IP2 16 D3
Buntingford Ct 2 CO2 136 A1
Bunyan Rd CM7 127 E3
Burdun Cl CM8 194 D8
Bure Dr CM8 176 D3
Buregate Rd IP11 221 D2
Bures CE Prim Sch CO8 79 F8
Bures Ct 16 CB9 8 E7
Bures Ho CO8 79 F8
Bures Rd
Great Cornard CO10 34 B3
Nayland CO6 81 B8
Bures Sta CO8 79 E8
Burgate Cl CO16 188 A4
Burgess Field CM2 205 F4
Burghley Ave CM23 145 C7
Burghley Cl
Great Notley CM77 154 B6
4 Ipswich IP2 17 A2
Burghley Way CM2 216 C8
Burgundy Ct CM2 205 C2
Burkitts Ct 8 CO10 33 E7
Burkitts La CO10 33 E7
Burley Rd CM23 146 A4
Burlington Ho IP2 17 B4
Burlington Rd
Colchester CO3 135 E6
Ipswich IP1 17 B6
Burmanny Cl CO15 188 C3
Burnell Gate CM1 206 A7
Burnells Way CM24 119 E7
Burnet Cl IP8 36 D8
Burnham Cl Ipswich IP4 17 F7
Trimley St M IP11 221 A7
Walton-on-t-N CO14 171 B8
Burnham Ct CO15 203 I8
Burnham Rd
Chelmsford CM1 205 D5
Woodham Mortimer CM9,
CM3 219 E5
Burns Ave CO3 134 F6
Burns Cl CM9 210 A1
Burns Cres CM2 216 C8
Burnsall Cl CB11 43 F8
Burnside Cres CM1 205 B7
Burnstie Rd CM6 152 F6
Burnt Dick Hill CO4 82 D7
Burnt Oak Cnr CO7 59 D1
Burnthouse Rd CO6 105 E2
Burr Cl CO12 90 C1
Burrell Rd IP2 17 C4
Burroughs Piece Rd
CO10 33 F7
Burrows Cl
Clacton-on-S CO16 188 D6
Lawford CO11 86 B4
Burrows Rd CO6 105 B7
Burrs Rd CO15 189 A7
Burrsville Com Inf Sch
CO15 188 F6
Burrswood Pl CM9 210 E3
Burstall Cl CO16 188 B4
Burstall La IP8 16 A6
Burton Cl CB9 8 E7
Burton End CB9 8 E7
Burton End Prim Sch CB9 8 D7
Burton Pl CM2 205 F4
Burton's Green Rd CO9 104 B4
Burwood Ct CM2 205 C1
Bury Cl Colchester CO1 136 A8
Marks Tey CO6 132 F4
Bury Fields CM6 152 A5
Bury Gdns CB11 20 A4
Bury La Chrishall SG8 19 D1
Great Waltham CM3 190 D8
Hatfield Peverel CM3 193 F4
Bury Lodge La
Great Hallingbury CM22 147 C7
Stansted Mountfitchet
CM24 120 A2
Bury The CO16 187 A4
Bury Water La CB11 42 E1
Burywater Cotts CB11 42 F1
Burywoods CO4 109 B3
Bush Gr CO10 33 C6
Bush La CB10 46 D2
Bush Rd CB10 46 E2
Bushell Way CO13 170 E6
Bushey Cl IP9 35 A1
Bushey Ley CM7 128 D3
Butcher's Hill CB10 3 A4
Butcher's View CO5 182 E6
Butchers La
Capel St M IP9 35 B1
Walton-on-t-N CO14 171 B7
Butchers Pasture CM6 122 F5
Butchers Row CB10 22 D1
Bute Ct CB9 8 F6
Butler Cl CB11 22 E1
Butler Rd CO9 76 D2
Butler's Hall La CM23 145 B3
Butler's La CO11 88 E1
Butlers Cl CM1 191 B2
Butlers La CB10 23 C5
Butlers Way CO9 30 A1
Butley Cl IP2 36 F8
Butley Ct 1 CB9 8 E6
Butley Rd IP11 221 C3
Butt La Maldon CM9 210 A3
Manuden CM23 92 E2
Butt Rd Colchester CO3 135 E5
Great Cornard CO10 34 B6
Stoke-by-N CO6 56 C5
Butt's Green Rd CM2 217 F3
Butter Market IP1 17 C6
Buttercup Cl IP8 16 C2
Buttercup Wlk CM8 176 E4
Butterfield Rd CM3 206 E8
Butterfly Gdns IP4 18 E5
Buttermarket Sh Ctr 3
IP1 17 C5
Buttermere CM77 154 C7
Buttleys La CM6 149 F8
Butts La CM3 218 F7
Butts Way CM2 215 E3
Buxey Cl CO5 201 B7
Buxton Cotts CO6 132 A3
Buxton Rd
Coggeshall CO6 130 F3
Colchester CO2 136 A3
Bylam La IP9 63 C6
Byland Cl IP2 17 A2
Bylands Cl CM23 145 D6
Byng Cres CO16 142 B1
Byng Ct CO2 136 A1
Byng Gdns CM7 128 C4
Byng Ho CO16 142 B1
Bypass Rd CO16 187 B5
Byrd's Farm La CB10 22 E3
Byron Ave CO3 134 F7
Byron Cl CM7 155 A8
Byron Dr CM8 195 E5
Byron Rd CM2 205 D2
Byrony Cl CM8 176 D4

C

Cadenhouse Mews CO3 134 E7
Cadmus Rd IP1 16 D7
Caernarvon Wlk CB9 8 E8
Cage La Boxted CO4 83 B4
Felixstowe IP11 221 D5
Cairns Rd CO2 136 B2
Caithness Cl IP4 18 B8
Calamint Rd CM8 176 D3
Caldbeck Way CM77 154 C6
Caledonia Rd IP9 91 B8
Calford Dr CB9 8 C8
California Cl CO4 110 B4
California Rd CO11 87 A4
Callis Ct CO10 12 C8
Callis St CO10 12 B8
Callowood Croft CM3 220 D1
Calverley Cl CM23 145 E4
Calves La CO6 56 B8
Cam Way CM8 176 D2
Camberley Rd IP4 18 D7
Camberton Rd CM7 127 E6
Camborne Cl CM1 205 E5
Cambrai Rd CO2 135 D4
Cambria Cl CO11 87 B3
Cambridge Ave CO9 75 E8
Cambridge Ct
Clacton-on-S CO15 188 E4
Frinton-on-S CO13 171 A5
Cambridge Dr IP2 16 F1
Cambridge Ho CB9 9 B6
Cambridge Rd
Clacton-on-S CO15 188 E4
Colchester CO3 135 C5
Felixstowe IP11 221 F4
Frinton-on-S CO13 171 A5
Littlebury CB11 21 F4
Newport CB11 43 A2
Stansted Mountfitchet
CM24 119 E8
Cambridge Way CO8 79 F8
Camden Rd IP3 18 B4
Camellia Ave CO16 188 C4
Camellia Cl 2 CM1 205 F6
Camellia Cres CO16 188 C5
Camellia Ct 5 CO4 136 D8
Camelot Cl CM1 204 F5
Cameron Cl
Braintree CM7 127 F8
Long Melford CO10 15 C6
Camoise Cl CO9 50 B7
Camomile Way CO4 109 C2
Camp Rd CO7 139 A7
Campbell Cl CM2 216 A7
Campbell Ct CO3 135 D6
Campbell Dr CO4 110 E2
Campbell Rd Ipswich IP3 18 C1
Witham CM8 176 F5
Campernell Cl CO7 185 F8
Campion Rd
Colchester CO2 136 A5
Ipswich IP2 16 F4
Campion Way CM8 176 E3
Campions Hill CO6 81 D8
Campions The CM24 119 E8
Camps Rd Bartlow CB1 6 B7
Haverhill CB9 8 F7
Helions Bumpstead CB9 8 B1
Camulodunum Way
CO2 135 C1
Camulus Cl
Braintree CM7 128 A2
Colchester CO2 135 A2
Camwood Gdns IP3 18 B4
Can Bridge Way CM2 205 C1
Canberra Cl
Chelmsford CM1 204 E5
9 Colchester CO2 136 A1
Ipswich IP4 18 D6
Candlet Gr IP11 221 D5
Candlet Rd IP11 221 D6
Candytuft Rd CM1 205 F6
Canes Mill Ct CM7 128 A5
Canfield CM23 145 E8
Canfield Rd CM6 149 D1
Canford Cl CM2 216 E7
Cangle Junc CB9 9 A8
Canham St 8 IP1 17 B6
Canhams Rd CO10 34 C5
Cann Hall Prim Sch
CO16 188 D6
Canning St CO12 91 D5
Cannock Mill Ct CO2 136 C4
Cannon Circ CM7 73 D6
Cannon Leys CM2 216 D3
Cannon Rd CO1 136 B6
Cannon St CO1 136 B6
Cannons Cl
Bishop's Stortford CM23 119 A1
Colchester CO2 135 D4
Cannons Mead CM24 119 D7
Cannons Mill La CM23 119 A1
Cannons The CO2 135 D4
Canonium Mews CO5 158 C2
Canons Cl CM3 218 E1
Cansey La CO11 114 E6
Cant Way CM7 128 C1
Canterbury Cl IP2 36 F8
Canterbury Grange
CM7 127 F8
Canterbury Rd
Colchester CO2 136 A5
Holland-on-S CO15 189 E5
Sudbury CO10 15 C2
Canterbury Way CM1 204 E4
Canuden Rd CM1 204 E2
Canvey Wlk CM1 205 E6
Canwick Gr CO2 136 C4
Cap Pillar Cl CO7 137 B2
Cape Cl CO3 134 F5
Capel Cl Chelmsford CM1 205 B7
Rayne CM77 126 F2
Capel Dr IP11 221 A4
Capel Ho CO4 109 F4
Capel Pk CO13 170 E7
Capel Rd Colchester CO3 135 C5
Rayne CM77 126 F2
Capel St Mary CE Prim Sch
IP9 35 A1
Caper La CO2 160 F4
Capons La CM3 219 A5
Capstan Pl CO4 136 D5
Captains Rd CO5 201 B6
Captains Wood Rd CM8,
CM9 196 A3
Caracalla Way CO4 110 B6
Card's Rd CM2 217 C6
Cardiff Ave IP2 17 B2
Cardigan St IP1 17 B7
Cardinal Cl CO4 137 A7
Cardinal Pk IP1 17 C5
Cardinal St IP1 17 C5
Cardinals Ct IP11 221 E3
Careless Ct 21 CM23 145 F7
Carisbrooke Ave CO15 189 A7
Carleton Ct CO5 163 E8
Carlisle Cl CO1 136 A8
Carlton Cl CO9 30 A2
Carlton Rd CO15 189 B5
Carlton Way IP4 17 E8
Carmarthen Cl IP2 17 A2
Carmel St CB10 3 D2
Carmelite Way CM9 209 F2
Carmen St CB10 3 D3
Carnarvon Rd CO15 188 F3
Carnation Cl CM1 205 F5
Carnation Dr CB10 22 F2
Carolbrook Rd IP2 16 E1
Carolina Way CO5 179 D5
Caroline Cl CO7 137 C3
Carpenters Dr CM77 154 B7
Carpenters The CM23 145 B5
Carr St IP4 17 D6
Carraways CM8 195 B8
Carriage Cl IP11 221 A8
Carriage Dr CM1 205 E7
Carriers Cl CO5 201 A7
Carriers Ct CO7 59 D3
Carrigans CM23 145 E8
Carrington Ct CO5 201 D7
Carrington Ho CO5 201 D7
Carrington Way CM7 127 F8
Carringtons Rd CO7 112 D4
Carrs Rd CO15 188 D3
Carsey Hill CB1 7 B6
Carshalton End CO3 134 F4
Carsons Dr CO10 34 D5
Carstone Pl CM1 204 F2
Cartbridge Cl CO14 171 B8
Carters Cl CO16 188 B3
Carters Croft CB10 6 B1
Carters Hill Boxted CO4 83 A6
Manuden CM23 93 A1
Carters La Henham CM22 94 F5
Wickham Bishops CM8 195 F6
Carters Leys CM23 145 D8

Carters Vineyard★ CO4 ..82 E5
Cartwright Wlk CM2 ...205 F2
Case La IP9 ....60 D7
Cassino Rd
  Chelmsford CM1 ....204 E6
  Colchester CO2 ......135 C3
Castle Cl CB9 ....8 E7
Castle Bailey 15 CO1 ..135 F7
Castle Camps CE Prim Sch
  CB1 ....7 E3
Castle Cl
  Castle Hedingham CO9 ...51 E4
  Great Leighs CM3 ....173 F6
Castle Cross CB10 .....22 E2
Castle Ct CO15 ....188 E3
Castle Hill Dedham CO7 ..84 F4
  Saffron Walden CB10 ..22 D2
Castle Hill Mid Sch CB9 ..8 D7
Castle Hill Pk CO16 ...188 E7
Castle Ho★ CO7 ....85 A5
Castle La
  Castle Hedingham CO9 ...51 E4
  Haverhill CB9 ....8 F8
Castle Manor Upper Sch
  CB9 ....8 F8
Castle Mdw CO9 ....51 D2
Castle Rd
  Clacton-on-S CO15 ...188 E3
  Colchester CO1 ......136 A7
Castle St
  Bishop's Stortford CM23 .145 F6
  Saffron Walden CB10 ..22 D2
Castle View CM23 .....146 A7
Castle Way CO16 .....187 A4
Castle Wlk Haverhill CB9 ..8 E8
  Stansted Mountfitchet
  CM24 ....119 E6
Castlefields CM3 .....173 F7
Castlegate St CO12 ....91 E6
Castleward Cl CO7 ....164 C8
Caswell Mews CM2 ...205 F2
Cat's La CO10 ....34 A7
Catchpole Ct 12 CO10 ..33 E7
Catchpole La CM9 ....196 A4
Catchpool Rd CO1 ....135 E8
Caterham Ct CO16 ....188 C6
Cates Cnr CB10 ....22 E1
Cathedral CE Prim Sch The
  CM1 ....205 C3
Cathedral Wlk CM1 ...205 B3
Catherine Cl CO15 ....189 A5
Catherine Hunt Way
  CO2 ....135 C2
Catherine May Ct CO15 .188 F3
Catherines Cl CM3 ...174 A6
Catons La CB10 ....22 D2
Cattawade St CO11 ....86 C7
Cattermole Ct CO16 ..188 B3
Catts Cl IP9 ....61 F2
Cattsfield IP9 ....61 F2
Cauldwell Ave IP4 .....17 F7
Cauldwell Hall Rd IP4 ..18 A6
Causeway CM3 ....152 F1
Causeway Bsns Ctr The 23
  CM23 ....145 F7
Causeway Cl CO10 ......2 C5
Causeway End CO16 ...86 B5
Causeway End Rd CM6 .152 C4
Causeway Reach CO15 .188 E7
Causeway The
  1 Bishop's Stortford
  CM23 ....146 A7
  Braintree CM7 ......127 F4
  Colchester CO4 .....110 C1
  Finchingfield CM7 ....72 D6
  Great Baddow CM2 ..216 F7
  Great Dunmow CM6 ..123 D2
  Great Horkesley CO6 ..82 B2
  Halstead CO9 ....76 E1
  Harkstead SG9 ......64 B1
  Haverhill CB9 ....8 E7
  Henham CB11 ....68 B7
  Langley CB11 ....40 C3
  Maldon CM9 ....210 A4
  Ridgewell CO9 ......28 F8
  Toppesfield CO9 .....50 B7
  Ulting CM9 ....208 D5
Causton Jun Sch IP9 ..221 C6
Causton Rd CO1 .....135 E8
Caustons Cl CO10 .....34 C5
Cavendish Ave CO2 ...136 C3
Cavendish CE Prim Sch
  CO10 ....1 C2
Cavendish Ct
  2 Haverhill CB9 ......8 E6
  8 Saffron Walden CB10 ..22 F2
Cavendish Dr
  Clacton-on-S CO16 ...188 A4
  Lawford CO11 ....86 B3
Cavendish Gdns
  Braintree CM7 ......128 C5
  Chelmsford CM2 ....205 E3
Cavendish La CO10 .....3 A6
Cavendish Rd Clare CO10 .12 D7
  Felixstowe IP11 .....221 D3
Cavendish St IP3 ......17 F5
Cavendish Way CO10 ..33 F7
Cawkell Cl CM24 .....119 D7
Cawkell Cl CM2 ......206 A4
Caxton Cl CO5 ....179 D4
Caxton Pl CO9 ....76 E2
Cecil Cl CM23 ....146 D7
Cecil Rd IP1 ....17 B7
Cecilia St IP1 ....17 C5
Cedar Ave
  Brightlingsea CO7 ...185 E7
  Chelmsford CM1 ....205 A3
  Tiptree CO5 ....179 C7

Cedar Ave W CM1 ....205 A3
Cedar Chase CM9 ....210 C5
Cedar Cl Brantham CO11 ..60 D1
  Great Dunmow CM6 ..123 A1
  Walton-on-t-N CO14 ..171 A7
Cedar Cres CO11 ......86 C3
Cedar Ct
  Bishop's Stortford CM23 .118 F1
  West Bergholt CO6 ...108 D5
Cedar Dr CM8 ....177 A5
Cedar Pk CM23 ......145 D4
Cedars Rd 13 CO2 ....135 F6
Cedars The CO9 ......102 E7
Celandine Ct CO4 ....109 C2
Cemetery La
  East Bergholt CO7 ....59 B2
  Ipswich IP4 ....17 E8
Cemetery Rd
  Bishop's Stortford CM23 .145 F6
  Ipswich IP4 ....17 E6
Centaury Cl CO3 .....134 C7
Centenary Way CO15,
  CO16 ....168 E1
Central Arc CB10 ......22 D1
Central Ave
  Frinton-on-S CO13 ...171 A6
  Ipswich IP3 ....38 E8
Central Ho CO12 ......91 D4
Central Maltings The 5
  CO11 ....86 D4
Central Par CO15 ....188 F2
Central Sq 7 CM1 ....205 B2
Centre The
  2 Colchester CO4 ...136 E7
  Halstead CO9 ....76 E2
  Ipswich IP2 ....17 A1
  Tiptree CO5 ....179 D5
Centurian Ho 2 CO2 ..135 F6
Centurion Way CO2 ..135 A3
Chadburn Rd CO10 ....15 D8
Chaffinch Dr CO12 ....90 E1
Chaffinch Gdns CO4 ..136 F8
Chaffinch Way CO9 ....77 A1
Chaffix CM6 ....152 C6
Chaffix Cl CM6 ......152 C6
Chainey Pieces 12 CB9 ..8 F7
Chalfont Rd CO4 .....110 C3
Chalfont Sq 15 IP4 ....17 D6
Chalklands
  Howe Green CM2 ....217 D3
  Saffron Walden CB10 ..22 E3
Chalks Rd CM8 ....177 A5
Chalkstone Way CB9 ...9 D7
Chalky La SG8 ....19 D2
Challenge Way CO1 ..136 B6
Challis La CM7 ....155 A3
Chalon St IP1 ....17 A1
Chamberlain Ave CO14 .171 B7
Chamberlain Way IP8 ..16 C2
Chamley Ct CO15 ....189 D5
Chancellor Ave CM2 ..206 B4
Chancery Gr CO2 .....163 A8
Chancery Pl CM1 .....204 B1
Chancery Rd IP1 ......17 B5
Chandlers Cl
  Bishop's Stortford CM23 .145 C4
  Clacton-on-S CO16 ..188 B3
  West Mersea CO5 ...201 C7
Chandlers Quay CM9 .210 A3
Chandlers Row CO1 ..136 C5
Chaney Rd CO7 ......137 A2
Chant Ct CO4 ....110 D3
Chanterelle CO4 .....110 D3
Chantry Cl
  Bishop's Stortford CM23 .145 E8
  Clacton-on-S CO16 ..188 E7
Chantry Dr CO6 ....80 E4
Chantry Gn IP2 ....16 D3
Chantry High Sch & Sixth
  Form Ctr IP2 ....16 F3
Chantry Jun & Inf Sch
  IP2 ....16 E3
Chantry La CM3 .....193 A3
Chantry Mount CM23 .145 E8
Chantry Rd CM23 ....145 E8
Chantry The
  6 Bishop's Stortford
  CM23 ....145 F8
  Colchester CO1 .....135 C7
Chantry View CM8 ...195 A4
Chantry Villas CM3 ..193 A4
Chanute Ave CM7 .....73 D7
Chapel Cl IP9 ....35 A1
Chapel Croft CO7 ....111 E7
Chapel Cut CO11 ......87 A4
Chapel Dr CM3 ......191 B6
Chapel End Way CO9 ..28 B2
Chapel Hill
  Belchamp Walter CO10 ..31 D4
  Braintree CM7 ......128 B2
  Halstead CO9 ....76 D2
  Stansted Mountfitchet
  CM24 ....119 E6
Chapel Hill Bsns & Ret Pk
  CM77 ....128 C1
Chapel Hill Prim Sch
  CM7 ....128 B2
Chapel La Belstead IP8 ..36 C7
  Boxted CO4 ....83 A3
  Colchester CO7 .....111 B1
  Elmstead CO7 ......138 A6
  Great Bromley CO7 ..139 A5
  Great Cornard CO10 ..34 C2
  Heybridge Basin CM9 .210 E2
  Kirby Cross CO13 ...170 A6

Chapel La continued
  Little Baddow CM3 ..207 B3
  Newport CM11 ......67 A8
  St Osyth CO16 ......187 A4
  Tendring CO16 .....140 E8
  Thorington Street CO6 ..57 D6
  Thorrington CO7 ....166 B5
  Washbrook IP8 ......16 A1
  West Bergholt CO6 ...108 E3
Chapel Mews 18 IP4 ...17 D6
Chapel Rd
  Beaumont CO16 .....141 E7
  Boxted CO4 ....83 A3
  Brightlingsea CO7 ...186 A7
  Colchester CO3 .....134 C6
  Great Totham CM9 ..196 D6
  Langham CO4 ....83 D4
  Ridgewell CO9 ......29 B7
  Tiptree CO5 ....179 E4
  Tolleshunt D'arcy CM9 .198 F4
  West Bergholt CO6 ...108 E4
  Wivenhoe CO7 ......164 B8
Chapel Rise CM7 .....129 D2
Chapel Row 3 CM23 ..145 F6
Chapel St Halstead CO9 ..76 E2
  Rowhedge CO5 .....164 A8
  Steeple Bumpstead CB9 ..27 C7
  Stoke by Clare CO10 ..11 A3
Chapel St N 2 CO2 ...135 E6
Chapel St S 3 CO2 ...135 E6
Chapelfields CO13 ...170 E6
Chaplin Cl CM2 ......216 B2
Chaplin Dr CO4 ......110 D1
Chaplin Rd CO7 ......59 D3
Chaplin Wlk CO10 .....34 D5
Chaplins CO13 ....170 F7
Chapman Rd CO15 ...188 F3
Chapmans Cl CO5 ....201 E6
Chappel & Wakes Colne Sta
  CO6 ....106 D6
Chappel CE Prim Sch
  CO6 ....106 D5
Chappel Cnr CO6 ....106 D6
Chappel Hill CO6 ....106 C5
Chappel Rd
  Bures CO6, CO8 ......79 E3
  Fordham CO6 ....107 D7
  Great Tey CO6 ......106 C1
Charlecote Rd CM77 ..154 C7
Charles Ct
  Colchester CO3 .....134 D6
  Wivenhoe CO7 ......137 C3
Charles Cvn Pk CO16 .167 E8
Charles Hall CO4 ....109 F4
Charles Pell Rd CO4 ..136 F4
Charles Rd
  Brightlingsea CO7 ...185 F6
  Felixstowe IP11 .....221 C3
Charles St
  Colchester CO1 .....136 A6
  Ipswich IP1 ....17 C6
Charleston Ct CO5 ...201 E6
Charlotte Dr CO13 ...170 E6
Charlotte Way CM8 ..177 B2
Charnock Cl CO3 ....170 F6
Charnwood Ave CM1 ..204 E1
Charnwood Ct IP2 ....17 B4
Charrington Cl CB9 ....9 C6
Charter Ct CO4 ......110 C6
Charter Ho CM9 .....210 A2
Charter Way
  Braintree CM77 .....128 C1
  Colchester CO4 .....109 F4
Charters The CM6 ...123 D2
Chartfield Dr CO13 ...170 D8
Chartwell Cl
  Braintree CM7 ......127 E7
  Ipswich IP4 ....18 A5
Chase Ct CO4 ....136 D7
Chase La CO12 ....90 E2
Chase Lane Prim Sch
  CO12 ....90 E2
Chase Rd E CO7 .....139 C8
Chase Rd W CO7 ....139 A6
Chase The Aldham CO6 .133 B8
  Barnston CM6 ......151 A4
  Bishop's Stortford CM23 .145 F6
  Boreham CM3 ......206 E8
  Braintree CM7 ......128 A7
  Brantham CO11 ......60 F1
  Colchester CO1 .....136 B7
  6 Colchester,Greenstead
  CO1 ....136 D7
  Elmstead CO7 ......138 B6
  Felixstowe IP11 .....221 D4
  Foxearth CO10 ......14 C6
  Goldhanger CM9 ....212 A1
  Great Baddow CM2 ..216 F6
  Great Notley CM77 ..154 C5
  Great Tey CO6 ......132 C8
  Great Totham CM9 ..196 A4
  Henham CB11 ....94 F6
  Holland-on-S CO15 ..189 E5
  Kelvedon CO5 ......158 C2
  Manningtree CO11 ...86 D3
  Steeple Bumpstead CB9 ..27 B7
  Tollesbury CM9 .....199 D2
  Tolleshunt D'arcy CM9 .198 B4
  West Mersea CO5 ...201 C6
Chase Way The
  Colchester CO3 .....109 C1
  Colchester,Lexden CO3 .109 B1
Chaser Cl IP3 ....38 C8
Chaseway CM8 ......176 F5
Chaseway The CM7 ..128 C2
Chaters Hill CB10 .....22 E2
Chatham Gn CM3 ....173 D3
Chatham Hall La CM3 .191 B8

Chatley Rd CM3 .....173 F7
Chatsworth Ave CM77 .154 B7
Chatsworth Cl CM23 ..145 C7
Chatsworth Cres
  Ipswich IP2 ....17 B2
  Trimley St M IP11 ...221 A6
Chatsworth Dr IP4 ....18 E5
Chatsworth Gdns CO15 .188 D2
Chatsworth Rd CO5 ..201 C7
Chatter End CM23 ...118 C7
Chattisham Rd IP8 ....35 C8
Chaucer Cl CO15 ....188 A1
Chaucer Cres CM7 ...155 A1
Chaucer Rd
  Chelmsford CM2 ....205 D1
  Felixstowe IP11 .....221 D3
  Sudbury CO10 ....15 D2
Chaucer Way CO3 ...134 F6
Chauntry Rd CB9 ......8 F7
Chauntry The 2 CB9 ...9 A7
Chedburgh Pl 3 CB9 ...9 A8
Chedworth Pl IP9 .....61 D7
Chelmer Ave CM3 ...191 B5
Chelmer Cl
  Kirby Cross CO13 ...170 F7
  Little Totham CM9 ..197 B4
Chelmer Dr CM6 .....150 E8
Chelmer Lea CM2 ...216 B2
Chelmer Pl CM2 .....205 D3
Chelmer Rd
  Braintree CM7 ......128 D1
  Chelmsford CM2 ....205 E2
  Haverhill CB9 ....9 B8
  Witham CM8 ....176 F2
Chelmer Terr CM9 ...210 B2
Chelmer Valley High Sch
  CM1 ....191 A2
Chelmer Valley Rd CM1 .205 B5
Chelmer Village Ret Pk
  CM2 ....205 E2
Chelmer Village Way
  CM2 ....206 A3
Chelmerton Ave CM2 .216 E7
Chelmondiston CE Prim Sch
  IP9 ....63 C7
Chelmsford & Essex
  Regiment Mus★ CM2 .216 A8
Chelmsford Coll
  Chelmsford CM2 ....216 A8
  Chelmsford CM2 ....216 C7
Chelmsford Cty High Sch for
  Girls CM1 ....205 A4
Chelmsford Ho CM6 ..150 E7
Chelmsford Rd
  Barnston CM6 ......151 A4
  Felsted CM6 ....152 B4
  Great Dunmow CM6 ..150 E7
  Great Waltham CM3 ..191 A6
  Holland-on-S CO15 ..189 D6
  Purleigh CM3 ......220 C3
  Woodham Mortimer CM9 .219 C6
  Writtle CM1 ....204 C1
Chelmsford Road Ind Est
  CM6 ....150 E7
Chelmsford Sta CM1 ..205 B3
Chelsea Ct CO10 ......33 F7
Chelsea Mews 6 CM7 .127 F2
Chelsea Rd CO10 .....33 F7
Chelsworth Ave CO10 ..34 B7
Chelsworth Rd IP11 ..221 B3
Chelwater CM2 ......216 D8
Chenies Gn CM23 ...145 D6
Chepstow Rd IP11 ...221 D5
Chequers CM23 .....145 C8
Chequers Ct CM8 ....177 B2
Chequers La
  Glemsford CO10 ......2 C6
  Great Dunmow CM6 ..150 D8
  Maldon CM9 ....210 A2
Chequers Rd CO11 ...113 C6
Chequers The CO7 ...165 A7
Cheriton Rd CM7 ....128 C1
Cherry Bglws CM7 ...127 F3
Cherry Blossom Cl IP8 ..16 B2
Cherry Chase CO5 ...179 D4
Cherry Garden La
  Danbury CM3 ......219 B2
  Newport CB11 ......66 F8
Cherry Garden Rd
  Great Waltham CM3 ..190 E7
  Maldon CM9 ....209 E2
Cherry Gdns
  Bishop's Stortford CM23 .146 A8
  Great Notley CM77 ..154 D8
  Haverhill CB9 ....9 B5
Cherry La CO9 ....51 A8
Cherry Lane Gdns IP4 ..18 B7
Cherry Row CO3 .....134 F5
Cherry Tree Ave CO15 .188 C1
Cherry Tree Cl
  Halstead CO9 ....77 A2
  Little Oakley CO12 ..117 B7
Cherry Tree Ho CO5 .158 C3
Cherry Tree La
  Abberton CO2 ......162 F6
  Blackheath CO2 ....163 A7
Cherry Tree Prim Sch
  CO2 ....163 A8
Cherry Trees CO15 ..188 F2
Cherrygarden La 1
  CM2 ....216 B2
Cherrytree Ct CO3 ...134 F5
Cherrytree Rd CO10 ..34 B7
Cherrytree Rise CM8 .177 A5
Cherrywood Dr CO3 ..134 F5
Cherrywoods CO7 ...166 D8
Chervil Cl CO5 ......179 C4
Cherwell Dr CM1 ....204 C5

Car – Chu 227

Cheryl Ct CO15 ......188 D1
Chesapeake Cl IP9 ....63 F7
Chesapeake Rd IP3 ...38 A8
Chesfield Cl CM23 ...145 F5
Chesham Rd IP2 ......17 B4
Chess La CM8 ....177 A2
Chessington Gdns IP1 ..16 F5
Chester Camp CO16 ..188 A4
Chester Ct 4 CB9 ......8 E6
Chester Pl CM1 ......205 A5
Chester Rd IP11 .....221 D5
Chesterton Cl IP2 .....16 F1
Chestnut Ave
  Blackheath CO2 ....163 A8
  Clacton-on-S CO15 ..188 C3
  Gosfield CO9 ....102 E8
  Great Notley CM77 ..154 C7
  Hatfield Peverel CM3 .194 A3
  Heybridge CM9 .....210 C6
  Jaywick CO16 ......188 A2
  Kirby Cross CO13 ...170 C6
  Littlebury CB11 ......21 C1
Chestnut Cl
  Bishop's Stortford CM23 .145 E6
  Haverhill CB9 ....8 F8
Chestnut Ct CB11 .....67 A8
Chestnut Gr CM7 ....127 C2
Chestnut Rd
  Alresford CO7 ......165 B8
  Glemsford CO10 ......2 B5
Chestnut Terr CO10 ..15 C8
Chestnut View CM6 ..123 C1
Chestnut Way
  Brightlingsea CO7 ...185 E7
  Takeley CM22 ......148 C3
  Tiptree CO5 ....179 C7
Chestnut Wlk
  Chelmsford CM1 ....205 A5
  Felsted CM6 ....152 C6
  Little Baddow CM3 ..207 E1
  Witham CM8 ....177 B4
Chestnuts The IP2 ....16 C2
Chevalier Rd IP11 ...221 F4
Chevallier St IP1 .....17 A7
Cheveley IP11 ....221 E4
Cheveling Rd CO2 ...136 D2
Cheviot Dr CM1 .....204 D6
Chevy Ct CO12 ....90 C2
Cheyne Ct CO10 ......33 E7
Chichester Ct CO3 ...135 A7
Chichester Dr CM1 ..205 C4
Chichester Rd CB11 ..43 E8
Chickney Rd CM22 ...95 C7
Chigborough Rd CM9 .210 F6
Chignall Rd CM1 .....204 D5
Chilburn Rd CO15 ...189 A7
Childers Field IP11 ...221 B5
Childwell Alley CO1 ..136 A6
Chilford Ct CM7 .....127 D3
Chiltern Cl IP1 ......109 E1
Chilton Cl
  Chelmsford CM2 ....216 D7
  Great Horkesley CO6 .109 B7
Chilton Cotts CO6 .....80 E4
Chilton Ct Ipswich IP2 ..17 B3
  Sudbury CO10 ....34 A6
Chilton Ind Est CO10 ..34 B8
Chilton Lodge Rd CO10 ..34 A7
Chilton Rd IP3 ....18 C4
Chimney Pot La CM3 .219 E3
Chimswell Way CB9 ...8 C8
Chinery Cl CM1 .....205 D4
Chingford Ave CO15 .188 F8
Chinnel La CB11 ......42 D5
Chinnery Hill CM23 ..145 F5
Chinook CO4 ....110 B4
Chippetts La CO3 ...133 C7
Chipping Hill
  2 Halstead CO9 ......76 F2
  Witham CM8 ....176 F3
Chipping Hill Inf Sch
  CM8 ....176 F3
Chippingdell CM8 ...176 F4
Chipstead Wlk CO16 .188 C6
Chishill Rd SG8 ......19 A4
Chislett Row CM2 ...216 C8
Chittock Cl CO16 ....188 B3
Chitts Hill CO3 ......108 D1
Chivers Rd CB9 ....8 D7
Choat's Cotts CO6 ...107 E1
Choats Wood CO3 ...107 F1
Chrismund Way CO6 .106 C1
Christ Church Ct CO3 .135 D5
Christchurch Ct 4 IP4 ..17 D6
Christchurch Mansion
  (Mus)★ IP4 ....17 D6
Christchurch Park Hospl
  (private) IP1 ....17 C7
Christchurch St IP4 ...17 D6
Christian Sch The CM2 .148 B7
Christies Warehouse 15
  IP4 ....17 D5
Christina Rd CM8 ....194 B4
Christine Chase CO3 .134 F5
Christmas Field CO9 ..51 D2
Christopher Ct 9 CO10 ..33 E7
Christopher Dr CO16 .168 D1
Christopher Jolly Ct
  CO2 ....135 F4
Christopher La CO10 ..33 E7
Christy Ave CM1 .....204 F4
Church Ave CM1 .....191 A2
Church Chase CM8 ..178 A3
Church Cl Cavendish CO10 ..1 D2
  Sproughton IP8 ......16 A6

Church Cl continued
West Bergholt CO6 ....108 E4
Wickham Bishops CM8 ...195 D5
Church Cnr CM9 ......208 D2
Church Cotts CM8 ......195 D5
Church Cres
Clacton-on-S CO15 ......188 F2
Sproughton IP8 ....16 A6
Church Dr CM23 ....92 B8
Church End
Great Dunmow CM6 ......123 E2
Panfield CM7 ....127 B7
Church End Villas CM6 .123 E3
Church Farm Way CO4 ..109 E4
Church Field CB11 ......43 E7
Church Field Rd CO10 ..34 C8
Church Fields CO9 ......29 F2
Church Gdns CM6 ......123 D2
Church Gn Boreham CM3 206 F8
Broomfield CM1 ....191 B1
Coggeshall CO6 ....131 A3
Hinxton CB10 ....3 B7
Little Yeldham CO9 ....30 D4
Wickham Bishops CM8 ...195 D5
Church Gr CO6 ....133 B8
Church Hill Ashdon CB10 .24 A8
Earls Colne CO6 ....105 C6
Finchingfield CM7 ....72 D6
Harwich CO12 ....90 B1
Helions Bumpstead CB9 ..26 C8
Lawford CO11 ....85 F3
Little Waltham CM3 ......191 C6
Purleigh CM3 ....220 E1
Rowhedge CO5 ....163 F8
White Notley CM8 ....175 F8
Woodham Walter CM9 ...208 D2
Church Housen CM3 ...190 F7
Church La
Beaumont CO16 ....142 A6
Belstead IP8 ....36 A7
Bishop's Stortford CM23 .145 D3
Braintree CM7 ....127 F6
Brantham CO11 ....60 E1
Castle Camps CB1 ....7 E3
Castle Hedingham CO9 ...51 E4
1 Chelmsford, Moulsham
CM1 ....205 B2
Chelmsford, Springfield
CM1 ....205 D4
Clare CO10 ....12 B7
Colchester, Lexden CO3 .135 A6
Colchester,Stanway CO3 .134 A4
Debden CB11 ....68 A7
East Mersea CO5 ....184 E1
Elsenham CM22 ....120 E8
Felixstowe IP11 ....221 D6
Ford End CM3 ....172 B6
Great Henny CO10 ....54 D8
Great Holland CO13 .....170 A3
Great Leighs CM3 ....173 D7
Great Tey CO6 ....132 C4
Great Wigborough CO5 ..181 F4
Harkstead IP9 ....63 B3
Harwich CO12 ....91 E6
Little Totham CM9 ......197 B1
Marks Tey CO6 ....133 A4
Mistley CO11 ....86 E4
Nayland CO6 ....56 B1
Ridgewell CO9 ....29 B6
Sproughton IP8 ....16 B6
Takeley,Brewer's End
CM22 ....148 B7
Takeley,Little Canfield
CM6 ....149 B7
Toppesfield CO9 ....50 B7
Washbrook IP8 ....35 D8
Washbrook,Copdock IP8 .35 F7
Weeley Heath CO16 .....168 A7
Widdington CB11 ....67 D4
Writtle CM1 ....204 B1
Church Manor CM23 ...146 B8
Church Mdws CM7 .....127 F6
Church Mead CM8 .....155 F1
Church Mews CO6 .....56 B1
Church Path Hadstock CB1 .5 B6
Saffron Walden CB10 ....22 D2
Church Pk CO10 ....11 C3
Church Rd
Alphamstone CO10 ......54 C6
Alresford CO7 ....165 B7
Bentley IP9 ....60 F7
Black Notley CM77 ......155 A6
Boxted CO4 ....82 E6
Bradwell CM7 ....129 E1
Brightlingsea CO7 ......185 E8
Bulmer CO10 ....32 F4
Capel St M IP9 ....35 F1
Chrishall SG8 ....19 D3
Clacton-on-S CO15 .....189 A3
Copford CO6 ....133 E2
Cressing CM77 ....156 A5
Elmstead CO7 ....138 A7
Fordham CO6 ....107 D5
Frating CO7 ....138 D2
Gosfield CO9 ....102 E8
Great Cornard CO10 .....34 A5
Great Hallingbury CM22 .146 D3
Great Notley CM77 .....154 F6
Great Totham CM9 .....196 E3
Great Yeldham CO9 .....29 F2
Greenstead Green CO9 ..104 A5
Hatfield Peverel CM3 ...194 A3
Hempstead CB10 ....46 F8
Holbrook IP9 ....62 D5
Kelvedon CO5 ....158 C2

Church Rd continued
Layer-de-l-H CO2 ....161 F4
Little Baddow CM3 .....207 A6
Little Bentley CO7 ......140 A5
Little Bromley CO11 ....113 B4
Pattiswick CM7 ....129 F5
Peldon CO5 ....182 D6
Rivenhall CM8 ....157 B1
Shudy Camps CB1 ......7 C5
Stambourne CO9 ....28 D2
Stansted Mountfitchet
CM24 ....119 F5
Stutton IP9 ....62 A2
Tattingstone IP9 ....61 C7
Terling CM3 ....175 B2
Thorrington CO7 ....166 A6
Tiptree CO5 ....179 D5
Tolleshunt Major CM9 ..197 F2
Ulting CM9 ....208 C6
Walton-on-t-N CO14 ...171 C8
West Mersea CO5 ......201 B6
Wickham Bishops CM8 ..195 E5
Wickham St P CO9 ......53 B6
Wormingford CO6 ....80 E5
Wrabness CO11 ....88 F4
Church Rise CB9 ......26 C8
Church Sq Bures CO8 ..55 F1
St Osyth CO16 ....187 A4
Church St
Belchamp St P CO10 ....13 B3
Bishop's Stortford CM23 .145 F7
Boxted CO4 ....82 F7
Braintree CM7 ....102 B1
Chelmondiston IP9 ......63 E7
Chelmsford CM1 ....205 B2
Clare CO10 ....12 B7
Coggeshall CO6 ....131 A2
Colchester CO1 ....135 E7
Colne Engaine CO6 .....78 A1
Gestingthorpe CO9 ......31 E1
Goldhanger CM9 ....211 E7
Great Baddow CM2 .....217 A6
Great Chesterford CB10 ..3 D2
Great Dunmow CM6 .....123 D2
Great Maplestead CO9 ...52 D1
Great Yeldham CO9 .....52 D1
Harwich CO12 ....91 E6
Henham CM22 ....94 F6
Ickleton CB10 ....3 B4
Kelvedon CO5 ....158 B2
Maldon CM9 ....210 B2
Newport CB11 ....43 A1
Rowhedge CO5 ....164 A8
Saffron Walden CB10 ....22 D2
Sible Hedingham CO9 ...51 D1
Steeple Bumpstead CB9 .27 B7
Stoke-by-N CO6 ....56 D5
Sudbury CO10 ....33 D6
Tollesbury CM9 ....199 D1
Tolleshunt D'arcy CM9 ..198 D4
Wendens Ambo CB11 ...42 E5
Witham CM8 ....176 F4
Church Terr CO10 .....10 C2
Church View
Ardleigh CO7 ....111 E7
Colne Engaine CO6 ......77 F1
Stoke by C CO10 ....10 D3
Church Wlk
Colchester CO1 ....135 E7
Littlebury CB11 ....21 F4
Maldon CM9 ....209 F3
Sturmer CB9 ....9 E4
5 Sudbury CO10 ....33 E7
Churchacre CM9 ......199 D1
Churchfield Rd
Coggeshall CO6 ....131 A3
Walton-on-t-N CO14 ...171 C8
Churchfields
Stansted Mountfitchet
CM24 ....119 F6
Steeple Bumpstead CB9 .27 B6
West Mersea CO5 ......201 B6
Churchfields Ave CO3 .134 C4
Churchfields Dr CB9 ...27 B6
Churchgate
Glemsford CO10 ....2 C5
Thorpe-le-S CO16 .....141 F1
Churchill Ave
Halstead CO9 ....77 A3
Ipswich IP4 ....18 B5
Churchill Cl CO7 ......185 F8
Churchill Ct CO12 .....91 A4
Churchill Dr CO10 .....15 E2
Churchill Rd
Braintree CM7 ....127 E7
Tiptree CO5 ....179 F5
Churchill Rise CM1 ....205 E7
Churchill Terr CM7 ....127 E6
Churchill Way CO2 ....136 B4
Churchmans Ho IP1 ...17 B5
Churchponds CO9 ......51 E4
Churchwell Ave CO5 ..160 A7
Churchwood Cl CO4 ...110 D1
Churchwood Rd CO4 ..110 D1
Chuzzlewit Dr CM1 ...204 E7
Cinnabar Cl IP8 ....36 E8
Cinque Port Rd CO7 ..185 E7
Circular Rd E CO2 .....135 E5
Circular Rd N CO2 .....135 E5
Circular Rd S CO2 .....135 E4
Circular Rd W CO2 ....135 E5
City Rd CO5 ....201 A6
Civic Dr IP1 ....17 B6
Civic Ind Est CB9 ......8 F5
Clachar Cl CM2 ....206 A3
Clacton & District Hospl
CO15 ....188 E1
Clacton Comm CO15 ..169 A1

Clacton Cty High Sch
CO15 ....189 A4
Clacton Rd
Bradfield CO11 ....114 A6
Elmstead CO7 ....138 C5
Great Holland CO13 ....170 A2
Holland-on-S CO15 ....189 F7
Little Oakley CO12 .....117 B5
Mistley CO11 ....86 E2
St Osyth CO16 ....187 B4
Thorrington CO7 ....166 C4
Weeley Heath CO16 ....168 A6
Wivenhoe CO7 ....137 C5
Wix CO11 ....115 C5
Wix,Stones Green CO12 115 D1
Clacton Sta CO15 .....188 F3
Claire Cl CO5 ....201 C7
Claire Rd CO15 ....170 B6
Clairmont Cl **11** CM7 .127 F2
Clairmont Rd CO3 ....134 E5
Clandon Ho CO13 .....170 F4
Clapgate Dr CO16 ....168 C2
Clapgate La IP3 ....18 A2
Clapton Hall La
Great Dunmow CM6 ....150 D5
Great Dunmow CM6 ....150 E6
Clara Reeve Cl CO3 ...134 F4
Clare Ancient House Mus★
CO10 ....12 C7
Clare Castle Ctry Pk★
CO10 ....12 C7
Clare Cl CO3 ....103 D7
Clare Com Prim Sch
CO10 ....12 B8
Clare Ct CM6 ....69 F3
Clare Mid Sch CO10 ...12 C8
Clare Rd Braintree CM7 127 E2
Ipswich IP1 ....17 F8
Clare Way CO16 ....188 B5
Claremont Hts CO1 ...109 E1
Claremont Rd CO7 ....164 C8
Clarence Cl CM2 ......206 A4
Clarence Rd Clare CO10 .12 B8
Ipswich IP3 ....18 B1
Stansted Mountfitchet
CM24 ....119 E7
Sudbury CO10 ....15 E1
Clarendon Pk CO15 ...189 B5
Clarendon Rd Haverhill CB9 8 F6
Takeley CM6 ....148 E7
Clarendon Way CO1 ..109 E1
Clark Way CM1 ....191 A1
Clarke's Rd CO2 ....90 F3
Clarkesmead CO5 ....179 C4
Clarkia Wlk CO4 ......136 D7
Clarks Farm Rd CM3 ..218 F8
Clarks Field Cotts CM3 219 E2
Clarks Wood Dr CM7 ..128 D3
Clarkson St IP1 ....17 B6
Clatterbury La
Arkesden CB11 ....41 E1
Clavering CB11 ....65 D5
Claud Ince Ave CM77 .155 E6
Claude Oliver Cl CO11 .86 A2
Claude St IP1 ....17 C6
Claudian Cl CB9 ....9 D7
Claudius Rd CO2 ......136 A5
Claudius Way CM8 ....194 E8
Clavering Prim Sch CB11 65 C4
Clavering Rd CM7 .....127 F6
Claverton Way IP4 ....18 E4
Clay Hill CO10 ....54 C8
Clay La St Osyth CO16 .187 C7
Stebbing CM6 ....124 D7
Clay Lane Gr CO4 .....110 D4
Clay Pit Piece CB11 ...43 E6
Clay Pits CM7 ....128 D3
Clay Pits Way CM7 ...128 D3
Claydon Cl CB1 ....7 A4
Claypit Hill CM22 .....120 E5
Claypits Ave CO8 ......80 A8
Claypits La CO10 ......14 D5
Claypits Rd CM3 ......192 F1
Claypits Villas CM6 ...70 B2
Clayponds CM23 .....146 B7
Clays Mdw CB11 ......21 F4
Clays Rd CO14 ....171 B7
Clayshotts Dr CM8 ...195 B8
Clayton Rd CO12 ......90 C2
Claywall Bridge CB9 ..27 C7
Claywall Cotts CB9 ...27 C7
Clear Springs Chalet Site
CO12 ....91 A1
Clearing CI IP8 ....36 E8
Clearwater CO2 ....136 B3
Clematis Tye **3** CM1 .205 E7
Clematis Way CO4 ....136 E7
Clement Mellish Ho **10**
CO1 ....135 F7
Clement's La CB9 .....8 F7
Clementine Gdns IP4 ..18 B5
Clements Cl
Chelmsford CM2 ....206 B3
Haverhill CB9 ....8 F7
Clements Dr CB9 ......8 F7
Clements Prim Sch CB9 .8 F7
Clench Cl **8** IP4 ....17 D6
Clench Rd IP9 ....62 D7
Clermont Ave CO10 ..15 E2
Clevedon Cl CM7 .....154 C7
Cleveland Cl CO4 .....110 C4
Cleves Ct CM3 ....192 E1
Cleves Rd CB9 ....8 D6
Clicket Hill CO8 ....80 B8
Cliff Cres CM7 ....100 E7
Cliff Ct CO15 ....171 B6

Cliff La IP3 ....17 F3
Cliff Lane Prim Sch IP3 .17 E3
Cliff Par CO14 ....144 E2
Cliff Rd Harwich CO12 .91 D3
Holland-on-S CO15 ....189 E5
Ipswich IP3 ....17 E3
Cliff Way CO13 ....171 B5
Cliffield CM7 ....100 E7
Clifford Cl **10** CM23 .146 A7
Clifford Rd IP4 ....17 F5
Clifford Road Prim Sch
IP4 ....17 F5
Clifton Terr CO7 ......164 B8
Clifton Way IP7 ....16 D2
Clifton Wood IP9 ......62 D6
Cliftons Farm Dr CO10 .12 B7
Clingoe Ct CO4 ....136 E5
Clive Rd CO1,CO2 .....136 A6
Cliveden Cl CM1 ......204 E3
Clobbs Yd CM1 ....205 B8
Clockhouse Way CM8 .128 C2
Cloes La CO16 ....188 B4
Cloisters The
Braintree CM7 ....128 A5
Kelvedon CO5 ....158 B1
Cloncurry Gdns IP11 ..221 B3
Clopton Dr CO10 ......15 C6
Close The
Clacton-on-S CO15 ....203 H7
Cressing CM77 ....155 E6
Debden CB11 ....68 B7
Frinton-on-S CO13 ....170 E5
Great Dunmow CM6 ....150 E7
Great Holland CO13 ....170 A3
Harwich CO12 ....91 A3
Sudbury CO10 ....33 F8
Tattingstone IP9 ....61 D7
Clouded Yellow Cl CM7 .154 E8
Clough Rd CO4 ....110 C6
Clovelly Cl IP4 ....18 F4
Clover Ave CM23 .....145 B6
Clover Cl IP2 ....16 F4
Clover Ct Colchester CO3 134 D5
Great Cornard CO10 ....34 C8
Clover Dr CO7 ....166 A5
Clover Field CB9 ......8 D8
Clover Way CO7 ....111 B5
Cloverlands CO4 ......110 C2
Clovers **5** CO9 ....76 D1
Cluanie Orch CO10 ....1 E1
Club Par CO16 ....203 B6
Clump Field IP2 ....16 F2
Clunford Pl CM1 ......205 F7
Clyde Cres CM1 ......204 D4
Clydesdale Rd CM7 ...127 E2
Coach House Way **10**
CM8 ....177 A2
Coach La CM9 ....209 F3
Coach Rd Alresford CO7 .165 B8
Great Horkesley CO6 ..109 A7
Hempstead CB9 ....25 F2
Coachman's Paddock
IP9 ....62 D6
Coachmans Ct **6** IP4 .17 C5
Coachmans Mead CM7 .72 C6
Coan Ave CO15 ....188 D1
Coast Rd CO5 ....201 A6
Coastguard Cotts CO14 .144 A1
Coates Cl CM9 ....210 B4
Coates Quay CM2 ....205 C2
Coats Hutton Rd CO2 .135 B3
Cobble Row CO1 ......134 E6
Cobbold Mews **16** IP4 .17 D6
Cobbold Rd IP11 .....221 E4
Cobbold St IP4 ....17 D6
Cobbs La CM22 ......121 F3
Cobbs Pl CM1 ....205 D3
Cobden Pl IP4 ....17 D6
Cobham Rd IP3 ....18 C2
Cock & Bell La CO10 ..15 C8
Cock & Pye Ct CO1 ...135 E7
Cock La CB11 ....64 F3
Cock Rd CO9 ....53 B1
Cockaynes La CO7 ....138 A1
Cockett Wick La CO16 .187 C1
Cockrell's Rd CO6 ....81 B4
Codham Little Park Dr
CM7 ....101 C6
Cody Rd IP3 ....18 C1
Coeur De Lion CO4 ...109 F2
Coggeshall Rd
Ardleigh CO7 ....84 F2
Braintree CM7 ....128 C3
Coggeshall CO6 ....131 F7
Coggeshall,Marks Tey CO6 131 F3
Earls Colne CO6 ....105 B3
Great Tey CO6 ....132 B7
Kelvedon CO5 ....158 B5
Marks Tey CO6 ....132 C3
Coggeshall Rd (Feering)
CO5 ....158 D7
Coggeshall Road (Feering)
CO6 ....131 B1
Coggeshall Way CO9 .77 A2
Cogmore CB11 ....41 B8
Cohen Cl CM77 ......155 B5
Cohort Dr CO2 ....135 A2
Coke St CO12 ....91 D5
Cokers Cl CM77 ......155 C5
Colam La CM3 ....207 C3
Colbayns High Sch
CO15 ....188 D4
Colchester Boys High Sch
CO3 ....135 E6
Colchester Bsns Pk
CO4 ....110 C6
Colchester Castle★
CO1 ....135 F7

Colchester Castle Mus★
CO1 ....135 F7
Colchester General Hospl
CO4 ....109 E3
Colchester High Sch for Girls
CO3 ....135 B6
Colchester Inst
Clacton-on-S CO15 ....189 A2
Colchester CO3 ....135 D8
Colchester Natural History
Mus★ CO3 ....135 F7
Colchester Oaks Hospl
CO3 ....135 D7
Colchester Rd
Abberton CO5 ....163 B1
Ardleigh CO7 ....111 C6
Bures CO8 ....79 F8
Chappel CO6 ....106 E5
Chelmsford CM2 ....206 A6
Coggeshall CO6 ....131 D2
Dedham CO7 ....84 E6
Elmstead CO7 ....137 F6
Frating CO7 ....139 E3
Great Bentley CO7,CO16 186 F8
Great Bromley CO7 ....112 A3
Great Totham CM9 .....196 D7
Great Wigborough CM9,
CO5 ....181 C2
Halstead CO9 ....77 A1
Heybridge CM9 ....210 B5
Holland-on-S CO15 ....189 D6
Ipswich IP4 ....18 B8
Lawford CO11 ....86 C3
Little Horkesley CO6 ...81 B1
Peldon CO5 ....183 B6
Salcott-cum-virley CM9 199 A5
St Osyth CO16 ....187 A5
Thorpe-le-S CO16 .....141 D2
Tiptree CO5 ....179 D7
Weeley CO16 ....140 C2
West Bergholt CO6 .....108 D6
West Mersea CO5 .....201 C7
White Colne CO6 ......105 E6
Witham CM8 ....177 B3
Wivenhoe CO7 ....137 B4
Wix CO12 ....115 B3
Wix,Goose Green CO11 .114 E4
Wormingford CO8 .....80 A6
Colchester Ret Pk CO1 .135 E7
Colchester Royal Gram Sch
CO3 ....135 D6
Colchester Sta CO1 ...109 E1
Colchester Town Sta
CO1 ....136 A6
Cold Hall Chase CO7 .138 E6
Cold Store Rd IP11 ....221 A1
Coldnailhurst Ave CM7 .127 F5
Cole End La CB10 .....44 D5
Cole Gn CO10 ....13 A1
Cole Hill CM3 ....174 B5
Cole Ness Rd IP3 .....38 A8
Colehills CB11 ....65 C4
Colehills Cl CB11 ......65 C4
Coleman Ct CO15 ....188 F3
Colemans La CM3 ....218 D7
Coleridge Rd CM9 ....210 A1
Coles La CO14 ....144 A1
Coles Oak La CO7 .....84 C6
College Cl CM23 ......145 D7
College Ct CO11 ......86 C4
College Ho CM7 ......127 E2
College Rd
Braintree CM7 ....127 E2
Clacton-on-S CO15 ....189 A3
College St IP4 ....17 C5
Coller Rd CO12 ....90 F5
Colles Brook Rd CO7 .166 F4
Colletts Chase CO6 ...80 F4
Colley Rd CM2 ....217 A6
Collier Row CB10 .....6 B1
Colliers The CM9 .....210 E3
Collimer Cl IP9 ....63 E7
Collimer Ct IP11 ......221 C6
Collindale Gdns CO15 .189 C5
Collingwood Ave IP3 ..18 B3
Collingwood Cl CM7 ..128 C5
Collingwood Fields CO7 .59 B4
Collingwood Rd
Clacton-on-S CO15 ....188 D1
Colchester CO3 ....134 E6
Witham CM8 ....177 A2
Collins Cl **7** CM7 .....127 F2
Collins Cross CM23 ...119 B1
Collins Rd CO9 ....53 D1
Collinson's IP2 ....16 D5
Collops Villas CM6 ...125 A4
Colne Bank Ave CO3 .135 D8
Colne Chase CM8 ....176 E2
Colne Com Sch & Colne Coll
The CO7 ....185 E8
Colne Cswy CO2 .....136 D5
Colne Ct CM7 ....136 C1
Colne Engaine CE Prim Sch
CO6 ....78 A2
Colne Park Rd CO6 ...105 C4
Colne Rd
Brightlingsea CO7 .....185 E6
Bures CO8 ....79 E8
Clacton-on-S CO15 ....188 F2
Coggeshall CO6 ....131 A6
Halstead CO9 ....77 A2
Sible Hedingham CO9 ..75 E8
Colne Rise CO5 ....163 F8
Colne Springs CO9 ...29 B6
Colne Terr CO7 ....164 B8
Colne Valley Cl CO9 ..76 D2
Colne Valley Rd CB9 ..9 A7

Colne Valley Rly★ CO9 ..51 C5
Colne View
  Colchester CO2 ......136 D2
  Point Clear B CO16 ....186 A2
Colne View Ret Pk C01 ..110 A1
Colne Way CO16 ....185 F4
Colne Wlk CM7 ....128 D1
Colneford Hill CO6 .....105 D7
Colneis Jun Sch IP11 ..221 F6
Colneis Rd IP11 ......221 F6
Colneys Cl CO10 ......15 D1
Colthorpe Rd CO15 ....188 F8
Colts The CM23 ....145 E4
Coltsfield CM24 ....119 E8
Coltsfoot Ct CO4 ......109 C2
Coltsfoot Rd IP2 ......16 E4
Columbine Gdns
  Ipswich IP2 ....16 E5
  Walton-on-t-N CO14 ...171 B7
Columbine Mews CO3 ..134 C7
Columbines The CO10 ...1 E2
Colville Cl CM77 ......154 C4
Colvin Chase CM2 .....216 B1
Colvin Cl CO3 ....134 F7
Colyers Reach CM2 ....206 A2
Colyn Pl CB10 ....22 E3
Comac Yd CO15 ....188 E5
Comma Cl CM7 ....127 E1
Commerce Pk CO2 .....136 D4
Commerce Way
  Colchester CO2 ....136 D4
  Lawford CO11 ....86 C5
Commercial Rd IP1 ....17 B4
Common Hill CB10 .....22 D2
Common La
  Duddenhoe End SG8 ...40 B7
  Little Baddow CM3 ....207 E2
  Woodham Walter CM9 ..208 B3
Common Quay IP2 .....17 D5
Common St CO10 ......12 B8
Common The CM3 .....218 E6
Commons The CO3 ....135 A5
Compasses Rd CM7 ....129 F5
Compton Mews 5 CO4 .136 C8
Compton Rd CO4 ......136 C8
Comyns Cl CO4 ....110 A6
Comyns Pl CM1 ....204 B1
Conan Doyle Cl CM7 ...155 A8
Conder Way CO2 ......136 D4
Conduit La CM9 ......219 E6
Coney Acre CB11 ......93 D8
Conies Rd CO9 ....103 D7
Conifer Cl Alresford CO7 .164 F7
  Colchester CO4 ....136 E8
Conifer Ct 7 CM23 ...145 F8
Coniston Cl CM77 .....154 D6
Coniston Rd IP3 ......18 B2
Coniston Sq IP3 ......18 B2
Connaught Ave CO13 ..170 F4
Connaught Cl CO15 ...189 B3
Connaught Ct CO15 ...189 B3
Connaught Gdns CM7 ..128 B4
Connaught Gdns E
  CO15 ....189 B4
Connaught Gdns W
  CO15 ....189 B3
Connaught Ho
  Clacton-on-S CO15 ....189 B4
  Frinton-on-S CO13 ....170 F5
Connaught Rd
  Haverhill CB9 ....8 E7
  Little Clacton CO16 ...168 C5
Conquerors Cl CM3 ...194 B3
Conrad Rd CM8 ....176 F5
Constable Ave CO16 ...188 C6
Constable Cl
  Lawford CO11 ....86 B4
  West Mersea CO5 .....201 D7
Constable Ct CO2 .....135 B3
Constable Ho CM7 ....127 E3
Constable Rd
  Felixstowe IP11 ......221 F4
  Ipswich IP4 ....17 D8
  Sudbury CO10 ....33 E8
Constable View CM1 ...205 F6
Constable Way CM77 ..155 B5
Constance Cl
  Broomfield CM1 ......191 A3
  Witham CM8 ....195 B8
Constantine Rd
  Colchester CO3 ....135 D5
  Ipswich IP1 ....17 B5
  Witham CM8 ....194 E8
Constitution Hill
  Ipswich IP1 ....17 B8
  Sudbury CO10 ....33 F8
Convalescent Hill IP11 .221 E4
Convent Hill CM7 .....128 A5
Convent La CM7 ......128 A5
Conway Cl Halstead CO9 103 D8
  Haverhill CB9 ....8 E8
  Ipswich IP2 ....17 B2
  Wivenhoe CO7 ....164 C8
Conyer Cl CM9 ....220 F8
Cook Cl CO12 ....90 F1
Cook Cres CO4 ....136 E7
Cook Pl CM2 ....205 F3
Cook's Cnr CO11 ......88 E2
Cook's Hall Rd CO6 ...108 C3
Cook's La Colchester CO3 134 F7
  Colchester,West Bergholt
  CO3 ....134 E8
  Great Bardfield CM7 ...71 E4
Cooks Cl CO9 ....103 F8
Cooks Hill CO4 ....83 B6
Coolyne Way CO15 ....189 B7
Coombe Lodge CM6 ...105 B6
Coombe Rise CM1 ....205 B7

Cooper Dr CM7 ......127 D4
Cooper Pk CM7 ......127 D4
Cooper's La CO7 ......84 F5
Cooper's Row CM1 ....205 A5
Coopers CM3 ....206 E8
Coopers Ave CM9 .....210 D5
Coopers Cl CM23 .....145 B4
Coopers Cres
  Great Notley CM77 ...154 C8
  West Bergholt CO6 ....108 E4
Coopers End Rd CM24 .121 A3
Coopers End Rdbt
  CM24 ....121 B3
Coopers La
  Clacton-on-S CO15 ....188 C3
  Great Leighs CM3 .....173 F7
Coopers Villas CM22 ..121 B2
Coopers Wlk CO4 .....136 D8
Copdock Prim Sch IP8 .35 F8
Copford CE Prim Sch
  CO6 ....133 D2
Copford Ct CO6 ......133 C4
Copland Cl
  Broomfield CM1 ......191 A1
  Great Baddow CM2 ...216 F8
Copleston High Sch IP4 .18 C5
Copleston Rd IP4 .....18 B5
Coploe Rd CB10 ......3 A2
Copper Beeches CO3 ..134 D5
Copper Ct CM7 ....127 E1
Copper Gr IP8 ....36 E8
Copperas Rd CO7 .....185 F5
Copperfield Rd
  Chelmsford CM1 .....204 E7
  Ipswich IP2 ....16 E5
Copperfields CB11 ....43 C8
Coppice Cl CM6 ......123 D1
Coppice End CO4 .....110 B3
Coppice Rd CO7 ......165 B8
Coppice The CO15 ....188 D1
Coppingford End CO6 .133 D5
Coppins Cl CM2 ......205 E4
Coppins Green Prim Sch
  CO15 ....188 E5
Coppins Rd CO15 .....188 D4
Copse The
  Bishop's Stortford CM23 .146 C8
  Colchester CO4 ....109 F3
  Felsted CM6 ....152 F6
Copt Hall La CO5 .....182 C3
Copt Hill CM3 ....218 E6
Copthall Cl CM22 .....146 E4
Copthall La CM6 ......70 B3
Copy Hill CB9 ....8 E3
Coral Dr IP1 ....16 B8
Coralin Wlk CO3 .....134 C6
Cordell Cl CO10 ......15 D8
Cordell Pl CO10 ......15 D8
Cordell Rd CO10 .....15 D8
Corder Rd IP4 ....17 D8
Cordwinders CO7 .....59 F1
Coriander Rd CO5 ....179 C4
Corinda Ho CO13 .....170 F4
Coriolanus Cl CO2 ....135 A3
Cormorant Wlk CM2 ..216 C5
Corn Mill Ct CB11 ....43 E8
Cornard Rd CO10 .....33 F7
Cornel Cl CM8 ....176 D4
Cornelius Vale CM2 ...206 B4
Cornells La CB11 .....67 E3
Corner Pk CB10 ......22 E3
Cornerth Cres CO10 ..34 B6
Cornflower Cl
  Colchester CO3 ....134 C7
  Ipswich IP2 ....16 E4
Cornflower Dr CM1 ...205 F6
Cornflower Rd CO15 ..203 G7
Cornford Way CO11 ..86 B4
Cornhill
  4 Chelmsford CM1 ...205 B2
  16 Ipswich IP1 ......17 C6
Corniche The CM7 ....72 A1
Cornish Hall End Rd
  Stambourne CO9 ......28 A1
  Steeple Bumpstead CO9 .48 E8
Cornwall Cl CO11 .....86 B3
Cornwall Cres CM1 ...205 A7
Cornwall Gdns CM7 ..128 B4
Cornwall Ho CM23 ...145 E4
Cornwall Rd IP11 .....221 D5
Cornwallis Dr CO6 ...132 F3
Cornwallis Pl CB10 ...22 E3
Cornwallis Rd CB9 ...8 F6
Coronation Ave
  Braintree CM7 ....127 F2
  Colchester CO2 ....136 A2
Coronation Dr IP11 ...221 C3
Coronation Rd
  Bishop's Stortford CM23 .145 E5
  Clacton-on-S CO15 ...188 C3
  Ipswich IP4 ....18 B5
Coronation Villas CO16 .141 F7
Coronation Way CM77 .155 D5
Corporation Ave IP2 ..37 A8
Corporation Rd CM1 ..205 A4
Corriander Dr CM22 ..94 D2
Corry Ct 7 CO4 .....136 D8
Corton Rd IP3 ....18 B1
Cortoncroft Cl CO13 ..170 F7
Cotman Ave CO11 ....86 B4
Cotman Lodge CM1 ...205 F6
Cotman Rd
  Clacton-on-S CO16 ...188 D6
  Colchester CO3 ....135 A5
  Ipswich IP3 ....18 A1
Cotswold Cres CM1 ...204 D6

Cotswold Ct
  Clacton-on-S CO15 ...189 A3
  Highwoods CO4 ....110 C4
Cotswold Dr CO10 ....15 C6
Cotswold Rd CO15 ...188 F5
Cottage Dr CO2 ......136 D3
Cottage Gn CO16 .....188 C6
Cottage Gr CO16 .....188 C6
Cottage Pl
  Chelmsford CM1 .....205 B3
  3 Ipswich IP1 ....17 B6
Cottage Wlk CO16 ....188 C6
Cottey Ho CM2 ......216 B2
Cottingham Rd IP8 ...16 B1
Cottonwood Cl CO2 ..135 D3
Coulsdon Cl CO16 ....188 C6
Council Bglws CM7 ...127 F7
Council Cotts
  Great Holland CO13 ..169 F3
  Helions Bumpstead CB9 ..8 E1
Council Hos
  Bicknacre CM3 ....218 F1
  Great Bromley CO7 ...139 A6
  Hadstock CB1 ....5 B6
  Holbrook IP9 ....62 D6
  Peldon CO5 ....182 E5
  Shudy Camps CB1 ....7 B6
  Thorington Street CO6 .57 B3
  Thorpe-le-S CO16 ....141 E2
  Tolleshunt Major CM9 .197 D3
  Wakes Colne CO6 ....79 C1
Council Houses
  Cressing CM77 ....156 A4
  Great Bentley CO7 ...166 F5
Counting House La
  CM6 ....123 D1
County Pl CM2 ....205 B1
Coupals Cl CB9 ......9 C6
Coupals Ct CB9 ......9 C6
Coupals Prim Sch CB9 .9 D7
Coupals Rd CB9 .....9 E6
Court Cl CM23 ....145 E4
Court Eight CM8 .....176 F5
Court Eighteen CM8 ..176 F5
Court Eleven CM8 ....176 F5
Court Farm CO11 .....61 A1
Court Fifteen CM8 ....176 F5
Court Five CM8 ......176 E5
Court Four CM8 ......176 F5
Court Fourteen CM8 ..176 F5
Court Ind Est CM2 ...205 C2
Court Nine CM8 ......176 F5
Court Nineteen CM8 ..176 F5
Court One CM8 ......176 F5
Court Rd CM1 ....191 A3
Court Seven CM8 .....176 F5
Court Seventeen CM8 .176 F5
Court Six CM8 ....176 F5
Court Sixteen CM8 ...176 F5
Court Ten CM8 ......176 F5
Court Thirteen CM8 ..176 F5
Court Three CM8 .....176 F5
Court Twelve CM8 ....176 F5
Court Twenty CM8 ...176 F5
Court Two CM8 ......176 F5
Courtauld Cl CO9 ....76 C1
Courtauld Homes of Rest
  CO9 ....76 E3
Courtauld Rd CM7 ...128 A4
Courtenay Cl CO10 ...15 D2
Courtland Mews CM9 .220 F8
Courtland Pl CM9 ....220 F8
Courtlands
  Chelmsford CM1 .....205 A6
  Halstead CO9 ....103 D8
Courts The IP11 .....221 F4
Courtyard The
  Braintree CM7 ....128 A4
  Maldon CM9 ....209 F2
Coval Ave CM1 ......205 A3
Coval La CM1 ....205 A2
Coval Wells CM1 ....205 A2
Covehite Ct 3 CB9 ..8 E6
Coventry Cl CO1 .....136 A8
Coverdale CM8 ......176 E4
Coverts The
  West Mersea CO5 ....201 D6
  Writtle CM1 ....204 B1
Cow La
  Great Chesterford CB10 ..4 A5
  Point Clear B CO16 ...186 C3
Cowdray Ave CO1 ....109 F1
Cowdray Cres CO1 ...135 F7
Cowdray Ctr The CO1 .110 A1
Cowdrie Way CM2 ...206 B4
Cowell Ave CM1 .....204 E5
Cowell St IP2 ....17 C3
Cowels Farm La CM6 .97 E5
Cowley Rd IP11 ......221 E4
Cowpar Mews CM7 ..155 A8
Cowper St IP4 ....18 B6
Cowslip Cl IP2 ......16 E4
Cowslip Ct CO3 .....134 C7
Cox La IP4 ....17 D5
Cox Rd CO7 ....165 B8
Coxhall Rd IP9 ......36 E1
Coxs Cl CB9 ....8 D7
Coytes Gdns 2 IP1 ..17 C5
Crabb's Hill CM3 ....193 F2
Crabb's La CO5 ......178 A8
Crabbe St IP4 ....18 A6
Crabs Croft CM7 ....128 D3
Crabtree CO13 ......170 C4
Crabtree Hill CB11 ...67 C3
Crabtree La CO6 .....81 C1
Cracknell Cl CO7 ....137 B2

Crafton Gn CM24 ....119 E7
Craig Ct CO2 ....135 B3
Craig Ho CM7 ....128 A3
Craig's Hill CO8 .....79 E6
Craigfield Ave CO15 ..189 A6
Craigs La CO8 ....79 E6
Craiston Way CM2 ...216 F5
Cramphorn Wlk CM1 .204 F3
Cramswell Cl CB9 ....8 E6
Cranborne Cl CM2 ...109 F2
Cranbrook La CO10 ..2 F1
Crane Ave CO3 ......134 B4
Crane Hill IP2 ....16 E4
Crane's La CO5 ......157 F1
Cranford Cl CO13 ....170 E5
Cranham Rd CO6 ....95 F3
Cranleigh Cl CO16 ...188 B6
Cranmer Ho CM2 ....215 F7
Cranmer's La CO6 ...131 E6
Cranmere Ct CO1 ....136 A7
Cranmore CM22 .....94 C2
Craven Dr CO4 ......110 C3
Crawley End CB10 ...19 D4
Crayfields CM6 ......123 E1
Crayford Cl CM9 ....220 E8
Crayford Rd CO10 ...15 D2
Creance Ct CM2 .....205 A2
Creasen Butt Cl CM9 .210 A4
Credon Cl CO15 .....188 F7
Credon Dr CO15 .....188 F7
Creek Cotts CO14 ...144 E4
Creek View CO5 .....181 F2
Creekhurst Cl CO7 ...186 A6
Creffield Rd CO3 ....135 D6
Crepping Hall Dr IP9 .61 F1
Crescent Ct CM9 ....209 F5
Crescent Rd
  Bishop's Stortford CM23 .146 A6
  Felixstowe IP11 ......221 E4
  Great Baddow CM2 ...217 A7
  Heybridge CM9 ......209 F6
  Ipswich IP1 ....17 B6
  Tollesbury CM9 ......199 E1
  Walton-on-t-N CO14 ..171 C8
Crescent The
  Clacton-on-S CO15 ...189 B7
  Colchester CO4 ......110 C7
  Frinton-on-S CO13 ...170 A4
  Great Holland CO13 ..170 A4
  Great Horkesley CO6 .82 B1
  Great Leighs CM3 ....173 E5
  Marks Tey CO6 ......133 A3
  Steeple Bumpstead CB9 .27 B7
  Thorpe-le-S CO16 ....141 F2
  West Bergholt CO6 ...108 D5
Cress Croft CM7 ....128 D1
Cressages Cl CM6 ...152 F6
Cressing Cty Prim Sch
  CM77 ....155 E6
Cressing Rd
  Braintree CM7 ....128 C2
  Witham CM8 ....176 D6
Cressing Sta CM77 ..155 D5
Cressing Temple Barns★
  CM77 ....156 B2
Crestlands CO7 ......165 B7
Cricket Hill Rd IP11 ..221 B5
Cricketers Cl
  Broomfield CM1 .....191 C1
  Sudbury CO10 ....33 E6
Cricketfield La CM23 .145 E8
Crispin Cl CB9 ......8 D7
Critchett Terr 1 CM1 .205 A3
Crittall Cl CM8 ......156 E4
Crittall Dr CM7 ......127 D4
Crittall Rd CM8 .....177 B3
Crix Green Villas CM6 .153 D6
Croasdaile Cl CM24 ..119 E8
Croasdaile Rd CM24 ..119 E8
Crocklands CO9 .....104 A5
Crocus Cl
  Clacton-on-S CO16 ...188 C4
  Ipswich IP2 ....16 E4
Crocus Fields CB10 ..22 E3
Crocus Way CM1 ....205 E7
Croft Cl CM7 ....128 A3
Croft Ct CM1 ....205 E8
Croft Ho CB9 ....9 B6
Croft La CB9 ....9 B6
Croft Rd
  Clacton-on-S CO15 ...188 D4
  Kelvedon CO5 ....158 D2
  Sudbury CO10 ....33 E8
Croft St IP2 ....17 C3
Croft The
  Bures CO8 ....55 F1
  Earls Colne CO6 .....105 A6
  Elsenham CM22 ......94 C1
  Glemsford CO10 .....2 C4
  Great Yeldham CO9 ..30 A2
Croft Way CM8 ......177 A3
Crofters Wlk CM77 ..154 D8
Crofton Cl IP4 ......18 B7
Crofton Rd IP4 ......18 B7
Croftside CO8 ......55 F1
Cromar Way CM1 ...204 F1
Cromarty Rd IP4 ....18 B8
Crome Cl CO3 ......135 A5
Crome Rd CO16 .....188 D5
Cromer Rd IP1 ......16 F8
Cromhurst Ct CO3 ...135 E7
Crompton Rd IP2 ....16 F2
Crompton St CM1 ...204 F1
Cromwell Cl
  Bishop's Stortford CM23 .145 B7
  Boreham CM3 ....206 D8

Col – Cur 229

Cromwell Ct
  11 Ipswich IP1 ......17 C5
  Maldon CM9 ....210 A3
Cromwell Ctr CM8 ...177 B2
Cromwell Hill CM9 ...209 F3
Cromwell Ho CO4 ...109 F4
Cromwell La CM9 ....209 F3
Cromwell Pk CM6 ...152 B5
Cromwell Rd
  16 Colchester CO2 ...135 F6
  Saffron Walden CB11 ..43 E7
Cromwell Sq 8 IP1 ..17 C5
Cromwell Way CM8 ..176 F2
Croquet Gdns CO7 ...137 C1
Cross Cotts CO4 .....83 B6
Cross End CO9 ......78 C8
Cross Field Way CO4 .83 B5
Cross Hill CO12 .....116 D1
Cross La CO5 ....201 F7
Cross Rd Maldon CM9 .210 A1
  Witham CM8 ....176 F1
Cross St Felixstowe IP11 .221 C6
  Saffron Walden CB10 ..22 D1
  Sudbury CO10 ....33 D7
Cross The
  West Mersea CO5 ....201 E7
  Wivenhoe CO7 ....137 B2
Cross Way CO5 ......201 E7
Crossfield Rd CO15 ..188 E3
Crossfield Way CO13 .170 B6
Crossfields CO6 .....56 C5
Crossgate Field IP11 .221 C5
Crossley Ave CO15 ..203 E7
Crossroads CO9 .....31 E2
Crosstree Wlk CO2 ..136 A3
Crossways
  Chelmsford CM2 .....216 C7
  Clacton-on-S CO15 ...203 G8
  Colne Engaine CO6 ...77 F1
Crotchets Cl IP9 .....35 A1
Crouch Ct CM7 .....128 D1
Crouch Dr CM8 .....176 E2
Crouch St CO3 ......135 E6
Crouchman's Farm Rd
  CM9 ....208 C7
Croutel Rd IP11 .....221 F5
Crow La CO16 ......141 A3
Crow Pond Rd CM3 ..175 C3
Crow St CM22 ......94 F5
Crowe Hall La IP9 ...62 A1
Crowhall La CO11 ...87 E1
Crowhurst Rd CO3 ..135 E7
Crowland Cl 7 IP2 ..17 A2
Crowland Rd CB9 ...8 F8
Crown Bays Rd CO4 .136 C8
Crown Gate CO4 ....110 D6
Crown Hill CB10 ....6 B1
Crown La Harwich CO12 .91 D4
  Tendring CO16 ......140 D3
Crown La N CO7 ....110 F7
Crown La S CO7 ....111 A4
Crown Mdw CM7 ...128 C4
Crown Rd CO15 .....188 C1
Crown St
  Castle Hedingham CO9 .51 E4
  Dedham CO7 ....84 F6
  Felixstowe IP11 ......221 C6
  Great Bardfield CM7 ..72 B2
  Ipswich IP1 ....17 C6
Crown Terr CM23 ...146 A7
Crownfield Rd CO10 .2 B6
Crownfields CO7 ....84 F6
Croxall Ct CM8 .....176 F2
Crozier Ave CM23 ...145 C8
Crozier Terr CM2 ...206 B4
Cruce Way CO16 ....185 F3
Crummock Cl CM77 .154 C6
Crunch Croft CB9 ...9 E5
Crusader Way CM7 ..128 D2
Crushton Pl CM1 ....204 F6
Cuckfield Ave IP3 ...18 E3
Cuckoo Hill Bures CO8 .55 F1
  Sible Hedingham CO9 .75 B8
Cuckoo Way CM77 ..154 C7
Cuckoos La
  Great Canfield CM6 ..149 A3
  Takeley CM6 ....148 F2
Cudmore Grove Ctry Pk★
  CO5 ....185 A1
Culford Pl IP3 ......17 F4
Culford Wlk IP11 ....221 A3
Cullingham Rd IP1 ..17 A5
Culver St E CO1 .....135 F7
Culver St W CO1 ....135 F7
Culver Wlk 21 CO1 ..135 F7
Culvert Cl CO6 ......130 F2
Cumberland Ave CM9 .209 E1
Cumberland Cl CM7 ..128 B4
Cumberland Cres CM1 .205 A7
Cumberland Ct
  Clacton-on-S CO15 ...189 B5
  Colchester CO3 ......135 D6
Cumberland St IP1 ..17 B7
Cumberland Twrs IP1 .17 A7
Cunningham Cl CO2 .136 A4
Cunnington Rd CM7 .128 C3
Cunobelin Way CO2 .135 A2
Cuppers Cl CM8 ....176 E1
Curds Rd CO6 ......105 A4
Curlew Cl
  Clacton-on-S CO15 ...188 F6
  Heybridge CM9 ......210 C5
  Kelvedon CO5 ....158 D2
Curlew Croft CO4 ...136 C6
Curlew Rd IP2 ......16 D4

Curling Tye La
  Maldon CM9 ....209 A3
  Woodham Walter CM9 ..208 F3
Currants Farm Rd CM7 .127 E5
Currents La CO12 ....91 E6
Curriers' La IP1 ....17 C5
Curtis Cl
  Clacton-on-S CO16 .....188 B3
  Ipswich IP8 ....16 C1
Curzon Rd CO10 ....34 B8
Curzon Way CM2 ....206 A2
Cusak Rd CM2 ....205 F3
Custerson Ct CB11 ......22 D1
Custerson Dr CM77 .....155 B5
Custom House La CO12 ..91 D6
Cut Hedge CM77 ....154 C6
Cut The CO5 ....179 C5
Cut Throat La CM8 .....177 A4
Cut-A-Thwart La CM9 ...209 C4
Cuthedge La CO6 ....157 D7
Cutler St IP1 ....17 C5
Cutlers Cl CM23 ....145 D6
Cutlers La CO7 ....59 D5
Cutmaple CO9 ....75 E4
Cutmore Pl CM2 ....215 F8
Cuton Hall La CM2 .....206 A5
Cutting Dr CO9 ....76 E1
Cygnet Ct
  [11] Bishop's Stortford
  CM23 ....145 F6
  Sible Hedingham CO9 ...51 E1
Cygnet Wlk CO3 ....134 C4
**Cymbeline Way (Colchester
  By Pass)** CO3 ....135 B8
Cypress Cl CO15 ....188 E7
Cypress Ct CM6 ....123 B1
Cypress Dr CM2 ....216 C6
Cypress Gr [5] CO4 ....136 F8
Cypress Mews CO5 .....201 B7
Cypress Rd CM8 ....177 A4
Cyril Child Cl CM8 .....136 C7
Cyril Dowsett Ct CM9 ..209 E2

D

D'arcy Ave CM9 ....210 B1
D'arcy Cl CO13 ....170 F6
D'arcy Ho CO14 ....144 D2
D'arcy Hts CO2 ....136 C3
D'arcy Rd Colchester CO2 136 C3
  St Osyth CO16 ....187 B4
  Tiptree CO5 ....179 F2
D'arcy Way
  Brightlingsea CO7 ......185 E7
  Tolleshunt D'arcy CM9 ..198 E4
Daen Ingas CM3 ....218 D7
Daffodil Cl IP2 ....16 E3
Daffodil Way CM1 ......205 E4
Dagnets La CM77 ....154 D3
Dahlia Cl
  [2] Chelmsford CM1 .....205 F5
  Clacton-on-S CO16 .....188 C4
Dahlia Wlk CO4 ....136 D7
Daimler Ave CO15 ......203 D6
Dains Pl IP11 ....221 A7
Dairy Rd CM2 ....205 F4
Dairyhouse La CO11 ....114 F7
Daisleys La CM3 ....174 A2
Daisy Ct CM1 ....206 A6
Daisy Green Rd CO3 ....133 E8
Daisley Rd CM6 ....98 B4
Dale Cl Colchester CO3 .134 B7
  Elmstead CO7 ....138 A6
Dale Hall La IP1 ....17 C8
Dale Ho CM7 ....127 E4
Dale The CO7 ....164 C8
Dales The CO12 ....90 F1
Dales View IP8 ....35 E8
Dales View Rd [1] IP1 ..17 A8
Dalham Pl [4] CB9 .....9 A8
Dallwood Way CM7 .....128 B3
Dalrymple Cl CM1 ......205 D3
Daltes La CO10 ....187 C3
Dalton Rd IP1 ....17 B6
Damant's Farm La CO16 142 D1
Damases La CM3 ....193 C1
Damask Mews CM7 .....128 A2
Damask Rd CO3 ....134 C7
Dame Elizabeth Ct CM1 190 F3
Dame Johane Bradbury's Sch
  CB10 ....22 F2
Dammant Ct [8] CO4 ...136 D8
Dampier Rd CO4 ....130 F3
Damselfly Rd IP3 ....38 C8
Danbury Cl CO6 ....132 F3
Danbury Ctry Pk ★ CM3 218 B7
Danbury Park Com Prim Sch
  CM3 ....218 C7
Danbury Vale CM3 ......219 A6
Dancing Dicks La CM8 .176 A2
Dandalan Cl IP1 ....16 E8
Dane Acres CM23 ......145 D8
Dane Ho CM23 ....145 D8
Dane O'Coys Rd CM23 .118 C1
Dane Pk CM23 ....145 D8
Dane Rd CM1 ....204 E2
Dane St CM23 ....146 A7
Danes Ct CO10 ....34 B4
Daneum Holt CO10 .....12 A6
Daniel Cole Rd CO2 ....135 F4
Daniel Way CM8 ....156 E4
Daniell Cl CO16 ....188 C6

Daniell Dr CO2 ....135 B2
Daniells Ho CO6 ....108 F4
Dansie Ct [7] CO4 .....136 C8
Daphne Cl CM77 ....154 C7
Daphne Ct [4] CO4 ....136 D8
Dapier Dr CM7 ....128 D3
Darcy Rise CM3 ....207 E1
Darina Ct CM3 ....134 B7
Darkhouse La CO5 ......164 A8
Darnay Rise CM1 ......204 D6
Darnel Way CO3 ....134 B7
Darnet Rd CM9 ....199 E1
Darrell Cl CM1 ....205 B6
Darrell Rd IP11 ....221 B1
Darsham Cl IP11 ....221 B1
Dart Cl CM8 ....176 D2
Darter Cl IP3 ....38 C8
Dartmouth Rd CM1 .....205 E6
Darwin Cl
  [5] Braintree CM7 ......127 F1
  Colchester CO2 ....136 B1
Darwin Rd IP4 ....17 F5
Dashwood Cl IP8 ....16 D1
Datchet Ho CO3 ....134 F7
Daundy Cl IP2 ....16 D5
Davall Cl CO12 ....90 C1
Davey Cl Colchester CO1 136 D6
  Ipswich IP8 ....17 F1
Davidson Cl CO10 ......34 D4
Davies Ct CM7 ....128 A2
Davy Rd CO15 ....189 C8
Daw St Birdbrook CO9 ..28 B7
  Finchingfield CM7 ....72 E4
Daw's Hall (Wildfowl Farm) ★
  CO8 ....55 B6
Dawes La CO5 ....201 E8
Dawlish Rd CO15 ....203 I8
Dawnbrook Cl [1] IP2 ..16 E1
Dawnford Cl CO3 ....134 C7
Dawnford Ct CO3 ....134 C7
Daws Cross CO8 ....78 F6
Dawson Cl CB10 ....22 F2
Dawson Dr IP11 ....221 A8
Days Cl CM1 ....205 B8
Dazeley's La CO7 ....85 F8
De Bohun Ct CB10 ......22 E2
De Burgh Rd CO3 ....134 E6
De Greys Cl CO10 ......34 C5
De Mandeville Rd CM22 .94 C2
De Staunton Cl CO7 ....165 B7
De Vere Ave CM9 ......210 B1
De Vere Cl
  Hatfield Peverel CM3 ...194 B3
  Wivenhoe CO7 ....164 B8
De Vere Est CO7 ....166 B8
De Vere La CO7 ....164 B8
De Vere Prim Sch CO9 ..51 E4
De Vere Rd
  Colchester CO3 ....135 A5
  Earls Colne CO6 ....104 F7
De Vere Way CO12 .....90 F2
De Veres Rd [7] CO9 ...76 D1
De Vigier Ave CB10 ....23 A2
De-Marci Cl CM7 ....128 D3
Dead La Ardleigh CO7 ..111 C8
  Great Bentley CO7 ......166 F2
  Lawford CO11 ....86 C2
  Little Clacton CO16 .....168 B2
Deadman's La CM2 .....216 C4
Deal Cl Braintree CM7 ..127 E6
  Clacton-on-S CO15 .....203 J8
Deal Way CO7 ....185 E8
Dean Rd CB1 ....6 B8
Dean Rogers Pl CM7 ....127 F7
Dean St CO7 ....185 E7
Dean Way CM1 ....204 E1
Deane's Cl CO12 ....91 A2
Deanery Gdns CM7 .....127 F7
Deanery Hill CM7 ......127 E7
Deanes Ct CO12 ....91 A2
Deanhill Ave CO15 .....189 C5
Deans Wlk CM7 ....127 F8
Debden CE Prim Sch
  CB11 ....68 B7
Debden Dr CB10 ....44 E2
Debden Gn Newport CB11 .67 C8
  Saffron Walden CB11 ....43 D8
  Saffron Walden CB11 ....43 E6
Debden Cl CM8 ....176 E2
Debden Ct CM7 ....128 D1
Debden Dr CO10 ....34 A8
Debden High Sch IP11 ..221 D4
Debden Rd Colchester CO4 110 F1
  Haverhill CB9 ....9 B8
Debden Way IP11 ......221 A5
Debden Wlk CO16 ......188 C6
Dedham Ave CO16 ......188 B5
Dedham CE Prim Sch
  CO7 ....85 A6
Dedham Ct CO2 ....136 B4
Dedham Meade CO7 ....84 F3
Dedham Pl [7] IP4 .....17 D5
Dedham Rd Ardleigh CO7 .84 D1
  Boxted CO4 ....83 B6
  Lawford CO11 ....85 A4
  Stratford St M CO7 .....58 E1
Deepdale Rd CO12 .....91 A4
Deeping Wlk CO16 .....187 B5
Deer Park Cl CO9 ......51 F3
Deerhurst Chase CM3 ..218 F1
Deerleap Way CM7 .....128 D4
Defoe Cres CO4 ....109 E4
Deford Rd CM8 ....194 D8
Delamere Rd
  Chelmsford CM1 ....204 E1
  Colchester CO4 ....110 D3
Delius Wlk CO4 ....136 E6

Dell La
  Bishop's Stortford, Hockerill
  CM23 ....146 A7
  Bishop's Stortford,
  Latchmore Bank CM22 ..146 B1
Dell The Colchester CO1 .136 A6
  Great Baddow CM2 .....216 F6
  Great Cornard CO10 ....34 A6
  Great Dunmow CM6 .....123 E1
Dellows La CM22 ....94 A2
Dells The [11] CM23 ....145 F7
Dellwood Ave IP11 .....221 F5
Delvyn's La CO9 ....52 C6
Demoiselle Cres IP3 ....38 C8
Dene Ct CM1 ....204 D5
Dengie Cl CM8 ....194 F8
Denham Cl CO7 ....164 C8
Denholm Ct CM8 ....194 F8
Denmark Gdns IP9 .....62 D6
Denmark Ho CM2 ....216 D8
Denny Ct CM23 ....119 B2
Denton Cl IP2 ....16 D2
Denton Cres CM77 .....155 B5
Denton's Terr CO7 .....164 B8
Derby Cl IP4 ....18 A5
Derby Rd IP3 ....18 A4
Derby Road Sta IP3 ....18 A4
Dereham Ave IP3 ....17 F3
Dereham Cl CO2 ....135 C3
Derwent Gdns CO15 ....189 C6
Derwent Rd
  Highwoods CO4 ....110 C4
  Ipswich IP3 ....18 A4
Derwent Way
  Chelmsford CM1 ....204 D4
  Great Notley CM77 .....154 C7
Desborough Path CM2 ..205 F8
Devereaux Cl CO14 .....170 F8
Devereaux Ct [17] IP4 ..17 D6
Devereaux Pl CO4 ......109 C3
Devereux Ct CO15 .....188 F3
Devereux Pl CO4 ....109 C3
Deverill Cl CM7 ....191 B2
Devlin Rd IP8 ....16 B1
Devoils La [8] CM23 ...145 F7
Devon Rd Colchester CO2 135 B3
  Felixstowe IP11 ....221 D5
Devon Way Harwich CO12 .90 D2
  Holland-on-S CO15 .....189 C7
Devonshire Cnr CM7 ...128 B4
Devonshire Rd IP3 .....17 F5
Dewberry Cl [3] CO4 ...136 D7
Dewes Green Rd
  Berden CM23 ....92 A8
  Clavering CM23 ....64 F1
Dewlands CM77 ....155 B6
Deynes Rd CB11 ....68 B7
Dhobi Pl IP1 ....16 F7
Dial Cnr CO7 ....166 E3
Dial La IP1 ....17 C6
Dial Rd CO7 ....166 E3
Diana Ho CO13 ....170 E5
Diana Way CO15 ....188 C2
Dickens Cl CM7 ....155 D8
Dickens Pl CM1 ....204 D7
Dickens Rd IP2 ....16 F5
Dicksons Cnr IP1 ......16 C7
Dicky Moors CM3 ......190 F7
Didsbury Cl IP2 ....16 D2
Digby Mews CO5 ....201 C6
Digby Rd IP4 ....18 C7
Dilbridge Rd E CO4 ....136 C8
Dilbridge Rd W CO4 ....136 C8
Dillestone Ct CB9 ......9 E5
Dillwyn St IP1 ....17 A6
Dillwyn St W IP1 ......17 A6
Dilston CM3 ....219 A6
Dimsdale Cres CM23 ...146 B6
Dinants Cres CO6 ......132 E3
Dinsdale Cl [1] CO4 ....136 C8
Dinsdale Ct IP11 ......221 D3
Dismals The CM3 ....175 B2
Distillery La CO2 ......136 C4
Ditchingham Gr IP5 ....18 F6
Dixon Ave
  Chelmsford CM1 ....204 F4
  Clacton-on-S CO16 .....188 C6
Dixon Cl CO11 ....86 B4
Dixon Way CO7 ....137 A2
Dobbies La CO6 ....132 F3
Dock Rd IP11 ....221 B2
Dock St IP2 ....17 C4
Docker Ct CO2 ....136 B4
Dockfield Ave CO12 ....90 F2
Dockwra La CM3 ....219 A7
Doctor's La CO10 ......11 D2
Docwra Rd CO5 ....158 C2
Doddenhill Cl CB10 ....22 E3
Dodmans [7] IP9 ....35 A1
Doe's Cnr Halstead CO9 .76 D5
  Hatfield Peverel CM9 ...194 F1
Dog Chase CM7 ....73 C3
Dogden La CM23 ....92 E2
Doggetts La CO6 ......132 F2
Doghouse Rd CM7 ......129 F4
Dogs Head St [4] IP4 ..17 C5
Dogwood Cl IP3 ....18 D2
Dolby Rise CM2 ....205 F2
Dolphin Ct CO13 ....171 B6
Dolphin Way CM23 .....146 A8
Dombey Cl CM1 ....204 F7
Dombey Rd IP2 ....16 F5
Domitian Cl CO4 ....110 B6
Doms La CM3 ....175 B2
Domsey Bank CO6 ......132 E3
Domsey Chase CO5 ....159 C8
Domsey La CM3 ....191 F5

Don Ct CM8 ....176 D2
Donald Way CM2 ....216 C7
Donard Dr CO6 ....108 D4
Donne Dr CO15 ....203 G8
Donyland Way CO5 .....163 F8
Dooley Rd
  Felixstowe IP11 ....221 A3
  Halstead CO9 ....76 D1
Dorchester End CO2 ....136 B3
Dorchester Rd IP3 .....18 D3
Dordell Ct CO9 ....50 B8
Dorewards Ave CM7 ....127 F7
Dorking Cres CO16 .....188 C6
Dorking Wlk CM2 ......216 F2
Dorothy Curtice Ct CO6 133 E5
Dorothy Sayers Dr CM8 177 A5
Dorset Ave CM2 ....216 C6
Dorset Cl
  Great Baddow CM2 .....216 E6
  Halstead CO9 ....76 E1
  Holland-on-S CO15 .....189 E6
Dorset Ho [13] CM23 ...145 F7
Dorset Rd CM9 ....220 F8
Dorvis La CB10 ....6 B1
Doubleday Dr CM9 .....209 F5
Doubleday Gdns CM7 ...128 B5
Doucecroft Sch CO5 ...158 C3
Douglas Cl CM2 ....216 D3
Douglas Gr CM8 ....176 D2
Douglas Rd
  Clacton-on-S CO15 .....188 C4
  Harwich CO12 ....91 B3
Douglas Wlk [3] CM2 ..216 A8
Dove Cl
  Bishop's Stortford CM23 .145 E3
  Stansted Mountfitchet
  CM24 ....119 E8
Dove Cotts CM22 ....93 F3
Dove Cres CO12 ....90 D2
Dove House Rd CB9 ....9 A8
Dove La CM2 ....216 A6
Dove St IP4 ....17 E5
Dove Tree Ct CO3 ......134 C5
Dovedale IP11 ....221 B3
Dovedale Gdns CO15 ...189 C6
Dover Cl Braintree CM7 .127 E6
  Clacton-on-S CO15 .....203 J8
Dover Rd
  Brightlingsea CO7 ......185 F8
  Ipswich IP3 ....18 B4
Dovercourt Caravan Pk
  CO12 ....91 A1
Dovercourt Sta CO12 ...91 D4
Doves Cl CM6 ....150 B2
Dowches Cotts CO5 ....158 C2
Dowches Dr CO5 ....158 C3
Dowches Gdns CO5 .....158 C3
Dowding Cl CO2 ....136 A4
Dowling Rd CO8 ....79 F3
Downham Bvd IP3 ......38 C3
Downing Cl IP2 ....16 F2
Downing Prim Sch IP2 ..16 F2
Downs Cres
  Great Dunmow CM6 .....123 C1
  Haverhill CB9 ....8 C8
Downs Pl [2] CB9 ......8 B8
Downs Rd CM9 ....210 B3
Downs Terr CM6 ....124 D6
Downs The
  Felixstowe IP11 ....221 B5
  Great Dunmow CM6 .....123 D1
Downside Cl IP2 ....36 F8
Downsway CM1 ....205 D6
Downton Dr CB9 ....8 E8
Downton Wlk CO5 ......179 D6
Dragon's Gn CB10 ......23 D1
Drake Ave IP3 ....18 B2
Drake Gdns CM7 ....128 C4
Drake Sq N IP3 ....18 B2
Drake Sq S IP3 ....18 B2
Drakes App CO15 ......188 A1
Drakes Cnr CO5 ....181 F2
Drakes La Boreham CM3 .192 B1
  Little Waltham CM3 .....191 F7
Drapers Chase
  Heybridge CM9 ....210 D4
  Rayne CM7 ....153 D6
Drapers La CB9 ....8 B2
Drapery Comm CO10 ...2 B4
Dray Ct CO6 ....108 F4
Drayman's Ct CM23 ....145 B5
Draymans Gr CM77 ....154 C8
Draymans Way IP3 .....17 E3
Drays The CO10 ....15 E5
Drayton Cl [4] CM9 ....210 A1
Dreys The CB10 ....44 E8
Driberg Way CM7 ......128 A1
Driffield Cl CO5 ....158 D4
Drift The
  East Bergholt CO7 ......60 C2
  Great Cornard CO10 ....34 C5
  Ipswich,Priory Heath IP3 .18 C1
  Ipswich,Rose Hill IP4 ...18 A6
  Stutton IP9 ....62 C2
Driftway The IP4 ....18 B6
Drive The
  Chelmsford CM1 ....205 A6
  Clacton-on-S CO15 .....189 B7
  Harwich CO12 ....91 B2
  Rivenhall CM8 ....177 C6
  Thaxted CM6 ....69 F3
Drood Cl CM1 ....204 F7
Drovers Way CM23 .....145 C5
Druce The CB11 ....65 D4
Drum Field CO7 ....58 D1
Drury Dr CO10 ....15 F2

Drury La
  [4] Braintree CM7 .....127 F3
  Ridgewell CO9 ....29 A6
Drury Rd CO2 ....135 C5
Dry Dock CO7 ....164 B8
Du Cane Pl [3] CM8 ...177 A2
Duchess Cl CM23 ......145 C7
Duck End CM23 ....119 F1
Duck St Little Easton CM6 122 F5
  Wendens Ambo CB11 ...42 A1
Duckend Farm La CM6 ..97 F6
Ducketts Wharf [10]
  CM23 ....145 F6
Duddery Cl CB9 ....9 B7
Duddery Hill CB9 ......9 A7
Duddery Rd CB9 ....9 A7
Dudley Cl Boreham CM3 .192 E1
  Colchester CO2 ....136 A4
Dudley Rd
  Clacton-on-S CO15 .....188 D3
  Earls Colne CO6 ....104 F7
  Fingringhoe CO5 ....163 E3
Duffield Dr CO4 ....136 E7
Duffield Rd CM2 ....216 D6
Duffries Cl CM3 ....190 E7
Duffs Hill CO10 ....2 B6
Dugard Ave CO3 ....134 E4
Duggers La CM7 ....128 A1
Dugmore Ave CO13 ....170 C8
Duke St
  Brightlingsea CO7 ......185 E6
  Chelmsford CM1 ....205 B2
  Ipswich IP3 ....17 E4
Dukes La [5] CM2 ......205 F4
Dukes Orch CM1 ....204 B1
Dukes Park Ind Est CM2 205 F4
Dukes Priory Hospl The
  CM1 ....205 D4
Dukes Rd CM7 ....127 F7
Dukes Ride CM23 ......145 C7
Dulverton Cotts CO3 ...134 C4
Dulwich Cl CO15 ......189 D4
Dulwich Rd CO15 ......189 D5
Dumbarton Rd IP4 .....18 C8
Dumfries Rd IP4 ....18 C8
Dumney La
  Braintree, Hornells Corner
  CM3 ....153 E2
  Braintree, Thistley Green
  CM6 ....153 B3
  Great Leighs CM3 ......173 E8
Dumont Ave CO16 .....186 B2
Duncan Rd CO2 ....135 B4
Duncan Rise CO9 ......29 F2
Dunlin Cl CM9 ....210 C5
Dunlin Ct CO5 ....158 C2
Dunlin Rd IP2 ....16 E2
Dunlop Rd IP2 ....16 F6
Dunmore Rd CM2 ......206 A3
Dunmow Rd
  Bishop's Stortford CM23 .146 C7
  Felsted CM6 ....125 C7
  Great Bardfield CM7 ....98 F8
  Great Canfield CM6 ....149 F1
  Great Hallingbury CM22 .147 C7
  Rayne CM77 ....126 B2
  Takeley CM22 ....148 C7
  Thaxted CM6 ....97 A7
Dunning Cl CO11 ......114 C8
Dunnock Way CO4 .....137 A7
Dunoon Cl CM7 ....128 D4
Dunster Dr CB9 ....8 E8
Dunthorne Rd CO4 .....110 E2
Dunthorpe Rd CO16 ...188 D6
Duntons Almshouses
  CO7 ....84 F6
Dunwich Ct
  Colchester CO2 ....135 F4
  Haverhill CB9 ....8 C8
  Ipswich IP1 ....16 E8
Dupont Cl CO16 ....188 D6
Durham Cl CM7 ....72 A1
Durham Sq CO1 ....136 A7
Duxford Rd CB10 ......3 A7
Dyehouse Mdw CO10 ..15 B7
Dyer's Rd Colchester CO3 134 C3
  Maldon CM9 ....210 A2
Dyers Ct CM23 ....145 C5
Dyers Rd CO9 ....28 E1
Dyke Rd IP11 ....221 A2
Dyke St IP1 ....17 C7
Dykes Chase CM9 .....209 F3
Dyne's Hall Rd CO9 ....76 C8

E

Eagle Ave CO14 ....144 D1
Eagle La CM7 ....127 F6
Eagle St [3] IP4 ....17 D5
Eaglegate CO1 ....136 A7
Eagles Cl IP11 ....221 D4
Earlhams Cl CO12 .....90 F1
Earls Cl CM23 ....145 D6
Earls Colne Prim Sch
  CO6 ....105 C6
Earls Colne Rd CO6 ....106 A1
Earls Gn CO9 ....8 C8
Earls Hall Dr CO16 ....187 E5
Earlsfield Dr CM2 ......205 F3
Earlsmead CM8 ....176 F3
Earlswood Way CO2 ...135 D2
East Anglian Rly Mus ★
  CO6 ....106 D6
East Area IP1 ....16 C7
East Bay CO1 ....136 B7
East Bergholt CE Prim Sch
  CO7 ....59 B3

East Bergholt High Sch
  CO7 . . . . .59 D3
East Bergholt Place Gdn★
  CO7 . . . . .59 F1
East Court Ho CO1 . . . .136 C7
East Dock Rd CO12 . . . . .90 F6
East End La CO7 . . . . . . .60 C2
East End Rd CO7 . . . . . . .60 A3
East Essex Aviation Mus★
  CO16 . . . . .185 E4
East Gores Rd CO6 . . . .131 F5
East Hanningfield Rd
  CM2 . . . . .217 E2
East Haven CO15 . . . . . .188 E5
East Hill CO1 . . . . .136 A7
East La CO7 . . . . .85 B5
East Lawn IP4 . . . . .18 C8
East Mersea Rd CO5 . . .183 E1
East Mill CO9 . . . . .76 D7
East Mill Gn IP9 . . . . . . .60 E6
East Rd
  Bishop's Stortford CM23 .146 B7
  East Mersea CO5 . . . . . .184 D1
  West Mersea CO5 . . . . .201 E7
East Row IP9 . . . . .62 D6
East Side CO4 . . . . .83 A4
East St Braintree CM7 . . .128 A3
  Coggeshall CO6 . . . . . . .131 A2
  Colchester CO1 . . . . . . .136 B7
  Harwich CO12 . . . . .91 D4
  Saffron Walden CB10 . . . .22 E1
  Sudbury CO10 . . . . .33 F8
  Tollesbury CM9 . . . . . . .199 D1
  Wivenhoe CO7 . . . . . . .164 B7
East Stockwell St CO1 . .135 F7
East Terr CO14 . . . . .144 D1
East View CM22 . . . . . . .148 C8
East View CI CB10 . . . . . .45 F8
East Ward Mews CO1 . .136 C7
Eastcate CB10 . . . . .22 E2
Eastby CI CB11 . . . . .43 F8
Eastcliff Ave CO15 . . . . .189 B4
Eastcliff Ho CO14 . . . . .144 D1
Easten Greene CO6 . . . . .80 E4
Eastend La CM6,CM22 . .121 C8
Easterford Rd CO5 . . . . .158 C2
Easterling Ct CO12 . . . . . .91 A4
Eastern App CM2 . . . . . .205 D7
Eastern Ave CB9 . . . . .8 F8
Eastern CI IP4 . . . . .18 F4
Eastern Cres CM1 . . . . . .204 D5
Eastern Prom CO16 . . . .185 F3
Eastern Rd CO7 . . . . . . .185 E6
Eastgate
  Great Chesterford CB10 . . .3 D2
  ⬛ Ipswich IP4 . . . . .17 D6
Eastgate St CO12 . . . . . . .91 D6
Easthorpe Rd
  Feering CO5 . . . . .159 D7
  Messing CO5 . . . . .159 F5
Eastland Ct IP11 . . . . . .221 E7
Easton Rd CM8 . . . . .177 A3
Easton Way CO13 . . . . . .171 B6
Eastway Ent Ctr IP1 . . . . .16 D8
Eastways CM8 . . . . .177 B4
Eastwood Dr CO4 . . . . . .110 B3
Eaton CI IP11 . . . . .221 A4
Eaton Cotts CO5 . . . . . .179 D7
Eaton Gdns IP11 . . . . . .221 C2
Eaton Ho ⬛ CM23 . . . . .146 B8
Eaton Mews CO2 . . . . . .136 B3
Eaton Way CM9 . . . . . . .196 F2
Ebenezer CI CM8 . . . . . .176 E5
Ebenezer Terr CM2 . . . .216 F7
Ebony CI CO2 . . . . .135 D2
Eccles Rd IP2 . . . . .16 D1
Eckersley Rd CM1 . . . . .205 C3
Eden CI CM8 . . . . .176 E3
Eden Rd Haverhill CB9 . . . .9 A7
  Ipswich IP4 . . . . .18 B5
Eden Way CM1 . . . . .204 C5
Edens CI CM23 . . . . .146 B7
Edenside CO13 . . . . .170 E7
Edgefield Ave CO11 . . . . .86 B3
Edgeworth Rd IP2 . . . . . .16 E2
Edgware Rd CO16 . . . . .188 D5
Edgworth Rd CO10 . . . . .33 E7
Edinburgh CI CM8 . . . . .195 A8
Edinburgh Gdns
  Bishop's Stortford CM23 .145 E5
  Braintree CM7 . . . . .128 C4
Edison CI ⬛ CM7 . . . . .127 F1
Edison Gdns CO4 . . . . . .110 C1
Edison Rd CO15 . . . . . . .189 F6
Edith Borthwick Sch The
  CM7 . . . . .127 F8
Edith Cavell Way CB9 . . .27 C6
Edith Rd
  Clacton-on-S CO15 . . . . .188 E2
  Kirby-le-S CO13 . . . . . . .170 D8
Edmund CI CB9 . . . . .8 E7
Edmund Gn CO9 . . . . . .102 E8
Edmund Rd CM8 . . . . . .194 E8
Edward Ave CO7 . . . . . .185 F7
Edward Bowden Ct CB10 22 D1
Edward Bright CI CM9 . .210 A2
Edward CI Ipswich IP1 . . . .16 E4
  Little Clacton CO16 . . . . .168 E5
Edward Cordy Ho IP11 . .221 E3
Edward Dr CM2 . . . . . . .216 C2
Edward Marke Dr CO5 . .163 B3
Edward Rd CO16 . . . . . .168 F7
Edward St CO12 . . . . .90 E5
Edward Terr CO16 . . . . .168 E5
Edwards Wlk CM9 . . . . .209 F3
Egerton Green Rd CO2 . .135 A3
Egglestone CI IP2 . . . . . .16 F1
Eggshall La CM7 . . . . . . .27 E2

Eglinton Dr CM2 . . . . . .206 B4
Egremont St CO10 . . . . . .2 B3
Egremont Way CO3 . . . .134 C4
Egret Cres CO4 . . . . . . .137 A8
Ehringshausen Way CB9 . .9 B7
Eight Acre La CO2 . . . . .135 C2
Eight Ash Green & Aldham
  CE Prim Sch CO3 . . . . . .107 F1
Eld La CO1 . . . . .135 F7
Elder Field CM7 . . . . . . .154 B5
Elderberry Gdns CM8 . . .177 B4
Eldon CI CO4 . . . . .110 E1
Eldred Ave CO2 . . . . . . .135 B3
Eldred Dr CO10 . . . . .34 C4
Eleanor CI CO5 . . . . .179 D6
Eleanor Wlk CO5 . . . . . .179 D6
Eleventh Ave CM24 . . . .120 B2
Elgar Dr CM8 . . . . .194 F7
Elgin Ave CM1 . . . . .205 A2
Elianore Rd CO3 . . . . . . .135 B7
Eliot Way CM9 . . . . .210 A1
Elizabeth Ave CM8 . . . . .195 A8
Elizabeth CI
  Highwoods CO4 . . . . . . .110 C4
  Saffron Walden CB10 . . . .22 C7
Elizabeth Ct CO14 . . . . .144 E3
Elizabeth Rd
  Bishop's Stortford CM23 .145 E5
  Harwich CO12 . . . . .91 A3
Elizabeth Villas CO5 . . . .180 A3
Elizabeth Way
  Brightlingsea CO7 . . . . .185 F6
  Felixstowe IP11 . . . . . . .221 C3
  Halstead CO9 . . . . .76 C2
  Hatfield Peverel CM3 . . .194 A4
  Heybridge CM9 . . . . . . .210 A5
  Saffron Walden CB10 . . . .22 F2
  Sudbury CO10 . . . . .33 C5
  Wivenhoe CO7 . . . . . . .137 C3
Ellen Friend Ho CM23 . .146 B6
Ellen Way CM7 . . . . .154 D7
Ellenborough CI CM23 . .145 D5
Ellenbrook Gn IP2 . . . . . .16 D1
Ellenbrook Rd IP2 . . . . . .16 D1
Elliot PI CM7 . . . . .128 C3
Elliots Dr CO14 . . . . .171 B8
Elliott St IP1 . . . . .17 A6
Ellis Rd Boxted CO4 . . . . .82 F3
  Bradfield CO11 . . . . . . .114 D8
  Clacton-on-S CO15 . . . . .188 E2
Elm Ave CM9 . . . . .210 C5
Elm Bglws CM7 . . . . . . .127 D4
Elm CI Alresford CO7 . . . .165 B8
  Brantham CO11 . . . . .60 D1
  Chelmsford CM1 . . . . . .205 A8
  Elsenham CM22 . . . . .94 C2
  Great Baddow CM2 . . . .216 F6
  Great Bentley CO7 . . . . .166 E8
  Haverhill CB9 . . . . .8 F8
  Sible Hedingham CO9 . . . .51 D2
  Takeley CM22 . . . . .148 C7
  Tiptree CO5 . . . . .179 C7
Elm Close Extension
  CM22 . . . . .148 C7
Elm Cres CO4 . . . . .136 D7
Elm Ct Elmdon CB11 . . . . .20 B4
  Sturmer CB9 . . . . .9 E5
Elm Dr Brightlingsea CO7 185 D7
  Halstead CO9 . . . . .76 F1
  Harwich CO12 . . . . .91 B3
Elm Est CO7 . . . . .59 C3
Elm Gdns IP11 . . . . .221 A7
Elm Gr
  Bishop's Stortford CM23 .146 B7
  Clacton-on-S CO15 . . . . .188 F6
  Jaywick CO16 . . . . .188 A2
  Kirby Cross CO13 . . . . . .170 D6
  Saffron Walden CB10 . . . .22 D1
  Wivenhoe CO7 . . . . . . .137 B1
Elm Green La CM3 . . . . .218 C8
Elm Green Prep Sch
  CM3 . . . . .207 D3
Elm Ho IP11 . . . . .221 C4
Elm La Capel St M IP9 . . . .35 A1
  Marks Tey CO5,CO6 . . . . .132 B2
  Washbrook IP8 . . . . .35 E8
Elm Rd
  Bishop's Stortford CM23 .145 F8
  Chelmsford CM2 . . . . . .216 A8
  East Bergholt CO7 . . . . . .59 C3
  Little Clacton CO16 . . . . .168 C3
  Rushmere St A IP5 . . . . . .18 F7
  Sudbury CO10 . . . . .34 A7
Elm Rise CM8 . . . . .177 A5
Elm St IP1 . . . . .17 C6
Elm Tree Ave CO13 . . . . .170 F7
Elm Tree CI CO13 . . . . . .170 F7
Elm Way CM3 . . . . .192 E1
Elm Wlk CM77 . . . . .126 F2
Elmbrook Dr CM23 . . . . .145 E3
Elmcroft CO7 . . . . .138 A6
Elmdale Dr CO11 . . . . . . .86 D3
Elmden Ct CO15 . . . . . . .188 E5
Elmdon PI ⬛ CB9 . . . . . . .9 B8
Elmfield CI CO15 . . . . . .189 E7
Elmhurst CI CB9 . . . . .9 B7
Elmhurst Dr IP3 . . . . .17 F3
Elmhurst Rd CO12 . . . . . .91 C3
Elms Dr CM1 . . . . .205 A4
Elms Hall Rd CO6 . . . . . .104 E8
Elms The
  East Bergholt CO7 . . . . . .60 C3
  Frinton-on-S CO13 . . . . .170 F6
  Great Chesterford CB10 . . .3 E3
Elmstead Prim Sch CO7 137 F6
Elmstead Rd
  Colchester CO4 . . . . . . .136 E5
  Wivenhoe CO7 . . . . . . .137 D4

Elmwood CO3 . . . . .134 D6
Elmwood Ave CO2 . . . . .135 B2
Elmwood Dr CO5 . . . . . .201 D7
Elsenham CE Prim Sch
  CM22 . . . . .94 D1
Elsenham Cross CM22 . . .94 D1
Elsenham Sta CM22 . . . . .94 C3
Elsham Dr CM77 . . . . . . .154 B6
Elsmere Rd IP1 . . . . .17 C8
Elthorne Pk CO16 . . . . . .188 B5
Elton Park Bsns Ctr IP2 . .16 E6
Elton Pk IP2 . . . . .16 D6
Elton Wlk CO5 . . . . .179 D6
Elvina Ho CO15 . . . . . . .203 F6
Elwes CI CO4 . . . . .110 D1
Elwin Rd CO5 . . . . .179 D5
Elysian Gdns CM9 . . . . .199 C3
Embassy Ct CM9 . . . . . .210 A2
Emberson Ct CM2 . . . . .205 F4
Emblems CM6 . . . . .123 C1
Embra Ct CO2 . . . . .136 B5
Emily May CO12 . . . . .91 A3
Emlen St IP1 . . . . .17 A6
Emmanuel CI IP2 . . . . . . .16 F3
Emperor Circ IP3 . . . . . . .38 C8
Empire Ct CO15 . . . . . . .188 E3
Empire Rd CO15 . . . . .91 D3
Empire Wlk ⬛ CM2 . . . .205 C2
Empress Ave CO5 . . . . . .201 E6
Empress Dr CO5 . . . . . . .201 D6
Emson CI CB10 . . . . .22 D2
Endean St CO7 . . . . .137 A2
Endeavour CI CM9 . . . . .199 D2
Endsleigh Ct CO3 . . . . . .135 C7
Endway The
  Great Easton CM6 . . . . .122 F7
  Steeple Bumpstead CM7 . .27 C8
Engaines Prim Sch
  CO16 . . . . .168 C2
Engleric SG8 . . . . .19 D5
Enid Way CO3 . . . . .109 D2
Ennerdale Ave CM77 . . .154 C6
Enterprise Ct
  Braintree CM7 . . . . .128 B2
  Witham CM8 . . . . .177 A3
Enville Way CO4 . . . . . . .110 A4
Epping CI
  Chelmsford CM1 . . . . . .204 D1
  Clacton-on-S CO15 . . . . .188 F8
Epping Way CM8 . . . . . .176 E1
Epsom Ct CO16 . . . . . . .188 D6
Erbury PI CO10 . . . . .12 B8
Erica Wlk CO3 . . . . .136 D7
Erick Ave CM1 . . . . .205 B7
Eridge CI CM1 . . . . .205 D7
Eriswell Rd CB9 . . . . .9 B8
Erle Havard Rd CO6 . . . .108 E4
Ernalds CI CO6 . . . . .105 B7
Ernest Rd CO7 . . . . .137 C1
Ernleigh Rd IP4 . . . . .18 B6
Errington Rd CO3 . . . . . .135 D5
Erskine Rd CO11 . . . . . . .86 D4
Esplanade
  Frinton-on-S CO13 . . . . .170 F3
  Harwich CO12 . . . . .91 E4
Esplanade Ct
  Frinton-on-S CO13 . . . . .171 A5
  Harwich CO12 . . . . .91 E6
Esplanade The CO15 . . .189 G6
Essex Ave
  Chelmsford CM1 . . . . . .205 A7
  Clacton-on-S CO15 . . . . .203 E6
  Sudbury CO10 . . . . .15 F2
Essex County Cricket Club★
  CM2 . . . . .205 B2
Essex Cty Hospl CO3 . . .135 D6
Essex Hall Rd CO1 . . . . .109 E1
Essex Hill CB11 . . . . .20 B2
Essex Knowle CO8 . . . . . .55 F1
Essex Rd Braintree CM7 . .128 B4
  Maldon CM9 . . . . .209 F1
Essex Regiment Way
  CM3 . . . . .191 D5
Essex Show Ground CM3 . .154
  A2
Essex Way IP3 . . . . .18 E1
Essex Yeomanry Way
  CO3 . . . . .134 C7
Estate Yd The CM3 . . . . .175 C2
Estella Mead CM1 . . . . .204 E7
Estuary CI CO4 . . . . .109 E4
Estuary Cres
  Clacton-on-S CO15 . . . . .188 D3
  Shotley Gate IP9 . . . . .91 B8
Estuary Mews CM9 . . . . .199 D2
Estuary Park Rd CO5 . . .201 E6
Estuary Rd IP9 . . . . .91 B8
Eton Ct CO13 . . . . .171 A5
Eton Rd
  Clacton-on-S CO15 . . . . .188 F4
  Frinton-on-S CO13 . . . . .171 A5
Eudo Rd CO2 . . . . .135 C4
Euro Ret Pk IP3 . . . . .18 E1
Europa Pk CM8 . . . . . . .177 A3
Europa Way Harwich CO12 90 F4
  Ipswich IP1 . . . . .16 D7
Eustace Rd IP1 . . . . .16 E8
Euston Ave IP4 . . . . .18 F6
Euston Ct IP11 . . . . .221 A4
Evabrook CI IP2 . . . . .16 E1
Evelyn PI CM1 . . . . .204 F1
Evelyn Rd CM3 . . . . .153 D4
Evelyn Wood Rd CM7 . . .155 E6
Everest Gdns CM23 . . . .145 E6
Everest Way CM9 . . . . . .210 B5
Everett Ho CO1 . . . . .136 B6
Evergreen Dr CO4 . . . . . .110 D4
Everitt Rd CB10 . . . . .22 F2

Everitt Way CO9 . . . . . . .51 E2
Eves Cnr CM3 . . . . .218 E7
Eves Cres CM1 . . . . .205 A5
Eves Ct CO12 . . . . .90 D1
Eves Orch CO8 . . . . .55 F1
Evesham CI IP2 . . . . .17 A2
Ewan CI CO3 . . . . .134 C6
Ewan Way CO3 . . . . .134 C7
Ewell Hall Chase CO5 . .158 C1
Ewer Ct CO1 . . . . .136 A6
Exchange Way ⬛ CM1 . .205 B2
Exeter CI Braintree CM7 . .128 B5
  Great Horkesley CO6 . . . .109 C7
Exeter Ct ⬛ CB9 . . . . . . .8 E6
Exeter Dr CO1 . . . . .136 A7
Exeter Rd
  Chelmsford CM1 . . . . . .205 E5
  Felixstowe IP11 . . . . . . .221 D5
  Ipswich IP3 . . . . .18 A4
Exmoor CI CM1 . . . . . . .204 D1
Exmoor Rd IP11 . . . . . . .221 D6

F

Faber Rd CM8 . . . . .194 E8
Fabians CI CO6 . . . . .131 A3
Factory Hill CO5 . . . . . . .179 E3
Factory La CO11 . . . . .86 C7
Factory La E CO9 . . . . . . .76 E1
Factory La W CO9 . . . . . .76 E1
Factory Terr CO9 . . . . . . .76 E2
Faggot Yd CM7 . . . . .127 F5
Fair CI CO7 . . . . .186 A6
Fair Gn CO10 . . . . .2 B5
Fair Leas CB10 . . . . .22 E3
Fairbrother Ct ⬛ CO4 . .136 D7
Fairclough Ave CO16 . . .188 B3
Fairfax Hall CO4 . . . . . . .109 F4
Fairfax Mead CM2 . . . . .206 A2
Fairfax Rd ⬛ CO2 . . . . .135 F6
Fairfield Ave IP11 . . . . . .221 E5
Fairfield CI CO7 . . . . .139 A7
Fairfield Gdns ⬛ CO4 . .136 C8
Fairfield Inf Sch IP11 . . .221 E5
Fairfield Rd
  Braintree CM7 . . . . .127 D7
  Chelmsford CM1 . . . . . .205 A3
  Clacton-on-S CO15 . . . . .188 E4
  Ipswich IP3 . . . . .18 A2
Fairfield Way CO9 . . . . . .76 F1
Fairfields CM3 . . . . .220 D1
Fairhaven Ave CO5 . . . . .201 E6
Fairhead Rd N CO4 . . . . .136 C8
Fairhead Rd S ⬛ CO4 . .136 C8
Fairleads CM3 . . . . .218 F8
Fairlop CI CO15 . . . . . . .188 F8
Fairstead Hall Rd CM3 . .175 A5
Fairstead Rd CM3 . . . . . .175 C5
Fairway
  Bishop's Stortford CM23 .146 C6
  Chelmsford CM2 . . . . . .216 D7
Fairways CO2 . . . . .109 B3
Fairways The IP4 . . . . . . .18 E5
Fairy Hall La CM77 . . . . .127 A1
Fairycroft Rd CB10 . . . . .22 E1
Fal Dr CM8 . . . . .176 E2
Falcon CI CB9 . . . . .9 C8
Falcon Cres CO1 . . . . . . .136 B5
Falcon Fields CM9 . . . . . .220 F8
Falcon Mews CM9 . . . . .220 F8
Falcon Sq CO9 . . . . .51 F4
Falcon St Felixstowe IP11 221 C6
  Ipswich IP1 . . . . .17 C5
Falcon Way
  Chelmsford CM2 . . . . . .216 A6
  Clacton-on-S CO15 . . . . .188 F6
Falconer Rd CB9 . . . . . . .9 C5
Falconer St CM23 . . . . . .145 C5
Falcons Mead CM2 . . . . .205 A1
Falkland CI CM3 . . . . . . .206 E8
Falkland Ct CM7 . . . . . . .128 B4
Falkland Gn CM9 . . . . . .219 E6
Falklands Dr ⬛ CO11 . . . .86 D4
Fallowden La CB10 . . . . . .23 F8
Fallowfield CI CO12 . . . . .90 F3
Fallowfield Ct ⬛ CB9 . . . .8 E7
Fallowfield Rd CO2 . . . . .135 C2
Falmouth Rd CM1 . . . . . .205 E5
Falstaff Cotts IP9 . . . . . . .60 F8
Fambridge Chase CM8 . .155 F2
Fambridge Ct CM9 . . . . .210 A1
Fambridge Rd CM9 . . . . .209 F2
Fanner's Green Cotts
  CM3 . . . . .190 C5
Fanny's La CO16 . . . . . . .167 D2
Faraday CI Braintree CM7 127 F1
  Clacton-on-S CO15 . . . . .169 A1
Faraday Rd IP4 . . . . .17 F5
Farford Field CO10 . . . . .34 C5
Farina CI IP1 . . . . .16 F7
Farm Rd CO12 . . . . .116 D3
Farm Wlk CO7 . . . . .185 E8
Farmadine Ct ⬛ CB11 . .22 E1
Farmadine Gr CB11 . . . . .22 E1
Farmadine Ho ⬛ CB11 . .22 E1
Farmers Way CO16 . . . . .188 B3
Farmfield Rd CO6 . . . . . .106 C3
Farmleigh Ave CO5 . . . . .188 F8
Farnham CE Prim Sch
  CM23 . . . . .118 D6
Farnham Gn CM23 . . . . .118 B7
Farriers Chase CO5 . . . . .201 D6
Farriers End CO3 . . . . . . .134 D5
Farriers Way CM77 . . . . .154 D7
Farriers Went IP11 . . . . .221 B7
Farrington CI ⬛ CO1 . . .136 C6

Farrow Rd CM1 . . . . . . .215 E7
Farthing CI CM7 . . . . . . .128 D4
Farthing Rd IP1 . . . . .16 C7
Farthing Road Ind Est
  IP1 . . . . .16 C7
Farthings Chase CO5 . . .201 E7
Farthings Went IP9 . . . . .35 B2
Fastnet CI CB9 . . . . .9 D8
Faulds Wlk CO4 . . . . . . .136 A3
Faulkbourne Rd CM8 . . .176 D4
Faulkeners Way IP11 . . .221 A8
Fawkner CI CM2 . . . . . . .205 F2
Fawley CI IP4 . . . . .18 C7
Feathers Field IP11 . . . . .221 B5
Feedhams CI CO7 . . . . . .137 C3
Feering CE Prim Sch
  CO5 . . . . .158 E4
Feering Hill CO5 . . . . . . .158 D3
Feering Mus★ CO5 . . . . .158 B1
Feering Rd CO6 . . . . . . .131 B1
Felaw St IP2 . . . . .17 D4
Felbrigg CI CM77 . . . . . .154 B7
Felix Rd Felixstowe IP11 . .221 F4
  Ipswich IP3 . . . . .18 C2
Felixstowe Beach Cvn Pk
  IP11 . . . . .221 C2
Felixstowe Ct CO16 . . . .188 A4
Felixstowe General Hospl
  IP11 . . . . .221 F4
Felixstowe Rd IP3 . . . . . .18 B3
Felixstowe Sta IP11 . . . .221 E5
Fell Christy CM1 . . . . . . .205 B5
Fell Rd CO9 . . . . .28 B8
Fellbrigg Ave IP5 . . . . . . .18 F6
Fellowes CI CO4 . . . . . . .109 F2
Felnor Wlk IP11 . . . . . . .221 E4
Felstead CI CO2 . . . . . . .163 A8
Felsted Almshouses
  CM6 . . . . .152 B6
Felsted Prep Sch CM6 . .152 B5
Felsted Prim Sch CM6 . .152 D7
Felsted Sch CM6 . . . . . . .152 C6
Felsted Vineyard★ CM6 151 C7
Feltwell PI ⬛ CB9 . . . . . .9 B8
Fen La CO7 . . . . .84 D1
Fen Mdw IP11 . . . . .221 A8
Fen St CO6 . . . . .56 B1
Fen View IP8 . . . . .35 E8
Fenbridge La CO7 . . . . . .59 B1
Fenman Ct CM22 . . . . . . .94 C2
Fenn CI CO7 . . . . .139 A3
Fenn Rd CO9 . . . . .77 A1
Fennell CI CO5 . . . . .179 C5
Fennels CI CB9 . . . . .9 A7
Fennes Rd CM7 . . . . . . .102 A3
Fennings Chase CO1 . . .136 A7
Fenno CI CO3 . . . . .134 F4
Fenton Rd CB9 . . . . .9 B8
Ferdinand Wlk CO4 . . . .136 F7
Ferguson CI CB11 . . . . . .23 A2
Fern Gr CB9 . . . . .8 E8
Fern Hill CO10 . . . . .2 B7
Fern Way CO15 . . . . . . .203 F7
Ferndale CI CO15 . . . . . .188 F7
Ferndale Rd CO12 . . . . . .91 D5
Ferndown Rd CO13 . . . .170 C5
Ferndown Way CM3 . . . .194 B4
Fernhayes CI IP2 . . . . . . .17 A2
Fernie Rd CM7 . . . . .127 D2
Fernlea CO4 . . . . .109 C2
Fernlea Rd CO12 . . . . . . .91 D5
Fernwood Ave CO15 . . .189 F5
Ferry La IP11 . . . . .221 A3
Ferry Rd CO5 . . . . .164 B6
Festival Gdns CM9 . . . . .198 D4
Feverills Rd CO16 . . . . . .168 D4
Fiat Ave CO15 . . . . .203 D6
Fiddlers Folly CO3 . . . . .107 E1
Fiddlers Hill CO3 . . . . . . .107 E2
Fiddlers La CO7 . . . . .59 C3
Field Ct CO4 . . . . .136 E8
Field Gate La CM22 . . . . .94 A3
Field View Dr CM9 . . . . .197 C4
Field Way CO7 . . . . .137 C2
Field Wlk CO14 . . . . .171 A8
Fieldgate Dock CO7 . . . .185 E5
Fields CI CO15 . . . . .167 F6
Fields Farm Rd CO2 . . . .162 B4
Fields View CO10 . . . . . . .33 F8
Fieldside CB11 . . . . .43 E7
Fieldview CI CO4 . . . . . .109 F4
Fifth Ave Chelmsford CM1 205 B6
  Frinton-on-S CO13 . . . . .170 E5
  Halstead CO9 . . . . .77 B1
  Stansted Mountfitchet
  CM24 . . . . .120 B2
Finbars Wlk IP4 . . . . .17 F5
Finborough CI IP4 . . . . . .18 F6
Finch Dr Braintree CM7 . .127 D4
  Great Bentley CO7 . . . . .139 D1
Finch Hill CO10 . . . . .33 A7
Finch's CM8 . . . . .195 F6
Finchdale CO15 . . . . . . .188 F6
Finchingfield CE Prim Sch
  CM7 . . . . .72 D6
Finchingfield Guildhall Mus★
  CM7 . . . . .72 D6
Finchingfield Rd
  Stambourne CO9 . . . . . . .49 C7
  Steeple Bumpstead CM7 . .27 C6
Finchingfield Way CO2 . .163 A8
Finchley Ave CM2 . . . . . .216 A8
Finchley Rd IP4 . . . . .17 E6
Findley CI IP9 . . . . .61 F2
Finer CI CO16 . . . . .188 C5

Fingringhoe CE Prim Sch
CO5 ....163 F5
Fingringhoe Rd
Abberton CO5 .....163 B3
Colchester CO2,CO5 ....136 D1
Fingringhoe Wick Conservation Ctr★
CO5 ....164 D3
Fingringhoe Wick Nature Reserve & Visitor Ctr★
CO5 ....164 D3
Finham Cl CO4 ......136 C8
Finsbury Pl CO9 .....76 F2
Fir Tree Cl CO4 .....110 B4
Fir Tree La CM3 .....207 E1
Fir Tree Rise
Chelmsford CM2 ....216 B6
Ipswich IP8 ......16 C2
Fir Tree Wlk CM9 ....210 C5
Fir Way CO15 ....203 G6
Firebronds Rd IP9 ....62 D5
Firecrest Rd CM2 ....216 C5
Firefly Way IP3 .....38 B8
Firlands CM23 ......145 E6
Firlands Ho CM23 ....145 E6
Firlie Wlk CO2 ......136 A2
Firmins Ct CO6 ......108 D4
Firs Chase CO5 .....201 A6
Firs Chase Cvn Pk CO5 .201 A7
Firs Cvn Pk CO16 ....168 D2
Firs Dr CM1 ....204 B1
Firs Hamlet CO5 .....201 A6
Firs Jun & Mid Sch The
CM23 ....145 E6
Firs Rd Tiptree CO5 ..179 D4
West Mersea CO5 ....201 B7
Firs The Gosfield CO9 ..102 E8
Layer-de-l-H CO2 ...162 A6
First Ave Chelmsford CM1 205 B5
Clacton-on-S CO15 ...189 B4
Frinton-on-S CO13 ...170 E4
Glemsford CO10 .....2 C5
Halstead CO9 ......77 B1
Harwich CO12 ......91 C3
Seawick CO16 ......203 C6
Stansted Mountfitchet
CM24 ....120 B2
Walton-on-t-N CO14 ..144 E3
Weeley CO16 ......140 F1
Firstore Dr CO3 .....134 E7
Firwood's Rd CO9 ....103 E8
Fish Pond Hill IP9 ....63 C3
Fish St CM9 ....211 E6
Fishbane Cl IP3 .....38 B8
Fisher Cl CB9 ......9 E8
Fisher Way CM7 .....128 C4
Fisher's La CO7 .....60 C3
Fishmarket St CM6 ...70 A2
Fishponds Hill CO6 ...81 F4
Fishponds La IP9 ....62 E5
Fisin Wlk CO3 ......134 E3
Fiske Ct CO15 ......188 F2
Fitches Cres CM9 ....210 B1
Fitches Croft CO6 ....133 C4
Fitches Mews CM9 ...210 B1
Fitzgerald Cl CO11 ...86 B4
Fitzgerald Cotts CO12 .90 F2
Fitzgerald Ct IP4 ....18 A5
Fitzgilbert Rd CO2 ...135 C4
Fitzmaurice Rd IP3 ...18 B3
Fitzpiers CB10 ......22 E2
Fitzroy St 2 IP1 ....17 C6
Fitzwalter La CM3 ...218 D6
Fitzwalter Pl
Chelmsford CM1 ....204 E1
Great Dunmow CM6 ..150 D8
Fitzwalter Rd
Boreham CM3 ......206 F8
Colchester CO3 .....135 B6
Little Dunmow CM6 ...151 E7
Fitzwilliam Cl IP2 ....16 F2
Fitzwilliam Rd CO3 ...135 B7
Five Acres Bicknacre CM3 218 F3
Holbrook IP9 ......62 D5
Stansted Mountfitchet
CM24 ....119 E8
Walton-on-t-N CO14 ..171 B8
Five Fields CO4 .....136 E7
Five Ways CO3 ......134 D4
Fiveash La CM7 .....129 E1
Flag Hill CO7 ....186 F8
Flagstaff Rd CO2 ....135 F6
Flail Cl CO7 ....137 F6
Flanders Cl CM7 ....127 E6
Flanders Field CO2 ...136 B3
Flatford Dr CO16 ....188 B5
Flatford Mill (Field Ctr)★
CO7 ....85 D7
Flatford Rd
East Bergholt CO7 ...85 C8
Haverhill CB9 ......8 C8
Flavian Cl CB9 .....9 D7
Flax La CO10 ....2 C3
Fleetwood
Felixstowe IP11 ....221 F5
Holland-on-S CO15 ..189 E7
Fleetwood Cl CO15 ...189 E7
Fleetwood Rd IP11 ...221 F5
Fleming Cl 7 CM7 ...127 F1
Flemish Cotts The CO7 .84 F6
Flemish Ct CO1 .....135 F8
Fletcher Rd IP3 .....18 A1
Flint Cl IP2 ....17 B2
Flintwich Manor CM1 .204 E7

Flitch Ind Est The CM6 .150 D7
Flitch La CM6 ......150 E7
Flixton Cl CO16 .....188 A4
Flood La CO4 ....110 C6
Flora Rd CM8 ......176 D4
Florence Cotts CO7 ..185 F6
Florence Rd CO14 ...144 E2
Florence Wlk 8 CM23 .145 F8
Florie's Rd CO6 .....131 F8
Flowers Way CO15 ...203 G7
Foley Cotts CM7 ....102 D3
Folkards La CO7 ....185 F8
Folley The CO3 .....134 D5
Folly La IP8 ....35 D4
Folly Mill La CM6 ...96 E6
Folly The
Layer-de-l-H CO2 ...162 A5
Tiptree CO5 ....179 F2
Wivenhoe CO7 .....164 C7
Fonnereau Rd IP1 ...17 C6
Ford End CE Prim Sch
CM3 ....172 B6
Ford La CO7 ....165 A5
Ford Rd CO15 ......188 D3
Ford Road Ind Est CO15 188 D3
Ford St CO7 ....107 C2
Fordham All Saints CE Prim Sch CO6 ....107 D4
Fordham Pl IP4 .....18 F5
Fordham Rd
Bures CO6, CO8 .....79 D3
Wormingford CO6 ...80 E2
Fords La CO4 ......109 D5
Fordson Rd CM2 ....206 B6
Fordstreet Hill CO6 ..107 C2
Fordwater Cl CO9 ...10 B3
Fordwich Rd CO7 ...165 E1
Fore Field CM7 .....128 D3
Fore Hamlet IP3 ....17 E5
Fore St IP4 ....17 D5
Forefield Gn CM1 ...205 F7
Foremans CM1 .....204 E3
Foresight Rd CO2 ...136 D2
Forest Dr CM1 ......204 E1
Forest Park Ave CO15 .188 F7
Forest Rd
Colchester CO4 .....136 D7
Witham CM8 ......177 A5
Forester Cl IP8 .....36 E8
Foresters Ct CO7 ...137 E1
Foresthall Rd CM24 ..119 E4
Forfar Cl IP4 ....18 B8
Forfields Way CM77 ..155 E6
Forge Cotts CO10 ...13 E6
Forge Cres CM7 ....129 D3
Forge St CO7 ......85 A6
Forges Cnr CO10 ...13 E6
Forres CO13 ....170 F4
Forsyth Dr CM7 ....155 A8
Forsythia Cl CM1 ...205 E7
Forties Cl CB9 .....9 D8
Fortinbras Way CM2 .216 B8
Fortis CM8 ....194 E8
Fortune Cl CM3 ....174 A7
Fossetts La CO6 ....107 F4
Foster Ct 2 CM8 ...177 A2
Foster Rd
Great Totham CM9 ..196 A4
Harwich CO12 .....90 E5
Foster's Cotts CM7 ..129 D2
Foundation St 18 IP4 .17 C5
Foundry La Copford CO6 133 D5
Earls Colne CO6 ....105 B6
Ipswich IP2 ......17 C5
Fountain Ct Harwich CO12 91 E5
West Mersea CO5 ...201 D7
Fountain La Copford CO6 134 A1
Easthorpe CO6 .....160 F8
Fountain Rd IP2 ....16 F1
Four Acres
Great Chesterford CB10 ...3 E3
Saffron Walden CB11 ..22 C1
Four Ash Hill CO9 ...10 E1
Four Ashes CM7 ....74 C1
Four Sisters CO7 ...59 B5
Fourth Ave
Chelmsford CM1 ....205 B5
Clacton-on-S CO15 ..189 C4
Frinton-on-S CO13 ..170 F4
Glemsford CO10 ....2 B5
Halstead CO9 ......77 B1
Seawick CO16 ......203 B6
Stansted Mountfitchet
CM24 ....120 B2
Fourways CM22 ....94 C1
Fowe's La CO10 ....31 B8
Fowler Ct CM2 .....216 A4
Fowlers Arc CO13 ...170 F4
Fowlmere Rd SG8 ...19 A6
Fox Burrows La CM1 .204 E4
Fox Cres CM1 ......204 F4
Fox Yd CO7 ....53 C5
Foxburrow Rd IP3 ...18 F1
Foxdells La CM23 ...118 F2
Foxden CM8 ....177 D6
Foxendale Folly CO3 .134 C7
Foxes Cnr CO6 .....107 D1
Foxes La
Aldham CO3,CO6 ...133 D8
Ashen CO10 ....11 D1
Foxes Rd CO10 .....11 E1
Foxglove Cl
Bishop's Stortford CM23 .145 C6
Clacton-on-S CO15 ..188 F7
Witham CM8 ......176 D3
Foxglove Cres IP3 ...18 C1
Foxglove Way CM1 ..205 F6
Foxglove Wlk 4 CO4 .136 E7

Foxgrove La IP11 ...221 F5
Foxhall Cl CO7 .....59 C4
Foxhall Fields CO7 ..59 C3
Foxhall Rd IP3,IP4 ..18 D5
Foxholes Rd CM2 ...216 F6
Foxley Dr CM23 ....146 B8
Foxmead CM8 ......177 D6
Foxtail Rd IP3 ......38 E8
Foxwood Cl CO11 ...85 C2
Foxwood Cres IP4 ...18 F5
Frambury La CB11 ...66 F8
Framlingham Ct 5 IP1 .17 A8
Framlingham Way
CM7 ....154 C7
Frances Cl CO7 .....137 B2
Frances Gn CM1 ....206 A7
Francis Cl Haverhill CB9 .8 F1
Tiptree CO5 ....179 C4
Francis Ct CM8 ....156 C5
Francis Rd
Braintree CM7 .....127 D2
14 Sudbury CO10 ....33 E7
Francis St CO7 .....185 F5
Francis Way
Colchester CO4 .....110 D1
Silver End CM8 ....156 C4
Franciscan Way IP1 ..17 C5
Frank Clater Cl CO4 .136 C8
Frank Naylor Ct 11 CO1 .135 F7
Franklin Rd IP3 .....18 B2
Fraser Cl CM2 .....216 C8
Fraser Rd IP1 ......16 F7
Frating Abbey Farm Rd
CO7 ....166 C6
Frating Cross CO7 ..166 B7
Frating Ct CM7 .....128 C1
Frating Hill CO7 ....138 D3
Frating Rd Ardleigh CO7 .111 F6
Great Bromley CO7 ..138 F6
Thorrington CO7 ...166 A7
Frederick Dr CO5 ...179 C4
Fredrick J French Meml Homes CM1 ......205 B6
Fredricks Cl CO11 ..115 B5
Freebournes Ct 5 CM8 177 A2
Freebournes Rd CM8 .177 B2
Freehold Rd IP4 ....18 B6
Freeland Rd CO15 ...188 E1
Freelands CO7 .....186 C6
Freeport Designer Outlet
CM77 ....128 C1
Freewood La CB11 ..20 B3
Freezes Barns CB9 ..27 B7
Fremantle Rd CO2 ..136 B1
French's Wlk 4 CM2 .205 C2
Frensham Cl CO3 ...134 D7
Frere Ct CM23 .....118 F1
Frere Way CO5 .....164 B6
Freshfields CO12 ...90 F1
Freshwater Cres CM9 .210 B4
Freshwater La CO15 .188 F1
Freshwell Gdns CB10 .22 C2
Freshwell St CB10 ..22 D1
Fresian Cl CM7 .....127 D2
Freston Hill IP9 ....37 E4
Freston Rd IP3 .....38 C8
Freston St IP9 .....37 E3
Friars CO9 ....60 B8
Friars Bridge Rd IP1 .17 B5
Friars Cl
Clacton-on-S CO15 ..188 E6
Colchester CO4 ....110 C4
Sible Hedingham CO9 .51 D2
Wivenhoe CO7 .....164 C8
Friars Ct CO2 ......136 C3
Friars Ctyd 1 IP1 ...17 C5
Friars Grove Jun & Inf Schs
CO4 ....110 C2
Friars La Braintree CM7 .127 F4
Maldon CM9 ......209 F2
Friars St Ipswich IP1 ..17 C5
Sudbury CO10 .....33 E7
Friars Wlk CM2 ....205 B1
Friars Wood CM23 ..146 C8
Friary Fields CM9 ...210 A2
Friday Wood Gn CO2 .162 F8
Friedberg Ave CM23 .145 D4
Friends Field CO8 ...55 F1
Friends Sch CB11 ...43 D8
Friends Wlk CB11 ..43 D7
Frietuna Rd CO13 ...170 E6
Frinton Ct CO13 ....170 F3
Frinton Park Ct CO14 .171 A6
Frinton Rd
Holland-on-S CO15 ..189 C6
Kirby Cross CO13 ...170 D6
Thorpe-le-S CO16 ...142 B1
Frinton Sta CO13 ...170 F5
Frinton-on-Sea Prim Sch
CO13 ....170 E5
Fritillary Cl IP8 .....36 E8
Fritton Cl IP2 ......17 A1
Fritton Ct 19 CB9 ...8 E7
Frobisher Dr CO15 ..187 F1
Frobisher Prim Sch
CO15 ....187 F1
Frobisher Rd
Harwich CO12 .....90 F1
Ipswich IP3 ....17 E1
Frobisher Way CM7 ..128 C4
Frog Hall Cl CO5 ...164 B6
Frog Mdw CO7 .....84 F7
Frogge St CB10 ....3 B3
Fronk's Ave CO12 ...91 C2
Fronk's Rd CO12 ...91 B2
Front Rd IP3 ....38 D8
Frowick La CO16 ...167 B2

Fryatt Ave CO12 ....91 A4
Fuchsia Ct 6 CO4 ..136 D8
Fuchsia La IP4 .....18 A5
Fuchsia Way CO16 ..188 C5
Fulcher Ave CM2 ...205 F3
Fulfen Way CB11 ...43 D7
Fullbridge CM9 ....210 A3
Fuller Ct 3 CM23 ...146 A7
Fuller's Cl CO5 .....158 B2
Fullers Gate CO5 ...158 B2
Fullers Rd CO2 .....136 D2
Fulmar Cl CM23 ....146 C8
Fulton Cres CM23 ..146 C8
Furneaux La CO5 ...163 F5
Furness Cl IP2 .....36 F8
Furriers Cl CM23 ...145 C5
Furrow Cl CO3 .....134 E5
Further Mdw CM1 ..215 A8
Furze Cres CO7 ....165 A7
Furze La CO7 ......139 A5

G

Gablefields CM2 ....217 D6
Gables The CB9 ....9 F4
Gaces Acre CB11 ...43 A1
Gadwall Reach CO5 .158 D2
Gage's Rd
Belchamp St P CO10 ..13 A1
Little Yeldham C10 ..30 F8
Gager Dr CO5 ......179 E5
Gaiger Cl CM1 .....205 D7
Gainsborough Cl
Clacton-on-S CO16 ..188 B6
West Mersea CO5 ...201 D6
Gainsborough Cres
CM2 ....205 E3
Gainsborough Dr CO11 .86 C5
Gainsborough La IP3 .37 F7
Gainsborough Rd
Black Notley CM77 ..155 A4
Colchester CO3 ....135 B5
Felixstowe IP11 ....221 C5
Ipswich IP4 ....17 D8
Sudbury CO10 .....33 D8
Gainsborough St CO10 .33 E7
Gainsborough's House Mus★
CO10 ....33 E7
Gainsford Ave CO15 .189 B4
Gainsford End Rd CO9 .50 B6
Galiots CO5 ....201 A6
Gall End La CM24 ..119 F7
Galleydene Ave CM2 .216 C3
Gallewood Inf Sch
CM2 ....216 C2
Galleywood Rd
Chelmsford CM2 ...216 A6
Great Baddow CM2 ..216 E5
Galliford Rd CM9 ...210 A4
Galliford Road Ind Est
CM9 ....210 A4
Galloway Cl 1 CM23 .145 F8
Galloway Dr CO16 ..168 B3
Gallows Green Rd CM6 .97 C2
Gallows Hill CB11 ...43 C7
Galsworthy Cl CM7 ..155 A7
Gandish Cl CO7 ....59 D1
Gandish Rd CO7 ...59 E2
Ganges Rd IP9 .....91 B8
Gannet Cl CB9 .....9 C8
Gannet Rd IP2 .....16 E3
Gaol La CO10 ......33 E7
Gap The
Clacton-on-S CO15 ..189 G6
Holland-on-S CO15 ..189 G6
Garden Ct CO13 ....170 F3
Garden Dr CO3 ....134 E6
Garden Farm CO5 ..201 D4
Garden Field
Felixstowe IP11 ....221 C5
Hatfield Peverel CM3 .193 D6
Garden Field Cotts CO6 .81 E5
Garden Fields
Great Tey CO5 .....132 C8
Stebbing CM6 ......124 D3
Garden Pl CO10 ....33 D7
Garden Rd
Clacton-on-S CO15 ..203 G7
Walton-on-t-N CO14 .171 A4
Garden Terr CO9 ...76 F2
Gardeners Rd CO9 ..76 F1
Gardeners Row CO6 .131 A2
Gardenia Pl CO16 ..188 B4
Gardenia Wlk CO4 ..136 E7
Garfield Cl IP11 ....221 D3
Garfield Rd IP11 ...221 D3
Garland Rd CO12 ...90 E5
Garling Wlk CO6 ...108 E3
Garnets Mead CM3 ..175 B3
Garnetts CM22 .....148 B8
Garnetts Bglws CM6 .152 C5
Garnetts La CM6 ...152 C5
Garnetts Villas CM6 .152 C5
Garnons Chase CO6 .81 A5
Garret Pl CO6 ......108 F4
Garrettlands CM2 ...217 F6
Garrison La IP11 ...221 D3
Garrod Ct CO2 .....163 B7
Garrods IP9 ....35 E4
Garthwood Cl CO6 ..108 E4
Gascoigne Rd CO4 ..136 C8
Gasfield 14 CO11 ..86 D4
Gasgoine Ho CO4 ..109 F4
Gaston End CO7 ...59 C3
Gaston St CO7 .....59 C3
Gatacre Ct CO2 ....135 B3

Gatacre Rd IP1 .....17 A7
Gate St CM9 ....209 F3
Gate Street Mews CM9 .209 F3
Gatefield Cl CO14 ..170 F7
Gatekeeper Cl
8 Braintree CM7 ...127 F1
Ipswich IP8 ......36 E8
Gatwick Cl CM23 ...119 B1
Gauden Rd CM7 ....127 F7
Gavin Way
Colchester CO4 ....110 B5
Colchester,Brinkley Gr
CO4 ....110 A5
Gawlers CM23 .....92 B8
Gay Bowers La CM3 .218 F6
Gay Bowers Rd CM3 .218 F4
Gay Bowers Way CM8 .195 A7
Gaye St 1 IP1 .....17 B6
Gazelle Cl CO4 ....110 C4
Generals La CM3 ...192 B2
Generals Mews IP11 .221 B5
Genesta CM9 ......199 D2
Geneva Rd IP1 .....17 B7
Genevyll Cl CO10 ...1 D2
Gentian Ct CO4 ....109 C2
Geoff Seaden Cl 2 CO1 136 C6
George Ave CO7 ...185 F7
George Cl CO15 ....188 C2
George Ct CM2 .....205 B1
George Cut CO7 ...185 F6
George Frost Cl IP4 ..17 D7
George Gent Cl CB9 .27 B6
George La CO10 ....2 B3
George Rd CM7 ....127 D2
George St
Chelmsford CM2 ...205 B1
12 Colchester CO1 ..135 F7
Harwich CO12 .....91 D6
Saffron Walden CB10 .22 D1
George Williams Way
CO1 ....136 A6
George Yd 7 CM7 ..127 F3
Georgian Ct IP11 ...221 D5
Gepp Pl CM2 ......206 B4
Geralds Ave IP4 ....18 A5
Geranium Cl CO16 ..188 C4
Geranium Wlk CO4 ..136 D7
Gerard Ave CM23 ..145 E4
Gerard Rd CO16 ...188 C6
Gernon Cl CM1 ....191 B3
Gernon Rd CO7 ....111 E7
Gershwin Bvd CM8 ..195 A7
Gestingthorpe Rd CO10 .31 F4
Gibbons Ct CM6 ...123 D1
Gibbons St 3 IP1 ...17 A6
Gibbs Field CM23 ..145 D5
Gibson Cl CB10 ....22 D1
Gibson Gdns CB10 ..22 D1
Gibson Rd CO9 ....51 D1
Gibson Vale CM1 ...205 B8
Gibson Way CB10 ..22 D1
Giffins Cl CM7 .....127 F1
Gifford Cl IP9 ......62 D5
Giffords Pl IP4 .....18 F6
Gilberd Cl CO4 ....110 C6
Gilberd Ho CO3 ....135 A7
Gilberd Rd CO2 ....136 B4
Gilberd Sch The CO4 .110 B5
Gilbert Rd CO10 ...12 B8
Gilbert Way CM7 ...128 C5
Gilbey Ave CM23 ...146 B6
Gilbey Cotts CM22 ..94 C1
Gilbey Cres CM24 ..119 E8
Gilbey Gn CM11 ...42 F1
Gilchrist Way CM7 ..127 F4
Gilda Terr CM77 ...127 B2
Gilderdale Cl CO4 ..110 D3
Gilders Way CO16 ..188 C5
Gill Cl CM9 ....209 F6
Gilmore Way CM2 ..217 B6
Gilpin Way CM77 ...154 C7
Gilson Cl CM2 .....205 F2
Gilwell Park Cl CO3 .135 A4
Gimson Cl CM8 ....176 F2
Gippeswyk Ave IP2 ..17 A4
Gippeswyk Rd IP2 ..17 B4
Gipping Cl CB9 ....8 E6
Gipping Way IP8 ...16 B6
Gipsy La CM23,CM24 .119 C4
Girling St CO10 ....33 E8
Girton Rd CB9 .....9 B7
Girton Way IP2 ....16 F1
Glade The CO4 ....110 C4
Gladeview CO15 ...188 F7
Gladiator Way CO2 ..135 A2
Gladstone Ct CM2 ..205 B1
Gladstone Rd
Colchester CO1 ....136 B5
Ipswich IP3 ....17 F5
Tiptree CO5 ....179 D4
Gladwin Rd CO2 ...135 D4
Glamis Cl CB9 .....8 D8
Glamorgan Rd IP2 ..17 B1
Glastonbury Cl IP2 ..16 F1
Glebe Ave CM7 ....127 F6
Glebe Cl Elmstead CO7 .138 A6
Sproughton IP8 ....16 B6
Tattingstone IP9 ...61 C7
Wix CO11 ....115 C5
Glebe Cres
Broomfield CM1 ....191 B1
Witham CM8 ......176 E4
Glebe Ct CM23 ....146 B8
Glebe End Capel St M IP9 .35 B2
Elsenham CM22 ....94 D1
Glebe Gdns CO5 ...158 E5
Glebe La
Chelmondiston IP9 ..63 A8

Glebe La continued
Little Easton CM6 . . . . . . .122 F5
Woolverstone IP9 . . . . .38 B1
Glebe Mdw CM3 . . . . .190 E7
Glebe Rd
Chelmsford CM1 . . . . .205 B3
Colchester CO2 . . . . .135 C2
Heybridge CM9 . . . . .210 C5
Kelvedon CO5 . . . . .158 B2
Tiptree CO5 . . . . .179 C5
Glebe The Elmdon CB11 . . . .20 A4
Elsenham CM22 . . . . .94 C1
Peldon CO5 . . . . .182 E5
Purleigh CM3 . . . . .220 D1
Saffron Walden CB11 . . . . . .43 E7
Glebe View CM2 . . . . . . .216 B3
Glebe Way
Clacton-on-S CO15 . . . . . .203 G7
Frinton-on-S CO13 . . . . . .170 F5
Glebefield Rd CM3 . . . . .194 B4
Glebelands CO6 . . . . .82 B1
Glemham Dr IP4 . . . . .18 F4
Glemsford Cl IP11 . . . . . .221 B3
Glemsford Com Prim Sch
CO10 . . . . .2 B5
Glemsford Pl 3 CB9 . . . . . .9 B8
Glen Ave CO3 . . . . .135 B7
Glenavon Rd IP4 . . . . .18 D7
Glencoe Rd IP4 . . . . .18 C8
Glendale Gr CO4 . . . . . . .110 C3
Gleneagles Dr IP4 . . . . . . .18 D5
Gleneagles Way CM3 . . . .194 B4
Glenhurst Ave IP4 . . . . . . .18 B8
Glenside CO10 . . . . .34 A6
Glentress Cl CO4 . . . . . . .110 D3
Glenway Ct CO6 . . . . .82 B1
Glisson Sq CO2 . . . . .135 B4
Globe Cl CO5 . . . . .179 D6
Globe Cres CM23 . . . . . . .118 D6
Globe Wlk CO5 . . . . .179 D6
Globe Yd 4 CO10 . . . . . . .33 E8
Gloucester Ave
Chelmsford CM2 . . . . .216 C6
Colchester CO2 . . . . .135 C3
Maldon CM9 . . . . .209 F1
Gloucester Cres CM1 . . . .205 A5
Gloucester Gdns CM7 . . . .128 C6
Gloucester Ho IP11 . . . . .221 C6
Gloucester Rd
Haverhill CB9 . . . . .8 F6
Ipswich IP3 . . . . .18 B2
Gloucester Way CO10 . . . . .15 D2
Glovers CM3 . . . . .173 F7
Goat Hall La
Chelmsford CM2 . . . . .215 F3
Galleywood CM2 . . . . .216 A3
Goat House La CM3 . . . . . .219 F4
Goat Lodge Rd CM8,
CM9 . . . . .196 A5
Goda Cl CM8 . . . . .194 D8
Goddard Way
Chelmsford CM2 . . . . .205 F2
Saffron Walden CB10 . . . . . .22 E3
Godfrey Way CM6 . . . . . . .123 C1
Godfreys Mews CM2 . . . . .205 B1
Godlings Way CM7 . . . . . .127 F2
Godmans La CO6 . . . . . . .132 E3
Godric Pl CM7 . . . . .127 C1
Godric Rd CM8 . . . . .194 E8
Godwin Cl CO9 . . . . .76 D1
Godwit Ct CO5 . . . . .158 D2
Goff's La CO16 . . . . .141 F8
Goings La CO5 . . . . .201 D6
Gold Cl CM22 . . . . .94 B3
Gold St CB10 . . . . .22 D1
Goldcrest Cl CO4 . . . . . . .137 A8
Goldcrest Ct IP2 . . . . .16 D3
Goldcrest Rd IP2 . . . . .16 C3
Golden Dawn Way CO4 . . .109 E2
Golden La Radwinter CB10 . .25 A2
Thorpe-le-S CO16 . . . . . . .141 F3
Golden Lion La CO12 . . . . .91 E6
Golden Noble Hill CO1 . . .136 A6
Goldenacres CM1 . . . . . . .205 F8
Goldenlond CO6 . . . . .56 C5
Goldfinch Cl CO4 . . . . . . .136 F7
Goldhanger Ct CM7 . . . . . .128 D1
Goldhanger Rd CM9 . . . . .210 D4
Golding Thoroughfare
CM2 . . . . .205 F3
Golding Way
Glemsford CO10 . . . . .2 B4
St Osyth CO16 . . . . .187 A5
Goldingham Dr CM7 . . . . .155 A7
Goldings CM23 . . . . .146 B8
Goldlay Ave CM2 . . . . . . .216 C6
Goldlay Gdns CM2 . . . . . .205 C1
Goldlay Rd CM2 . . . . .205 C1
Golds Nursery Bsns Pk
CM22 . . . . .94 C3
Golf Green Rd CO15 . . . . .203 G8
Goodchild Way CO9 . . . . . .30 A2
Goodey Cl CO1 . . . . .136 A6
Goodier Rd CM1 . . . . .204 F4
Goodlake Ct CO12 . . . . . . .90 F2
Goodliffe Pk CM23 . . . . . .119 B2
Goodmans La CM3 . . . . . .173 F4
Goodwin Cl CM2 . . . . . . .216 D8
Goodwin Stile CM23 . . . . .145 D5
Goodwins Cl CB11 . . . . . . .21 E3
Goojerat Rd CO2 . . . . . . .135 D5
Gordian Wlk CO4 . . . . . . .110 B5
Gordon Dr CO4 . . . . .110 C5
Gordon Rd
Chelmsford CM2 . . . . .216 A6
Harwich CO12 . . . . .91 B2
Ipswich IP4 . . . . .18 A7

Gordon Way CO12 . . . . . . .91 B2
Gore La CM77 . . . . .127 A2
Gore Rd CM77 . . . . .127 A2
Gore Terr CM77 . . . . .127 A2
Gorefield Rd CM22,CM24 .121 B5
Gorefield Rdbt CM24 . . . .121 B4
Goring Ho CO4 . . . . .109 E4
Goring Rd
Colchester CO4 . . . . .110 C1
Ipswich IP4 . . . . .18 C6
Gorse La
Clacton-on-S CO15 . . . . . .189 A8
Tiptree CO5 . . . . .179 D4
Gorse Lane Ind Est
CO15 . . . . .189 B8
Gorse Rd IP3 . . . . .18 B2
Gorse Way
Clacton-on-S CO15 . . . . . .203 F7
Colchester CO3 . . . . .134 D4
Gorse Wlk CO4 . . . . .136 D7
Gorsehayes IP2 . . . . .17 B3
Gosbecks Prim Sch
CO2 . . . . .135 A3
Gosbecks Rd CO2 . . . . . . .135 A2
Gosbecks View CO2 . . . . .135 A2
Gosfield Com Prim Sch
CO9 . . . . .102 E8
Gosfield Hall ★ CO9 . . . . .102 C8
Gosfield Rd
Blackheath CO2 . . . . .163 A8
Braintree CM7 . . . . .102 D3
Gosfield Sch CO9 . . . . . . .75 F2
Gosford Cl CO10 . . . . .12 B8
Goshawk Dr CM2 . . . . . . .216 B5
Goslings The CM8 . . . . . .156 C5
Goul La CB10 . . . . .22 D1
Gouldings Ave CO14 . . . . .171 B8
Goulds Rd CO8 . . . . .54 F2
Goulton Rd CM1 . . . . .191 A1
Government Ct CO12 . . . . . .91 E5
Gower St IP2 . . . . .17 C4
Gowers Ave CM2 . . . . . . .216 E6
Gowers End CO10 . . . . .2 C5
Goyfield Ave IP11 . . . . . . .221 D4
Grace Gdns CM23 . . . . . . .145 F4
Grace's Cross CM2 . . . . . .217 C7
Graces Cl CM8 . . . . .195 A7
Graces La CM3 . . . . .207 B1
Graces Wlk CO13 . . . . . . .171 A6
Grafton Pl CM2 . . . . .206 A4
Grafton Rd CO12 . . . . .91 D4
Grafton Way IP1 . . . . .17 C5
Graham Ave IP1 . . . . .17 B8
Graham Rd
Felixstowe IP11 . . . . .221 D5
Ipswich IP1 . . . . .17 B7
Grailands CM23 . . . . .145 D8
Grammar School Pl 11
CO10 . . . . .33 E7
Grampian Gr CM1 . . . . . .204 D6
Granary Barn Mus The ★
CO7 . . . . .85 D7
Granary Ct CM6 . . . . .150 D7
Granary The CO10 . . . . . . .12 B6
Grand Ct CO13 . . . . .170 F3
Grand The CO13 . . . . . . .170 F3
Grange Cl
Felixstowe IP11 . . . . .221 C5
Halstead CO9 . . . . .103 E7
Walton-on-t-N CO14 . . . . .171 A7
Grange Com Prim Sch
IP11 . . . . .221 B4
Grange Ct
Chelmsford CM2 . . . . .215 F7
Clacton-on-S CO16 . . . . . .188 A4
Grange Farm CO2 . . . . . . .136 D3
Grange Farm Ave IP11 . . .221 B5
Grange Farm Rd CO2 . . . .136 D4
Grange Hill CO6 . . . . .130 F1
Grange La CM6 . . . . .151 C7
Grange Mill CO6 . . . . .130 F2
Grange Pk CM23 . . . . .118 F1
Grange Rd
Bishop's Stortford CM23 . . .146 A7
Felixstowe IP11 . . . . .221 B4
Great Horkesley CO6 . . . . .109 B7
Harwich CO12 . . . . .91 A3
Ickleton CB10 . . . . .20 A8
Ipswich IP4 . . . . .17 E6
Lawford CO11 . . . . .85 F1
Little Bromley CO11 . . . . . .112 E7
Tiptree CO5 . . . . .179 A6
Wickham Bishops CM8 . . . .195 E4
Grange The CM23 . . . . . . .118 F1
Grange Way CO2 . . . . . . .136 D3
Grange Way Bsns Pk
CO2 . . . . .136 D3
Grange Wlk CM23 . . . . . . .146 A7
Granger Ave CM9 . . . . . . .209 F1
Granger Row CM1 . . . . . . .204 F6
Grangeside CM23 . . . . . . .119 A2
Granta Cl CB10 . . . . .3 D1
Granta Cotts CB10 . . . . . . .3 C2
Grantham Ave CM77 . . . . .154 B7
Grantham Cres IP2 . . . . . . .17 A4
Grantham Ct CO1 . . . . . . .136 A7
Grantham Rd CO6 . . . . . . .109 B7
Grantley Cl CO6 . . . . .133 D5
Grants Ct CO14 . . . . .171 C8
Granville Cl CO6 . . . . .108 E3
Granville Rd
Clacton-on-S CO15 . . . . . .188 F3
Colchester CO1 . . . . .136 B5
Felixstowe IP11 . . . . .221 D3
Granville St 2 IP1 . . . . . . .17 B6
Granville Way CO7 . . . . . .186 A7
Grasby Cl CO7 . . . . .137 C2

Grasmere Cl
Great Notley CM77 . . . . . .154 C6
Ipswich IP3 . . . . .18 B1
Grasmere Gdns CO13 . . . .170 F7
Grassfields CO13 . . . . . . .170 E6
Grassmere CO4 . . . . .110 B5
Gravel Hill CO6 . . . . .56 A2
Gravel Hill Way CO12 . . . . .90 F1
Gravel Pit La CO11 . . . . . . .60 E2
Gravel The CO6 . . . . .130 F2
Gray Rd CO3 . . . . .135 D6
Gray's Cotts CO1 . . . . . . .136 B7
Gray's La CM7 . . . . .73 E4
Grayling Cl CM7 . . . . .127 E1
Grayling Dr CO4 . . . . .110 F1
Grayling Rd IP8 . . . . .36 E8
Grays Cl CO5 . . . . .201 C6
Grays Ct CM23 . . . . .145 E8
Grays Mead CO9 . . . . .51 D2
Great Baddow High Sch
CM2 . . . . .216 D6
Great Bardfield Cage ★
CM7 . . . . .72 B2
Great Bardfield Cottage
Mus ★ CM7 . . . . .72 A1
Great Bardfield Prim Sch
CM7 . . . . .72 B2
Great Bentley Prim Sch
CO7 . . . . .166 E7
Great Bentley Rd CO7 . . . .166 A8
Great Bentley Sta CO7 . . .166 E7
Great Bradfords Jun & Inf
Schs CM7 . . . . .128 B4
Great Canfield Rd
CM22 . . . . .148 D5
Great Chesterford CE Prim
Sch CB10 . . . . .3 D2
Great Chesterford Ct
CB10 . . . . .3 C2
Great Chesterford Sta
CB10 . . . . .3 C1
Great Cob CM1 . . . . .205 E5
Great Colman St 14 IP4 . . .17 D6
Great Cornard Ctry Pk ★
CO10 . . . . .34 C4
Great Cornard Mid Sch
CO10 . . . . .34 C4
Great Cornard Upper Sch &
Tech Coll CO10 . . . . . . .34 B4
Great Dunmow CE Jun Sch
CM6 . . . . .150 C8
Great Dunmow Inf Sch
CM6 . . . . .123 D1
Great Eastern Cl CM23 . . .146 A6
Great Eastern Cl CO14 . . .171 C7
Great Eastern Rd CO10 . . .33 F7
Great Eastern Sq IP11 . . .221 E5
Great Easton CE Prim Sch
CM6 . . . . .123 A8
Great Field IP11 . . . . .221 A8
Great Gibcracks Chase
CM2 . . . . .218 A2
Great Gipping St IP1 . . . . . .17 B5
Great Hadham Rd CM23 . .145 C4
Great Harrods CO14 . . . . .171 A4
Great Holland Common Rd
CO13 . . . . .169 D2
Great Holland Ct CO13 . . .170 A3
Great Leighs Prim Sch
CM3 . . . . .174 A7
Great Notley Ave CM77 . . .154 C5
Great Oak St CO9 . . . . .30 A1
Great Pitchers CO6 . . . . . .105 A4
Great Sampford Prim Sch
CB10 . . . . .47 A3
Great Sq 9 CM7 . . . . .127 F3
Great Tey CE Prim Sch
CO6 . . . . .106 C1
Great Tey Rd CO6 . . . . . . .132 C4
Great Totham Prim Sch
CM9 . . . . .196 A5
Great Totham Rd CM8 . . . .195 F5
Great Tufts IP9 . . . . .35 B1
Great Waltham CE Prim Sch
CM3 . . . . .190 E7
Great Whip St IP2 . . . . .17 C4
Great Yeldham Rd CO9 . . . .50 D7
Greate House Farm Rd
CO2 . . . . .162 A5
Grebe Cl IP2 . . . . .16 E2
Green Acres Rd CO2 . . . . .162 A5
Green Cl Chelmsford CM1 205 D4
Hatfield Peverel CM3 . . . . .194 C3
Writtle CM1 . . . . .204 B1
Green Cnr CO7 . . . . .139 E1
Green Ct CO6 . . . . .104 F7
Green End La CO13 . . . . . .170 B5
Green Farm Rd CO6 . . . . . .78 B2
Green La Aldham CO6 . . . .107 C1
Ardleigh CO7 . . . . .111 D6
Black Notley CM8 . . . . . . .155 A2
Boxted CO4 . . . . .82 D5
Colchester CO4 . . . . .110 A4
Colchester, Crockleford Heath
CO7 . . . . .111 C1
Great Dunmow CM6 . . . . .150 C8
Great Horkesley CO6 . . . . .109 C6
Great Notley CM8 . . . . . . .154 F2
Little Totham CM9 . . . . . . .197 C4
Stratford St M CO7 . . . . . . .58 C4
Tattingstone IP9 . . . . .61 D7
Tiptree CO5 . . . . .179 D6
Tolleshunt Knight's CO5 . . .179 E1
Walton-on-t-N CO14 . . . . .144 D2
Weeley Heath CO16 . . . . . .168 A6
Green Man La CM8 . . . . . .195 F7
Green Mdws CM3 . . . . . . .219 A6
Green Oak Glade IP8 . . . . .36 D8

Green St CM6 . . . . .148 F2
Green The
Bishop's Stortford CM23 . . .145 F4
Chelmsford CM1 . . . . .204 F4
Chrishall SG8 . . . . .19 D3
Clacton-on-S CO16 . . . . . .188 B5
Feering CO5 . . . . .158 E5
Great Bentley CO7 . . . . . . .166 D8
Little Totham CM9 . . . . . . .197 C4
Mistley CO11 . . . . .86 F4
Saffron Walden CB10 . . . . . .22 D3
Seawick CO16 . . . . .203 B6
Stanstead CO10 . . . . .2 E7
Writtle CM1 . . . . .204 B1
Green Way CO6 . . . . .78 A2
Green's Yd CO1 . . . . .135 E7
Greenacres
Clacton-on-S CO15 . . . . . .189 A5
Coggeshall CO6 . . . . .130 F1
Colchester CO4 . . . . .109 E3
Greene View CM7 . . . . . . .155 B8
Greenfield CM8 . . . . .177 A1
Greenfield Cotts CO4 . . . . .82 E6
Greenfield Dr CO6 . . . . . .106 B1
Greenfields
Galleywood CM2 . . . . .216 C2
Gosfield CO9 . . . . .102 F7
Stansted Mountfitchet
CM24 . . . . .119 E7
Greenfields Way CB9 . . . . . .8 E6
Greenfinch Ave IP2 . . . . . . .16 D3
Greenfinch End CO4 . . . . .136 F8
Greenford Rd CO15 . . . . . .188 E4
Greengates Mobile Home Pk
CO16 . . . . .168 C4
Greenhill Pk CM23 . . . . . .145 F6
Greenhurst Rd CO7 . . . . . .186 A6
Greenhythe Ct CO4 . . . . . .136 D6
Greenland Gr CO16 . . . . . .186 D3
Greenlawns Cvn Pk
CO16 . . . . .168 C2
Greens The IP4 . . . . .18 F4
Greens Yd CO13 . . . . .170 F5
Greensmill CO11 . . . . .86 C5
Greenspire Gr IP8 . . . . . . .16 B5
Greenstead Ct CO1 . . . . . .136 D6
Greenstead Rd CO1 . . . . . .136 D7
Greenstead Rdbt CO4 . . . .136 D6
Greenview Pk CO15 . . . . . .189 A7
Greenway
Bishop's Stortford CM23 . . .146 A7
Frinton-on-S CO13 . . . . . .170 F5
Greenway Cl CO15 . . . . . .189 B7
Greenway Gdns CM77 . . . .154 C7
Greenway The CO15 . . . . .189 B7
Greenways
Chelmsford CM1 . . . . .205 B6
Feering CO5 . . . . .158 E5
Gosfield CO9 . . . . .102 F7
Maldon CM9 . . . . .209 F2
Saffron Walden CB11 . . . . . .43 F2
Greenways Cl IP1 . . . . .17 B8
Greenways The CO6 . . . . .131 C4
Greenwich Bsns Pk IP3 . . . .17 E2
Greenwich Cl IP3 . . . . .17 E2
Greenwich Rd IP3 . . . . .17 E2
Greenwood Cl CB9 . . . . . . .8 E7
Greenwood Gr CO4 . . . . . .110 C3
Gregory St CO10 . . . . .33 E7
Grenadier Rd CB9 . . . . . . .8 C8
Grendel Way CO15 . . . . . .189 F6
Grenfell Ave CO15 . . . . . .189 E6
Grenfell Cl CO4 . . . . .110 C1
Grenville Rd
Braintree CM7 . . . . .127 E2
Sudbury CO10 . . . . .15 F2
Gresley Cl CO4 . . . . .109 F2
Gresley Dr CM7 . . . . .128 A2
Gresley Gdns IP2 . . . . .17 C3
Gretna Gdns IP4 . . . . .18 B8
Greville Ct CO14 . . . . .144 E2
Grey Friars Rd 10 IP1 . . . . .17 C5
Grey Ladys CM2 . . . . .216 B2
Greyhound Hill CO4 . . . . . .83 E5
Greyhound Rd CO10 . . . . . .2 B3
Greys Cl CO10 . . . . .1 C1
Greys Hollow CB11 . . . . . . .93 D8
Greystones Cl CO3 . . . . . .135 A3
Grieves Ct CO3 . . . . .134 C4
Griffin Ct IP2 . . . . .17 D3
Grimston Rd CO2 . . . . . . .136 A4
Grimston Way CO14 . . . . .171 B7
Grimwade Cl CO1 . . . . . . .136 D7
Grimwade St IP4 . . . . .17 D5
Grindle The IP8 . . . . .16 A7
Groom Ho CO15 . . . . .188 E4
Groom Pk CO15 . . . . .188 E4
Groome Ct 2 CO4 . . . . . . .136 D7
Grooms La CM8 . . . . .156 E4
Groomside CM7 . . . . .128 A2
Grosvenor Cl
Bishop's Stortford CM23 . . .145 D4
Chelmsford CM2 . . . . .216 D7
Ipswich IP4 . . . . .17 E8
Tiptree CO5 . . . . .179 D5
Grosvenor Ct IP3 . . . . .18 B1
Grosvenor Ho 4 CM23 . . .146 B8
Grosvenor Rd CO10 . . . . . .15 D2
Grove Ave
Walton-on-t-N CO14 . . . . .171 B8
West Mersea CO5 . . . . . . .201 C5
Grove Cotts 1 CM8 . . . . . .177 A2
Grove Ctr The CM8 . . . . . .177 A1
Grove Farm Rd
Little Totham CM9 . . . . . . .197 C7
Tiptree CO5,CM9 . . . . . . .179 A1
Grove Field CM7 . . . . .102 C1

Grove Hill Belstead IP8 . . . .36 C7
Dedham CO7 . . . . .84 D4
Ipswich IP8 . . . . .16 E1
Langham CO4 . . . . .83 F5
Stansted Mountfitchet
CM24 . . . . .119 E7
Grove La
Chelmondiston IP9 . . . . . . .63 E5
Ipswich IP4 . . . . .17 E5
Grove Lea CM9 . . . . .194 F1
Grove Orch CM7 . . . . .102 C1
Grove Pl 19 CM23 . . . . . . .145 F7
Grove Rd Bentley IP9 . . . . . .60 E6
Brantham CO11 . . . . .86 D8
Chelmsford CM2 . . . . .205 B1
Felixstowe IP11 . . . . .221 E6
Little Clacton CO16 . . . . . .168 D5
Tiptree CO5 . . . . .179 B5
Grove The Bicknacre CM3 . .218 F1
Clacton-on-S CO15 . . . . . .188 F2
Earls Colne CO6 . . . . .105 B6
Great Hallingbury CM22 . . .146 F4
Witham CM8 . . . . .177 A2
Grove Villas CM7 . . . . .126 A8
Grove Wlk IP8 . . . . .36 D8
Gryme's Dyke Ct CO3 . . . .134 D6
Gryme's Dyke Way CO3 . . .134 E3
Guelph's La CM6 . . . . .70 A3
Guernsey Ct CM7 . . . . . . .209 F2
Guernsey Way CM7 . . . . . .127 D2
Guildford Rd CO1 . . . . . . .136 A8
Guildhall Way CB10 . . . . . .24 A7
Guinea Cl CM7 . . . . .128 D4
Guisnes Ct CM9 . . . . .199 A4
Guithavon Ct CM8 . . . . . . .176 F2
Guithavon Rd CM8 . . . . . . .176 F1
Guithavon Rise CM8 . . . . .176 F2
Guithavon St CM8 . . . . . . .176 F2
Guithavon Valley CM8 . . . .176 F2
Gull Cotts CO16 . . . . .142 D4
Gull Ct CO16 . . . . .141 F1
Gull's La CO7 . . . . .85 A3
Gulls Croft CM7 . . . . .128 D3
Gulpher Bsns Pk IP11 . . . .221 D8
Gulpher Rd IP11 . . . . .221 E8
Gun Hill CO7 . . . . .84 C7
Gunfleet Cl CO5 . . . . .201 B7
Gunfleet Ct CO15 . . . . . . .189 C4
Gunson Gate CM2 . . . . . . .216 D7
Gurdon Rd CO2 . . . . .135 F3
Gurney Benham Cl CO2 . . .135 B4
Gurton Rd CO6 . . . . .131 A3
Gusford Com Prim Sch
IP2 . . . . .16 D1
Gutteridge Hall La
CO16 . . . . .167 E7
Gutters La CM1 . . . . .205 C7
Guy Cook Cl CO10 . . . . . . .34 C4
Guys Farm CM1 . . . . .204 B1
Gwendoline Cl IP4 . . . . . . .18 F4
Gwyn Cl CM3 . . . . .192 E1
Gwynne Rd CO12 . . . . .91 D4
Gymnasium St IP1 . . . . . . .17 B7
Gypsy La CO5 . . . . .159 C6

H

Ha'penny Field IP9 . . . . . .62 D5
Ha'penny Gdns IP9 . . . . . .62 D5
Hackmans La CM3 . . . . . . .219 E2
Haddon Pk CO1 . . . . .136 C6
Hadfelda Sq CM3 . . . . . . .194 A4
Hadfield Dr CM77 . . . . . . .155 B5
Hadham Ct CM23 . . . . . . .145 C8
Hadham Gr CM23 . . . . . . .145 C8
Hadham Rd CM23 . . . . . . .145 D8
Hadleigh Ct
Clacton-on-S CO15 . . . . . .189 A3
4 Saffron Walden CB10 . . .22 C4
Hadleigh Rd
Clacton-on-S CO16 . . . . . .188 B4
East Bergholt CO7 . . . . . . .59 B3
Frinton-on-S CO13 . . . . . .171 A5
Ipswich IP2 . . . . .16 D5
Stratford St M CO7 . . . . . . .58 A6
Hadleigh Road Ind Est
IP2 . . . . .16 F7
Hadleigh Way CO13 . . . . . .170 F5
Hadley Cl CM7 . . . . .102 B1
Hadrian Cl
Colchester CO4 . . . . .110 B6
Haverhill CB9 . . . . .9 D7
Hadrians Cl CM8 . . . . .194 E8
Hadrians Way CM9 . . . . . .210 A4
Hadstock Rd CB1 . . . . .5 B8
Haggars La CO7 . . . . .138 F3
Haggers Cl CO10 . . . . .3 D2
Haglemere Dr IP4 . . . . . . .17 E7
Haig Ct CM2 . . . . .205 A1
Hailes Wood CM22 . . . . . . .94 D1
Hailes Wood Cl CM22 . . . . .94 D1
Hainault Gr CM1 . . . . .204 E1
Hakewill Way CO4 . . . . . . .109 E3
Hale Cl IP2 . . . . .16 D2
Hale Way CO4 . . . . .110 B6
Halesowen Cl IP2 . . . . .36 F8
Half Acres CM23 . . . . .145 C4
Half Moon Yd CO10 . . . . . .12 B7
Halfacres CM8 . . . . .195 A7
Halford Ct 6 IP8 . . . . .16 C2
Halfway Cotts CO5 . . . . . .158 B4
Halifax Prim Sch IP2 . . . . .17 B2
Halifax Rd IP2 . . . . .17 B2
Halifax Way CO6 . . . . .104 F2

Hall Barn CO5 . . . .**201** B6
Hall Bridge Rise CM9 . .**210** C4
Hall Chase CO6 . . . .**133** B3
Hall Cl
　Great Baddow CM2 . . . .**217** A6
　Henham CM22 . . . .**94** F5
Hall Cres CO15 . . . .**189** F6
Hall Cut CO7 . . . .**185** E4
Hall Dr CO9 . . . .**102** D8
Hall Est CM9 . . . .**211** E7
Hall Farm Ct CO5 . . . . .**158** E4
Hall Field IP11 . . . .**221** C5
Hall La Chelmsford CM2 ..**217** C6
　Harwich CO12 . . . .**91** A2
　Ridgewell CO9 . . . .**29** B6
　Thorpe-le-S CO16 . . . . .**169** B8
　Walton-on-t-N CO14 . . .**144** D2
Hall Pond Way IP11 . . .**221** C5
Hall Rd
　Belchamp Walter CO10 . .**32** A6
　Borley CO10 . . . .**15** A3
　Bures CO8 . . . .**79** E5
　Copford CO6 . . . .**133** E4
　Elsenham CM22 . . . .**94** D1
　Fordham CO6 . . . .**107** D5
　Great Bromley CO7 . . . .**112** C2
　Great Totham CM9 . . . .**196** C3
　Maldon CM9 . . . .**210** B4
　Panfield CM7 . . . .**127** A6
　Tiptree CO5 . . . .**179** C3
　Tollesbury CM9 . . . .**199** D1
　West Bergholt CO6 . . . .**108** D5
Hall Rise Sudbury CO10 . .**33** C6
　Witham CM8 . . . .**194** F8
Hall Road Cotts CO6 . .**108** D6
Hall St Chelmsford CM2 .**205** B1
　Long Melford CO10 . . . . .**15** C8
Hall View Rd CO7 . . . . .**166** E7
Hall Villas CM7 . . . .**72** B1
Hallcroft Chase CO4 . . .**110** C4
Hallett Rd CM6 . . . .**151** E6
Hallingbury Cl CM22 . . .**146** B1
Hallingbury Rd CM22,
　CM23 . . . .**146** B4
Halliwell Rd IP4 . . . .**18** B6
Halstead Hospl CO9 . . . .**76** E3
Halstead Rd
　Braintree CM7 . . . .**102** E3
　Colchester CO3 . . . .**134** D7
　Earls Colne CO6 . . . . . .**104** F7
　Eight Ash G CO6 . . . . . .**134** A8
　Fordham CO6 . . . .**107** B3
　Fordham Heath CO6 . . .**107** E1
　Gosfield CO9 . . . .**75** F1
　Kirby Cross CO13 . . . . .**170** F7
　Kirby-le-S CO13 . . . . . .**170** C8
　Sible Hedingham CO9 . . .**76** B6
Halston Pl CM9 . . . .**220** F8
Halton Cres IP3 . . . .**18** C1
Hamble Cl CM8 . . . .**176** E2
Hamel Way CB11 . . . .**67** D4
Hamford Cl CO14 . . . . . .**144** D2
Hamford Dr CO12 . . . . .**116** C3
Hamford Prim Sch
　CO13 . . . .**170** F7
Hamilton Ct
　Brightlingsea CO7 . . . . .**186** A7
　Chelmsford CM1 . . . . . .**204** D6
　Clacton-on-S CO15 . . . .**189** E6
Hamilton Gdns IP11 . . .**221** F3
Hamilton Ho IP4 . . . .**18** A7
Hamilton Mews 3 CB10 . .**22** F2
Hamilton Prim Sch CO3 **135** D5
Hamilton Rd
　Colchester CO3 . . . .**135** D5
　Felixstowe IP11 . . . . . .**221** E4
　Great Holland CO13 . . .**170** A5
　Ipswich IP3 . . . .**18** B3
　Sudbury CO10 . . . .**33** C4
　Takeley CM22 . . . .**148** F7
　Wivenhoe CO7 . . . .**164** B8
Hamilton St
　Felixstowe IP11 . . . . . .**221** C5
　Harwich CO12 . . . .**90** F5
Hamlet Ct CO8 . . . .**79** E8
Hamlet Dr CO4 . . . .**136** F7
Hamlet Rd
　Chelmsford CM2 . . . . . .**205** B1
　Haverhill CB9 . . . .**9** B7
Hammonds Rd CM3 . . . .**206** B3
Hampit Rd CB11 . . . .**41** D2
Hampstead Ave CO16 . .**188** D5
Hampton Rd
　Great Baddow CM2 . . . .**216** E6
　Ipswich IP1 . . . .**16** F7
Hamsters Cl CO9 . . . . . .**77** F8
Hanbury Gdns CO4 . . . .**110** B5
Hanbury Rd CM1 . . . . . .**215** E8
Hance La CM77 . . . .**126** F2
Hanchetts Orch CM6 . . .**70** A3
Handel Wlk CO4 . . . .**136** E6
Handford Cut IP1 . . . . . .**17** A6
Handford Hall Prim Sch
　IP1 . . . .**17** A6
Handford Rd IP1 . . . .**17** A6
Handley's La CM8 . . . . .**195** F6
Handy Fisher Ct CO3 . .**135** B4
Hankin Ave CO12 . . . . . .**90** C1
Hanlee Brook CM2 . . . .**216** F6
Hanningfield Way CO4 ..**110** B5
Hanover Bridge CO5 . . .**158** F5
Hanover Ct
　Braintree CM7 . . . .**127** F8
　Ipswich IP4 . . . .**17** C6
　Sudbury CO10 . . . .**33** D6

Hanover Ct continued
　Walton-on-t-N CO14 . . . .**171** A8
　Witham CM8 . . . .**177** B1
Hanover Pl CB10 . . . .**22** C1
Hanover Sq CO5 . . . . . .**158** F6
Hanwell Ct CO16 . . . . . .**188** D5
Happy Gdns CO5 . . . . . .**179** A8
Harborough Hall Rd
　CO5 . . . .**159** E2
Harbour Cres CO12 . . . .**91** E5
Harcourt Ave CO12 . . . .**91** A4
Hardings Cl CO16 . . . . .**188** D8
Hardings Yd CO7 . . . . . .**164** B7
Hardwick Cl
　Great Notley CM77 . . . .**154** B7
　Rushmere St A IP4 . . . . .**18** E5
Hardwick Rd CB9 . . . .**9** B8
Hardy Cl Braintree CM7 .**155** A8
　Brantham CO11 . . . .**86** C7
Hardy Ct CO10 . . . .**15** F2
Harebell Cl CO4 . . . .**110** B3
Harebell Dr CM8 . . . . . .**176** E3
Harebell Rd IP2 . . . .**16** F4
Hares Wlk CO10 . . . .**33** F8
Harewood Rd CM1 . . . .**204** E1
Harewood Terr 20 CB9 . . .**8** E7
Harfred Ave CM9 . . . . . .**210** E3
Hargrave Cl CM24 . . . . .**119** E6
Harkilees Way CM7 . . . .**127** F5
Harkstead La
　Chelmondiston IP9 . . . . .**63** A7
　Woolverstone IP9 . . . . . .**38** A1
Harkstead Rd IP9 . . . . . .**62** F3
Harlings Gr CM1 . . . . . .**205** C3
Harman Wlk CO16 . . . . .**188** C5
Harness Cl CM1 . . . .**205** E7
Harnham Dr CM77 . . . . .**154** C7
Harold Cl CO9 . . . .**76** F1
Harold Gr CO13 . . . .**170** F4
Harold Rd Braintree CM7 .**127** E4
　Clacton-on-S CO15 . . . .**188** F3
　Frinton-on-S CO13 . . . .**170** F4
Harold Rise CM9 . . . . . .**209** F5
Harold Way CO13 . . . . .**170** F4
Harp Close Rd CO10 . . . .**33** F8
Harp Mdw La CO2 . . . . .**135** D4
Harpur's Rd CO10 . . . . . .**2** B4
Harrier Cl IP3 . . . .**18** B1
Harrington Cl
　8 Bishop's Stortford
　CM23 . . . .**146** A7
　Tiptree CO5 . . . .**179** B5
Harris Gn CM6 . . . .**150** E4
Harrison Ct CM1 . . . . . .**204** F3
Harrison Dr CM7 . . . . . .**128** A1
Harrison Rd CO2 . . . . . .**135** F3
Harrisons CM23 . . . .**119** D2
Harrold Ct CO15 . . . . . .**189** A2
Harrow Cl IP4 . . . .**18** B5
Harrow Hill CO9 . . . .**49** F6
Harrow Rd
　Clacton-on-S CO15 . . . .**188** F4
　Haverhill CB9 . . . .**8** E7
Harrow Way CM2 . . . . .**217** A6
Harsnett Rd CO1 . . . . . .**136** B5
Hart St CM2 . . . .**205** A1
Hart's La CO7 . . . .**84** B2
Hartest Way CO10 . . . . .**34** B6
Hartley Cl CM2 . . . .**206** A4
Hartley St IP2 . . . .**17** C4
Harvard Ct CO4 . . . .**110** B4
Harvest Cl CO6 . . . .**133** B4
Harvest Ct Feering CO5 .**158** E4
　Felixstowe IP11 . . . . . .**221** F4
Harvest End CO3 . . . . . .**134** D5
Harvest Ho IP11 . . . .**221** F4
Harvest Way
　Elmstead CO7 . . . .**137** F6
　Maldon CM9 . . . .**209** F5
Harvesters CM9 . . . .**198** D4
Harvesters' Way CO6 . .**132** B8
Harvey Cl CO11 . . . .**86** C4
Harvey Cres CO3 . . . . . .**134** C4
Harvey Ct CO15 . . . .**203** F4
Harvey Rd
　Colchester CO2 . . . .**135** B2
　Great Totham CM9 . . . .**196** A4
　Wivenhoe CO7 . . . .**137** C1
Harvey St CO9 . . . .**76** F1
Harvey Way
　Hempstead CB10 . . . . . .**25** F1
　Saffron Walden CB10 . . .**22** F2
Harwell Cl CM7 . . . .**128** C4
Harwich & District Hospl
　CO12 . . . .**91** A3
Harwich Com Prim Sch
　CO12 . . . .**91** E4
Harwich Crane The★
　CO12 . . . .**91** E5
Harwich Ct CO4 . . . .**136** F4
Harwich Ind Est CO12 . . .**90** F5
Harwich International Port
　CO12 . . . .**90** F6
Harwich Parkeston Quay Sta
　CO12 . . . .**90** F6
Harwich Rd Ardleigh CO7 **111** F8
　Beaumont CO16 . . . . . .**141** F7
　Bradfield CO11 . . . .**87** C2
　Colchester CO7 . . . .**110** F3
　Colchester,Greenstead
　CO1 . . . .**136** C7
　Dedham CO7 . . . .**84** F1
　Great Bromley CO7 . . . .**139** C4
　Great Oakley CO12 . . . .**116** D5
　Lawford CO11 . . . .**85** C7
　Little Bentley CO7 . . . . .**113** E1
　Little Clacton CO16 . . . .**168** E6
　Little Oakley CO12 . . . .**117** C7

Harwich Rd continued
　New Mistley CO11 . . . . . .**87** B3
　Ramsey CO11 . . . .**89** A2
　Wix CO11,CO12 . . . .**116** A7
　Wix,Wix Green CO11 . . .**115** D5
　Wrabness CO11 . . . .**88** D2
Harwich Sch The CO12 . .**91** A2
Harwich Town Sta CO12 . .**91** D5
Harwood Cl CO2 . . . .**136** A4
Haselfoot Rd CM3 . . . . .**206** F8
Haselmere Gdns CO13 .**170** F7
Haskell Mews CM7 . . . .**155** A8
Haslemere CM23 . . . . . .**146** A4
Haslemere Dr IP4 . . . . . .**17** E6
Haslemere Ind Est
　CM23 . . . .**146** A4
Hasler Rd CM9 . . . .**199** D2
Haslers La CM6 . . . .**150** D8
Hastings Ave CO15 . . . .**203** J8
Hastings Pl CO7 . . . .**185** F8
Hastings Rd CO3 . . . . . .**135** A4
Hatchcroft Gdns CO7 . .**138** A6
Hatcher Cres CO2 . . . . .**136** C5
Hatchfields CM3 . . . . . .**190** F7
Hatfield Forest (Ctry Pk)★
　CM22 . . . .**147** D6
Hatfield Forest Nature Trail★
　CM22 . . . .**147** E5
Hatfield Gr CM1 . . . .**204** D1
Hatfield Peverel Sta
　CM3 . . . .**193** F5
Hatfield Rd
　Hatfield Peverel CM8 . . .**194** F4
　Ipswich IP3 . . . .**18** A3
　Langford CM9 . . . .**209** B2
　Terling CM3 . . . .**175** D2
　Witham CM8 . . . .**194** F7
Hatherley Ct CB10 . . . . . .**22** E2
Haubourdin Ct CO9 . . . . .**77** A2
Haughley Dr IP4 . . . .**18** F4
Hauliers Rd IP11 . . . . . .**221** B2
Haven Ave CO15 . . . . . .**189** G6
Haven Cl IP11 . . . .**221** B4
Haven Ct CM3 . . . .**193** F4
Haven Rd CO2 . . . .**136** D4
Haven The CO12 . . . .**90** F3
Havencourt CM1 . . . . . .**205** B3
Havencroft Ct 3 CO14 . .**171** C6
Havengore CM1 . . . .**205** F5
Havens The IP3 . . . .**38** E7
Havergate Rd IP3 . . . . . .**38** D8
Haverhill Rd
　Castle Camps CB1 . . . . . .**7** E5
　Helions Bumpstead CB9 . .**8** D1
　Steeple Bumpstead CB9 . .**27** C8
Havering Cl
　Clacton-on-S CO15 . . . .**188** E7
　Colchester CO4 . . . .**110** B1
Havers Inf Sch CM23 . . .**145** F5
Havers La CM23 . . . .**145** F5
Havers Par CM23 . . . . . .**145** F5
Havisham Way CM1 . . . .**204** E7
Hawbridge IP9 . . . .**35** A2
Hawbush Gn CM77 . . . . .**155** F5
Hawes St IP2 . . . .**17** D3
Hawfinch Rd CO2 . . . . . .**162** A5
Hawfinch Wlk CM2 . . . .**216** B5
Hawke Rd IP3 . . . .**17** E1
Hawkendon Rd CO16 . . .**188** A4
Hawkes La IP11 . . . .**221** B6
Hawkes Rd CO6 . . . .**130** F3
Hawkesway CO15 . . . . .**188** F6
Hawkhurst Cl CM1 . . . . .**204** E2
Hawkins Cl CM3 . . . .**219** E2
Hawkins Ct CO10 . . . . . .**15** F2
Hawkins Rd
　Alresford CO7 . . . .**165** B8
　Colchester CO2 . . . .**136** D5
Hawkins Way CM7 . . . . .**128** C4
Hawks Cl CM3 . . . .**219** A6
Hawkwood Rd CO9 . . . . .**75** D8
Hawlmark End CO6 . . . .**132** E3
Hawthorn Ave CO4 . . . .**136** E7
Hawthorn Cl
　Chelmsford CM2 . . . . . .**216** C6
　Halstead CO9 . . . .**77** A2
　Takeley CM22 . . . .**148** C7
Hawthorn Dr IP2 . . . .**16** E3
Hawthorn Rd
　Clacton-on-S CO15 . . . .**188** E6
　Great Cornard CO10 . . . .**34** B7
　Hatfield Peverel CM3 . . .**194** A5
　Tolleshunt Knights CM9 ..**180** A2
Hawthorn Rise CM23 . . .**145** F3
Hawthorn Rise CM8 . . . .**177** A5
Hawthorns CM3 . . . .**220** D1
Hawthorns
　Kirby Cross CO13 . . . . . .**170** F7
　Sible Hedingham CO9 . . .**51** D2
Hawthorns The CM3 . . . .**219** A4
Hay Gn CM3 . . . .**218** F8
Hay La N CM7 . . . .**128** C3
Hay La S CM7 . . . .**128** C3
Haycocks La CO5 . . . . . .**183** F1
Haycroft CM23 . . . .**146** C7
Haye La CO5 . . . .**163** C4
Hayes Cl CM2 . . . .**205** B1
Hayes Rd CO15 . . . .**188** E3
Hayhill Rd IP4 . . . .**17** E7
Hayhouse Rd CO6 . . . . .**105** A6
Hayley Bell Gdns CM23 .**145** F3
Hayman Rd IP3 . . . .**17** F1
Haymeads La CM23 . . . .**146** C6
Haynes Green Rd CO5 . .**180** A8
Haytor Cl CM7 . . . .**128** C2
Haywain The CO3 . . . . . .**134** D5
Hayward Ct CO1 . . . .**136** C7
Hayward Sch The CM1 . .**205** A4

Hazel Cl Haverhill CB9 . . . .**8** E7
　Thorrington CO7 . . . . . .**166** A5
　Witham CM8 . . . .**177** A4
Hazel Dr IP3 . . . .**18** F1
Hazel Gr CM7 . . . .**127** E1
Hazel Mews CO7 . . . . . .**185** E7
Hazeldon Cl CM3 . . . . . .**190** F7
Hazeleigh Hall La CM3 .**220** C6
Hazelend Rd CM23 . . . . .**119** B4
Hazell Ave CO2 . . . .**135** B2
Hazelton Rd CO4 . . . . . .**110** D1
Hazelville Cl CO12 . . . . . .**90** E1
Hazelwood Cres CO16 . .**168** C1
Hazelwood Ct CM9 . . . . .**210** B6
Hazlemere Jun & Inf Schs
　CO4 . . . .**136** E8
Hazlemere Rd CO15 . . . .**189** C4
Head Cl CO10 . . . .**34** B5
Head St Colchester CO1 ..**135** E7
　Goldhanger CM9 . . . . . .**211** E6
　Halstead CO9 . . . .**76** F2
　Rowhedge CO5 . . . .**163** F8
Headgate CO1 . . . .**135** E6
Headgate Bldg 1 CO2 . .**135** E6
Headingham Cl 3 IP2 . . .**17** A2
Headland Ave CO3 . . . . . .**8** E7
Heard's La CM7 . . . .**48** D5
Heards La CM7 . . . .**48** C5
Hearsall Ave CM1 . . . . .**205** B7
Heath Cl CO7 . . . .**59** D3
Heath Cotts CO3 . . . . . .**107** F1
Heath Dr CM2 . . . .**216** B6
Heath La IP4 . . . .**18** C5
Heath Rd Alresford CO7 ..**165** B8
　Bradfield CO11 . . . .**114** D8
　Colchester CO3 . . . .**134** F5
　Colchester,Stanway Green
　CO3 . . . .**134** D4
　East Bergholt CO7 . . . . .**59** D3
　Fordham Heath CO3 . . .**108** A1
　Ipswich IP4 . . . .**18** D6
　New Mistley CO11 . . . . . .**87** B2
　Rowhedge CO5 . . . .**163** F8
　St Osyth CO16 . . . .**167** E1
　Tendring CO16 . . . .**140** E7
　Wivenhoe CO7 . . . .**137** B2
Heath Row CM23 . . . . . .**119** B1
Heath Sch The CO3 . . . .**134** D5
Heath The Dedham CO7 . .**85** A4
　Layer-de-l-H CO2 . . . . .**162** A6
Heathcote Sch CM3 . . . .**218** E7
Heather Ave IP3 . . . .**18** C3
Heather Cl
　Bishop's Stortford CM23 .**145** D6
　Clacton-on-S CO15 . . . .**189** B7
　Layer-de-l-H CO2 . . . . .**161** F5
Heather Ct 10 CM1 . . . . .**205** F6
Heather Dr CO3 . . . .**134** F6
Heatherhayes IP2 . . . . . .**17** A3
Heathfield Rd
　Chelmsford CM1 . . . . . .**205** B7
　Holbrook IP9 . . . .**62** D5
Heathfields CO6 . . . .**134** B8
Heathfields Ho CO2 . . . .**136** C3
Heathgate CM8 . . . .**195** D6
Heathgate Piece IP11 . .**221** A8
Heathgate Rd CO4 . . . . .**166** A5
Heathlands CE Prim Sch
　CO6 . . . .**108** E4
Heathlands Pk IP4 . . . . . .**18** E4
Heathside CO6 . . . .**108** E4
Heathside Inf Sch IP4 . . .**18** D6
Heatley Way CO4 . . . . . .**136** F8
Heaton Way CO5 . . . . . .**179** D6
Heckford's Rd CO7 . . . . .**139** E2
Heckworth Cl CO4 . . . . .**110** C6
Hedge Dr CO2 . . . .**135** B3
Hedgelands CO6 . . . .**133** D5
Hedgerows CO3 . . . .**134** D6
Hedgerows Bsns Pk
　CM2 . . . .**206** A6
Hedgerows The CM23 . .**146** B6
Hedingham Castle (remains
　of)★ CO9 . . . .**51** F4
Hedingham Rd
　Bulmer Tye CO10 . . . . . .**32** C1
　Gosfield CO9 . . . .**75** E3
　Halstead CO9 . . . .**76** B3
　Wickham St P CO9 . . . . .**53** A7
Hedingham Sch CO9 . . . .**51** D3
Hedingham Pl CO9 . . . . . .**51** D3
Heights The CM3 . . . . . .**218** D7
Helen How CM3 . . . .**173** F7
Helena Rd IP3 . . . .**17** E3
Helena Romanes Sch & Sixth
　Form Ctr CM6 . . . .**123** C3
Helford Ct CM8 . . . .**176** D2
Helions Bumpstead Rd
　CB9 . . . .**9** A5
Helions Park Ave CB9 . . . .**9** A7
Helions Park Gdns CB9 . . .**9** A7
Helions Park Gr CB9 . . . . .**9** A7
Helions Rd CB9 . . . .**27** A6
Helions Service Rd CB9 . . .**9** A7
Helions Wlk CB9 . . . .**9** A7
Helm Cl CO6 . . . .**109** C7
Helston Rd CM1 . . . .**205** E6
Hemingway Rd CM8 . . . .**176** F5
Hemlock Cl CM8 . . . .**177** A4
Hemmings Ct CM9 . . . . .**220** E8
Hendon Cl CO16 . . . .**188** D5
Hengrave Cl CO2 . . . . . .**135** F7
Henham & Ugley Prim Sch
　CM22 . . . .**94** F5
Henham Rd Debden CB11 .**68** E3
　Elsenham CM22 . . . .**94** E2
Henley Ct Colchester CO3 **134** F6
　Manningtree CO11 . . . . . .**86** C4

Henley Rd IP1 . . . .**17** C8
Henniker Gate CM2 . . . .**206** A4
Henniker Rd IP1 . . . .**16** D8
Henny Back Rd CO8 . . . . .**54** E4
Henny Rd CO8 . . . .**55** B5
Henrietta Cl CO7 . . . . . .**137** C3
Henry Cl CO15 . . . .**188** C2
Henry Dixon Rd CM8 . . .**177** D6
Henry Rd
　Chelmsford CM1 . . . . . .**205** B4
　Ipswich IP3 . . . .**18** B1
Henslow Rd IP4 . . . .**18** B5
Henstead Gdns IP3 . . . . .**18** A2
Herald Cl CM23 . . . .**145** D6
Herbage Park Rd CM9 . .**208** D1
Herbert Rd CO15 . . . . . .**188** E3
Hereford Ct
　Clacton-on-S CO15 . . . .**189** E5
　Great Baddow CM2 . . . .**217** A5
Hereford Dr CM7 . . . . . .**128** D5
Hereford Rd
　Colchester CO1 . . . .**136** A8
　Holland-on-S CO15 . . . .**189** E6
Hereward Cl CO7 . . . . . .**137** C3
Hereward Way CM7 . . . . .**73** C3
Heriot Way CM9 . . . .**196** B4
Hermitage Ct CM24 . . . .**119** D7
Hermitage Ho CM24 . . . .**119** D7
Heron Ct CM23 . . . .**146** A7
Heron Glade CO15 . . . . .**188** F7
Heron Rd Ipswich IP2 . . . .**16** E3
　Kelvedon CO5 . . . .**158** D2
Heron Way
　Frinton-on-S CO13 . . . .**170** C6
　Heybridge CM9 . . . .**210** C5
Heronsgate CO13 . . . . . .**170** F6
Herrick Pl CO3 . . . .**135** A6
Herring's Way CO6 . . . .**107** D6
Herringham Gn CM2 . . . .**206** A4
Hertford La SG8,CB11 . . . .**19** E5
Hertfordshire & Essex High
　Sch The CM23 . . . .**146** B7
Herts & Essex Hospl
　CM23 . . . .**146** B6
Hervey St IP4 . . . .**17** D7
Hervilly Way CO14 . . . . .**171** B7
Heseltine Ct CO15 . . . . .**189** B3
Hesper Rd CO2 . . . .**136** C5
Hetherington Cl CO2 . . .**163** A8
Hewes Cl CO4 . . . .**136** F7
Hewitt Rd CO12 . . . .**90** C1
Hewitt Wlk 6 CM8 . . . . .**177** A2
Hexham Cl 6 IP2 . . . .**17** A2
Heybridge App CM9 . . . .**209** F5
Heybridge Ct CO15 . . . . .**189** B3
Heybridge House Ind Est
　CM9 . . . .**210** B4
Heybridge Prim Sch
　CM9 . . . .**210** C5
Heybridge St CM9 . . . . .**210** B5
Heycroft Dr CM77 . . . . .**155** E5
Heycroft Way
　Great Baddow CM2 . . . .**216** F5
　Tiptree CO5 . . . .**179** D6
Heydon La Chrishall SG8 . .**19** B5
　Elmdon CB11 . . . .**19** F4
Heymeads Ct CM9 . . . . .**210** A5
Heythrop The CM2 . . . . .**205** D4
Heywood Cl IP2 . . . .**16** E1
Heywood Cres CM9 . . . .**210** B6
Heywood La CM6 . . . . . .**150** D7
Heywood Way CM9 . . . . .**210** B6
Hickford Hill CO10 . . . . . .**12** D6
Hickory Ave CO4 . . . . . .**136** D7
Hicks Way CB9 . . . .**9** E5
Hidcote Way CM77 . . . . .**154** B7
High Bridge Rd CM2 . . . .**205** C1
High Chelmer 8 CM1 . . .**205** B2
High Cl SG8 . . . .**19** A5
High Croft CO6 . . . .**78** A2
High Cross La CM6 . . . . .**149** B5
High Cross La E CM6 . . .**149** E6
High Cross Villas CM6 . .**149** E6
High Easter Rd CM6 . . . .**150** F2
High Fields CM6 . . . .**150** D8
High Garrett CM7 . . . . . .**102** C2
High La
　Bishop's Stortford CM24 .**119** F8
　Stansted Mountfitchet
　CM24 . . . .**93** E1
High Lift Villas CO4 . . . . .**83** D8
High Mdw CM6 . . . .**150** C8
High Oaks CO12 . . . .**90** B2
High Pasture CM3 . . . . .**207** D3
High Rd CO2 . . . .**161** F5
High Rd E IP11 . . . .**221** F5
High Rd W IP11 . . . .**221** D5
High Ridge CM8 . . . .**196** C8
High St
　Bishop's Stortford CM23 .**145** F7
　Braintree CM7 . . . .**127** F3
　Brightlingsea CO7 . . . . .**185** F6
　Bures CO8 . . . .**55** F1
　Castle Camps CB1 . . . . . .**7** E3
　Cavendish CO10 . . . .**1** D2
　Chelmsford CM1 . . . . . .**205** B2
　Chrishall SG8 . . . .**19** D3
　Clacton-on-S CO15 . . . .**188** F2
　Clare CO10 . . . .**12** B7
　Clavering CB11 . . . .**65** D4
　Colchester CO1 . . . .**135** F7
　Debden CB11 . . . .**68** B7
　Dedham CO7 . . . .**84** F7
　Earls Colne CO6 . . . . . .**105** B6
　Elsenham CM22 . . . .**94** D1
　Felixstowe IP11 . . . . . .**221** C6
　Great Baddow CM2 . . . .**216** F6
　Great Bardfield CM7 . . . .**72** A1

High St continued
Great Chesterford CB10 . . .3 E2
Great Chesterford,Little
  Chesterford CB10 . . . . . . .21 F8
Great Dunmow CM6 . . . .150 D8
Great Oakley CO12 . . . . . .116 C4
Great Yeldham CO9 . . . . . .30 A1
Halstead CO9 . . . . .76 D1
Harwich CO12 . . . . .91 D4
Haverhill CB9 . . . . .9 A7
Hempstead CB10 . . . . .25 F1
Henham CM22 . . . . .94 F5
Hinxton CB10 . . . . .3 B7
Ipswich IP1 . . . . .17 C6
Kelvedon CO5 . . . . .158 C2
Langham CO4 . . . . .83 D4
Littlebury CB11 . . . . .21 F4
Maldon CO9 . . . . .210 A2
Manningtree CO11 . . . . . . .86 D4
Mistley CO11 . . . . .86 F4
Nayland CO6 . . . . .56 B1
Newport CB11 . . . . .67 A8
Rowhedge CO5 . . . . .164 A8
Saffron Walden CB10 . . . . .22 D1
Sproughton IP8 . . . . .16 A6
Stebbing CM6 . . . . .124 E5
Thorpe-le-S CO16 . . . . . .141 F1
Tollesbury CM9 . . . . .199 D1
Walton-on-t-N CO14 . . . .171 C8
West Mersea CO5 . . . . . .201 B6
Wethersfield CM7 . . . . . . .73 C3
Widdington CB11 . . . . .67 D4
Wivenhoe CO7 . . . . .164 B8
High St N CO5 . . . . .201 C7
High Stile CM6 . . . . .150 C8
High Tree La CO14 . . . . .144 D2
High View CM23 . . . . . . .119 D3
High View Ave CO15 . . . .188 E6
High View Cl CO15 . . . . .188 E6
High View Rd IP1 . . . . . . .16 D8
High Woods Country Park
  Visitor Ctr★ CO4 . . . . .109 F3
High Woods Ctry Pk★
  CO4 . . . . .110 A4
Higham Hill CO7,IP7 . . . .58 A8
Higham Rd CO7 . . . . .58 B3
Highams Chase CM9 . . .212 A8
Highbank CO10 . . . . .2 B5
Highbirch Rd CO16 . . . .167 D3
Highbury Terr 1 CO9 . . .76 F2
Highbury Way CO10 . . . . .34 B5
Highclere Rd
  Colchester CO4 . . . . . . .110 B4
  Great Notley CM77 . . . . .154 B6
Highfield CO10 . . . . .12 D7
Highfield Ave
  Bishop's Stortford CM23 .146 C6
  Harwich CO12 . . . . .91 B3
Highfield Cl
  Braintree CM7 . . . . .128 A6
  Danbury CM3 . . . . .218 D6
Highfield Ct CO12 . . . . . .91 B3
Highfield Dr CO3 . . . . . .135 C7
Highfield Holiday Pk
  Clacton-on-S CO16 . . . .188 E8
  Little Clacton CO15 . . . .168 F1
Highfield Rd
  Chelmsford CM1 . . . . . .204 E4
  Felixstowe IP11 . . . . . . .221 E4
  Sudbury CO10 . . . . .34 A8
Highfield Stile Rd CM7 .128 A6
Highfields Bentley IP9 . . .60 E6
  Debden CB11 . . . . .68 B7
  Great Yeldham CO9 . . . . .30 A2
  Halstead CO9 . . . . .103 F8
  Henham CM22 . . . . .94 F6
  Langley CB11 . . . . .40 D2
  Saffron Walden CB10 . . . .22 E2
Highfields La CO5 . . . . .178 E7
Highfields Prim Sch
  CO11 . . . . .86 C4
Highfields Rd CM8 . . . . .176 E1
Highland Rd CM23 . . . .145 F3
Highlands CO9 . . . . .75 E1
Highlands Chalet Pk
  CO15 . . . . .188 F7
Highlands Dr CM9 . . . . .209 E2
Highmead CM24 . . . . . . .119 E8
Highview Cl CO10 . . . . . .15 E2
Highwoods App CO4 . . . .110 C4
Highwoods Prim Sch
  CO4 . . . . .110 B4
Highwoods Sq CO4 . . . .110 B4
Hildabrook Cl 2 IP2 . . . .16 F7
Hill Cl CO10 . . . . .15 D8
Hill Cotts CO4 . . . . .166 E1
Hill Cres CM2 . . . . .205 D2
Hill Farm La IP9 . . . . . . .63 F7
Hill House Ct CO7 . . . . .186 A4
Hill House Rd IP3 . . . . . .17 E5
Hill La CB9 . . . . .9 F4
Hill Rd Chelmsford CM2 .205 D2
  Clacton-on-S CO15 . . . .188 E6
  Coggeshall CO6 . . . . . . .131 B2
  Harwich CO12 . . . . .91 C4
  Hempstead CB10 . . . . . . .46 D8
  Ramsey CO12 . . . . .116 E8
Hill Rd S CM2 . . . . .205 D2
Hill St CB10 . . . . .22 D1
Hill Terr CO10 . . . . .12 C8
Hill Top La CB11 . . . . . . .43 E7
Hill View CM3 . . . . .218 F1
Hill View Rd CM1 . . . . . .205 C4
Hillary Cl Bradwell CM7 . .129 D2
  Chelmsford CM1 . . . . . .205 D4
  Heybridge CM9 . . . . . . .210 B5
  Ipswich IP4 . . . . .18 A5

Hillcrest
  Clacton-on-S CO15 . . . .189 A6
  Kirby-le-S CO13 . . . . . .170 D8
Hillcrest Cotts CO4 . . . . .83 E6
Hillcrest Ct CO12 . . . . . .91 C3
Hillcrest Rd CO10 . . . . . .15 E2
Hillfield CO5 . . . . .158 D4
Hillhouse La CO16 . . . .141 B3
Hilliards Rd CO7 . . . . . .113 C2
Hillie Bunnies CO6 . . . .105 B7
Hillman Ave CO15 . . . . .203 E6
Hillmead Prim Sch
  CM23 . . . . .145 C7
Hillridge CO4 . . . . .110 B3
Hills Cl CM7 . . . . .127 F4
Hills Cres CO3 . . . . .135 A5
Hills Rd CO9 . . . . .75 D8
Hillside CO13 . . . . .170 E4
Hillside Ave CM23 . . . . .146 A7
Hillside Com Prim Sch
  IP2 . . . . .17 C3
Hillside Cotts
  Birchanger CM23 . . . . . .119 C3
  Sudbury CO10 . . . . .34 A7
  Thorpe-le-S CO16 . . . . .142 A7
Hillside Cres
  Holland-on-S CO15 . . . .189 C5
  Ipswich IP3 . . . . .18 C3
Hillside End CM23 . . . . .119 C3
Hillside Gdns CM7 . . . . .127 F1
Hillside Gr CM2 . . . . . . .216 A7
Hillside Ho 2 CM7 . . . . .127 F1
Hillside Mews CM2 . . . .216 A7
Hillside Rd CO10 . . . . . . .34 A7
Hillside Specl Sch CO10 .15 F1
Hillside Terr 1 CM7 . . . .127 F1
Hillsleigh Mews CO1 . . .136 A7
Hillston Cl CO2 . . . . . . .136 B2
Hilltop Cl CO2 . . . . .136 D4
Hilltop Cres CO16 . . . . .140 F1
Hilltop Rise CO16 . . . . .140 E1
HillView Cl CO5 . . . . . . .163 F8
Hillybroom Gdns CO5 . .201 D6
Hilton Cl CO11 . . . . .86 D4
Hilton Rd IP3 . . . . .18 C1
Hilton Way CO9 . . . . .75 E8
Hilton Wlk CO9 . . . . .75 E8
Hines Cl CO6 . . . . .133 B8
Hines Rd IP3 . . . . .18 A4
Hintesham Cl CM4 . . . . . .18 F5
Hintlesham Dr IP11 . . . .221 B5
Hinxton Rd CB10 . . . . .3 A7
Hipkins CM23 . . . . .145 E4
Histon Cl IP5 . . . . .18 F1
Hitch Common Rd CB11 .66 F8
Hitcham Rd CO6 . . . . . . .130 F3
Hitchcock Pl CO10 . . . . . .15 E1
Hitchin Mews CM7 . . . . .155 B8
Hitherwood Rd CO2 . . . .135 C2
HMS Ganges Association
  Mus★ IP9 . . . . .91 C8
Hobart Cl CM1 . . . . .204 E5
Hobbs Dr CO4 . . . . .83 A5
Hobbs La CO10 . . . . .2 D2
Hoblongs Ind Est CM6 . .150 E6
Hockerill Anglo-European
  Sch CM23 . . . . .146 B7
Hockerill Ct 7 CM23 . . .146 A7
Hockerill St CM23 . . . . .146 A7
Hockley Cl CB1 . . . . .7 B5
Hockney Gdns IP3 . . . . . .38 A8
Hodges Holt CM8 . . . . . .195 A7
Hodgkinson Rd IP11 . . . .221 A3
Hoe Dr CO3 . . . . .135 A5
Hoe La
  Great Waltham CM3 . . . .190 A6
  Pentlow CO10 . . . . .13 F8
Hoe Mill Rd CM9 . . . . . .208 E4
Hoffmanns Way CM1 . . .205 B4
Hog's La SG8 . . . . .19 D3
Hogarth Cl CO5 . . . . . . .201 D6
Hogarth Ct CM1 . . . . . . .205 E6
Hogarth End CO13 . . . . .170 E7
Hogarth Rd IP3 . . . . .18 A1
Hogarth Sq IP3 . . . . .18 A1
Holborough Cl CO4 . . . .136 F7
Holbrook Cl CO16 . . . . .188 B4
Holbrook Cres IP11 . . . .221 B4
Holbrook High Sch IP9 . .62 D6
Holbrook Prim Sch IP9 . .62 D6
Holbrook Rd
  Harkstead IP9 . . . . .63 A2
  Haverhill CB9 . . . . .8 E6
  Ipswich IP3 . . . . .17 F1
  Stutton IP9 . . . . .62 A2
Holbrooke Wlk CO5 . . . .179 E5
Holcombe Cres IP2 . . . . .16 D2
Holden Cl Braintree CM7 .128 A2
  Ipswich IP2 . . . . .17 D3
Holden Rd CO4 . . . . .109 C2
Holdsworth Cl CO10 . . . . .2 B3
Holkham Cl IP4 . . . . .18 F5
Holland Haven Ctry Pk
  CO15 . . . . .189 I8
Holland Haven Prim Sch
  CO15 . . . . .189 E6
Holland Ho CO15 . . . . . .189 A3
Holland Lodge CO15 . . .188 F3
Holland Park Prim Sch
  CO15 . . . . .189 B5
Holland Pk CO15 . . . . . .189 B4
Holland Rd
  Clacton-on-S, Holland on S
    CO15 . . . . .189 B4
  Clacton-on-S, Rush Green
    CO15 . . . . .188 F2
  Felixstowe IP11 . . . . . .221 D3
  Frinton-on-S CO13 . . . .170 E3

Holland Rd continued
  Ipswich IP4 . . . . .17 F6
  Kirby Cross CO13 . . . . .170 B6
  Little Clacton CO16 . . . .168 E2
Hollands Rd CB9 . . . . .9 A6
Holledge Cres CO13 . . . .170 A6
Hollesley Ave CB9 . . . . . .8 C8
Hollies Rd CM7 . . . . . . .129 C3
Holliland Croft CO6 . . . .132 C8
Hollingtons Gr CO2 . . . .161 A3
Hollis Lock CM2 . . . . . .206 A3
Holliwel Cl CO3 . . . . . . .134 D6
Hollow La Ashen CO10 . . .11 E3
  Broomfield CM1 . . . . . . .204 E8
  Bures CO8 . . . . .55 F3
  Chelmondiston IP9 . . . . .63 F7
Hollow Rd Braintree CM6 153 B4
  Chrishall SG8 . . . . .19 D2
  Elmdon CB11 . . . . .20 A4
  Kelvedon CO5 . . . . .157 F2
  Washbrook IP8 . . . . .35 D8
  Widdington CB11 . . . . . .67 C3
Holloway Rd CM9 . . . . . .210 A5
Holly Blue Cl IP8 . . . . . . .36 E8
Holly Bush Cnr CO7 . . . . .58 C5
Holly Cl Colchester CO2 .135 C2
  Ipswich IP3 . . . . .18 F1
Holly Cotts CO7 . . . . .60 C1
Holly Ct CO15 . . . . .188 E4
Holly La Belstead IP8 . . . . .36 C7
  Great Horkesley CO6 . . . .82 C4
  Stutton IP9 . . . . .61 E3
Holly Oaks CO6 . . . . .80 E4
Holly Rd Colchester CO3 .134 C4
  Ipswich IP1 . . . . .17 B7
  Rushmere St A IP5 . . . . .18 F7
Holly Way
  Chelmsford CM2 . . . . . .216 D7
  Elmstead CO7 . . . . .138 A6
  Tiptree CO5 . . . . .179 C5
Holly Wlk CM8 . . . . .177 B5
Hollybank CM8 . . . . .176 F1
Hollybush Hill CO7 . . . . .166 E3
Hollycroft CM2 . . . . . . .217 B6
Hollyhock Rd CB10 . . . . .22 E2
Hollymead Cl CO4 . . . . .109 F3
Hollytree Ct CO2 . . . . . .135 C3
Hollyview Cl CM2 . . . . . .140 F5
Hollywood Cl CM2 . . . . .216 E6
Holm Oak CO2 . . . . .136 A3
Holman Cres CO3 . . . . . .135 A4
Holman Rd CO9 . . . . . . .103 E8
Holmans CM3 . . . . .206 E8
Holmbrook Way CO13 . . .170 E5
Holmes Rd CO9 . . . . . . .103 E8
Holmoak IP2 . . . . .62 D6
Holmswood House Prep Sch
  CO3 . . . . .134 D8
Holmwood Cl CO16 . . . .188 B6
Holmwood House Prep Sch
  CO3 . . . . .134 D8
Holst Ave CM8 . . . . .194 F7
Holt Dr Blackheath CO2 . .163 A7
  Wickham Bishops CM8 . .195 E5
Holt's Rd CO6 . . . . .81 B3
Holy Family RC Prim Sch
  CM8 . . . . .194 F7
Holy Trinity & St Nicholas CE
  Prim Sch SG8 . . . . .19 C3
Holy Trinity CE Prim Sch
  CO9 . . . . .76 D2
Holybread La CM3 . . . . . .207 C4
Holyrood CO12 . . . . .90 F2
Holyrood Cl IP2 . . . . .16 F2
Holywells Cl IP3 . . . . . . .17 E4
Holywells High Sch IP3 . .18 C1
Holywells Rd IP3 . . . . . . .17 E3
Home Cl CB9 . . . . .27 C7
Home Farm La
  Ardleigh CO7 . . . . .112 A8
  Dedham CO7 . . . . .85 A1
Home Farm Prim Sch
  CO3 . . . . .134 F6
Home Mead
  Galleywood CM2 . . . . . .216 C2
  Writtle CM1 . . . . .204 A1
Homebridge CM8 . . . . . . .47 A3
Homedale Cotts CO4 . . . .83 B6
Homefield IP9 . . . . .35 B1
Homefield Cl CM1 . . . . .204 D5
Homefield Rd
  Colchester CO2 . . . . . . .135 C1
  Haverhill CB9 . . . . .8 F5
  Witham CM8 . . . . .177 A4
Homefield Road Units CB9 8 F5
Homefield Way
  Cressing CM77 . . . . . . .155 D7
  Earls Colne CO6 . . . . . .105 B7
Homelands CO14 . . . . . .171 A7
Homelye Chase CM6 . . . .124 B1
Homeorr Ho IP11 . . . . . .221 F4
Homerton Ct CO15 . . . . .188 F8
Homestead CM1 . . . . . . .205 B7
Homestead Sch CO4 . . . .83 E4
Homey Bridge Rd CO6 . . .56 C8
Homing Rd CO16 . . . . . .168 C4
Honey Cl CM2 . . . . .216 D6
Honey La CB5 . . . . .64 F3
Honey Pot Hall CO15 . . .188 F3
Honeybourne CM23 . . . .145 E4
Honeycroft CO11 . . . . . . .86 B3
Honeypot La
  Little Clacton CO16 . . . .168 A4
  Tolleshunt Knights CM9 . .180 B1
  Weeley Heath CO16 . . . .168 B4
  Wix CO11 . . . . .114 F3
Honeypots CM2 . . . . . . .216 C6
Honeysuckle Cl CM23 . . .145 C6

Honeysuckle Gdns IP2 . . .16 E4
Honeysuckle Path 9
  CM1 . . . . .205 F6
Honeysuckle Way
  Colchester CO4 . . . . . . .136 E8
  Thorrington CO7 . . . . . .166 A5
  Witham CM8 . . . . .176 D4
Honeywood Ave CO6 . . . .131 A3
Honeywood Rd CO9 . . . . .77 A3
Honor Link CM1 . . . . . . .206 A7
Honorius Dr CO4 . . . . . .110 B6
Honywood Cl CO6 . . . . . .132 E3
Honywood Com Sch The
  CO6 . . . . .131 A3
Honywood Rd CO3 . . . . .135 D6
Honywood Way CO13 . . .170 F7
Hood Gdns CM7 . . . . . . .128 C4
Hood Rd IP3 . . . . .17 E1
Hop Gardens La CM9 . . .208 F1
Hop View CO7 . . . . .59 B2
Hopgrounds The CM7 . . .72 D6
Hopkin's La CO12 . . . . . .91 D6
Hopkins Cl
  Chelmsford CM2 . . . . . .206 A3
  Kirby Cross CO13 . . . . .170 F6
Hopkins Mead CM2 . . . .206 A3
Hopkirk Cl CM3 . . . . . . .218 F8
Hopping Jacks La CM3 . .218 F7
Hoppit Mead CM7 . . . . .127 F1
Hopton Rise CB9 . . . . .8 B8
Horace Eves Cl 1 CB9 . . .8 F8
Hordle Pl CO12 . . . . .91 D4
Hordle St CO12 . . . . .91 D4
Horkesley Hill CO6 . . . . .82 A7
Horkesley Rd
  Great Horkesley CO4 . . .109 E8
  Nayland CO6 . . . . .56 A1
Horley IP2 . . . . .16 E4
Horley Cl CO16 . . . . .188 C6
Horn Book CB10 . . . . . . .22 F1
Horn Hill CO9 . . . . .75 C5
Hornbeam Cl
  Chelmsford CM2 . . . . . .216 A6
  Colchester CO2 . . . . . . .135 D2
Hornbeam Wlk CM8 . . . .177 A4
Hornbeams The CO12 . . .117 B7
Horne Row CM3 . . . . . . .218 D5
Horner Pl 4 CM8 . . . . . .177 A2
Hornsea Villas CM6 . . . .124 D7
Horrocks Cl CO2 . . . . . .136 A4
Horse & Groom La CM2 216 A3
Horse Pond Cl CO10 . . . . .34 C4
Horsehoe Cl CB11 . . . . . .20 B4
Horseshoe La CB9 . . . . . . .8 E7
Horsey Rd CO13 . . . . . . .170 C8
Horsham Ave IP3 . . . . . . .18 D3
Horsley Cross CO11 . . . .114 A3
Horsley Ho IP11 . . . . . . .221 F4
Hospital App CM1 . . . . . .191 B3
Hospital Field CM77 . . . .155 B5
Hospital La CO3 . . . . . . .135 D6
Hospital Rd CO3 . . . . . . .135 D6
Hossack Rd IP3 . . . . .38 A8
Houblon Dr CM2 . . . . . .216 C2
Houchin's La CO6 . . . . . .131 E3
Houghton Pl IP4 . . . . . . .18 F5
House Martins The
  IP11 . . . . .221 D6
Hove Ct CO15 . . . . .189 F6
Howard Ave CO12 . . . . . .90 F2
Howard Cl Braintree CM7 .128 C3
  Haverhill CB9 . . . . .8 D7
Howard Dr CM2 . . . . . . .206 A2
Howard Rd
  Holland-on-S CO15 . . . .189 C4
  Saffron Walden CB10 . . . .22 C2
Howard St IP4 . . . . .18 B6
Howard Vyse Ct CO15 . . .188 E5
Howards Cl CM3 . . . . . . .206 E8
Howards Croft CO4 . . . .109 D5
Howbridge CE Jun Sch
  CM8 . . . . .194 F8
Howbridge Hall Rd
  Witham CM8 . . . . .194 F6
  Witham CM8 . . . . .194 F7
Howbridge Inf Sch The
  CM8 . . . . .194 F8
Howbridge Rd CM8 . . . . .194 F8
Howe Ave IP3 . . . . .18 C3
Howe Chase CO9 . . . . . . .76 E4
Howe Cl CO4 . . . . .136 D7
Howe Green House Sch
  CM22 . . . . .146 D2
Howe La CB10 . . . . .47 A5
Howlets Terr IP9 . . . . . . .63 E7
Hoxter Way CO10 . . . . . .15 E2
Hoxton Cl CO16 . . . . . . .188 D5
Hoynors CM3 . . . . .219 A7
Hubbards Chase CO14 . .171 B8
Hubert Rd CO3 . . . . .135 B8
Hucklesbury Ave CO15 . .189 E7
Hudson Cl
  Clacton-on-S CO16 . . . .188 C5
  Harwich CO12 . . . . .91 A1
  Haverhill CB9 . . . . .9 C6
Hudson's Hill CM7 . . . . . .73 D4
Hudsons La CO6 . . . . . . .57 B5
Hugh Dickson Rd CO4 . .109 E2
Hugh Villas CM23 . . . . . .146 A5
Hughes Cnr CO7 . . . . . . .59 A4
Hughes Rd CO7 . . . . .59 A4
Hughes Stanton Way
  CO11 . . . . .86 B4
Hull La CM3 . . . . .175 A2
Hull's La CM2 . . . . .217 D4
Hulton Cl CM3 . . . . .206 E8
Hulver Ct IP3 . . . . .18 B2
Humber Ave CO15 . . . . .203 E6

Humber Doucy La IP4 . . .18 D8
Humber Rd
  Chelmsford CM1 . . . . . .205 C5
  Witham CM8 . . . . .176 D2
Humphrey's Farm La
  CM3 . . . . .190 C7
Humphry Rd CO10 . . . . . .33 E8
Hundon Pl 4 CB9 . . . . . . .9 B8
Hundred La CO4 . . . . .83 C4
Hungerdown La CO11 . . . .85 E1
Hunnable Rd CM7 . . . . . .127 E2
Hunt Ave CM9 . . . . .210 B5
Hunt Cl CO5 . . . . .158 D4
Hunt Dr CO16 . . . . .188 D6
Hunt Rd CO6 . . . . .105 A6
Hunt Way CO13 . . . . . . .170 E6
Hunt's Cl CM1 . . . . .215 B8
Hunt's Dr CM1 . . . . .215 B8
Hunter Dr Braintree CM7 128 C2
  Lawford CO11 . . . . .86 A3
Hunter Rd IP3 . . . . .38 C8
Hunter's Chase CO7 . . . .84 E2
Hunters Cnr CO3 . . . . . .134 F5
Hunters Ct CM22 . . . . . . .94 C2
Hunters End IP11 . . . . . .221 A7
Hunters Ridge CO4 . . . .110 B4
Hunters Way
  Chelmsford CM1 . . . . . .205 F7
  Saffron Walden CB11 . . . .43 D7
Hunting Gate CO1 . . . . . .136 C7
Huntingdon Way CO15 . .188 E6
Huntley's Cvn Pk (E)
  CO16 . . . . .203 C6
Huntley's Cvn Pk (W)
  CO16 . . . . .203 B6
Hunts Farm Cl CM9 . . . .199 D2
Hunts Hill CO10 . . . . .2 B4
Hunts La CO10 . . . . .3 B7
Hunwicke Rd CO4 . . . . .136 E7
Hurnard Dr CO3 . . . . . . .135 A7
Hurrell Down
  Boreham CM3 . . . . .192 F1
  Highwoods CM3 . . . . . .110 A4
Hurrells La CM3 . . . . . . .206 F3
Hurricane Pl IP3 . . . . . . .18 C1
Hurst Cl
  Bishop's Stortford CM23 .145 E7
  Brightlingsea CO7 . . . . .186 A6
Hurst Way CM2 . . . . . . .205 F2
Hutchinson Cl CO5 . . . . .179 D4
Hutland Rd IP4 . . . . .17 F7
Huxtables La CO3 . . . . . .108 A1
Hyacinth Cl
  Clacton-on-S CO16 . . . .188 C4
  Tollesbury CM9 . . . . . . .199 E1
Hyacinth Ct 4 CM1 . . . . .205 E7
Hyam's La IP9 . . . . .61 F1
Hyams La IP9 . . . . .62 D5
Hyde Chase
  Danbury CM3 . . . . .219 B4
  Woodham Mortimer CM9 .219 D4
Hyde Gn CM3 . . . . .219 B7
Hyde Hall Danbury CM3 . .219 B6
  Wethersfield CM7 . . . . . .74 B2
Hyde Rd CO10 . . . . .33 E7
Hyde The CB11 . . . . .65 C4
Hydewood Rd CO9 . . . . . .30 B3
Hyem's La IP11 . . . . .221 F7
Hylands Cl CM6 . . . . . . .151 A4
Hylands Par CM2 . . . . . .216 A6
Hylands Sch CM2 . . . . . .204 D1
Hyldon Ct IP11 . . . . .221 E3
Hyll Cl CB10 . . . . .3 D3
Hyntle Cl IP2 . . . . .16 E5
Hythe Cl Braintree CM7 . .127 E6
  Clacton-on-S CO15 . . . .203 J8
Hythe Gr CO7 . . . . .165 E1
Hythe Hill CO1 . . . . .136 C6
Hythe Quay CO2 . . . . . . .136 D5
Hythe Sta CO4 . . . . .136 D6
Hythe Station Rd CO2 . .136 D6
Hythe The CM9 . . . . .210 B2

I

Iceni Way CO2 . . . . .135 B3
Ickleton Pl 5 CB9 . . . . . . .9 B8
Ickleton Rd Elmdon CB11 .20 A4
  Great Chesterford CB10 . . .3 C2
  Hinxton CB10 . . . . .3 B6
Icknield Cl CB10 . . . . .3 A3
Ickworth Cl CM77 . . . . .154 C7
Ickworth Cres IP4 . . . . . .18 F5
Ickworth Cl IP11 . . . . . .221 A3
Ilex Cl CO2 . . . . .135 D2
Imogen Cl 4 CO4 . . . . . .136 F8
Imphal Cl CO2 . . . . .135 C1
Ingarfield Rd CO15 . . . . .189 E6
Ingelrica Ave CM3 . . . . .194 B3
Ingestre St CO12 . . . . . . .91 D4
Ingham Rd CB9 . . . . .9 B8
Inglenook CO15 . . . . . . .189 B7
Ingleside Ct CB11 . . . . . .22 D1
Inglis Rd CO3 . . . . .135 D6
Ingram Mews CM7 . . . . .155 B8
Ingram's Piece CO7 . . . .111 E8
Ingram's Well CO10 . . . . .33 F7
Ingram's Well Rd CO10 . .33 F7
Inkerman Row 3 CO10 . . .33 E8
Inkerpole Pl CM2 . . . . . .205 F4
Innes End 4 IP8 . . . . . . .16 C2
Innham Hill CO9 . . . . .75 C6
Inverness Cl CO1 . . . . . .136 A8
Inworth La CO6 . . . . .79 D2

Inworth Rd CO5 ....158 E3
Inworth Wlk **5** CO2 ...136 A1
Iona Wlk CO5 ....164 A8
Ipswich High Sch IP9 ...38 C2
Ipswich Hospl IP4 ....18 C6
Ipswich Mus★ IP1 ......17 C6
Ipswich Pre Prep Sch
  IP1 ....17 B7
Ipswich Rd Ardleigh CO7 .83 F1
  Brantham CO11 ....60 E2
  Colchester CO4 ....110 C3
  Dedham CO7 ....84 B6
  Harkstead IP9 ....63 B3
  Holbrook IP9 ....62 E6
  Holland-on-S CO15 ....189 D6
  Ipswich IP10 ....38 E2
  Stratford St M CO7 ....58 E2
Ipswich Sch IP1 ....17 C7
Ipswich Sta IP2 ....★17 B4
Ipswich Transport Mus★
  IP3 ....18 C2
Ireland Rd IP3 ....17 F1
Ireton Ho CO4 ....109 F4
Ireton Rd CO3 ....135 C5
Iris Cl Chelmsford CM1 ..205 F5
  Ipswich IP2 ....16 F5
Irlam Rd IP2 ....16 D1
Iron Latch La CO3 .....134 C8
Irvine Rd CO3 ....135 C5
Irving Cl CM23 ....145 D4
Isaac Sq CM2 ....217 B6
Isbourne Rd CO4 ......136 F7
Ishams Chase CM8 .....195 C7
Island Cl CM23 ....146 A5
Island La CO13 ....143 E1
Island Rd CO14 ....143 E4
Ivor Brown Ct CO4 ....110 B4
Ivry St IP1 ....17 B7
Ivy Cotts CM6 ....123 B4
Ivy La CO5 ....185 B3
Ivy Lodge Rd CO6 .....109 C8
Ivy Todd Hill CB11 .....68 A8
Ixworth Rd CB9 ....8 E6

J

Jacaranda Cl CM1 .....206 A6
Jack Andrews Dr CO4 ..110 C5
Jack Branch Ct CO15 ..188 E2
Jack Hatch Way CO7 ...137 A3
Jack's La CM22 ....148 D7
Jackson Ho CO4 ....110 B6
Jackson Pl CM2 ....216 D6
Jackson Rd CO15 .....188 E2
Jackson Sq **10** CM23 ..145 F7
Jackson Wlk CO2 ......136 B3
Jackson's La CB10 ......3 D3
Jackson's Sq CB10 ......3 D3
Jacobs Ct CO7 ....185 F6
Jacquard Way CM7 ....128 A2
Jacqueline Ct CO3 ....135 A7
Jaggard's Rd CO6 .....131 A5
James Boden Cl IP11 ..221 C5
James Carter Rd CO3 ..134 F3
James Cl CO7 ....137 C3
James Croft CM2 ......216 B2
James Gdns CO16 .....187 B5
James Hatfield Ho IP2 ..17 D4
James Rd CO15 ....188 C2
James St
  Brightlingsea CO7 .....185 F6
  Colchester CO1 ....136 A6
Jameson Pl **5** CO10 ...33 D8
Jameson Rd CO15 .....188 C3
Janebrook Rd IP2 ......16 E2
Janmead CM8 ....177 A3
Janus Cl CB9 ....9 D6
Japonica Ct CO15 .....189 C4
Jaques Cl CO10 ....2 C5
Jarmin Rd CO1 ....135 F2
Jarndyce CM1 ....204 F6
Jarvis Field CM3 ......207 D5
Jasmin Cl CM23 ....145 C6
Jasmine Cl
  2 Chelmsford CM1 ....205 E7
  Colchester CO4 ....136 C6
  Ipswich IP2 ....16 F3
Jasmine Way CO3 .....203 G7
Jaspers Green CM7 ....100 E2
Jay Cl Great Notley CM77 154 D8
  Haverhill CB9 ....9 C7
Jaymar Ct **9** CM7 ....127 F2
Jayrest Ctr CO3 ......134 E4
Jays La CO6 ....132 F3
Jays The CO4 ....110 C3
Jaywick La CO15,CO16 .188 A3
Jaywick Rd CB9 ....9 A8
Jeans La CM23 ....145 E7
Jeffcut Rd CM2 ....205 E2
Jefferies Rd IP4 ....17 E6
Jefferson Cl CO3 ......134 E5
Jeffery Rd CM2 ....217 A4
Jeffrey Cl CO3 ....134 F5
Jeffrey's Rd CM77 ....155 C6
Jekylls La CM7 ....48 D4
Jellicoe Way CM7 .....128 C4
Jenkins Dr CM22 ....94 C3
Jenkins La CM7 ....146 C5
Jenner Cl CM7 ....127 F1
Jenner Mead CM2 .....206 A3
Jennings Cl **1** CO1 ..136 C5
Jermyns Cl IP9 ....35 B2
Jersey Rd CM9 ....210 B3
Jersey Way CM7 ......127 D2

Jervis Cl IP9 ....62 D5
Jervis Rd CM23 ....145 F6
Jessica Cl CO4 ....136 F7
Jessop Cl CO15 ....189 B8
Jimmy's La CO11 ......60 F2
Joes Rd CO10 ....34 F6
John Ball Wlk **2** CO1 ..135 F7
John Bird Ct CO1 .....109 F1
John Bramston Sch The
  CM8 ....176 F1
John Bunyan Jun & Inf Schs
  CM7 ....127 E4
John Dane Player Ct **4**
  CB10 ....22 E1
John English Ave CM7 .127 E4
John Harper St **4** CO1 .135 E8
John Henry Keene Meml
  Homes CM1 ....205 A4
John Kavanagh Ct **1**
  CO1 ....136 A6
John Kent Ave CO2 ....135 B2
John King Ct CO7 .....185 F6
John Raven Ct CO3 ...158 D3
John Ray Gdns CM77 ..155 B5
John Ray Jun & Inf Schs
  CM7 ....154 F8
John Ray St CM7 .....128 A3
John St CO7 ....185 F6
John Tibauld Ct CB9 ...27 B6
Johns Rd CM23 ....119 A1
Johnson Cl
  Halstead CO9 ....103 F8
  Holland-on-S CO15 ...189 E5
Jollyboys La N CM6 ...152 C6
Jollyboys La S CM6 ...152 C4
Jonathan Feedham Ct
  CO7 ....137 B1
Jonquil Way CO4 .....110 B6
Joseph Gdns CM8 .....156 E4
Josse Lyns The IP11 ..221 A6
Josselin Cl CO6 ......105 B7
Jovian Way CO4 .....110 B6
Joyce's Chase CM9 ...212 A8
Jubilee Ave
  Broomfield CM1 ....191 B2
  Clacton-on-S CO16 ...188 E8
Jubilee Cl
  Colchester CO3 ....134 D6
  Harwich CO12 ....90 E2
Jubilee Ct
  Great Dunmow CM6 ...123 C1
  Sible Hedingham CO9 ..75 E8
  Walton-on-t-N CO14 ..171 C7
Jubilee End CO11 ......86 C5
Jubilee La CO7 ....111 C3
Jubilee Rd CO10 ....33 F8
Jubilee Rise CM3 ....219 A6
Jubilee Terr CM1 .....205 A4
Jubilee Way CO3 .....134 F4
Jubilee Wlk **3** CB9 ....9 A7
Judge Rd CM2 ....206 B4
Julian Ave CO4 ......110 B6
Julian Cl Broomfield CM1 191 B1
  Haverhill CB9 ....9 D7
Julien Court Rd CM7 ..128 A4
Juniper Cl CO9 ....103 D8
Juniper Cres CM8 .....177 A4
Juniper Ct CM6 ....123 B1
Juniper Dr CM2 ......216 B6
Juniper Rd Boreham CM3 206 F8
  Colchester CO3 ....134 D5
Juniper Way CO4 .....136 D8
Juno Mews CO2 ......135 C1
Jupe's Hill CO6 ....79 D1
Jupes Hill CO7 ....85 C4
Jupiter Cl CB9 ....9 D6
Jupiter Rd IP4 ....18 B7
Justinian Cl CB9 ......9 D6
Juvina Cl CM8 ....194 F7

K

Kale Croft CO3 ....134 D5
Kangels The CB11 .....40 D7
Kate Daniels Ho CO16 .140 F1
Kate's La CB10 ....24 C8
Katherine Semar Inf Sch
  CB11 ....43 E6
Katherine Semar Jun Sch
  CB11 ....43 E6
Kay Cl CM3 ....174 A7
Kayla Ct **6** CO3 .....135 E6
Keable Rd CO6 ......132 E3
Keating Cl CO11 ....86 B4
Keats Ave CM7 ......154 F8
Keats Rd CO3 ....134 F6
Kebbles CO10 ....2 B6
Keble Cl CO3 ....135 D6
Kedington Hill CO10 ...34 B2
Keeble Cl CO5 ....179 E5
Keeble Pk CM9 ......220 F8
Keeble Way CM7 .....128 A3
Keeble's Yd **7** CB9 ...9 A8
Keelars La CO7 ......137 E2
Keelers Way CO6 ....109 B7
Keene Way CM2 .....216 B3
Keep The **3** CB9 ......8 E7
Keepers Gn CO4 .....109 B3

Keith Cl CO15 ....189 B8
Kelly Rd IP2 ....16 E5
Kelso Cl CO6 ....109 C6
Kelvedon Cl CM1 .....205 A6
Kelvedon Dr IP4 ......18 F5
Kelvedon Hall La CO5 .178 E5
Kelvedon Rd
  Coggeshall CO6 ......158 A8
  Messing CO5 ....159 C2
  Tiptree CO5 ....179 B3
  Tolleshunt D'arcy CM9 .198 C6
  Wickham Bishops CM8 .195 F5
Kelvedon St Mary's CE Prim
  Sch CO5 ....158 C2
Kelvedon Sta CO5 ....158 C3
Kelvin Ct CO13 ......170 F3
Kemball St IP4 ....18 A5
Kempe Rd CM7 ....72 D6
Kempson Dr CO10 .....34 C5
Kempsters The CM23 ..221 B7
Kempton Pk CO16 ....168 B5
Kemsley Rd
  Earls Colne CO6 ......105 A6
  Felixstowe IP11 ......221 A6
Ken Cooke Ct **4** CO1 .135 F7
Kendall CE Prim Sch
  CO1 ....136 C4
Kendall Rd CO1 ......136 A6
Kendall Terr CO1 .....136 A6
Kendall's Almshouses **3**
  CO1 ....136 A6
Kenilworth Rd CO16 ..142 A2
Kenilworth Rd CO15 ..189 E6
Kennedy Cl IP4 ....18 A6
Kennedy Way CO15 ..189 A5
Kennet Way CM1 ....204 D5
Kensington Rd IP1 ....17 A8
Kenston Ct CO5 ......201 B6
Kent Cl CO7 ....185 F6
Kent Cres CM23 ......145 E4
Kent Gdns CM7 ......128 B4
Kent Ho IP11 ....221 C6
Kent's Ave CO15 .....189 E6
Kentford Rd IP11 .....221 A6
Kentings The CM7 ....127 E2
Kentmere CO4 ....110 E2
Kents Grass CM9 ....199 D2
Kents Yd CB11 ....21 F4
Kentwell Cl IP4 ....18 F4
Kenworthy Rd CM7 ...127 F2
Kenyon Cl CO7 ....58 D1
Kenyon St IP2 ....17 C4
Kerby Rise CM2 ......205 F2
Kerridge's Cut CO11 ...87 A4
Kerry Ct CO1 ....136 C2
Kersey Ave CO10 .....34 B6
Kersey Ct CO2 ....135 C3
Kersey Dr CO16 ......188 B5
Kersey Rd IP11 ......221 B3
Kessler Ave CM7 .....73 D7
Kesteven Rd IP4 ......18 A4
Kestrel Gdns CM23 ..145 C6
Kestrel Rd
  Haverhill CB9 ....9 C7
  Ipswich IP2 ....16 D3
Kestrel Rise CO9 .....76 F1
Kestrel Way CO15 ....188 F6
Kestrel Wlk CM7 .....128 A3
Keswick Cl CO13 .....170 F7
Ketley Cl CO5 ....179 E5
Ketleys CM2 ....216 C3
Ketleys View CM7 ....127 A7
Kettlebaston Way IP4 ..17 D8
Kew La CO13 ....170 A4
Key Rd CO15 ....188 E3
Key St IP4 ....17 C5
Keyes Way CM7 ......128 C4
Keymer Way CO3 ....134 F4
Keynes Way CO10 .....90 F1
Khartoum Rd IP4 ......17 F7
Khartoum Villas CO7 ..111 E8
Kidder Rd CM7 ......126 F1
Kilburn Gdns CO16 ...188 B5
Kildermorie Cl CO4 ...110 D3
Kilmaine Rd CO12 .....90 F2
Kiln Barn Ave CO15 ..188 F7
Kiln Cotts
  Danbury CM3 ....218 D6
  Dedham CM3 ....84 F5
Kiln Dr CO10 ....34 B6
Kiln Field IP11 ......221 B5
Kiln La CO11 ....86 D4
Kilns Hill CO6 ....130 F5
Kiltie Rd CO5 ....179 E5
Kimberley Cl CM23 ...146 A5
Kimberley Rd CO1 ...136 B5
Kincaid Rd CO16 .....187 A4
King Charles Rd CO5 ..201 D6
King Coel Rd CO3 ...134 D7
King Edward Ct CM1 ..205 A3
King Edward Ind Pk
  CO2 ....135 D5
King Edward Quay CO2 136 D5
King Edward Rd IP3 ...18 B3
King Edward IV's Almshouses
  CB11 ....22 D1
King Edward Quay CO2 .136 D5
King Edward VII Dr IP9 .91 C8
King Edward Way CM8 .194 E8
King George Rd CO2 ..135 F4
King George V Memorial
  Homes IP9 ....17 F3
King George's Ave CO12 91 B4
King George's Pl CM9 .210 A2
King Harold Rd CO3 ..135 A4

King St
  Bishop's Stortford CM23 .145 F7
  Bradfield CO11 ......114 C8
  Castle Hedingham CO9 ..51 F4
  Felixstowe IP11 ......221 C6
  14 Ipswich IP1 ......17 C6
  Maldon CM9 ....210 A1
  Saffron Walden CB10 ..22 D1
  Sudbury CO10 ....33 E7
King Stephen Rd CO1 .136 B6
King Street Mews **1**
  CM23 ....145 F7
King's Cl CO16 ......187 A3
King's Cotts CM23 ...146 A6
King's Ct CM6 ....123 D1
King's Ford Jun & Inf Schs
  CO2 ....135 C3
King's Head St CO12 ..91 E6
King's La Elmdon CB11 ..20 A3
  Long Melford CO10 ...15 F7
King's Quay St CO12 ..91 E6
King's Rd
  Clacton-on-S CO15 ...188 D1
  Harwich CO12 ....91 B3
King's Way IP3 ....18 C2
Kingfisher Ave IP2 ....16 E3
Kingfisher Cl
  Colchester CO4 ......136 F8
  Haverhill CB9 ....9 C8
  Heybridge CM9 ......210 C5
Kingfisher Dr CO12 ....90 E1
Kingfisher Gate CM7 ..128 A5
Kingfisher Lodge CM2 .216 F7
Kingfisher Mdws CO9 ..76 F1
Kingfisher Way
  Bishop's Stortford CM23 .146 A7
  Kelvedon CO5 ....158 C2
Kingfishers CO15 ....188 F6
Kings Acre CO6 .....130 F2
Kings Ave
  Clacton-on-S CO15 ...189 D5
  Ipswich IP4 ....17 E5
Kings Chase CM8 ....177 A1
Kings Cl CO11 ....86 C5
Kings Ct
  Bishop's Stortford CM23 .146 A8
  Harwich CO12 ....91 B3
  Holland-on-S CO15 ...189 D5
Kings Fleet Rd IP11 ..221 C3
Kings Ford Ct CO2 ...135 B3
Kings Head Ct **1** CO1 .135 E8
Kings Head Wlk **6** CM2 205 D2
Kings Hill CO10 ....34 A6
Kings Ho CO13 ......171 A4
Kings La CM7 ....129 A6
Kings Mead CO9 .....78 A7
Kings Meadow CO10 ..34 A6
Kings Meadow Ct CO5 158 C3
Kings Meadow Rd CO5 135 F8
Kings Mews CO7 .....137 C4
Kings Par CO5 ....189 E5
Kings Prom CO15 ....203 J8
Kings Quay St CO12 ..91 E6
Kings Rd Braintree CM7 127 C6
  Chelmsford CM1 ......204 F4
  Glemsford CO10 ....2 B5
  Great Totham CM9 ...196 D7
  Halstead CO9 ....76 E1
Kings Reach CO14 ....144 D1
Kings Road Prim Sch
  CM1 ....204 F4
Kings Wlk CM1 ......199 E1
Kingsbridge Cl CM7 ..127 F8
Kingsbridge Rd CM23 .146 A8
Kingsbury Cl CO6 ....132 F3
Kingsbury Rd IP11 ...221 A7
Kingsbury Wlk CO10 ..34 C5
Kingsdale Ind Est The
  CM1 ....205 C3
Kingsfield Ave IP1 ....17 D8
Kingsford Dr CM2 ....206 B4
Kingsgate Dr IP4 .....17 E7
Kingsland Beach CO5 .201 C5
Kingsland Cl CO5 ....201 C6
Kingsland Hts CO5 ...201 C6
Kingsland Rd CO5 ...201 D6
Kingsman Dr CO5 ....188 C5
Kingsmead Rd CM23 .146 A8
Kingsmere Cl CO5 ...201 D7
Kingston Ave CM2 ...205 E3
Kingston Chase CM9 .209 F5
Kingston Cres CM2 ..205 E3
Kingston Mews CO15 .188 C3
Kingston Rd IP1 ......16 F8
Kingsway Harwich CO12 .91 D4
  Tiptree CO5 ....179 C6
Kingswode Hoe Sch
  CO3 ....135 C7
Kingswood Rd CO4 ..109 F4
Kingwell Ave CO15 ..188 E5
Kinlett Cl CO4 ....110 B4
Kinloch Chase CM8 ..194 F7
Kino Rd CO14 ....171 D8
Kipling Cl CM1 ......205 A5
Kipling Way CM7 ....155 A8
Kirby Cl CO5 ....18 A7
Kirby Cross Sta CO13 .170 B6
Kirby Hall Rd CO9 ....51 D3
Kirby Prim Sch CO13 .170 B7
Kirby Rd
  Great Holland CO13 ..170 B5
  Walton-on-t-N CO14 ..171 B8
Kirby St IP4 ....18 A6
Kirk Pl CM2 ....205 F3
Kirkbaye CO13 ......170 E6
Kirkham Cl IP2 ....17 A2
Kirkhurst Cl CO7 ....186 A6
Kirklees CM1 ....204 F4

Kirkley Ct CB9 ....8 C8
Kirkmans Rd CM2 ...216 D3
Kirkton Cl IP9 ....91 A8
Kirtling Pl **12** CB9 ....9 B8
Kitchen Field CM7 ...128 D3
Kitchen Rd IP1 ....16 F8
Kitchener Rd IP1 ......16 F8
Kitchener Way IP9 ....91 A8
Kittiwake Cl IP2 ......16 E3
Kittiwake Dr CM9 ...210 C5
Knapton Cl CM1 .....205 D7
Knebworth Ct CM23 ..145 C6
Knevett Cl CO4 .....109 E3
Knight's Ct **2** CB9 ....8 E7
Knights Cl
  Bishop's Stortford CM23 .145 C8
  Lawford CO11 ....86 C4
  Tiptree CO5 ....179 F3
Knights Rd
  Braintree CM7 ....128 D1
  Coggeshall CO6 .....130 F2
Knights Way CM6 ....123 D1
Knightsbridge Cl CO2 .135 C3
Knightsbridge Ct CO15 189 B3
Knole Cl CO3 ....41 A7
Knowles Cl CO9 ......76 E1
Knox Ct CO15 ....188 E5
Knox Gdns CO15 ....188 E5
Knox Rd CO15 ....188 E5
Knutsford Cl IP8 ......16 C1
Kohima Rd CO2 .....135 B1
Kreswell Gr CO12 .....91 B2
Kynaston Pl CM8 ....177 B2
Kynaston Rd CM7 ...127 A7

L

La Salle Cl IP2 ....17 B3
Laburnum Cl
  Clacton-on-S CO15 ...188 C3
  Great Bentley CO7 ...166 F8
  2 Ipswich, Chantry IP8 ..16 C2
  Ipswich,Warren Heath IP3 .18 C2
Laburnum Cres CO13 .170 D6
Laburnum Dr CM2 ...216 B6
Laburnum Gr CO4 ...136 E8
Laburnum Way
  Hatfield Peverel CM3 .194 A3
  Witham CM8 ....177 A5
Lacewing Cl IP8 ......36 E8
Lacey St IP4 ....17 E6
Ladbrook Dr CO2 ....136 A3
Ladbrooke Rd CO16 ..188 D6
Ladell Cl CO3 ....134 E3
Lady D'Arcy Charity
  Almshouses **3** CO1 ..135 F6
Lady La Chelmsford CM2 216 C8
  6 Ipswich IP1 ....17 B6
Ladygate CB9 ....8 E6
Ladysmith Ave CO7 ..185 E6
Ladysmith Cotts CM6 .152 C4
Ladywell La CM2 ....217 B5
Ladywood Rd IP4 .....18 C7
Laing Rd CO4 ....136 E6
Lake Ave CO15 .....188 E5
Lake Way CO15 .....203 F6
Lake Wlk CO15 .....188 E5
Lakes Ind Pk CM7 ..128 B2
Lakes Mdw CO6 ....131 A2
Lakeside Cl IP2 ....16 E2
Lakeside Rd IP2 ......16 E2
Lakeside Wlk CO3 ...134 C4
Lakforth CO10 ....15 D8
Lakin Cl CO2 ....206 A3
Lamarsh Hill Bures CO8 ..55 E1
  Lamarsh CO8 ....55 B6
Lamarsh Rd CO8 ......55 A4
Lamb La CO9 ....75 D7
Lambert Cross CB10 ..22 E3
Lambert's Rd CO6 ...105 F3
Lambeth Cl IP1 ....16 F8
Lambeth Wlk CO15 ..188 E5
Lambourne Cl
  Clacton-on-S CO15 ...188 F8
  Colchester CO3 ......134 D4
Lambourne Gr CM9 ..220 F8
Lammas Dr CM7 .....128 D3
Lammas Way CO7 ....137 C2
Lancaster Gdns E CO15 189 A3
Lancaster Gdns W CO15 189 A3
Lancaster Ho IP11 ...221 C5
Lancaster Rd
  6 Ipswich IP4 ....17 E6
  Sudbury CO10 ....15 D2
Lancaster Way
  Bishop's Stortford CM23 .145 C8
  Braintree CM7 ....127 C4
  Earls Colne CO6 .....104 F2
Lanchester Ave CO15 .203 D6
Lancing Ave IP4 .....18 A8
Land Cl CO16 ....188 C5
Land La CO1 ....136 A7
Landermere Rd CO16 .142 B2
Landermere View CO16 142 A2
Landers Ct CM1 .....204 E5
Landisdale CM3 ......219 A7
Landscape View CB11 ..43 D6
Landsdown Rd CO10 ..34 A8
Landseer Cl IP3 ......18 A1
Landseer Ct
  Clacton-on-S CO15 ...188 F2
  Haverhill CB9 ....8 F6
Landseer Rd
  Colchester CO3 ......135 B5
  Ipswich IP3 ....17 F2
Lane Rd CO6 ....106 B7

Lane The Mistley CO11 ....86 F4
West Mersea CO5 .....201 A7
Lanercost Way IP2 .....17 A1
Langdale CM77 ....154 C7
Langdale Dr CO4 ......110 B4
Langdale Gdns CM2 ...216 D8
Langenhoe Com Prim Sch CO5 ....163 B2
Langenhoe Hall La CO5 183 C7
Langenhoe Pk CO5 ....163 B2
Langer Park Ind Est IP11 ....221 D3
Langer Prim Sch IP11 .221 C2
Langer Rd IP11 ....221 C2
Langford Rd
Heybridge CM9 ....209 F6
Wickham Bishops CM8, CM9 ....195 C2
Langham Dr CO16 .....188 B4
Langham La CO4 ....83 B2
Langham Prim Sch CO4 .83 F4
Langham Rd CO4 ......82 F1
Langley Ave
Felixstowe IP11 ......221 C4
Wethersfield CM7 .....73 D7
Langley Cl
Felixstowe IP11 ......221 C4
Harwich CO12 ....91 C3
Langley Hill CO8 ......55 C3
Langleys CO6 ....106 C1
Langstons IP11 ....221 B7
Langton Ave CM1 .....204 E5
Languidic Cl CO10 .....34 C6
Langwood CO5 ....201 C7
Lanham Green Rd CM77 ....156 A7
Lansdowne Cl CO5 ....179 C4
Lansdowne Rd
Felixstowe IP11 ......221 F6
Ipswich IP4 ....18 A5
Lanvalley Rd CO3 .....134 C4
Lanyards IP11 ....221 F4
Lapwing Dr
Heybridge CM9 ....210 C5
Kelvedon CO5 ....158 D2
Lapwing Rd IP2 ....16 D3
Larch Cl CO4 ....136 D8
Larch Gr Chelmsford CM2 216 C6
Witham CM8 ....177 A5
Larch Ho IP11 ....221 C4
Larch Way CM6 ....123 B1
Larch Wlk CM9 ....210 C6
Larches The CM3 .....206 E8
Larchwood CM3 ....145 D5
Larchwood Cl IP2 .....16 C5
Lark Rise CO10 ....33 D5
Lark's La Broomfield CM3 191 A6
Great Waltham CM3 ...190 F5
Larkfield Rd CO7 .....139 D1
Larkhill Rise IP4 ......18 E5
Larkhill Way IP11 .....221 C6
Larkrise Prim Sch CM2 .216 E6
Larks Cl CB9 ....9 C7
Larks Rise CO9 ....77 A1
Larksfield Cres CO12 ..91 B4
Larksfield Rd IP9 .....62 A2
Larkspur Cl
Bishop's Stortford CM23 .145 D6
Witham CM8 ....176 E4
Larkspur Ct 3 CM1 ...205 F6
Larkspur Rd IP2 ......16 F3
Larksway
Bishop's Stortford CM23 .145 C6
Felixstowe IP11 ......221 B3
Larkway CO13 ....170 E7
Larman Ct CO11 ......86 C7
Larneys The CO13 ....170 E7
Latchmore Bank CM22 .146 B2
Lathcoates Cres CM2 ..216 E8
Lattice Ave IP4 ....18 C6
Launceston Cl CO2 ....136 B1
Laundry Gdns CO10 ...33 D6
Laurel Ave CO12 .....90 F2
Laurel Cl CO15 ....189 B7
Laurel Ct CO4 ....136 E8
Laurel Dr
Great Dunmow CM6 ...123 B1
Long Melford CO10 ...15 C7
Laurel Gr 4 CM2 .....216 A8
Laurelhayes IP2 ......17 A3
Laurels The
Braintree CM7 ....128 A3
Great Notley CM77 ...154 C8
Laurence Ave CM8 ...195 A8
Laurence Cl CO7 .....137 F6
Laurence Croft CM1 ..204 B1
Lauriston Bglws CM9 ..212 C6
Lavender Cl
Bishop's Stortford CM23 .145 C4
Tiptree CO5 ....179 C4
Witham CM8 ....176 E4
Lavender Ct 1 CM1 ...205 F5
Lavender Field
Haverhill CB9 ....8 D8
6 Saffron Walden CB10 ..22 F2
Lavender Hill IP2 .....16 F4
Lavender Way CO4 ...109 C2
Lavender Wlk CO15 ...203 G7
Lavenham Cl CO16 ...188 B4
Lavenham Ct CO2 ....135 C2
Lavenham Rd IP2 .....16 E5
Lawford CE Prim Sch CO11 ....86 B2
Lawford La
Chelmsford CM1 .....204 D3
Writtle CM1 ....204 C1
Lawford Mead Inf Sch CM1 ....204 D5

Lawford Mead Jun Sch CM1 ....204 D5
Lawford Pl IP4 ....18 F5
Lawling Ave CM9 .....210 C5
Lawn Chase CM8 .....176 F1
Lawn La CM1 ....205 D6
Lawn Way IP11 ....221 C5
Lawns Cl CO5 ....201 C7
Lawns The
Chelmsford CM1 .....205 D5
Ipswich IP4 ....18 C8
Laws Cl CB11 ....43 D7
Lawshall's Hill CO6 ...78 D1
Laxton Ct CO3 ....135 A4
Laxton Gr CO13 ......170 A5
Laxton Rd CO7 ....165 B8
Layer Breton Hill CO2 .161 B1
Layer Cross CO2 .....161 F5
Layer Ct CO2 ....135 D4
Layer Marney Twr★ CO5 ....180 D8
Layer Rd Abberton CO5 162 E4
Abberton CO5 ....163 A3
Colchester CO2 ......135 C3
Great Wigborough CO5 .181 E5
Haverhill CB9 ....8 E7
Layer-de-la-Haye CE Prim Sch CO2 ....161 E1
Layzell Croft CO10 ...34 C4
Le Cateau Rd CO2 ....135 E6
Lea Cl
Bishop's Stortford CM23 .119 B1
Braintree CM7 ....128 D1
Lea Gr CM23 ....119 B1
Lea La CM8 ....177 F2
Lea Side CO5 ....201 D6
Leach Cl CM2 ....217 B7
Leam Cl CO4 ....136 F7
Leapingwell Cl CM2 ..206 A3
Leas La CO2 ....161 D6
Leas Rd
Clacton-on-S CO15 ...188 D2
Colchester CO2 ......135 C1
Leas Sch The CO15 ..188 D2
Leas The CO13 ......171 B6
Leather La
5 Braintree CM7 ....127 F3
Great Yeldham CO9 ..30 A1
Haverhill CB9 ....8 E7
Lee Ct CM2 ....216 E7
Lee Rd Harwich CO12 .91 C3
Ipswich IP3 ....17 F3
Lee Wick La CO16 ...186 D2
Leech's La CO4 ......109 D4
Leeford CM1 ....204 F6
Leeward Ct IP11 .....221 E5
Leeway The CM3 ....218 F7
Leez La CM8 ....152 E2
Leez Priory★ CM3 ...153 A2
Legerton Cotts CO6 ..79 C1
Legg St CM1 ....205 B3
Legions Way CM23 ..146 A8
Leicester Cl
Colchester CO1 .....136 A8
Ipswich IP2 ....16 F1
Jaywick CO15 ....187 F1
Leicester Ct CM8 ....156 D3
Leigh Dr Elsenham CM22 .94 C1
Wickham Bishops CM8 .195 D5
Leighs Rd CM3 ......191 E6
Leighton Rd IP3 .....38 A8
Leighton Sq IP3 .....38 A8
Leiston Rd CB9 ......8 E7
Lely Rd IP3 ....37 F8
Lemons Hill IP9 .....61 D8
Leonard Mews CM7 ..155 B8
Leopold Gdns IP4 ....18 B8
Leopold Rd
Felixstowe IP11 .....221 E4
Ipswich IP4 ....18 A8
Les Bois CO2 ....162 A5
Leslie Newnham Ct 1 CM9 ....210 A1
Leslie Rd IP3 ....18 D1
Lethe Gr Blackheath CO2 .163 A8
Colchester CO2 ......162 F8
Letton Cl IP9 ....35 A1
Levels Gn CM23 .....118 C5
Levens Way CM77 ...154 C6
Levington Rd
Felixstowe IP11 .....221 C1
Ipswich IP3 ....18 A3
Lewes Cl IP3 ....18 E3
Lewin Cl CM3 ....206 E8
Lewis Dr CM2 ....216 B6
Lewis La IP9 ....61 E2
Lexden Ct CO3 ......135 C7
Lexden Gr CO3 ......134 F7
Lexden Mews CO3 ...134 F7
Lexden Park Ho CO3 .135 A7
Lexden Pl CO3 ......134 E7
Lexden Prim Sch CO3 .134 E6
Lexden Rd
Colchester CO3 ......135 B7
West Bergholt CO6 ..108 D4
Lexden Springs Sch CO3 ....134 E7
Ley Field Marks Tey CO6 .132 E3
Takeley CM22 ....148 C7
Ley The CM7 ....128 D1
Leybourne Dr CM1 ...205 E7
Leyfields CM77 ......126 F1
Leys Dr CO16 ....168 C1
Leys Rd CO7 ....139 C3
Leys The Chelmsford CM2 205 F5
Wimbish CB10 ......45 C3
Leyside CM77 ....126 F2
Leyton Ct CO15 .....188 F8

Leywood Cl CM7 .....128 D2
Lichfield Cl
Chelmsford CM1 .....204 E4
Colchester CO1 ......136 A8
Lidgate Ct IP11 ......221 A4
Lidius Dr CO4 ....110 A5
Lie Field Cl CM7 .....128 D3
Lifchild Cl CM8 ......195 A7
Lilac Ave CO16 ......203 B6
Lilac Cl CM2 ....216 C6
Lilac Ct CO7 ....137 A2
Lilac Tree Ct CM4 ...136 E8
Lilian Impey Dr CO4 ..110 B5
Lilley's La CO7 ......112 D4
Lillies The CM7 ......102 B1
Lilly Cnr CB9 ....27 B6
Lily Cl CM1 ....205 F6
Limbourne Dr CM9 ..210 D5
Lime Ave Colchester CO4 136 D8
Harwich CO12 ....91 B3
Lime Cl
Clacton-on-S CO15 ...188 C3
Witham CM8 ....177 A5
Lime Gr Haverhill CB9 ..9 C5
Sudbury CO10 ......33 C5
Lime St CO7 ....185 F5
Lime Tree Hill CM6 ..123 D2
Lime Wlk CM2 ......216 C6
Limebrook Way CM9 .220 E7
Limefields CB10 .....22 D4
Limekiln La CM24 ...119 C5
Limes Cres 4 CM1 ..204 A1
Limes The Ardleigh CO7 .111 F7
Clacton-on-S CO15 ..189 A3
Galleywood CM2 ....216 B2
Gosfield CO9 ....102 C2
Long Melford CO10 ..15 C7
Tattingstone IP9 ....61 B6
Limetree Dr IP3 .....18 D2
Lincoln Ave CO15 ...203 D6
Lincoln Cl CM23 ....145 D5
Lincoln La CO6 .....82 C1
Lincoln Terr IP11 ...221 D3
Lincoln Way CO1 ...136 A8
Lindbergh Rd IP3 ...18 C2
Linden Cl
Chelmsford CM2 ....216 C7
Colchester CO4 .....110 E1
Lawford CO11 ......86 B3
Linden Dr CO15 .....188 E7
Lindens The
Bishop's Stortford CM23 .145 F6
Braintree CM7 ......128 A1
Colchester CO3 .....135 B7
Halstead CO9 ......103 F8
Lindisfarne Cl IP2 ...17 A1
Lindisfarne Cl CM9 ..220 E8
Lindsell La CM6 .....98 B2
Lindsey Ave CO10 ...34 B6
Lindsey Cl CM23 ....118 F1
Lindsey Rd
Bishop's Stortford CM23 .118 F1
Ipswich IP4 ....18 C7
Line Cotts CO4 .....83 A4
Linfold Cl CM7 ......128 D4
Linford Mews CM9 ..220 E8
Ling's La IP9 ....63 D5
Lingwood Cl CM3 ...218 E2
Link Cl CO4 ....109 E4
Link La IP9 ....60 D6
Link Rd
Bishop's Stortford CM23 .145 F8
Brightlingsea CO7 ..186 A6
Capel St M IP9 .....35 A1
Clacton-on-S CO15 ..188 D2
Halstead CO9 ......103 D8
Link The IP9 ....60 D6
Link Way CM23 .....145 E6
Links Ave IP11 ......221 B7
Links Bsns Ctr The CM23 ....146 C7
Links Cl CO10 ......2 C5
Links Dr CM2 ....215 F7
Links Rd Cressing CM77 .156 C7
Seawick CO16 ......203 B6
Linksfield IP5 ....18 E7
Linksfield Gdns IP5 ..18 F7
Linkside CO13 ......170 E3
Linkside Rd CM23 ..146 C6
Linley Gdns CO15 ..188 D2
Linnet Dr CM2 ......216 B6
Linnet Rd IP2 ....16 D4
Linnet Way CO7 ....166 D8
Linnets CO15 ....188 F6
Linnetts La CB9 ....10 A4
Linstead Cl CO16 ...188 A4
Linton Cl CB11 .....43 F8
Linton Pl 13 CB9 ...9 B8
Linton Rd CB1 ......5 B7
Lintons The CM2 ...217 D6
Lion Mdw CB9 ......27 B7
Lion Rd CO10 ......2 B5
Lion St IP1 ....17 C6
Lion Wlk 20 CO1 ...135 F7
Lionel Hurst Cl CO10 .34 C5
Lionfield Terr CM1 ..205 D3
Lisle Ho
Colchester,Lexden CO3 .135 A7
Colchester,Mile End CO4 .109 E4
Lisle Rd CO2 ....136 A5
List Ho CO10 ....15 C8
Lister Rd CM7 ......154 F8
Lister Tye CM2 .....216 C7
Liston La CO10 .....15 B6
Listonhall Chase CO9 .75 B5
Litchborough Pk CM3 .218 F7
Litchfield CO12 .....90 E2
Litchfield Cl CO15 ..188 E5

Littell Tweed CM2 ...206 A3
Little & Great Sir Hughes La CM2 ....217 B2
Little Baddow Rd
Danbury CM3 ....218 E7
Woodham Walter CM9 208 C3
Little Bakers CO14 ..171 A7
Little Bentley Rd CO16 .114 B1
Little Bradfords CM7 .128 A4
Little Braxted La CM8 .177 C3
Little Bromley Rd
Ardleigh CO7 ....112 B7
Great Bromley CO7 ..112 F3
Little Bentley CO7 ..112 B7
Little Chishill Rd SG8 ..39 C8
Little Clacton Rd
Clacton-on-S CO15 ..188 B7
Great Holland CO13 ..169 E2
Little Croft St IP2 ...17 C3
Little Dorrit CM1 ....204 E7
Little Fields CM3 ....219 D4
Little Gipping St 7 IP1 .17 B6
Little Gr 4 IP9 .....35 A1
Little Gulls 6 IP9 ...35 A1
Little Harrods CO14 .171 A7
Little Hills CM8 .....209 D8
Little Hyde Cl CO9 ..30 A2
Little Hyde Rd CO9 ..30 A2
Little Larchmount CB11 .43 D8
Little London Hill CM7 .72 D8
Little London La CM9 .208 D4
Little Mdw CM1 ....204 A1
Little Nell CM1 .....204 E7
Little Orch IP9 .....62 D5
Little Paddocks CM77 .126 F1
Little Sq 6 CM7 ....127 F3
Little St Mary's CO10 ..15 C7
Little Stile CM1 ....215 A8
Little Stone Ct CO15 .203 J8
Little Tey Rd CO5 ...158 F7
Little Totham Rd CM9 .211 D8
Little Tufts IP9 .....35 B1
Little Walden Rd CB10 .22 E5
Little Waltham CE Prim Sch CM3 ....191 B8
Little Waltham Rd CM1 .191 D1
Little Whip St 2 IP2 .17 C4
Little Wood CO13 ...170 E6
Little Yeldham Rd CO9 .30 C3
Little's Cres IP2 ....17 C4
Littlebury Gdns CO2 .136 C4
Littlebury Green Rd CB11 ....21 D3
Littlecotes CO4 ....109 D4
Littlefield Rd CO2 ...135 C2
Littlegarth Sch CO6 .82 B7
Livery Mews CM6 ...124 E5
Llewellyn Cl CM1 ...205 D3
Lloyd Rd IP3 ....91 A8
Lloyds Ave 7 IP1 ...17 C6
Loamy Hill Rd
Little Totham CM9 ..197 A3
Tiptree CO5 ....178 F1
Loates Pasture CM24 .119 D8
Lobelia Cl CM1 .....206 A6
Locarno Rd IP3 ....18 B3
Lock Hill CM9 ......210 E2
Lock Rd CO9 ....103 E8
Lockhart Ave CO4 ..135 C7
Lockram La Witham CM8 176 F2
7 Witham CM8 ....177 A2
Lockside Marina CM2 .205 D1
Lodge Ave CM2 ....216 F7
Lodge Cl
Clacton-on-S CO15 ..188 C4
Little Oakley CO12 ..117 C8
Lodge Cres CM3 ...206 E7
Lodge Ct CO6 ......108 F4
Lodge Farm La CO16 .187 D4
Lodge Farm Rd CO10 ..2 C3
Lodge La Abberton CO5 .163 D1
Ardleigh CO7 ....111 B6
Ardleigh CO7 ....111 C6
Brightlingsea CO7 ..185 E7
Langham CO4 ......110 D8
Peldon CO5 ....182 E7
Purleigh CM3 ......220 C2
Tendring CO16 .....140 F6
Lodge Rd Braintree CM7 .127 F1
Brightlingsea CO7 ..185 E8
Little Clacton CO16 .169 A5
Little Oakley CO12 ..117 C8
Maldon CM9 ....209 F3
Messing CO5 ....159 D3
Thorpe-le-S CO16 ..168 F5
Woodham Mortimer CM3, CM9 ....220 B5
Wrttle CM1 ....215 A8
Lodge The CO15 ...189 F6
Loftin Way CM2 ....216 D7
Lombard Ct IP4 ....17 F7
Lombardy Pl CM1 ..205 B3
Lombardy Rd CO10 ..15 D2
Lonbarn Hill CO11 ..88 A2
London Hill
Chelmsford CM2 ...215 F2
Galleywood CM2 ...216 A2
London Land Cotts CO6 .80 E4
London Rd
Bishop's Stortford CM23 .146 A5
Braintree CM7 .....127 E1
Capel St M IP9 ....35 B1
Chelmsford CM2 ...215 E6
Clacton-on-S CO15 ..188 E7
Colchester CO3 ....134 D6

London Rd continued
Copford CO3,CO6 ....133 D4
Feering CO5 ....159 B7
Great Chesterford CB10 ..3 D2
Great Horkesley CO6 ..81 F2
Great Notley CM77 ..154 D6
Ipswich IP1 ....17 A6
Ipswich,Chantry IP2 ..16 C3
Ipswich,Chantry IP2 ..16 F5
Kelvedon CO5 ......158 B1
Littlebury CB11 .....21 F2
Maldon CM9 ....209 D3
Marks Tey CO6 .....133 A3
Newport CB11 .....67 A6
Saffron Walden CB11 ..43 D8
Washbrook IP8 .....35 E6
Wendens Ambo CB11 ..42 F4
Wendens Ambo,Littlebury CB11 ....42 F7
London Stansted Airport CM24 ....121 A4
Lone Barn Ct IP1 ...16 B8
Long Acres CO5 ....158 F6
Long Border Rd
Great Hallingbury CM22, CM24 ....147 C8
Takeley CM24 ......120 E1
Long Brandocks CM1 .204 A1
Long Comm CM9 ...209 F5
Long Croft CM24 ...119 D8
Long Field IP11 .....221 B6
Long Gdns CO9 ....53 F5
Long Gn CM77 .....155 E8
Long Green La CM7 ..99 C2
Long Horse Croft CB11 .43 E7
Long La Arkesden CB11 ..41 E5
Great Holland CO13 .170 C3
Rayne CM7 ....153 F8
Long Ley CB11 .....40 D2
Long Mdw
Bishop's Stortford CM23 .145 D6
Great Notley CM77 ..154 B5
Long Mdws CO12 ..90 F2
Long Melford CE Prim Sch CO10 ....15 C7
Long Pastures CO10 ..2 C3
Long Perry IP9 .....35 B1
Long Rd CO11 .....86 C3
Long Rd E CO7 ....85 B3
Long Rd W CO7 ...84 E3
Long St IP3 ....17 E5
Long Wyre St CO1 ..135 F7
Longacre
Chelmsford CM1 ...215 E8
Colchester CO4 ....109 E2
Longacre Rd CM77 .155 E6
Longacres CM7 ....128 A1
Longcroft
Felixstowe IP11 ....221 C6
Hempstead CB10 ...46 E8
Takeley CM22 .....148 C7
Longcroft Rd CO4 ..136 C8
Longedryve CO2 ...135 C4
Longfellow Rd CM9 .210 A1
Longfield CM8 .....176 E5
Longfield Rd
Capel St M IP9 ....35 B2
Great Baddow CM2 ..216 E8
Longfields CO16 ...187 B4
Longhedges CB11 ..22 E1
Longleaf Dr CM7 ...155 A8
Longleat Cl CM1 ...204 F7
Longmead Ave CM2 .216 F8
Longmeads CM8 ...195 E5
Longmeads Cl CM1 .204 A1
Longmore Ave CM2 .216 E8
Longridge CO4 ....136 F8
Longs La CM3 .....173 F1
Longship Way CM9 .220 E8
Longshots Cl CM1 ..191 A1
Longstomps Ave CM2 .216 A7
Longstraw Cl CO3 ..134 D6
Lonsdale 4 IP2 ....17 C4
Lonsdale Cl IP4 ....17 F7
Lonsdale Rd CO16 ..142 A2
Looe Rd IP11 ......221 F5
Loompits Way CB11 .43 D7
Loppys Hill 1 CM24 .119 E6
Loraine Way IP8 ...16 A8
Lord Holland Rd CO2 .135 F3
Lord Mews IP3 .....18 A2
Lord's Croft La CB9 ..9 A8
Lords Ave CM23 ...145 B7
Lords Cl CB10 .....23 D1
Lordship Rd CM1 ..204 B3
Lordsland La CM77 .103 C1
Lordswood Rd CO2 .135 C2
Lorkin Way CO6 ...108 F4
Lorkin's La CO10 ..54 C4
Lott's Rd CO16 ....168 B4
Lotus Way CO15 ..203 E7
Louise Cl CO14 ...144 E3
Louse La CO7 .....84 E4
Louvain Dr CM1 ...205 F7
Louvain Rd CO12 ..91 A1
Love La CO7 ......185 F8
Love Way CO16 ...188 C6
Loveday Cl SG8 ...19 D3
Lover's La CO7 ....167 A7
Lovers La IP9 .....63 C4
Loves Wlk CM1 ...204 B1
Lovibond Pl 4 CM2 .205 F4
Low Lighthouse Maritime Mus★ CO12 ....91 E5
Low Rd CO12 .....90 E1

Low St CO10 . . . . .2 C6
Lowe Chase CO14 . . . . . .171 B8
Lowefields CO6 . . . . .105 D5
Lower Anchor St CO2 . . .205 A1
Lower Brook Mews IP1 . .17 C5
Lower Brook St IP4 . . . . . .17 C5
Lower Cotts SG9 . . . . .64 A2
Lower Dales IP1 . . . . .16 F8
Lower Dales View Rd **3**
 IP1 . . . . .17 A8
Lower Downs Slade CB9 . .9 A8
Lower Farm Rd CO4,CO6 . .57 B1
Lower Gn
 Galleywood CM2 . . . . . . .216 C2
 Stoke by Clare CO10 . . . . .11 C4
 Wakes Colne CO6 . . . . . . .79 C1
Lower Harlings IP9 . . . . . .91 A8
Lower Holt St CO6 . . . . . .105 D6
Lower Houses Rd IP9 . . . .63 D2
Lower King CM7 . . . . . . .128 D1
Lower Langley CO6 . . . . .106 C1
Lower Marine Par CO12 . .91 C3
Lower Mill Field CM6 . . .150 E7
Lower Orwell St IP4 . . . . .17 D5
Lower Park Cres CM23 . .145 F5
Lower Park Rd CO7 . . . . .185 E6
Lower Rd Birch CO2 . . . .181 A8
 Borley CO10 . . . . .15 B3
 Glemsford CO10 . . . . .2 B2
 Peldon CO5 . . . . .182 D3
 Wormingford CO8,CO6 . . . .80 B5
Lower Sq CB10 . . . . .22 D2
Lower St Cavendish CO10 . .1 D1
 Sproughton IP8 . . . . .16 A7
 Stanstead CO10 . . . . .2 E6
 Stansted Mountfitchet
 CM24 . . . . .119 F7
 Stutton IP9 . . . . .62 B2
Lowry Gdns IP3 . . . . .38 A4
Luard Way Birch CO2 . . .161 A3
 Witham CM8 . . . . .176 F1
Lubberhedges La CM6 .125 B8
Lucas Ave
 Chelmsford CM2 . . . . . . .216 C6
 Fordham CO6 . . . . .107 D5
Lucas Hall CO4 . . . . .109 F4
Lucas Ho CO3 . . . . .135 A7
Lucas Rd
 18 Colchester CO2 . . . . .135 F6
 Sudbury CO10 . . . . .33 F7
Lucas's La CO16 . . . . . . .141 D6
Lucerne Rd CO7 . . . . . . .138 A6
Lucerne Way CM1 . . . . . .215 B8
Luces La CO9 . . . . .51 F4
Lucius Cres CO4 . . . . . . .110 B6
Luck's La CM3 . . . . .172 F4
Lucksfield Way CM2 . . . .216 F5
Lucy Cl CO3 . . . . .134 C6
Lucy La N CO3 . . . . .134 B7
Lucy La S CO3 . . . . .134 C7
Ludgores La CM3 . . . . . .218 D5
Ludham Hall La CM77 . .154 D7
Luff Way CO14 . . . . .170 F7
Lufkin Rd CO4 . . . . .109 F3
Lugar Cl CO4 . . . . .136 E6
Lukin's Dr CM6 . . . . .150 D7
Lulworth Ave IP3 . . . . . . .18 D3
Lulworth Cl CO15 . . . . . .203 I8
Lulworth Ct CB9 . . . . .8 E8
Lumber Leys CO14 . . . . .171 A4
Lundy Cl CB9 . . . . .9 D7
Lunnish Hill CO12 . . . . . .89 F2
Lupin Dr CM1 . . . . .205 F6
Lupin Mews **1** CM1 . . .205 F6
Lupin Rd IP2 . . . . .16 E5
Lupin Way CO16 . . . . . . .188 C4
Lushington Ave CO13 . . .170 E6
Lushington Rd CO11 . . . .86 C4
Luther Dr CO5 . . . . .179 C5
Luther Rd IP2 . . . . .17 C4
Lutus Cl CO10 . . . . .12 A6
Lydgate Cl CO11 . . . . . . .86 B4
Lydia Dr CO16 . . . . .186 A2
Lymington Ave CO15 . . .189 A8
Lyndhurst Ave IP4 . . . . . .18 D5
Lyndhurst Dr CM3 . . . . . .218 F1
Lyndhurst Rd CO15 . . . . .189 C4
Lynmouth Ave CM2 . . . .205 C1
Lynmouth Gdns CM2 . . .205 C1
Lynne Cl CO13 . . . . .170 E6
Lynton Cl CO12 . . . . .91 B4
Lynton Ct CM23 . . . . . . .145 E4
Lynton Dr CM1 . . . . .205 E5
Lynwood Ave IP11 . . . . .221 F5
Lyon Cl
 Clacton-on-S CO15 . . . . .189 A4
 Galleywood CM2 . . . . . . .216 B3
Lyons Hall Prim Sch
 CM7 . . . . .128 D4
Lyons Hall Rd CM7 . . . . .128 D8
Lysander Rd IP3 . . . . .38 C8
Lyster Ave CM2 . . . . .217 A7

M

Mabbitt Way CO4 . . . . . .110 B5
Maberly Ct CB10 . . . . . . .22 D2
Macbeth Cl CO4 . . . . . . .136 F7
MacDonough Cotts CO12 .91 E5
Mace Wlk CM1 . . . . .204 F3
Mackay Ct CO2 . . . . .136 B1
Maclarens CM8 . . . . .196 A6
Macmillan Ct **4** CM2 . .205 B1
Madeira Rd CO15 . . . . . .189 D4

Madeline Pl CM1 . . . . . . .204 E6
Madgements Rd CM7 . . .129 C8
Magazine Farm Way
 CO3 . . . . .135 A6
Magdalen Cl CO15 . . . . .188 E4
Magdalen Ct CO15 . . . . .188 E4
Magdalen Gn
 Colchester CO1 . . . . .136 B6
 Thaxted CM6 . . . . .70 B2
Magdalen Rd CO15 . . . . .188 E4
Magdalen St CO1 . . . . . .136 A6
Magdalene Cl IP2 . . . . . . .16 F2
Magdalene Cres CM8 . . .156 D3
Maginley Cres IP5 . . . . . .18 F6
Magnaville Rd CM23 . . .145 E4
Magnolia Cl
 Chelmsford CM2 . . . . . . .216 B6
 Witham CM8 . . . . .177 A5
Magnolia Dr CO4 . . . . . .136 F8
Magnus Dr CO4 . . . . .110 B6
Magpie Cl Harwich CO12 . .90 C1
 Ipswich IP8 . . . . .16 C2
Magwitch Cl CM1 . . . . . .204 F7
Maidenburgh St CO1 . . .135 F7
Maidenhall App IP2 . . . . .17 B3
Maidenhall Gn IP2 . . . . . .17 B2
Maidment Cres CM8 . . . .194 F8
Maidstone Inf Sch IP11 .221 C5
Maidstone Rd IP11 . . . . .221 C5
Mailers La CM23 . . . . . . .92 F2
Main Rd Boreham CM3 . .192 F1
 Braintree CM3 . . . . .153 D4
 Broomfield CM1 . . . . .191 B2
 Chelmondiston IP9 . . . . . .63 D7
 Chelmsford CM2 . . . . . . .217 F2
 Danbury CM3 . . . . .218 A7
 Danbury CM3 . . . . .218 D7
 Frating CO7 . . . . .138 E3
 Great Holland CO13 . . . . .170 A3
 Great Leighs CM3 . . . . . .173 F7
 Harwich, Bath Side CO12 . .91 E5
 Harwich, Dovercourt CO12 . .91 B3
 Ramsey CO12 . . . . .90 A1
 Rushmere St A IP5 . . . . . . .18 F8
 Woolverstone IP9 . . . . . . .38 B2
 Wormingford CO6 . . . . . . .80 F4
Main St CB1 . . . . .6 F4
Mais Ct IP2 . . . . .16 F2
Maitland Ct CO13 . . . . . .170 F4
Maitland Rd CM24 . . . . .119 E6
Majendie La CO9 . . . . . . .51 F4
Makemores CM77 . . . . . .126 F2
Makins Rd CO12 . . . . .90 F5
Maldon Court Sch CM9 .209 F3
Maldon Ct
 8 Colchester CO3 . . . . .135 E6
 Great Cornard CO10 . . . . .34 B7
Maldon District Mus★
 CM9 . . . . .210 B2
Maldon Prim Sch CM9 . .210 A2
Maldon Rd Birch CO2 . . .160 E4
 Bradwell Waterside CM0 . .214 F1
 Colchester, Abbey Field
 CO3 . . . . .135 D5
 Colchester,Stanway Green
 CO3 . . . . .134 D1
 Danbury, Gay Bowers CM3 .219 B5
 Danbury, Runsell Green
 CM3 . . . . .219 B7
 Goldhanger CM9 . . . . . . .211 E2
 Great Baddow CM2 . . . . .217 C7
 Great Totham CM9 . . . . . .196 B4
 Great Wigborough CO5 . .181 E2
 Hatfield Peverel CM3,CM9 .194 D3
 Kelvedon CO5 . . . . .158 C1
 Langford CM9 . . . . .209 D6
 Tiptree CO5 . . . . .179 B3
 Witham CM8 . . . . .195 A6
 Woodham Mortimer CM9 .219 E6
Maldon Way CO16 . . . . .188 B4
Malin Cl CB9 . . . . .9 D7
Mallard Cl
 Great Notley CM77 . . . . .154 C5
 Kelvedon CO5 . . . . .158 C3
 Layer-de-l-H CO2 . . . . . . .162 A5
 Tollesbury CM9 . . . . .199 D2
Mallard Rd CM2 . . . . . . .216 A5
Mallard Way
 Great Cornard CO10 . . . . .34 C5
 Ipswich IP2 . . . . .16 E3
Mallow Wlk CB9 . . . . .8 D8
Mallowhayes Cl IP2 . . . . .17 B3
Mallows Field CO9 . . . . . .76 F2
Mallows Green Rd CM23 .92 D1
Mallows La CO9 . . . . .49 F3
Malmesbury Cl IP2 . . . . .17 A1
Maltese Rd CM1 . . . . . . .205 A4
Malthouse Rd CO11 . . . . .86 D4
Malthouse The CO10 . . . .15 B5
Malting Cotts CB9 . . . . . . .9 F4
Malting Farm La CO7 . . . .84 D2
Malting Green Rd CO2 . .162 A5
Malting La Clare CO10 . .12 B7
 Kirby-le-S CO13 . . . . .143 C1
Malting Rd
 Colchester CO2 . . . . .135 C1
 Peldon CO5 . . . . .182 E6
Malting Terr IP2 . . . . .17 D4
Malting Yd CO7 . . . . .164 B8
Maltings Cl CO8 . . . . .55 E1
Maltings Cl CM8 . . . . . . .194 F8
Maltings La CM8 . . . . . . .194 F8
Maltings Rd
 Brightlingsea CO7 . . . . . .165 E1
 Great Baddow CM2 . . . . .217 A5
Maltings The
 Cavendish CO10 . . . . .1 D2

Maltings The continued
 Great Dunmow CM6 . . . . .123 D1
 Great Easton CM6 . . . . . . .96 A2
 Ramsey CO12 . . . . .116 E8
 Rayne CM77 . . . . .127 A2
 Saffron Walden CB10 . . . . .22 D1
 Thaxted CM6 . . . . .70 A2
Maltings View CM7 . . . . .128 A3
Maltings Wharf CO11 . . . .86 D4
Maltings Park Rd CO6 . .108 F4
Malvern Cl
 Chelmsford CM1 . . . . . . .204 D6
 Ipswich IP3 . . . . .18 A4
 Rushmere St A IP5 . . . . . . .18 F7
Malvern Way CO6 . . . . . .109 B7
Malyon Rd CM8 . . . . .194 F8
Man's Cross CO9 . . . . . . .29 E2
Manchester Rd
 Holland-on-S CO15 . . . . .189 E6
 Ipswich IP2 . . . . .16 D2
Mandeville Rd
 Marks Tey CO6 . . . . .132 E3
 Saffron Walden CB11 . . . . .43 D8
Mandeville Way
 Broomfield CM1 . . . . .191 B3
 Kirby Cross CO13 . . . . . . .170 F6
Mandy Cl IP4 . . . . .18 A6
Manfield Gdns CO16 . . . .187 B5
Manning Rd IP11 . . . . . . .221 D3
Mannings Cl CB11 . . . . . .43 E7
Mannings La IP9 . . . . .38 A2
Mannington Cl IP4 . . . . . .18 F5
Manningtree Ct CO7 . . . .136 F4
Manningtree High Sch
 CO11 . . . . .86 B3
Manningtree Mus★
 CO11 . . . . .86 D4
Manningtree Rd
 Brantham CO11 . . . . .86 A8
 Dedham CO7 . . . . .85 B6
 East Bergholt CO7 . . . . . . .59 F1
 Little Bentley CO7 . . . . . .139 F8
 Stutton IP9 . . . . .61 F2
Manningtree Sta CO11 . . .86 A5
Manor Cl Cavendish CO10 . .1 C2
 Great Horkesley CO6 . . . .109 C7
Manor Cres CM3 . . . . . . .191 B5
Manor Dr CM2 . . . . .216 F7
Manor Farm Cl CB9 . . . . . .9 B7
Manor Fields Prim Sch
 CM23 . . . . .145 D5
Manor Ho CM3 . . . . .219 A5
Manor House Way CO7 .185 E8
Manor La
 Great Chesterford CB10 . . .3 D2
 Harwich CO12 . . . . .91 B2
 Stutton IP9 . . . . .61 E2
Manor Links CM23 . . . . .146 C7
Manor Pl CM7 . . . . .128 A3
Manor Rd
 Bishop's Stortford CM23 . .146 A2
 Chelmsford CM2 . . . . . . .205 C1
 Colchester CO3 . . . . .135 E7
 Felixstowe IP11 . . . . .221 C1
 Great Holland CO13 . . . . .170 A3
 Harwich CO12 . . . . .91 B3
 Hatfield Peverel CM3 . . . .194 C1
 Haverhill CB9 . . . . .9 B7
 Ipswich IP4 . . . . .17 D8
 Little Easton CM6 . . . . . .122 F5
 Maldon CM9 . . . . .209 A4
 Stansted Mountfitchet
 CM24 . . . . .119 E5
 Sudbury CO10 . . . . .15 L1
 West Bergholt CO6 . . . . . .108 E5
 Witham CM8 . . . . .177 A4
 Wivenhoe CO7 . . . . .137 C1
 Woodham Walter CM9 . . .208 E5
Manor St CM7 . . . . .128 A3
Manor Way CO15 . . . . . .189 G6
Manors CM8 . . . . .156 D4
Manors Way CM8 . . . . . .156 C4
Mansard Ct CO15 . . . . . .189 C5
Mansbrook Bvd IP3 . . . . .38 D7
Manse Chase CM9 . . . . .210 A1
Mansfield Twrs CO15 . . .188 F2
Manston Dr CM23 . . . . . .119 B1
Manuden Prim Sch
 CM23 . . . . .93 A2
Manwick Rd IP11 . . . . . .221 D2
Maple Ave
 Bishop's Stortford CM23 . .145 D8
 Braintree CM7 . . . . .127 D8
 Heybridge CM9 . . . . .210 C6
Maple Cl
 Bishop's Stortford CM23 . .145 D8
 Clacton-on-S CO15 . . . . .188 C3
 Halstead CO9 . . . . .77 A2
 Harwich CO12 . . . . .91 B3
 Ipswich IP2 . . . . .17 A3
Maple Dr
 Chelmsford CM2 . . . . . . .216 B6
 Kirby Cross CO13 . . . . . . .170 D6
 Witham CM8 . . . . .177 A5
Maple Gr CM23 . . . . .145 D8
Maple Ho IP11 . . . . .221 C4
Maple La CB10 . . . . .45 C5
Maple Leaf CO5 . . . . .179 C7
Maple Rd CO10 . . . . .34 B5
Maple Spring CM23 . . . .145 D8
Maple Way CO2 . . . . .136 A4
Maples The IP4 . . . . .18 E8
Maplin Ct CO15 . . . . .189 D4
Marasca End CO2 . . . . . .163 A7
Maraschino Cres CO2 . . .163 A7
Marbled White Dr IP8 . . .36 E8
Marconi Rd CM1 . . . . . . .205 B3

Marcus Cl
 Colchester CO4 . . . . .110 B6
 Haverhill CB9 . . . . .9 D7
Marennes Cres CO7 . . . .185 E7
Mareth Rd CO2 . . . . .135 C2
Margaret Cl CO7 . . . . . . .186 A6
Margaret Rd CO1 . . . . . .135 F8
Margaret St
 Felixstowe IP11 . . . . .221 C5
 Thaxted CM6 . . . . .70 A3
Margaret Way CB10 . . . . .22 D1
Margaretting Rd
 Chelmsford CM2 . . . . . . .215 F1
 Galleywood CM2 . . . . . . .216 A2
 Writtle CM1 . . . . .215 A6
Margate Rd IP3 . . . . .18 C3
Margery Allingham Pl
 CM9 . . . . .198 D4
Margrave Gdns **4**
 CM23 . . . . .145 E5
Marguerite Way CM23 . .145 C6
Maria Ct CO2 . . . . .136 C5
Maria St CO12 . . . . .91 D5
Marigold Ave
 Clacton-on-S CO16 . . . . .188 C4
 Ipswich IP2 . . . . .16 E3
Marigold Cl
 Chelmsford CM1 . . . . . . .205 F6
 Colchester CO4 . . . . .136 E8
Marina Gdns
 Clacton-on-S CO15 . . . . .189 C5
 Felixstowe IP11 . . . . .221 C2
Marina Mews **1** CO14 .171 C8
Marina Point CO15 . . . . .188 D1
Marina Rd CM3 . . . . .194 A4
Marine Ct
 Clacton-on-S CO15 . . . . .188 E1
 Frinton-on-S CO13 . . . . . .170 F4
Marine Par CO12 . . . . . . .91 D3
Marine Par E CO15 . . . . .189 B3
Marine Par W CO15 . . . .188 E1
Maritime Ave CO15 . . . . .188 E6
Maritime Ave CM9 . . . . .210 E3
Maritime Ct **12** IP4 . . . .17 D5
Market Cl CO15 . . . . .135 E8
Market End CO6 . . . . .130 F2
Market Field Sch CO7 . . .138 A5
Market Gr CO9 . . . . .30 A1
Market Hill Clare CO10 . .12 B7
 Coggeshall CO6 . . . . .131 A2
 Halstead CO9 . . . . .76 E2
 Haverhill CB9 . . . . .9 A8
 Maldon CM9 . . . . .210 A3
 Saffron Walden CB10 . . . . .22 D2
 Sudbury CO10 . . . . .33 E7
Market Hill Ct CM9 . . . . .210 A3
Market Pl
 11 Braintree CM7 . . . . .127 F3
 Great Dunmow CM6 . . . . .123 D1
 Maldon CM9 . . . . .209 F2
 Saffron Walden CB10 . . . . .22 D2
Market Rd CM1 . . . . .205 B2
Market Row CB10 . . . . . . .22 D1
Market Sq
 6 Bishop's Stortford
 CM23 . . . . .145 F7
 6 Chelmsford CM1 . . .205 B2
Market St
 7 Bishop's Stortford
 CM23 . . . . .145 F7
 10 Braintree CM7 . . . . .127 F3
 Harwich CO12 . . . . .91 E6
 Saffron Walden CB10 . . . . .22 D1
Market Wlk CO10 . . . . . . .22 D1
Marking's Field CB10 . . . .22 E2
Markland Cl CM2 . . . . . . .216 C3
Markland Dr CM9 . . . . . .209 E1
Marks Gdns CM7 . . . . . . .128 C3
Marks Hall Ctry Est★
 CO6 . . . . .130 E7
Marks Hall Rd CO6 . . . . .130 E6
Marks Tey Rdbt CO6 . . . .133 B4
Marks Tey Sta CO6 . . . . .133 B4
Markwells CM22 . . . . .94 D2
Marlborough Cl
 Bishop's Stortford CM23 . .145 F5
 Clacton-on-S CO15 . . . . .188 C3
Marlborough Ct
 Felixstowe IP11 . . . . .221 D2
 Haverhill CB9 . . . . .8 E7
Marlborough Dr CO10 . . .33 F8
Marlborough Rd
 Braintree CM7 . . . . .128 A4
 2 Chelmsford CM2 . . .205 A1
 Ipswich IP4 . . . . .18 A6
Marlborough Terr CM1 . .205 A1
Marlowe Cl CM7 . . . . . . .155 A8
Marlowe Rd
 Clacton-on-S CO15 . . . . .203 G8
 Jaywick CO15 . . . . .188 A1
Marlowe Way CO3 . . . . . .134 F6
Marlpits Rd CM3,CM9 . . .219 E4
Marne Rd CO2 . . . . .135 E4
Marney Cl CM2 . . . . .216 E8
Marney Way CM13 . . . . .171 B6
Marquis Cl CM23 . . . . . .145 B7
Marram Cl CO3 . . . . .134 B6
Marsden Ct CO3 . . . . . . .134 E4
Marsh Cres CO5 . . . . . . .164 A8
Marsh Farm La CO7 . . . .166 D3
Marsh Rd CO6,CO7 . . . . .57 E6
Marsh Way CO7 . . . . . . .185 E6
Marshall Cl CO5 . . . . . . .158 D4
Marshalls Piece CM6 . . .124 D6
Marshalls Rd CM7 . . . . . .127 E1
Marshbarns CM23 . . . . . .145 C8
Marshy La CO9, C10 . . . . .30 C7
Marston Beck CM2 . . . . .206 A2

Martello Cvn Pk CO14 . .171 C8
Martello Rd **8** CO14 . .171 C8
Marten's La CO6 . . . . . . .56 F8
Martens Mdw CM7 . . . . .128 D3
Martin End CO2 . . . . .162 A5
Martin Rd IP2 . . . . .17 C4
Martin's Rd CO9 . . . . .76 E1
Martinet Gn IP3 . . . . .18 C1
Martingale Dr CM1 . . . . .205 F7
Martinsdale CO15 . . . . . .188 F6
Martyns Rise CO10 . . . . . .15 C5
Marvens CM2 . . . . .216 D3
Marvens The IP8 . . . . .16 A1
Mary La N CO7 . . . . .139 A8
Mary La S CO7 . . . . .139 B6
Mary McArthur Pl CM24 .119 E8
Mary Park Gdns CM23 . .145 F4
Mary Ruck Way CM77 . .155 B5
Mary Warner Rd CO7 . . .111 E7
Maryborough Gr CO2 . . .136 B2
Maryland Ct **1** CO2 . . .136 A1
Maryon Rd IP3 . . . . .18 B1
Mascalls The CM2 . . . . . .216 E8
Mascalls Way CM2 . . . . .216 E8
Mascot Ct CO15 . . . . . . .188 E5
Mascot Sq CO4 . . . . .136 D5
Masefield Dr CO3 . . . . . .134 F6
Masefield Rd CM7 . . . . . .155 A8
Mashay Rd CO9 . . . . .30 D5
Mason Cl CO2 . . . . .135 B3
Mason Rd
 Clacton-on-S CO16 . . . . .188 B3
 Colchester CO1 . . . . .109 F1
Masons Cl IP4 . . . . .17 F6
Masons Ct CM23 . . . . . . .145 E7
Masterman Wharf **12**
 CM23 . . . . .145 F7
Matchett Dr CO4 . . . . . . .110 B6
Matching La CM23 . . . . .145 B6
Matfield Cl CM1 . . . . . . .205 D7
Mathams Dr CM23 . . . . .145 D5
Mather Way IP2 . . . . .17 D4
Mathews Cl CO9 . . . . .77 A3
Matlock Cl **8** IP2 . . . . . .16 C2
Matson Rd IP1 . . . . .16 F8
Matthews Cl CO7 . . . . . . .58 C1
Maudlyn Rd CO1,CO4 . . .136 C6
Maximus Dr CO4 . . . . . . .110 B6
May Rd IP3 . . . . .18 C2
May Wlk Chelmsford CM2 .216 C7
 Elsenham CM24 . . . . .94 A1
May's La CO7 . . . . .84 E4
Mayberry Wlk CO2 . . . . .136 A3
Maybury Cl CO6 . . . . . . .132 F3
Maybury Rd IP3 . . . . .18 B1
Mayda Cl CO9 . . . . .76 D1
Mayes Cl CM23 . . . . .146 D8
Mayes La
 Chelmsford CM2 . . . . . . .217 E5
 Danbury CM3 . . . . .218 E6
 Harwich CO12 . . . . .90 C1
Mayes Pl CM6 . . . . .97 A6
Mayfield Cl CO4 . . . . .110 C2
Mayfield Pk CM23 . . . . . .145 D3
Mayfield Rd Ipswich IP4 . .18 C7
 Writtle CM1 . . . . .204 A2
Mayflower Ave CO12 . . . .91 E5
Mayflower Cl CO3 . . . . . .134 D6
Mayflower Gdns CM23 . .145 B6
Mayflower Ho CO12 . . . . .91 D6
Mayflower Prim Sch
 CO12 . . . . .91 B4
Mayflower Way CO10 . . . .15 F2
Mayfly Cl IP8 . . . . .36 E8
Mayford Way CO16 . . . . .188 B6
Mayland Cl CM3 . . . . . . .210 D4
Mayland Rd CM8 . . . . . . .177 A2
Maylands Dr CM77 . . . . .154 D8
Maynard Cl CM6 . . . . . . .123 D1
Maynards Villas CM6 . . .122 F5
Mayne Crest CM1 . . . . . .205 E6
Maypole Cl CB11 . . . . . . .43 C7
Maypole Dr CO16 . . . . . .187 B4
Maypole Green Rd CO2 .135 C1
Maypole Green Rd Tiptree CO5 .179 C6
 Wickham Bishops CM8,
 CM9 . . . . .195 F2
Maypole The CM6 . . . . . . .69 F3
Mays Ct IP11 . . . . .221 D3
Maysent Ave CM7 . . . . . .127 F5
Maytree Gdns CM22 . . . . .94 B3
Maze Green Hts CM23 . .145 C7
Maze Green Rd CM23 . . .145 D7
Mazers Cl **5** CM7 . . . . .127 F2
Mazoe Cl CM23 . . . . .145 F5
Mazoe Rd CM23 . . . . . . .145 F5
Meachen Rd CO2 . . . . . . .136 C5
Mead Ct
 Clacton-on-S CO15 . . . . .188 E3
 Stansted Mountfitchet
 CM24 . . . . .119 D7
Mead Pastures CM9 . . . .208 D3
Mead Path CM2 . . . . .215 F8
Mead The
 Brightlingsea CO7 . . . . . .185 F8
 Great Cornard CO10 . . . . .34 B4
 Great Dunmow CM6 . . . . .123 C2
 Thaxted CM6 . . . . .70 A3
Meadgate Ave CM2 . . . . .216 D8
Meadgate Prim Sch
 CM2 . . . . .216 E8
Meadgate Terr CM2 . . . .216 D8
Meadow Brown Ct CM7 .127 E1
Meadow Cl
 Chelmondiston IP9 . . . . . .63 D7
 Clacton-on-S CO15 . . . . .189 B7
 Elmstead CO7 . . . . .137 F6
 Great Bromley CO7 . . . . .139 A6

Meadow Cl *continued*
Halstead CO9 103 F8
Panfield CM7 127 A7
Meadow Cres IP3 18 F1
Meadow Grass Cl CO3 134 B6
Meadow La Sudbury CO10 33 E7
West Mersea CO5 201 C5
Meadow Rd
Colchester CO2 135 D1
Great Chesterford CB10 3 D3
Meadow Side CM1 205 B3
Meadow View
Bicknacre CM3 218 E1
Great Bardfield CM7 72 B2
Kirby-le-S CO13 143 D1
St Osyth CO16 187 B4
Tiptree CO5 179 B5
Meadow View Cl CO3 134 E5
Meadow View Rd CO10 33 D5
Meadow Way
Abberton CO5 163 B2
Black Notley CM77 155 C5
Clacton-on-S CO15 203 G7
Meadow Wlk 5 CM2 205 C2
Meadowbrook Ct CO1 136 B7
Meadowcroft CM24 119 E7
Meadowcroft Way CO13 170 F7
Meadowford CB11 42 F1
Meadowlands CM23 119 A2
Meadows The
Bishop's Stortford CM23 145 E5
3 Chelmsford CM2 205 C2
Meadowside
Braintree CM7 127 E5
Chelmsford CM2 205 C3
Meadowside Ct CM3 192 E1
Meadowside Gdns IP4 18 E8
Meadowsweet Cl CM23 145 C6
Meadowvale Cl IP4 17 F7
Meads The
Chelmsford CM2 205 A1
Stansted Mountfitchet CM24 119 F6
Wicken Bonhunt CB11 66 A7
Meadside CM7 73 B3
Meadway Gosfield CO9 102 E8
Lawford CO11 86 B3
Maldon CM9 210 B1
Mearns Pl 3 CM2 205 F4
Mede Way CO7 137 C3
Medlar Cl CM8 177 A4
Medley Rd CM77 126 F2
Medusa Ct Harwich CO12 91 B2
Holland-on-S CO15 189 E5
Medway Ave CM8 176 D2
Medway Cl CM1 204 D4
Medway Rd IP3 17 F2
Meekings Rd CO10 34 B8
Meers The CO13 170 E6
Meeson Mdws CM9 220 E8
Meeting Field CO10 15 C7
Meeting La
East Mersea CO5 184 C1
Ridgewell CO9 29 B7
Meeting Wlk CB9 9 B7
Meggy Tye CM2 206 B5
Megs Way CM7 128 B2
Melba Ct CM1 204 C1
Melbourne Ave CM1 204 E5
Melbourne Chase CO2 136 B1
Melbourne Ct CM1 204 E5
Melbourne Par CM1 204 E5
Melbourne Park Prim Sch CM1 204 F6
Melbourne Rd
Clacton-on-S CO15 188 E4
Ipswich IP4 18 D7
Melford Cl IP4 18 F5
Melford Gr CM77 154 B7
Melford Rd Cavendish CO10 1 E2
Sudbury CO10 15 D2
Melford Way IP11 221 A3
Mell Rd CM9 199 E1
Mellis Ct IP11 221 B5
Mellor Chase CO3 134 E7
Melplash Cl IP3 18 E4
Melplash Rd IP3 18 E4
Melrose Gdns
Clacton-on-S CO15 189 C5
Ipswich IP4 18 B8
Melrose Rd CO5 201 C6
Melton Cl CO16 188 A6
Melville Rd IP4 17 F5
Menai Ct IP1 17 B7
Mendip Dr IP5 18 F6
Mendip Rd CM1 204 D6
Mendlesham Cl CO16 188 B4
Menin Rd CO2 135 D4
Menish Way CM2 206 A3
Meon Cl CM1 205 C6
Meopham Ct CO2 136 B4
Mercantile Ho 1 CO1 135 F6
Mercers Ave CM23 145 B4
Mercers Row CB10 22 D1
Mercers Way 2 CO1 135 E8
Mercia Cl CM2 217 A5
Mercury Cl CO2 135 A3
Mercury Pl CM9 209 F5
Merdle Sq CM1 204 F6
Mere Gdns IP4 18 F4
Meredith Rd CO15 188 E3
Merediths Cl CO7 164 B8
Meres Cl CM8 176 F1
Meriden Ct CO15 189 A5
Merivale Cl CO11 86 C3
Merivale Rd CO11 86 B3
Merlin End CO4 110 F1
Merlin Pl CM1 204 F5
Merlin Rd IP2 16 C3
Merriam Cl CO11 86 D8
Merrilees Cres CO15 189 D6
Merrill Pl 2 CM23 145 E5
Merrion Cl 7 IP2 16 C2
Merrymount Gdns CO15 189 B5
Mersea Ave CO5 201 B6
Mersea Ct CO5 201 B7
Mersea Fleet Way CM7 128 C1
Mersea Island Sch CO5 201 C6
Mersea Mus★ CO5 201 B6
Mersea Point Nature Reserve★ CO5 185 C3
Mersea Rd
Abberton CO2,CO5 163 B5
Colchester CO2 136 A3
Peldon CO5 182 F5
Mersea View CO16 186 A3
Mersey Rd Ipswich IP3 17 F2
Witham CM8 176 E2
Mersey Way CM1 204 C5
Merstham Dr CO16 188 C6
Merton Ct CO2 163 A7
Messines Rd CO2 135 D5
Messing Gn CO5 159 D2
Messing-cum-Inworth Prim Sch CO5 159 C2
Meteor Way CM1 204 F2
Mews Ct CM2 205 B1
Mews The
Bishop's Stortford CM22 146 A3
Felixstowe IP11 221 E4
Frinton-on-S CO13 171 A5
Harwich CO12 91 C3
Panfield CM7 126 A7
Stansted Mountfitchet CM24 119 F7
Meyrick Cres CO2 135 F5
Micawber Way CM1 204 D7
Michaels Rd CM23 119 A2
Michaelstowe Cl CO12 90 C2
Michaelstowe Dr CO12 90 C2
Mickfield Mews IP11 221 B5
Micklegate Rd IP11 221 C1
Middle Gn CO6 79 C1
Middle King CM7 128 D1
Middle Mill Rd CO1 135 F8
Middle Row 5 CM23 145 F6
Middle St CB11 65 C4
Middle Way CO10 15 D8
Middleborough CO1 135 E8
Middlefield CO9 76 F1
Middlefield Rd CO11 87 A3
Middleton Cl
Clacton-on-S CO16 188 D6
Ipswich IP2 16 D2
Middleton Rd CO10 33 D5
Middlewick Cl 4 CO2 136 A1
Midguard Way CM9 220 F8
Midland Cl CO2 135 F4
Midway CO15 203 E6
Midway Rd CO2 135 C2
Milbank CM2 206 B4
Milburn Cres CM1 204 D1
Milch La CM3 153 E6
Milden Rd IP2 16 E5
Mildenhall Pl 14 CB9 9 B8
Mildmay Cl CM6 151 E7
Mildmay Ct 2 CM2 205 B1
Mildmay Jun & Inf Schs CM2 216 B5
Mildmay Rd
Chelmsford CM2 205 B1
Ipswich IP3 18 B1
Mildmays CM3 218 C7
Mile End IP1 17 A6
Mile End Rd CO4 109 E3
Miles Cl CO3 134 C6
Milestones The CM3 194 A4
Milford Cl CO7 137 D1
Military Ct 10 CO1 136 A6
Military Rd CO1 136 A5
Military Way CO12 90 C1
Mill Chase Halstead CO9 76 F2
Steeple Bumpstead CB9 27 C5
Mill Cl Elsenham CM22 94 C1
Felixstowe IP11 221 B4
Great Bardfield CM7 72 B2
Harwich CO12 91 C4
Tiptree CO5 179 C6
Mill Cotts CM2 217 C8
Mill Croft CM23 119 A1
Mill Cswy SG8 19 C5
Mill Ct Braintree CM7 128 B2
Takeley CM6 149 B7
Mill End CM6 70 A2
Mill Field Barnston CM6 151 A4
Chelmondiston IP9 63 E8
Mill Hill Braintree CM7 128 B2
Chelmsford CM2 215 F2
Farnham CM23 118 E5
Harwich CO12 91 C3
Haverhill CB9 9 A7
Lawford CO11 85 D4
Manningtree CO11 86 C4
Purleigh CM3 220 C1
Stansted Mountfitchet CM24 119 E6
Sudbury CO10 33 D7
Wormingford CO6 80 E6
Mill House Cotts CO12 116 D4
Mill La Ardleigh CO7 112 B4
Birch CO2 161 A3
Bradfield CO11 87 D2
Broomfield CM1 191 C1
Cavendish CO10 13 B8
Chelmondiston IP9 63 E7
Coggeshall CO5 131 F1
Mill La *continued*
Colne Engaine CO6 105 B8
Cressing CM77 155 D5
Danbury CM3 219 A6
Dedham CO7 84 F7
Felixstowe IP11 221 C4
Finchingfield CM7 48 F3
Ford End CM3 172 D7
Great Dunmow CM6 123 D1
Great Holland CO13 169 E3
Great Leighs CM3 174 B7
Great Maplestead CO9 76 E8
Harkstead SG9 64 A5
Harwich CO12 91 D3
Hinxton CB10 3 A7
Ickleton CB10 3 B4
Layer-de-l-H CO2 162 B5
Little Baddow CM3 207 E3
Little Yeldham CO9 30 A3
Littlebury CB11 21 F4
Maldon CM9 210 A3
Manningtree CO11 86 D4
Pebmarsh CO9 78 A7
Purleigh CM3 220 C1
Rayne CM7 153 E8
Saffron Walden CB10 22 F2
Salcott-cum-virley CM9 199 B8
Stebbing CM6 124 E5
Stoke-by-N CO6 56 D7
Sudbury CO10 33 D7
Terling CM3 175 A3
Thorington Street CO6 57 C4
Thorpe-le-S CO16 141 F1
Tolleshunt Major CM9 197 E3
Walton-on-t-N CO14 171 C8
Washbrook IP8 16 A1
Weeley Heath CO16 168 A6
Witham CM8 176 F1
Mill Lane Cl CO16 168 A6
Mill Park Dr CM7 128 B1
Mill Rd Birdbrook CO9 10 E2
Boxted CO4 82 F4
Clare CO10 12 C7
Colchester CO4 109 F4
Debden CB11 68 B8
East Bergholt CO7 59 E2
Elder Street CB10 45 B3
Felsted CM6 152 A4
Finchingfield CM7 72 D5
Fordham CO6 107 D4
Foxearth CO10 14 C5
Great Bardfield CM7 72 B2
Great Totham CM9 196 D7
Haverhill CB9 9 A7
Helions Bumpstead CB9 26 C8
Henham CM22 94 E4
Maldon CM9 210 B2
Marks Tey CO6 133 C4
North End CM6 151 F2
Ridgewell CO9 29 B6
Stambourne CO9 28 C3
West Mersea CO5 201 D7
Mill Rise IP9 62 D5
Mill Road Cotts CB10 45 B3
Mill Road Dr IP3 18 F1
Mill Side CM24 119 E6
Mill St
Bishop's Stortford CM23 146 A5
Brightlingsea CO7 186 A6
Colchester CO1 136 A6
Nayland CO6 56 B1
St Osyth CO16 186 F4
Stoke-by-N CO6 56 D8
Mill Tye CO10 34 A4
Mill Vale Lo CM8 176 F2
Mill View CM7 129 D3
Mill Vue Rd CM2 205 F2
Mill Wlk CO5 179 C6
Millars The CM1 191 A3
Millbridge Rd CM8 176 F2
Milldene Prim Sch CO5 179 D6
Millennium Way CM7 155 D8
Miller's Barn Rd CO15 188 A1
Miller's Cl CM6 151 A4
Millers Cl
Bishop's Stortford CM23 145 C5
Braintree CM7 128 A8
Colchester CO3 134 C6
Great Horkesley CO6 109 B7
Millers Croft
Great Baddow CM2 216 F6
Great Dunmow CM6 123 E1
Millers Dr CM77 154 C7
Millers La CO3 134 D6
Millers Mead CO5 158 E4
Millers Reach CO11 87 A4
Millers Row CM7 48 C6
Millers View IP1 16 F7
Millfield Gdns IP4 18 A6
Millfields CO5 179 C6
Millfields Danbury CM3 219 A6
Stansted Mountfitchet CM24 119 E6
Writtle CM1 204 A1
Millfields Prim Sch CO7 137 D1
Millfields Way CB9 9 B8
Millhouse Villas CM6 151 A4
Milligans Chase CM2 216 B1
Milliners Way CM23 145 C4
Mills La CO10 15 C4
Mills Rd CO10 34 A8
Mills The IP4 18 E8
Millside CM23 146 A5
Millson Bank CM2 206 A4
Millways CM9 196 B4
Millwrights CO5 179 C6
Milner Rd CO10 34 B8
Milner St IP4 17 E5
Milnrow IP2 16 C2
Milton Ave CM7 155 A8
Milton Cl CO3 134 F6
Milton Ct CO15 189 E6
Milton Pl CM1 205 A5
Milton Rd Harwich CO12 91 D4
Lawford CO11 86 B2
Witham CM8 176 F5
Milton St IP4 18 B6
Mimosa Cl CM1 205 F6
Mimosa Ct CO4 136 E8
Minden Rd CO10 33 F7
Minerva Cl Harwich CO12 90 F1
Haverhill CB9 9 D6
Minerva End CO2 135 C1
Minos Way IP1 16 D8
Minsmere Dr CO16 188 C6
Minsmere Rd IP3 38 D8
Minsmere Way CO10 34 C6
Minster Way CM9 220 E8
Minters Cotts CO11 115 C5
Miranda Wlk CO4 136 E7
Mirosa Dr CM9 210 B1
Mission La CO7 60 B3
Mistley Norman CE Prim Sch CO11 87 A4
Mistley Place Pk★ CO11 86 E4
Mistley Sta CO11 86 F4
Mistley Twrs★ CO11 86 F4
Mitchell Ave CO9 76 E1
Mitchell Circ CM7 73 C6
Mitre Gdns CM23 146 A4
Mitre Way IP3 17 F4
Mitton Vale CM2 205 F2
Moat Farm CO9 28 B7
Moat Farm Chase CM8 176 F3
Moat Farm Cl IP4 17 F8
Moat Fields CO6 107 D6
Moat La CO8 55 A4
Moat Rd Birdbrook CO9 28 C7
Fordham CO6 107 D6
Moat Wlk CB9 8 E8
Modlen Rd CO14 171 B7
Moffat Ave IP4 18 B8
Mole Hall La CB11 67 F3
Mole Hall Wildlife Pk★ CB11 67 F3
Molehill Green Cotts CM22 121 C6
Molehill Green Rdbt CM22 121 C5
Molrams La CM2 217 B6
Monarch Cl CB9 8 C8
Monarch Way IP8 36 D8
Monk's Cnr CB10 47 B4
Monk's La CO7 84 D4
Monkdowns Rd CO6 131 B3
Monklands Ct 2 CO9 76 D1
Monks Ct CM8 176 E3
Monks Gate IP8 16 A6
Monks Hill CB11 43 F8
Monks Lodge Rd CO9 52 D2
Monks Mead CM3 218 F2
Monks Rd CO6 105 B7
Monks Wlk CM9 213 E8
Monkswood Dr CM23 145 D6
Monkwick Ave CO2 135 F1
Monkwick Jun & Inf Schs CO2 136 A2
Monmouth Cl IP2 17 B1
Mons Rd CO2 135 D4
Montagu Gdns CM1 205 F7
Montague Rd IP11 221 E4
Montbretia Cl CO3 134 D6
Montbretia Ct CO16 188 C4
Montfort Ct 8 CB9 8 F7
Montgomery Cl
Chelmsford CM1 205 E7
Colchester CO2 136 B4
Montgomery Jun & Inf Sch CO2 135 D2
Montgomery Rd IP2 17 B1
Monton Rise IP2 16 D2
Montrose Ct IP3 17 F4
Montrose Rd CM2 206 A4
Moon Hall La CB9 9 A6
Moonhall Bsns Pk CB9 9 A5
Moor Hall La
Bishop's Stortford CM23 145 C3
Bishop's Stortford,Thorley CM23 145 B3
Danbury CM3 218 E2
Moor Rd Great Tey CO6 132 C8
Langham CO4 83 D4
Moor's Farm Chase CM9 197 A3
Moor's La CO7 139 E1
Moorfield Ct CM8 176 F1
Moorhouse Gn CO7 111 E8
Moorings The CM23 146 A5
Moors Cl Feering CO5 158 E5
Great Bentley CO7 139 E1
Moors Croft CM7 128 D3
Moors La
Little Dunmow CM6 151 D7
Rayne CM77 126 D3
Moors The CM6 151 D7
Moorsfield CO10 34 B4
Moorside CO1 136 B7
Mope La CM8 195 D6
Moran Ave CM1 205 B7
Morant Rd CO1 136 B5
Morebarn Rd CO7 112 E2
Morecambe Ct IP4 18 A7
Morella Cl CO7 166 E8
Morello Ct CO2 163 A7
Moretons CM2 216 B2
Morland Ct CO6 82 B1
Morland Prim Sch IP3 38 A8
Morland Rd IP3 37 F8
Morley Rd Halstead CO9 76 F2
Tiptree CO5 179 D4
Morleys Rd CO6 105 A6
Mornington Ave 2 IP1 17 A8
Morris Ave CO15 203 E6
Morris Harp CB10 22 E3
Morris Rd CM2 205 D2
Morrow La CO7 112 A6
Mors End CO7 58 D2
Morses La CO7 165 F1
Morten Rd CO1 135 E8
Mortimer Rd CM3 194 A4
Morton Rd CM9 196 A4
Morton Way CO9 77 A3
Moss Path CM2 216 C3
Moss Rd Colchester CO3 134 E4
Witham CM8 177 B3
Moss Way CO6 108 E3
Moss Wlk CM2 216 B6
Mossfield Cl CO3 135 C6
Mott's La CO6 132 D4
Mottram Cl 9 IP2 16 C2
Motts Cl CM7 127 E4
Motts La CM8 177 B4
Motts Yd CM6 124 E5
Moules La CB1 5 C6
Moulsham Chase CM2 216 C8
Moulsham Dr CM2 216 B8
Moulsham Hall La
Braintree CM3 153 F2
Great Leighs CM3 154 A1
Moulsham High Sch CM2 216 B7
Moulsham Jun & Inf Schs CM2 216 B7
Moulsham St
Chelmsford CM1 205 B2
Chelmsford,Moulsham CM2 205 B1
Moulsham Thrift CM2 216 A6
Moulton Cl CO10 33 F8
Mount Dr Ipswich IP3 18 F1
Stansted Mountfitchet CM24 119 E5
Mount Hill CO9 76 D1
Mount Lodge Chase CM9 196 E6
Mount Pleasant
Halstead CO9 76 E1
Maldon CM9 209 F2
Mount Pleasant Cotts CB11 43 D8
Mount Pleasant Est CM9 196 E6
Mount Pleasant Rd CB11 43 E8
Mount Rd Braintree CM7 128 A3
Coggeshall CO6 131 B2
Haverhill CB9 9 B7
Mount Rise 4 CO9 76 D1
Mount The
Colchester CO3 134 F6
Tollesbury CM9 199 D1
Mountain Ash Cl CO4 110 C2
Mountain's Farm Rd CM6 150 C3
Mountains Rd CM8,CM9 196 C7
Mountbatten Cl CO10 15 F2
Mountbatten Ct 7 IP1 17 A7
Mountbatten Dr CO2 136 B4
Mountbatten Rd
Braintree CM7 128 C4
Sudbury CO10 15 F2
Mountbatten Way CM1 205 E7
Mountfitchet Castle & Norman Village★ CM24 119 F6
Mountfitchet High Sch CM24 119 F4
Mountfitchet Rd CM24 119 E5
Mounthill Ave CM2 205 D3
Mountview Rd CO15 189 A5
Moverons La CO7 165 C2
Mowden Hall La
Hatfield Peverel CM3 193 D1
Ulting CM3 208 A8
Mowlands IP9 35 B1
Moy Rd CO2 136 A1
Moze Cross CO12 116 D1
Mulberries The CM7 128 A2
Mulberry Ave CO2 136 A4
Mulberry Ct CM23 146 A5
Mulberry Gdns CM8 177 A4
Mulberry Harbour Way CO7 164 B8
Mulberry Way CM1 205 D4
Mullins Rd CM7 127 F6
Multon Lea CM1 206 A7
Mumford Cl CO6 108 E4
Mumford Rd Ipswich IP1 16 E8
West Bergholt CO6 108 D4
Mumfords La CO13 170 A7
Mundon Rd CM7 128 D1
Munnings Cl IP3 38 B8
Munnings Dr CO16 188 D6
Munnings Rd CO3 135 A5
Munnings Way CO11 86 B5
Munro Rd CM8 176 F5
Murchison Cl CM1 204 E5
Murray Cl CM7 127 F6
Murray Rd IP3 18 A3
Murrayfield Com Prim Sch IP3 18 A2

Murrell Lock CM2 ......206 A4
Murrills Rd IP3 ....18 F1
Murton Slade **6** CB9 .....9 A8
Mus of Power★ CM9 .209 D6
Muscade Cl CO5 ......179 D6
Museum St
  14 Colchester CO1 .....135 F7
  Ipswich IP1 ....17 C6
  Saffron Walden CB10 ....22 D2
Musgrave Cl CO12 ......90 F1
Musk Cl CO3 ....134 D7
Muswell Wlk CO16 .....188 D5
Mutlow Cl CB11 ....42 F5
Mutlow Hill CB11 ....42 F5
Mychett Cl CO16 ......188 B6
Myddlyton Pl CB10 .....22 D2
Myland Hall Chase CO4 110 C3
Myland Prim Sch CO4 ..109 E4
Mynards Way CM3 .....218 C1
Myneer Pk CO6 ....131 B2
Myrtle Gr CO2 ....136 B5
Myrtle Rd IP3 ....17 E4
Myson Way CM23 .....146 B7

N

Nabbott Rd CM1 ....204 E2
Nacton Cres IP3 ....18 B2
Nacton Rd
  Felixstowe IP11 ....221 C1
  Ipswich,Racecourse IP3 .18 A2
  Ipswich,Rose Hill IP3 ...18 A3
Nails La **15** CM23 .....145 F7
Nalla Gdns CM7 ....205 A6
Nancy Smith Cl CO2 ..135 F5
Nansen Rd
  Holland-on-S CO15 .....189 D6
  Ipswich IP3 ....18 B2
Napier Ave CO15 ....203 D6
Napier Ct CM1 ....204 E5
Napier Rd CO2 ....135 F6
Narvik Cl CM9 ....220 E8
Nash Cl Colchester CO3 .135 B5
  Lawford CO11 ....86 B5
Nash Dr CM1 ....191 A3
Nash Gdns IP3 ....38 B8
Nassau Rd CO16 ....187 B4
Nathan Ct CO2 ....163 B8
Nats La CB11 ....42 E6
Navarre St **4** IP1 .....17 C6
Navigation Pl CM9 .....210 B4
Navigation Rd CM2 ....205 C2
Nayland Dr CO16 ......188 B4
Nayland Prim Sch CO6 ..56 A1
Nayland Rd Bures CO8 ..79 F8
  Colchester CO6 ....109 D6
  Felixstowe IP11 ....221 A4
  Great Horkesley CO6 ....82 B4
  Haverhill CB9 ....8 E6
  Little Horkesley CO6 ....81 F6
  West Bergholt CO6 ....108 D7
Nayling Rd CM7 ....127 C2
Naze Ct CO14 ....144 E3
Naze Nature Reserve The★
  CO14 ....144 D6
Naze Nature Trail The★
  CO14 ....144 E4
Naze Park Rd CO14 ....144 E2
Neale Rd CO9 ....76 F1
Neale St IP1 ....17 C6
Neasden Ave CO16 ....188 D5
Neath Dr IP2 ....17 A1
Needle Cnr IP9 ....63 D1
Nelson Ct CO7 ....186 A7
Nelson Gdns CM7 .....128 C4
Nelson Gr CM1 ....204 F3
Nelson Rd
  Bishop's Stortford CM23 .146 A5
  Clacton-on-S CO15 .....188 E1
  Colchester CO3 ....134 E6
  Harwich CO12 ....91 D4
  Ipswich IP4 ....18 A6
Nelson St CO7 ....185 F6
Neptune Ct
  Chelmsford CM1 ....204 F4
  5 Colchester CO1 ....136 C6
Neptune Quay IP4 ......17 D5
Neptune Sq IP4 ....17 D5
Ness Wlk IP4 ....176 D2
Nether Ct CO9 ....77 A1
Nether Hill CO9,CO10 ...31 D5
Nether Rd CO10 ....1 D2
Nethergate St CO10 ....12 B7
Netley Cl IP2 ....36 F8
Nettleditch CB11 ....21 E4
Neville Rd CB10 ....22 E2
New Barn La CM22 ....146 D1
New Bowers Way CM1 .205 F6
New Captains Rd CO5 .201 B6
New Cardinal St IP1 ....17 B5
New Church Rd CO6 ...108 E4
New Cotts Great Tey CO6 132 C8
  Wakes Colne CO6 .....106 C6
New Cut Bures CO8 .....79 E8
  Glemsford CO10 ....2 B3
  Great Bentley CO7 ....166 E8
  Layer-de-l-H CO7 ....161 F5
New Cut E IP2,IP3 ......17 D4
New Cut W IP2 ....17 D4
New Dukes Way CM2 ..205 F4
New England Cl CM3 ..218 F1
New Farm Lodge CO3 .134 D5
New Farm Rd CO3 ....134 D6
New Hall Cotts CO7 ....58 F7
New Hall Sch CM3 .....192 A1
New Hall Vineyard★
  CM3 ....220 D2
New House La CB10 ....24 C3
New Kiln Rd CO1 .....135 C7
New La Feering CO5 ...158 F5
  Holbrook IP9 ....63 A5
New Lodge Chase CM3 .207 B2
New London Rd CM2 ..205 A1
New Nabbotts Way CM1 205 E7
New Orleans Flats CO5 .201 B5
New Park Gdns CO7 ...185 F7
New Park St CO1 ......136 B6
New Pier St **7** CO14 ..171 C8
New Pk CO9 ....51 F3
New Place Ho IP2 ......17 A4
New Pond La CB10 .....22 C2
New Queens Rd CO10 ..15 E1
New Rd Aldham CO6 ..107 B2
  Broomfield CM1 ....191 B1
  Colchester CO3 ....134 D6
  Elsenham CM22 ....94 C2
  Gosfield CO9 ....102 E5
  Great Baddow CM2 ....217 A6
  Hatfield Peverel CM3 ...194 A4
  Hinxton CB10 ....3 B6
  Kelvedon CO5 ....158 C2
  Long Melford CO10 .....15 C7
  Messing CO5 ....159 C1
  Mistley CO11 ....86 E4
  Rayne CM77 ....127 A1
  Saffron Walden CB10 ....22 E1
  Shudy Camps CB1 ......7 C7
  Terling CM3 ....175 C3
  Tiptree CO5 ....179 D5
  Tollesbury CM9 ....199 D2
  Trimley St M IP11 .....221 C1
New Road Terr CM7 ...126 F1
New St Braintree CM7 ..127 F2
  Brightlingsea CO7 .....185 F6
  Chelmsford CM1 ......205 B3
  Glemsford CO10 ....2 A5
  Great Dunmow CM6 ...150 D8
  Halstead CO9 ....76 E1
  21 Ipswich IP4 ....17 D5
  Maldon CM9 ....209 F2
  Sudbury CO10 ....33 E8
New Street Fields CM6 .150 D8
New Thorpe Ave CO16 .142 A2
New Town Rd
  Colchester CO1 ....136 A6
  Thorpe-le-S CO16 .....141 F2
New Village CO11 ....86 C7
New Way Ipswich IP2 ...16 F6
  Point Clear B CO16 ....185 F3
New Writtle St CM2 ....205 B1
Newark Cl IP2 ....16 F1
Newbarn Rd CM6 .....106 B1
Newbourne Gdns IP11 .221 B3
Newbridge Hill CO6 ....108 D2
Newbridge Rd Birch CO5 180 A6
  Tiptree CO5 ....179 F5
Newbury Cl CM23 .....145 E8
Newbury Ho IP4 ....18 B6
Newbury Rd IP4 ....18 C6
Newby Dr IP4 ....18 F5
Newcastle Ave CO3 ...134 F4
Newcomen Way CO4 ..110 C6
Newcourt Rd CM2 ....205 D3
Newcroft **1** CB10 .....22 E1
Newgate St **5** CO14 ..171 C8
Newhaven Cl CO12 .....91 D6
Newhouse Rd CO6 ....104 F5
Newhythe CO3 ....134 E7
Newington Gdns CO15 .188 F8
Newland Ave CM7 .....72 B6
Newland Pl CM8 ......177 A1
Newland St CM8 ......177 A2
Newlands Dr CM8 .....177 A2
Newlands La CO6 ......56 B1
Newlands Prec **8** CM8 .177 A2
Newlands Spring Prim Sch
  CM1 ....204 D1
Newman Dr CO4 ....83 A4
Newman's Rd CO10 ....33 F8
Newmarket Rd CB10 ....3 C3
Newmill La
  Brantham CO11 ....61 A1
  Stutton CO11 ....87 A8
Newnham Cl CM7 .....127 E2
Newnham Ct IP2 ....16 E2
Newnham Gn CM9 ....209 E3
Newpasture La CM6 ...125 C5
Newport Cl
  Great Baddow CM2 ....217 B6
  Harwich CO12 ....91 A1
Newport Dr
  Clacton-on-S CO15 ....189 A7
  Rickling Green CB11 ....66 F4
Newport Free Gram Sch
  CB11 ....42 F1
Newport Prim Sch CB11 .66 F7
Newport Rd CB11 ......43 C7
Newport Sta CB11 ......67 A8
Newport Way CO13 ...171 A6
Newpots Cl CO5 ......182 D5
Newpots La CO5 ......182 E5
Newquay Cl IP5 ....18 F6
Newry Ave IP11 ......221 D4
Newson St IP1 ....17 B7
Newton Cl **4** CM7 ...127 F1
Newton Croft CO10 ....34 A7
Newton Gdns CO16 ...187 A5
Newton Gn CM6 ......123 C1
Newton Gr CM6 ......123 B1
Newton Pl **19** CB9 ....9 B8
Newton Rd Harwich CO12 91 A3

Newton Rd continued
  Ipswich IP3 ....18 A4
  Sudbury CO10 ....34 A7
Newton St **10** IP4 .....17 D6
Newton Way CO16 ....187 B5
Newtown Rd CM23 ....145 D6
Nexus The CO1 ....135 E8
Nicholas Cl CM1 ......204 B1
Nicholas Ct
  Chelmsford, Scot's Green
  CM1 ....204 D6
  Witham CM8 ....176 F2
Nicholas Rd IP11 .....221 A4
Nichols Cl CO11 ....86 B3
Nichols Cnr CO7 ......112 A5
Nichols Ct **1** CM1 ....205 A1
Nichols Gr CM7 ......128 C3
Nickleby Rd CM1 .....204 D6
Nicholsons Gr CO1 ...136 A6
Nien-Oord CO16 ......188 C4
Nightingale Cl
  Clacton-on-S CO15 ....188 F5
  Colchester CO4 ....137 A8
  Harwich CO12 ....90 F1
  Witham CM8 ....194 E8
Nightingale Cnr **2** CM9 210 A1
Nightingale Ct CO2 ...163 A8
Nightingale Hill CO4 ...83 F6
Nightingale Mews **2**
  CB10 ....22 F2
Nightingale Pl CO3 ...134 C4
Nightingale Rd IP3 .....38 A8
Nightingale Sq IP3 .....38 A8
Nightingale Way CO15 .188 F5
Nine Acres IP2 ....16 D5
Nineacres CM7 ....128 A1
Ninth Ave CM24 ......120 B2
Noah's Ark La CO10 ....33 D7
Noak's Cross CM8 ....178 B2
Noakes Ave CM2 .....216 E6
Noaks Rd IP7 ....58 D8
Nobles The CM23 .....145 D6
Nonsuch Mdw CO10 ...33 E7
Nook The CO7 ....164 C8
Norbury Cl IP6 ....132 F3
Norbury Rd IP4 ....18 B8
Nordic Lodge CM9 ....220 F8
Norfolk Ave
  Clacton-on-S CO15 ....189 E7
  West Mersea CO5 .....201 D7
Norfolk Cl CM9 ....209 E1
Norfolk Cres CO4 .....110 B1
Norfolk Dr CM1 ......205 A7
Norfolk Rd Ipswich IP4 ..17 D6
  Maldon CM9 ....209 E1
Norfolk Way CM23 ....145 F5
Norman Ave CM23 ....145 D6
Norman Cl
  Marks Tey CO6 ....132 E3
  St Osyth CO16 ....187 A4
Norman Cres IP3 ....18 A2
Norman Ct CM24 ......119 E2
Norman Hill CM3 .....175 B2
Norman Rd
  Clacton-on-S CO15 ....189 E6
  Manningtree CO11 .....86 D4
Norman Way
  Colchester, Lexton CO3 ..135 B6
  Colchester, Shrub End CO3 135 B4
  Point Clear B CO16 ....185 F3
Norman's Way CM24 ..119 E2
Normandie Way CO8 ...79 E8
Normandy Ave CO2 ...136 A3
Normanhurst CO15 ....188 E1
Normansfield CM6 ....150 E7
Norris Cl
  Bishop's Stortford CM23 .146 C7
  Braintree CM7 ....128 C5
North Ave
  Chelmsford CM1 ......204 F5
  Haverhill CB9 ....8 E8
North Cl IP4 ....17 E8
North Cres CB9 ....27 B7
North Dell CM1 ....205 E7
North Dr CM2 ....216 F7
North End Rd
  Gestingthorpe CO9,CO10 ..31 C2
  Hinxton CB10 ....3 B8
  Little Yeldham CO9 .....30 E2
North Hall Rd CB11 ....67 A2
North Hill Colchester CO1 135 E7
  Little Baddow CM3 ....207 B3
North Hill Gdns **11** IP4 .17 E6
North Hill Rd CO13 ...170 F4
North Ho CO13 ....170 F4
North La CO6 ....133 B5
North Lawn IP4 ....18 C8
North Mill Pl CO9 ......76 E3
North Prim Sch CO1 ..135 E8
North St
  4 Bishop's Stortford
  CM23 ....145 F7
  Great Dunmow CM6 ...123 D1
  Maldon CM9 ....210 B2
  Manningtree CO11 .....86 D4
  Steeple Bumpstead CB9 .27 B7
  Sudbury CO10 ....33 E8
  Tolleshunt D'arcy CM9 .198 E5

North St continued
  Walton-on-t-N CO14 ...171 C8
North Station Rd CO1 ..135 E8
North Street Par **1** CO10 33 E7
North Terr **5** CM23 ...145 F8
North View Cotts CO6 ..109 B7
North Wall CO1 ....135 F8
Northampton Cl CM7 ..128 D5
Northampton Mdw CM7 ..72 B2
Northbourne Rd CM7 ..188 F4
Northcroft CO10 ....33 E7
Northend CB11 ....22 A4
Northern Rd CO10 .....34 B8
Northfield CM7 ....72 B3
Northfield Gdns CO4 ..110 A4
Northfield Rd CB11 ....43 E8
Northgate End CM23 ..145 F8
Northgate Prim Sch
  CM23 ....145 E8
Northgate St
  Colchester CO1 ....135 F8
  Ipswich IP1 ....17 C6
Northolt Ave CM23 ....119 B1
Northumberland Cl
  CM7 ....128 B4
Northumberland Ct **1**
  CM2 ....205 F4
Norton Rd
  Chelmsford CM1 ......205 A3
  Haverhill CB9 ....8 E6
Norway Cres CO12 .....90 F3
Norwich Cl
  Clacton-on-S CO16 ....188 E6
  Colchester CO1 ....136 A8
Norwich Ct **2** IP1 ....17 A7
Norwich Rd IP1 ....17 A7
Norwood Ave CO15 ...189 B5
Norwood Way CO14 ..171 A7
Notcutts CO7 ....59 E1
Notley Gn CM77 ......154 B6
Notley Green Prim Sch
  CM77 ....154 C8
Notley High Sch The
  CM7 ....154 F8
Notley Rd CM7 ....154 F8
Nottage Cl CO7 ......164 C8
Nottidge Rd IP4 ....17 E6
Nottingham Rd CO15 .189 E6
Nounsley Rd CM3 ....194 B1
Nun's Mdw CO9 ......102 E7
Nunn's Rd CO1 ......135 E7
Nunnery St CO9 ....51 D4
Nunns Cl CO6 ....131 A2
Nuns Wlk CO9 ....29 F1
Nunty's La
  Greenstead Green CO9 .104 A1
  Pattiswick CM7 ....129 F8
Nursery Cl
  Bishop's Stortford CM23 .145 F6
  Colchester CO3 ....134 C5
Nursery Dr CM7 ......128 A5
Nursery La CM3 ......218 F8
Nursery Rd
  Bishop's Stortford CM23 .145 F6
  Chelmsford CM2 ......216 B8
  Great Cornard CO10 ...34 B5
Nursery Rise CM6 ....150 D7
Nursery Wlk IP11 .....221 D5

O

Oak Ave CO16 ....188 A2
Oak Bglws CM7 ......127 E3
Oak Cl Felixstowe IP11 .221 C4
  Rushmere St A IP4 .....18 E7
  Thorpe-le-S CO16 .....142 A1
  West Bergholt CO6 ....108 E4
Oak Cotts CM3 ....86 E8
Oak Eggar Chase IP8 ...36 D8
Oak Fall CM8 ....177 A5
Oak Farm Rd CM9 ....208 E1
Oak Gr IP8 ....16 A6
Oak Hall CM23 ....145 E8
Oak Haven CO12 ....90 F1
Oak Hill Beazley End CM7 101 A8
  Wethersfield CM7 .....73 F1
Oak Hill La IP2 ....17 B3
Oak Ho IP2 ....16 D2
Oak Ind Pk CM6 ......150 F6
Oak Lodge Tye CM1 ..206 A6
Oak Rd Chappel CO6 ..106 B3
  Great Cornard CO10 ...34 B6
  Halstead CO9 ....103 D7
  Heybridge CM9 ....210 B6
  Little Maplestead CO9 ..77 A8
  Pebmarsh CO9 ....77 F8
  Rivenhall CM8 ....177 C6
  Tiptree CO5 ....179 C7
Oak Ridge CO12 ......117 B7
Oak Sat CM23 ....145 F6
Oak Tree Cotts CO6 ..133 B8
Oak Tree Rd CO7 .....165 B8
Oak Wlk CO9 ....51 D2
Oak Yd CO9 ....76 E2
Oakapple Cl CO2 .....135 D1
Oakfield CM6 ....125 A4
Oakfield Dr CO4 ....83 A5
Oakfield La CM3 ......175 A2
Oakfield Rd Belstead IP8 .36 A7
  Washbrook IP8 ....35 F6
Oakfield Wood★ CO11 ..88 D4
Oakland Rd CO12 ......91 C3
Oaklands Ave CO3 ....134 E5
Oaklands Cl
  Bishop's Stortford CM23 .119 B2

Oaklands Cl continued
  Great Notley CM77 ....154 D8
Oaklands Cres CM2 ...216 B8
Oaklands Dr CM23 ....119 B2
Oaklands Inf Sch CM2 .216 B8
Oaklands Pk CM23 ....119 B2
Oaklands Way CM3 ...207 E2
Oaklea Ave CM2 ......205 E3
Oaklee IP2 ....17 A1
Oakleigh Ct CM23 ....145 D8
Oakleigh Rd CO15 ....188 F8
Oakley Cross CO12 ....117 B7
Oakley Rd Braintree CM7 127 F7
  Harwich CO12 ....90 D1
  Wix CO11 ....115 E5
Oakmead Rd CO16 ...186 B3
Oakroyd Ave CM6 ....150 E8
Oaks Dr CO3 ....135 D7
Oaks Hospl The CO4 ..109 E3
Oaks Pl CO4 ....109 E2
Oaks The CO13 ....170 F6
Oaksmere Gdns IP2 ...17 A2
Oakstead Cl IP4 ....18 A6
Oaktree Cl **14** CM23 ..145 F7
Oaktrees CM9 ....197 B5
Oakview CO12 ....90 F1
Oakwood Ave
  Clacton-on-S CO15 ....189 E7
  West Mersea CO5 .....201 D7
Oakwood Cl CO13 ....170 E6
Oakwood Dr CO5 .....201 D7
Oakwood Gdns CO5 ..201 D7
Oakwood Inf Sch CO15 .188 D2
Oasis Ct CM1 ....205 F5
Oast House Spinney
  CM7 ....127 F6
Oasthouse Ct CB10 ....22 D1
Oatfield Cl CO3 ......134 D6
Oatlands CO7 ....137 C6
Oban St IP1 ....17 B7
Oberon Cl CO4 ....136 F7
Obrey Way CM23 .....145 E3
Observation Ct IP1 ....17 B5
Observer Way CO5 ...158 C4
Ockelford Ave CM1 ..204 F5
Ockendon Way CO14 .171 A8
Octavia Dr CM8 ......194 E7
Oddcroft CO6 ....77 F1
Odin Lodge CM9 .....220 F8
Office La CM9 ....197 A4
Old Barn Rd CO8 ......80 A6
Old Bell Cl CM24 .....119 D6
Old Burylodge La CM24 120 A4
Old Cattle Market **5** IP4 17 C5
Old Church La
  Bulmer CO10 ....32 F3
  Bulmer Tye CO10 .....32 F2
  West Bergholt CO6 ...108 D5
Old Clements La CB9 ...8 F7
Old Coach Rd CO1 ...136 B7
Old Coastguard Cotts
  CM0 ....214 E4
Old Convent The CO5 .158 B1
Old Court Rd CM2 ....205 D3
Old Ct Chelmsford CM2 .205 D3
  Long Melford CO10 .....15 D8
Old Ferry Rd CO7 ....164 B8
Old Forge CO7 ....137 C2
Old Forge Rd
  Boreham CM3 ....206 E8
  Layer-de-l-H CO2 .....161 F5
Old Foundry Rd IP4 ...17 D6
Old Hall Cl CB9 ....27 C7
Old Hall La Capel St M IP9 35 F3
  Tollesbury CM9 ....199 C5
  Walton-on-t-N CO14 ...144 E3
Old Heath Prim Sch
  CO2 ....136 D3
Old Heath Rd CO1,CO2 .136 C4
Old House La CO4 ......83 B2
Old House Rd CO6 ....109 A8
Old Ipswich Rd CO7 ..110 E7
Old London Rd
  Capel St M IP9 ....59 F7
  Woodham Walter CM9 .208 E1
Old Maltings The **2**
  CM23 ....146 A7
Old Market Ct **3** CO10 .33 E7
Old Market Pl **2** CO10 .33 E7
Old Mead La CM22 ....94 D4
Old Mead Rd CM22 ....94 C5
Old Mill Chase CM7 ...73 C4
Old Mill La CO5 ......158 D7
Old Mill Rd Langham CO4 83 D5
  Saffron Walden CB11 ..43 E8
Old Parsonage Ct CM8 .176 F2
Old Parsonage Way
  CO13 ....170 F5
Old Pier St CO14 .....171 C8
Old Rd Clacton-on-S CO15 188 E4
  Coggeshall CO6,CO5 ..131 E1
  Frinton-on-S CO13 ....170 F4
  Pattiswick CM7 ....129 F5
  Wickham St P CO9 .....53 D5
Old River La CM23 ....145 F7
Old Rope Wlk CB9 ......8 F1
Old Rose Gdns CO4 ..109 D4
Old School Cl CO16 ..187 A4
Old School Ct CM3 ...194 B3
Old School Field CM1 .205 C4
Old School Ho IP9 .....91 B8
Old School Ho The CO5 164 A8
Old School La CO7 ....138 A6
Old School Yd CB11 ...43 D8
Old St The IP9 ....35 B1
Old Vicarage Rd CO12 .91 C3
Old Vicarage The CM7 .72 D6
Old Way CO13 ....170 F4

Oldbury Ave CM2 . . . . . .216 F8
Olde Forge CO7 . . . . . . .165 E1
Oldfield Rd IP8 . . . . .16 B1
Oldhouse Villas CM22 . . .148 C8
Olive Gr CO2 . . . . .135 D2
Oliver Pl CM8 . . . . .177 B2
Oliver Way CM1 . . . . . . .204 F7
Olivers Cl
　Clacton-on-S CO15 . . . . .188 E4
　Long Melford CO10 . . . . . .15 D7
Olivers Ct CO15 . . . . . . .188 E4
Olivers Dr CM8 . . . . .195 A7
Olivers La CO2 . . . . .135 A1
Olivers Rd CO15 . . . . . . .188 E4
Oliveswood Rd CM6 . . . . .150 D7
Olley Wlk CO5 . . . . .179 E6
Ongar Cl CO16 . . . . .188 E4
Ongar Rd
　Great Dunmow CM6 . . . . .150 D6
　Writtle CM1 . . . . .204 B1
Ongar Road Trad Est
　CM6 . . . . .150 E7
Onslow Cotts CO5 . . . . . .160 A7
Onslow Cres CM2 . . . . . .136 B1
Opal Ave IP1 . . . . .16 D8
Ophir Rd CO7 . . . . .185 F5
Orange St CM6 . . . . .70 A2
Orange Tree Cl CM2 . . . . .216 C6
Orchard Ave CO9 . . . . . . .76 D2
Orchard Cl
　Chelmsford CM2 . . . . . . .216 C6
　Clacton-on-S CO16 . . . . .188 C5
　Copford CO6 . . . . .133 D2
　Elmstead CO7 . . . . .138 A6
　Great Oakley CO12 . . . . .116 C3
　Hatfield Peverel CM3 . . . .194 A4
　Haverhill CB9 . . . . .8 F7
　Maldon CM9 . . . . .209 F2
　Newport CB11 . . . . .66 F8
　Ramsey CO12 . . . . .90 A2
　Ridgewell CO9 . . . . .29 B6
　Saffron Walden CB11 . . . . .43 D7
　Thaxted CM6 . . . . .70 A3
　Tollesbury CM9 . . . . .199 E1
　Writtle CM1 . . . . .204 B1
Orchard Cotts
　Boreham CM3 . . . . .193 A2
　Langham CO4 . . . . .83 F3
　Little Horkesley CO6 . . . . .81 E5
Orchard Ct CO3 . . . . . . .135 C7
Orchard Dr
　Braintree CM7 . . . . .128 A1
　Great Holland CO13 . . . . .170 A4
Orchard Field Ct CO5 . . . .201 E6
Orchard Gate IP2 . . . . . . .16 C5
Orchard Gdns CM4 . . . . .136 B8
Orchard Gr IP5 . . . . .18 F7
Orchard Lodge CO5 . . . . .179 D4
Orchard Mews CO5 . . . . .179 D4
Orchard Pightle CB1 . . . . . .5 C6
Orchard Rd
　Alresford CO7 . . . . .165 B8
　Bishop's Stortford CM23 . .119 B1
　3 Colchester CO1 . . . . .135 E8
　Kelvedon CO5 . . . . .158 C3
　Maldon CM9 . . . . .209 F2
Orchard St
　Chelmsford CM2 . . . . . . .205 B1
　9 Ipswich IP4 . . . . .17 D5
Orchard The CM6 . . . . . .152 C5
Orchard Way CO10 . . . . . . .2 B3
Orchards CM8 . . . . .176 F1
Orchid Ave CM8 . . . . . . .176 E4
Orchid Cl IP2 . . . . .16 E4
Orford Cres CM1 . . . . . . .205 D5
Orford Rd
　Felixstowe IP11 . . . . . . .221 C1
　Haverhill CB9 . . . . .8 F6
Orford St IP1 . . . . .17 B7
Oriel Cl CO10 . . . . .34 B6
Oriole Way CM23 . . . . . .145 C6
Orion Way CM7 . . . . .128 B4
Orkney Cl CB9 . . . . .9 D7
Orlando Ct CO14 . . . . . . .171 C8
Ormonde Cl CO6 . . . . . . .108 E4
Orpen Cl CO6 . . . . .108 D4
Orpen's Hill CO2 . . . . . . .161 A5
Orplands Cotts CM0 . . . . .214 F1
Orsino Wlk CO4 . . . . . . .136 F7
Orvis La CO7 . . . . .59 E1
Orwell Bsns Ctr IP3 . . . . . .17 E2
Orwell Cl CO4 . . . . .110 C1
Orwell Country Pk★
　IP3 . . . . .38 B6
Orwell Ct **1** IP4 . . . . .17 D5
Orwell Gdns IP2 . . . . .17 A3
Orwell High Sch IP11 . . . .221 C5
Orwell Ho IP11 . . . . .221 A4
Orwell Hts IP2 . . . . .16 E2
Orwell Pl
　Chelmondiston IP9 . . . . . .63 F7
　2 Ipswich IP4 . . . . .17 D5
Orwell Rd
　Clacton-on-S CO15 . . . . .188 F2
　Felixstowe IP11 . . . . . . .221 D3
　Harwich CO12 . . . . .91 D4
　Ipswich IP3 . . . . .18 A4
Orwell Ret Pk IP2 . . . . . . .16 F5
Orwell Rise IP9 . . . . .63 F8
Orwell Way CO16 . . . . . .188 C6
Orwell Wlk CM8 . . . . . . .176 E4
Osbert Rd CM8 . . . . .194 E8
Osborne Cl CO15 . . . . . . .189 A7
Osborne Rd Ipswich IP3 . . .18 A4
　West Mersea CO5 . . . . . .201 C6
Osborne St CO2 . . . . . . .135 F6
Osbourne Gdns **5**
　CM23 . . . . .145 E5

Osbournes Ct CO7 . . . . . .185 F6
Osea Rd CM9 . . . . .211 B3
Osea Way CM1 . . . . .205 F5
Osier Pl **3** CB9 . . . . .8 F8
Osmond Cl CM77 . . . . . .155 B5
Osprey Rd CB9 . . . . .9 C7
Osprey Way CM2 . . . . . . .216 A5
Ospreys CO15 . . . . .188 F6
Ostler Cl CM23 . . . . .145 C4
Othello Cl CO4 . . . . .136 F8
Otho Dr CO4 . . . . .110 A6
Otley Cl IP11 . . . . .221 B5
Otten Rd CO10 . . . . .13 B1
Ottershaw Way CO16 . . . .188 B6
Oulton Cl CO12 . . . . .90 F3
Oulton Rd IP3 . . . . .17 E2
Our Lady Immaculate RC
　Prim Sch CM2 . . . . .205 A1
Ouse Chase CM8 . . . . . . .176 D2
Outpart Eastward CO12 . . .91 E6
Over Hall La CB10 . . . . .6 D2
Overchurch Cl CB9 . . . . . . .8 F7
Overhall Hill CO6 . . . . .78 C2
Overstone Ct CO2 . . . . . .135 C3
Ovington Pl **16** CB9 . . . . . .9 B8
Owen Ward Cl CO2 . . . . .135 A3
Owl's Hill CM3 . . . . .175 B3
Owls Retreat **1** CO4 . . . .136 F8
Ox Yd CO9 . . . . .102 E7
Oxborrow Cl CO13 . . . . .170 A6
Oxcroft CM23 . . . . .145 F3
Oxenford Cl CO12 . . . . . . .90 F1
Oxford Cl CO10 . . . . .34 A6
Oxford Cres CO15 . . . . . .188 F4
Oxford Ct
　Chelmsford CM2 . . . . . . .205 E4
　Earls Colne CO6 . . . . . . .105 B6
Oxford Ho CB9 . . . . .9 B6
Oxford La CO9 . . . . .51 D2
Oxford Mdw CO9 . . . . . . .51 D2
Oxford Pl CO6 . . . . .105 B6
Oxford Rd
　Clacton-on-S CO15 . . . . .188 F4
　Colchester CO3 . . . . .135 D6
　Frinton-on-S CO13 . . . . .171 A5
　Halstead CO9 . . . . .76 D1
　Ipswich IP4 . . . . .17 E5
　Manningtree CO11 . . . . . .86 D4
Oxley Hill Abberton CO5 . .163 A3
　Tollesbury D'arcy CM9 . . .198 B8
　Tollesbury Knights CM9 . .180 A1
Oxley Ho CM77 . . . . .155 B5
Oxley Parker Dr CO4 . . . .110 A6
Oxlip Rd CM8 . . . . .176 E4
Oxney Villas CM6 . . . . . .152 D6
Oxton Cl CO5 . . . . .164 A8
Oyster Bsns Ctr CM9 . . . .199 F2
Oyster Cl CO5 . . . . .201 C7
Oyster Cotts CM0 . . . . . .213 C1
Oyster Pk CO1 . . . . .136 C6
Oyster Pl CM2 . . . . .205 F4
Oyster Tank Rd CO7 . . . . .185 E5
Ozier Ct CB11 . . . . .43 E7
Oziers CM22 . . . . .94 C2

P

Packard Ave IP3 . . . . .18 B2
Packards La CO6 . . . . .80 F1
Packe Cl CO5 . . . . .158 D4
Paddock Cl CO12 . . . . . . .91 C4
Paddock Dr CM1 . . . . . . .205 E8
Paddock The CM23 . . . . .145 D3
Paddock Way CO7 . . . . . .137 C3
Paddocks The
　Abberton CO5 . . . . .163 A4
　Ashen CO10 . . . . .11 D1
　Bures CO8 . . . . .79 E8
　Great Bentley CO7 . . . . .166 F5
　Great Totham CM9 . . . . .196 A4
　West Mersea CO5 . . . . . .201 D6
　Witham CM8 . . . . .177 A2
Paeony Chase CO5 . . . . . .201 C8
Page Cl CM8 . . . . .194 D8
Page Rd CO15 . . . . .188 E3
Pages Cl CM23 . . . . .145 D5
Pages La CM9 . . . . .198 F1
Paget Ct CM22 . . . . .94 C1
Paget Rd Ipswich IP1 . . . . .17 B7
　Rowhedge CO5 . . . . .163 F8
　Wivenhoe CO7 . . . . .164 C8
Paignton Ave CM1 . . . . . .205 D5
Pakenham Pl **18** CB9 . . . . . .9 B8
Palace Gdns CM23 . . . . . .145 E6
Palfrey Hts CO11 . . . . . . .86 D8
Palm Cl Chelmsford CM2 . .216 C6
　Witham CM8 . . . . .177 A5
Palmers Croft CM2 . . . . .206 A2
Palmers La
　8 Bishop's Stortford
　CM23 . . . . .145 F7
　Chrishall SG8 . . . . .22 A6
Palmerston Lodge CM2 . .216 F7
Palmerston Rd
　Ipswich IP4 . . . . .17 E6
　Thorpe-le-S CO16 . . . . . .142 A2
Palmerswent Cl CO10 . . . .15 D8
Pamela Gdns CM23 . . . . .145 F3
Pampas Cl CO4 . . . . .110 A4
Pan Wlk CM1 . . . . .204 D5
Panfield La CM7 . . . . .127 E5
Pannells Ash CO10 . . . . . .11 D1
Pannels Cl CO10 . . . . .2 B4
Pantile Cl CM8 . . . . .195 A7
Pantlings La CO5 . . . . . . .158 A5

Panton Cres **7** CO4 . . . . . .136 E7
Panton Mews CM7 . . . . . .155 A8
Papermill Cotts CO9 . . . . .76 C2
Papillon Rd CO3 . . . . .135 E7
Parade Dr CO12 . . . . .90 C1
Parade Rd IP4 . . . . .17 F7
Parade The
　Colchester CO2 . . . . . . .136 A1
　Kirby Cross CO13 . . . . . .170 B6
　Walton-on-t-N CO14 . . . .171 C8
Paradise Rd CM1 . . . . . . .215 B8
Pardoe Pl IP3 . . . . .18 E5
Park Ave
　Bishop's Stortford CM23 . .145 F4
　Chelmsford CM1 . . . . . . .204 F4
　Felixstowe IP11 . . . . . . .221 F5
Park Bvd CO15 . . . . .189 E6
Park Chase CO16 . . . . . . .187 C5
Park Cl CO10 . . . . .34 A8
Park Cotts Gosfield CO9 . .102 E8
　Manningtree CO11 . . . . . .86 D3
　St Osyth CO16 . . . . .187 A5
Park Ct Felixstowe IP11 . . .221 D2
　Sible Hedingham CO9 . . . .51 D1
Park Dr Braintree CM7 . . . .155 A8
　Brightlingsea CO7 . . . . . .185 E7
　Halstead CO9 . . . . .76 E1
　Maldon CM9 . . . . .210 B1
Park Drive Par CO7 . . . . .185 E7
Park Farm Ind Est SG8 . . .39 C2
Park Farm La SG8 . . . . . . .39 C2
Park Gate Cotts CM7 . . . .101 C6
Park Gate Rd CM7 . . . . . .157 B3
Park La
　Bishop's Stortford CM23 . .145 F4
　Bulmer Tye CO10 . . . . . . .32 F2
　Castle Camps CB1 . . . . . . .7 F3
　Earls Colne CO6 . . . . . . .105 B6
　Glemsford CO10 . . . . .2 D4
　Langham CO4 . . . . .83 E3
　Langley CB11 . . . . .40 A3
　Saffron Walden CB10 . . . .22 D1
　Tolleshunt Knights CM9 . .180 B3
　Toppesfield CO9 . . . . . . .50 B7
Park Lane Cl CO6 . . . . . . .105 B6
Park N IP4 . . . . .17 D8
Park Rd Ardleigh CO7 . . . .111 F3
　Chelmsford CM1 . . . . . . .205 B2
　Clacton-on-S CO15 . . . . .188 D2
　Colchester CO3 . . . . .135 C6
　East Bergholt CO7 . . . . . .60 B2
　Elsenham CM22 . . . . .94 D1
　Ford End CM3 . . . . .172 A3
　Great Chesterford CB10 . . .3 E5
　Harwich CO12 . . . . .91 D4
　Haverhill CB9 . . . . .8 D8
　Ipswich IP1 . . . . .17 C8
　Little Bentley CO7 . . . . . .139 D8
　Little Easton CM6 . . . . . .122 F3
　Little Horkesley CO6 . . . . .82 B8
　Maldon CM9 . . . . .209 F2
　Rivenhall CM8 . . . . .157 A2
　Stansted Mountfitchet
　CM24 . . . . .119 E6
　Stoke-by-N CO6 . . . . . . .56 E4
　Sudbury CO10 . . . . .34 A8
　Wivenhoe CO7 . . . . .164 C8
　Wivenhoe, Wivenhoe Park
　CO4 . . . . .137 A4
Park Side CM6 . . . . .124 D6
Park Sq E
　Clacton-on-S CO15 . . . . .203 G8
　Jaywick CO15 . . . . .188 A1
Park Sq W
　Clacton-on-S CO15 . . . . .203 F8
　Jaywick CO15 . . . . .187 F5
Park St Stoke-by-N CO6 . . .56 D5
　Thaxted CM6 . . . . .70 A2
Park Terr Harwich CO12 . . .91 D4
　Long Melford CO10 . . . . . .15 C7
Park The CO11 . . . . .86 D3
Park Vale Cl CO9 . . . . .51 E4
Park View CO10 . . . . .12 C7
Park View Cres CM2 . . . . .216 F5
Park View Rd IP1 . . . . .17 B8
Park Way CO15 . . . . .188 D1
Park Wood La CM9 . . . . .197 A3
Parkdale CM3 . . . . .218 C7
Parker Ct CM0 . . . . .214 F4
Parker Rd CM2 . . . . .205 C1
Parker Way CO9 . . . . .103 E8
Parker's Way CO6 . . . . . . .56 A1
Parkeston Rd
　Felixstowe IP11 . . . . . . .221 B4
　Harwich, Parkeston CO12 . .90 F4
　Harwich, Upper Dovercourt
　CO12 . . . . .91 A4
Parkfield St CO5 . . . . . . .163 F7
Parkfields CO9 . . . . .51 D1
Parkgate Cnr CO16 . . . . .169 A2
Parkhall Rd
　Beazley End CM7 . . . . . .101 E2
　Gosfield CO9 . . . . .102 B7
Parkins The IP9 . . . . .35 C2
Parkinson Dr CM1 . . . . . .204 F1
Parkland Ct CO1 . . . . . . .136 C5
Parklands Braintree CM7 . .155 A8
　Coggeshall CO6 . . . . . . .131 C4
Parklands Cl CO10 . . . . . . .2 C5
Parklands Cl CO16 . . . . . .188 B3
Parklands Dr CM1 . . . . . .205 D3
Parklands Way CM2 . . . . .216 C6
Parkside Haverhill CB9 . . . . .8 F6
　Saffron Walden CB10 . . . .22 C1
Parkside Ave IP4 . . . . .17 D7
Parkside Quarter CO1 . . . .135 E8

Parkway
　Chelmsford CM1 CM2 . . . .205 B2
　Shudy Camps CB1 . . . . . . .7 C6
Parkway Mid Sch CB9 . . . . .8 D8
Parkwood IP1 . . . . .17 C7
Parkwood Ave CO7 . . . . .137 B1
Parkwood Dr CO10 . . . . . .15 E2
Parliament Rd IP4 . . . . . . .18 B5
Parmenter Dr CO10 . . . . . .34 C5
Parnell Cl CO2 . . . . .136 A2
Parnham Pl IP4★ 18 F5
Parr Cl CM7 . . . . .128 D4
Parr Dr CO3 . . . . .134 E4
Parr Rd CB9 . . . . .8 D6
Parrington Way CO11 . . . . .86 A3
Parry Dr CO16 . . . . .188 C5
Parson's Field CO7 . . . . . .85 A6
Parson's Heath CO4 . . . . .110 E2
Parson's Hill CO3 . . . . . . .135 A6
Parsonage Cl
　Broomfield CM1 . . . . . . .191 A1
　Felixstowe IP11 . . . . . . .221 B4
Parsonage Downs CM6 . . .123 C3
Parsonage Farm La CB10 47 B4
Parsonage Farm Trad Est
　CM24 . . . . .119 F3
Parsonage Gdns **6** CB9 . . . .8 E8
Parsonage Gr CO8 . . . . . . .79 E8
Parsonage La
　Barnston CM6 . . . . .151 D3
　Bishop's Stortford CM23 . .146 C8
　Clavering CB11 . . . . .65 B3
　Elder Street CB10 . . . . . . .44 F3
　Howe Street CM3 . . . . . .172 F2
　Little Baddow CM3 . . . . .207 D2
　Stansted Mountfitchet
　CM24 . . . . .119 F4
　Tendring CO16 . . . . .140 E8
Parsonage Rd CM22 . . . . .148 C8
Parsonage St CO9 . . . . . . .76 F1
Parsons Cl **4** CO9 . . . . . . .76 F2
Parsons Heath CE Prim Sch
　CO4 . . . . .110 E2
Parsons Hill CO7 . . . . . . .138 F8
Parsons La CO1 . . . . .136 C6
Parsons Yd **10** CO11 . . . . . .86 D4
Partridge Ave CM1 . . . . . .204 F6
Partridge Cl CO12 . . . . . .116 D4
Partridge Dr CO6 . . . . . . .107 D5
Partridge Rd IP2 . . . . .16 E3
Partridge Way CO3 . . . . . .134 C4
Paschal Way CM2 . . . . . . .216 F8
Pashlers Alley CO10 . . . . . .12 B7
Paske Ave CO9 . . . . .8 F7
Pastures The IP4 . . . . .18 F5
Patching Hall La CM1 . . . .205 A6
Paternoster Row **6**
　CO14 . . . . .171 C8
Path The CO7 . . . . .166 E8
Pathfields Rd CO15 . . . . . .188 D4
Pathway The CO13 . . . . . .170 E6
Patmore Cl CM23 . . . . . . .145 C8
Patmore Fields CM22 . . . . .93 E6
Patmore Rd CO4 . . . . . . .110 D1
Patricia Gdns CM2 . . . . . .145 E5
Patten Cl CO6 . . . . .132 F3
Pattern Bush Cl CO11 . . . . .86 D8
Patterson Rd IP3 . . . . .17 E4
Patticroft CO10 . . . . .2 B3
Pattison Cl CM8 . . . . .195 A8
Pattock's La CO6 . . . . . . .106 C2
Pattrick's La CO12 . . . . . . .91 C4
Paul Spendlove Ct CO4 . .110 E1
Paul's Rd IP2 . . . . .16 F5
Pauline Cl CO15 . . . . .189 B6
Pauline St **8** IP2 . . . . .17 C4
Pauls Cres CO7 . . . . .137 F6
Pauls Way CO15 . . . . .188 A1
Pavilion Ct CB9 . . . . .9 B7
Pavitt Mdw CM2 . . . . . . .216 C2
Pawle Cl CM2 . . . . .217 A7
Paxman Ave CO2 . . . . . . .135 A3
Paxton Rd CO15 . . . . .189 B8
Paycocke Way CO6 . . . . . .131 C4
Paycocke's Ho★ CO6 . . . .130 F1
Payne's La CO13 . . . . . . .113 C3
Peace Rd CO3 . . . . .134 D7
Peacehaven CO13 . . . . . . .171 A5
Peacock Cl
　Braintree CM7 . . . . .127 F1
　5 Ipswich IP8 . . . . .16 C2
Peacocks Cl CO10 . . . . .1 C2
Peacocks Rd CO10 . . . . . . .1 C2
Peake Ave CO13 . . . . . . .170 A6
Peakes Cl CO5 . . . . .179 B4
Peal Rd CB11 . . . . .43 F7
Pear Tree Cl CO9 . . . . . . .77 A3
Pearce Manor CM2 . . . . . .215 F8
Pearce Rd IP3 . . . . .18 A5
Pearl Dr CM7 . . . . .128 C3
Pearl Rd IP1 . . . . .16 D8
Pearmain Way CO3 . . . . . .134 C4
Pearmain Wlk CB9 . . . . . . .8 C8
Pearmains CM3 . . . . .173 F7
Pearse Way IP3 . . . . .18 E1
Pearson Rd IP3 . . . . .18 C5
Pearsons Cl CO10 . . . . .2 B4
Peartree Bsns Ctr CO3 . . .134 E4
Peartree Cl
　Braintree CM7 . . . . .128 A1
　Goldhanger CM9 . . . . . . .211 E6
Peartree Hill CO8 . . . . . . .80 A5
Peartree La CM3 . . . . . . .218 F3
Peartree Rd CO3 . . . . . . .134 E4
Peartree Way CO16 . . . . . .168 C2
Peaslands Rd CB11 . . . . . .43 E8
Pebmarsh Cl CO2 . . . . . . .163 A8

Pebmarsh Rd
　Alphamstone CO8 . . . . . . .54 E2
　Colne Engaine CO6 . . . . . .77 F2
Pecockes Cl CO10 . . . . . . .34 C5
Peddars Ct CO10 . . . . .15 C7
Pedder's Cl CO3 . . . . .134 F3
Pedlars Cl CM3 . . . . .219 A6
Pedlars Path CM3 . . . . . . .219 A6
Pedler''s Cnr CO11 . . . . . . .86 D2
Peek's Cnr CO6 . . . . .105 D5
Peel Cres CM7 . . . . .127 E3
Peel Rd CM2 . . . . .205 F4
Peel St **5** IP1 . . . . .17 C6
Peers Sq CM2 . . . . .206 A4
Peerswood Rd CO2 . . . . . .135 D2
Peewit Ct IP11 . . . . .221 B3
Peewit Cvn Pk IP11 . . . . . .221 C2
Peewit Hill IP11 . . . . .221 B3
Peewit Rd IP2 . . . . .16 C3
Peg Millar's La CM3 . . . . .175 E5
Pegasus Way
　Braintree CM7 . . . . .127 E6
　Colchester CO4 . . . . . . .110 C1
Peggotty Cl CM1 . . . . . . .204 F6
Peldon Cres CO5 . . . . . . .182 E5
Peldon Rd Abberton CO5 . .182 E7
　Great Wigborough CO5 . . .182 A3
Pelham Cl CO12 . . . . .90 F2
Pelham Rd CB11 . . . . .65 C4
Pelham's La **18** CO1 . . . . . .135 F7
Pelican Cl IP2 . . . . .16 E3
Pelly Ave CM8 . . . . .195 A8
Pembroke Ave CM9 . . . . .209 F1
Pembroke Cl
　Colchester CO3 . . . . .136 C3
　Ipswich IP2 . . . . .17 B3
Pembroke Gdns CO15 . . . .189 E6
Pembroke Pl
　Chelmsford CM1 . . . . . . .205 B7
　Sudbury CO10 . . . . .15 D2
Pendleton Rd IP2 . . . . . . .16 D1
Penfold Rd
　Clacton-on-S CO15 . . . . .188 E2
　Felixstowe IP11 . . . . . . .221 E4
Penhaligon Ct **9** CM8 . . . .177 A2
Penlan Hall La CO6 . . . . . .107 B5
Penn Cl IP9 . . . . .35 B2
Penn Mews CM7 . . . . . . .155 A8
Pennine Rd CM1 . . . . . . .204 D5
Pennington La CM22,
　CM24 . . . . .93 D2
Penningtons CM23 . . . . . .145 C5
Pennsylvania La CO5 . . . .179 C5
Penny Cnr IP1 . . . . .16 C8
Penny La IP3 . . . . .18 F1
Penny Mdw IP9 . . . . .35 A1
Penny Royal Rd CM3 . . . .218 D6
Pennypot Cnr CO9 . . . . . .103 B6
Pennypot Cotts CO9 . . . . .103 B5
Pennyroyal Cres CM8 . . . .176 E4
Pennyroyal Gdns IP2 . . . . .16 E4
Pennystone Rd CB11 . . . . .43 E8
Penrice Cl CO4 . . . . .136 E6
Penrice Ct CO14 . . . . . . .144 D1
Penrose Mead CM1 . . . . . .215 B8
Penshurst Pl CM77 . . . . . .154 B6
Penshurst Rd IP3 . . . . .18 D4
Penticton Rd CM7 . . . . . .127 D2
Pentland Ave CM1 . . . . . .205 A6
Pentlow Dr CO10 . . . . .1 F1
Pentlow Hawke Cl CB9 . . . . .9 B7
Pentlow Hill CO10 . . . . . . .14 A8
Pentlow Ridge CO10 . . . . . .13 F6
Penzance Cl
　Chelmsford CM1 . . . . . . .205 E5
　Clacton-on-S CO15 . . . . .203 I8
Penzance Rd IP5 . . . . .18 F6
Pepper's Rd CO4 . . . . .82 E1
Peppercorn Cl CO4 . . . . . .109 F2
Peppercorn Way IP2 . . . . .17 D3
Pepples La Debden CB10 . . .69 A8
　Elder Street CB10 . . . . . . .45 A1
Pepys St CO12 . . . . .91 D5
Percival Rd
　Kirby-le-S CO13 . . . . . . .143 D1
　Walton-on-t-N CO14 . . . .144 D2
Peregrine Cl
　Bishop's Stortford CM23 . .145 D6
　Clacton-on-S CO15 . . . . .188 F7
Peregrine Ct CO4 . . . . . . .136 F8
Peregrine Dr CM2 . . . . . . .216 A4
Perkins Way IP3 . . . . .17 F1
Perriclose CM1 . . . . .205 D7
Perrin Pl CM2 . . . . .205 A1
Perry Hill CM1 . . . . .205 D3
Perry La CO4 . . . . .84 A4
Perry Rd Tiptree CO5 . . . .179 C5
　Witham CM8 . . . . .177 B1
Perry Way CM7 . . . . .177 B1
Perryfield CO10 . . . . .34 B4
Perryfields Jun & Inf Sch
　CM1 . . . . .205 D6
Persardi Ct CO2 . . . . .163 A7
Pershore End CO3 . . . . . .134 E5
Perth Cl CO2 . . . . .136 A1
Pertwee Cl CO7 . . . . .185 E8
Pertwee Dr CM2 . . . . . . .216 F6
Pertwee Way CO5 . . . . . .163 B2
Pertwees Ct CO1 . . . . . . .136 C6
Pesthouse La CO12 . . . . . .116 D3
Peter Bruff Ave CO16 . . . .188 C5
Peter's Gr IP9 . . . . .35 A1
Peterfield's La CO9 . . . . . .102 F5
Peterhouse Cl IP2 . . . . . . .16 F2

Peters Ho C05 ....158 C2
Petersfield CM1 ......205 B7
Peto Ave C04 ....109 F2
Petrebrook CM2 ....206 A3
Petrel Way CM2 ....216 C6
Petrolea Cl C04 ....109 F1
Petronius Way C04 ...110 B5
Pettit La CM77 ....156 A4
Petts La CB10 ....4 E1
Petunia Cres CM1 ....205 F6
Petworth Cl
  Great Notley CM77 ......154 B7
  Wivenhoe C07 ....164 C8
Pevensey Dr C015 ....203 I8
Peverel Ave CM23 .....194 C1
Peverells Rd CB10 ......44 D1
Pewterers Ave CM23 ..145 C4
Pharos La IP9 ....201 C6
Pheasant Rd IP2 ....16 E3
Pheasant Rise IP8 ......35 F8
Philip Ave IP11 ....221 B3
Philip Cl C014 ....171 A8
Philip Morant Sch C03 .135 B5
Philip Rd Ipswich IP2 ...17 C4
  Witham CM8 ....194 E8
Philips Cl CM77 ....126 F2
Philips Rd CM77 ......126 F2
Phillip Rd C07 ....164 B8
Phillips Chase CM7 ...128 A5
Phillips Field Rd C010 ..34 A5
Philpot End La CM6 ...150 B4
Phoenix Gr CM2 ....136 D5
Phoenix Gr CM2 ....216 A8
Phoenix Gr IP4 ....18 A7
Piccotts La CM7 ......126 B8
Pickers Way C015 ....189 E7
Pickford Wlk C04 .....136 F7
Pickpocket La CM77 ..154 D6
Pickwick Ave CM1 ....204 D6
Pickwick Rd IP2 ....16 E5
Pier App C014 ....171 C4
Pier Ave C015 ....188 E2
Pier Gap C015 ....188 F2
Pier Rd IP11 ....221 A1
Pierce Glade C05 .....179 C5
Pierrefitte Way CM7 ..127 E3
Pig La CM22 ....146 A3
Pigeon's La IP8 ....16 A3
Pightle The Capel St M IP9 35 B2
  Finchingfield CM7 ....72 B6
  Haverhill CB9 ....9 A8
Pightle Way C014 ....171 A4
Pigotts Way CM23 ....145 E5
Pilborough Way C03 ..134 E3
Pilcox Hall La C016 ...140 D8
Pilgrim Cl CM7 ....127 F5
Pilgrims Cl CB10 ....3 D2
Pimblett Row CM22 ....94 F5
Pimpernel Rd IP2 .....16 F3
Pin Mill Cl IP2 ....16 C1
Pincey Rd CM24 ......120 F3
Pincey Robin C04 ....121 A3
Pinchpools Rd CM23 ...93 A3
Pine Ave
  Great Dunmow CM6 ....123 B1
  Ipswich IP1 ....17 B8
Pine Cl Brantham C011 ..86 D8
  Great Bentley C07 .....166 F8
Pine Gr
  Bishop's Stortford CM23 .146 B6
  West Mersea C05 ....201 B7
  Witham CM8 ....177 A5
Pine Ho IP11 ....221 C4
Pine Tree Ct C04 .....136 E8
Pine View Rd IP1 ......17 A8
Pinecroft Gdns C04 ..110 B3
Pinecroft Rise C010 ...33 D5
Pinelands CM23 ......118 F1
Pines Hill CM24 ......119 D5
Pines Rd CM1 ....204 D5
Pines The CM3 ....194 A5
Pinetree Cl IP5 ....18 F7
Pinewood Cl
  Clacton-on-S C015 ....188 E7
  Kirby Cross C013 .....170 D6
Pink La CM3 ....175 D7
Pinkeneys SG8 ....19 E5
Pinkham Dr CM8 .....194 F8
Pinkney Cl CB10 ......44 E2
Pinkuah La C010 ......13 F6
Pinmill Rd IP9 ....63 F8
Pinner's Cross SG8 ....39 A7
Pintail Cl IP2 ....16 E3
Pintail Cres CM77 ....154 C6
Pioneer Pl **8** C01 ...136 A6
Pipchin Rd CM1 ......204 F6
Piper Rd C03 ....135 B7
Piper's Tye CM2 ......216 D3
Piper's Vale Com Prim Sch
  IP3 ....17 F1
Piperell Way CB9 ....9 A5
Piperell Way Units CB9 .9 A5
Pipers Cl CB9 ....9 C6
Pipers Vale Cl IP3 .....17 E1
Pippins The
  Glemsford C010 ....2 C4
  Halstead C09 ....76 D2
Pirie Rd C06 ....108 E3
Pit La C05 ....179 C6
Pitcairn Rd IP1 ....16 E8
Pitmire La C08 ....55 B6
Pitt Ave CM8 ....195 A8
Pitt Chase CM2 ......216 E5
Pitt Gn CM8 ....195 A8

Pitts End C07 ....59 D3
Place Farm Ct C02 ...136 D2
Place Farm Prim Sch CB9 .8 F8
Plains Farm Cl C07 ...110 D6
Plains Field CM7 .....128 D1
Plains Rd
  Great Totham CM9 .....196 F6
  Little Totham CM9 .....197 A6
Plaistow Green Rd C09 103 C5
Plaiters Way CM7 ....128 D3
Plane Tree Cl CM2 ...216 B6
Plane View Cl C016 ..188 B2
Plantation Cl CB11 ....43 E6
Plantation Rd CM3 ...192 F1
Planton Way C07 .....185 E6
Platters Cl IP3 ....38 B7
Platters Rd IP11 .....221 C2
Plaw Hatch Cl CM23 .146 B8
Plaw Hatch Cnr CM23 146 D8
Players Ct CM6 ....152 C6
Playford Ct **2** C010 ...33 E8
Playford Rd IP4 ....18 E8
Playle Chase CM9 ....196 B4
Pleasant Rd C015 ....145 E8
Pleasant Row **13** IP4 ..17 D5
Pleasant Valley CB11 ..43 D7
Pleasants Mews C05 ..201 C6
Pleshey Rd CM3 ......172 B5
Plough Cnr C016 .....168 C4
Plough Dr C03 ....135 A5
Plough La C010 ....33 D7
Plough Rd C07 ....166 E6
Plough St IP3 ....17 E4
Ploughmans Cl CM23 .145 C5
Ploughmans Headland
  C03 ....134 C5
Ploughmans La CM77 154 C8
Plover Cl C013 ......170 E6
Plover Rd IP2 ....16 E2
Plover Wlk CM2 .....216 B5
Plowright Ho **5** C01 135 B8
Plum St C010 ....2 A6
Plume Ave
  Colchester C03 ....135 A4
  Maldon CM9 ....209 F1
Plume Sch (Lower)
  CM9 ....210 A2
Plume Sch (Upper)
  CM9 ....209 F2
Plummers Rd C06 ....107 E7
Plumptre La CM3 ....218 D5
Plums La CM7 ....99 E4
Plumtree Ave CM2 ...216 F6
Plymouth Rd
  Chelmsford CM1 ......205 E5
  Clacton-on-S C015 ...203 J8
  Felixstowe IP11 ......221 D6
Pochard Way CM77 ..154 C5
Pocklington Cl CM2 ..206 A3
Pod's Brook Rd CM7 .127 D2
Pods La CM77 ....126 D2
Point Clear Bay Holiday Cvn
  Pk C016 ....185 F3
Point Clear Rd C016 ..186 D3
Pointwell La C06 .....158 A8
Pole Barn La C013 ...170 F5
Pole La CM8 ....155 C3
Polecat Rd CM77 ....155 F5
Pollard Ct IP2 ....16 D2
Pollard Wlk C016 ....188 C5
Pollard's Gn CM2 ....205 F2
Pollards Villas CM7 ...99 C3
Polley Cl C013 ......170 E7
Polstead St C06 ......56 D5
Polstead Way C016 ..188 B4
Pond Chase C03 .....135 B4
Pond Cl IP11 ....221 B5
Pond Cotts IP9 ....61 E2
Pond Cross Cotts CB11 .67 A8
Pond Cross Farm CB11 .67 A8
Pond Cross Way CB11 ..67 A8
Pond House La C015 .189 D8
Ponders Rd C06 ......107 C4
Pondfield Rd C04 ....110 D1
Pondholton Dr CM8 ..194 F7
Ponds Rd CM2 ....216 B1
Pondtail Ct C013 ....170 C6
Poney Chase CM8 ....195 F5
Poney's CM8 ....195 F5
Pontisbright Cotts C06 .106 C6
Poole Cl IP3 ....18 D3
Poole St Cavendish C010 ..1 C1
  Great Yeldham C09 .....51 B6
Poore St CB11 ....65 B8
Poors' Piece Nature Trail★
  CM3 ....207 F1
Pope's La C03 ....135 E7
Pope's Rd C06 ....106 D4
Poperinghe Rd C02 ..135 F4
Popes Ct CB9 ....9 E5
Poplar Ave C016 .....188 A2
Poplar Cl
  Chelmsford CM2 ......216 B6
  Clacton-on-S C015 ...188 B2
  Great Yeldham C09 ....30 A1
  Halstead C09 ....103 F8
  Witham CM8 ....177 A5
Poplar Cotts C05 ....160 C1
Poplar Ct C010 ....34 B7
Poplar Grove Chase
  CM9 ....210 B8
Poplar Hall Cl C01 ..109 E1
Poplar La IP8 ....16 B3
Poplar Rd C010 ......34 B7
Poplar Way C013 ....170 D6
Poplars Cl C07 ....165 B7

Poplars The
  Brantham C011 ....60 D2
  Great Dunmow CM6 ...123 C2
  Great Hallingbury CM22 146 F4
Poppy Cl IP2 ....16 F4
Poppy Gdns C02 .....136 C3
Poppy Gn CM1 ....206 A6
Pork La C013 ....169 E5
Port La
  Bishop's Stortford CM22 146 B2
  Colchester C01 ....136 B5
Port Of Felixstowe Rd
  IP11 ....221 A4
Portal Prec C01 .....135 F7
Porter Rd IP3 ....18 F1
Porter Way C016 ....188 B3
Porter's Cl C03 ......107 F2
Porter's Cotts C03 ...107 F1
Porter's La C03 ......107 F2
Porters Brook Wlk C04 110 C2
Porters Pk CM3 .....193 A2
Portland Ave C012 ...91 C3
Portland Cl CM7 .....128 B3
Portland Cres C012 ..91 C3
Portland Ho C015 ...170 F5
Portland Pl **17** CM23 145 F7
Portland Rd
  Bishop's Stortford CM23 .145 F7
  15 Colchester C02 ...136 F6
Portlight Cl C011 .....87 A4
Portman Rd IP1 ......17 B6
Portman Road (Ipswich Town
  FC) IP1 ....17 B5
Portman's Wlk IP1 ...17 A5
Portmans Walk Ind Ctr
  IP1 ....17 A5
Portobello Rd C014 .171 C8
Portreath IP11 ....205 A7
Portsmouth Rd C015 .203 J8
Portway CM2 ....206 B4
Portway Ct C09 ......76 F3
Posford Ct C04 .....109 F4
Post Mill Cl IP4 ......17 F6
Post Office Cnr IP9 ...61 F2
Post Office La
  Glemsford C010 ....2 B5
  Little Totham CM9 .....197 B4
Post Office Rd
  Chelmsford CM1 ......205 B8
  Woodham Mortimer CM9 219 E6
Postman's La CM3 ...207 E3
Pot Kiln Chase C09 ...31 F2
Pot Kiln Prim Sch C010 34 B6
Pot Kiln Rd C010 .....34 B6
Pot Kilns The C010 ...34 C6
Potash Cotts IP9 ......60 E8
Potash La IP9 ....60 E8
Potter St
  Bishop's Stortford CM23 .145 F7
  Sible Hedingham C09 ...75 E7
Potters Cl CM3 ......219 A6
Pottery La
  Castle Hedingham C09 ..51 F3
  Chelmsford CM1 ......205 A5
Poulk Hall La CM3 ...174 A5
Poulteney Rd CM24 ..119 E8
Pound Farm Dr C012 ..91 A3
Pound Fields CM1 ...215 B8
Pound Gate CM6 ....124 D6
Pound Hill Villas CM6 151 E8
Pound La IP9 ....59 F8
Pound Wlk CB10 ......22 C2
Poundfield Cl C07 ...165 B7
Poundfield Ho C07 ..138 A5
Powell Cl C05 ....179 E5
Powers Hall End CM8 176 B3
Powers Hall Inf & Jun Sch
  CM8 ....176 B3
Powling Rd IP3 ....18 A2
Pownall Cres C02 ....135 F4
Poynter Pl C013 .....170 E7
Prail Ct C06 ....130 F2
Pratt's La IP9 ....38 A2
Pratts Farm La CM3 .191 D4
Prentice Hall La CM9 213 B8
President Rd C03 ....134 E5
Preston Rd C015 ....189 D5
Prestwick Dr CM23 ..119 B1
Pretoria Rd C09 ......76 F2
Prettygate Jun & Inf Sch
  C03 ....135 B4
Prettygate Rd C03 ..135 A4
Pretyman Rd
  Felixstowe IP11 ......221 C1
  Ipswich IP3 ....18 B3
Prime's Cl CB10 ......22 D1
Primrose Cl CM23 ...145 C6
Primrose Hill
  Chelmsford CM1 ......204 F3
  Haverhill CB9 ....8 F7
  Holbrook IP9 ....62 D4
  Ipswich IP2 ....16 F4
Primrose La Ramsey C012 89 A1
  Tiptree C05 ....179 C6
Primrose Pl CM8 .....176 E4
Primrose Rd C015 ...189 E6
Primrose Wlk
  Colchester C04 ......136 E7
  Maldon CM9 ....210 B1
Primula Cl C016 .....188 C4
Primula Way CM1 ...206 A6
Prince Albert Rd C05 .201 D6
Prince Charles Cl
  Clacton-on-S C015 ...188 C1
  Sudbury C010 ....33 F8
Prince Charles Rd C02 136 A2
Prince Of Wales Dr IP2 .17 B2

Prince Of Wales Rd
  CM8,CM9 ....196 A3
Prince of Wales Rdbt
  C06 ....133 B4
Prince Philip Ave C015 188 C1
Prince Philip Rd C04 .136 A1
Prince St C010 ....33 E8
Prince's Espl C014 ..144 D1
Princel La C07 ....84 F7
Princel Mews C07 ....84 F7
Princes Ct CM23 ....145 C7
Princes Gate C02 ...145 C7
Princes Gdns IP11 ..221 D4
Princes Rd
  Chelmsford CM2 ......216 B7
  Clacton-on-S C015 ...189 D5
  Felixstowe IP11 ......221 C6
  Harwich C012 ....91 B3
  Maldon CM9 ....210 A2
Princes St IP1 ....17 B5
Princes Well CB10 ....45 F7
Princess Anne Cl C015 188 C1
Princess Dr C04 .....110 C5
Princess St C012 .....90 F5
Princess Way CB9 .....8 E8
Princethorpe Rd IP3 ..18 C1
Princeton Mews C04 .119 E5
Prior Cl C09 ....103 D8
Prior Way C04 ....109 E2
Prior's Hall Barn★ CB11 .67 D4
Prior's Wood Rd CM22 148 C7
Priors **9** CM23 ....146 A7
Priors Way C06 ......131 A3
Priory Ave CB9 ....8 F7
Priory Cl Chelmsford CM1 204 E2
  Hatfield Peverel CM3 .194 B1
  Ickleton CB10 ....3 A3
  Seawick C016 ....203 A6
Priory Ct
  Bishop's Stortford CM23 .145 F7
  Colchester C01 ....135 F7
  Hatfield Peverel CM3 .194 A4
  Ipswich IP10 ....38 C6
Priory Dr CM24 .....119 E5
Priory Farm Rd CM3 .194 B2
Priory Heath Prim Sch
  IP3 ....18 C1
Priory La Bicknacre CM3 218 E1
  Great Notley CM77 ...154 C8
Priory Mews CM3 ...194 C2
Priory Pk C016 ......187 A4
Priory Prim Sch CM3 194 C2
Priory Rd Bicknacre CM3 218 E1
  Chappel C06 ....106 B3
  Clacton-on-S C015 ...188 E3
  Sudbury C010 ....15 D1
  Tiptree C05 ....178 F3
Priory St Colchester C01 136 A7
  Earls Colne C06 ....105 B7
Priory The CM1 .....215 B8
Priory Wlk
  23 Colchester C01 .135 F7
  Sudbury C010 ....33 E7
Priory Wood C09 .....51 E4
Priory Wood Rdbt
  CM22 ....147 A8
Prittlewell Cl IP2 ....16 F1
Proctor Cl C015 .....163 B2
Proctor Way C06 ....132 E3
Proctors Way CM23 .146 A4
Progress Ct CM7 ....127 E3
Progress Way C016 ..168 C1
Promenade
  Clacton-on-S C015 ...203 D6
  Harwich C012 ....91 A4
  Harwich,Dovercourt C012 .91 C2
Promenade Way C07 .185 E5
Prospect Cl CM3 .....194 A3
Prospect Hill C010 ...34 D3
Prospect Pl CB11 ....22 F1
Prospect Rd IP1 .....17 A7
Prospect St **1** IP1 .17 A6
Prospero Cl C04 .....136 F8
Provence Cl C04 ....134 C7
Providence La IP1 ...17 A7
Providence Pl C01 ..136 B6
Providence St **6** IP1 17 C6
Prunus Ct C02 ....163 A2
Prykes Dr CM1 ......205 A2
Pryor Cl CM8 ....177 A1
Pryors Cl CM23 .....146 A6
Pryors Rd CM2 ......216 C2
Pudding La C02 .....161 B3
Puffinsdale C015 ....188 F5
Pulford Pl CM6 ......124 D7
Pulpitfield Cl C014 .171 A8
Pump Hill
  Great Baddow CM2 ...216 F6
  Harkstead SG9 ....64 A2
  St Osyth C016 ....187 D4
Pump Hill Cvn Pk C016 187 C4
Pump La Chelmsford CM1 205 E6
  Danbury CM3 ....218 D5
  Purleigh CM3 ....220 D1
Punchard Way IP11 ..221 A8
Punders Field CM7 ..128 D1
Purbeck Ct
  4 Colchester C01 ...136 D7
  Great Baddow CM2 ...216 E6
Purcell Cl Colchester C04 136 E6
  Writtle CM1 ....204 A1
Purdis Ave IP3 ....18 F2
Purdis Farm La IP3 ..18 F2
Purleigh Prim Sch CM3 220 D1
Purley Way C016 ....188 B6
Purplett Ho IP2 ......17 D4
Purplett St IP2 ....17 D4
Purvis Way C04 .....110 B5

Putticks La C07 ....59 E3
Pye Cnr C09 ....51 E4
Pyecat's Cnr C07 ....137 C7
Pyefleet Cl
  Brightlingsea C07 ....185 E7
  Fingringhoe C05 ......164 C6
Pyefleet Ho C05 .....201 D7
Pyefleet View C05 ...163 B3
Pyesand C013 ....170 C6
Pygot Pl CM7 ....127 E4
Pyms Rd CM2 ....216 B3
Pynchbek CM2 ......145 E3
Pynchon Mews CM1 205 D3
Pyne Gate CM2 .....216 B1

QM Ind Pk IP3 ....18 C1
Quadling St IP1 ......17 C5
Quadrangle Ctr The IP3 .18 C1
Quaker's La CB9 ....9 A7
Quale Rd C02 ....206 B4
Quantock Cl IP5 ......18 F7
Quay Ctyd **2** C011 ..86 D4
Quay La Beaumont C016 .142 B5
  Kirby-le-S C013 ......143 D1
  Sudbury C010 ....33 E6
Quay St
  1 Manningtree C011 .86 D4
  Wivenhoe C07 ....164 B8
Quay The Harwich C012 .91 D6
  Wivenhoe C07 ....164 B7
Quay Theatre C010 ...33 E6
Quayside Ind Est CM9 .210 A4
Queech La IP9 ....87 C8
Queech The IP9 ......35 B2
Queen Anne Dr C05 ..201 D6
Queen Anne Gdns C05 201 D6
Queen Anne Rd C05 .201 D7
Queen Edith Dr CB9 ..27 B6
Queen Elizabeth Ave
  C015 ....188 C1
Queen Elizabeth Way
  C02 ....136 A2
Queen Mary Ave C02 135 F4
Queen St
  Brightlingsea C07 ....185 F6
  Castle Hedingham C09 .51 E3
  Chelmsford CM2 ......205 A1
  Coggeshall C06 ....131 A2
  Colchester C01 ....135 F7
  Felixstowe IP11 ......221 C6
  Great Oakley C012 ...116 C4
  Haverhill CB9 ....9 A8
  Ipswich IP1 ....17 C5
  Maldon CM9 ....210 A2
  Sible Hedingham C09 ...75 F6
Queen Victoria Dr IP9 .91 B8
Queen's Ave C09 ....210 A1
Queen's Cotts C06 ..105 B7
Queen's Ct
  Clacton-on-S C015 ...189 D4
  6 Haverhill CB9 .....8 A7
Queen's Gdns CM7 ..127 B7
Queen's Head Rd C04 .82 C5
Queen's Ho C013 ...170 F4
Queen's Rd
  Chelmsford CM2 ......205 D2
  Clacton-on-S C015 ...188 D1
  Colchester C03 ....135 C6
  Earls Colne C06 ......105 B7
  Felixstowe IP11 ......221 E4
  Frinton-on-S C013 ...170 F4
  Harwich C012 ....91 A4
  West Bergholt C06 ...108 C3
  Wivenhoe C07 ....164 C8
Queen's Sq IP3 ....18 B2
Queen's Way IP3 .....18 B2
Queenborough Gr
  CM77 ....154 C8
Queenborough La
  Great Notley CM77 ...154 C8
  Rayne CM77 ....154 B8
Queenbury Cl C05 ..201 E6
Queens Cl
  Stansted Mountfitchet
  CM24 ....119 E8
  Sudbury C010 ....33 E8
Queens Cnr C05 .....201 D7
Queens Cres CM23 ..145 E5
Queens Ct C05 ......201 D7
Queens Mews C05 ..201 B6
Queens Rd
  Braintree CM7 ....127 F5
  Sudbury C010 ....33 E8
Queens Sq **5** CB9 ...9 A8
Queens Terr C010 ...34 A7
Queensberry Rd IP3 ..18 A1
Queensbury Ave C06 133 D5
Queenscliffe Rd IP3 ..17 A3
Queensgate Dr IP4 ..17 F8
Queensland Cres CM1 204 E5
Queensland Dr C02 ..136 A1
Queensway
  Clacton-on-S C015 ...189 D5
  Great Cornard C010 ...34 B5
  Haverhill CB9 ....8 E8
  Lawford C011 ....86 C4
  Tiptree C05 ....179 C6
Quendon Pl **17** CB9 ...9 B8
Quendon Way C013 ..171 A6
Quentin Cl IP1 ....16 E8
Quickset Rd CB11 ...20 C5
Quicksie Hill CB11 ...41 E2
Quilp Dr CM1 ....204 F7
Quilter Dr IP8 ....16 C1
Quilter Rd IP11 .....221 F4

Quilters Cl CO15 . . . . .189 F6
Quince Cl CO11 . . . . .60 D1
Quinion Cl CM1 . . . . .204 D7
Quinton's La IP11 . . . . . .221 F7
Quintons Cnr CO7 . . . . . . .59 D4
Quintons Rd CO7 . . . . . . .59 D4

R

R A Butler Jun & Inf Schs
CB11 . . . . .22 E1
Rachael Ct **1** CM2 . . . .205 B1
Rachael Gdns CM8 . . . .156 E4
Rachel Ct **6** IP4 . . . . . .17 D6
Radcliffe Dr IP2 . . . . . . .16 D2
Radiator Rd CO10 . . . . . .34 A5
Radwinter Prim Sch
CB10 . . . . .45 F7
Radwinter Rd
Ashdon CB10 . . . . .24 B7
Saffron Walden CB10 . . . .23 B1
Sewards End CB10 . . . . . .23 F1
Raeburn Cl CO13 . . . . . .170 F7
Raeburn Rd IP3 . . . . .18 A1
Raeburn Rd S IP3 . . . . . . .17 F1
Raglan Mews CO15 . . . .188 C3
Raglan Rd CO13 . . . . . . .171 A5
Ragley Cl CM77 . . . . . . .154 B6
Raile Wlk CO10 . . . . .15 D8
Railey Rd CB11 . . . . .43 E8
Railway App IP11 . . . . . .221 E5
Railway Cotts CB11 . . . . .42 F1
Railway Sq CM1 . . . . . . .205 A3
Railway St Braintree CM7 128 A3
Chelmsford CM1 . . . . . .205 A3
Manningtree CO11 . . . . . .86 D4
Railway Terr
Clacton-on-S CO15 . . . .188 F3
11 Manningtree CO11 . . . .86 D4
Rainbow Ct CO12 . . . . . . .91 D4
Rainbow Mead CM3 . . . .194 A5
Rainbow Mews CM9 . . . .209 F5
Rainbow Rd CO5 . . . . . .201 D6
Rainbow Way CO6 . . . . . .77 F1
Raine Ave CB9 . . . . .8 D8
Rainham Way CO13 . . . .171 B6
Rainsborowe Rd CO2 . . .135 C4
Rainsford Ave CM1 . . . . .204 F3
Rainsford La CM1 . . . . . .204 F2
Rainsford Rd
Chelmsford CM1 . . . . . .204 F3
Stansted Mountfitchet
CM24 . . . . .119 E8
Rambler Cl CO3 . . . . . . .134 D7
Rampart Cotts CO6 . . . . .109 B7
Ramparts Cl CO6 . . . . . .109 B7
Ramplings Ave CO15 . . . .188 C5
Ramsden Cl CO15 . . . . . .189 A5
Ramsey Cl
Heybridge CM9 . . . . . . .210 D4
Ipswich IP2 . . . . .17 A1
Ramsey Mews CO2 . . . . .136 A4
Ramsey Rd Halstead CO9 103 D8
Harwich CO12 . . . . .90 C2
Ramsey Sch (Priory Hall) The
CO9 . . . . .77 A2
Ramsey Sch The CO9 . . . .77 A2
Ramsgate Dr IP3 . . . . . . .18 B3
Ramshaw Dr CM2 . . . . . .205 F3
Rana Ct CM7 . . . . .127 F4
Rana Dr CM7 . . . . .127 F4
Randall Cl CM6 . . . . . . .123 D1
Randolph Ave CM7 . . . . . .73 C6
Randolph Cl Ipswich IP4 . .18 B5
Maldon CM9 . . . . .220 F8
Rands Way IP3 . . . . .18 B2
Randulph Terr CM1 . . . . .205 D3
Randwell Cl IP4 . . . . .18 B5
Ranelagh Ct IP11 . . . . . .221 E4
Ranelagh Prim Sch IP2 . .16 F5
Ranelagh Rd
Felixstowe IP11 . . . . . . .221 E4
Ipswich IP2 . . . . .17 A5
Ranger Wlk CO2 . . . . . . .136 B3
Rangoon Cl CO2 . . . . . . .135 B1
Ransom Cl CO5 . . . . . . .179 C5
Ransome Cl IP8 . . . . .16 A4
Ransome Cres IP3 . . . . . .18 B2
Ransome Rd IP3 . . . . .18 B3
Ransomes Europark IP3 .38 E8
Ransomes Way
Chelmsford CM1 . . . . . .205 B4
Ipswich IP3 . . . . .38 D8
Ranulph Way CM3 . . . . .194 B3
Raphael Dr CM1 . . . . . . .205 F7
Rapier St IP2 . . . . .17 C3
Rat Hill IP9 . . . . .63 F7
Ratcliffe Ct
Frinton-on-S CO13 . . . . .170 F5
Kelvedon CO5 . . . . .158 B2
Ratcliffe Rd CO3 . . . . . . .134 E6
Ravel Ave CM8 . . . . .194 F7
Raven Way CO4 . . . . . . .109 E4
Ravens Ave CO9 . . . . . . .76 F1
Ravens Cres CM6 . . . . . .152 E6
Ravensbourne Dr CM1 . .204 E2
Ravenscroft Prim Sch
CO16 . . . . .188 B4
Ravensdale CO15 . . . . . .188 F6
Ravenswood **11** CO1 . . .136 A6
Ravenswood Ave IP3 . . . .38 C8
Ravenswood Com Prim Sch
IP3 . . . . .38 C8
Ravenswood Way IP3 . . .38 B8
Rawden Cl CO12 . . . . . . .91 B4
Rawlings Cres CO4 . . . . .110 B5
Rawstorn Rd CO3 . . . . . .135 E7

Ray Ave CO12 . . . . .91 A3
Ray Ho CO5 . . . . .201 D7
Ray La Harwich CO12 . . . .90 E5
Ramsey CO12 . . . . .90 A3
Ray Mead CM3 . . . . .190 F7
Ray The CM1 . . . . .205 E5
Raycliff Ave CO15 . . . . . .188 E7
Raydon Way CO10 . . . . . .34 C6
Rayfield Cl CM6 . . . . . . .151 A4
Rayhaven CO2 . . . . .90 D2
Rayleigh Cl
Braintree CM7 . . . . .128 C4
Colchester CO4 . . . . . . .110 B1
Rayleigh Mans CO2 . . . .135 C5
Rayleighs The CO2 . . . . .135 C5
Rayments Bglws CB10 . . .45 E3
Rayne Prim Sch CM77 . .126 F2
Rayne Rd CM7 . . . . .127 D3
Rayner Rd CO2 . . . . .135 B4
Rayner Way CO9 . . . . . . .76 E1
Raynham Cl CM23 . . . . .146 C7
Raynham Rd CM23 . . . . .146 B8
Raynhams CB10 . . . . .22 D1
Reaburn Ct CM1 . . . . . . .205 E6
Reade Rd IP9 . . . . .62 D5
Reader's Cnr CM2 . . . . . .216 E5
Readers Ct CM2 . . . . . . .216 E6
Reading Rd IP4 . . . . .18 B7
Reaper Rd CO3 . . . . .135 A5
Rebecca Gdns CM8 . . . .156 E4
Rebecca Meade CM6 . . .152 C8
Rebow Rd Harwich CO12 . .91 A2
Wivenhoe CO7 . . . . .164 B8
Rebow St CO1 . . . . .136 B6
Reckitts Cl CO15 . . . . . . .189 B4
Recreation Cl IP11 . . . . .221 D6
Recreation Ground
CM24 . . . . .119 E6
Recreation La IP11 . . . . .221 D6
Recreation Rd
Clacton-on-S CO15 . . . .188 F3
Colchester CO1 . . . . . . .136 C5
Haverhill CB9 . . . . .8 F7
Sible Hedingham CO9 . . . .75 D8
Recreation Way
Brightlingsea CO7 . . . . .185 F7
Ipswich IP3 . . . . .18 B2
Recreation Wlk CO10 . . .34 B5
Rectory Dr CM23 . . . . . .118 D6
Rectory Field IP9 . . . . . . .63 E7
Rectory Hill
East Bergholt CO7 . . . . . .59 C1
Stoke-by-N CO6 . . . . . . .56 D7
Wivenhoe CO7 . . . . .137 C1
Rectory La Abberton CO5 163 A3
Ashdon CB10 . . . . .6 A1
Brantham CO11 . . . . .60 E1
Chelmsford CM1 . . . . . .205 B4
Farnham CM23 . . . . .118 D6
Great Leighs CM3 . . . . . .173 D7
Ramsey CO12 . . . . .90 A1
Rivenhall CM8 . . . . .177 A6
Wickham St P CO9 . . . . . .53 C6
Woodham Mortimer CM9 .219 F6
Rectory Mdw CM7 . . . . .129 C2
Rectory Mdws CM7 . . . . .51 B4
Rectory Rd Aldham CO6 .132 F7
Copford CO6 . . . . .133 C1
Frating CO7 . . . . .138 F1
Great Henny CO10 . . . . . .33 E4
Great Holland CO13 . . . .170 A3
Harkstead IP9 . . . . .63 C2
Ipswich IP2 . . . . .17 C4
Langham CO4 . . . . .83 F7
Little Bentley CO7 . . . . . .139 E8
Little Oakley CO12 . . . . .117 A7
Rowhedge CO5 . . . . .163 E8
Sible Hedingham CO9 . . . .51 D1
Stisted CM7 . . . . .129 B7
Tiptree CO5 . . . . .179 C5
Tolleshunt Knights CM9 . .180 C1
Weeley Heath CO16 . . . .167 F3
Wivenhoe CO7 . . . . .137 C2
Woodham Walter CM9 . . .208 D3
Wrabness CO11 . . . . .89 A3
Writtle CM1 . . . . .215 B8
Red Barn La CO12 . . . . .116 B2
Red Barn Rd CO7 . . . . . .185 F8
Red House La
Great Cornard CO10 . . . .34 A4
Sudbury CO10 . . . . .33 E7
Red La IP9 . . . . .60 A8
Red Lion Ct **5** CM23 . . .146 A7
Red Lion Yd **17** CO1 . . . .135 F7
Red Sleeve **5** IP9 . . . . .35 A1
Redan St IP1 . . . . .17 B7
Redbridge Rd CO15 . . . .188 F8
Redcliffe Rd **3** CM2 . . .205 A1
Reddells **3** CO10 . . . . . .33 F8
Rede Way CO10 . . . . .34 C6
Redgate La IP9 . . . . .37 D5
Redgates La CB10 . . . . . .23 E3
Redgates Pl CM2 . . . . . .205 D4
Redhouse La CO4 . . . . . . .82 D2
Redmayne Dr CM2 . . . . .215 F8
Redmill CO3 . . . . .135 A3
Redrose Wlk CO16 . . . . .188 C4
Redruth Cl CM1 . . . . . . .205 E5
Redshank Cl CB9 . . . . . . .9 C7
Redshank Dr CM9 . . . . . .210 C5

Redvers Cl CM23 . . . . . .119 A2
Redwing Cl IP2 . . . . .16 D3
Redwood Cl
Colchester CO4 . . . . . . .110 E1
Witham CM8 . . . . .177 A6
Redwood Ct **2** CO4 . . .136 E8
Reed Cl CO16 . . . . .188 C5
Reed Hall Ave CO2 . . . . .135 D3
Reedland Way IP11 . . . . .221 B5
Reeds La CB9 . . . . .9 A8
Refinery Rd CO12 . . . . . . .90 E5
Regal Ct CM2 . . . . .216 D8
Regency Cl
Bishop's Stortford CM23 .145 D4
Chelmsford CM2 . . . . . .205 D3
Regency Ct
Heybridge CM9 . . . . . . .210 A5
Ipswich IP3 . . . . .17 F5
Regency Gn CO3 . . . . . . .135 A4
Regent Cl CO7 . . . . .185 F8
Regent Ct CO5 . . . . .164 A8
Regent Rd CO7 . . . . .185 F7
Regent St Ipswich IP4 . . . .17 E6
9 Manningtree CO11 . . .86 D4
Rowhedge CO5 . . . . .164 A8
Regents Cl CO4 . . . . .110 C5
Regimental Way CO12 . . .90 C1
Regina Cl IP4 . . . . .18 B5
Regina Rd CM1 . . . . .205 C3
Reigate Ave CO16 . . . . . .188 D6
Reigate Cl IP3 . . . . .18 B3
Rembrandt Gr CM1 . . . . .205 E6
Rembrandt Way CO3 . . .135 B5
Rembrow Rd IP9 . . . . . . .35 A1
Remembrance Ave CM4 .194 A3
Remercie Rd CO11 . . . . . .87 A4
Remus Cl CO4 . . . . .109 F5
Rendlesham Ct **8** IP1 . .17 A7
Rendlesham Rd
Felixstowe IP11 . . . . . . .221 B5
Ipswich IP1 . . . . .17 A6
Renfrew Rd IP4 . . . . .18 B8
Rennie Pl CM2 . . . . .206 B3
Renoir Pl CM1 . . . . .205 F7
Retreat The
West Bergholt CO6 . . . . .108 D3
Witham CM8 . . . . .177 A1
Reverdy Ho CO2 . . . . . . .135 E2
Reydon Cl CB9 . . . . .8 C8
Reydon Ho IP3 . . . . .18 A2
Reymead Cl CO5 . . . . . .201 C6
Reynard Copse CM23 . . .118 F1
Reynard Ct CM2 . . . . . . .216 F6
Reynard Hts CO4 . . . . . .136 C8
Reynards Cl CO13 . . . . . .170 D6
Reynards Copse CO4 . . .110 A5
Reynolds Ave
Colchester CO3 . . . . . . .135 B5
Ipswich IP3 . . . . .38 A8
Reynolds Ct IP11 . . . . . .221 B5
Reynolds Rd IP3 . . . . . . .18 A1
Rhodes Ave CM23 . . . . .145 F5
Riby Rd IP11 . . . . .221 D3
Rice Bridge Ind Est
CO16 . . . . .169 A7
Rich Cl CM3 . . . . .173 F7
Richard Ave
Brightlingsea CO7 . . . . .185 F6
Wivenhoe CO7 . . . . .137 C3
Richard Burn Way CO10 .15 E2
Richard de Clare Com Prim
Sch CO9 . . . . .76 F1
Richard Whittington Prim
Sch The CM23 . . . . . .145 E4
Richards Wlk CO15 . . . . .188 E6
Richardson Pl CM1 . . . . .204 F4
Richardson Rd CO7 . . . . .59 D3
Richardson Wlk
Colchester CO4 . . . . . . .134 F5
Witham CM8 . . . . .177 B2
Richardsons La IP9 . . . . .63 D8
Riche Cl CM6 . . . . .152 B5
Richmond Cl CM23 . . . . .145 C7
Richmond Cres CO12 . . .91 B2
Richmond Dr CO15 . . . . .188 A1
Richmond Ho **20** IP4 . . .17 D5
Richmond Rd
Chelmsford CM2 . . . . . .206 A4
Ipswich IP1 . . . . .16 F8
West Mersea CO5 . . . . . .201 D6
Rickling CE Prim Sch
CB11 . . . . .93 E8
Rickling Green Rd
Quendon CB11 . . . . .66 E1
Rickling Green CB11 . . . .93 E8
Rickling Rd CB11 . . . . . . .66 B6
Rickstones Rd CM8 . . . . .177 A6
Rickstones Sch The
CM8 . . . . .176 F6
Riddiford Dr CM1 . . . . . .204 F4
Riddles Dr CO4 . . . . .109 F2
Ridge The Braintree CM7 .128 B6
Little Baddow CM3 . . . . .207 B6
Walton-on-t-N CO14 . . . .171 B8
Ridgeway CO4 . . . . .110 A4
Ridgeway The
Braintree CM7 . . . . .128 A1
Harwich CO12 . . . . .91 B3
Ridgewell Ave CM1 . . . . .204 F4
Ridgewell CE Prim Sch
CO9 . . . . .29 B6
Ridgewell Rd
Birdbrook CO9 . . . . .10 E2
Great Yeldham CO9 . . . . .29 E3
Ridgewell Way CO2 . . . .135 F1
Ridings Ave CM77 . . . . . .154 B7

Ridings The
Bishop's Stortford CM23 .145 D4
Great Baddow CM2 . . . . .216 D7
Ridlands Cl CM77 . . . . . .155 E6
Ridley Gdns CM22 . . . . . .94 C2
Ridley Rd CM1 . . . . .205 B8
Riffhams Chase CM3 . . . .207 D2
Riffhams Dr CM2 . . . . . .217 A7
Riffhams La
Danbury CM3 . . . . .218 C8
Little Baddow CM3 . . . . .207 C8
Rifle Hill CM7 . . . . .127 F1
Rifle Hill Works CM7 . . . .127 F1
Rigby Ave CO11 . . . . .87 A3
Rigby Rd CO11 . . . . .87 A4
Rignal's La CM2 . . . . . . .216 D3
Riley Ave CO15 . . . . .203 E6
Rimini Cl CO2 . . . . .135 C3
Ringham Rd IP4 . . . . .18 A6
Ripley Cl CO16 . . . . .188 B6
Ripple Way CO4 . . . . . . .110 B1
Risby Cl
Clacton-on-S CO16 . . . . .188 A4
Ipswich IP4 . . . . .18 B6
Rise The CO6 . . . . .134 A8
Ritabrook Rd IP2 . . . . . . .16 E1
Rivenhall CE Prim Sch
CM8 . . . . .177 B8
River Blackwater Chalet Site
CM9 . . . . .210 C3
River Cl CO9 . . . . .76 F1
River Cotts CM3 . . . . . . .206 F8
River Hill CM3 . . . . .175 B3
River Mead CM7 . . . . . . .128 A4
River View Braintree CM7 127 F1
Holbrook IP9 . . . . .62 D5
Manningtree CO11 . . . . . .86 C4
Witham CM8 . . . . .195 A8
River View Rd IP9 . . . . . . .63 B2
Riverbank Cl CO10 . . . . . .12 C7
Riverdale Ct IP11 . . . . . .221 D3
Rivermead Gate CM1 . . .205 B4
Rivermead Ind Est CM1 .205 B4
Rivers Ho CO14 . . . . . . .144 D2
Rivers St IP4 . . . . .17 F7
Riverside
Bishop's Stortford CM23 .145 F7
Bradwell CM7 . . . . .129 A3
Chelmsford CM1 . . . . . .205 C3
Great Dunmow CM6 . . . .123 C1
Riverside Ave E CO11 . . . .86 C5
Riverside Ave W CO11 . . .86 C5
Riverside Bsns Pk
Earls Colne CO6 . . . . . . .104 F8
Stansted Mountfitchet
CM24 . . . . .119 E6
Riverside Cotts CO11 . . . .86 C5
Riverside Ct CO7 . . . . . . .76 E2
Riverside Ind Pk IP2 . . . .17 D3
Riverside Pk CM1 . . . . . .205 C3
Riverside Rd IP1 . . . . . . .16 F7
Riverside Way CO5 . . . . .158 C2
Riverside Wlk
16 Bishop's Stortford
CM23 . . . . .145 F7
Colchester CO1 . . . . . . .135 E8
Riverton Dr CM0 . . . . . . .213 B1
Rivish La CO10 . . . . .15 C7
Roach Vale CO4 . . . . . . .110 E1
Roach Vale Prim Sch
CO4 . . . . .110 E1
Robeck Rd IP3 . . . . .17 F1
Robert Cl CM2 . . . . .205 F4
Robert Suckling Ct CB9 . .27 B6
Robert Wallace Cl
CM23 . . . . .118 F1
Robert Way CO7 . . . . . . .137 C3
Robert's Hill CO8 . . . . . . .79 F3
Roberts Ct CM2 . . . . . . .216 E7
Roberts Rd CO1,CO2 . . . .136 A5
Robin Cl
Great Bentley CO7 . . . . .166 D8
Haverhill CB9 . . . . .9 C7
Robin Cres CO3 . . . . . . .134 B4
Robin Dr IP2 . . . . .16 D3
Robin Hood Rd CM22 . . . .94 C1
Robin Way
Chelmsford CM2 . . . . . .216 B5
Sudbury CO10 . . . . .33 C5
Robinia Ct **1** CO4 . . . . .136 E7
Robinsbridge Rd CO6 . . .130 F2
Robinsdale CO15 . . . . . .188 F6
Robinson Cl CM23 . . . . .145 F5
Robinson Rd CO7 . . . . . .186 A7
Robjohns Rd CM1 . . . . . .215 B8
Robletts Way CO6 . . . . . .80 E4
Rochdale Way CO4 . . . . .136 E6
Rochelle Cl CM6 . . . . . . .70 A3
Rochester Ct CM7 . . . . . .128 D4
Rochester Ct CB10 . . . . .22 F2
Rochester Way CO10 . . . .15 D2
Rochford Ct CM24 . . . . .119 E5
Rochford Rd
Bishop's Stortford CM23 .119 C1
Chelmsford CM2 . . . . . .205 C1
St Osyth CO16 . . . . .187 B4
Rochford Way
Frinton-on-S CO13 . . . . .170 F7
Walton-on-t-N CO14 . . . .171 A7
Rockall Cl CM3 . . . . .9 D7
Rockhampton Wlk **10**
CO2 . . . . .136 A1
Rockingham Cl CO4 . . . .110 D3
Rodbridge Hill CO10 . . . .15 B5
Rodbridge Nature Reserve*
CO10 . . . . .15 B4
Roddam Cl CO3 . . . . . . .135 C6
Roding Ct CM7 . . . . .128 D1

Rodney Gdns CM7 . . . . .128 C4
Rodney Way CM1 . . . . . .215 E7
Rogation Cl CO3 . . . . . . .134 D6
Rogers Cl IP11 . . . . .221 D6
Rokell Way CO13 . . . . . .170 F6
Rolands Cl CM1 . . . . . . .205 B7
Rollerworld* CO1 . . . . . .136 B7
Rolley La CO5 . . . . .158 C2
Rolph CE Prim Sch
CO16 . . . . .141 F1
Rolph Cl CO16 . . . . .142 A2
Roman Ct Braintree CM7 128 C1
Saffron Walden CB11 . . . .43 E7
Roman Ho **3** CM2 . . . .205 B1
Roman La CM24 . . . . . . .120 B2
Roman Rd
Colchester CO1 . . . . . . .136 A7
Little Waltham CM3 . . . .191 B5
Roman Way
Great Dunmow CM6 . . . .123 C1
Haverhill CB9 . . . . .9 D7
Littlebury CB11 . . . . .21 F4
Long Melford CO10 . . . . .15 C6
Point Clear B CO16 . . . . .186 A3
Romans Pl CM1 . . . . . . .204 B1
Romans Way CM1 . . . . .204 B1
Romanshurst CM9 . . . . .210 A4
Romford Cl CO4 . . . . . . .136 B8
Romney Cl
Braintree CM7 . . . . .127 E6
Brightlingsea CO7 . . . . .165 E4
Clacton-on-S CO16 . . . .188 D3
Kirby Cross CO13 . . . . . .170 E7
Romney Rd IP3 . . . . .38 A8
Romulus Cl CO4 . . . . . . .109 F5
Ronald Rd CO9 . . . . .103 E8
Rook End La CB11 . . . . . .68 B5
Rookeries The CO6 . . . . .133 B4
Rookery Chase CO7 . . . . .84 C2
Rookery Cl
Great Chesterford CB10 . . .3 D3
Hatfield Peverel CM3 . . . .194 A5
Rookery La
Great Totham CM9 . . . . .196 E7
Tiptree CO5 . . . . .179 C7
Wendens Ambo CB11 . . . .42 E4
Rookery The
Lawford CO11 . . . . .86 C4
Stansted Mountfitchet
CM24 . . . . .119 E8
Rookes CB10 . . . . .22 D3
Rookes Cres CM1 . . . . . .215 F8
Rookwood Cl CO15 . . . . .188 D7
Rookwood Way CB9 . . . . .9 A6
Roos Hill Debden Rd
CB11 . . . . .43 E5
Roosevelt Way CO2 . . . . .136 B4
Roothings The CM9 . . . . .210 B5
Roots La CM8 . . . . .195 E5
Rope Wlk Ipswich IP4 . . . .17 E5
Maldon CM9 . . . . .210 A1
Roper Ct IP4 . . . . .18 C5
Roper's Chase CM1 . . . . .215 A7
Ropers La CO10 . . . . .15 B5
Rosabelle Ave CO7 . . . . .137 B1
Rosalind Cl CO4 . . . . . . .136 E6
Rose & Crown Wlk CB10 .22 D2
Rose Acre CO7 . . . . .58 F6
Rose Ave CO3 . . . . .134 C4
Rose Cotts
Great Sampford CM7 . . . .47 E5
Harkstead SG9 . . . . .64 A5
Rose Cres CO9 . . . . .109 D2
Rose Ct CO2 . . . . .163 B8
Rose Gdns
Braintree CM7 . . . . .128 A2
Seawick CO16 . . . . .203 B6
Rose Glen CM2 . . . . .216 C7
Rose Green Cotts CO6 . .106 E5
Rose Hill CM7 . . . . .128 A2
Rose Hill Prim Sch IP3 . .18 A4
Rose Ho **12** CO1 . . . . . .136 A6
Rose La
Great Chesterford CB10 . . .3 E2
Ipswich IP1,IP4 . . . . .17 C5
Salcott-cum-virley CM9 . .199 B8
Wivenhoe CO7 . . . . .164 B7
Rose Wlk CO9 . . . . .29 B6
Roseacres CM22 . . . . . . .148 C7
Rosebank CO12 . . . . .91 A3
Rosebank Cl CO15 . . . . .189 A2
Rosebank Rd CO5 . . . . . .201 B6
Rosebay Cl CM8 . . . . . . .176 D3
Rosebery CM23 . . . . . . .146 C6
Rosebery Ave CO1 . . . . .136 A7
Rosebery Rd
Chelmsford CM2 . . . . . .216 B8
Felixstowe IP11 . . . . . . .221 F6
Ipswich IP4 . . . . .17 F5
Rosecroft Cl CO15 . . . . .188 E6
Rosedale Cotts CO3 . . . .133 F5
Rosefinch Cl CB9 . . . . . . .9 C7
Rosehill Cres IP3 . . . . . . .17 F4
Rosehill Rd IP3 . . . . .17 F4
Roselawn Fields CM1 . . .205 B8
Rosemary Ave
Braintree CM7 . . . . .127 E4
Felixstowe IP11 . . . . . . .221 F6
Rosemary Cl
Great Dunmow CM6 . . . .123 C1
Tiptree CO5 . . . . .179 C5
Rosemary Cotts CM3 . . .192 E1
Rosemary Cres
Clacton-on-S CO15 . . . .188 F2

Rosemary Cres *continued*
Great Dunmow CM6 ....**123** C1
Tiptree CO5 ....**179** C5
Rosemary Ct 2 CO4 ....**136** D8
Rosemary Gdns CO10 ....**15** F2
Rosemary La
Castle Hedingham CO9 ...**52** A5
Great Dunmow CM6 ....**123** C1
Halstead CO9 ....**76** E2
Stebbing CM6 ....**124** C7
Thorrington CO7 ......**166** B5
Rosemary Rd CO15 .....**188** F2
Rosemary Rd W CO15 ...**188** E2
Rosemary Way CO15 ...**203** G7
Rosemount Ct IP11 ....**221** F4
Rosery Mews CO13 ....**170** A4
Rosetta Cl CO7 ....**137** B2
Rosewood Cl CO4 .....**110** A4
Roslings Cl CM1 ......**204** D5
Ross Cl Haverhill CB9 ....**9** D7
Saffron Walden CB11 ....**43** E6
Rossendale CM1 ......**204** E1
Rossendale Cl CO4 ....**110** D3
Rossland Ct CO15 .....**188** F3
Rosslyn Terr CO5 .....**158** C3
Rothbury Rd CM1 ....**204** D1
Rothesay Ave CM2 ....**216** A8
Rothmans Ave CM2 ...**216** E6
Roughtons CM2 ....**216** C3
Round Cl CO3 ....**135** B7
Round Coppice Rd
Great Hallingbury CM24 ..**147** A8
Stansted Mountfitchet
CM24 ....**120** B1
Roundacre CO9 ....**103** E8
Roundbush Cnr
Birch CO5 ....**160** D3
Great Totham CM9 ......**196** D6
Roundbush Rd CO5 ....**160** D2
Roundridge Rd IP9 ....**35** B2
Roundwood Rd IP4 .....**18** A7
Rous Chase CM2 ......**216** B1
Routh Ave IP3 ....**18** F1
Rover Ave CO15 ......**203** E6
Row The Hadstock CB1 ...**5** D1
Stratford St M CO7 .....**58** C2
Rowallan Cl CO3 ......**135** A3
Rowan Chase CO5 ....**179** C5
Rowan Cl
Clacton-on-S CO15 .....**188** C3
Colchester CO3 ....**134** D4
Great Bentley CO7 .....**166** F6
Harwich CO12 ....**91** B3
Ipswich IP3 ....**18** D2
Rowan Dr CM9 ....**210** C5
Rowan Pl CO1 ....**109** E1
Rowan Way
Hatfield Peverel CM3 ....**194** A3
Witham CM8 ....**177** A5
Rowanhayes Cl IP2 .....**17** B3
Rowhedge Cl CO7 ....**136** F4
Rowhedge Ferry Rd
CO7 ....**164** A8
Rowhedge Rd CO2,CO5 .**136** E1
Rowherns La CO7 .....**139** F4
Rowland Ho IP11 .....**221** B5
Rowland's Yd CO12 ....**90** E2
Rowley Cl CO11 ....**86** D8
Rowley Ct CB9 ....**9** E5
Rowley Hill CB9 ....**9** E5
Rowney Ave CO10 .....**44** E2
Rowntree Way CB11 ....**43** D7
Roxborough Cl CO6 ...**132** E3
Roxburghe Rd CO16 ...**167** F6
Roxwell Ave CM1 .....**204** D3
Roxwell Rd
Chelmsford CM1 ......**204** C4
Writtle CM1 ....**204** A4
Roy Ave IP3 ....**18** B5
Royal Cl Colchester CO4 ..**110** E1
Maldon CM9 ....**210** A1
Royal Hospital Sch IP9 ..**62** D3
Royal Oak Gdns 6
CM23 ....**145** F6
Royal Sq CO7 ....**84** F7
Roydon Way CO13 ....**170** F6
Royston Dr IP2 ....**16** D2
Royston La CB11 ......**20** C5
Royston Rd CB11 ......**42** C5
Ruaton Dr CO16 ......**188** C4
Rubens Gate CM1 ....**205** F7
Rubens Rd IP3 ....**18** A1
Rudd Ct CO4 ....**110** F1
Rudkin Rd CO4 ....**109** F5
Rudlands IP8 ....**16** C1
Rudsdale Way CO3 ....**134** F5
Rue De Jeunes 2 CM7 .**127** C7
Ruffels Field CM6 .....**124** E4
Ruffles Rd CB9 ....**9** C7
Rugby Rd CO10 ....**34** B4
Rugosa Cl CO3 ....**134** C7
Rumballs Cl CM23 ....**145** C4
Rumsey Fields CM3 ...**218** F2
Rumsey Row CM1 ....**204** B1
Runnacles St CM7 ....**156** C5
Runnacles Way IP11 ...**221** B5
Running Mare La CM2 ..**216** A3
Runsell Cl CM3 ......**218** F8
Runsell La CM3 ......**218** F8
Runsell View CM3 ....**219** A4
Rurik Ct CM9 ....**220** F8
Rush Cl IP4 ....**18** F4
Rush Green Rd CO16 ..**188** B2
Rush La CM22 ....**94** C1
Rushbury Cl IP4 ......**18** B8

Rushes Ct CM23 ......**146** A5
Rushleigh Gn CM23 ...**145** D4
Rushleydale CM1 .....**205** E5
Rushmere Cl CO5 ....**201** D6
Rushmere Pl CB9 ......**9** B8
Rushmere Rd IP4 .....**18** B7
Rushmere St
Ipswich IP4,IP5 ....**18** D8
Rushmere St A IP5 .....**18** E8
Rushmoor Dr CM7 ....**128** B1
Ruskin Cl CO13 ......**170** E7
Ruskin Rd
Chelmsford CM2 ......**205** E2
Ipswich IP4 ....**17** F5
Ruskins The CM77 ....**126** F1
Russell Ct
Colchester CO2 ......**136** B4
Felixstowe IP11 ......**221** C1
Russell Gdns CM2 ....**216** A4
Russell Rd
Clacton-on-S CO15 ....**189** A3
Felixstowe IP11 ......**221** D2
Ipswich IP1 ....**17** B5
Russell Way CM1 .....**215** D2
Russell's Rd Gosfield CO9 ..**76** A1
Halstead CO9 ....**103** B8
Russet Cl CM7 ....**128** A1
Russets CM2 ....**216** D3
Russett Cl CB9 ....**8** C8
Rustic Cl CM7 ....**128** C3
Rutherfords CM1 .....**191** B1
Rutland Ave CO2 .....**135** B3
Rutland Cl CM7 ......**128** A4
Rutland Pl 11 CB9 .....**8** E7
Rutland Pl CM7 ....**72** B2
Rutland Rd CM1 ......**205** A7
Rydal Way CM77 .....**154** C6
Rydal Wlk IP3 ....**18** C2
Ryde Ave CO15 ......**189** A8
Rye Cl Brightlingsea CO7 .**165** E1
Colchester CO3 ......**134** E5
Hatfield Peverel CM3 ...**194** A3
Ipswich IP3 ....**18** D4
Rye Ct 3 CB9 ....**8** F7
Rye Field The CM3 ....**207** D3
Rye Grass Way CM7 ..**128** B1
Rye Hills CO9 ....**103** F8
Rye La CO2 ....**162** A4
Rye Mill La CO5 ......**158** D4
Rye St CM23 ....**118** F1
Ryes La CO10 ....**33** A2
Rygate Rd CO1 ....**135** F7
Rylands IP9 ....**35** A2
Ryle The CM1 ....**215** A8
Rylstone Way CB11 ...**43** F8
Rysley CM3 ....**207** D4

S

Sackett's Grove Caravan Pk
CO16 ....**188** A2
Sacketts Grove Cvn Pk
CO15 ....**187** F2
Sackville Cl CM1 .....**204** E3
Sackville Way CO6 ....**108** D4
Saddle Mews CO3 ....**134** E6
Saddle Rise CM1 .....**205** E8
Saddlers Cl
Bishop's Stortford CM23 .**145** C4
Great Notley CM77 ....**154** B7
Sadds Yd CO15 ......**188** F3
Sadler Cl CO2 ....**136** B4
Sadlers Cl CO13 .....**170** C6
Saffron Bsns Ctr CB10 ..**22** F7
Saffron Cl CM7 ....**73** C3
Saffron Croft CM9 ...**209** E2
Saffron Ct CB11 ......**22** D1
Saffron Gdns CM7 ....**73** C3
Saffron Walden Cty High Sch
CB11 ....**43** C8
Saffron Walden Mus★
CB10 ....**22** D2
Saffron Walden YH★
CB10 ....**22** D2
Saffron Waldon Hospl
CB11 ....**23** A2
Saffron Way CO5 ....**179** C4
Saffron Wlk CM7 .....**73** B3
Sage Rd CO2 ....**136** A2
Sage Wlk CO5 ....**179** C4
Sagehayes IP2 ....**17** B3
Sages End Rd CB9 ....**26** B8
Sages CM22 ....**94** F5
Sainty Cl CO7 ....**164** C8
St Agnes Way IP5 .....**18** F6
St Alban's RC High Sch
IP4 ....**18** C7
St Alban's Rd
Clacton-on-S CO15 ....**189** A3
Colchester CO3 ......**135** D7
St Andrew's Ave CO4 ..**137** A5
**St Andrew's Ave (Colchester
By-Pass Rd)** CO4 ....**136** D7
**St Andrew's CE Jun Sch &
Hatfield Peverel Inf Sch**
CM3 ....**194** B3
St Andrew's CE Prim Sch
Bulmer CO10 ....**32** E4
Great Yeldham CO9 ....**29** F2
Halstead CO9 ....**77** A3
Marks Tey CO6 ....**132** E3
Weeley CO16 ....**167** F8
Wormingford CO6 ......**80** E5
St Andrew's Cotts CM3 .**194** B3
St Andrew's Dr IP9 ....**63** E7
St Andrew's Jun & Inf Schs
CO4 ....**136** D7

St Andrew's Rd
Clacton-on-S CO15 ....**188** E3
Felixstowe IP11 ......**221** E6
Hatfield Peverel CM3 ...**194** A4
Weeley CO16 ....**140** F1
St Andrew's Rise CO10 ..**32** E5
St Andrews Cl
Alresford CO7 ....**165** A7
Ipswich IP4 ....**18** D5
St Andrews Ct 3 CO4 .**136** C8
St Andrews Gdns CO4 .**136** C8
St Andrews Pl CO7 ...**165** E1
St Andrews Rd
Boreham CM3 ....**192** F1
Great Cornard CO10 ....**34** A6
Halstead CO9 ....**76** F1
St Anne's Prim Sch CO4 **110** C1
St Anne's Rd CO4 ....**136** C8
St Anne's Sch CM2 ...**205** A1
St Annes Cl CO6 .....**131** B2
St Annes Ct CM1 ....**205** C3
St Anns Rd CO15 ....**188** E4
St Anthony's Dr CM2 ..**216** C7
St Aubins Cl CO15 ....**189** B4
St Aubyns Rd IP4 .....**18** A5
St Augustine Cl CM6 ..**151** F6
St Augustine Mews
CO1 ....**136** A7
St Augustine Rd IP3 ....**18** D4
St Augustine's Rd IP3 .**18** C3
St Austell Rd CO4 ....**110** D2
St Austin's La CO12 ...**91** E6
St Barbara's Rd CO2 ..**135** D4
St Bartholomew Cl CO4 **110** C3
St Bartholomews La
CO10 ....**15** D2
St Benedict RC Coll
CO3 ....**135** B6
St Bernard Rd CO4 ...**110** D2
St Botolph's Church Wlk 7
CO2 ....**135** F6
St Botolph's Cir 8 CO2 .**135** F6
St Botolph's Pl 5 CO2 ...**8** F7
St Botolph's St 6 CO2 .**135** F6
St Botolph's Terr 11
CO13 ....**171** C8
St Botolph's Way CB9 ...**8** F7
St Brelades Ct CO15 ..**189** B5
St Bride Ct CO4 ......**110** D2
St Catherine's Ct IP2 ..**16** E1
St Catherine's Rd
Chelmsford CM1 ......**204** E2
Long Melford CO10 ....**15** C7
St Catherines Cl CO2 ..**135** D1
St Catherines Ct CM23 .**145** E7
St Cedd's Sch CM2 ...**205** A4
St Christopher Ct CO4 .**110** D2
St Christopher Rd CO4 **110** D2
St Christophers Way
CO15 ....**203** G7
St Clair Cl CO15 .....**188** F8
St Clair's Dr CO16 ....**187** B5
St Clair's Rd CO16 ...**187** B5
St Clare Dr CO3 ......**135** A7
St Clare Rd CO3 .....**135** A6
St Clare's RC Prim Sch
CO16 ....**188** B4
St Clement Rd CO4 ...**110** D2
St Clement's Church La 19
IP4 ....**17** D5
St Clement's Ct CO16 .**188** B5
St Clement's Hospl IP3 .**18** B4
St Clements CM6 .....**70** A2
St Cleres Hall La CO16 .**187** B3
St Cleres Way CM3 ...**218** D2
St Columb Ct CO4 ....**110** C2
St Cyrus Rd CO4 .....**110** D3
St David's Rd IP3 .....**18** B3
St Davids Cl CO4 .....**136** C7
St Denis Cl CO12 .....**91** A1
St Dominic Rd CO4 ...**110** D2
St Edmund's Ct CO4 ..**136** C8
St Edmund's Hill CO8,
CO10 ....**55** D6
St Edmund's Pl IP1 ...**17** C8
St Edmund's Rd
Felixstowe IP11 ......**221** D2
Ipswich IP1 ....**17** B8
St Edmunds Cl CO12 ...**91** A1
St Edmunds Croft CM6 **123** E1
St Edmunds Fields CM6 **123** E2
St Edmunds Ho CO4 ..**110** C2
St Edmunds La Bures CO8 **55** F1
Great Dunmow CM6 ....**123** E1
St Edmundsbury Ho IP4 .**17** F6
St Fabian's Dr CM1 ...**204** E4
St Faith Rd CO4 ......**110** D2
St Felix RC Prim Sch CB9 **.8** D7
St Fillan Rd CO4 .....**110** D2
St Francis RC Prim Sch
Braintree CM7 ....**127** E4
Maldon CM9 ....**209** F3
St George's CE Prim Sch
CO7 ....**112** E1
St George's Cl CO7 ...**112** E1
St George's Inf Sch CO2 **136** A4
St George's Jun Sch
CO2 ....**136** A5
St George's St IP1 ....**17** C6
St Georges Cl CM9 ...**210** E3
St Giles CE Prim Sch
CO9 ....**52** D2
St Giles Cl
Great Maplestead CO9 ..**52** D2
Maldon CM9 ....**209** E2
St Giles Cres CM9 ...**209** E2

St Gregory CE Prim Sch
CO10 ....**33** D7
St Gregory's Ct CO10 .**33** D8
St Helen's Church La 5
IP4 ....**17** E6
St Helen's Gn CO12 ...**91** E5
St Helen's La 7 CO1 ..**135** F7
St Helen's Prim Sch IP4 **17** E6
St Helen's St IP4 .....**17** D6
St Helena Mews CO3 .**135** D5
St Helena Rd CO3 ....**135** D5
St Helena Sch CO3 ...**135** D8
St Helens Ave CO15 ..**189** A8
St Helier Ct CO15 ....**189** B4
St Ives Cl CO16 ......**188** B3
St Ives Rd CO5 ......**182** E6
St James Ct
Brightlingsea CO7 .....**185** E6
Clacton-on-S CO15 ....**188** E1
Haverhill CB9 ....**8** E8
5 Saffron Walden CB10 ..**22** F2
St James Pk CM1 ....**204** D4
St James Rd CM7 ....**127** F5
St James Way CM23 ..**145** C3
St James' CE Prim Sch
CO1 ....**136** B7
St James's St CO9 ....**51** F4
St Jean Wlk CO5 ....**179** D6
St John Gdns CO15 ..**188** E6
St John Payne RC Comp Sch
CM1 ....**204** F6
**St John The Baptist CE Prim
Sch** CO9 ....**78** B8
St John's Ave
Chelmsford CM2 ......**216** B8
12 Colchester CO2 .....**135** F6
St John's CE Prim Sch
Colchester CO4 ......**110** D4
Ipswich IP4 ....**18** A7
St John's Cl CO4 .....**110** D4
St John's Cres CM24 ..**119** E7
St John's Ct Ipswich IP4 .**18** B6
Tollesbury CM9 ......**199** C1
**St John's Danbury CE Prim
Sch** CM3 ....**218** E2
St John's Gn CM1 ....**204** B1
St John's Green Prim Sch
CO2 ....**135** F6
St John's Hospl CM2 ..**215** F6
St John's La CO4 .....**119** E7
St John's Pl 14 CO2 ..**135** F6
St John's Rd
Chelmsford CM2 ......**216** B8
Clacton-on-S CO16 ....**188** C5
Colchester CO4 ......**110** D3
Ipswich IP4 ....**18** A6
Stansted Mountfitchet
CM24 ....**119** E7
Wivenhoe CO7 ....**164** C7
Writtle CM1 ....**204** B1
St John's St
Colchester CO2 ......**135** F6
Tollesbury CM9 ......**199** C1
St Johns Ave CM7 ....**127** F3
St Johns Cl
Great Chesterford CB10 ...**3** D2
Saffron Walden CB11 ....**43** D7
St Johns Ct IP11 .....**221** D4
St Joseph Rd CO4 ....**110** C3
St Joseph's Coll IP2 ...**17** A3
St Joseph's Prim Sch
CO10 ....**33** E8
St Joseph's RC Prim Sch
Bishop's Stortford CM23 .**145** E6
Harwich CO12 ....**91** B2
St Jude Gdns CO4 ....**110** E2
St Judes Cl CO4 ......**110** D2
St Julian Gr CO1 .....**136** A6
St Lawrence CE Prim Sch
CO2 ....**163** F8
St Lawrence Ct 3 CM7 .**127** F3
St Lawrence Dr CM0 ..**213** B1
St Lawrence Rd CO4 ..**110** D2
St Lawrence St 11 IP1 ..**17** D6
St Leonard's Hospl CO10 **33** F7
St Leonard's Rd CO1 ..**136** C6
St Leonards Cl CB11 ...**43** A2
St Leonards Rd IP3 ...**18** B3
St Leonards School Ho 8
CO1 ....**136** C6
St Leonards Terr 7
CO1 ....**136** C6
St Luke's CE Prim Sch
CO5 ....**179** D5
St Luke's Chase CO5 ..**179** D5
St Luke's Cl CO4 .....**110** D2
St Margaret's CE Prim Sch
Ipswich IP4 ....**17** D6
Toppesfield CO9 ......**50** C7
St Margaret's Gn 2 IP4 .**17** D6
St Margaret's Plain 1
IP4 ....**17** D6
St Margaret's Rd CM2 .**205** E3
St Margaret's Sch CO2 .**102** D8
St Margaret's St IP4 ...**17** D6
St Mark Dr CO4 ......**110** D2
St Marks RC Prim Sch
IP2 ....**16** F3
St Marks Rd CO15 ....**188** E4
St Martins CO15 ......**188** E4
St Mary Magdalen Ho
CO1 ....**136** B6
St Mary's Art Ctr★ CO1 **135** B7
St Mary's Cath★ CM1 .**205** B2
St Mary's CE Foundation
Prim Sch CM24 ......**119** E7

St Mary's CE Prim Sch
Ardleigh CO7 ....**111** E7
Saffron Walden CB10 ...**22** D2
St Mary's Cl
Great Baddow CM2 ....**216** F6
Panfield CM7 ....**127** B7
St Mary's Cres IP11 ...**221** D6
St Mary's Dr CM24 ...**119** F5
St Mary's La CM9 ....**210** B2
St Mary's Pl CM6 ....**151** D7
St Mary's RC Prim Sch
IP4 ....**17** F7
St Mary's RC Sch CM23 **145** E7
St Mary's Rd
Braintree CM7 ....**128** B3
Clacton-on-S CO15 ....**188** E4
Frinton-on-S CO13 ....**171** A5
Great Bentley CO7 ....**166** F6
Ipswich IP4 ....**17** F7
St Mary's Rd
Kelvedon CO5 ....**158** C2
Rivenhall CM8 ....**177** B7
St Mary's Sch
Colchester CO3 ......**135** C7
Copford CO3 ....**133** F5
St Mary's Sq CO5 ....**158** B1
St Mary's Villas CM7 ...**72** B1
St Mary's Wlk CB9 ....**27** B6
St Marys Mead CM1 ..**191** A1
St Marys Mews
Frinton-on-S CO13 ....**171** A5
Tollesbury CM9 ......**199** D2
St Marys View CM9 ...**22** E4
St Mathew's Ho 4 IP1 .**17** B6
St Matthew's CE Prim Sch
IP1 ....**17** B6
St Matthew's St IP1 ...**17** B6
St Michael's CE Prim Sch
Bishop's Stortford CM23 .**145** F7
Braintree CM7 ....**127** F2
St Michael's Chase CO6 **133** D2
St Michael's Ct 4 CM7 .**127** F2
St Michael's Hospl CM7 **127** E3
St Michael's La 1 CM7 .**127** F2
St Michael's Prim Sch
Bishop's Stortford CM23 .**145** E7
Colchester CO2 ......**135** C1
St Michael's Rd
Braintree CM7 ....**127** F2
Chelmsford CM2 .....**216** B8
Harwich CO12 ....**91** B2
Thorpe-le-S CO16 ....**141** F2
St Michaels Ct 6 CO11 .**86** D4
St Michaels Rd CO4 ...**135** D1
St Michaels Wlk CM2 .**216** C2
St Mildreds Rd CM2 ..**216** B8
St Monance Way CO4 .**110** D2
St Nazaire Rd CM1 ...**204** E6
St Neots Cl CO4 .....**110** D2
St Nicholas Cl CM8 ...**176** F4
St Nicholas Cl CO12 ...**91** D6
St Nicholas Field CO3 ..**92** B8
St Nicholas Pas 16 CO1 **135** F7
St Nicholas Rd CM8 ..**176** F4
St Nicholas St
22 Colchester CO1 .....**135** F7
Ipswich IP1 ....**17** C5
St Nicholas Way CO6 .**131** A3
St Nicholas' Gdns CM7 **127** F8
St Osyth CE Prim Sch
CO16 ....**187** B4
St Osyth CE Sch CO15 .**188** E3
St Osyth Cl IP2 ....**16** F8
St Osyth Priory★ CO16 **187** A4
St Osyth Rd
Alresford CO7 ....**165** D7
Clacton-on-S CO15 ....**188** D3
Little Clacton CO16 ...**168** B1
St Osyth Rd E CO16 ..**168** C2
St Osyth Rd W CO16 ..**168** C1
St Paul's Rd
Clacton-on-S CO15 ....**189** A3
Colchester CO1 ......**135** E8
St Peter's Ave CM9 ...**209** F2
St Peter's CE Prim Sch
Coggeshall CO6 ......**131** B2
Sible Hedingham CO9 ...**75** D8
St Peter's Cl CM7 ....**127** F4
St Peter's Hospl CM9 .**209** F2
St Peter's Rd
Braintree CM7 ....**127** F4
Chelmsford CM1 ......**204** E2
Coggeshall CO6 ......**131** B2
West Mersea CO5 ....**201** B6
St Peter's St
Colchester CO1 ......**135** F8
Ipswich IP1 ....**17** C5
St Peter's Wlk CM7 ...**127** F3
St Peter's-In-the-Fields
CM7 ....**127** F4
St Peters Cl CM9 .....**211** E6
St Peters Ct
Clacton-on-S CO15 ....**189** B5
Clare CO10 ....**12** B7
Colchester CO1 ......**135** E8
10 Sudbury CO10 ....**33** E7
St Peters View CO9 ...**51** D1
St Philip's Priory Sch
CM2 ....**216** A8
St Philomena's Sch
CO13 ....**170** F5
St Pius X RC Prim Sch
CM1 ....**204** F6
St Runwald St 9 CO1 ..**135** F7
St Saviour Cl CO4 ....**110** D2
St Stephens La 13 IP1 ..**17** C6
St Swithins Cotts CM2 .**217** C3

St Teresa's RC Prim Sch
CO3 ....134 E5
St Thomas Cl CO4 ....110 E4
St Thomas More RC Prim Sch
CB11 ....128 C1
St Thomas More's RC Prim
Sch CO1 ....136 A7
St Valery CM22 ......148 C7
St Vincent Chase CM7 .128 B5
St Vincent Rd CO15 ...188 E1
St Vincents Dr CM2 ...216 B8
Salary Cl CO4 ....110 E1
Salcombe Rd CM7 ....128 C1
Salcott Creek Ct CM7 .128 D1
Salcott St CM9 ....199 C8
Salehurst Rd IP3 ......18 E3
Salerno Cres CO2 ....135 C2
Salerno Way CM1 .....204 E6
Saling Hall Gdns★ CM7 126 A8
Salisbury Ave CO3 ....135 E6
Salisbury Cl CM23 ....145 F5
Salisbury Ct
  Clacton-on-S CO15 ...189 D5
  2 Haverhill CB9 ....8 F7
Salisbury Rd
  Clacton-on-S CO15 ...189 D5
  Ipswich IP3 ....18 A4
Salisbury Terr 1 CO10 .33 E8
Sallows Cl IP1 ....16 F7
Salmon Cl CO3 ....134 C4
Salmon Par CM1 .....205 B3
Salmon's Cnr CO6 ...132 A3
Salmon's La CO6 .....132 A4
Salmons Cl CM6 .....151 A5
Saltcote Maltings CM9 .210 E4
Salter Pl CM2 ....205 F2
Salter's Mdw CM9 ....198 D4
Salters CM23 ....145 C4
Salters Hall Mews CO10 .33 D7
Salthouse St 17 IP4 ...17 D5
Salvia Cl CO16 ....188 C4
Samford Cl IP9 ....62 D7
Samford Ct IP9 ....61 D7
Samford Pl IP8 ....16 B6
Samian Cl CM9 ......209 F5
Samphire Cl CM8 ....176 D3
Sampson Dr CO10 .....15 D8
Sampson's La CO5 ...182 F3
Samson's Cnr CO7 ...165 D1
Samson's Rd CO7 ....165 E1
Samsons Cl CO7 .....185 E8
Samuel Ct IP4 ....17 D6
Samuel Manor CM2 ...205 F3
Sanderling Gdns CM9 .210 C5
Sanders Cl CM24 ....119 D7
Sanders Dr CO3 .....135 B7
Sanderson Mews CO5 .163 F8
Sandford Cl CO7 .....164 C8
Sandford Mill Rd
  Chelmsford CM2 .....205 F2
  Chelmsford CM2 .....206 B2
  Great Baddow CM2 ..217 C8
Sandford Rd CM2 ....205 E3
Sandhurst Ave IP3 .....17 F4
Sandle Rd CM23 .....146 A7
Sandling Cres IP4 .....18 E5
Sandlings The IP3 .....18 E5
Sandmartin Cres CO3 .134 C4
Sandon Brook Pl CM2 .217 B6
Sandon Cl CO6 ......109 C7
Sandon Hall Bridleway
  CM2 ....217 D4
Sandon Hill CM3 .....172 A6
Sandon Sch The CM2 .217 B6
Sandown Cl CO15 ....189 A8
Sandpiper Cl
  Colchester CO4 .....137 A8
  Haverhill CB9 ....9 C8
  Heybridge CM9 .....210 C5
Sandpiper Rd IP2 .....16 E2
Sandpiper Wlk CM2 ..216 C6
Sandpit Cl IP4 ....18 F5
Sandpit La 8 CM7 ...127 F3
Sandra Ct 5 CO2 ....135 E6
Sandringham Cl IP2 ...16 A7
Sandringham Ct CO10 .34 A7
Sandringham Dr CO2 ..136 A4
Sandringham Gdns 6
  CM23 ....145 E5
Sandringham Pl CM2 .205 C2
Sandwich Cl CM7 ....127 E6
Sandwich Rd
  Brightlingsea CO7 ...185 F8
  Clacton-on-S CO15 ..203 J8
Sandy Hill CO6 ....80 D5
Sandy Hill La IP3 .....17 E1
Sandy La Bulmer CO10 .32 F5
  Sudbury CO10 ....33 B5
Sapling Pl IP4 ....18 E5
Sarah's Wlk CM22 ...148 B7
Saran Ct CO7 ....137 A2
Sarcel CM7 ....129 C6
Sargeant Cl CO2 .....136 B3
Sarre Way CO7 ......185 E8
Sassoon Way 3 CM9 .210 A1
Saul's Ave CM8 ......195 A8
Sauls Bridge Cl CM8 .195 A8
Saunders Ave CM7 ...127 E3
Saunders Cl CM22 ....94 C1
Savernake Rd CM1 ...204 E1
Savill Rd CM2 ....136 C2
Saville Cl CB11 ......65 C4
Saville St CO14 ......144 C1
Sawkins Ave CM2 ....216 D6
Sawkins Cl Abberton CO5 163 B2
  Chelmsford CM2 .....216 D6
Sawkins Gdns CM2 ...216 D6
Sawney Brook CM1 ...204 A1

Sawpit La CM23 ......92 D7
Sawston Cl IP2 ....17 A2
Sawyer's Rd CM9 ....197 C5
Sawyers Cl 3 IP9 .....35 A1
Saxmundham Way
  CO16 ....188 A3
Saxon Bank CM7 ....128 B2
Saxon Cl Colchester CO3 .134 F4
  Halstead CO9 ....76 F2
Saxon Ct CM9 ....210 A3
Saxon Dr CM8 ....176 E3
Saxon La IP8 ....35 D7
Saxon Way
  Chelmsford CM1 ....205 B7
  Holland-on-S CO15 ..189 F6
  Maldon CM9 ....210 B1
  Point Clear B CO16 ..185 F3
  Saffron Walden CB11 .22 C1
Saxstead Dr CO16 ...188 A4
Saywell Brook CM2 ..206 A2
Scarfe Way CO4 .....136 E6
Scarfe's Cnr CO6 ....82 B4
Scarletts Cl CM8 ....195 A7
Scarletts Rd CO1 ....136 C4
Sceptre Cl CM9 .....199 D2
School Barn Cotts CO10 .13 E7
School Chase CO9 ...103 E8
School Cl IP9 ....35 A1
School Ct CO12 ......91 D4
School Hill Birch CO2 .161 A4
  Washbrook IP8 ....35 F8
School Ho
  13 Colchester CO1 ...136 A6
  Shalford CM7 ....100 E5
School La Birch CO2 ..161 A3
  Brantham CO11 ......60 D1
  Broomfield CM1 .....191 B1
  Chelmsford CM1 ....204 F8
  Dedham CO7 ....84 F7
  Duddenhoe End CB11 .41 A7
  East Bergholt CO7 ....59 B3
  Great Bentley CO7 ..166 A8
  Great Horkesley CO6 .82 A2
  Great Leighs CM3 ...173 F8
  Great Wigborough CO5 .181 F3
  Haverhill CB9 ....8 E7
  Henham CM22 ....94 F5
  Lawford CO11 ....86 A2
  Little Horkesley CO6 .81 D5
  Mistley CO11 ....86 F4
  Newport CB11 ....42 F1
  Stratford St M CO7 ...58 D2
  Takeley CM22 ......121 D6
  West Bergholt CO6 ..108 E4
School Mews CO6 ....130 C7
School Rd
  Colchester CO2 .....136 A2
  Copford CO6 ....133 D3
  Elmstead CO7 ......138 A4
  Frinton-on-S CO13 ..170 E5
  Great Oakley CO12 ..116 C4
  Great Totham CM9 ..196 B3
  Langham CO4 ....83 E4
  Little Horkesley CO6 .81 D4
  Little Maplestead CO9 .77 B8
  Little Totham CM9 ...197 B3
  Little Yeldham CO9 ...30 D3
  Messing CO5 ....159 D2
  Pentlow CO10 ....13 F6
  Rayne CM7 ....153 E8
  Shotley Gate IP9 .....91 B8
  Sible Hedingham CO9 .75 D8
  Silver End CM8 .....156 E3
  Tattingstone IP9 ....36 D1
  Tendring CO16 ......140 E6
  Wickham Bishops CM8 .195 F5
  Wickham St P CO9 ...53 C5
School St Foxearth CO10 .14 D6
  Great Chesterford CB10 .3 D2
  Stoke-by-N CO6 ......56 D5
  Sudbury CO10 ....33 E7
School View CM7 ....127 E2
School View Rd CM1 .204 F3
School Villas
  Great Easton CM6 ...123 A8
  Henham CM6 ....95 F2
  Lindsell CM6 ....97 F4
  Takeley CM22 ......121 C6
School Wlk CM7 .....127 E6
Schoolfield Birdbrook CO9 28 A6
  Glemsford CO10 ......2 B5
Schreiber Rd IP4 .....18 B7
Scofield Ct CO10 .....34 A6
Scotland St CO6 .....56 E6
Scott Ave CM7 ....73 D6
Scott Cl CM7 ....155 A8
Scott Dr CO3 ....134 F6
Scott Rd
  Bishop's Stortford CM23 .145 E6
  Ipswich IP3 ....18 B1
Scotts Wlk CM1 .....204 D5
Scraley Rd CM9 .....210 E6
Scrip's Rd CO6 ......158 A7
Scrivener Dr IP2 .....16 C2
Scurvy Hall La
  Howe Street CM3 ...173 C1
  Little Waltham CM3 .191 B8
Scylla Cl CM9 ....210 C6
Scythe Way CO3 ....134 F4
Sea Cornflower Way
  CO15 ....203 G7
Sea Cres CO15 ......203 G7
Sea Flowers Way CO15 .203 G7
Sea Glebe Way CO15 .203 G7
Sea Holly Way CO15 .203 G6
Sea King Cres CO4 ..110 B4
Sea Lavender Way
  CO15 ....203 G7

Sea Pink Way CO15 ..203 G6
Sea Rd IP11 ....221 D2
Sea Rosemary Way
  CO15 ....203 G7
Sea Shell Way CO15 .203 G6
Sea Thistle Way CO15 .203 G7
Sea View Par CM0 ...213 C1
Sea View Prom CM0 .213 B1
Sea Way CO15 ....203 F6
Seabrook Gdns CM3 .192 C1
Seabrook Rd CM2 ...217 A6
Seafield Ave CO11 ....87 B4
Seafield Rd CO12 ....91 B2
Seafields Gdns CO15 .189 C5
Seafields Rd CO15 ..189 C5
Seagers CM9 ....196 B4
Searle Way CO6 .....108 B1
Seaton Cl CO11 ......86 B3
Seaton Rd IP11 .....221 D5
Seaview Ave
  Little Oakley CO12 ..117 C7
  West Mersea CO5 ..201 E6
Seaview Ct CO15 ....189 A2
Seaview Cvn Pk CO5 .201 F6
Seaview Gdns CO7 ..185 F7
Seaview Hts CO14 ..171 C7
Seaview Rd
  Brightlingsea CO7 ..185 F7
  Seawick CO16 ......203 B7
Seaview Terr CO16 ..186 A3
Seawick CO16 ......203 B6
Sebastian Cl CO4 ...136 F7
Seckford Cl IP4 ......18 F5
Second Ave
  Chelmsford CM1 ....205 B5
  Clacton-on-S CO15 ..189 B4
  Frinton-on-S CO13 ..170 E3
  Glemsford CO10 .....2 C5
  Halstead CO9 ....77 B4
  Harwich CO12 ....91 C3
  Seawick CO16 ......203 C6
  Stansted Mountfitchet
  CM24 ....120 B2
  Sudbury CO10 ....15 F1
  Trimley St M IP11 ...221 A2
  Walton-on-t-N CO14 .144 E3
  Weeley CO16 ....167 F8
Seden Ct CO15 ......169 B1
Sedgefield Way CM7 .128 B1
Sedop Cl CB11 ....43 D7
Seedbed Ctr CO4 ....110 C6
Seedfield The CO5 ..201 B6
Selby Cl CO2 ....135 D1
Seldon Rd CO5 .....179 D5
Selhurst Ct CO14 ....170 F7
Selkirk Rd IP4 ....18 B8
Selsey Ave CO15 ....203 I8
Selvale Way IP11 ....221 C4
Selwyn Cl IP2 ....17 C4
Septimus Dr CO4 ....110 A5
Serpentine Rd IP3 ....18 C2
Serpentine Wlk CO1 .109 E1
Servite Ho IP4 ....17 F6
Seven Ash Gn CM1 ..205 C5
Seven Devils La CB11 .43 D6
Seventh Ave
  Chelmsford CM1 ....205 B6
  Stansted Mountfitchet
  CM24 ....120 B2
Severalls Hospl CO4 .109 E5
Severalls La CO4 ....110 B6
Severn Rd
  Clacton-on-S CO15 ..188 F5
  Ipswich IP3 ....17 F3
Sewell's La CO10 .....13 B1
Sexton Cl CO2 ......163 B8
Sextons La CM8 .....178 B1
Seymore Dr CB9 ......9 D7
Seymour Rd Ipswich IP2 .17 C4
  Jaywick CO15 ......187 F1
Seymour St CM2 ....205 A1
Shackleton Cl CO12 ..90 F1
Shackleton Gdns CM23 .145 E6
Shackleton Rd IP3 ....18 B3
Shackleton Sq IP3 ...18 B3
Shaftenhoe End Rd SG8 .39 B8
Shaftesbury Ave CO12 .91 B4
Shaftesbury Ct 10 CB9 .8 E7
Shaftesbury Sq 4 IP4 .17 D5
Shafto Rd IP1 ....16 E8
Shair La
  Great Bentley CO7 ..167 B8
  Weeley CO16 ....140 B2
Shakespeare Cl CM7 .155 A7
Shakespeare Rd CO3 .134 F6
Shakeston Cl CM1 ...215 B8
Shalfleet Ct CO15 ...188 F8
Shalford Lodge CM1 .205 B8
Shalford Prim Sch CM7 100 E5
Shalford Rd CM77 ...126 E3
Shamrock Ave IP2 ....16 E4
Shamrock Cl CM9 ...199 D3
Shamrock Ho CO15 .203 J8
Shangani Rd CM23 ..145 F5
Shanklin Cl CO15 ...189 A8
Shannon Cl CB9 ......9 D7
Shannon Rd IP3 ......38 A8
Shardelow Ave CM1 .206 A8
Sharlands Row CM9 .199 A8
Sharpington Cl CM2 .216 C3
Shatters Rd CO2 ....161 A1
Shaw Cl CO13 ....170 F7
Shaw Dr CM7 ....73 D7
Shaw Rd
  Long Melford CO10 ..15 D8
  Witham CM8 ....176 F5
Shearers The CM23 .145 C4

Shearers Way CM3 ..192 F1
Shearman Ct 1 CB9 ...9 A7
Shears Cres CO5 ....201 D5
Shears Ct CO5 ......201 D5
Sheds La CB10 ....22 E2
Sheene Gr CM7 .....128 D5
Sheepcoates La CM9 .196 F2
Sheepcot La CM23 ...92 E3
Sheepcotes CM2 ....206 B5
Sheepcotes La
  Little Waltham CM3 .191 C7
  Silver End CM8 .....156 E5
Sheepen Pl CO3 ....135 E8
Sheepen Rd CO3 ....135 D8
Sheepshead Hill CO10 .34 C6
Sheering Wlk CM2 ...135 F2
Sheerwater Mews CO4 .137 A8
Sheldrake Dr IP2 .....16 E2
Sheldrick Link CM2 .206 B4
Shellcroft CO6 ....77 F1
Shellduck Cres CM77 .154 C5
Shelley Ave
  Great Cornard CO10 .34 B6
  Tiptree CO5 ....179 E5
Shelley La CO16 .....168 F2
Shelley Rd
  Chelmsford CM2 ....205 D2
  Clacton-on-S CO16 ..188 A5
  Colchester CO3 .....134 F6
Shelley St 6 IP2 .....17 C4
Shelley Wlk CM7 ....155 A8
Sheltons The CO13 ..170 B6
Shenley Rd IP3 ......18 B1
Shepherd Dr IP8 .....16 C2
Shepherds Cl CM23 .145 C4
Shepherds Croft CO3 .134 D5
Shepherds Ct 15 CB9 ..8 E7
Shepherds La CO10 ...2 A6
Shepherds Way CB10 .22 F2
Sheppard Cl CO16 ..188 D6
Sheppard Dr CM2 ...206 A4
Sherborne Rd CM1 ..205 D5
Sherbourne Cl CO13 .170 F7
Sherbourne Rd CO4 .136 F7
Sheriffs Way CO15 ..188 E7
Sheriidan Wlk CO3 ..134 F6
Sheringham Dr CM77 .154 C7
Sherrington Rd IP1 ...17 A8
Sherwood Cl CO4 ...136 F7
Sherwood Ct 20 CM23 .145 F7
Sherwood Dr
  Chelmsford CM1 ....204 D1
  Clacton-on-S CO15 ..188 E6
Sherwood Way CO5 .158 D4
Shetland Cl IP4 ......18 A8
Shetland Rd CB9 ......9 D8
Shewell Wlk CO1 ....135 E7
Shillito Cl CO3 ......134 F3
Ship La CO11 ....87 E3
Ship Launch Rd IP3 ..17 E3
Shipwrights The CO7 .164 B8
Shipyard Est CO7 ...185 F5
Shire Cl CM1 ....205 F7
Shire Ct 13 CB9 ......8 E7
Shire Hall Yd 10 IP4 ...17 D5
Shire Hill CB11 ......22 F1
Shire Hill La CB10 ...44 A1
Shire La CO6 ....108 F4
Shires Cl CO15 .....188 A1
Shirley Ct CO15 .....188 A1
Shoebridge's Hill CO7 .84 E6
Shop La CO5 ....184 F3
Shop Rd CO11 ......113 B6
Shops The CM8 .....156 D4
Shore La Bradfield CO11 .87 E3
  Harkstead IP9 ....63 C3
Shoreham Rd CO15 .203 I8
Short Cut Rd CO1 ...135 C2
Short Wyre St 24 CO1 .135 F7
Shortcroft CM23 ....146 D7
Shortlands IP8 ......16 D1
Shortlands Pl CM23 .145 F8
Shortridge Ct CM8 ..194 F8
Shotley Cl
  Clacton-on-S CO16 ..188 A3
  Felixstowe IP11 .....221 B4
  Ipswich IP2 ....16 C2
Shotley Mews CB9 ....8 C8
Shropshire Cl CM2 ..216 F5
Shrub End Rd CO3 ..135 B4
Shrubbery Cl IP11 ..221 C4
Shrubland Dr CO15 .189 B5
Shrubland Pr IP4 .....18 F5
Shrubland Rd
  6 Colchester CO2 ..136 A6
  New Mistley CO11 ...87 A4
Shrublands CB10 ....22 E2
Shrublands Cl CM2 .205 C2
Shums Hill CO13 ....170 C8
Shut La CO6 ....105 B6
Siam Pl CO10 ....33 E7
Sidegate Ave IP4 .....18 A8
Sidegate La IP4 ......18 A8
Sidegate Prim Sch IP4 ..18 A8
Sidings Pl CM7 .....128 A2
Sidmouth Rd CM1 ..205 D6
Sidney Pl CM1 ......206 A7
Sidney Terr CM23 ...145 F6
Siena Mews CO1 ....136 B4
Siggin's La CB1 ......5 D7
Silcock Cl CO4 ......110 C2
Silcott St CO7 ......185 E6
Silent St 3 IP1 ......17 C5
Silk Factory Row CO10 .2 B6
Silk Mus★ CM7 ......127 F2
Silks Way CM7 .....127 F2
Sillett Cl CO16 ......188 D6

St T – Sno 245

Silvanus Cl CO3 .....135 D6
Silver Dawn Touring Pk
  CO16 ....188 A4
Silver End Prim Sch
  CM8 ....156 E3
Silver Leys IP9 ......60 E6
Silver Row CB11 ....42 F5
Silver St Maldon CM9 .209 F3
  Silver End CM8 .....156 D4
Stansted Mountfitchet
  CM24 ....119 D6
  Wethersfield CM7 ...73 B3
Silverdale Cl CO15 ..189 B5
Silverthorne Cl CO2 .136 A3
Silvester Way CM2 ..206 B4
Simmonds Way CM3 .218 F8
Simons Flats CO5 ...179 C7
Simons La CO1 .....136 B6
Simpson Cl IP3 ......17 F1
Simpsons La CO5 ...179 A3
Sims Cl CO6 ....105 B7
Sinclair Cl CO4 .....109 F2
Sinclair Dr IP2 ....17 C3
Singer Ave CO15 ...203 E7
Singleton Ct CO10 ...34 A5
Sinnington End CO4 .110 C4
Sioux Cl CO4 ....110 C4
Sir Alf Ramsey Way IP1 .17 B5
Sir Charles Lucas Comp Sch
  CO4 ....136 E8
Sir Isaac's Wlk CO1 .135 F7
Sirdar Rd IP1 ....17 A7
Siskin Cl CO2 ....136 F8
Sittang Cl CO2 ......135 C1
Sitwell Cl CO11 ......86 B4
Siward Rd CM8 .....194 D8
Six Bells Ct CM7 ....127 F5
Sixth Ave
  Chelmsford CM1 ....205 B6
  Stansted Mountfitchet
  CM24 ....120 C3
Sixth Form Coll The
  CO1 ....135 E7
Skate's Hill CO10 .....2 B2
Skeins Way CB11 ....65 C4
Skelmersdale Rd CO15 .188 F3
Skelton Cl CO11 .....86 C4
Skerry Rise CM1 ....205 B7
Skiddaw Cl CM77 ...154 D7
Skinner's La CM2 ...216 B3
Skinners St CM23 ...145 C4
Skipper Ct CM7 .....154 F8
Skipper Rd IP8 ......36 E8
Skitts Hill CM7 ......128 A1
Skitts Hill Ind Est CM7 .128 B1
Skreens Ct CM1 ....204 D4
Sky Hall Hill CO4 ....83 D7
Skylark La IP8 ....16 C2
Skylark Wlk CM2 ....216 B5
Skyrmans Fee CO13 .170 E6
Sladbury's La CO15 .189 C6
Sladburys La CO15 .189 D8
Slade Rd CO15 .....189 C6
Slade St 14 IP4 ......17 D5
Slade The CB10 .....22 F7
Slade's La CM2 .....216 A3
Slades Cl CO10 ......2 C5
Slate CO9 ....76 F1
Slaters Cl CO13 ....170 E6
Sleaford Cl IP2 ......17 A3
Sloe Hill CO9 ....76 C2
Slough Farm Rd CO9 .76 D2
Slough House Cl CM7 .128 D1
Slough La Ardleigh CO7 .111 D4
  Cock Clarks CM3 ...219 D3
  Elmstead CO7 .....137 B6
Slough Rd
  Brantham CO7,CO11 .60 D2
  Danbury CM3 ......219 C3
Slushy La IP9 ....63 B3
Smaley La CO10 .....15 C8
Smallbridge Entry CO8 ..80 D8
Smallwood Rd CO2 .135 B3
Smart St 11 IP4 .....17 D5
Smeaton Cl CO4 ....110 C4
Smeetham Hall La CO10 .32 E6
Smith's End La SG8 ..39 A8
Smithers Cl IP9 .....35 A1
Smithers Dr CM2 ...217 A6
Smiths Cotts CM22 ..93 E4
Smiths Field
  Colchester CO1 ....136 C5
  Rayne CM77 ....126 F2
Smiths Gn CB11 .....68 A8
Smythe Cl CO16 ....188 C6
Smythies Ave CO1 ..136 A7
Snakes La
  Stansted Mountfitchet CM24 93 F2
  Ugley CM22 ....94 A2
Snape Cl CO16 .....188 A4
Snape Way CO13 ...170 F7
Sneating Hall La CO13 .169 E8
Snelling Gr CM2 ....216 F6
Sniveller's La CO5 ..157 D3
Snow Hill La CO6 ....57 D5
Snowberry Ct CM7 ..128 D4
Snowberry Gr CO2 ..136 A3
Snowcroft IP9 ......35 A1
Snowdon Ct 5 CB9 ..8 E6
Snowdon Rd IP2 .....17 B2
Snowdrop Cl
  Bishop's Stortford CM23 .145 C6
  Chelmsford CM1 ....205 E7
  Witham CM8 ....176 E4
Snowley Par CM23 ..119 B1

Snows Way CO11 ......86 D8
Soane St IP4 ....17 D6
Soft Rd CO10 ....31 F5
Soils The CO12 ....116 E5
Solway Ct **3** CO4 ....136 E8
Somers Rd CO3 ....135 A4
Somerset Cl CO2 ......135 B3
Somerset Ct **9** CB9 ....8 E7
Somerset Pl CM1 .....205 A7
Somerset Rd IP4 ......17 E8
Somerset Way CO15 ...187 F1
Somme Rd CO2 ....135 E4
Sonell Ct CO7 ....137 B2
Songers Cotts CO4 ....83 B6
Sorrel Cl Colchester CO4 .109 C2
  Ipswich IP2 ....16 F3
Sorrel Gr CM77 ....154 B7
Sorrel Horse Mews **22**
  IP4 ....17 D5
Sorrel Wlk CB9 ....8 D8
Sorrell Cl
  Goldhanger CM9 .....211 E7
  Little Waltham CM3 ..191 B6
South Area IP1 ....16 C7
South Cl Halstead CO9 .103 E8
  Ipswich IP4 ....17 E8
  St Osyth CO16 ....187 B4
South Gn CB11 ....67 D4
South Green Rd CO5 ..163 F4
South Heath Rd CO7 ..166 F3
South Hill IP11 ....221 D3
South Hill Cl CM3 ....218 D6
South Ho CO13 ....170 F4
South Primrose Hill
  CM1 ....204 F3
South Rd
  Bishop's Stortford CM23 .146 A5
  Saffron Walden CB11 ..22 C1
  Takeley CM22 ......148 C8
South St
  Bishop's Stortford CM23 .145 F6
  Braintree CM7 ......127 F4
  Colchester CO2 .....135 E6
  Great Chesterford CB10 ..3 D3
  Great Waltham CM3 ..190 E7
  Ipswich IP1 ....17 B7
  Manningtree CO11 ...86 D4
  Tolleshunt D'arcy CM9 .198 D4
South St Commercial Ctr **1**
  CM23 ....145 F6
South Strand CO11 ....86 C5
South Suffolk Bsns Pk
  CO10 ....34 A7
South View CM6 ......150 C8
South View Gn IP9 .....60 E6
Southborough Rd CM2 .216 A8
Southcliff CO14 ....171 C7
Southcliff Ct
  Clacton-on-S CO15 ...189 B4
  Walton-on-t-N CO14 ..171 C7
Southcliff Hall CO15 ..188 F2
Southcliff Pk CO15 ....189 A4
Southcliff Prom CO14 .171 C7
Southcote Rd CM8 ....176 F4
Southcroft Cl CO13 ...170 C6
Southend Rd
  Great Baddow CM2 ...217 B4
  Howe Green CM2 ....217 D2
  Woodham Mortimer CM9 .219 C5
Southey Ct CM9 ....210 C4
Southfield CB10 ....3 A3
Southfields CO7 ....84 F6
Southgate Cres CO5 ..179 C6
Southgate Gdns CO10 ..15 C6
Southgate Rd IP8 .....16 B1
Southgate St CO10 ....15 C6
Southgates Ind Pk CB10 .43 F7
Southgreen Gdns CO16 .188 C4
Southland Cl CO4 ....110 C1
Southlands Chase CM2 .217 E2
Southmill Rd CM23 ...146 A5
Southmill Trad Ctr
  CM23 ....146 A6
Southview Dr
  Holland-on-S CO15 ...189 F6
  Walton-on-t-N CO14 ..171 C7
Southview Rd CM3 ....218 D4
Southview Sch CM8 ...176 F6
Southview Terr CM3 ..218 D6
Southway
  Brightlingsea CO7 ...185 F7
  Colchester CO1, CO3 .135 E6
Southwold Way CO16 .188 A5
Southwood Chase CM3 .219 A4
Sovereign Cl CM7 ....128 D4
Sovereign Cres CO3 ..135 C6
Sovereign Dr IP1 ......16 C7
Sowerberry Cl CM1 ...204 F7
Spa Dr CM0 ....213 B1
Spa Rd Feering CO5 ..158 E4
  Witham CM8 ....176 E2
Spalding Ave CM1 ....204 E5
Spalding Cl CM7 .....127 E4
Spalding Ct CM1 .....205 A3
Spalding Way CM2 ...216 F8
Spanbies Rd CO7 ......58 D2
Spansey Ct **1** CO9 ...76 D1
Spar La CM3 ....220 C3
Sparepenny La N CB10 .47 A4
Sparepenny La S CB10 .47 B4
Sparkey Cl CM8 ......195 A7
Sparks La CO9 ....29 A6
Sparling Cl CO2 ......135 C2
Sparlings The CO13 ...170 C8

Sparrow Cl CO9 ......75 D8
Sparrow Rd CO10 .....34 B6
Sparrows Cnr CO12 ..116 E5
Sparrows Herne CO15 .188 F6
Sparrowsend Cotts CB11 43 A4
Sparrowsend Hill CB11 .43 A5
Spartan Cl CB9 ....8 C8
Speckled Wood Cl IP8 .36 D8
Speckled Wood Ct CM7 154 E8
Speedwell Cl CM8 ....176 D4
Speedwell Rd
  Colchester CO2 .....136 D2
  Ipswich IP2 ....16 F4
Spencer Cl
  Elsenham CM22 ......94 C3
  Stansted Mountfitchet
    CM24 ....119 E6
Spencer Rd
  Great Chesterford CB10 ..3 D3
  Thorpe-le-S CO16 ...142 A2
Spencer Sq CM7 .....127 F8
Spencers Piece CO4 ...83 E4
Spendells Cl CO14 ...144 D2
Spenlow Dr CM1 .....204 D5
Spennells The CO16 ..142 A2
Spenser Way CO15 ...187 F1
Spicers La CO10 ......15 C8
Spike The **7** CB10 ...22 F7
Spindle Rd CB9 ....8 D8
Spindle Wood CO4 ...110 B4
Spindrift Way CO7 ...164 B8
Spinks La CM8 ....176 F1
Spinnaker Cl CO15 ...203 J8
Spinnaker Dr CM9 ...210 E3
Spinnel's Hill CO11 ...88 B1
Spinnel's La Wix CO11 .115 D7
  Wrabness CO11 ......88 C1
Spinner Cl IP1 ....16 D8
Spinney The
  Braintree CM7 ......128 C1
  Earls Colne CO6 .....105 A6
  Newport CB11 ....67 A7
  Rushmere St A IP4 ...18 F4
  Stansted Mountfitchet
    CM24 ....119 E6
Spinneyfields CO5 ...179 D6
Spires The
  Bishop's Stortford CM23 .145 D7
  Great Baddow CM2 ..216 F6
Spital Rd Maldon CM9 .209 F2
  Maldon CM9 ....220 D7
Spitfire Ct IP3 ....18 B1
Sporehams La
  Danbury CM3 ....218 C4
  Howe Green CM2, CM3 .217 F4
Sportsmans La CM3 ..194 A2
Sportsway CO1 ......135 F8
Spots Wlk CM2 ......216 D3
Spout La CO10 ....55 D7
Spratts La CO11 .....113 A4
Spring Chase
  Brightlingsea CO7 ...185 E7
  Wivenhoe CO7 ......137 B2
Spring Cl
  Clacton-on-S CO16 ..188 C5
  Colchester CO4 .....110 C5
  Little Baddow CM3 ..207 D5
Spring Cotts CB9 ......9 C6
Spring Elms La CM3 ..207 F3
Spring Gardens Rd CO6 106 E6
Spring Gdns CO10 ....15 C8
Spring Hill CB11 ......22 A1
Spring La Colchester CO3 135 A7
  Colchester, Lexden Bridge
    CO3 ....135 A8
  Eight Ash G CO3 ....108 B1
  Great Totham CM9 ..196 C6
  Hatfield Peverel CM3, CM9 194 F2
  Maldon CM9 ....210 B4
  West Bergholt CO6 ..108 E3
  Witham CM8 ....195 A7
  Wivenhoe CO7 ......137 B2
Spring Lane Rdbt CO3 .135 A7
Spring Mdw CO10 .....2 B6
Spring Meadow Prim Sch
  CO12 ....91 A3
Spring Pond Cl CM2 ..216 E8
Spring Rd
  Brightlingsea CO7 ...185 F7
  Ipswich IP4 ....18 A6
  St Osyth CO16 ......187 A3
  Tiptree CO5 ....179 C4
Spring Rise
  Galleywood CM2 ....216 C2
  Haverhill CB9 ....9 C6
Spring Sedge Cl CO3 .134 C7
Spring Way CO9 ......51 E1
Springbank Ave CO11 .86 B3
Springbok Ho CM2 ...216 F5
Springett's Hill CO8 ...55 D2
Springfield Ave IP11 .221 E5
Springfield Basin CM2 .205 C2
Springfield Cotts CM9 .210 B5
Springfield Ct CM23 ..145 E8
Springfield Gn CM1 ..205 E4
Springfield Inf Sch IP1 .16 F8
Springfield Jun Sch IP1 .16 F8
Springfield La IP1 .....16 F8
Springfield Lyons App
  CM2 ....206 A5
Springfield Park Ave
  CM2 ....205 E2
Springfield Park Hill
  CM2 ....205 D2
Springfield Park La
  CM2 ....205 E2
Springfield Park Par
  CM2 ....205 D2

Springfield Park Rd
  CM2 ....205 E2
Springfield Pl CM1 ...205 E5
Springfield Rd
  Chelmsford CM1 ....205 E4
  Sudbury CO10 ......15 E1
Springfield Terr **2** CO10 .33 F8
Springfields
  Braintree CM77 .....127 C2
  Brightlingsea CO7 ...185 F7
  Great Dunmow CM6 .150 D8
Springfields Dr CO2 ..135 A3
Springhill Cl CO7 .....138 E8
Springhill Rd CB11 ....43 E8
Springhurst Cl IP4 ....17 F6
Springland Cl IP4 .....18 A6
Springlands Way CO10 .15 F2
Springmead CM77 ....154 D7
Springtail Rd IP8 .....36 E8
Springvalley La CO7 ..111 C4
Springwell Rd CB10, CB11 .22 A5
Springwood Ct CM7 ..127 D3
Springwood Dr CM7 ..127 C4
Springwood Ind Est
  CM7 ....127 D3
Sprites End IP11 .....221 B7
Sprites Jun & Inf Sch
  IP2 ....16 C2
Sprites La IP8, IP2 .....16 C2
Spriteshall La IP11 ...221 B7
Sproughton Bsns Pk IP1 16 C8
Sproughton CE Prim Sch
  IP8 ....16 B6
Sproughton Ct IP8 ....16 A6
Sproughton Rd IP1 ...16 D7
Spruce Ave
  Colchester CO4 .....136 E8
  Great Dunmow CM6 .123 B1
Spruce Cl
  West Mersea CO5 ...201 B7
  Witham CM8 ....177 A4
Spurgeon Cl CO9 .....51 E1
Spurgeon Pl CO5 ....158 C2
Spurgeon St CO1 ....136 C6
Square The
  Colchester CO2 .....135 B3
  Heybridge CM9 .....210 A5
  Stansted Mountfitchet CM22 93 F3
  West Mersea CO5 ...201 B6
  Widdington CB11 ....67 D4
Squire's Ct **1** CB9 ...8 E7
Squires Cl CO10 .....145 C8
Squirrells Ct CM1 ....204 F5
Squirrels Cl **2** CM23 ..145 F8
Squirrels Field CO4 ..109 F5
Squirrels The IP9 .....35 A2
Stable Cl Colchester CO3 .134 E6
  West Mersea CO5 ...201 E7
Stable Mews CO5 ....201 E8
Stablecroft CM1 .....205 E8
Stablefield Rd CO14 ..171 A7
Stacey Ct **9** CM23 ..145 F6
Stackyard The CB10 ....3 A3
Stafford Cl CO13 .....170 E6
Stafford Cres CM7 ...128 D4
Stafford Ho CM23 ....145 C5
Stainers CM23 ....145 C5
Stalin Rd CO2 ....136 B4
Stallards Cres CO13 ..170 E6
Stambourne Rd
  Great Yeldham CO9 ..29 D3
  Ridgewell CO9 ......28 F5
  Toppesfield CO9 .....50 B8
Stambridge Rd CO15 .188 C4
Stamford Cl IP2 ......36 F8
Stammers Rd CO4 ...109 F4
Standard Ave CO15 ..203 D6
Standard Rd **9** CO1 ..136 C6
Standley Rd CO14 ...144 D1
Standrums CM6 ......150 D8
Stane Cl CM23 ....118 F1
Stane Field CO6 .....132 E3
Stanes Rd CM7 ......127 F6
Stanfield Cl CO3 .....134 C3
Stanfield Mdw CM8 ..155 F1
Stanier Cl CM8 ......194 F7
Stanley Ave
  Brightlingsea CO7 ...186 A7
  Ipswich IP3 ....18 A4
Stanley Rd
  Clacton-on-S CO15 ..188 C2
  Felixstowe IP11 .....221 E3
  Great Chesterford CB10 ..3 E3
  Halstead CO9 ....76 D2
  Sudbury CO10 ......33 E8
  Wivenhoe CO7 ......137 C1
Stanley Rise CM2 ....205 F3
Stanley Wood Ave CO10 .15 F1
Stanley Wooster Way
  CO4 ....136 E7
Stanleys Farm Rd CB11 .43 F8
Stanmore Cl CO16 ...188 D5
Stanmore Way CO16 .187 B4
Stannard Way CO10 ..34 A6
Stansted Rd CO9 ....103 F8
Stansted Airport Sta
  CM24 ....121 B4
Stansted Cl CM1 .....204 E1
Stansted Mountfitchet Sta
  CM24 ....119 E6
Stansted Rd
  Birchanger CM23 ....119 B2
  Bishop's Stortford CM23 .119 B2
  Colchester CO2 .....136 A1
  Elsenham CM22 ......94 C1
Stansted Way CO13 ..171 A6
Stanstrete Field CM77 154 B5
Stanton Pl **9** CB9 ....9 B8

Stanway Cl CO10 ......2 C5
Stanway Fiveways Prim Sch
  CO3 ....134 C6
Stanway Prim Sch CO3 .134 C6
Stanway Sch The CO3 .134 D5
Stanwell St **9** CO2 ..135 F6
Stanwyn Ave CO15 ..188 E3
Stapleford Cl CM2 ...205 A1
Staplers Cl CM9 .....196 B4
Staplers Heath CM9 ..196 B4
Staplers Wlk CM9 ...196 B4
Star La
  Great Dunmow CM6 .123 D1
  Ipswich IP4 ....17 D5
Star Mead CM6 ....70 A2
Starfield Cl IP4 ....18 B6
Starling's Hill CO9 ....75 E4
Starr Rd CM22 ....94 F5
Start Hill CM22 ......147 A7
Station App
  Braintree CM7 ......128 A2
  Frinton-on-S CO13 ..170 F5
Station Cotts CO6 ...133 D2
Station Hill CO8 ......79 E8
Station La CO12 ......91 E5
Station Rd Alresford CO7 165 A8
  Ardleigh CO7 ....111 E7
  Bentley IP9 ....60 E6
  Birdbrook CO9 ......10 D1
  Bishop's Stortford CM23 .146 A7
  Bradfield CO11 ......87 E3
  Braintree CM7 ......127 F2
  Brightlingsea CO7 ...185 E6
  Clacton-on-S CO15 ..188 F3
  Clare CO10 ....12 C7
  Colne Engaine CO6 ..77 F1
  Cressing CM8 ......156 A3
  Earls Colne CO6 ....105 A7
  Elsenham CM22 .....94 C2
  Felsted CM6 ....151 F6
  Great Bentley CO7 ..166 E8
  Great Dunmow CM6 .150 E8
  Harwich, Bath Side CO12 .91 E5
  Harwich, Dovercourt CO12 .91 D4
  Harwich, Parkeston CO12 .90 F5
  Hatfield Peverel CM3 .193 F5
  Haverhill CB9 ....9 A8
  Kelvedon CO5 ......158 C3
  Kirby Cross CO13 ...170 B6
  Long Melford CO10 ..15 C5
  Maldon CM9 ....210 A3
  Manningtree CO11 ..86 C5
  Marks Tey CO6 .....133 B4
  Newport CB11 ......67 A8
  Rayne CM77 ....126 F1
  Saffron Walden CB11 ..22 D1
  Sible Hedingham CO9 .51 E2
  Stansted Mountfitchet
    CM24 ....119 E6
  Sudbury CO10 ......33 E7
  Takeley CM22 ....148 C7
  Thorpe-le-S CO16 ..168 F8
  Thorrington CO7 ...166 A6
  Tiptree CO5 ....179 C4
  Tollesbury CM9 .....199 D2
  Tolleshunt D'arcy CM9 .198 E5
  Trimley St M IP11 ..221 A7
  Wakes Colne CO6 ..106 D6
  Wendens Ambo CB11 .42 F5
  White Colne CO6 ...105 E8
  White Notley CM8 ..155 F2
  Wivenhoe CO7 .....164 B8
  Wrabness CO11 ......88 F3
Station Road Ind Est
  Great Dunmow CM6 .150 E7
  Tolleshunt D'arcy CM9 .198 E5
Station St Ipswich IP2 ..17 C3
  Saffron Walden CB11 .22 D1
  Walton-on-t-N CO14 .171 C8
Station Terr CM3 .....193 F5
Station Way CO1 .....109 E1
Station Yd IP2 ....17 B4
Steadman Ct CO15 ..203 D6
Steam Mill Rd CO11 .114 B8
Steamer Terr **2** CM1 .205 A3
Stebbing Prim Sch CM6 124 E5
Stebbing Rd CM6 ...152 B7
Steeds Mdw CO10 ....15 C8
Steele Cl CO6 ....132 F3
Steele Ho CO12 ......91 C5
Steeple Bumpstead Prim Sch
  CB9 ....27 B6
Steeple Bumpstead Rd
  CB9 ....26 E7
Steeple Cl CM9 ......210 D5
Steeple View CM23 ..145 F8
Steerforth St CM1 ...204 D7
Stella Maris IP2 ......16 D5
Stepfield CM8 ....177 B2
Stephen Cl Haverhill CB9 .8 F8
  Long Melford CO10 .15 B5
Stephen Cranfield Cl
  CO5 ....164 A7
Stephen Marshall Ave
  CM7 ....72 C6
Stephen Neville Ct CB11 .43 D8
Stephen's Ct IP4 .....18 B6
Stephenson Rd
  Braintree CM7 ......128 A1
  Clacton-on-S CO15 ..189 B8
  Colchester CO4 .....110 D6
Stephenson Rd W CO15 189 A1
Sterling Cl CO3 ......134 E5
Sterling Complex IP1 ..16 D7
Stevens Cl CO4 ......109 E3
Stevens La CM6 ......152 F6

Stevens Rd CM8 .....176 E1
Stevens Wlk CO4 ....136 F7
Stevenson Rd IP1 .....17 B6
Stewards Cl CO13 ...170 F7
Stewart Rd CM2 .....216 A6
Stewarts The CM23 ..145 E6
Stewarts Way CM23 ..92 F2
Stilemans Wood CM7 .128 C3
Stiles The CM9 ......210 E3
Stirling Dr CB9 ....8 C8
Stirrup Cl CM1 ......205 E7
Stirrup Mews CO3 ...134 E6
Stisted CE Prim Sch
  CM7 ....129 B6
Stivvy's Rd CM9 ....208 C3
Stock Chase CM9 ...210 B5
Stock Rd CM2 ......216 B2
Stock Terr CM9 .....210 B5
Stockhouse Cl CM9 ..180 B2
Stockhouse Rd CO5 .180 B7
Stocking La SG8 ......39 C1
Stockley Cl CB9 ....9 C7
Stockman Terr CM77 .154 C8
Stockmen Field CM23 .145 C5
Stockmers End **1** IP9 .35 A1
Stockwell **5** CO1 ...135 F7
Stoke Coll CO10 ......11 C3
Stoke Hall Rd IP2 ....17 C4
Stoke High Sch IP2 ...17 C2
Stoke Park Dr IP2 ....17 A1
Stoke Park Gdns IP2 ..17 A1
Stoke Quay IP2 ......17 D4
Stoke Rd Clare CO10 ..12 A6
  Nayland CO6 ....56 B2
Stoke St IP2 ....17 C4
Stoke-by-Nayland Mid Sch
  CO6 ....56 C6
Stoke-by-Nayland Prim Sch
  CO6 ....56 C5
Stokeash Cl CO16 ...188 A3
Stokebridge Maltings **1**
  IP2 ....17 C4
Stokes The CO14 ....171 B8
Stone Cl CM7 ....127 F2
Stone Cotts CO9 .....52 D2
Stone Hall CO10 .....12 B7
Stone La Tiptree CO5 .179 A4
  Wrabness CO11 ......88 F5
Stone Lodge La IP2 ..17 A3
Stone Lodge La W IP2 .17 F3
Stone Lodge Wlk IP2 .17 B3
Stone Path Dr CM3 ..193 F3
Stone Rd CO7 ....113 B1
Stone's Green Rd CO12 .115 E2
Stonebridge Hill CO6 .104 E7
Stonechat Rd IP2 .....16 D2
Stonecrop CO4 ......109 C2
Stonegrove Rd IP11 ..221 B1
Stonehall Dr CO16 ...168 D1
Stonehall La CO12 ...115 B1
Stoneham St CO6 ...130 F2
Stonehill Way CO5 ..201 A6
Stoneleigh Pk CO3 ..134 F4
Stoney Brook CM24 ..119 E5
Stoney Comm CM24 .119 E5
Stoney Common Rd
  CM24 ....119 D5
Stoney La CO7 ......186 A8
Stoney Pl CM24 .....119 E5
Stoneyfield Dr CM24 .119 E6
Stonham Ave CO16 ..188 A4
Stony La CM6 ....70 A2
Stopford Ct **2** IP1 ...17 A6
Storelands Ho IP11 ..221 B6
Stores Rd CO5 ......179 C6
Stores The CO11 .....86 F4
Storms Way CM2 ...206 B2
Stort Lodge CM23 ...145 D8
Stort Rd CM23 ......145 F6
Stort Valley Ind Pk
  CM23 ....119 B2
Stortford Hall Ind Pk
  CM23 ....146 B7
Stortford Hall Pk CM23 .146 B8
Stortford Hall Rd **3**
  CM23 ....146 B8
Stortford Rd
  Clavering CB11 ......65 C4
  Great Dunmow CM6 .123 C1
  Takeley CM6 ....149 D7
Stour Ave IP11 ......221 C3
Stour Cl Glemsford CO10 ..2 C2
  Harwich CO12 ......90 D2
Stour Ct CM7 ....128 D1
Stour Estuary Nature
  Reserve★ CO12 ....89 C3
Stour Gdns CO10 ....34 B4
Stour Gn CO10 ....12 B6
Stour Rd CO12 ....91 D5
Stour St Cavendish CO10 .13 C8
  Manningtree CO11 ..86 D4
  Sudbury CO10 ......33 E7
Stour Vale Clare CO10 .12 A6
  Stoke by C CO10 ....10 D2
Stour Valley Rd CB9 ...9 B7
Stour View Ct CO12 ..91 D5
Stour Wlk CO4 ......110 E2
Stourdale Cl CO11 ....86 A3
Stourside IP9 ....91 A8
Stourton Rd CM8 ...176 E3
Stourview Ave CO11 ..87 A4
Stourview Cl CO11 ...87 A4
Stow Ct CO4 ....109 F5
Stradbroke Rd IP4 ...18 A7
Straight Rd Boxted CO4 ..82 F2
  Bradfield CO11 ......87 C1
  Colchester CO3 .....134 F5
  Great Bentley CO7 ..167 A4

Straight Way CO2 ......161 A2
Strand The IP2 ....37 C8
Strasbourg Sq 6 CB9 ....9 B8
Stratford Pl 4 CO14 ...171 C8
Stratford Rd
Clacton-on-S CO15 ......189 D6
Dedham CO7 ....84 D7
Stratford St Mary Prim Sch
CO7 ....58 C1
Straw La CO10 ....33 D7
Strawberry Cl CM7 .....128 A1
Strawberry Fields CB9 ....8 D7
Strawberry La CO5 .....179 F3
Strawbrook Hill CM3 ...173 E4
Street Farm Bglws CO11 .61 A2
Street The Ardleigh CO7 .111 E8
Ashen CO10 ....11 D1
Belchamp Walter CO10 ....31 C8
Belstead IP8 ....36 C6
Berden CM23 ....92 B8
Birdbrook CO9 ....28 B7
Bradfield CO11 ....87 E1
Bradwell CM7 ....129 D3
Brantham CO11 ....61 A1
Bulmer CO10 ....32 E5
Capel St M IP9 ....35 A1
Chappel CO6 ....106 D5
Cressing CM77 ....156 A6
East Bergholt CO7 ......59 B2
Feering CO5 ....158 E5
Foxearth CO10 ....14 C6
Galleywood CM2 ....216 B2
Gosfield CO9 ....102 E7
Great Hallingbury CM22 ..147 B4
Great Henny CO10 ....33 E3
Great Tey CO6 ....132 C8
Harkstead IP9 ....63 B2
Hatfield Peverel CM3 ...193 F4
Holbrook IP9 ....62 D6
Kirby-le-S CO13 ....143 B1
Little Clacton CO16 ....168 C3
Little Dunmow CM6 .....151 D7
Little Totham CM9 .....197 B5
Little Waltham CM3 ....191 B6
Manuden CM23 ....92 F2
Messing CO5 ....159 D2
Pebmarsh CO9 ....78 A8
Pentlow CO10 ....14 A8
Purleigh CM3,CM9 ......220 F1
Ramsey CO12 ....90 A1
Rayne CM77 ....126 F2
Salcott-cum-virley CM9 ..199 B8
Shalford CM7 ....100 E7
Stisted CM7 ....129 C6
Stoke by Clare CO10 .....11 B3
Stratford St M CO7 ......84 C8
Tendring CO16 ....140 E5
Terling CM3 ....175 C2
Tiptree CO5 ....179 A8
Toppesfield CO9 ....50 B7
Washbrook IP8 ....35 F8
Weeley CO16 ....140 F1
Wherstead IP9 ....37 B6
White Notley CM8 ......155 E1
Wickham Bishops CM8 ...195 F5
Woodham Walter CM9 ...208 D2
Stretford Ct CM8 ......156 D3
Strethall Rd CB11 ....21 C4
Strickmere CO7 ....58 D2
Strood Cl CO5 ....201 B7
Strood The CO5 ....183 C3
Strudwick Cl 10 CM7 ...127 F2
Strutt Cl CM3 ....194 A4
Stuart Cl
Great Baddow CM2 ......217 B6
Ipswich IP4 ....17 F7
Stuart Pawsey Ct CO7 ..137 C1
Stuarts Way CM7 ....128 B2
Stubbs Cl Ipswich IP3 ....18 A1
Kirby Cross CO13 ......170 E7
Lawford CO11 ....86 B4
Stubbs La CM7 ....128 C1
Studd's La CO4 ....109 D4
Stump Cross CB10 ....3 C5
Stump La CM1 ....205 D4
Stump's Cross CO9 ....29 A2
Sturdee Ave IP3 ....18 B3
Sturmer Ct 3 CO2 .....136 A1
Sturmer End Ind Est CB9 .9 C6
Sturmer Rd Haverhill CB9 ..9 C6
Haverhill, Calford Green CB9 .9 F7
Sturrick La CO7 ....139 D1
Stutton CE Prim Sch IP9 62 A2
Stutton Cl IP9 ....62 A2
Stutton Gn IP9 ....62 C1
Stutton La IP9 ....61 C5
Stutton Rd CO11 ....61 A2
Stylemans La CM22 .....146 B5
Styles CM7 ....71 D2
Sub-Station Rd IP11 ...221 B2
Sudbourne Ave CO16 ...188 A4
Sudbourne Rd IP11 ....221 B5
Sudbury Rd Bulmer CO10 .32 F6
Bures CO8 ....55 F1
Castle Hedingham CO9 ....52 B4
Felixstowe IP11 ....221 A4
Gestingthorpe CO9 ....31 F2
Great Cornard CO10 ......34 F7
Great Maplestead CO9 ....53 C2
Halstead CO9 ....76 F3
Long Melford CO10 ....15 C3
Stoke-by-N CO6 ....56 C6
Sudbury Sta CO10 ....33 F7
Sudbury Upper Sch CO10 15 A1
Sue Ryder Mus* CO10 .....1 D1
Suffolk Ave CO5 ....201 D7
Suffolk Cl
Clacton-on-S CO15 ......189 E7
Suffolk Cl *continued*
Colchester CO4 ....110 B1
Suffolk Coll IP4 ....17 E5
Suffolk Coll (Argyll St Annexe) IP4 ....17 D6
Suffolk Cres CM9 ......209 E1
Suffolk Dr CM2 ....206 A4
Suffolk Ent Pk IP1 ......17 B5
Suffolk Knowle CO8 ......55 F1
Suffolk Rd Ipswich IP4 ...17 D7
Maldon CM9 ....209 E1
Sudbury CO10 ....33 E8
Suffolk Ret Pk IP1 ......17 A6
Suffolk Ski Ctr* IP2 .....37 B8
Suffolk Sq CO10 ....33 E8
Suffolk St CO14 ....171 C8
Sugar La CO9 ....74 E7
Sulleys Hill IP7 ....58 B8
Sullivan Cl CO4 ....136 E6
Summer Hill Rd CB11 ....43 D8
Summercroft Inf Sch
CM23 ....146 C8
Summercroft Jun Sch
CM23 ....146 C8
Summerfield Cl IP4 ......18 D8
Summerfield Ct IP4 ......18 D8
Summerfields CO9 ....51 E1
Summerleaze Ct CM77 .154 D7
Sun Lido Square Gdns
CM77 ....127 C2
Sunbank CM6 ....150 E7
Sunbeam Ave CO15 .....203 E6
Sunbeam Cl CO5 ....164 A8
Sunbury Way CM9 ......220 F8
Sundale Cl CO15 ....189 F6
Sunfield Cl IP4 ....18 B6
Sunflower Cl 5 CM1 ...205 F6
Sunningdale CM23 .....145 E6
Sunningdale Ave
Felixstowe IP11 ....221 F6
Ipswich IP4 ....18 D5
Sunningdale Dr IP11 ...221 F6
Sunningdale Fall CM3 .194 B4
Sunningdale Rd CM1 ...204 E4
Sunningdale Way CO13 .170 E7
Sunny Point CO14 ......144 E3
Sunnyfields Rd CM7 ...102 D2
Sunnyside Braintree CM7 127 E3
Stansted Mountfitchet
CM24 ....119 E6
Sunnyside Rd CO6 .....107 D5
Sunnyside Way CO16 ...168 C1
Sunnyway Cotts CM3 ...218 E3
Sunray Ave IP11 ....221 F6
Sunrise Ave CM1 ....205 A5
Surbiton Rd IP1 ....16 F8
Surrey Ct CO15 ....189 A2
Surrey La CO5 ....179 C4
Surrey Rd
Felixstowe IP11 ....221 D4
Ipswich IP1 ....17 A6
Sussex Cl CM3 ....206 F8
Sussex Gdns CO15 .....189 E6
Sussex Rd CO3 ....135 C7
Sutherland Ho CM1 ....205 A4
Sutor Cl CM8 ....176 E1
Sutton Mead CM2 ......206 A4
Sutton Park Ave CO3 ..135 A3
Swains Ct CO10 ....32 E5
Swallow Cl Harwich CO12 .90 E1
Layer-de-l-H CO2 ......162 A5
Swallow Field CO6 ....105 B6
Swallow Path CM2 .....216 B5
Swallow Rd IP2 ....16 C3
Swallow Wlk CO9 ....76 F1
Swallow's Row CO7 ....167 B8
Swallow's Row CO7 ....140 B1
Swallowdale
Clacton-on-S CO15 ......188 F6
Colchester CO2 ....136 C3
Swallowtail Cl IP8 ....36 E8
Swan Chase CO9 ....75 E8
Swan Cl Colchester CO4 .136 E5
Hatfield Peverel CM3 ...193 F4
Swan Cotts CM3 ....193 F4
Swan Ct
2 Bishop's Stortford
CM23 ....145 F6
Maldon CM9 ....210 B4
New Mistley CO11 ....87 A3
Sible Hedingham CO9 .....75 E8
Swan Dale CO15 ....188 F7
Swan Farm Mews IP8 ....16 A1
Swan Gr CO6 ....106 C5
Swan Hill IP8 ....16 A2
Swan La Haverhill CB9 ....9 A8
Long Melford CO10 ....15 C7
Swan Mdw CO7 ....58 C1
Swan Pas 13 CO1 ......135 F7
Swan Rd CO16 ....141 D5
Swan Side CM7 ....127 F3
Swan St Chappel CO6 ..106 C3
Kelvedon CO5 ....158 D3
Sible Hedingham CO9 .....51 E1
Swan Yd CO6 ....131 A2
Swanfield CO10 ....15 C7
Swans Pasture CM1 ....205 D6
Swanscomb Rd CO6 ....105 F5
Swansea Ave IP2 ....17 B1
Swatchway Cl IP3 ....38 B8
Swaynes CO7 ....58 C2
Sweden Cl CO12 ....90 F4
Swedish Est CO11 ......115 B5
Sweet Briar CM23 .....145 B6
Sweet Briar Rd CO3 ...134 C7
Sweet Mead CB10 ....22 E3
Swift Ave
Clacton-on-S CO15 ......203 F6
Swift Ave *continued*
Colchester CO3 ....134 C4
Swift Cl CM7 ....155 A7
Swinbourne Dr CM7 ...127 D3
Swinton Cl IP2 ....16 D1
Swiss Ave CM1 ....205 A4
Sworders Yd 3 CM23 ..145 F7
Sycamore Cl Ipswich IP8 .16 C1
Takeley CM22 ....148 C7
Witham CM8 ....177 A5
Sycamore Gr CM7 ......127 E1
Sycamore Pl CO7 ......166 E8
Sycamore Rd
Colchester CO4 ....136 D8
Great Cornard CO10 ......34 B7
Heybridge CM9 ....210 C6
Sycamore Way
Brantham CO11 ....60 D1
Chelmsford CM2 ....216 C6
Clacton-on-S CO15 .....188 C3
Kirby Cross CO13 .....170 D6
Sycamores The CM23 ..146 B6
Sydner Cl CM2 ....217 A5
Sydney St
Brightlingsea CO7 .....185 F6
Colchester CO2 ....136 B1
Syers Field CM7 ....74 B2
Sylvan Cl CM2 ....216 B6
Symmons Cl CM77 .....126 F1
Syringa Ct 6 CO4 .....136 E7

T

Taber Pl CM8 ....177 B3
Tabor Ave CM7 ....127 E3
Tabor Cl CO7 ....185 F8
Tabor High Sch CM7 ...127 D4
Tabor Rd CO1 ....136 C7
Tabor's Hill CM2 ......216 F7
Tabors Ave CM2 ....216 F8
Tacket St IP4 ....17 D5
Tacon Ct IP11 ....221 C1
Tacon Rd IP11 ....221 C1
Tailors CM23 ....145 B5
Tailors Cl CM77 ....154 C8
Tait Mews CM9 ....210 A2
Takeley Pk CM22 ......148 C6
Takeley Prim Sch CM22 148 C8
Talbot Ave CO15 ......203 F6
Talbot Rd
Little Clacton CO16 ....168 C4
Sudbury CO10 ....15 F2
Talbot St CO12 ....91 D5
Talbots IP11 ....221 D3
Talcott Rd CO2 ....136 A2
Talisman Cl CO5 ....179 D6
Talisman Wlk CO5 .....179 D6
Tall Trees CO4 ....109 E3
Tally Ho CO4 ....110 B4
Tally Ho Cnr CO7 ....58 D1
Talmash Gdns IP2 ....17 A4
Tamar Ave CM8 ....176 E2
Tamar Rise CM1 ....205 C6
Tamarisk Way
Clacton-on-S CO15 .....203 F6
Colchester CO4 ....136 E8
Tambour Cl CO6 ....132 C8
Tamdown Way CM7 .....127 C4
Tamworth Chase CO2 ..136 A2
Tan La CO16 ....168 F4
Tangerine Cl CO4 .....136 D6
Tanner Cl CO16 ....188 B3
Tanners Mdw CM7 .....128 D2
Tanners View IP1 ....16 F7
Tanners Way CB10 ......22 E1
Tanyard The CM6 ....70 A2
Tapestry Ct CO6 ....105 B6
Tapestry Wlk CM7 .....128 D2
Tapley Rd CM1 ....204 F7
Tapsworth Cl CO16 ....188 D5
Tapwoods CO3 ....135 A7
Tara Cl CO4 ....110 D1
Tarragon Cl CO5 ......179 C4
Tarragona Mews CO2 ..136 B4
Tasman Ct CM1 ....204 E5
Tasman Rd CB9 ....9 C7
Tasmania Rd IP4 ....18 D6
Tattersall Way CM1 ...215 E7
Tattingstone CE Prim Sch
IP9 ....61 D7
Taunton Rd
Chelmsford CM1 ....205 E5
Felixstowe IP11 ....221 D6
Tavern St IP1 ....17 C6
Taverners Wlk CM8 ....176 F4
Tavistock Rd CM1 .....205 E5
Tawell Mews CO5 ......179 D5
Tawney Cl IP9 ....35 A1
Tawneys Ride CO8 ....80 A8
Taylor Ave CM1 ....204 E5
Taylor Ct CO1 ....135 F7
Taylor Dr CO11 ....86 C4
Taylor's Rd CO5 ......163 F8
Taylors End Rd CM24 ..120 E1
Tayspill Ct CO2 ......135 B3
Teak Wlk CM8 ....177 A4
Teal Cl Colchester CO4 ..137 A8
Great Notley CM77 .....154 B5
Ipswich IP2 ....16 D3
Teal Way CO5 ....158 D2
Teapot Cnr IP7 ....57 E8
Tedder Cl CO2 ....136 A4
Tees Cl CM8 ....176 E2
Tees Rd CM1 ....205 C6
Teign Dr CM8 ....176 D2
Telford Pl CM1 ....205 D4
Telford Rd
Braintree CM7 ....128 A1
Clacton-on-S CO15 .....189 C8
Telford Way CO4 ......110 D6
Temperance Yd CO6 ...105 B6
Templar Rd CM7 ......128 D2
Templar's Ct CB9 ....8 E7
Templars Cl CM8 .....176 F4
Templars Jun Sch CM8 .176 F5
Temple Cl CO13 ......171 A6
Temple Ct CO4 ....110 D2
Temple La CM8,CM77 ..156 C3
Temple Pattle CO11 .....86 C7
Temple Rd
Colchester CO2 ....135 A2
Ipswich IP3 ....18 C4
Temple Way CM9 ......209 F5
Templemead CM8 .....176 F3
Templewood Rd CO4 ..110 E1
Ten Acre App CM9 .....209 F5
Tenby Rd IP2 ....17 B1
Tendring Prim Sch
CO16 ....140 F6
Tendring Rd
Little Bentley CO7 .....140 A8
Tendring CO12 ....114 E2
Thorpe-le-S CO16 .....141 D4
Tendring Tech Coll
Thorpe-le-S CO16 .....142 A1
Walton-on-t-N CO13 ...171 A7
Tennyson Cl CM7 .....154 F8
Tennyson Rd
Chelmsford CM1 ....204 F5
Ipswich IP4 ....17 F5
Tenpenny Hill CO7 ....165 E5
Tenter Cl CM7 ....127 F5
Tenter Field CO7 ....58 D1
Tenterfield CM6 ......150 E8
Tenterfield Rd CM9 ...210 A2
Tenterfields CB11 ....42 F1
Tenth Ave CM24 ......120 C2
Terling CE Prim Sch
CM3 ....175 C3
Terling Cl CO2 ....136 A1
Terling Hall Rd CM3 ..193 C7
Terling Rd
Hatfield Peverel CM3 ...193 F6
Witham CM8 ....176 B3
Terminal Rd N CM22,
CM24 ....121 B4
Terminal Rd S CM22,
CM24 ....121 B4
Termitts Chase CM3 ...194 A7
Tern Cl Haverhill CB9 ......9 C7
Kelvedon CO5 ....158 D3
Tern Mews CO7 ....164 B8
Tern Rd IP2 ....16 E2
Terndale CO15 ....188 F6
Terra Cotta Pl CO10 ......2 E8
Terrace Hall Chase
CO6 ....109 D6
Terrace The
Cavendish CO10 ....1 D1
Felsted CM6 ....152 B5
Hatfield Peverel CM3 ...194 B5
Tew Cl CO5 ....179 D5
Tewkesbury Rd CO15 ..188 F4
Tey Rd Aldham CO6 ...106 E1
Coggeshall CO6 ....131 C4
Earls Colne CO6 ......105 D4
Tey Road Cl CO6 .....105 D6
Thackeray Cl CM7 ....155 A8
Thames Ave CM1 .....204 D4
Thames Cl CM7 ....128 D1
Thanet Rd IP4 ....18 B6
Thanet Wlk CO5 ......164 A8
Thatchers Dr CO7 .....137 F6
Thatchers The CM23 ..145 C5
Thatchers Way CM77 ..154 C8
Thaxted Prim Sch CM6 ..70 A2
Thaxted Rd Debden CB11 .68 C6
Elder Street CB10 ....44 C4
Saffron Walden CB10 .....43 F8
Thaxted CB10 ....69 E8
Thaxted Wlk CO2 .....163 A8
The Bglws CM7 ....100 F5
Theberton Rd IP3 ....18 B1
Thelsford Wlk CO4 ...136 F7
Thetford Ct CM1 ......204 E1
Thetford Rd 1 IP1 ......17 A7
Thieves' Cnr CM1 .....204 A4
Third Ave
Chelmsford CM1 ....205 B5
Clacton-on-S CO15 .....189 C4
Frinton-on-S CO13 ....170 E4
Glemsford CO10 ....2 C5
Halstead CO9 ....77 B1
Harwich CO12 ....91 C3
Seawick CO16 ....203 B6
Stansted Mountfitchet
CM24 ....120 B2
Walton-on-t-N CO14 ...144 E3
Thirlmere Cl CM77 ...154 D7
Thirslet Dr CM9 ......210 C4
Thirtieth St CM24 ....120 F3
Thirtle Cl CO16 ......188 D6
Thistle Cl IP2 ....16 F4
Thistledown
Highwoods CO4 ....110 B3
Panfield CM7 ....127 A7
Thistley Cl CM9 ......211 E6
Thistley Cres CB11 .....66 E1
Thistley Green Rd CM7 .128 B7
Thomas Ave IP11 .....221 A8
Thomas Bell Rd CO6 ..105 A6
Thomas Cl CM2 ....205 F3
Thomas Heskin Ct 11
CM23 ....146 A7
Thomas Rd CO15 ......188 D4
Thomas St CO7 ....185 F6
Thomas Wakley Cl CO4 .109 F5
Thomas Wlk CB11 ....20 F1
Thomas, Lord Audley Sch
CO2 ....135 F2
Thompson Ave CO3 ...134 F6
Thompson Rd IP1 ....16 F8
Thorington Cl CM77 ..154 C6
Thorley High CM23 ...145 F2
Thorley Hill CM23 ....145 F5
Thorley Hill Prim Sch
CM23 ....145 F4
Thorley La CM23 .....145 F3
Thorley La E CM23 ...145 D3
Thorley La W CM23 ...145 B4
Thorley Neighbourhood Ctr
CM23 ....145 D4
Thorley Park Rd CM23 .145 F4
Thorn Gr CM23 ....146 B6
Thorn Grove Prim Sch
CM23 ....146 B6
Thorn Way IP11 ......221 C4
Thornbera Cl CM23 ...145 F4
Thornbera Gdns CM23 .145 F4
Thornbera Rd CM23 ...145 F4
Thornberry Ave CO16 ..140 F1
Thornbury Rd CO15 ...188 F4
Thornbush La IP8 ....16 A8
Thorncroft CB10 ....22 F2
Thorndon Cl CO16 ....188 A4
Thorne Rd CO5 ....158 B2
Thorney Rd IP9 ....35 A1
Thornfield Ct CO2 ....136 D2
Thornfield Rd CM23 ..145 E8
Thornhayes Cl IP2 ......17 A3
Thornhill CM3 ....220 D1
Thornhill Cl CO13 ....170 F7
Thornley Dr IP4 ....18 C8
Thorns Way CO14 .....171 A8
Thornton Dr CO4 .....109 F2
Thornton Rd CM6 .....148 F7
Thornwood CO4 ....109 F4
Thornwood Cl CO5 ....201 D6
Thoroughfare 9 IP1 .....17 C6
Thoroughgood Rd CO15 188 F3
Thorpe Cross CO16 ...169 D8
Thorpe Park La CO16 ..169 B7
Thorpe Rd
Beaumont CO16 ....141 B5
Clacton-on-S CO15 .....188 F7
Kirby Cross CO13 .....169 E7
Weeley CO16 ....141 A2
Thorpe Wlk CO4 ......136 F7
Thorpe-le-Soken Sta
CO16 ....168 F7
Thorrington Cross CO7 .165 F5
Thorrington Rd
Great Bentley CO7 .....166 C8
Little Clacton CO16 ....168 C4
Thorrington Tide Mill*
CO7 ....165 E3
Thracian Cl CO2 ......135 A3
Threadneedle St
2 Chelmsford CM1 .....205 B2
Dedham CO7 ....84 F7
Three Acres CO16 ....187 A4
Three Crowns Rd CO4 .109 E2
Three Gates Cl CO9 ..103 D8
Three Mile Hill CM4 ..215 C2
Thremhall Ave
Bishop's Stortford CM23 .146 F8
Great Hallingbury CM22,
CM24 ....147 C8
Takeley CM24 ....121 A2
Threshelfords Bsns Pk
CO5 ....158 E3
Thresher Cl CM23 ....145 C5
Thresher Rise CM77 ..154 C8
Threshers End CO3 ...134 D5
Thrift Wood CM3 .....218 F1
Thriftwood Sch CM2 ..216 B3
Thrimley La CM23 ....118 C6
Thrushdale CO15 .....188 F6
Thurlow Pl 10 CB9 ....9 B8
Thurlston Cl CO4 .....110 D1
Thurstable Cl CM9 ...199 E2
Thurstable Rd CM9 ...199 D2
Thurstable Sch CO5 ..179 D6
Thurstable Way CM9 ..199 E2
Thurston Ct IP11 .....221 A3
Thyme Mews CM8 .....176 E3
Thyme Rd CO5 ....179 C5
Tiberius Cl
Colchester CO4 ....110 B6
Haverhill CB9 ....9 D7
Tiberius Gdns CM8 ...194 E8
Tideswell Cl CM7 .....128 D4
Tidings Hill CO9 ......103 E8
Tiffin Dr CO5 ....179 E5
Tilbury Rd
Great Yeldham CO9 ......30 A3
Ridgewell CO9 ....29 C7
Tildesley Cl CO13 ....170 A6
Tile Barn La CO11 ......85 C2
Tile House Rd CO6 ...109 B8
Tilkey Rd CO6 ....130 F3
Tillwicks Cl CO6 .....105 A7
Timber Hill CO1 ......136 C6
Timbers Cl CM77 .....154 B7
Timsons La CM2 ......205 E4
Tinabrook Cl IP2 ....16 E1
Tindal Sq 3 CM1 .....205 B2
Tindal St CM1 ....205 B2
Tindon End Rd CB10 ....46 D2

Tinker Ave CM7 . . . . .73 C6
Tinker St CO12 . . . . .116 D8
Tinnocks La CM0 . . . . .213 B1
Tintagel Way CM9 . . . . . . .220 E8
Tintern Cl IP2 . . . . .17 A2
Tippett Cl CO4 . . . . .136 E6
Tiptree Hall La CO5 . . . . .179 B2
Tiptree Heath Prim Sch
CO5 . . . . .179 B3
Tiptree Mus★ CO5 . . . . . .179 E4
Tiptree Rd
Great Braxted CM8,CM9 . .196 B8
Wickham Bishops CM8 . . .195 F6
Titania Cl CO4 . . . . .136 E6
Titchwell Dr IP3 . . . . .38 D7
Tithe Cl CM8 . . . . .176 E3
Titus Way CO4 . . . . .110 B6
Tobruk Rd
Chelmsford CM1 . . . . . .204 F6
Colchester CO2 . . . . . . .135 D3
Tofts Chase CM3 . . . . . . .207 E5
Tofts Wlk 12 CM7 . . . . . .127 F3
Tog La
Great Horkesley CO6 . . . . .82 A3
Little Horkesley CO6 . . . . .81 B3
Toga Cl CO2 . . . . .135 A2
Tokely Rd CO7 . . . . .139 A3
Tokio Rd IP4 . . . . .18 A6
Toll Gate Rd IP9 . . . . .35 A1
Toller Rd IP3 . . . . .17 E3
Tollesbury Rd CM9 . . . . . .198 F3
Tollesbury Sch CM9 . . . . .199 D1
Tolleshunt D'arcy Prim Sch
CM9 . . . . .198 D4
Tolleshunt D'arcy Rd
CM9 . . . . .197 F3
Tollgate Ct CO3 . . . . . . .134 C6
Tollgate Dr CO3 . . . . . . .134 B6
Tollgate E CO3 . . . . .134 C6
Tollgate Rd CO3 . . . . . . .134 C5
Tollgate Rdbt CO3 . . . . . .134 C6
Tollgate W CO3 . . . . .134 B5
Tolliday Cl CO7 . . . . .137 A2
Tolly Cobbold Brewery Tours
& Brewery★ IP3 . . . . . . .17 E3
Tolworth Rd IP4 . . . . .18 A6
Tom Davies Ho 8 CM7 . . .127 F2
Tom Tit La CM9 . . . . .219 E2
Tom's La CM7 . . . . .72 A6
Tomline Rd
Felixstowe IP11 . . . . . . .221 E4
Ipswich IP3 . . . . .18 A4
Tony Webb Cl CO4 . . . . . .110 C4
Tooley's Ct (Almshouses) 9
IP4 . . . . .17 D5
Top Rd
Tolleshunt Knights CM9 . .180 A2
Wimbish CB10 . . . . .45 E3
Woodham Walter CM9 . . .208 D2
Toppesfield Rd CO9 . . . . . .50 F8
Torquay Rd CM1 . . . . . . .205 D5
Torrington Cl CM1 . . . . . .205 E5
Tortoiseshell Cl IP8 . . . . . .36 E8
Tortoiseshell Way CM7 . . .127 E1
Tortosa Cl CO2 . . . . .136 B4
Torver Cl CM77 . . . . .154 C6
Tot La CM23,CM24 . . . . . .119 D4
Totham Hill Gn CM9 . . . . .196 B6
Totlands Dr CO15 . . . . . . .189 A7
Totnes Wlk CM1 . . . . . . .205 E6
Totteridge Cl CO16 . . . . . .188 D5
Toucan Way CO15 . . . . . .188 F6
Toulmin Rd CM3 . . . . . . .194 A4
Tovell's Rd IP4 . . . . .17 F6
Tower Ave CM1 . . . . .204 F4
Tower Cl 4 CB9 . . . . .8 E7
Tower Cut CO7 . . . . .185 F6
Tower Cvn Pk CO15 . . . . .203 D6
Tower Est CO16 . . . . .185 E4
Tower Hill Redoubt Fort★
CO12 . . . . .91 E5
Tower Mill Rd IP1 . . . . . . .16 F7
Tower Ramparts IP1 . . . . . .17 C6
Tower Ramparts Ctr 8
IP1 . . . . .17 C6
Tower Rd
Clacton-on-S CO15 . . . . .188 E1
Felixstowe IP11 . . . . . . .221 D3
Wivenhoe CO7 . . . . .137 B2
Tower St
Brightlingsea CO7 . . . . . .185 F6
Ipswich IP1 . . . . .17 C6
Towers Rd CM9 . . . . .210 C5
Towers The CO15 . . . . . . .189 A4
Town Croft CM1 . . . . .205 A5
Town End Field CM8 . . . . .194 F8
Town St CM6 . . . . .70 A2
Townfield St CM1 . . . . . . .205 B3
Townsend CM2 . . . . .206 B5
Townsend Rd CO5 . . . . . .179 C7
Towse Cl CO16 . . . . .188 C5
Traddles Ct CM1 . . . . . . .204 F6
Trafalgar Cl IP4 . . . . .17 F6
Trafalgar Cotts CO12 . . . . .90 F3
Trafalgar Ct CM7 . . . . . . .128 B4
Trafalgar Rd
Clacton-on-S CO15 . . . . .188 E1
Colchester CO3 . . . . . . .134 C6
Trafalgar Way CM7 . . . . . .128 B4
Trajan Cl CO4 . . . . .110 B6
Tredgetts CB10 . . . . .6 B1
Tree Cl CO15 . . . . .188 F7
Treetops IP11 . . . . .221 C6
Treetops Ct CO4 . . . . . . .109 F5
Trefoil Cl IP2 . . . . .16 F4

Trefoil Ct 4 CB9 . . . . .8 F7
Trelawn CM3 . . . . .206 E8
Trenchard Cres CM1 . . . . .205 D8
Trenchard Lodge CM1 . . . .205 D7
Trent Rd Chelmsford CM1 .204 D5
Ipswich IP3 . . . . .17 F2
Witham CM8 . . . . .176 E2
Trevose IP11 . . . . .221 F4
Trews Gdns CO5 . . . . . . .158 C3
Triangle Garage CM9 . . . .210 B5
Triangle Sh Ctr CO14 . . . . .170 F7
Trickett Ct CO7 . . . . .137 B1
Trimley Cl CO16 . . . . .188 B4
Trimley St Mary Prim Sch
IP11 . . . . .221 A7
Trimley St Pll 221 A7
Trinity Ave IP11 . . . . .221 A4
Trinity Cl
Bishop's Stortford CM23 . .145 F6
Chelmsford CM2 . . . . . .205 D3
Manningtree CO11 . . . . . .86 D3
Rushmere St A IP5 . . . . . .18 F7
West Mersea CO5 . . . . . .201 C7
Wivenhoe CO7 . . . . .137 C1
Trinity Ct CO9 . . . . .76 E2
Trinity Farm Ct 12 CO11 . . .86 D1
Trinity Mews CO5 . . . . . .201 C7
Trinity Rd
Chelmsford CM2 . . . . . .205 D2
Halstead CO9 . . . . .76 D1
Manningtree CO11 . . . . . .86 D3
Trinity Road Prim Sch
CM2 . . . . .205 D2
Trinity Sq 19 CO1 . . . . . . .135 F7
Trinity St
Bishop's Stortford CM23 . .145 F6
Colchester CO1 . . . . . . .135 F7
Halstead CO9 . . . . .76 D2
Ipswich IP4 . . . . .17 E4
Trinity Terr 3 CO9 . . . . . .76 D1
Trinity Way CM23 . . . . . . .145 F6
Trinovantian Way CM7 . . .128 A2
Triumph Ave CO15 . . . . . .203 E7
Triumph Cl CO4 . . . . . . .136 E5
Troon Gdns IP4 . . . . .18 B8
Trotters Field CM7 . . . . . .128 B3
Trotwood Cl CM1 . . . . . . .204 E7
Troys Chase CM3 . . . . . . .175 C6
Trunette Rd CO15 . . . . . .188 C3
Trusses Rd CM0 . . . . .214 F3
Tryon Ct 6 CO9 . . . . .76 D1
Tucker Dr CM8 . . . . .176 F1
Tucker's Row 4 CM23 . . . .145 F6
Tuddenham Ave IP4 . . . . . .17 E7
Tuddenham Rd IP4 . . . . . . .17 E8
Tudor CE Prim Sch CO10 . 15 F1
Tudor Cl
Brightlingsea CO7 . . . . . .185 E8
Jaywick CO15 . . . . .188 A1
Sudbury CO10 . . . . .15 E1
Walton-on-t-N CO14 . . . .144 D2
Witham CM8 . . . . .176 F1
Tudor Ct CO5 . . . . .201 C7
Tudor Gn
Clacton-on-S CO15 . . . . .203 F8
Jaywick CO15 . . . . .187 F1
Sudbury CO10 . . . . .15 E2
Tudor Par CO15 . . . . .203 G8
Tudor Pl 3 IP4 . . . . .17 D6
Tudor Rd CO10 . . . . .15 E1
Tudor Rose Cl CO3 . . . . . .134 C7
Tudwick Rd CM9 . . . . . . .197 E6
Tudor Works 12 IP4 . . . . . .17 C5
Tufnell Way CO4 . . . . . . .109 D2
Tufted Cl CM77 . . . . .154 C5
Tugby Pl CM1 . . . . .204 E6
Tukes Way CB11 . . . . .43 F7
Tulip Cl CM1 . . . . .205 E7
Tulip Way CO16 . . . . .188 C4
Tulip Wlk CO4 . . . . .136 D7
Tumulus Way CO2 . . . . . .135 A3
Tunstall Cl CO16 . . . . . . .187 B5
Tupman Cl CM1 . . . . .204 D6
Turin St IP2 . . . . .17 C4
Turkentine Cl CO10 . . . . . .34 D5
Turkey Cock La CO3,
CO6 . . . . .133 E7
Turkey Oaks CM1 . . . . . . .205 D3
Turner Ave CO11 . . . . .86 B5
Turner Cl
Black Notley CM77 . . . . .155 B4
Wivenhoe CO7 . . . . .137 C1
Turner Rd Colchester CO4 .109 F3
Ipswich IP3 . . . . .38 A8
Turners Cres CM23 . . . . . .145 C4
Turnpike Cl CO7 . . . . .110 E8
Turnpike Pl CM7 . . . . . . .128 A3
Turnstone End 3 CO4 . . . .136 E8
Turpins Ave CO15 . . . . . . .189 C5
Turpins Cl CO15 . . . . .189 C5
Turpins Ct CO15 . . . . . . .189 C5
Turpins La
Kirby Cross CO13 . . . . . .170 E7
Kirby-le-S CO13 . . . . . . .170 E8
Turret Green Ct 7 IP1 . . . .17 C5
Turret Ho CO15 . . . . .189 A2
Turret La IP4 . . . . .17 C5
Turstan Rd CM8 . . . . .194 E8
Tusser Cl CM8 . . . . .177 B7
Tusser Ct CM2 . . . . .216 D8
Tusset Mews CO3 . . . . . .134 E7
Tweed Cl CO9 . . . . .103 D8
Twelve Acres CM7 . . . . . .128 D3
Twenty First St CM24 . . . .120 F3
Twin Oaks CM2 . . . . .206 A4
Twining Rd CO3 . . . . .134 E4
Twitten La CM2 . . . . .216 B2

Twitty Fee CM3 . . . . .219 A8
Two Acres IP9 . . . . .35 B2
Twyford Bsns Ctr The
CM23 . . . . .146 A4
Twyford Bury La CM22,
CM23 . . . . .146 A4
Twyford Cl CM23 . . . . . . .146 A5
Twyford Gdns CM23 . . . . .145 F4
Twyford Mill CM22 . . . . . .146 A3
Twyford Rd CM23 . . . . . . .146 A5
Tyburn Hill CO6 . . . . .106 A6
Tydeman Cl CO3 . . . . . . .134 C4
Tye Cnr CO10 . . . . .32 F2
Tye Gn CO10 . . . . .2 B5
Tye Green Paddocks CO10 2 B5
Tye Green Rd CM22 . . . . .120 D6
Tye La CO7 . . . . .137 E3
Tye Rd CO7 . . . . .137 E2
Tye Rd The CO7 . . . . .167 B7
Tyed Croft CO3 . . . . .134 D6
Tyehurst Cres CO4 . . . . . .110 C2
Tyler Ave CO16 . . . . .188 B3
Tyler St Harwich CO12 . . . .90 F5
Ipswich IP2 . . . . .17 D4
Tylers CB10 . . . . .23 E1
Tylers Cl CM2 . . . . .216 B6
Tylers Gn IP11 . . . . .221 A7
Tylneys Rd CO9 . . . . .77 A3
Tymperley Ct 9 CO1 . . . . .136 A6
Tymperleys Clock Mus★
CO1 . . . . .135 F7
Tyndale Dr CO15 . . . . . . .188 A1
Tyndales La CM3 . . . . . . .219 B5
Tyne Way CM1 . . . . .204 D5
Tynedale Ct CO4 . . . . . . .110 B4
Tynedale Sq CO4 . . . . . . .110 B4
Tyrells Cl CM2 . . . . .205 E4
Tyrells Way CM2 . . . . . . .216 F7
Tyrrells Sch The CM1 . . . .205 E5
Tyssen Mead CM3 . . . . . .206 E8
Tythe Cl CM1 . . . . .205 E8
Tythings The CM9 . . . . . .103 D8

U

Ufford Pl 8 CB9 . . . . .9 B8
Ullswater Cl CM77 . . . . . .154 C6
Ulting Hall Rd CM9 . . . . . .208 E7
Ulting La CM9 . . . . .208 E6
Ulting Rd
Hatfield Peverel CM3 . . . .194 C2
Ulting CM9 . . . . .208 C8
Una Rd CO2 . . . . .90 F5
Undercliff Rd W IP11 . . . . .221 D3
Union Rd CO15 . . . . .203 G8
Union St 11 IP4 . . . . .17 D6
Unity Cl CO2 . . . . .136 B4
Unity St IP3 . . . . .17 E4
Univ of Essex CO4 . . . . . .136 F4
Upland Cres CO5 . . . . . . .201 C7
Upland Dr CO4 . . . . .110 C2
Upland Rd Ipswich IP4 . . . .18 A6
West Mersea CO5 . . . . . .201 C7
Uplands Com Mid Sch
CO10 . . . . .15 F1
Uplands Cres CO10 . . . . . .15 E1
Uplands Cl CO15 . . . . . . .188 D1
Uplands Dr CM1 . . . . .205 D7
Uplands Rd
Clacton-on-S CO15 . . . . .188 D1
Sudbury CO10 . . . . .15 E1
Upper Acres CM8 . . . . . . .176 F5
Upper Barclay St 12 IP4 .17 D6
Upper Branston Rd
CO15 . . . . .188 D4
Upper Bridge Rd CM2 . . . .205 A1
Upper Brook St IP4 . . . . . .17 D5
Upper Cavendish St IP3 . . .18 A5
Upper Chapel St CO9 . . . . .76 E2
Upper Chase 2 CM2 . . . . .216 A8
Upper East St CO10 . . . . . .33 F8
Upper Farm Rd CO9 . . . . . .29 D8
Upper Fenn Rd CO9 . . . . . .77 A2
Upper Fourth Ave CO13 170 F5
Upper High St 1 IP1 . . . . .17 C6
Upper Holt St CO6 . . . . . .105 C6
Upper Mill Field CM6 . . . . .150 E7
Upper Moors CM3 . . . . . . .190 F7
Upper Orwell St 1 IP4 . . . .17 D5
Upper Park Rd
Brightlingsea CO7 . . . . . .185 E7
Clacton-on-S CO15 . . . . .188 D3
Upper Rd CO10 . . . . .55 E8
Upper Roman Rd CM2 . . . .205 B1
Upper Second Ave
CO13 . . . . .170 E5
Upper Sq CB10 . . . . .22 D2
Upper St Stanstead CO10 . . .2 E8
Stratford St M CO7 . . . . . .58 C1
Upper Third Ave CO13 . . . .170 E5
Upper Trinity Rd CO9 . . . . .76 E1
Upperfield Dr IP11 . . . . . .221 F6
Upsheres CB11 . . . . .43 F8
Upton Cl Ipswich IP4 . . . . .17 E6
West Bergholt CO6 . . . . .108 D4
Urban Rd CM23 . . . . .146 B7
Usterdale Rd CB10 . . . . . .22 E3
Uxbridge Cres IP3 . . . . . . .18 C1

V

Valance Rd CB11 . . . . .65 A7
Vale Cl CO4 . . . . .110 C2
Vale End CM2 . . . . .216 C3
Vale La IP9 . . . . .61 B4
Valens Cl CO4 . . . . .110 A6

Valenta Cl CO1 . . . . .136 C6
Valentine Ct CM7 . . . . . . .127 E4
Valentine Way CM8 . . . . . .156 D3
Valentines Dr CO4 . . . . . .110 C1
Valfreda Way CO7 . . . . . .137 B2
Valkyrie Cl CM9 . . . . .199 D5
Valletta Cl CM1 . . . . .205 A3
Valley Bridge CM1 . . . . . .205 B6
Valley Cl Brantham CO11 . . .60 D1
Colchester CO3 . . . . . . .134 E3
Valley Cres CO6 . . . . .108 E3
Valley Ct CO3 . . . . .145 E5
Valley Farm Camping Ground
CO15 . . . . .189 B6
Valley La Tattingstone IP9 . .36 F4
Wherstead IP9 . . . . .37 A3
Valley Rd Braintree CM7 . .128 A4
Clacton-on-S CO15 . . . . .189 A5
Colchester CO4 . . . . . . .136 F4
Harwich CO12 . . . . .90 D2
Ipswich IP1 . . . . .17 B8
Sudbury CO10 . . . . .34 F8
Wivenhoe CO7 . . . . .164 C8
Valley View
Finchingfield CM7 . . . . . . .72 D6
Stanstead CO10 . . . . .2 F7
West Bergholt CO6 . . . . .108 E3
Valley View Cl CO4 . . . . . .110 A4
Valley Wlk
Felixstowe IP11 . . . . . . .221 D5
Walton-on-t-N CO14 . . . .171 A7
Valleybridge Rd CO15 . . . .189 A5
Valleyview Dr IP4 . . . . . . .18 F5
Vallis Way CO5 . . . . .179 E5
Valonia Dr CO7 . . . . .164 B8
Van Dieman's La CM2 . . . .216 C8
Van Dieman's Rd CM2 . . . .216 C8
Van Dyck Rd CO3 . . . . . . .135 B5
Vandenburg Circ CM7 . . . .73 D6
Vandyck Rd IP3 . . . . .38 A8
Vane Ct CM8 . . . . .177 A5
Vane La CO6 . . . . .131 A2
Vanessa Dr CO7 . . . . .137 B1
Vange Pl 7 CB9 . . . . .9 B8
Vanguard Way CM7 . . . . . .128 B4
Vanners Rd CB9 . . . . .9 A7
Vansittart St CO12 . . . . . . .91 D5
Varden Cl CM1 . . . . .204 F6
Vaughan Cl CM77 . . . . . . .126 F2
Vaughan St 9 IP2 . . . . . . .17 C4
Vaux Ave CO12 . . . . .90 F1
Vauxhall Ave CO15 . . . . . .203 E6
Vauxhall Dr CM7 . . . . . . .127 C2
Vega Cl CO1 . . . . .136 C6
Vellacotts CM1 . . . . .205 B7
Venmore Dr CM6 . . . . . . .150 E8
Ventnor Dr CO15 . . . . . . .189 A8
Ventris Cl IP2 . . . . .16 D5
Ventura Dr CO1 . . . . .136 C6
Vermont Cl CO15 . . . . . . .189 A4
Vermont Cres IP4 . . . . . . .17 D7
Vermont Rd IP4 . . . . .17 D7
Vernon Ct CM23 . . . . .145 E4
Vernon St IP2 . . . . .17 C4
Vernon Way CM7 . . . . . . .128 C5
Vernon's Cl CM22 . . . . . . .94 F4
Vernons Rd CO6 . . . . .106 E5
Veronica Wlk CO4 . . . . . . .136 E7
Vesta Cl CO6 . . . . .130 F2
Veyses End CO7 . . . . .58 D2
Viaduct Rd CM1 . . . . .205 A2
Viborg Gdns CM9 . . . . . . .220 E8
Vica Cotts CM3 . . . . .207 D5
Vicarage Ave CM8 . . . . . . .155 F1
Vicarage Cl
18 Bishop's Stortford
CM23 . . . . .145 F7
Panfield CM7 . . . . .126 A8
Tolleshunt D'arcy CM9 . . .198 D4
Vicarage Cres CM3 . . . . . .194 B4
Vicarage Ct CO9 . . . . .76 D2
Vicarage Field CO10 . . . . . .34 B5
Vicarage Gdns CO15 . . . . .188 E2
Vicarage La Berden CM23 . .92 B8
Great Baddow CM2 . . . . .216 F7
Thaxted CM6 . . . . .70 A3
Thorpe-le-S CO16 . . . . . .141 F2
Ugley CM22 . . . . .93 D5
2 Walton-on-t-N CO14 . .171 C8
Wherstead IP9 . . . . .37 B5
Vicarage Mdw CO9 . . . . . .76 E1
Vicarage Mead CM6 . . . . . .70 A3
Vicarage Mews CM2 . . . . .216 F7
Vicarage Rd
Belchamp St P CO10 . . . . .13 A1
Chelmsford CM2 . . . . . .216 B8
Felixstowe IP11 . . . . . . .221 C4
Finchingfield CM7 . . . . . . .72 D6
Vicars Orch CO10 . . . . . . .32 E5
Vicerons Pl CM23 . . . . . . .145 D4
Viceroy Cl CO2 . . . . .136 B3
Victor Rd CO1 . . . . .136 B6
Victoria Ave
Kirby-le-S CO13 . . . . . . .170 D8
Saffron Walden CB11 . . . .22 E1
Victoria Chase CO1 . . . . . .135 E8
Victoria Cl CO7 . . . . .137 B2
Victoria Cotts CM9 . . . . . .210 A5
Victoria Cres
Chelmsford CM1 . . . . . .205 A3
Lawford CO11 . . . . .86 C5
Victoria Ct
Braintree CM7 . . . . .128 A2
Clacton-on-S CO15 . . . . .188 F3
Colchester CO3 . . . . . . .134 F7
Harwich CO12 . . . . .91 C3
Victoria Espl CO5 . . . . . . .201 E5

Victoria Gdns
Colchester CO4 . . . . . . .110 B3
Saffron Walden CB11 . . . .22 E1
Victoria Ho
Felixstowe IP11 . . . . . . .221 E4
Ipswich IP2 . . . . .17 B4
Victoria Pl
Brightlingsea CO7 . . . . . .185 F6
Colchester CO1 . . . . . . .136 B6
Victoria Rd
Chelmsford CM1 . . . . . .205 B3
Clacton-on-S CO15 . . . . .189 A3
Colchester CO3 . . . . . . .135 C6
Felixstowe IP11 . . . . . . .221 D3
Haverhill CB9 . . . . .8 D7
Maldon CM9 . . . . .210 A2
Walton-on-t-N CO14 . . . .171 C8
Weeley Heath CO16 . . . .168 B5
Victoria Rd S CM1 . . . . . .205 B2
Victoria St
Braintree CM7 . . . . .128 A2
Felixstowe IP11 . . . . . . .221 E4
Harwich CO12 . . . . .91 D4
Ipswich IP1 . . . . .17 A6
Victory Ct CO3 . . . . .134 E6
Victory Gdns CM7 . . . . . . .128 B4
Victory Rd
Clacton-on-S CO15 . . . . .188 D3
Ipswich IP4 . . . . .18 A7
West Mersea CO5 . . . . . .201 A6
Vienna Cl CO12 . . . . .91 A1
Viking Rd CM9 . . . . .209 E1
Viking Way CO15 . . . . . . .189 F6
Villa Cl 4 CO1 . . . . .136 C6
Villa Ho CO3 . . . . .134 C6
Villa Rd CO3 . . . . .134 C5
Village Cl
Kirby Cross CO13 . . . . . .170 D7
Little Clacton CO16 . . . . .168 D1
Village Gate CM2 . . . . . . .206 A2
Village Sq CM2 . . . . .206 A3
Village Way CO13 . . . . . . .170 D6
Villiers Pl CM3 . . . . .206 E8
Villiers-Sur-Marne Ave
CM23 . . . . .145 C4
Vince Cl CO5 . . . . .201 C6
Vincent Cl IP1 . . . . .16 E8
Vine Dr CO7 . . . . .137 C3
Vine Farm Rd CO7 . . . . . .137 C3
Vine Par CO7 . . . . .137 C3
Vine Rd CO5 . . . . .179 C6
Vine St CM7 . . . . .72 B2
Vine Wlk IP9 . . . . .35 A1
Vinesse Rd CO6 . . . . .81 D3
Vineyard Gate 4 CO2 . . . .135 F6
Vineyard St CO2 . . . . .135 F6
Vineyards The★
Braintree CM7 . . . . .153 D6
Great Baddow CM2 . . . . .216 F7
Vinnicombe Ct 3 IP2 . . . . .16 E1
Vint Cres CO3 . . . . .135 C6
Viola Wlk CO4 . . . . .136 E7
Violet Cl Chelmsford CM1 . 205 E7
Ipswich IP2 . . . . .16 F4
Virgil Rd CM8 . . . . .176 F5
Virginia Cl CO15 . . . . .188 A1
Virley Cl CM9 . . . . .210 D4
Viscount Dr CO4 . . . . . . .110 C5
Visitor Ctr & Country Wlk★
CB9 . . . . .9 C6
Vista Ave CO13 . . . . .143 D1
Vista Rd CO15 . . . . .189 A3
Vitllus Ct CO4 . . . . .110 B6
Vivian Ct CO14 . . . . .171 C8
Volwycke Ave CM9 . . . . . .220 F8

W

Waddesdon Rd CO12 . . . .91 D4
Wade Rd CO15 . . . . .189 B8
Wade Reach CO14 . . . . . .171 B8
Wadgate Rd IP11 . . . . . . .221 C4
Wadhurst Rd IP3 . . . . .18 D3
Wadley Cl CO5 . . . . .179 E5
Wagtail Dr CM9 . . . . .210 C5
Wagtail Pl CO5 . . . . .158 C2
Wainsfield Villas CM6 . . . . .70 B2
Wainwright Ave CM7 . . . . .154 D8
Wainwright St CM23 . . . . .145 C5
Wakefield Cl
Colchester CO1 . . . . . . .136 A8
Great Chesterford CB10 . . .3 D3
Wakelin Way CM8 . . . . . . .177 B2
Wakes St CO6 . . . . .106 C6
Wakeshall La CO10 . . . . . .30 C8
Waldeck Ct CB11 . . . . .43 D7
Waldegrave Cl CO11 . . . . . .86 B3
Waldegrave Rd CO11 . . . . .86 C3
Waldegrave Way CO11 . . . .86 B3
Waldegraves Farm Cvn Site
CO5 . . . . .201 G6
Waldegraves La CO5 . . . . .201 G7
Waldegraves The CO8 . . . . .79 F8
Walden Ave CB10 . . . . . . .44 E2
Walden Castle★ CB10 . . . . .22 D2
Walden Cl CM9 . . . . .196 A4
Walden Ho CO13 . . . . .170 F4
Walden House Rd CM8,
CM9 . . . . .196 A4
Walden Pl CB10 . . . . .22 D2
Walden Rd Ashdon CB10 . .23 E6
Great Chesterford CB10 . . .3 E3
Hadstock CB1 . . . . .5 B6
Littlebury CB10 . . . . .21 F4
Radwinter CB10 . . . . .45 D7
Sewards End CB10 . . . . . .23 D1

Walden Rd continued
Thaxted CM6 ....69 F5
Wendens Ambo CB11 ...42 F6
Wendens Ambo CB11 ...43 A6
Walden Way CO13 ....171 A6
Waldgrooms CM6 ....123 C1
Waldingfield Rd CO10 ..33 F8
Walford Cl CO6 ......131 A2
Walford Pl CM2 .....205 F2
Walford Way CO6 ....131 A2
Walk The
Eight Ash G CO6 ......134 A8
Felixstowe IP11 ....221 C5
10 Ipswich IP1 ......17 C6
Walker Cl IP3 ....18 C5
Walkers CM1 ....205 D7
Wall Ct 6 CM7 ......127 F1
Wall La CO11 ....88 D4
Wall St CO16 ....202 D6
Wallace Binder Cl CM9 .209 F1
Wallace Cres CM2 ...216 D8
Wallace La CM3 .....172 B7
Wallace Rd
Colchester CO4 ....109 E3
Ipswich IP1 ....16 E8
Wallace's La CM3 ...192 F4
Wallasea Gdns CM1 ..205 F5
Waller's Gr IP2 .....16 F4
Wallflower Ct 11 CM1 ..205 F6
Wallis Ct CO3 ......134 E3
Walls The CO11 ......86 E4
Walnut Dr
Bishop's Stortford CM23 .145 D3
Witham CM8 ....177 A4
Walnut Gr CM7 ......127 E2
Walnut Tree Cotts CM3 .190 E5
Walnut Tree La
Harkstead IP9 ....63 B2
Sudbury CO10 ....33 D7
Walnut Tree Way
Colchester CO2 ......135 B3
Tiptree CO5 ....179 C7
Walnuttree Hospl CO10 ..33 D7
Walsingham Cl CO10 ...34 C5
Walsingham Ct IP2 ....37 A8
Walsingham Rd CO2 ..135 F6
Walter Porter Ct CO4 .110 D1
Walter Radcliffe Way
CO7 ....164 C7
Walter Way CM8 ....156 D4
Walters Cl CM2 .....216 C3
Walters Yd 6 CO1 ..135 F7
Waltham Cl IP2 ......17 A2
Waltham Glen CM2 ..216 C7
Waltham Rd
Boreham CM3 ....193 A3
Terling CM3 ....175 A2
Waltham Way CO13 ..171 A5
Walton Ave IP11 ....221 A2
Walton Ct Colchester CO4 136 F4
Felixstowe IP11 ....221 D6
Walton Hall La CM3 ..220 B1
Walton Ho 4 Ipswich IP1 17 A6
Walton-on-t-N CO14 ....171 B8
Walton Maritime Mus★
CO14 ....144 D1
Walton Rd
Clacton-on-S CO15 ...189 A3
Frinton-on-S CO13 ...170 F6
Kirby-le-S CO13 ......170 E8
Thorpe-le-S CO13, CO16 .142 D2
Walton-on-t-N CO13,CO14 .171 B7
Walton-On-Naze Sta
CO14 ....171 C7
Walton-on-the-Naze Prim
Sch CO14 ....144 D1
Wantz Chase CM9 ...210 A2
Wantz Haven CM9 ...210 A2
Wantz Rd CM9 ......210 A2
Wapping La CO7 .....165 B2
Warburton Ave CO9 ..75 D8
Ward Cres CM23 ....145 E6
Ward Path CM2 .....206 B4
Ward Rd IP8 ....16 B2
Warde Chase CO14 ..171 B8
Warder Cl CM6 ......123 E1
Wardle Way CM1 ....204 E7
Wardley Cl IP2 ....16 D1
Wards Croft CB11 ....43 D7
Wareham Ave IP3 .....18 D3
Warehouse Rd CM6 ..124 F4
Warehouse Villas CM6 .125 D4
Wargrave Rd CO15 ..188 D4
Warham Rd CO12 .....90 F1
Warley Cl CM7 ......128 C3
Warley Way CO13 ...171 B6
Warner Cl CM77 .....126 F1
Warner Dr CM7 .....127 D4
Warner Way CO10 ....34 A8
Warners CM6 ....150 D8
Warnham Cl CO16 ...188 B6
Warren Cl
Broomfield CM1 ....191 B3
Takeley CM22 ....148 D7
Warren Ct 12 CB9 .....8 E7
Warren Heath Ave IP3 .18 D2
Warren Heath Rd IP3 ..18 D2
Warren La CO3 ......134 C2
Warren Lingley Way
CO5 ....179 E6
Warren Rd
Braintree CM7 ....128 C2
Halstead CO9 ....76 D1
Warrens The
Kirby Cross CO13 ....170 E6

Warrens The continued
Wickham Bishops CM8 ..195 F5
Warrenside CM7 .....155 A8
Warrington Rd IP1 ....17 B7
Warwick Bailey Cl CO4 .109 D2
Warwick Cl
Braintree CM7 ....128 B4
Little Easton CM6 ....122 F5
Maldon CM9 ....210 A1
Warwick Cres
Clacton-on-S CO15 ...188 E3
Maldon CM9 ....210 A1
Warwick Ct 2 CB9 .....8 E8
Warwick Dr CM9 ....210 A1
Warwick Rd
Bishop's Stortford CM23 .146 B6
Clacton-on-S CO15 ...188 E3
Ipswich IP4 ....17 E6
Takeley CM6 ....148 E7
Warwick Sq CM1 ....204 F4
Wash Cnr Aldham CO6 .107 C3
Ramsey CO12 ....89 E1
Wash La
Clacton-on-S CO15 ...188 D1
Goldhanger CM9 .....211 B7
Washall Dr CM77 ....154 D8
Washford Gdns CO15 .188 D2
Washington Cl CM9 ..209 E1
Washington Ct
Colchester CO3 ......134 E5
Maldon CM9 ....209 E1
Washington Rd
Harwich CO12 ....91 A2
Maldon CM9 ....209 F1
Wasses Cnr CO16 ....141 D5
Wat Tyler Wlk 1 CO1 .135 F7
Watch House Rd CM6 .124 F5
Watchouse Rd CM2 ..216 C3
Water Hall La CM7 ..100 F6
Water La
Bishop's Stortford CM23 .145 F8
Bures CO8 ....55 E1
Cavendish CO10 ....1 D2
Colchester CO3 ......135 D8
Debden CB11 ....44 B1
Great Easton CM6 ....122 C7
Helions Bumpstead CB9 ..26 D7
Little Horkesley CO6 ...81 F8
Newport CB11 ....43 A1
Pebmarsh CO9 ....78 A7
Radwinter CB10 ......45 E8
Shalford CM7 ....100 F3
Stansted Mountfitchet
CM24 ....119 E6
Steeple Bumpstead CB9 ..27 B6
Ststed CM7 ....129 C5
Stoke-by-N CO6 ....56 E8
Sturmer CB9 ....7 E7
Waterfront Terr CO14 .144 D1
Waterglade Ret Pk
CO15 ....188 E2
Waterhouse La
Ardleigh CO7 ....112 B5
Chelmsford CM1 .....204 F1
Waterhouse St CM1 ..204 F1
Waterloo La CM1 ....205 C2
Waterloo Rd IP1 .....17 A7
Watermill Rd CO5 ...158 E4
Waterside
Brightlingsea CO7 ....185 F5
Stansted Mountfitchet
CM24 ....119 E6
Waterside Bsns Pk CM8 177 B4
Waterside Rd CM0 ...214 F3
Waterson Vale CM2 ..216 C8
Waterville Mews CO2 .136 A3
Waterwick Hill CB11 ...40 B1
Waterworks Cl CO2 ..161 E5
Waterworks Cotts CO5 .179 A6
Waterworks Dr CO16 .188 B5
Waterworks Rd CM9 .199 D2
Waterworks St 6 IP4 ..17 D5
Watery La
Coggeshall CO6 ......130 A1
Great Dunmow CM6 ..150 A2
Manuden CM23 ....92 C1
Watling La CM6 ....69 F3
Watling St CM6 ....70 A3
Watsham Pl CO7 .....137 C2
Watson Rd CO15 ....188 B3
Watson's Cl CB10 .....47 B4
Watts Cl CM6 ....151 B4
Watts Ct 1P4 ....17 D5
Watts Rd CO2 ......135 B2
Watts Yd CM23 ....93 A2
Wavell Ave CO2 .....135 C4
Wavell Cl CM1 ......205 D8
Waveney Dr CM1 ....205 C6
Waveney Rd
Felixstowe IP11 ....221 C3
Ipswich IP1 ....16 E8
Waveney Terr CB9 .....9 A7
Waverley Bridge Ct
CM9 ....210 B5
Wavring Ave CO13 ...170 E7
Way Bank La CO10 ....10 E7
Wayback The CB10 ....22 E2
Wayletts Dr CM23 ...146 B7
Wayside CM3 ....218 E8
Waytemore Castle★
CM23 ....146 A7
Waytemore Rd CM23 .145 E6
Wear Dr CM1 ....205 D6
Weathervane Cotts CM7 .72 B1
Weaver Cl IP1 ....16 D8
Weaver St CO23 .....145 C4
Weaverhead Cl CM6 ...70 A3
Weaverhead La CM6 ...70 A3

Weavers Cl
Braintree CM7 ....127 F3
Colchester CO3 ......134 F5
Weavers Ct Halstead CO9 .76 E1
6 Sudbury CO10 ......33 E7
Weavers Dr CO10 ......2 B4
Weavers Gn CO6 ....107 D6
Weavers La CO10 .....33 C5
Weavers Row CO6 .....76 F1
Weavers Terr 7 CO10 ..33 E7
Weaversfield CM8 ...156 C5
Webb Cl CM2 ....206 B3
Webb St IP2 ....17 C3
Webster Cl CO9 ......75 D8
Weddell Rd CB9 ....9 C6
Wedgewood Dr CO4 ..109 E2
Wedow Rd CM6 ......70 A3
Weeley By-Pass Rd
CO16 ....140 E1
Weeley Rd
Great Bentley CO7 ...166 F8
Great Bentley,Aingers Green
CO7 ....166 F5
Little Clacton CO16 ..168 C4
Weeley Sta CO16 .....167 F8
Weggs Willow CO4 ..136 C7
Weighbridge Ct CB11 ..43 D8
Weight Rd CM2 .....205 C2
Weir La CO2,CO5 .....163 C7
Welhams Way CO11 ...86 B8
Well Field Halstead CO9 .103 F8
Writtle CM1 ....204 A1
Well La Clare CO10 ...12 B7
Danbury CM3 ....218 C7
Easthorpe CM6 ......160 A6
Galleywood CM2 .....216 A6
Well Side CO6 ......132 E3
Well St CO7 ....185 E7
Well Terr CM9 ......210 B5
Well's St 3 CM1 ....205 A4
Well-Green Cl CB11 ...43 E7
Welland Ave CM1 ...204 C5
Wellands CM8 ....195 E5
Wellands Cl CM8 ....195 D5
Weller Gr CM1 ......204 E7
Wellesley Ho 7 CO3 .135 E6
Wellesley Rd
Clacton-on-S CO15 ...188 E4
Colchester CO3 ......135 E6
Ipswich IP4 ....17 F5
Wellfield Way CO13 ..170 D7
Wellington Cl
Braintree CM7 ....128 C4
Chelmsford CM1 .....204 D5
Wellington Ct 5 IP1 ..17 A7
Wellington Rd
Harwich CO12 ....91 E6
Maldon CM9 ....209 F2
Wellington St
Brightlingsea CO7 ....185 F6
4 Colchester CO2 ..135 E6
Ipswich IP1 ....17 A7
Wellington Terr 7 CB9 ..8 E7
Wellmeads CM2 .....216 B8
Wells Cl 4 IP4 ....17 E6
Wells Ct Chelmsford CM1 205 D5
Great Dunmow CM6 ..123 C1
Wells Hall Com Prim Sch
CO10 ....34 B4
Wells Hall Rd CO10 ...34 C4
Wells Mead CB11 .....67 D4
Wells Rd CO1 ....136 B8
Wellum Cl 8 CB9 .....8 E7
Welshwood Park Rd
CO4 ....110 F2
Wenden Rd CB11 .....43 B7
Wendy Cl IP9 ....63 F7
Wenham La CO7 ......59 D6
Wenham Rd IP8 ......35 C7
Wenlock Rd CO16 ...167 F6
Wentford Ct CB9 ......8 C8
Wents Cl CO7 ....139 E1
Wentworth Cl CM3 ..194 B4
Wentworth Cres CM7 .127 F5
Wentworth Dr
Bishop's Stortford CM23 .145 D6
Ipswich IP8 ....16 C2
Wentworth Mdws CM9 .209 F2
Wentworth Prim Sch
CM9 ....209 F1
Wentworth Terr 5 CB9 ..8 E8
Wesel Ave IP11 .....221 B3
Wesley Ave CO4 ....136 C8
Wesley End Rd CO9 ...28 D4
Wesley Way IP1 ......16 F8
West Acre Ct CO3 ...135 B7
West Area IP1 ....16 C7
West Ave
Chelmsford CM1 .....204 F5
Clacton-on-S CO15 ...188 E2
West Bank Ferry Terminal
IP2 ....17 C2
West Belvedere CM3 .218 F7
West Bowers Rd CM9 .208 C4
West Chase CM9 ....209 F3
West Dock Rd CO12 ...90 E5
West Dr CM7 ....73 C3
West End La CO12 .....91 B2
West End Rd Ipswich IP1 .17 A5
Tiptree CO5 ....179 A3
West Fields CB11 .....43 B8
West Green Cotts CO11 .86 A7
West Hanningfield Rd
CM2 ....217 A3
West Lawn
Galleywood CM2 .....216 C2
Ipswich IP4 ....18 C8

West Lodge Rd CO3 ..135 D6
West Mill Gn IP9 .....60 E6
West Quay CO7 .....164 B7
West Rd
Bishop's Stortford CM23 .145 E6
Clacton-on-S CO15 ...203 H8
Halstead CO9 ....76 E1
Ipswich IP3 ....38 E8
Saffron Walden CB11 ..43 D8
Stansted Mountfitchet
CM24 ....119 E6
West Sq CM9 ....209 F3
West St Coggeshall CO6 .130 E1
Colchester CO3 ......135 E6
Harwich CO12 ....91 D6
Rowhedge CO5 ......163 F8
Tollesbury CM9 ......199 C1
Walton-on-t-N CO14 ..171 C8
Wivenhoe CO7 ......164 B8
West Station Ind Est
CM9 ....209 E1
West Station Rd CM9 .209 E1
West Stockwell St CO1 .135 F7
West View CM22 ....148 C8
West View CO4 .....110 B3
West Wood Hill CO4 .109 B3
West Yd CO9 ....103 E8
Westbourne Ct 1 CB9 ..9 A8
Westbourne Gr CM2 .216 D7
Westbourne Rd IP1 ...16 F4
Westbury Cl CO6 ....133 C5
Westbury Rd
Great Holland CO13 ..170 A5
Ipswich IP4 ....18 B8
Westcliff Ct CO15 ...188 E1
Westcott Cl CO16 ....188 D6
Westerdale CM1 ....205 D7
Westerfield Ct IP4 ....17 D7
Westerfield Rd IP4 ...17 D8
Westergreen Mdw CM7 .127 E1
Westerings
Bicknacre CM3 ....218 F2
Purleigh CM3 ....220 D1
Westerings The CM2 .216 F5
Westerlings The CM77 .155 E6
Western Cl
Rushmere St A IP4 ....18 F4
Silver End CM8 ......156 E3
Western Ho CO5 ....158 C2
Western La CM8 ....156 E3
Western Prom
Brightlingsea CO7 ....185 D5
Point Clear B CO16 ..185 E4
Western Rd
Brightlingsea CO7 ....185 E6
Silver End CM8 ......156 F3
Western's End CO11 ..86 D8
Westfield CO10 ....12 A6
Westfield Ave CM1 ..205 A4
Westfield Cl CM23 ..145 E8
Westfield Dr CO6 ...131 A3
Westfield Prim Sch CB9 ..9 B7
Westfield Rd CM23 ..145 E8
Westgate St IP1 ......17 C6
Westholme Rd IP1 ....17 A8
Westlake Cres CO7 ..137 A2
Westlands Com Prim Sch
CM1 ....204 E2
Westleton Way IP11 ..221 B6
Westley La CB10 ......22 D5
Westminster Cl IP4 ...18 B5
Westminster Ct
Clacton-on-S CO15 ...189 B3
Colchester CO2 ......136 C4
Westminster Gdns CM7 .128 B4
Westmorland Cl CO11 ..87 B3
Weston Rd CO2 .....136 B5
Westridge Rd CO15 ..189 A6
Westropps CO10 .....15 C5
Westside Ctr CO3 ....134 A5
Westway Chelmsford CM1 215 E8
Colchester CO1, CO3 ..135 E8
Westwood Ave IP1 ....17 A8
Westwood Ct IP1 .....17 A7
Westwood Dr CO5 ...201 E6
Wet La CO4 ....82 E5
Wetherfield CM24 ...119 D7
Wethersfield CE Prim Sch
CM7 ....73 C3
Wethersfield Rd
Blackheath CO2 ......163 A4
Shalford CM7 ....100 E8
Sible Hedingham CO9 ..51 C1
Wetzlar Ct CO2 .....136 B4
Weymouth Cl CO15 ..203 J8
Weymouth Rd
Chelmsford CM1 .....205 E6
Ipswich IP3 ....17 F6
Whalebone Cnr CO4 ...83 F7
Whaley Rd CO4 .....136 C7
Wharf La CO8 ....79 F8
Wharf Pl CM23 .....146 A6
Wharf Rd
12 Bishop's Stortford
CM23 ....145 F6
Chelmsford CM2 .....205 C2
Heybridge Basin CM9 .210 F4
Wharfe Cl CM8 .....176 E2
Wharton Dr CM1 ....206 A7
Wheat Croft CM23 ..145 E4
Wheater Ind Est CM8 .177 B1
Wheatfield Rd CO3 ..134 D5
Wheatfield Way CM1 .204 F3
Wheatlands Ardleigh CO7 111 F6
Elmstead CO7 ....137 F6
Wheatley Ave CM7 ..128 C3
Wheaton Rd CM8 ...177 B2
Wheatsheaf Cl CO11 ..88 D3

Wheatsheaf Ct 14 CO1 .136 A6
Wheatsheaf La CO11 ..88 D3
Wheeler Cl CO4 ....136 E6
Wheeler's Hill CM3 ..191 D6
Wheelwrights Cl CM23 .145 C4
Wheelwrights The IP11 221 A8
Wherry La 16 IP4 ....17 D5
Wherry Quay IP2 ....17 D5
Wherstead Rd
Ipswich,Maidenhall IP2 ..17 C2
Ipswich,Stoke IP2 .....17 C3
Whinchat Cl IP2 .....16 D3
Whinfield Ave CO12 ...90 F1
Whitbreads Farm La
CM3 ....173 D4
Whitby Rd IP4 ....17 D4
White Arch Pl CO4 ...83 B6
White Barns CM3 ...172 B6
White Bear CM24 ...119 E8
White Caville CB9 .....8 C8
White Cotts CM3 ....174 E5
White Court Prim Sch
CM77 ....154 C6
White Cross CO11 ....89 A2
White Elm Rd CM3 ..219 A2
White Elm St IP3 .....17 E4
White Hart Cotts CM2 .206 A6
White Hart La
Chelmsford CM1 .....205 F8
West Bergholt CO6 ..108 E5
White Horse Ave CO9 .103 D8
White Horse Hill IP9 ...36 D1
White Horse La
Maldon CM9 ....209 F2
Newport CB11 ....43 A1
Witham CM8 ....176 F3
White Horse Rd
Capel St M IP9 ....35 B1
East Bergholt CO7 ....59 E1
White Lodge Cres CO16 142 C1
White Mead CM1 ....191 B2
White Notley CE Prim Sch
CM8 ....155 F1
White Notley Sta CM8 ..155 F2
White Post Field CM6 .150 E8
White St CM6 ....150 D8
Whitebeam Cl
Chelmsford CM2 .....215 F7
Colchester CO4 ......109 D5
Whiteditch La CB11 ...42 F2
Whitefriars Way CO3 .135 A5
Whitegate Rd CO4 ...186 A6
Whitegates CM6 .....97 F4
Whitegates CM77 ...154 C6
Whitehall Cl CO2 ....136 C4
Whitehall Ct CM8 ...177 A2
Whitehall Ind Est CO2 .136 D4
Whitehall La
Bishop's Stortford CM23 .118 C1
Thorpe-le-S CO16 ....141 C3
Whitehall Rd
Bishop's Stortford CM23 .118 E1
Colchester CO2 ......136 D4
Whitehart Ct CO12 ...91 D6
Whitehead Cl CM1 ..215 B8
Whitehouse Cl CO4 ...83 D4
Whitehouse Cres CM2 .216 D8
Whitehouse Hill CM9 .199 A7
Whitehouse La
Belchamp St P CO10 ...13 B2
West Bergholt CO6 ..108 D3
Whitehouse Rd CM6 .124 F5
Whites Field CO7 .....59 B3
Whites La CM3 ......173 E6
Whitesbridge La CM4 .215 D1
Whiteshot Way CB10 ..22 F2
Whitethorn Cl CO4 ..136 D6
Whitethorn Gdns CM2 .216 C7
Whitethorn Rd IP3 ....18 F1
Whiteways CB10 ......3 C2
Whiteways Ct CM8 ..176 E3
Whitewell Rd 10 CO2 .135 F6
Whitfield Link CM2 ..216 D7
Whitland Cl IP2 ......37 A8
Whitlands CO10 ......2 B6
Whitlock Dr CO9 .....29 F1
Whitmore Cres CM2 ..206 B4
Whittaker Way CO5 ..201 B7
Whittington Way CM23 .145 F3
Whittle Rd IP2 ....16 F6
Whitworth Cl IP2 .....16 D2
Whybrews 4 CO4 ....136 C8
Whyverne Cl CM1 ...205 E6
Wick La Ardleigh CO7 .111 B8
Fingringhoe CO5 .....164 C3
Harwich CO12 ....91 B2
St Osyth CO7,CO16 ..167 C3
Wick Rd Colchester CO2 .136 D2
Great Bentley CO7 ...167 B5
Langham CO4 ....83 F3
Thorington Street CO4,CO6 .57 C2
Wicken Rd Arkesden CB11 .41 F1
Newport CB11 ....66 F8
Wickfield Ash CM1 ..204 D6
Wickham Bishop Rd
CM3 ....194 D4
Wickham Cres
Braintree CM7 ....128 A2
Chelmsford CM1 .....204 F6
Wickham Hall La CM8 .195 D3
Wickham Rd
Colchester CO3 ......135 D6
Witham CM8 ....194 F8
Wickham's Chase CM3 .219 C2
Wickhambrook Ct IP11 .221 A4

Wickhay Cotts CM3 ....207 D5
Wicklow Ave CM1 ....204 D6
Wicks Cl CM7 ....127 C6
Widford Chase CM2 .....215 F7
Widford Cl CM2 ....215 F7
Widford Gr CM2 ....215 F7
Widford Ind Est CM1 ...215 E8
Widford Lodge Sch
CM2 ....215 F7
Widford Park Pl CM2 ...215 F7
Widford Rd CM2 ....215 F7
Widgeon Cl IP2 ....16 F3
Widgeon Pl CO5 ....158 C2
Widleybrook La
Wethersfield CM7 ....73 F3
Wethersfield,Blackmore End
CM7 ....74 A2
Wigboro Wick La CO16 ..186 F2
Wigborough Rd
Layer-de-l-H CO2 ....161 E2
Peldon CO5 ....182 C5
Wigeon Cl CM77 ....154 C5
Wiggins View CM2 ......206 B4
Wigmore Cl IP2 ....16 F1
Wignall St CO11 ....85 F3
Wilberforce St IP1 ....17 A6
Wilbye Cl CO2 ....135 B4
Wilbye Ho CO3 ....135 A7
Wild Boar Field CM7 ...128 D3
Wilding Rd IP8 ....16 B1
Wilkin Cl CO3 ....135 A4
Wilkin Dr CO5 ....179 E5
Wilkinson Gr CM77 .....155 B5
Wilkinsons Mead CM2 ..206 B4
Will's Ayley La CB10 .....23 F2
Willets Pond CO7 ....59 E1
Willett Rd CO2 ....135 B3
Willetts Field CB10 ....47 A3
William Booth Way
IP11 ....221 B5
William Boys Cl **1** CO4 .136 D6
William Cl CO7 ....137 C4
William Dr CO15 ....188 D2
William Groom Ave CO12 .91 A2
William Ho **7** IP4 ....17 D6
William Julian Courtauld
Hospl CM7 ....127 E2
William Paul Housing Trust
3 IP2 ....17 C4
William Sparrow Ct
CO7 ....137 C2
William St **3** IP1 ....17 C6
William's Wlk **8** CO1 ..135 F7
Williams Dr CM7 ....127 F4
Williams Rd CM1 ....191 B1
Williamson Ho **2** CO1 .136 A6
Willingale Rd CM7 .....128 D4
Willingham Way CO4 ...136 E7
Willis Almshouses CM9 .196 B3
Willoughby Ave CO5 ...201 D6
Willoughby Dr CM2 ....205 F2
Willoughby Rd IP2 ......17 B4
Willoughby's La CM7 ..128 C8
Willow Ave
Kirby Cross CO13 ......170 D6
Seawick CO16 ....203 B6
Willow Cl Ardleigh CO7 .110 D6
Bishop's Stortford CM23 .145 E8
Brightlingsea CO7 ......185 D6
Broomfield CM1 ....191 B1
Sudbury CO10 ....33 E6
Willow Cres CM3 ......194 A3
Willow Dene CO9 ....51 D2
Willow Hall La CO11 ...115 D8
Willow Mdws CO9 ......75 E8
Willow Pk CO6 ....133 E5
Willow Rd CM6 ....123 C6
Willow Rise CM8 ....177 A5
Willow Springs CM23 ..145 D8
Willow Tree Ct **1** CO4 .136 E8
Willow Tree Way CO6 ..105 B6
Willow Way
Clacton-on-S CO15 ....203 G7
Halstead CO9 ....76 D1
Harwich CO12 ....90 F2
Willow Wlk
Heybridge CM9 ....210 C6
Tiptree CO5 ....179 C7
Weeley CO16 ....167 F8
Willowbank CM2 ....216 B3
Willows The
Boreham CM3 ....206 F8
Chelmsford CM1 ....205 A4
Colchester CO2 ....136 A3
Frinton-on-S CO13 .....170 F5
Great Chesterford CB10 ...3 D3
Wills Gn CO5 ....158 F6
Wilmington Rd CO4 ....110 C2
Wilmslow Dr CM2 ......16 C2
Wilshire Ave CM2 .....205 F3
Wilson Cl
Bishop's Stortford CM23 .145 F6
Wivenhoe CO7 ....137 A2
Wilson Ct CO15 ....189 B8
Wilson Marriage Rd
CO4 ....110 C1
Wilson Rd IP8 ....16 B1
Wilson's Ct CM9 ....210 B2
Wilson's La CO6 ....132 E3
Wilton Cl CM23 ....146 B7
Wimbish Prim Sch CB10 .45 C4
Wimbish Wlk CB10 .....44 E2
Wimborne Ave CM1 ....205 A4
Wimbourne Gdns CO13 .170 F7
Wimpole Cl IP5 ....18 F6

Wimpole Rd CO1 ......136 B5
Wimsey Ct CM8 ....177 A5
Wincelow Hall Rd CB10 .25 E3
Winchelsea Dr CM2 ....216 E7
Winchelsea Pl IP7 .....185 E8
Winchester Cl CM23 ...145 D4
Winchester Ct CO13 ...171 A5
Winchester Rd
Colchester CO2 ....136 B5
Frinton-on-S CO13 .....171 A5
Winchester Way IP2 ....36 F8
Winckford St CM1 ......36 C8
Windermere Cl IP3 ......38 B8
Windermere Dr CM77 ..154 C6
Windermere Rd
Clacton-on-S CO15 ....189 C6
Great Notley CM77 ....154 C7
Sudbury CO10 ....34 A8
Windham Rd CO10 .....34 B8
Windhill CM23 ....145 E7
Windhill Old Rd CM23 .145 E7
Winding Piece IP9 ......35 A1
Windley Tye CM1 ......204 E3
Windmill CI Boxted CO4 .82 F4
Great Dunmow CM6 ...123 C1
Ramsey CO12 ....89 F1
Windmill Ct
Clacton-on-S CO15 ....188 F5
Colchester CO4 ....109 E4
Copford CO6 ....133 D4
Windmill Fields CO6 ...130 F3
Windmill Gdns CM7 ...128 A8
Windmill Hill CB10,CB11 .22 B3
Windmill Pk CO15 .....188 F5
Windmill Rd
Bradfield CO11 ....87 C1
Halstead CO9 ....76 D1
Windmill Row CO10 .....2 C5
Windmill View CO5 ....179 C6
Windmills CO6 ....106 C1
Windmills The CM1 ....191 B3
Windrush Dr CM1 .....205 C6
Windsor Ave CO15 ....188 D3
Windsor Cl CO2 ....136 A2
Windsor Ct
Brightlingsea CO7 .....185 F6
6 Colchester CO1 ...136 C6
Windsor Gdns
Bishop's Stortford CM23 .145 C7
Braintree CM7 ....128 B4
Windsor Ho CO5 ......201 D7
Windsor Pl CO10 ....34 A7
Windsor Rd
Clacton-on-S CO15 ....188 D3
Felixstowe IP11 ....221 C3
Ipswich IP1 ....16 F7
West Mersea CO5 .....201 D7
Windsor Sch The CO15 .189 B4
Windsor Terr CB9 ....8 E8
Windsor Way CM1 ....204 E1
Winfield Terr CO14 ....144 D2
Winfrith Rd IP3 ....18 D4
Wingate Cl CM7 ....127 E5
Wingfield St IP4 ....17 D5
Wingrove Ct CM1 .....205 A6
Winnock Rd CO1 ......136 A6
Winnock's Almshouses **4**
CO1 ....136 A6
Winnocks **5** CO1 ....136 A6
Winsey Chase CM7 ....72 C6
Winsford Way CM2 ...206 C6
Winsgate Ho **6** IP1 ...17 A7
Winsley Rd CO1 ....136 B6
Winsley Sq CO1 ....136 B4
Winstanley Rd CB11 ...43 E7
Winston Ave
Colchester CO3 ....135 B4
Ipswich IP4 ....18 C8
Tiptree CO5 ....179 E5
Winston Cl
Braintree CM7 ....127 E6
Felixstowe IP11 ....221 B5
Winston Ct CO13 .....170 F4
Winston Way CO9 ......77 A3
Winstree Cl CO2 ......161 F5
Winstree Ct CO3 ......134 C4
Winstree Rd CO3 .....134 D5
Winter's Hill CO2 .....160 F1
Winter's Rd CO5 ......160 E1
Winterbournes CO14 ..171 A7
Wisdoms Gn CO6 .....131 B3
Wistaria Ct **3** CO4 ...136 E7
Wistaria Pl CO16 .....188 C3
Wisteria Lodge **7** CM1 .205 F6
Wiston Rd CO6 ....81 D8
Witch Elm CO12 ....90 F2
Witch La CO6 ....131 B8
Witchtree La CB10 .....25 F3
Witham Lodge CM8 ...194 D7
Witham Rd
Black Notley CM77,CM8 .155 B5
Cressing CM77 ....156 B3
Langford CM9 ....209 D7
Terling CM3 ....175 C2
Tolleshunt Major CM9 .197 D5
Wickham Bishops CM8 .195 E6
Witham Sta CM8 ......177 A3
Withersfield Rd CB9 .....8 F8
Withipoll St IP4 ....17 D6
Withrick Wlk CO16 ....187 A5
Witting Cl CO16 ......188 B5
Witton Wood Rd CO13 .170 E5
Wivenhoe Cross CO7 ..137 C2
Wivenhoe Rd
Alresford CO7 ....165 B7

Wivenhoe Rd continued
Colchester CO7 ....111 C1
Wivenhoe Sta CO7 ...164 B8
Wix & Wrabness Prim Sch
CO11 ....115 B5
Wix By-Pass CO11 ....115 C6
Wix Rd Beaumont CO16 .141 E8
Bradfield CO11 ....87 E1
Great Oakley CO12 ....116 B3
Ramsey CO12 ....89 F1
Tendring CO11 ....114 F8
Wix CO11 ....115 C3
Woburn Ave
Bishop's Stortford CM23 .145 C7
Kirby Cross CO13 .....170 D7
Woburn Ct CM2 ....205 A1
Wolfe Ave CO1,CO2 ...136 A5
Wolmers Hey CM3 ....190 F7
Wolseley Ave CO15 ...203 E6
Wolseley Rd CM2 .....205 A1
Wolsey Art Gall★ IP4 ..17 D6
Wolsey Ct IP11 ....221 E3
Wolsey Gdns IP11 ....221 E3
Wolsey St **9** IP1 .....17 C5
Wolton Rd CO2 ....135 B2
Wolves Hall La CO16 ..114 F1
Wood Barn La CO11 ....85 D1
Wood Cnr
Fordham Heath CO6 ...107 F1
Maldon CM9 ....209 B2
Wood Dale CM2 ......216 E6
Wood End CB11 ....67 D3
Wood Field End CO2 ..162 A5
Wood Green Est CO7 ..166 F5
Wood La
Birchanger CM23 ......119 E2
Fordham Heath CO3 ..107 F1
Harkstead SG9 ....64 A6
Heybridge CM9 ....210 A5
Wood Rd CM9 ....210 B6
Wood St CM2 ....216 A7
Wood Way CM77 .....154 B6
Woodberry Way CO14 .171 C7
Woodbridge Gr CO16 .188 A4
Woodbridge Rd
Ipswich IP4 ....17 E6
Ipswich,California IP5 ..18 B7
Rushmere St A IP5 .....18 E7
Woodbridge Rd E IP4 ..18 D7
Woodcock Cl
Colchester CO4 ....136 E6
Haverhill CB9 ....9 C7
Woodcock Rd IP2 ......16 E2
Woodfield Cl
Stansted Mountfitchet
CM24 ....119 E6
Walton-on-t-N CO14 ..171 A7
Woodfield Cotts CM9 .210 C6
Woodfield Dr CO5 ....201 B7
Woodfield La IP9 ....61 E3
Woodfield Rd CM7 ....128 A3
Woodfield Terr CO11 ..119 E6
Woodfield Way CM1 ..194 A4
Woodfields CM24 .....119 E6
Woodford Cl CO15 ....188 F8
Woodgates CO11 .....221 B6
Woodgates Rd CO7 ....59 D5
Woodhall Bsns Pk CO10 .15 F2
Woodhall Cl CO10 .....15 E1
Woodhall Com Prim Sch
CO10 ....15 F2
Woodhall Gr CM23 ...145 D6
Woodhall Hill CM1 ....190 C2
Woodhall Par CM1 ....205 A7
Woodhall Rd
Chelmsford CM1 ......205 A7
Sudbury CO10 ....15 E1
Woodham Dr CM3 ....194 B4
Woodham Mortimer Rd
CM9 ....219 E8
Woodham Walter CE Prim
Sch CM9 ....208 D3
Woodhill Common Rd
CM3 ....218 B5
Woodhill Rd
Chelmsford CM2 ......217 E6
Danbury CM3 ....218 B6
Woodhouse La CM3 ..191 A4
Woodhouse Sq **5** IP4 ..17 D5
Woodland Chase CO3 .107 F1
Woodland Cl CM3 ....194 A5
Woodland Dr CO3 ....134 F5
Woodland Rd CM1 ...205 A4
Woodland Way
Gosfield CO9 ....102 E8
Wivenhoe CO7 ....137 B1
Woodlands
Bishop's Stortford CM23 .146 C8
Braintree CM7 ....128 C4
Broomfield CM1 ....191 A4
Chelmondiston IP9 .....63 E7
Colchester CO4 ....110 F2
Great Oakley CO12 ...116 B2
Great Waltham CM1 ..190 F4
Ipswich IP8 ....16 C1
Jaywick CO16 ....188 A1
Woodlands Cl CO15 ..189 A8
Woodlands Park Dr
CM6 ....123 B1
Woodlands Rd IP9 .....62 D7
Woodlands Rise CO16 .140 F1
Woodlands Sch CM1 ..204 F6
Woodlands The CO7 ..185 E8
Woodlands Wlk CM6 .123 B1
Woodlark Cl IP2 ....16 E1
Woodlyn Cl CO15 ....189 E6
Woodpecker Cl
Bishop's Stortford CM23 .145 C6

Woodpecker Cl continued
2 Colchester CO4 ...136 F8
Woodpecker Rd IP2 ....16 D3
Woodroffe Cl CM2 ....206 A3
Woodrolfe Farm La
CM9 ....199 E1
Woodrolfe Pk CM9 ...199 F2
Woodrolfe Rd CM9 ...199 E2
Woodrose Lodge **6**
CM1 ....205 F6
Woodrow Way CO4 ...136 E7
Woodrows La CO16 ...188 B6
Woodrush End CO3 ...134 B6
Woodrush Rd IP3 ......18 E2
Woods Cl CB9 ....9 E5
Woods Rd CM3 ....172 B6
Woodside
Bishop's Stortford CM23 .146 D8
Great Totham CM9 ....196 B3
Little Baddow CM3 ...207 C1
Walton-on-t-N CO14 ..171 B7
Woodside Cl CO4 .....110 E1
Woodside Gn CO2 ....146 F1
Woodside Way CM6 ..123 A1
Woodspring Cl **2** IP2 ..17 A4
Woodstock CO5 ......201 C7
Woodstock Pl CM2 ...216 F5
Woodview Cl CO4 ....110 D4
Woodview Cotts CM3 .180 C8
Woodview Dr CM3 ...174 A7
Woodview Rd CM6 ...150 D8
Woodville Rd IP4 ......17 F5
Woodward Cl IP2 .....16 D5
Woodyards CM0 ......214 F3
Woollards Cl IP1 ....17 A6
Woollards Gdns CO10 ..15 C8
Woolner Rd CO16 ....188 D6
Woolnough Cl CB9 ....27 B6
Woolpack La CM7 ....127 F5
Woolpit Downs CO8 ...79 E8
Woolpit's Rd CM7 .....99 E1
Woolverstone Cl IP2 ..16 C1
Woolwich Rd CO16 ...188 C5
Worcester Cl CM7 ....128 A1
Worcester Cres CO7 ..165 B8
Worcester Ct
Clacton-on-S CO15 ...188 E1
Great Baddow CM2 ...217 A5
Worcester Ho CB9 .....9 B6
Worcester Rd
Colchester CO1 ....136 A8
Ipswich IP3 ....38 B8
Wordsworth Ct CM1 ..205 A5
Wordsworth Rd
Braintree CM7 ....127 F7
Colchester CO3 ....134 F6
Wordsworths Way
CO16 ....188 A5
Workhouse Cnr CO12 .116 C3
Workhouse Hill CO4 ...82 E4
Workhouse Rd CO6 ....81 C2
Worlds End La CO5 ...158 D3
Worrin Rd CM6 ....151 E6
Worsdell Way CO4 ...109 F2
Worsley Cl IP2 ....16 D2
Wortham Pl CB9 ....9 A8
Worthing Mews CO15 .203 I8
Worthington Way CO3 .134 F4
Wrabness Local Nature
Reserve★ CO11 ....88 D4
Wrabness Rd
Ramsey CO12 ....90 A2
Wrabness CO12 ....89 D3
Wrabness Sta CO11 ....89 A4
Wraglins The CM23 ...146 B5
Wratting Rd CB9 ....9 A8
Wren Ave IP2 ....16 D3
Wren Cl Colchester CO3 .134 C4
Great Bentley CO7 ....139 D1
Wrenbrook Rd CM23 .145 F6
Wrendale CO15 ....188 F6
Wright Ct **2** CM7 ...127 F3
Wright Mead CM2 ....206 B4
Wright Rd IP3 ....18 C2
Wright's Ave CM77 ...155 E6
Wright's Piece CM22 ..95 A6
Writtle Cl CO16 ......188 B4
Writtle Coll CM1 .....204 B3
Writtle Jun & Inf Schs
CM1 ....215 A8
Writtle Rd CM1 ....215 E8
Wroxham Cl CO3 .....135 B6
Wroxham Rd IP3 ......17 F3
Wryneck Cl CO4 .....109 F3
Wulvesford CM8 .....194 D8
Wyatts La CO10 ....55 D8
Wych Elm CO2 ....136 A3
Wycke Hill CM9 ......220 D8
Wycke Hill Bsns Pk
CM9 ....220 E8
Wycke La CM9 ....213 E8
Wycliffe Gr CO1 .....109 E1
Wye Rd IP3 ....18 A3
Wyedale Dr CO3 .....134 E5
Wykeham Rd CM1 ...204 B1
Wykes Bishop St IP3 ..17 E4
Wyncolls Rd CO4 ....110 D6
Wyndam Cl CO2 .....163 B8
Wyndham Cres CO15 .189 A5
Wynterton Cl IP3 ......18 B1
Wynyard Rd CB10 ....22 E2
Wyseman Pl CO11 ....86 C7
Wyvern Ct CO7 ......137 B1
Wyvern Rd IP3 ....18 C1
Wyverne CM6 ....151 A5

Y
Yale Bsns Pk IP3 ....38 E8
Yale Mews CO4 ......110 B4
Yard The CM7 ....128 A2
Yardley Hall La CM6 ...69 D6
Yare Ave CM8 ....176 D2
Yarmouth Cl CO16 ...188 E6
Yarmouth Pl CB9 ....9 A8
Yarmouth Rd IP1 ......17 A6
Yarwood Rd CM2 ....205 E2
Yeldham Lock CM2 ..206 A2
Yeldham Pl CB9 ....9 A8
Yeldham Rd CO9 ......51 D3
Yeoman Rd IP11 .....221 B3
Yeomans Cl CM23 ...145 D6
Yerril Gdn CB9 ....8 E7
Yew Cl CM8 ....177 B5
Yew Ct IP2 ....17 B3
Yew Tree Cl
Colchester CO4 ....136 E8
Hatfield Peverel CM3 .194 A5
Yew Tree Gdns CM2 .216 C6
Yew Tree Pl CM23 ...145 F8
Yew Way CO15 ......203 F6
Yewtree Gr IP5 ....18 F7
Yewtree Rise IP8 .....16 C1
Yonge Cl CM3 ....192 E1
Yorick Ave CO5 .....201 C6
Yorick Rd CO5 ......201 C6
York Cl CO10 ....33 E8
York Gdns CM7 .....128 B4
York Mews CO15 ....189 E5
York Pl CO1 ....136 A8
York Rd
Brightlingsea CO7 ....185 E6
Chelmsford CM2 .....216 A8
Clacton-on-S CO15 ..189 E5
Earls Colne CO6 .....105 B6
Felixstowe IP11 .....221 E4
Haverhill CB9 ....8 E7
Ipswich IP3 ....18 A4
Sudbury CO10 ....33 E8
York St **7** CO11 .....86 D4
Young Cl CO16 ......188 C5
Ypres Rd CO2 ....135 E4

Z
Zambesi Rd CM23 ...145 F5
Zinnia Mews CO16 ...188 C4

NG	NH	NJ	NK
NM	NN	NO	NP
NR	NS	NT	NU
NX	NY	NZ	
SC	SD	SE	TA
SH	SJ	SK	TF	TG
SM	SN	SO	SP	TL	TM
SR	SS	ST	SU	TQ	TR
SW	SX	SY	SZ	TV

Any feature in this atlas can be given a unique reference to help you find the same feature on other Ordnance Survey maps of the area, or to help someone else locate you if they do not have a Street Atlas.

The grid squares in this atlas match the Ordnance Survey National Grid and are at 500 metre intervals. The small figures at the bottom and sides of every other grid line are the National Grid kilometre values (**00** to **99** km) and are repeated across the country every 100 km (see left).

To give a unique National Grid reference you need to locate where in the country you are. The country is divided into 100 km squares with each square given a unique two-letter reference. Use the administrative map to determine in which 100 km square a particular page of this atlas falls.

The bold letters and numbers between each grid line (**A** to **F**, **1** to **8**) are for use within a specific Street Atlas only, and when used with the page number, are a convenient way of referencing these grid squares.

Example   The railway bridge over DARLEY GREEN RD in grid square B1

Step 1: Identify the two-letter reference, in this example the page is in **SP**

Step 2: Identify the 1 km square in which the railway bridge falls. Use the figures in the southwest corner of this square: Eastings **17**, Northings **74**. This gives a unique reference: **SP 17 74**, accurate to 1 km.

Step 3: To give a more precise reference accurate to 100 m you need to estimate how many tenths along and how many tenths up this 1 km square the feature is (to help with this the 1 km square is divided into four 500 m squares). This makes the bridge about **8** tenths along and about **1** tenth up from the southwest corner.

This gives a unique reference: **SP 178 741**, accurate to 100 m.

Eastings (read from left to right along the bottom) come before Northings (read from bottom to top). If you have trouble remembering say to yourself "Along the hall, THEN up the stairs"!

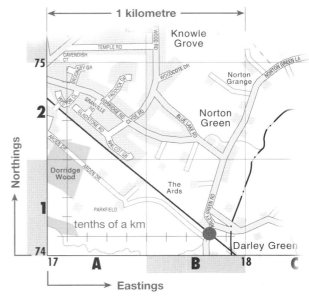

Addresses

Name and Address	Telephone	Page	Grid reference

Name and Address	Telephone	Page	Grid reference

Street Atlases from Philip's

Philip's publish an extensive range of regional and local street atlases which are ideal for motoring, business and leisure use. They are widely used by the emergency services and local authorities throughout Britain.

Key features include:

◆ Superb county-wide mapping at an extra-large scale of 3½ inches to 1 mile, or 2½ inches to 1 mile in pocket editions

◆ Complete urban and rural coverage, detailing every named street in town and country

◆ Each atlas available in two handy sizes – standard spiral and pocket paperback

'The mapping is very clear... great in scope and value'

★★★★ BEST BUY   AUTO EXPRESS

PHILIP'S — STREET ATLAS Cambridgeshire — With complete coverage of Peterborough — BEST BUY Auto Express — Unique comprehensive coverage — Plus Cambridge Town maps

PHILIP'S — STREET ATLAS Glasgow and West Central Scotland

PHILIP'S — STREET ATLAS Cardiff, Swansea and the Valleys — Unique comprehensive coverage

PHILIP'S — STREET ATLAS London — The definitive London atlas

PHILIP'S — STREET ATLAS East Sussex — With complete coverage of Brighton and Hove — BEST BUY — The definitive East Sussex atlas

PHILIP'S — STREET ATLAS North Yorkshire — Unique comprehensive coverage — BEST BUY Auto Express

PHILIP'S — STREET ATLAS Wiltshire and Swindon — Unique comprehensive coverage

PHILIP'S — STREET ATLAS Devon — Unique comprehensive coverage — BEST BUY Auto Express — with time-saving through-routes — Includes Lyme Regis, Saltash and Wellington, plus Exeter and Plymouth city centres at extra-large scale

1 Bedfordshire
2 Berkshire
3 Birmingham and West Midlands
4 Bristol and Bath
5 Buckinghamshire
6 Cambridgeshire
7 Cardiff, Swansea and The Valleys
8 Cheshire
9 Cornwall
10 Derbyshire
11 Devon
12 Dorset
13 County Durham and Teesside
14 Edinburgh and East Central Scotland

15 North Essex
16 South Essex
17 Glasgow and West Central Scotland
18 Gloucestershire
19 North Hampshire
20 South Hampshire
21 Herefordshire and Monmouthshire
22 Hertfordshire
23 East Kent
24 West Kent
25 Lancashire
26 Leicestershire and Rutland
27 Lincolnshire
28 London
29 Greater Manchester
30 Merseyside
31 Norfolk
32 Northamptonshire
33 Nottinghamshire
34 Oxfordshire
35 Shropshire
36 Somerset
37 Staffordshire
38 Suffolk
39 Surrey
40 East Sussex
41 West Sussex
42 Tyne and Wear and Northumberland
43 Warwickshire
44 Worcestershire
45 Wiltshire and Swindon
46 East Yorkshire and Northern Lincolnshire
47 North Yorkshire
48 South Yorkshire
49 West Yorkshire

How to order

The Philip's range of street atlases is available from good retailers or directly from the publisher by phoning 01903 828503